★ **Trajan's Markets** ⑩
See pages 88–9

★ **San Clemente** ⑫
See pages 186–7

★ **Santa Maria del Popolo** ⑥
See pages 138–9

★ **Santa Maria Maggiore** ⑬
See pages 172–3

Piazza di Spagna

Via Veneto

Quirinal

Esquiline

Capitol

Forum

Palatine

Lateran

Caracalla

Aventine

★ **San Giovanni in Laterano** ⑭
See pages 182–3

Santa Maria in Trastevere ⑤
pages 212–13

★ **Colosseum** ⑪
See pages 92–5

EYEWITNESS *TRAVEL GUIDES*

ROME

EYEWITNESS *TRAVEL GUIDES*

ROME

DORLING KINDERSLEY
LONDON • NEW YORK • STUTTGART

A DORLING KINDERSLEY BOOK

PROJECT EDITOR Fiona Wild
ART EDITOR Annette Jacobs
EDITORS Ferdie McDonald, Mark Ronan, Anna Streiffert
DESIGNER Lisa Kosky
DESIGN ASSISTANT Marisa Renzullo

MANAGING EDITOR Douglas Amrine
MANAGING ART EDITOR Geoff Manders
SENIOR EDITOR Georgina Matthews
SERIES DESIGN CONSULTANT Peter Luff
EDITORIAL DIRECTOR David Lamb
ART DIRECTOR Anne-Marie Bulat

PRODUCTION CONTROLLER Hilary Stephens
PICTURE RESEARCH Catherine O'Rourke
RESEARCH IN ROME Sam Cole
DTP EDITOR Siri Lowe

MAIN CONTRIBUTORS
Olivia Ercoli, Ros Belford, Roberta Mitchell

MAPS
Andrew Heritage, James Mills-Hicks, John Plumer,
Chez Picthall (Dorling Kindersley Cartography)

PHOTOGRAPHERS
John Heseltine, Mike Dunning, Kim Sayer

ILLUSTRATORS
Studio Illibill, Kevin Jones Associates,
Martin Woodward, Robbie Polley

•

This book was produced with the assistance of
Websters International Publishers.

Film outputting bureau PLS (London)
Reproduced by Colourscan (Singapore)
Printed and bound by Graphicom (Italy)

First published in Great Britain in 1993
by Dorling Kindersley Limited
9 Henrietta Street, London WC2E 8PS
Reprinted with revisions 1994 (twice), 1995, 1997

•

Every effort has been made to ensure that the information in this
book is as up-to-date as possible at the time of going to press.
However, details such as telephone numbers, opening hours,
prices, gallery hanging arrangements and travel information are
liable to change. The publishers cannot accept responsibility for
any consequences arising from the use of this book.

We would be delighted to receive any corrections and
suggestions for incorporation in the next edition. Please write to
the Managing Editor, Eyewitness Travel Guides
Dorling Kindersley
9 Henrietta Street, London WC2E 8PS.

CONTENTS

HOW TO USE
THIS GUIDE 6

Colosseum

INTRODUCING ROME

PUTTING ROME
ON THE MAP 10

THE HISTORY OF
ROME 14

ROME
AT A GLANCE 40

ROME THROUGH
THE YEAR 58

Moses by Michelangelo in
San Pietro in Vincoli

Fresco in Villa Farnesina

ROME AREA BY AREA

CAPITOL *64*

FORUM *76*

PALATINE *96*

PIAZZA DELLA ROTONDA *102*

The Tempietto

PIAZZA NAVONA *116*

PIAZZA DI SPAGNA *128*

CAMPO DE' FIORI *142*

QUIRINAL *154*

ESQUILINE *166*

LATERAN *176*

CARACALLA *188*

AVENTINE *198*

TRASTEVERE *206*

JANICULUM *214*

VATICAN *222*

VIA VENETO *250*

FURTHER AFIELD *256*

SIX GUIDED WALKS *272*

Arch of Titus

TRAVELLERS' NEEDS

WHERE TO STAY *288*

RESTAURANTS AND CAFÉS *302*

SHOPS AND MARKETS *322*

ENTERTAINMENT IN ROME *340*

CHILDREN'S ROME *352*

The basilica of St Peter's in the Vatican City

Mosaic in Santa Prassede

SURVIVAL GUIDE

PRACTICAL INFORMATION *358*

Roman antipasto

GETTING TO ROME *368*

GETTING AROUND ROME *374*

ROME STREET FINDER *380*

GENERAL INDEX *404*

ACKNOWLEDGMENTS *428*

PHRASE BOOK *431*

HOW TO USE THIS GUIDE

THIS EYEWITNESS TRAVEL GUIDE helps you get the most from your stay in Rome with the minimum of practical difficulty. The opening section, *Introducing Rome*, locates the city geographically, sets modern Rome in its historical context and explains how Roman life changes through the year. *Rome at a Glance* is an overview of the city's attractions. The main sightseeing section, *Rome Area by Area*, starts on page 62. It describes all the important sights with maps, photographs and detailed illustrations. In addition, six planned walks take you to parts of Rome you might otherwise miss.

Carefully researched tips for hotels, shops and markets, restaurants and cafés, sports and entertainment are found in *Travellers' Needs*, and the *Survival Guide* has advice on everything from posting a letter to catching the Metro.

ROME AREA BY AREA

The chapters covering the 16 central sightseeing areas are indicated by colour-coded bars. Each chapter opens with a portrait of the area and a list of the sights to be covered. These are located by numbers on an *Area Map*. This is followed by a large-scale *Street-by-Street Map* focusing on the most interesting part of the area. The main body of the chapter consists of detailed descriptions of all the sights. Finding your way about the chapter is made simple by a consistent numbering system used throughout for the sights. This refers to the order in which they are described in the chapter.

Sights at a Glance lists the sights in the area by category: Churches and Temples, Museums and Galleries, Historic Streets and Piazzas, Historic Buildings, Arches and Gates, Columns, Obelisks and Statues, Fountains, Ancient Sites and Parks and Gardens.

The area covered in greater detail on the *Street-by-Street Map* is shaded red.

1 Area Map

For easy reference, the sights in each area are numbered and located on a map of the area. To help the visitor, the map also shows Metro stations and parking areas.

Photographs of distinctive details of buildings help you to identify the sights.

Colour-coding on each page makes the area easy to find in the book.

Numbered circles pinpoint all the listed sights on the *Area Map*. Palazzo Doria Pamphilj, for example, is **6**.

2 Street-by-Street Map

This gives a bird's eye view of the heart of each sightseeing area. To help you locate and identify important sights as you walk around, these are picked out in stronger colour.

A locator map shows you exactly where you are in relation to surrounding areas. The area shown in the *Street-by-Street Map* is marked in red.

Palazzo Doria Pamphilj 6 is shown on this map as well.

A suggested route for a walk takes in the most interesting and attractive streets in the area.

Red stars indicate the sights that no visitor should miss.

Travel tips help you to reach the area quickly.

ROME AT A GLANCE
Each map in this section covers a specific theme: *Churches and Temples, Museums and Galleries, Fountains and Obelisks, Celebrated Visitors and Residents*. The top sights are shown on the map; other sights are described on the following two pages.

Each sightseeing area is colour-coded.

The theme is explored in greater detail on the two pages following the map.

3 Detailed information on each sight

All the important sights in each area are described individually. They are listed in order, following the numbering on the Area Map. *Practical information is also provided.*

PRACTICAL INFORMATION
Each entry provides all the information needed to visit the sight. A key to the symbols used is inside the back cover.

Map reference to *Street Finder* at back of book

Sight number

Address

Telephone number

Palazzo Doria Pamphilj 6

Palazzo del Collegio Romano 1A.
Map 5 A4 & 12 E3. 679 43 65.
56, 60, 62, 85, 90, 95, 160, 492.
Open 10am–1pm Tue, Fri, Sat & Sun.
Closed public hols. **Adm charge.**
compulsory for private apartments; notify attendant if you want tour.

Opening hours

Useful bus routes

Services and facilities available

4 Rome's major sights

These are given two or more full pages in the sightseeing area in which they are found. Historic buildings are dissected to reveal their interiors; and museums and galleries have colour-coded floorplans to help you find important exhibits.

The Visitors' Checklist provides the practical information you will need to plan your visit.

The facade of each major sight is shown to help you spot it quickly.

Red stars indicate the most interesting architectural details of the building, and the most important works of art or exhibits on view inside.

A timeline charts the key events in the history of the building.

INTRODUCING
ROME

PUTTING ROME ON THE MAP 10-13
THE HISTORY OF ROME 14-39
ROME AT A GLANCE 40-57
ROME THROUGH THE YEAR 58-61

Putting Rome on the Map

SINCE ITS FOUNDATION 2,700 years
ago on seven hills near the
banks of the River Tiber, Rome has
grown into a city of three million
people covering 1,500 sq km (580
sq miles) of southern Italy. Within
this area is the independent Vatican
City State. Rome was made capital of
the newly united Italy in 1870. It is
about 28 km (17 miles) from the sea and
has good rail and road links to many
other historic Italian towns and cities.

KEY

☐ Rome and Environs

— Main railway

✈ Airport

▰ Motorway

═ A road

0 kilometres   50

0 miles   25

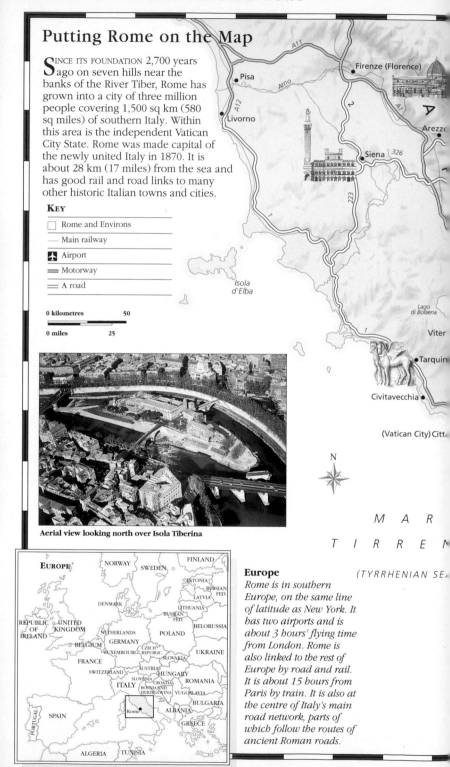

Aerial view looking north over Isola Tiberina

Pisa

Firenze (Florence)

Livorno

Arezzo

Siena

Isola
d'Elba

Lago
di Bolsena

Viter

Tarquin

Civitavecchia

N

(Vatican City) Citt

M A R

T I R R E N

(TYRRHENIAN SE

Europe

Rome is in southern
Europe, on the same line
of latitude as New York. It
has two airports and is
about 3 hours' flying time
from London. Rome is
also linked to the rest of
Europe by road and rail.
It is about 15 hours from
Paris by train. It is also at
the centre of Italy's main
road network, parts of
which follow the routes of
ancient Roman roads.

EUROPE
NORWAY SWEDEN FINLAND
ESTONIA
DENMARK LATVIA
LITHUANIA
RUSSIAN
FED.
RUSSIAN
FED.
REPUBLIC UNITED
OF KINGDOM
IRELAND NETHERLANDS BELORUSSIA
GERMANY POLAND
BELGIUM
LUXEMBOURG CZECH
REPUBLIC UKRAINE
FRANCE SLOVAKIA
SWITZERLAND AUSTRIA HUNGARY
SLOVENIA CROATIA ROMANIA
ITALY BOSNIA AND YUGOSLAVIA
HERZEGOVINA
Rome BULGARIA
PORTUGAL SPAIN ALBANIA
GREECE
ALGERIA TUNISIA

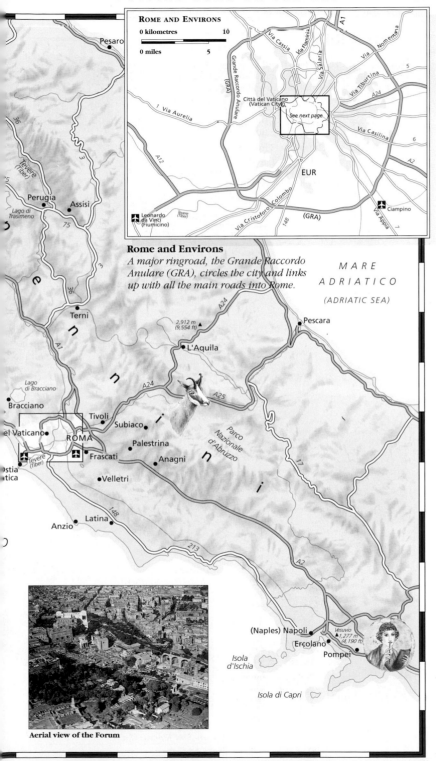

ROME AND ENVIRONS

0 kilometres 10

0 miles 5

Pesaro

Via Cassia
Via Flaminia
Via Salaria
Via Nomentana
A1
A24
Via Tiburtina
Grande Raccordo Anulare (GRA)
1 Via Aurelia
Città del Vaticano (Vatican City)
See next page
Via Casilina
A12
EUR
A2
Leonardo da Vinci (Fiumicino)
Tevere (Tiber)
Via Cristoforo Colombo
148
(GRA)
Via Appia
Ciampino

Rome and Environs
A major ringroad, the Grande Raccordo Anulare (GRA), circles the city and links up with all the main roads into Rome.

MARE
ADRIATICO
(ADRIATIC SEA)

Perugia

Assisi

Lago di Trasimeno

Tevere (Tiber)

75

36

Terni

A1

Lago di Bracciano

Bracciano

el Vaticano

ROMA

Tevere (Tiber)

Ostia Antica

Tivoli

Subiaco

Palestrina

Frascati

Anagni

Velletri

A24

2,912 m (9,554 ft)

L'Aquila

A24

A25

Parco Nazionale d'Abruzzo

Pescara

17

Latina

Anzio

148

213

A2

(Naples) Napoli

Ercolano

Pompei

Vesuvio 1,277 m (4,190 ft)

Isola d'Ischia

Isola di Capri

Aerial view of the Forum

Central Rome

MOST OF THE SIGHTS described in this book lie within the old city wall in 16 areas shown on the map below. Each of the areas has its own chapter. If you are on a short visit, you may have to restrict yourself to just a few of the central areas: the Forum to see ancient Rome; the Capitol, Piazza della Rotonda and Piazza Navona for the historic centre of the city; Campo de' Fiori for its grand Renaissance palazzi; Piazza di Spagna for its reminders of the 18th-century Grand Tour and its smart modern shops; and the Vatican to see St Peter's and the centre of Roman Catholicism.

PAGES 128–41
Street Finder maps
4, 5

0 metres   500

0 yards   500

N

Vatican

PAGES 222–49
Street Finder maps
3, 4

PAGES 116–27
Street Finder maps
4, 11, 12

PAGES 142–53
Street Finder maps
4, 8, 11, 12

Piazza di Spagna

Piazza della Rotonda

Piazza Navona

Campo de' Fiori

Janiculum

Trastevere

T I B E R

PAGES 214–21
Street Finder maps
3, 4, 7, 11

PAGES 206–13
Street Finder maps
4, 7, 8, 11

PAGES 102–15
Street Finder maps
4, 5, 12

PAGES 198–205
Street Finder maps
7, 8, 12

PAGES 154–65
Street Finder maps
5, 6, 12

PAGES 250–55
Street Finder maps
5, 6

PAGES 64–75
Street Finder maps
5, 12

PAGES 166–75
Street Finder maps
5, 6

PAGES 76–95
Street Finder maps
5, 8, 9, 12

PAGES 96–101
Street Finder map 8

Via Veneto

Quirinal

Esquiline

apitol

Forum

Palatine

Lateran

ventine

Caracalla

PAGES 188–97
Street Finder maps
8, 9

PAGES 176–87
Street Finder maps
6, 9, 10

THE HISTORY OF ROME

ONE OF THE most ancient cities in Europe, Rome was founded over 2,700 years ago. Since then it has been continuously inhabited, and, as the headquarters first of the Roman Empire and then of the Catholic Church, it has had an immense impact on the world. Many European languages are based on Latin; many political and legal systems follow the ancient Roman model; and buildings all round the world utilize styles and techniques perfected in ancient Rome. The city itself retains layers of buildings spanning over two millennia. Not surprisingly, all this history can seem a little overwhelming.

Roman eagle (2nd century AD)

Rome began as an Iron Age hut village, founded in the mid-8th century BC. In 616, the Romans' sophisticated Etruscan neighbours seized power, but were ousted in 509, when Rome became a Republic. It conquered most of the rest of Italy, then turned its attentions overseas, and by the 1st century BC, ruled Spain, North Africa and Greece. The expansion of the Empire provided opportunities for power-hungry individuals, and the clashing of egos led to the collapse of democracy. Julius Caesar ruled for a time as dictator, and his nephew Octavian became Rome's first emperor, assuming the title Augustus. During the reign of Augustus, Christ was born, and though Christians were persecuted until the 4th century, the new religion took hold and Rome became its main centre.

Even though it was the seat of the papacy, during the Middle Ages Rome went into decline. The city recovered spectacularly in the mid-15th century, and for over 200 years was embellished by the greatest artists of the Renaissance and the Baroque. Finally, in 1870, Rome became the capital of the newly unified Italy.

15th-century map of Rome from the north

Detail from 2nd-century AD Roman mosaic from the Temple of Fortune in Palestrina

Rome's Early Development

ACCORDING TO THE HISTORIAN Livy, Romulus founded
Rome in 753 BC. Sometime later, realizing his tribe
was short of females, he invited the neighbouring
Sabines to a festival, and orchestrated the mass
abduction of their women. Although Livy's account is
pure legend, there is evidence that Rome was founded
around the middle of the 8th century BC, and that the
Romans and Sabines united shortly afterwards.
Historical evidence also gives some support to Livy's
claim that after Romulus's death Rome was ruled by a
series of kings, and that in the 7th century BC it was
conquered by the Etruscans and ruled by the Tarquin
family. Last of the dynasty was Tarquinius Superbus
(Tarquin the Proud). His despotic rule led to the
Etruscans being expelled and the founding of a
Republic run by two annually elected consuls.
The uprising was led by Lucius Junius Brutus, the
model of the stern, patriotic Roman Republican.

EXTENT OF THE CITY

▨ 750 BC   ☐ Today

Ceremonial trumpets

Capitoline   Quirinal   Viminal

Palatine

Aventine   Celian   Esquiline

The Seven Hills of Rome
*By the 8th century BC, shepherds and
farmers lived on four of Rome's seven hills.
As the population grew, huts were built in the
marshy valley later occupied by the Forum.*

Iron Age Hut
*Early settlers lived
in wattle and
daub huts.
Traces of their
foundations
have been
found on the
Palatine.*

Augur, digging
foundation

TEMPLE OF JUPITER
*This Renaissance painting by Perin del
Vaga shows Tarquinius Superbus
founding the Temple of Jupiter on the
Capitol, the sacred citadel of Rome.*

TIMELINE

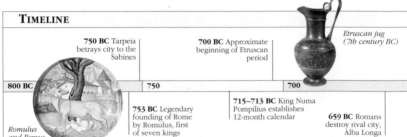

750 BC Tarpeia
betrays city to the
Sabines

700 BC Approximate
beginning of Etruscan
period

*Etruscan jug
(7th century BC)*

800 BC   750   700   6

*Romulus
and Remus*

753 BC Legendary
founding of Rome
by Romulus, first
of seven kings

715–713 BC King Numa
Pompilius establishes
12-month calendar

659 BC Romans
destroy rival city,
Alba Longa

☐   Rome's Early Development

The Legend of the She-Wolf
The evil King of Alba threw his baby nephews, Romulus and Remus, into the Tiber but they were washed ashore, and suckled by a she-wolf.

Raven, guardian of the citadel

Apollo of Veio
Etruscan culture and religion were influenced by the Greeks. This 5th- or 6th-century statue of the Greek god Apollo comes from Veio, a powerful, wealthy Etruscan city.

King Tarquin, holding stone worshipped as a thunderbolt

The Legend of Aeneas
Some Roman legends make the Trojan hero Aeneas the grandfather of Romulus and Remus.

WHERE TO SEE ETRUSCAN ROME

The Cloaca Maxima sewer still functions, but there are few other traces of Etruscan Rome. Most finds come from Etruscan sites outside Rome like Tarquinia, with its tomb paintings of sumptuous banquets *(see p271)*, but there are good collections in the Villa Giulia *(pp262–3)* and Vatican Museums *(p238)*. The most famous object, however, is a bronze statue of the legendary she-wolf in the Capitoline Museums *(p73)*. The Antiquarium Forense *(p87)* displays objects from the necropolis which once occupied the site of the Roman Forum.

Funeral urns shaped like huts were used for cremation from the mid-8th century BC.

Etruscan jewellery, like this 7th-century BC gold filigree brooch, was lavish. Treasures of this kind have given the Etruscans a reputation for luxurious living.

578 BC Servius Tullius Etruscan King

600 BC Possible date of construction of Cloaca Maxima sewer

565 BC Traditional date of the Servian Wall around Rome's seven hills

Statue of Jupiter

510 BC Temple of Jupiter consecrated on Capitoline

| 600 | 550 | 500 |

616 BC Tarquinius Priscus, first Etruscan king. Forum and Circus Maximus established

534 BC King Servius murdered

509 BC L J Brutus expels Etruscans from Rome and founds the Republic

L J Brutus

507 BC War against Etruscans. Horatius defends wooden bridge across Tiber

Kings, Consuls and Emperors

ROME HAD OVER 250 RULERS in the 1,200 years between its
foundation by Romulus and AD 476, when the last emperor
was deposed by the German warrior, Odoacer. Romulus was the
first of seven kings, overthrown in 509 BC when Rome became a
Republic. Authority was held by two annually elected consuls, but
provision was made for the appointment of a dictator in times of
crisis. In 494 BC, the office of Tribune was set up to protect the
plebeians from injustice at the hands of their patrician rulers.
Roman democracy, however, was always cosmetic. It was
discarded completely
in 27 BC, when
absolute power
was placed in
the hands of
the emperor.

70–63 BC Pompey

107–87 BC
Marius is
consul
seven times

205 BC Scipio
Africanus

218 BC Quintus Fabius
Maximus

*Romulus, his twin Remus and
the she-wolf who suckled them*

456 BC Lucius
Quintus
Cincinnatus

c753–715 BC
Romulus

800 BC	700	600	500	400	300	200	100
SEVEN KINGS			REPUBLIC				
800 BC	700	600	500	400	300	200	100

c715–673 BC
Numa
Pompilius

c673–641 BC
Tullus Hostilius

c641–616 BC
Ancus Marcius

396 BC Marcus
Furius Camillus

c509 BC Lucius
Junius Brutus and
Horatius Pulvillus

c534–509 BC
Tarquinius Superbus

c579–534 BC
Servius Tullius

616–579 BC
Tarquinius Priscus

133 BC Tiberius Gracchus

122–121 BC
Gaius Gracchus

82–80 BC
Sulla

63 BC
Cicero

60–50 BC Triumvirate
of Julius Caesar,
Pompey and Crassus

45–44 BC Julius
Caesar is sole ruler

*Julius Caesar,
whose rise to
power marked
the end of the
Roman Republic*

Tarquinius Priscus consulting an augur

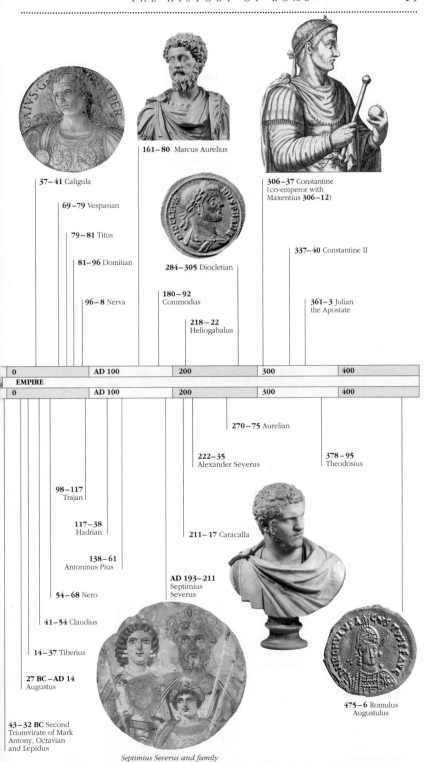

37–41 Caligula

161–80 Marcus Aurelius

69–79 Vespasian

79–81 Titus

81–96 Domitian

284–305 Diocletian

96–8 Nerva

180–92
Commodus

218–22
Heliogabalus

306–37 Constantine
(co-emperor with
Maxentius 306–12)

337–40 Constantine II

361–3 Julian
the Apostate

| 0 | AD 100 | 200 | 300 | 400 |

EMPIRE

| 0 | AD 100 | 200 | 300 | 400 |

270–75 Aurelian

222–35
Alexander Severus

378–95
Theodosius

98–117
Trajan

117–38
Hadrian

211–17 Caracalla

138–61
Antoninus Pius

AD 193–211
Septimius
Severus

54–68 Nero

41–54 Claudius

14–37 Tiberius

27 BC–AD 14
Augustus

475–6 Romulus
Augustulus

43–32 BC Second
Triumvirate of Mark
Antony, Octavian
and Lepidus

Septimius Severus and family

The Roman Republic

Bronze coin, showing Temple of Vesta (c57 BC)

BY THE MID-2ND CENTURY BC, Rome controlled the west Mediterranean, policing and defending it with massive armies. The troops had more loyalty to the generals than to distant politicians, giving men like Marius, Sulla, Pompey and Caesar the muscle to seize political power. Meanwhile, peasants, whose land had been destroyed during the invasion of Hannibal in 219 BC, had flooded into Rome. They were followed by slaves and freedmen from conquered lands such as Greece, swelling the population to half a million. There was plenty of work for immigrants, constructing roads, aqueducts, markets and temples, financed by taxes on Rome's expanding trade.

EXTENT OF THE CITY

▨ *400 BC*   ☐ *Today*

Cut stone blocks

Covered water channels

Arch spanning road

The gradient of an aqueduct was about 1 in 1,000.

How an Aqueduct Worked
Water from a spring in the hills was collected in a reservoir to build up pressure and ensure a steady supply to the city.

High ground

Cleaning vent

Reservoir

Underground water channel

Arches carrying water across low ground

Cicero Denounces Catiline
In 62 BC Catiline planned a coup. Cicero discovered the plot and persuaded the Senate to condemn the conspirators to death.

TIMELINE

499 BC Battle against Latin tribes; Temple of Castor and Pollux built to commemorate the victory

380 BC Servian Wall rebuilt

396 BC Definitive victory over rival Etruscan city, Veio

Via Appia

312 BC Construction of Via Appia and Rome's first aqueduct, the Aqua Appia

500 BC	450 BC	400 BC	350 BC	300 B◗

Relief of Capitoline geese

390 BC Rome invaded by Celtic Gauls: quacking geese on Capitoline hill warn of impending attack

264–241 BC First Punic War (against Carthage)

☐ **Roman Republic**

Roman Street
In the 1st century BC, most buildings in Rome were made from brick and concrete. Only a few public buildings used marble.

AQUEDUCT (2ND CENTURY BC)
Rome owed much of her prosperity to her skilled civil engineers. When the city's wells were no longer sufficient, aqueducts were built to bring water from surrounding hills. Some were over 80 km (50 miles) long.

Arches for maintaining a constant gradient over low-lying land

Temple of Juno
The ruins of this 197 BC temple are embedded in the church of San Nicola in Carcere (see p152). Romans consulted their gods before all important ventures.

Scipio Africanus
In 202 BC the Roman general Scipio defeated Hannibal. Rome replaced Carthage as master of the Mediterranean.

WHERE TO SEE REPUBLICAN ROME

This fresco depicting a gang of slaves building a wall can be seen at the Museo Nazionale Romano (see p163).

The Temple of Saturn, first built in 497 BC, now consists of eight majestic columns overlooking the Forum at the end of the Via Sacra (see p83).

Rome's loveliest Republican buildings are the two Temples of the Forum Boarium (see p203). Four more temples can be seen in the Area Sacra of Largo Argentina (p150). Most monuments from this period, however, lie underground. Only a few, like the Tomb of the Scipios (p195), have been excavated. One of the bridges leading to Tiber Island (p152), the Ponte Fabricio, dates from the 1st century BC and is still used by pedestrians.

Ponte Fabricio, built in 62 BC

220 BC Via Flaminia built, linking Rome to the Adriatic coast

168 BC Victory in Macedonian War completes Roman conquest of Greece

133–120 BC Gracchi brothers killed for trying to introduce land reforms

51 BC Caesar conquers Gaul

250 BC	200 BC	150 BC	100 BC

218–202 BC Second Punic War; Scipio Africanus defeats Carthaginians

Hannibal

149–146 BC Third Punic War; Carthage destroyed

71 BC Spartacus's slave revolt crushed by Crassus and Pompey

60 BC Rome has three joint rulers: Pompey, Crassus and Caesar

Imperial Rome

IN 44 BC Caesar became dictator for life, only to be assassinated a month later. The result was 17 years of civil war, which ended only in 27 BC when Augustus became Rome's first emperor. The Empire expanded in fits and starts, but by the late 3rd century was so huge that Diocletian decided to share it between four emperors. Thanks to trade and taxes from its vast domains, Rome was the most magnificent city in the world, studded with the lavish buildings of emperors keen to advertise their civic munificence and military triumphs.

Statue of Bacchus, god of wine

EXTENT OF THE CITY

AD 250   Today

Cross-vaulted ceiling with mosaic decoration

Natatio (swimming pool)

Apotheosis of Augustus
The first and perhaps the greatest Roman emperor, Augustus ruled for 27 years and was deified by the Senate after his death.

ROMA CAPVT MVNDI

The baths could hold up to 3,000 people. They met to gossip in the central *frigidarium* (cold room).

Area for exercise and gymnastics

The Roman Empire under Trajan
By the 2nd century AD, the Roman Empire stretched from Britain to Syria, and Rome was known as the Caput Mundi, *the head of the world.*

TIMELINE

49 BC Caesar crosses the Rubicon and takes Rome

27 Augustus becomes first emperor

Emperor Nero

64 Fire during Nero's rule destroys much of city

65 First persecution of Christians under Nero

72 Colosseum begun

50 BC | **0** | **AD 50** | **100**

44 Caesar becomes dictator for life, and is murdered by Brutus and Cassius

13 Ara Pacis is erected to celebrate the peace Augustus has secured in the Empire

AD 42 St Peter the Apostle comes to Rome

67 St Peter is crucified and St Paul executed in Rome

Statue of St Peter in San Paolo fuori le Mura

☐ **Imperial Rome**

Roman Revelry
Banquets could last for ten hours, with numerous courses. In order to continue eating, guests would retire to a small room to vomit between courses.

WHERE TO SEE IMPERIAL ROME
There are relics of Imperial Rome throughout the city centre, some hidden below churches and palazzi, others like the Forum (*see pp76–87*), the Palatine (*pp97–101*) and the Imperial Fora (*pp88–91*), fully excavated. The magnificence of the era, however, is best conveyed by the Pantheon (*pp110–11*) and the Colosseum (*pp92–5*).

BATHS OF DIOCLETIAN (AD 298)
Rome's public baths were not just places to keep clean. They also had bars, libraries, barbers' shops, brothels and sports facilities.

The Arch of Titus *(p87)*, erected in the Forum in AD 81, commemorates Emperor Titus's Sack of Jerusalem in AD 70.

Tepidarium (warm room)

A relief of Mithras, a popular Persian god (3rd century AD), can be seen beneath the church of San Clemente (*pp186–7*).

Virgil (70–19 BC)
Virgil was Rome's greatest epic poet. His most famous work is the Aeneid, *the story of the Trojan hero, Aeneas's journey to the future site of Rome.*

164–180 Plague rages in Roman Empire

212 Citizenship granted to virtually all inhabitants of the Empire

270 Aurelian Wall begun

Section of Aurelian Wall

150

200

250

125 Hadrian redesigns the Pantheon

216 Baths of Caracalla completed

247 Rome's Millennium is celebrated

284 Empire divided into West and East

Mosaic from the Baths of Caracalla

Early Christian Rome

Crucifixion in Santa Maria Antiqua

In the 1st century AD, during the reign of Tiberius, a rebellious pacifist was crucified in a distant corner of the Empire. This was nothing unusual, but within a few years Jesus Christ and his teachings became notorious in Rome, his followers were perceived as a threat to public order, and many were executed. This was no deterrent, and the new religion spread through all levels of Roman society. When the Apostles Peter and Paul arrived in Rome there was already a small Christian community, and in spite of continued persecution by the state, Christianity flourished. In AD 313 the Emperor Constantine issued an edict granting freedom of worship to Christians, and soon after founded a shrine on the site of St Peter's tomb. This secured Rome's position as a centre of Christianity, but in the 5th century the political importance of Rome declined and the city fell to Goths and other invaders.

EXTENT OF THE CITY

▨ *AD 395*   ☐ *Today*

St Paul

Youthful, beardless representation of Christ

Santo Stefano Rotondo
This 17th-century engraving shows how a Roman temple (top) might have been transformed (above) into the 5th-century round church of Santo Stefano.

Classical-style border decorated with fruit

4th-Century Mosaic, Santa Costanza
Beautiful mosaics, often with palm trees and other oriental motifs suggesting Jerusalem, helped spread the message of early Christianity.

The Good Shepherd
The pagan image of a shepherd sacrificing a lamb became a Christian symbol.

Timeline

Gold solidus of Theodosius

300	350	400	450

c320 Building of first St Peter's

356 Legendary founding of Santa Maria Maggiore

410 Rome sacked by Alaric's Goths

455 Rome sacked again by Vandals

312 Control of Empire won by Constantine after battle at Milvian Bridge

Battle of the Milvian Bridge

380 Emperor Theodosius makes Christianity the official religion of the Roman Empire

395 Division of the Empire between Ravenna and Constantinople

422 Founding of Santa Sabina

☐ **Early Christian Rome**

Epigraph of Peter and Paul
This is one of hundreds of early Christian graffiti housed in the Lapidary Gallery of the Vatican (see p237).

Crucifixion, Santa Sabina
This 5th-century panel on the door of Santa Sabina (see p204) is one of the earliest known representations of the Crucifixion. Interestingly, Christ's cross is not actually shown.

St Peter receiving peace from the Saviour

Lambs symbolizing the Christian flock

Constantine's Cross
Constantine's vision of the True Cross during the Battle of the Milvian Bridge made him convert to Christianity.

WHERE TO SEE EARLY CHRISTIAN ROME

There are traces of early Christianity all over Rome. Many ancient churches were built over early Christian meeting places and sites of martyrdoms: among them San Clemente *(see pp186–7)*, Santa Pudenziana *(p171)* and Santa Cecilia *(p211)*. Outside the walls of the old city are miles of underground catacombs *(pp265–6)*, many decorated with Christian frescoes, while the Vatican's Pio-Christian Museum *(p240)* has the best collection of early Christian art.

This statuette, carved out of bone, is embedded in the rock of the Catacombs of San Panfilo, just off the Via Salaria (**map** 2 F4).

The Cross of Justin, in the Treasury of St Peter's *(p232)*, was given to Rome by the Emperor Justin in AD 578.

A Byzantine image of St Paul

475 Fall of Western Roman Empire; Byzantium becomes seat of Empire

496 Anastasius II is first pope to assume title *Pontifex Maximus*

590–604 Pope Gregory the Great strengthens the papacy

609 Pantheon is consecrated as a Christian church

630 Sant'Agnese fuori le Mura is built in Roman Byzantine style

500   550   600

The Papacy

THE POPE is considered Christ's representative on earth, claiming his authority from St Peter, the first Bishop of Rome. Though some popes have been great thinkers and reformers, the role has rarely been purely spiritual. In the Middle Ages, many popes were involved in power struggles with the Holy Roman Emperor. Renaissance popes like Julius II and Leo X, the patrons of Raphael and Michelangelo, lived as luxuriously as any secular prince. The popes listed here include all those who exercised significant political or religious influence, up as far as the end of the Counter Reformation, when the power of the papacy began to wane.

St Ludovic Kneels before Boniface VIII *by Simone Martini*

314–35 St Sylvester I

222–30 St Urban I

217–22 St Callixtus I

590–604 St Gregory the Great

496–8 St Anastasius II

Gregory the Great leading a procession to end the plague

931–5 John XI

891–6 Formosus

955–64 John XII

1227–41 Gregory IX

1216–27 Honorius III Savelli

0	200	400	600	800	1000	1200

PAPACY BASED IN ROME

0	200	400	600	800	1000	1200

336–7 St Mark

352–66 Liberius

90–9 St Clement

42–67 St Peter

579–90 Pelagius II

608–15 St Boniface IV

731–41 St Gregory III

772–95 Adrian I

1047–8 Benedict IX

1073–85 St Gregory VII

1099–1118 Paschal II

1130–43 Innocent II

1154–9 Adrian IV

847–55 St Leo IV

817–24 St Paschal I

1198–1216 Innocent III

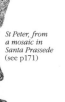

St Peter, from a mosaic in Santa Prassede (see p171)

795–816 St Leo III

Innocent III's Vision of the Church, *from a fresco by Giotto*

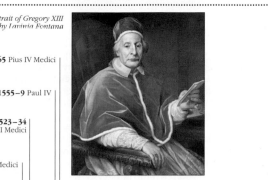

*Portrait of Gregory XIII
by Lavinia Fontana*

1559–65 Pius IV Medici

1555–9 Paul IV

1523–34
Clement VII Medici

1513–21 Leo X Medici

1492–1503
Alexander
VI Borgia

1572–85 Gregory XIII Boncompagni

1294–1303
Boniface VIII

1670–76 Clement X Altieri

1484–92
Innocent VIII Cybo

1667–9 Clement IX

1655–67
Alexander VII Chigi

1471–84 Sixtus IV della Rovere

1464–71 Paul II Barbo

1605 Leo XI
Medici

1700–21 Clement XI

1458–64
Pius II Piccolomini

1300	1400	1500	1600	1700
AVIGNON	PAPACY AGAIN BASED IN ROME			
1300	1400	1500	1600	1700

1644–55 Innocent X Pamphilj

1417–31
Martin V Colonna

1447–55
Nicholas V

1585–90
Sixtus V

1623–44 Urban VIII Barberini

Nicholas V Receiving a
Book, *illustration from a
contemporary manuscript*

1592–1605
Clement VIII
Aldobrandini

1503–13 Julius II della Rovere

1605–21 Paul V
Borghese

Urban VIII Approving a Building
Project *in the Vatican's Gallery
of Tapestries* (see p241)

Raphael's portrait of Julius II

1534–49 Paul III Farnese

Paul III Gives his Approval to
the Capuchin Order *by
Sebastiano Ricci*

Medieval Rome

Mosaic, San Clemente

Supplanted by CONSTANTINOPLE as capital of the Empire in the 4th century, Rome was reduced to a few thousand inhabitants by the early Middle Ages; its power was just a memory, its monuments little more than weed-covered ruins. In the 8th and 9th centuries, the growing importance of the papacy revived the city and made it once more a centre of power. But continual conflicts between the pope and the Holy Roman Emperor soon weakened the papacy. The 10th, 11th and 12th centuries were among the bleakest in Roman history: violent conflict with invaders left Rome poverty-stricken and the constantly warring local barons tore apart what remained of the city. In 1309 the papacy was forced to move to Avignon, leaving Rome to slide into further squalor and strife.

EXTENT OF THE CITY

■ 1300   □ Today

Charlemagne Crowned in St Peter's
On Christmas Day in 800, Charlemagne was made emperor of the Holy Roman Empire, a new Christian dominion to replace that of ancient Rome.

Madonna and Child Mosaic
The Chapel of St Zeno (817–24) in the church of Santa Prassede (see p171) has some of the best examples of Byzantine mosaics in Rome.

San Giovanni in Laterano

Aurelian Wall

Column of Trajan

Column of Marcus Aurelius

MEDIEVAL PLAN OF ROME
Maps like this one, illustrating the principal features of the city, were produced for pilgrims, the tourists of the Middle Ages.

TIMELINE

700	800	900	1000
725 King Ine of Wessex founds the first hostel for pilgrims in the Borgo	**852** The Vatican is fortified with walls following a raid by Saracens	*Emperor Otto I*	**961** King Otto the Great becomes first German Holy Roman Emperor
778 Charlemagne, King of the Franks, conquers Italy	**800** Charlemagne crowned emperor in St Peter's	**880–932** Rome is ruled by two women, Theodora and then her daughter, Marozia	

□ **Medieval Rome**

Stefaneschi Triptych *(1315)* *Giotto and his pupils painted this triptych for Cardinal Stefaneschi as an altarpiece for St Peter's. It is now in the Vatican Museums* (see p240).

WHERE TO SEE MEDIEVAL ROME

Among the most interesting churches of the period are San Clemente, with a fine apse mosaic and Cosmati floor *(see pp186–7)*, Santa Maria in Trastevere *(pp212–13)* and Santa Maria sopra Minerva, Rome's only Gothic church *(p108)*. Santa Cecilia in Trastevere *(p211)* has a Cavallini fresco, and there is fine Cosmati work in Santa Maria in Cosmedin *(p202)*.

Colosseum | Capitol | Pyramid of Caius Cestius

Old St Peter's

Castel Sant'Angelo

Pantheon

Cosmati Tabernacle *Marblework by the Cosmati family, like this tabernacle in Santa Sabina* (see p204), *decorates many of Rome's medieval churches.*

Charlemagne's Dalmatic in the Treasury of St Peter's *(p232)* was supposedly worn by the Holy Roman Emperor at his coronation. In fact the richly embroidered vestment probably dates from the 14th century.

Santa Sabina *(p204)* on the Aventine Hill has a medieval bell-tower.

| **1084** Rome is attacked by Normans | **1108** San Clemente is rebuilt | **1200** Rome an independent commune under Arnaldo di Brescia | **1300** First Holy Year proclaimed by Pope Boniface VIII | **1309** Pope Clement V moves the papacy to Avignon | **1348** Black Death strikes Rome |

| **1100** | **1200** | **1300** |

Mosaic facade, Santa Maria in Trastevere (pp212–13) | **1140** Santa Maria in Trastevere is restored | **1232** Cloister of San Giovanni in Laterano completed | *Cola di Rienzo* | **1347** Cola di Rienzo – an Italian patriot – tries to restore the Roman Republic |

Renaissance Rome

POPE NICHOLAS V came to the throne in 1447 determined to make Rome a city fit for the papacy. Among his successors, men like Julius II and Leo X eagerly followed his lead, and the city's appearance was transformed. The Classical ideals of the Renaissance inspired artists, architects and craftsmen, such as Michelangelo, Bramante, Raphael and Cellini, to build and decorate the churches and palaces of a newly confident Rome.

Detail of Botticelli's *Youth of Moses* (1480s)

EXTENT OF THE CITY

◻ 1500   ☐ Today

Hemispherical dome

Balustrade of small columns

Classical colonnade of 16 Doric columns

School of Athens by Raphael
In this fresco (see p243) Raphael complimented many of his peers by representing them as ancient Greek philosophers. The building shown is based on a design by Bramante.

THE TEMPIETTO
The Tempietto (1502) at San Pietro in Montorio (see p219) was one of Bramante's first works in Rome. A simple, perfectly proportioned miniature Classical temple, it is a model of High Renaissance architecture.

Cosmati-style mosaic floor

Palazzo Caprini
Bramante's design had a strong influence on later Renaissance palazzi. Parts of the building survive in Palazzo dei Convertendi (see p227).

TIMELINE

1377 Papacy returns to Rome from Avignon under Pope Gregory XI

1409–15 Papacy moves to Pisa

1452 Demolition of old St Peter's basilica begins

1444 Birth of Bramante

1350	1400	1450

1378–1417 The Great Schism, a division in the papacy in Avignon

1417 Pope Martin V ends the Great Schism in the papacy

Pope Martin V, reigned 1417–31

☐ Renaissance Rome

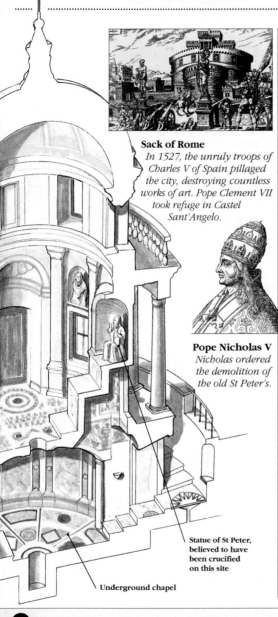

Sack of Rome
In 1527, the unruly troops of Charles V of Spain pillaged the city, destroying countless works of art. Pope Clement VII took refuge in Castel Sant'Angelo.

Pope Nicholas V
Nicholas ordered the demolition of the old St Peter's.

Statue of St Peter, believed to have been crucified on this site

Underground chapel

WHERE TO SEE RENAISSANCE ROME

The Campo de' Fiori area *(see pp142–53)* is full of grand Renaissance palazzi, especially along Via Giulia *(pp276–7)*. Across the river stands the delightful Villa Farnesina *(pp220–21)*. The most typical church of the period is Santa Maria del Popolo *(pp138–9)*, and the best collection of Renaissance art is in the Vatican Museums *(pp234–47)*. These include the Sistine Chapel *(pp244–7)* and the Raphael Rooms *(pp242–3)*.

The Madonna di Foligno by Raphael (1511–12) is one of the fine Renaissance paintings in the Vatican Pinacoteca *(p241)*.

The Pietà, commissioned for St Peter's in 1501, was one of Michelangelo's first sculptures executed in Rome *(p233)*.

1483 Birth of Raphael

1486 Building of Palazzo della Cancelleria

1519 Frescoes completed in Villa Farnesina

1527 Troops of Emperor Charles V sack Rome

Emperor Charles

1500

1550

1475 Birth of Michelangelo

1506 Pope Julius II orders start of work on new St Peter's

1508 Michelangelo begins painting the Sistine Chapel ceiling

Cumaean Sibyl, Sistine Chapel

1547 Pope Paul III appoints Michelangelo architect of St Peter's

Baroque Rome

Baroque putto

BY THE 16TH CENTURY, the Catholic Church had become immensely rich – one of the chief criticisms of the Protestant reformers. The display of grandeur and extravagance by the papal court contrasted sharply with the poverty of the people, and wealthy Roman society was characterized by sumptuous luxury and a ceaseless round of entertainment. To make the Catholic faith more appealing than Protestantism, scores of churches were built and monuments and fountains were erected to glorify the Holy See. The finest architects in the ornate, dramatic style of the Baroque were Bernini and Borromini.

EXTENT OF THE CITY

▇ 1645	☐ Today

Ceiling portraying heavenly scenes

Monument to Pope Alexander VII
This Bernini tomb in St Peter's (pp230–33) includes a skeleton brandishing an hour glass.

Gian Lorenzo Bernini *(1598–1680)*
The favourite artist of the papacy, Bernini transformed Rome with his churches, palaces, statues and fountains.

Holy Family fresco

Tapestry of Pope Urban VIII
Bernini's most devoted patron, Pope Urban VIII Barberini (1623–44), is shown here receiving the homage of the nations.

A marble rose marks the best place to stand to appreciate the illusion of space created by the artist.

TIMELINE

1568 The Jesuits build the Gesù, prototypical church of the early Baroque

Altar carving from the Gesù

1595 Annibale Carracci begins to fresco Palazzo Farnese

1624 Bernini's sculpture of *Apollo and Daphne*

1626 Work on St Peter's is completed

1550	1575	1600	1625

1571 Birth of Caravaggio

1585 Pope Sixtus V plans new streets

1600 Philosopher Giordano Bruno is burnt at the stake for heresy

Galileo

1633 Galileo condemned to death in Rome for heresy

☐ **Baroque Rome**

Illusionistic beams in ceiling

Chapel painted on flat slanting wall

Figures painted to be viewed from an angle

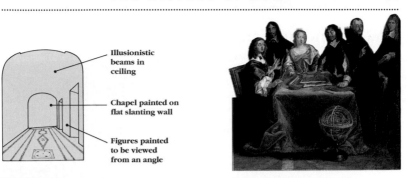

Queen Christina of Sweden
In a coup for Catholicism, Christina renounced Protestantism and abdicated her throne. In 1655 she moved to Rome, where she became the centre of a lively literary and scientific circle.

St Ignatius, founder of the Jesuits

Francesco Borromini
(1599–1667)
In the many churches he built in Rome, Borromini made use of revolutionary geometric forms.

San Carlo alle Quattro Fontane
One of Borromini's most influential designs was this tiny oval church (see p161) *on the Quirinal hill.*

POZZO CORRIDOR
The use of perspective to create an illusion of depth and space was a favourite Baroque device. Andrea Pozzo painted this illusionistic corridor in the 1680s in the Rooms of St Ignatius near the Gesù (see pp114–15).

1651 Bernini redesigns much of Piazza Navona

Bernini's Fontana dei Fiumi in Piazza Navona

1694 Palazzo di Montecitorio is completed

1735 Spanish Steps are designed

1732 Works start on Trevi Fountain

| 1650 | 1675 | 1700 | 1725 |

1657 Borromini completes Sant'Agnese in Agone

Bonnie Prince Charlie, pretender to the throne of England

1656 Work starts on Bernini's colonnade for St Peter's square

1721 Bonnie Prince Charlie is born in Rome

1734 Clement XII makes Palazzo Nuovo world's first public museum

Understanding Rome's Architecture

Arch of Titus

THE ARCHITECTURE of Imperial Rome kept alive the Classical styles of ancient Greece, at the same time developing new, uniquely Roman forms based on the arch, the vault and the dome. The next important period was the 12th century, when many Romanesque churches were built. The Renaissance saw a return to Classical ideals, inspired by the example of Florence, but in the 17th century Rome found a style of its own again in the flamboyance of the Baroque.

The entablature above these columns has both straight and arched sections (Hadrian's Villa).

CLASSICAL ROME

Most Roman buildings were of concrete faced with brick, but from the 1st century BC, the Romans started to imitate earlier Greek models, using marble to decorate temples and other public buildings.

Corinthian capital

Plain frieze

Triangular pediment

Cornice (projecting section along facade)

Architrave (horizontal section resting on columns)

Fluted column shaft

Podium

Cella (inner sanctuary)

Colonnade enclosing portico

Roman temples were usually built on a raised dais or podium, to make them prominent. Many were fronted by a portico, a roofed porch with columns.

Caryatids were sculpted columns, usually in the form of a female figure. Roman caryatids, like this one in the Forum of Augustus, were often copied in detail from earlier Greek examples.

The orders of Classical architecture were building styles, each based on a different column design. The three major orders were borrowed by the Romans from the Greeks.

Doric order   **Ionic order**   **Corinthian order**

Aedicules were small shrines, framed by two pillars, usually containing a statue of a god.

Coffers were decorative sunken panels that reduced the weight of domed and vaulted ceilings.

EARLY CHRISTIAN AND MEDIEVAL ROME

The first Christian churches in Rome were based on the basilica: oblong, with three naves, each usually ending in an apse. From the 10th to the 13th century, most churches were built in the Romanesque style, which used the rounded arches of ancient Rome.

Basilicas in Rome have, in most cases, kept their original rectangular shape. The nave of San Giovanni in Laterano retains its 4th-century floorplan.

The triumphal arch divides the nave of a church from the apse. Here, in San Paolo fuori le Mura, it is decorated with mosaics.

RENAISSANCE AND BAROQUE ROME

Renaissance architecture (15th–16th centuries) drew its inspiration directly from Classical models. It revived the use of strict geometric proportions. The Baroque age (late 16th–17th centuries) broke many established rules, favouring grandiose decoration over pure Classical forms.

Putti were a popular decorative feature in the Baroque. A putto is a painting or a sculpture of a child like a Cupid or cherub.

A loggia is an open-sided gallery or arcade. It may be a separate structure or part of a building, as here at San Saba.

A tabernacle is used to house the Sacrament for the mass. This 13th-century Gothic wall tabernacle is in San Clemente.

A baldacchino is a canopy, supported on columns, rising over the main altar. This Baroque example is in St Peter's.

Rusticated masonry decorates the exterior of many Renaissance palazzi. It consists of massive blocks divided by deep joints.

COSMATESQUE SCULPTURE AND MOSAICS

The Cosmati family, active in Rome during the 12th and 13th centuries, have given their name to a particularly Roman style of decoration. They worked in marble, producing all kinds of fittings for churches, including cloisters, episcopal thrones, tombs, pulpits, fonts and candlesticks. These were often decorated with

Cosmatesque floor, Santa Maria in Cosmedin

bands of colourful mosaic. They also left many fine floor mosaics, usually of white marble with an inlay of red and green porphyry. Ancient Roman columns were cut up to provide the materials. Several other families of stonemasons used a similar style, and their work is also described as Cosmatesque.

Rome during Unification

U NDER NAPOLEON, Italy had a brief taste
of unity, but by 1815 it was once more
divided into many small states and
papal rule was restored in Rome. Over
the next 50 years, patriots, led by
Mazzini, Garibaldi and others,
struggled to create an independent,
unified Italy. In 1848 Rome was
briefly declared a Republic, but
Garibaldi's forces were driven out by French troops.
The French continued to protect the pope, while the
rest of Italy was united as a kingdom under Vittorio
Emanuele of Savoy. In 1870, troops stormed
the city, and Rome became capital of Italy.

**Garibaldi in his
distinctive red shirt**

EXTENT OF THE CITY

▨ *1870* ▢ *Today*

Porta Pia

Tricoloured
flag of the
new Italian
kingdom

Plumed hat of
the Bersaglieri,
crack troops
from Savoy

Allegory of Italy's Liberty
*This patriotic poster from
1890 shows the king,
his chief minister
Cavour, Garibaldi and
Mazzini. The woman
in red represents Italy.*

Vittorio Emanuele II
*Vittorio Emanuele, King
of Piedmont, became the
first King of Italy in 1861.*

ROYALISTS STORM PORTA PIA
*On 20 September 1870, troops of the
kingdom of Italy put an end to the
papal domination of Rome. They
breached the city walls near Porta
Pia; the pope retreated and Rome
was made the Italian capital.*

TIMELINE

1751 Piranesi's *Views of Rome* revive interest in Classical ruins	**1762** Trevi Fountain is completed	*Napoleon Bonaparte*		**1797** Napoleon captures Rome	**1799** Napoleon expelled from Italy by Austrians and Russians
1750		**1775**			**1800**

*Piranesi etching of
Trajan's Forum*

1792 Canova creates
the Tomb of Pope
Clement XIII, St
Peter's

1800–1
Napoleon takes
Italy again

1807 Birth
of Garibaldi

▢ **Rome during Unification**

Garibaldi and Rome

The charismatic leader Giuseppe Garibaldi had taken much of Italy from foreign rule by 1860. Rome still remained a crucial problem. Here he declares "O Roma o morte" (Rome or Death).

Villa Paolina

Giuseppe Verdi (1813–1901)

Verdi, the opera composer, supported unification and in 1861 became a member of Italy's first national parliament.

Breach in Aurelian Wall

A Freed City

This marble plaque was set up at Porta Pia to commemorate the liberation of Rome.

Victor Emmanuel Monument

A vast monument to Italy's first king (see p74) stands at the end of Via del Corso.

S · P · Q · R ·
VRBE · ITALIAE · VINDICATA
INCOLIS · FELICITER · AVCTIS
GEMINOS · FORNICES · CONDIDIT

1816 Work begins on Piazza del Popolo

Fountain in Piazza del Popolo

1848 Nationalist uprising in Rome. Pope flees and a Republic is formed

1860 Garibaldi and his 1,000 followers take Sicily and Naples

1870 Royalist troops take Rome, completing the unification of Italy

1825

1850

1820 Revolts throughout Italy

1821 Keats dies in Piazza di Spagna

1849 Pope is restored to power, protected by a French garrison

Pope Pius IX

1861 Kingdom of Italy founded with capital in Turin

Twentieth-Century Rome

World Cup mania

The FASCIST DICTATOR, Mussolini, dreamed of recreating the immensity, order and power of the old Roman Empire: "Rome", he said, "must appear wonderful to the whole world." He planned to build a massive Palace of Fascism by the Forum. This came to nothing, though he did begin to build a grandiose new complex, EUR, in the suburbs, and razed 15 churches and many medieval houses to create space for wide new roads. Fortunately most of the old centre has survived, leaving the city with one of Europe's most picturesque historic cores.

EXTENT OF THE CITY

☐ 1960s   ☐ Today

Placido Domingo | José Carreras | Luciano Pavarotti

Mussolini's Plans for Rome
This propaganda poster reflects Mussolini's grandiose projects such as Via dei Fori Imperiali in the Forum area (see p76), and EUR (p267).

Pope John Paul II
John Paul II is the first non-Italian pope since the 1520s. A traditionalist, he exerts a tremendous influence on the lives of the world's Catholics.

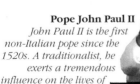

THREE TENORS CONCERT (1990)
Combining Italy's love for music and football, this opera recital at the Baths of Caracalla was broadcast live during the World Cup.

TIMELINE

1900	1912	1925	1938

1915 Italy enters World War I

1926 Opposition parties banned

1946 National referendum establishes Italy as a Republic; King Umberto II exiled

1944 Allies liberate Rome from Germans

1911 Victor Emmanuel Monument is completed

1922 Fascists march on Rome. Mussolini becomes Prime Minister

1929 Lateran Treaty creates a separate Vatican state

Poster for EUR

1940 Italy enters World War II; work begins on EUR zone

☐ **Twentieth-Century Rome**

Religion in the 20th Century

Rome has attracted pilgrims for centuries, and they continue to come, especially at Easter and for the ever more frequent beatifications. The city also hosts a large, cosmopolitan religious community.

Conductor Zubin Mehta

Poster for La Dolce Vita

In the 1950s and '60s Rome was Europe's Hollywood. Ben Hur, Quo Vadis? *and* Cleopatra *were made at the Cinecittà studios, as well as Italian films like Fellini's* La Dolce Vita.

Valentino Model

While not as important as Milan for fashion, Rome is still home to some of the industry's leading designers.

City-Centre Traffic

Rome's streets are congested, and many buildings have been damaged by pollution. There are plans to close the historic centre to traffic.

1960 Olympic Games are held in Rome

1981 Assassination attempt on Pope John Paul II in St Peter's Square

1993 Francesco Rutelli of the Green Party is elected mayor

1950

1962

1975

1988

1957 Treaty of Rome initiates European Common Market

1962 Second Vatican Council brings about Church reforms

1978 Premier Aldo Moro kidnapped, then killed by Red Brigades; Karol Wojtyla is elected Pope John Paul II

1990 World Cup is held in Rome

ROME AT A GLANCE

FROM ITS EARLY DAYS as a settlement of shepherds on the Palatine hill, Rome grew to rule a vast empire stretching from northern England to North Africa. Later, after the empire had collapsed, Rome became the centre of the Christian world and artists and architects flocked to work for the popes. The legacy of this history can be seen all over the city. The following pages are a time-saving summary of some of the best Rome has to offer. There are sections on churches, museums and galleries, fountains and obelisks, and celebrated visitors and residents in Rome. Below are the top attractions that no visitor should miss.

ROME'S TOP TOURIST ATTRACTIONS

Capitoline Museums
See pp70–73.

Colosseum
See pp92–5.

Sistine Chapel
See pp244–7.

Raphael Rooms
See pp242–3.

Trevi Fountain
See p159.

Spanish Steps
See p134.

Castel Sant'Angelo
See pp248–9.

Pantheon
See pp110–11.

St Peter's
See pp230–33.

Roman Forum
See pp78–87.

Piazza Navona
See p120.

Interior of the Pantheon, by Giovanni Paolo Pannini (1691–1765)

Rome's Best: Churches and Temples

As the centre of Christianity, Rome has a vast wealth of beautiful and interesting churches. These range from magnificent great basilicas built to assert the importance of the medieval and Renaissance Catholic church, to smaller, humbler buildings where the first Christians gathered, often in secret. Among the most fascinating early churches are those converted from ancient Roman temples. Additions to these over the years have resulted in some intriguing, many-layered buildings. A more detailed historical overview of Rome's churches is on pages 44–5.

Pantheon
This monumental 2,000-year-old building is one of the largest surviving temples of ancient Rome.

St Peter's
At 136 m (450 ft) high, Michelangelo's dome is the tallest in the world. Sadly, the artist died before seeing his work completed.

Santa Maria in Trastevere
Built over a very early Christian foundation, this church is famous for its ornate mosaics.

Vatican

Piazza di Spagna

Piazza della Rotonda

Piazza Navona

Janiculum

Campo de' Fiori

Capit

Trastevere

Santa Cecilia in Trastevere
This statue of Cecilia, showing her as she lay when her tomb was uncovered, was sculpted in 1599 by Stefano Maderno.

Santa Maria in Cosmedin
The decorations in this 6th-century church are 12th-century and earlier. A restored painting in the apse shows the Virgin, Child and saints.

Santa Maria Maggiore
Rich mosaics and relics contrast with the sober interior form of Santa Maria Maggiore. Among its treasures are vestments bearing the Borghese coat of arms.

Sant'Andrea al Quirinale
Bernini made maximum use of strong, dynamic curves in this oval interior (1658–70), creating a small masterpiece of the Roman Baroque.

Santa Prassede
Magnificent Byzantine mosaics cover the walls and ceilings of this 9th-century church. This Christ with angels is in the Chapel of St Zeno.

Santa Croce in Gerusalemme
Saints adorn the facade of Santa Croce. Inside are relics of the Cross, brought from Jerusalem by St Helena.

Via Veneto

Quirinal

Esquiline

Forum

alatine

Lateran

entine

Caracalla

0 metres   500

0 yards   500

San Clemente
Many archaeological layers lie beneath the 12th-century church. This sarcophagus dates from the 4th century.

San Giovanni in Laterano
The original church was built by Constantine, the first Christian emperor. The Chapel of St Venantius mosaics include the figure of St Venantius himself.

Exploring Churches and Temples

THERE ARE MORE CHURCHES in Rome than there are days of the year, so you'll have to be selective. Catholic pilgrims have always been drawn to the seven major basilicas: **St Peter's**, the heart of the Roman Catholic church, **San Giovanni in Laterano**, **San Paolo fuori le Mura**, **Santa Maria Maggiore**, **Santa Croce in Gerusalemme**, **San Lorenzo fuori le Mura** and **San Sebastiano**. These have a wealth of relics, tombs and magnificent works of art from many different periods. Smaller churches can be equally fascinating, especially those that have preserved their original character.

ANCIENT TEMPLES

ONE PAGAN TEMPLE survives virtually unaltered since it was erected in the 2nd century AD. The **Pantheon**, "Temple of all the Gods", has a domed interior quite different in structure from any other church in Rome. It was reconsecrated as a Christian church in the 7th century.

Other Roman temples have been incorporated into Christian churches at various times. Two of these are in the Forum; **Santi Cosma e Damiano** was established in the Temple of Romulus in 526, while San Lorenzo in Miranda

The impressive domed interior of the Pantheon, which became a church in 609

was built on to the ruins of the **Temple of Antoninus and Faustina** in the 11th century. The Baroque facade, built in 1602, looms behind the columns of the temple.

Another church that clearly shows its ancient Roman origins is **Santa Costanza**, built as a mausoleum for Constantine's daughter. It is a round church with some splendid 4th-century mosaics.

EARLY CHRISTIAN AND MEDIEVAL CHURCHES

SOME EARLY BASILICAS, the 5th-century **Santa Maria Maggiore** and **Santa Sabina** for example, retain much of their original structure. Other, even earlier churches such as the 4th-century **San Paolo fuori le Mura** and **San Giovanni in Laterano** still preserve their original basilica shape. San Paolo was rebuilt after a fire in 1823 destroyed the original building, and the San Giovanni of today dates from a 1646 reconstruction by Borromini. Both these churches still have their medieval cloisters.

13th-century fresco by Pietro Cavallini in Santa Cecilia

Santa Maria in Trastevere and **Santa Cecilia in Trastevere** were built over houses where the earliest Christian communities met and worshipped in secret, to avoid persecution. One church where the different layers of earlier structures can clearly be seen is **San Clemente**. At its lowest level, it has a Mithraic temple of the 3rd century AD. Other early churches include **Santa Maria in Cosmedin,** with its impressive Romanesque bell tower, and the fortified convent of **Santissimi Quattro Coronati**. Many Roman churches, most notably **Santa Prassede**, contain fine early Christian and medieval mosaics.

Cloister of San Giovanni in Laterano

UNUSUAL FLOORPLANS

The design of Rome's first churches was based on the ancient basilica, a rectangular building divided into three naves. Since then there have been many bold departures from the this plan, including round churches, square churches based on the shape of the Greek cross, as in Bramante's plan for St Peter's, and, in the Baroque period, even oval and hexagonal ones.

Pantheon (2nd century)

Santa Costanza (4th century)

RENAISSANCE

The greatest undertaking of the Renaissance popes was the rebuilding of **St Peter's**. Disagreements on the form it should take meant that, although work started in 1506, it was not completed until well into the 17th century. Fortunately, this did not prevent the building of Michelangelo's great dome. As well as working on St Peter's, Michelangelo also provided the **Sistine Chapel** with its magnificent frescoes.

On a completely different scale, another key work of Renaissance architecture is Bramante's tiny **Tempietto** (1499) on the Janiculum. **Santa Maria della Pace** has a Bramante cloister, some frescoes by Raphael and a charming portico by Pietro da Cortona. Also of interest is Michelangelo's imaginative use of the great vaults of the Roman Baths of Diocletian in the church of **Santa Maria degli Angeli**.

There are other churches worth visiting for the sake of

Michelangelo's dramatic dome crowning the interior of St Peter's

their outstanding paintings and sculptures. **Santa Maria del Popolo**, for example, has two great paintings by Caravaggio, the Chigi Chapel designed by Raphael, and a series of 15th-century frescoes by Pinturicchio. **San Pietro in Vincoli**, besides having the chains with which St Peter was bound in prison, also has Michelangelo's awe-inspiring statue of Moses, while **San Luigi dei Francesi** has three Caravaggios depicting St Matthew and frescoes by Domenichino.

BAROQUE

Interior of Rosati's dome in San Carlo ai Catinari (1620)

THE COUNTER REFORMATION inspired the exuberant, lavish style of churches such as the **Gesù** and **Sant' Ignazio di Loyola**. The best-loved examples of Roman Baroque are the later works associated with Bernini, such as the great colonnade and baldacchino he built for **St Peter's**. Of the smaller churches he designed, perhaps the finest is **Sant' Andrea al Quirinale**, while **Santa Maria della Vittoria** houses his truly astonishing Cornaro Chapel with its sculpture of the *Ecstasy of St Teresa*. The late Baroque was not all Bernini, however. You should also look out for churches such as **San Carlo**

ai Catinari with its beautiful dome by Rosato Rosati and the many churches by Bernini's rival, Borromini. **Sant'Agnese in Agone** and **San Carlo alle Quattro Fontane** are famed for the dramatic concave surfaces of their facades, while the complex structure of **Sant'Ivo alla Sapienza** makes it one of the miniature masterpieces of the Baroque.

WHERE TO FIND THE CHURCHES

Gesù *pp114–15*
Pantheon *pp110–11*
Sant'Agnese in Agone *p121*
Sant'Andrea al Quirinale *p161*
San Carlo ai Catinari *p150*
San Carlo alle Quattro Fontane *p161*
Santa Cecilia in Trastevere *p211*
San Clemente *pp186–7*
Santa Costanza *p264*
Santi Cosma e Damiano *p86*
Santa Croce in Gerusalemme *p181*
San Giovanni in Laterano *pp182–3*
Sant'Ignazio di Loyola *p106*
Sant'Ivo alla Sapienza *p122*
San Lorenzo fuori le Mura *p264*
San Luigi dei Francesi *p122*
Santa Maria degli Angeli *p163*
Santa Maria in Cosmedin *p202*
Santa Maria Maggiore *pp172–3*
Santa Maria della Pace *p121*
Santa Maria del Popolo *pp138–9*
Santa Maria in Trastevere *pp212–13*
Santa Maria della Vittoria *p255*
San Paolo fuori le Mura *p267*
St Peter's *pp230–33*
San Pietro in Vincoli *p170*
Santa Prassede *p171*
Santissimi Quattro Coronati *p185*
Santa Sabina *p204*
San Sebastiano *p265*
Sistine Chapel *pp244–7*
Tempietto *p219*
Temple of Antoninus and Faustina *p85*

Bramante's St Peter's (1503)

Sant'Andrea al Quirinale (1658)

Sant'Ivo alla Sapienza (1642)

Rome's Best: Museums and Galleries

THE MUSEUMS OF ROME are among the richest in the world; the Vatican alone contains incomparable collections of Egyptian, Etruscan, Greek, Roman and Early Christian artefacts, as well as frescoes by Michelangelo and Raphael, priceless manuscripts and jewels. Excavations in the 19th century added treasures from ancient Rome which are now on show in museums throughout the city. The finest Etruscan collections in the world can be enjoyed in the Villa Giulia. More details of Rome's museums and galleries are given on pages 48–9.

Villa Giulia
Etruscan treasures from Rome's early history are displayed in this beautiful Renaissance villa.

Vatican Museums
The galleries and long corridors hold priceless artefacts such as this 9th-century mosaic showing scenes from the life of Christ.

0 metres 500
0 yards 500

Vatican

Piazza Navona

Piazz
Spag

Piazz
dell
Roton

Campo de' Fiori

Galleria Spada
This collection's strength lies in its 17th- and 18th-century paintings. Earlier works include a Visitation *by Andrea del Sarto (1486–1530).*

Janiculum

Trastevere

Palazzo Corsini
Included here are works by Caravaggio, Rubens and Van Dyck, as well as a painting of the Baroque sculptor Bernini – a rare portrait by Il Baciccia (1639–1709).

Galleria Doria Pamphilj
Most of the great names of the Renaissance are represented on this gallery's crowded walls. Titian (1485–1576) painted Salomé *early in his career.*

Museo Borghese

The ground floor galleries house sculpture from ancient Greece and Rome as well as early Bernini masterpieces such as his David *(1619).*

Museo Nazionale Romano

This fresco, from Livia's Villa (1st century AD) outside Rome, is one of a huge collection of finds from archaeological sites throughout the city.

Palazzo Barberini

The works of art here date mainly from the 13th to the 16th centuries. This figure of Providence comes from Pietro da Cortona's The Triumph of Divine Providence *(1633–9).*

Palazzo Venezia

The highlights of Rome's most important museum of decorative arts are its Byzantine and medieval collections, including this Byzantine enamel of Christ dating from the 13th century.

Via Veneto

Quirinal

Esquiline

itol

Forum

Palatine

Caracalla

Lateran

ntine

Capitoline Museums: Palazzo dei Conservatori

Pietro da Cortona's Rape of the Sabine Women *(1629) is one of many Baroque paintings in the picture gallery.*

Capitoline Museums: Palazzo Nuovo

Among the sculptures is this head of Giulia Domna (wife of Septimius Severus) from the 2nd century AD.

Exploring Museums and Galleries

ROME'S MUSEUMS and galleries have two major strengths: Greek and Roman archaeological treasures, and paintings and sculptures of the Renaissance and the Baroque. The Vatican Museums have superb collections of both, as do, on a smaller scale, the Capitoline Museums. Fine paintings can also be found scattered throughout Rome in museums, galleries and churches *(see pp44–5)*.

Etruscan clay head, Villa Giulia

ETRUSCAN ARTEFACTS

5th-century BC Etruscan gold plate with inscription, Villa Giulia

THE ETRUSCANS inhabited an area stretching from Florence to Rome from the 8th century BC, and governed Rome from the late 7th century BC *(see pp16–17)*. It was the Etruscan custom to bury the dead along with their possessions, and as a result Etruscan artefacts have been excavated from tombs all over central Italy. Three main collections can be seen in Rome. The **Villa Giulia** has been the home of the Museo Nazionale Etrusco since 1889. The villa, designed by Vignola for Pope Julius III for summer outings, is one of Rome's prettiest Renaissance buildings. In addition to the collections, the villa gardens contain

Victory banner, Museo della Civiltà Romana

a reconstructed Etruscan temple. Not all of the finds are Etruscan; some of the pottery, statuettes and other artefacts are relics of the Faliscans, Latins and other tribes who inhabited central Italy before the Romans.

The Gregorian Etruscan Museum in the **Vatican Museums** was opened in 1837 to house Etruscan finds from tombs on church-owned land. The Museo Barracco in the **Piccola Farnesina** has statues from the much older civilizations of ancient Egypt and Assyria.

ANCIENT ROMAN ART

THE ARCHAEOLOGICAL zone in Rome forms a huge open-air museum of evidence of ancient Roman life, while the porticoes and cloisters of the city's churches are filled with ancient sarcophagi and fragments of statuary. The largest important collection can be seen in the **Museo Nazionale Romano** at the Baths of Diocletian in front of the station. The museum's many ancient artefacts include, most notably, a sarcophagus from Livia's Villa at Prima Porta just north of Rome. Much of this extensive collection is in store while the rooms are being reorganized. The most important statues are in the **Vatican Museums**, which also have the best of the great Greek works, such as the *Laocoön*, brought to Rome around the 1st century AD. It had tremendous influence on the subsequent

development of Roman art. Splendid copies of Greek originals can be seen in the **Capitoline Museums**.

In the Forum, occupying two floors of the church of Santa Francesca Romana, is the small but worthwhile **Antiquarium Forense**. For those who enjoy history, the large scale model at the **Museo della Civiltà Romana** in EUR gives an excellent idea of what ancient Rome looked like in the 4th century AD.

Centurion's breast-plate, Museo della Civiltà Romana

ART GALLERIES

Muses in Raphael's *Parnassus* (1508–11), Vatican Museums

IN THE PAST, many of Rome's great aristocratic families owned magnificent private collections of paintings and sculpture. Some of these are still housed in ancestral palazzi, which are open to the public. One is the **Galleria Doria Pamphilj**, which has the greatest concentration of paintings of any palazzo in Rome. It's well worth searching through the dimly lit rooms to find the pearls of the collection, which include works by Raphael, Filippo Lippi, Caravaggio, Titian and Claude Lorrain, as well as a portrait of Pope Innocent X Pamphilj by the Spanish artist Velázquez. The collection of the **Galleria Spada**, begun by Bernardino Spada in 1632, is still in the fine original gallery built for it. The paintings demonstrate 17th-century Roman taste: Rubens, Caravaggio, Guido Reni, Guercino, Domenichino and Jan Brueghel the Elder.

Hellenistic faun, Museo Borghese

The **Galleria Colonna** houses a collection of art from the same period.

Other old family residences are now showcases for state art collections. The Galleria Nazionale d'Arte Antica is divided between **Palazzo Barberini** and **Palazzo Corsini**. Palazzo Barberini, built between 1625 and 1633 by Bernini and others for the Barberini family, houses paintings from the 13th to the 16th centuries. It also has *objets d'art* acquired by the state from various private collections. At some future date, the 17th- and 18th-century paintings exhibited in the Palazzo Corsini, on the south side of the Tiber, will be transferred to join the Palazzo Barberini collection.

Another wonderful private collection was that of the Borghese family, also now managed by the state. The **Museo Borghese** is under repair and only the sculpture on the ground floor can be seen. But it's worth going to see the technically amazing *Apollo and Daphne* by the youthful genius Bernini and the famous statue of Pauline Borghese by Canova.

The **Capitoline Museums** hold collections that were gifts of the popes to the people of Rome. The Pinacoteca (art gallery) in the **Palazzo dei Conservatori** contains works by Titian, Guercino and Van Dyck. There is an art gallery at the **Vatican Museums**, but lovers of Renaissance art will head straight for the Sistine Chapel and the Raphael Rooms. Rome's main modern art collection is in the **Galleria Nazionale d'Arte Moderna**.

SMALLER MUSEUMS

THE MOST IMPORTANT of the smaller collections is the beautifully laid-out medieval museum in **Palazzo Venezia**, which has exhibits ranging from ceramics to sculpture. Rome has a wealth of small, specialist museums including a **Museum of Musical Instruments**, a **Museo del Folklore**, with tableaux showing life in Rome during the last century, and the **Burcardo Theatre Museum**.

For those with an interest in the English Romantic poets who lived in Rome in the 19th century, there is the **Keats-Shelley Memorial House**, a museum in the house where John Keats died. If you're keen on the French Empire, the **Museo Napoleonico** has relics and paintings of Napoleon and members of his family, many of whom lived in Rome. Finally, for

Laocoön (1st century AD) in the Vatican's Pio-Clementine Museum

those with a taste for the macabre there is a waxworks, the **Museo delle Cere**.

Portrait of Pauline Borghese painted by Kinson (c1805), now in the Museo Napoleonico

WHERE TO FIND THE MUSEUMS AND GALLERIES

Antiquarium Forense *p87*
Burcardo Theatre Museum *p149*
Capitoline Museums *pp70–73*
Galleria Colonna *p158*
Galleria Doria Pamphilj *p107*
Galleria Nazionale d'Arte Moderna *pp258–9*
Galleria Spada *p147*
Keats-Shelley Memorial House *p134*
Museo Borghese *pp260–61*
Museo delle Cere *p159*
Museo della Civiltà Romana *p267*
Museo del Folklore *p210*
Museo Nazionale Romano *p163*
Museo Napoleonico *p127*
Museum of Musical Instruments *p181*
Palazzo Barberini *p255*
Palazzo Corsini *p218*
Palazzo dei Conservatori *pp72–3*
Palazzo Venezia *p75*
Piccola Farnesina *p149*
Vatican Museums *pp234–47*
Villa Giulia *pp262–3*

The Deposition (1604) by Caravaggio, the Vatican

Rome's Best: Fountains and Obelisks

ROME HAS SOME of the loveliest fountains in the world.
Many of them are the work of the greatest sculptors of
the Renaissance and Baroque. Some fountains are
flamboyant displays, others restful trickles of water. Many
are simply drinking fountains, while a few cascade from
the sides of buildings. Obelisks date from far earlier in
the city's history. Although some of them were
commissioned by Roman emperors, many are even
older and were brought to Rome by triumphant,
conquering armies. A more detailed overview of
Rome's fountains and obelisks is on pages 52–3.

Piazza San Pietro
*Twin fountains give
life to the splendid
monumental piazza
of St Peter's. Maderno
designed the one on
the Vatican side in
1614; the other was
later built to match.*

Piazza del Popolo
*Nineteenth-century
marble lions and
fountains surround an
ancient obelisk in the
centre of the piazza.*

Vatican

Piazza
Navona

Piaz
delle
Roton

Campo
de' Fiori

Janiculum

TIBER

Trastevere

Fontana dei Fiumi
*The figures in the
fountain of the four
rivers by Bernini
represent the Ganges,
the Plate, the Danube
and the Nile.*

**Obelisk of Santa Maria
sopra Minerva**
*The Egyptian obelisk,
held up by Bernini's
marble elephant, dates
from the 6th century BC.*

Fontana delle Tartarughe
*One of Rome's more secret fountains,
this jewel of Renaissance sculpture
shows youths helping tortoises into a basin.*

Fontana della Barcaccia
This elegant fountain of 1627 is probably the work of Pietro Bernini, father of the more famous Gian Lorenzo.

Trevi Fountain
The Trevi, inspired by Roman triumphal arches, was designed by Nicola Salvi in 1762. Tradition has it that a coin thrown into the water guarantees a visitor's return to Rome.

N

0 metres 500
0 yards 500

azza
pagna

Via Veneto

Quirinal

Esquiline

apitol

Forum

Palatine

Lateran

Caracalla

ventine

Fontana delle Naiadi
When this fountain was unveiled in 1901, the realistically sensual bronze nymphs caused a storm of protest.

Obelisk of Piazza San Giovanni in Laterano
The oldest obelisk in Rome dates from the 15th century BC. It came to Rome in AD 357, brought here on the orders of Constantine II.

Piazza della Bocca della Verità Fountain
In this 18th-century fountain, built by Carlo Bizzaccheri for Pope Clement XI, water spills over a craggy rock formation where two Tritons hold aloft a large shell.

Exploring Fountains and Obelisks

THE POPES who restored the ancient Roman aqueducts used to build fountains to commemorate their deeds of munificence. As a result, fountains of all sizes and shapes punctuate the city, drawing grateful crowds on hot summer evenings. Ancient obelisks provide powerful reminders of the debt Roman civilization owed to the Egyptians. Architects have learnt to incorporate them into Roman piazzas in fascinating ways.

Fountain of the Amphorae (1920s)

FOUNTAINS

THE TREVI FOUNTAIN is one of the most famous of all. It is a *mostra*, a monumental fountain built to mark the end of an aqueduct – in this case the Acqua Vergine, built by Marcus Agrippa in 19 BC, although the Trevi itself was not erected until 1762. Other *mostre* are the **Fontana Paola,** built for Pope Paul V in 1612 on the Janiculum, and the less magnificent **Moses Fountain**, commemorating the opening of the Acqua Felice by Pope Sixtus V in 1587.

Almost all Rome's famous piazzas have fountains. In **Piazza San Pietro** there is a matching pair of powerful fountains. Piazza Navona has Bernini's wonderful Baroque **Fontana dei Fiumi** (fountain of the rivers) as its main attraction. The fountain's four figures each represent one of the four principal rivers then known. To the south of this is the smaller **Fontana del Moro** (the Moor), also by Bernini, showing an Ethiopian struggling with a dolphin. At the north end, Neptune wrestles with an octopus on a

19th-century fountain. In Piazza Barberini is the magnificent Bernini creation of 1642–3: the **Fontana del Tritone** with its sea god blowing through a shell.

More recently, large piazzas have been redesigned around fountains. Valadier's great design for **Piazza del Popolo** (1816–20) has marble lions and fountains surrounding the central obelisk plus two more

Fountain of the Four Tiaras located behind St Peter's

19th-century fountain. In Piazza Barberini is the magnificent Bernini creation of 1642–3: the **Fontana del Tritone** with its sea god blowing through a shell.

The Pantheon Fountain

fountains on the east and west sides of the square. The turn of the century saw the opening of the **Fontana delle Naiadi** (nymphs), in Piazza della Repubblica; its earthy figures caused great scandal at the time. The highly original **Fountain of the Amphorae** (map 8 D2) was erected in Piazza dell' Emporio during the 1920s. The same designer, Pietro Lombardi, also created the **Fountain of the Four Tiaras** (map 3 C3) behind the colonnade of St Peter's.

The city also has a number of smaller, and often very charming, fountains. At the foot of the Spanish Steps is the **Fontana della Barcaccia** (the leaking boat) of 1627; the **Fontana delle Tartarughe**

THE TREVI FOUNTAIN

Appropriately for a fountain resembling a stage set, the theatrical Trevi has been the star of many films set in Rome, including romantic films like *Three Coins in a Fountain* and *Roman Holiday*, but also *La Dolce Vita*, Fellini's satirical portrait of Rome in the 1950s. Whatever liberties Anita Ekberg took then, paddling in the fountains of Rome is now forbidden, however tempting it could be in the summer heat.

Anita Ekberg in *La Dolce Vita* (1960)

Fontana dei Cavalli Marini

(the tortoise fountain) has been in the tiny Piazza Mattei since 1581, and by Santa Maria in Domnica is the **Fontana della Navicella** (little boat), created out of an ancient Roman sculpture in the 16th century. In the forecourt of **Santa Sabina** (map 8 D2) water gushes from a huge mask set in an ancient basin. The **Pantheon Fountain** (map 4 F4), from 1575, is by Jacopo della Porta. **Le Quattro Fontane** (four fountains) have stood at the Quirinal hill crossroads since 1593.

Fountains in parks and gardens include the **Galleon Fountain** (1620–21) at the Vatican, and the **Fontana dei Cavalli Marini** (seahorses), of 1791, at Villa Borghese. The somewhat decayed 16th-century terraced gardens of the **Villa d'Este**, with their display of over 500 fountains, are still worth the journey.

Piazza Navona with Fontana dei Fiumi, by Pannini (1691–1765)

time of Augustus and also erected in the Circus Maximus. The slightly smaller **Obelisk of Piazza Montecitorio** was another of Augustus's trophies.

Other obelisks, such as the one at the top of the Spanish Steps, are Roman imitations of Egyptian originals. The **Obelisk of Piazza dell' Esquilino** and the one in **Piazza del Quirinale** (map 5 B4) first stood at the entrance to the Mausoleum of Augustus. When re-erected, most obelisks were mounted on decorative bases, often with statues and fountains at their foot. Others became integral parts of sculptures. Bernini was responsible for the marble elephant balancing the Egyptian **Obelisk of Santa Maria sopra Minerva** on its back, and for the **Fontana**

dei Fiumi, with an obelisk from the Circus of Maxentius. Another obelisk was added to the remodelled Pantheon Fountain in 1711. The obelisk in **Piazza San Pietro** is Egyptian but does not have the usual hieroglyphics.

The **Obelisk of Axum** was brought by Mussolini's army from Ethiopia in 1937 as a war trophy. It now stands by the United Nations building near the Circus Maximus.

Wall fountain at Villa d'Este

WHERE TO FIND THE FOUNTAINS AND OBELISKS

Fontana dei Cavalli Marini *p258*
Fontana dei Fiumi *p120*
Fontana del Moro *p120*
Fontana del Tritone *p254*
Fontana della Barcaccia *p133*
Fontana della Navicella *p193*
Fontana delle Naiadi *p164*
Fontana delle Tartarughe *p150*
Fontana Paola *p219*
Galleon Fountain *p225*
Moses Fountain *p162*
Obelisk of Piazza dell'Esquilino *p168*
Obelisk of Piazza di San Giovanni in Laterano *p178*
Obelisk of Piazza Montecitorio *p113*
Obelisk of Santa Maria sopra Minerva *p108*
Piazza della Bocca della Verità *p200*
Piazza del Popolo *p137*
Piazza San Pietro *p224–5*
Le Quattro Fontane *p162*
Trevi Fountain *p159*
Villa d'Este *p268*

The Ovato Fountain at Villa d'Este

OBELISKS

THE MOST ANCIENT and tallest of Rome's obelisks is the **Obelisk of Piazza di San Giovanni in Laterano**. Built of red granite, 31 m (100 ft) high, it came from the Temple of Ammon at Thebes, erected in the 15th century BC. It was brought to Rome in AD 357 by the order of Constantine II and put up in the Circus Maximus. In 1587 it was rediscovered, broken into three pieces, and was re-erected in the following year. Next in age is the obelisk in **Piazza del Popolo**, from the 12th or 13th century BC. It was brought to Rome in the

Obelisk in Piazza del Popolo

Celebrated Visitors and Residents

ROME EXERTS a powerful fascination and foreigners thoughout history have succumbed to its charms, often staying for long periods or even taking up permanent residence. The list of famous visitors is almost endless: painters, sculptors and architects from Rome's very earliest days; writers, poets, musicians, exiles, pilgrims, religious teachers, philosophers, aesthetes, archaeologists – all have passed through. Their orchestral works, operas, paintings, drawings, drama and literary journals testify to Rome's inspirational effect.

J W von Goethe *(1749–1832)*
The German poet, philosopher, artist, playwright, botanist and courtier lived at No. 20 Via del Corso, now a museum.

Martin Luther *(1483–1546)*
The religious reformer from Germany came to the convent at Santa Maria del Popolo in 1511. His horror at the corruption he saw led to the Reformation.

Vatican

Piazza del Popolo

Piazza della Roton

Piazza Navona

Janiculum

Campo de' Fior

Trastevere

Sant'Ignazio di Loyola *(1491–1556)*
He came to Rome from Spain in 1537 and founded the Jesuits near what is now the Gesù, the first Jesuit church.

Queen Christina *(1626–89)*
The Swedish queen abdicated in 1654, and came to live in Palazzo Corsini on Via Lungara.

St Dominic *(1170–1221)*
Founder of the Dominican order, St Dominic was born in Spain. The order's headquarters were at Santa Sabina on the Aventine.

Jean Auguste Ingres *(1780–1867)*
The 19th-century French painter, leader of the Neo-Classical tradition, lived in Rome from 1806 until 1820. He returned in 1834 as director of the French Academy at Villa Medici.

Pauline Borghese *(1780–1825)*
Napoleon's sister was the subject of scandal in 1805, when she posed semi-nude for a statue by Canova, which is now in Villa Borghese.

Via Veneto

The Exiled Stuarts
James Stuart (1688–1766), unsuccessful claimant to the British throne, came to Rome as an exile. He was presented with Palazzo Balestra by Pope Clement XI and died here.

Quirinal

Esquiline

itol

Forum

Palatine

Lateran

Caracalla

ventine

Lord Byron *(1788–1824)*
Though the English poet's stay in the city was brief, the influence on his work was long-lasting. Stanzas in Childe Harold's Pilgrimage *and* Manfred *were inspired by seeing the Colosseum in moonlight.*

0 metres	500
0 yards	500

Percy Bysshe Shelley *(1792–1822)*
The great English Romantic poet wrote his drama Prometheus Unbound *in the calm of the ruined Baths of Caracalla in 1819.*

Artists and Writers Inspired by Rome

ARTISTS AND WRITERS have been attracted to Rome since Classical times. Many came to work for the emperors; the poets Catullus, Horace, Virgil and Ovid, for example, all enjoyed the patronage of Emperor Augustus. Later on, especially in the Renaissance and Baroque periods, the greatest artists and architects came to Rome to compete for commissions from the popes. However, patronage was not the only magnet. Since the Renaissance, Rome's Classical past and its picturesque ruins have drawn artists, architects and writers from all over Italy and abroad.

The prolific love poet Ovid (43 BC–AD 17)

Self-portrait by the 18th-century artist Angelica Kauffmann, c1770

PAINTERS, SCULPTORS AND ARCHITECTS

Diego Velázquez, one of many great 17th-century artists to visit Rome

IN THE EARLY 16th century, artists and architects were summoned from all parts of Italy to realize the grandiose building projects of the popes. From Urbino came Bramante (1444–1514) and Raphael (1483–1520); from Perugia Perugino (1450–1523); from Florence Michelangelo (1475–1564) and many others. They worked in the Vatican, on the new St Peter's and the decoration of the Sistine Chapel. Artists were often well rewarded, but they also lived in dangerous times. Florentine sculptor and goldsmith Benvenuto Cellini (1500–71) helped defend Castel Sant' Angelo (see pp248–9) during the Sack of Rome (1527), but was later imprisoned there and made a dramatic escape. His memoirs tell the story.

Towards the end of the 16th century church patronage was generous to the

Milanese-born Caravaggio (1571–1610) despite his violent character and unruly life. The Carracci family from Bologna also flourished – especially brothers Annibale (1560–1609) and Agostino (1557–1602).

The work of Gian Lorenzo Bernini (1598–1680) can be seen all over Rome. He succeeded Carlo Maderno (1556–1629) as architect of St Peter's, and created its great bronze baldacchino, the splendid colonnade (see pp230–31) and numerous fountains, churches and sculptures. His rival for the title of leading architect of the Roman Baroque was Francesco Borromini (1599–1667), whose highly original genius can be appreciated in many Roman churches and palazzi.

In the 17th century it became more common for artists from outside Italy to come and work in Rome. Diego Velázquez (1599–1660), King Philip IV of Spain's court painter, came in 1628 to study

the art treasures of the Vatican. Rubens (1577–1640) came from Antwerp to study, and carried out various commissions. The French artists Nicolas Poussin (1594–1665) and Claude Lorrain (1600–82) lived here for many years.

The Classical revival of the 18th century attracted artists to Rome in unprecedented numbers. From Britain came the Scottish architect Robert Adam (1728–92) and the Swiss artist Angelica Kauffmann (1741–1807), who settled here and was buried with great honour in Sant'Andrea delle Fratte. After the excesses of the Baroque, sculpture also turned to the simplicity of Neo-Classicism. A leading exponent of this movement was Antonio Canova (1757–1821). Sculptors from all over Europe were influenced by him, including the Dane Bertel Thorvaldsen (1770–1844) who lived in Rome for many years.

Claude Lorrain's view of the Forum, painted in Rome in 1632

WRITERS

DANTE (1262–1321) visited Rome during his exile from Florence and in the *Inferno* describes the great influx of pilgrims for the first Holy Year (1300). The poet Petrarch (1304–74), born in Arezzo, came to the city in much happier circumstances to be crowned with laurels on the Capitol in 1341. The poet Torquato Tasso (1544–95), from Sorrento, was invited to receive a similar honour, but died soon after his arrival. He is buried in Sant'Onofrio *(see p219)* on the Janiculum.

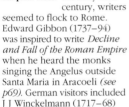

Two of the first writers from abroad to visit Rome were the French essayist Montaigne (1533–92) and English poet John Milton (1608–74). Then, by the early 18th century, writers seemed to flock to Rome. Edward Gibbon (1737–94) was inspired to write *Decline and Fall of the Roman Empire* when he heard the monks singing the Angelus outside Santa Maria in Aracoeli *(see p69).* German visitors included J J Winckelmann (1717–68)

Torquato Tasso

who wrote influential studies of ancient art, and the poet J W von Goethe (1749–1832).

In the Romantic period Rome teemed with English writers: poets Keats, Shelley and Byron, followed by the Brownings and the novelist Charles Dickens. Travel writers in the 19th century included Augustus Hare (1834–1903) and the German historian Ferdinand Gregorovius (1821–91). Much of *The Portrait of a Lady* by American Henry James (1843–1916) is set in Rome.

Modern life in Rome is brilliantly captured by the Roman-born novelist and short-story writer Alberto Moravia (1907–90).

MUSICIANS

GIOVANNI LUIGI da Palestrina (1525–94), from the town of that name, became choirmaster and organist to the Vatican and composed some of the greatest unaccompanied choral music ever written. In 1770 the 14-year-old Mozart heard Gregorio Allegri's unpublished *Miserere* in the Sistine Chapel and wrote it down from memory. Arcangelo

Portrait of the poet John Keats painted by his friend Joseph Severn in 1819

Corelli (1653–1713), the great violinist and composer of the Baroque age, worked in Rome under the patronage of Cardinal Ottoboni. One of his first commissions was to provide a festival of music for Queen Christina of Sweden.

During the 19th century the Prix de Rome brought many French musicians to study here at the Villa Medici *(see p135).* Hector Berlioz (1803–69) owed the inspiration for his popular *Roman Carnival,* the **Giacomo Puccini** overture to his opera *Benvenuto Cellini,* to his two-year stay in Rome. Georges Bizet (1838–75) and Claude Debussy (1862–1918) were also Prix de Rome winners. Franz Liszt (1811–86), after his 50th year, settled in Rome, took minor orders and became known as Abbé Liszt. He wrote *Fountains of the Villa d'Este* while staying at the villa in Tivoli.

More recent, 20th-century musical associations with Rome include the popular works by Ottorino Respighi (1870–1936): *The Fountains of Rome* and *The Pines of Rome,* while Giacomo Puccini (1858–1924) used Roman settings when creating his dramatic, tragic opera *Tosca.*

ROMAN CINEMA

The Cinecittà studios, built in 1937 just outside Rome, are most famous for the films made here in the 1940s, classics of Italian Neo-Realism such as Roberto Rossellini's *Roma Città Aperta* and Vittorio De Sica's *Sciùscià* and *Ladri di Bicicletta.* In the 1950s Cinecittà became a centre for international productions, including the epics *Ben Hur* and *Spartacus.*

The director most strongly associated with Roman cinema is Federico Fellini, whose films *La Dolce Vita* (1960) and *Roma* (1972) present a highly idiosyncratic portrait of the follies of the city. Of all the Roman-born filmmakers, perhaps the most famous is the controversial writer Pier Paolo Pasolini (1922–75), who became internationally known with his films *Teorema* (1968) and *Il Decamerone* (1971).

Pier Paolo Pasolini

ROME THROUGH THE YEAR

THE BEST TIMES to visit Rome are spring and autumn when the weather is usually warm, and sometimes even hot enough to sunbathe and swim at the beaches and lakes outside the city. November is best avoided as the weather tends to be grey and extremely rainy, while in high summer, most people (including Romans, who leave the city in their droves) find the heat unbearable.

Easter and Christmas are obviously very special in Rome, but there are other religious festivals worth seeing at other times in the year, as well as some enjoyable secular events like the Festa de Noantri in Trastevere and the Flower Festival in Genzano. In villages outside Rome, local celebrations are held to welcome new crops such as strawberries and beans in the spring, and grapes and truffles in the autumn.

SPRING

EASTER, falling in March or April, marks the official beginning of the tourist season in Rome. Catholics from all over the world flock into the city to make their pilgrimages to the main basilicas and to hear the pope's Easter Sunday address outside St Peter's, while the less devout come simply to take advantage of the mild weather. Meanwhile, Romans pile into their cars and head for the coast and countryside, so you can expect the roads, beaches, and the restaurants of the Castelli Romani and Lake Bracciano to be busy.

Temperatures tend to be around 18° C (66° F), but can hit 28° C (82° F), so by mid-May it's usually possible to lunch and dine outside. However, there can still be sudden downpours and temperature swings, so do bring warm clothes and an umbrella.

Crowds gathering in St Peter's square at Easter

In April tubs full of colourful azaleas are ranged on the Spanish Steps and along Via Veneto, and once the roses start to flower in the city's Rose Garden overlooking the Circus Maximus, it is opened to the public.

For a fortnight from mid-May Via dei Coronari is lit by candles, lined with plants and hung with banners for the street's antiques fair, while Via Margutta hosts an outdoor art show. In the first week of May the International Horse Show is held in the Villa Borghese, and towards the end of the month many world-class tennis players flock to Rome to compete in the International Tennis Championships held at the Foro Italico.

EVENTS

Festa di Santa Francesca Romana *(9 March)*, Santa Francesca Romana. Blessing of the city's cars, buses and trams *(see p87)*.
Festa di San Giuseppe *(19 March)*, in the Trionfale area. St Joseph's (and Father's) Day celebrated with street stalls, cream puffs and music.
Good Friday *(March/April)*, Colosseum. Procession of the Cross at 9pm led by the pope.
Easter Sunday *(March/April)*, St Peter's square. Address made by the pope *(see p231)*.
Rome's Birthday *(Sunday before 21 April)*, Piazza del Campidoglio.
Festa della Primavera *(March/April)*, Spanish Steps and Trinità dei Monti. Azaleas in the street and concerts.
Art exhibition *(April/May)*, Via Margutta *(see p339)*.
International Horse Show *(early May)*, Villa Borghese *(see p350)*.
Antiques Fair *(mid–late May)*, Via dei Coronari *(see p324)*.
International Tennis Championships *(late May)*, Foro Italico *(see p350)*.

Flowers for sale on the Piazza del Popolo

AVERAGE DAILY HOURS OF SUNSHINE

Hours

Sunshine Chart
*Rome is famous for
its light. June is the
sunniest month; but
it is also very dry,
and without the odd
shower the bright
heat can feel intense.
In autumn, Rome's
southerly position
means that the sun
can still be enjoyably
warm at midday.*

SUMMER

IN JUNE a summer season of
concerts begins, with performances in some of the
city's most beautiful palaces,
churches and courtyards. In
July and August opera is
usually staged in the Baths of
Caracalla and classical drama
at Ostia Antica. Throughout
the summer there are also
contemporary cultural events
– film, music of all kinds,
dance and theatre – staged as
part of the Cineporto and
Massenzio film festivals *(see
p346)* and RomaEuropa. On
midsummer evenings there
are stalls and amusements on
the Tiber embankments by
Castel Sant'Angelo, while in
the last two weeks of July

Flower-carpeted streets in Genzano

when the temperature often
soars to over 40° C (104° F),
virtually all Romans flee the
city for the seaside, and many
cafés, shops and restaurants
close for the month.

EVENTS

Flower Festival *(June, the
Sunday after Corpus Domini)*,
Genzano, Castelli Romani,
south of Rome. Streets are
carpeted with flowers.
Festa di San Giovanni
(23–24 June), Piazza di Porta
San Giovanni. Celebrated with
meals of snails in tomato
sauce, suckling pig, a fair and
firework display.
RomaEuropa *(late June–
late July)*, mainly in Villa
Medici. Films, dance, theatre
and concerts *(see p341)*.
Festa di San Pietro *(29 June)*,
many churches. Celebrations
mark the feast of St Peter.

Expo Tevere *(end
June–mid-July)*, along
the Tiber. Arts and
crafts, food and wine
stalls, folk music and
fireworks *(see p339)*.
Festa de Noantri *(last
two weeks in July)*, the
streets of Trastevere.
Feasting, processions
and entertainment *(see
p339 and p341)*.
Arts outdoors *(July/
August)*, Baths of
Caracalla, Villa Ada,
Ostia Antica, by the
Tiber, in parks. Opera,
concerts, drama and
film *(see p341)*.
**Festa della Madonna
della Neve** *(5 August)*,
Santa Maria Maggiore.
Legendary 4th-century
fall of snow re-enacted
with showers of white
flower petals *(see p172)*.
Ferragosto *(15 August)*,
Santa Maria in Trastevere.
Midsummer Roman holiday.
Almost everything closes
down. Celebrations are held
for the Feast of the Assumption.

Summer vegetables

Trastevere becomes an open-
air party as the Noantri
festival is celebrated with
trinket stalls, dining in the
street and fireworks. Mid-July
is good for shoppers as the
sales *(saldi)* begin.
Many Romans leave the city
at the end of June, when
schools close, but as June and
July are peak tourist months,
hotels, cafés, restaurants and
sights are packed. In August,

**The heat of an August afternoon
in front of St Peter's**

AVERAGE MONTHLY RAINFALL

Rainfall Chart

Autumn is Rome's rainiest season, with heavy downpours, sometimes lasting for days, especially in November. Rain in summer tends to come in violent – but often extremely refreshing – storms. In winter and early spring expect a few dull, drizzly days.

AUTUMN

SEPTEMBER AND OCTOBER are the best – and among the most popular – months to visit Rome. The fiery heat of July and August will have cooled a little, but midday can be very hot, and you can still eat and drink outside without feeling chilly until late at night. Visiting Rome in November is not recommended: it is the wettest month of the year and Roman rainstorms are often very strong and heavy.

At the beginning of October an artisans' fair is held on Via dell'Orso and adjacent streets, while nearby the antiques galleries of Via dei Coronari hold open house. There are also October antiques fairs in Orvieto and Perugia, two of the loveliest Umbrian hill towns, which are about an hour's drive north of Rome. In November, there's yet another prestigious antiques fair at the papal palace of Viterbo, 65 km (40 m) north of Rome *(see p271).*

Autumn is, of course, the season of harvest festivals, and it can be fun to head out to the small towns around Rome to sample local cheeses, sausages, chestnuts

A roast chestnut stall in autumn

and mushrooms. Perhaps the most spectacular of these is the wine festival in Marino (in the Castelli Romani, south of Rome) where wine flows freely from the fountain in the central piazza. In Rome itself, there's a grape festival in early September, the Sagra dell'Uva, held in the Basilica of Constantine in the Forum, where there are grapes for sale as well as street entertainment. Throughout the autumn and winter, freshly roasted chestnuts can be bought from vendors on street corners, and there is usually a stand on Campo de' Fiori where you can sample the new season's wine, *vino novello,* for free.

On All Souls and All Saints days, which fall on 1 and 2 November, the Romans make pilgrimages to the tombs of relatives who are buried in the cemeteries of Prima Porta and Verano. Chrysanthemums are then traditionally placed on their graves and for this reason they should definitely not be given to friends, hosts and hostesses as thank you presents for their hospitality. On a much happier note, the classical concert and opera seasons begin again in October and November. Details of performances can be found in *Trovaroma (see p340)* and on posters dotted around the city.

EVENTS

Art fair *(September)*, Via Margutta *(see p339).*
Sagra dell'Uva *(early September)*, Basilica of Constantine. Harvest festival with grapes selling at bargain prices and lots of folksy street entertainment.
Crafts fair *(last week September/first week October)*, Via dell'Orso, near Piazza Navona *(see p339).*
Marino Wine Festival *(first Sunday in October)*, Marino. Celebrations include tastings, street entertainment and wine spouting from the fountain in the main piazza.
Antiques Fair *(mid-October)*, Via dei Coronari *(see p339).*
Festa di Santa Cecilia *(22 November)*, Santa Cecilia in Trastevere and Catacombs of San Callisto.
Vino Novello tasting *(late November)*, Campo de' Fiori.

Autumn in the Villa Doria Pamphilj park

AVERAGE MONTHLY TEMPERATURE

Temperature Chart
The chart shows the average minimum and maximum monthly temperatures. July and August can be unbearably hot, making sightseeing a chore. The fresher days of spring and autumn are ideal to visit Rome, but there are some dull and rainy spells.

WINTER

DURING THE WINTER Rome is bracingly chilly but the temperature rarely drops below freezing. Not all buildings are centrally heated so if you're staying in a small hotel bring warm clothes and request extra blankets as soon as you arrive, as they are often in short supply. Warm up in cafés with hot chocolate and frothy cappuccino.

The run-up to Christmas is great fun in Rome, especially if you have children. Manger scenes, *presepi*, are set up in many churches, piazzas and public places and from mid-

Rome during one of its rare snowfalls

February, celebrated largely by children with fancy-dress parties and parades along Via Nazionale, Via Cola di Rienzo and the Pincio. Keep out of the way of teenagers with shaving cream spray cans and water-filled balloons.

EVENTS

Festa della Madonna Immacolata *(8 December)*, Piazza di Spagna. Firemen climb up a ladder to place a wreath on the statue of the Virgin Mary.
Befana *(mid-December – mid-January)*, Piazza Navona. Christmas and children's market *(see p120)*.
Nativity scenes *(mid-December – mid-January)*, many churches. Life-size scene in St Peter's square, collection at Santi Cosma e Damiano.
Midnight Mass *(24 December)*, at most churches.
Christmas Day *(25 December)*, St Peter's square. Blessing by the pope.
New Year's Eve *(31 December)*, all over city. Firework displays, furniture thrown out.

The Befana on Piazza Navona

December to Twelfth Night Piazza Navona hosts the Befana, a Christmas market where you can buy manger scenes, decorations and toys. Unless you have friends in Rome, Christmas itself can be rather lonely, as it is very much a family event. On New Year's Eve, however, everyone is out on the street to drink sparkling wine and let off fireworks. Watch out for flying wardrobes as there's a tradition of throwing out old furniture in the New Year.

The Carnival season runs from late January through to

PUBLIC HOLIDAYS
New Year's Day (1 Jan)
Epiphany (6 Jan)
Easter Monday
Liberation Day (25 April)
Labour Day (1 May) .
Ferragosto (15 Aug)
All Saints (1 November)
Immaculate Conception (8 December)
Christmas Day (25 December)
Santo Stefano (26 December)

Via Condotti at Christmas

ROME AREA
BY AREA

CAPITOL 64–75

FORUM 76–95

PALATINE 96–101

PIAZZA DELLA ROTONDA 102–115

PIAZZA NAVONA 116–127

PIAZZA DI SPAGNA 128–141

CAMPO DE' FIORI 142–153

QUIRINAL 154–165

ESQUILINE 166–175

LATERAN 176–187

CARACALLA 188–197

AVENTINE 198–205

TRASTEVERE 206–213

JANICULUM 214–221

VATICAN 222–249

VIA VENETO 250–255

FURTHER AFIELD 256–271

SIX GUIDED WALKS 272–285

CAPITOL

THE TEMPLE OF JUPITER on the Capitol, the southern summit of the Capitoline hill, was the centre of the Roman world. Reached by a zig-zag path up from the Forum, the temple was the scene of all the most sacred religious and political ceremonies. The hill and its temple came to symbolize Rome's authority as *caput mundi*, head of the world, and the concept of a "capital" city is derived from the Capitol. Throughout the city's history, the Capitol, or Campidoglio as it is called in Italian, has remained the seat of municipal government.

Hand of colossal statue in Palazzo dei Conservatori

Today's city council, the Comune di Roma, meets in the Renaissance splendour of Palazzo Senatorio. Rome's position as a modern capital is forcefully expressed in the enormous white Victor Emmanuel Monument, which unfortunately blots out the view of the Capitol from Piazza Venezia. The present arrangement of the buildings on the hill dates from the 16th century, when Michelangelo created a beautiful piazza reached by a dramatic flight of steps, the Cordonata. Two of the three buildings around the piazza are now home to the Capitoline Museums.

SIGHTS AT A GLANCE

Churches and Temples
Santa Maria in Aracoeli ❼
Temple of Jupiter ❽
San Marco ⓬

Museums and Galleries
Capitoline Museums:
Palazzo Nuovo pp70–71 ❶
Capitoline Museums:
Palazzo dei Conservatori
pp72–3 ❷
Palazzo Venezia
and Museum ⓫

Historic Buildings
Roman Insula ❺

Historic Streets and Piazzas
Piazza del Campidoglio ❸
Cordonata ❹
Aracoeli Staircase ❻

Ancient Sites
Tarpeian Rock ❾

Monuments
Victor Emmanuel
Monument ❿

GETTING THERE
All the sights in this area are within walking distance of Piazza Venezia. Bus routes converge here from all parts of the city, as do many thousands of motorists. From Termini station you can catch the 64, 65, 70, 75 or 170; from Piazza Barberini the 56, 60 or 492. From St Peter's and the Vatican the only bus is the 64. Other useful routes include the 44, 46, 57, 90 and 90b.

KEY

▨ Street-by-Street map

0 metres 200
0 yards 200

N

SEE ALSO
• *Street Finder*, maps 5, 12

Michelangelo's Piazza del Campidoglio

Street-by-Street: The Capitol and Piazza Venezia

THE CAPITOL, citadel of ancient Rome, is a must for every visitor. A broad flight of steps (the Cordonata) leads up to Michelangelo's spectacular Piazza del Campidoglio. This is flanked by the Palazzo Nuovo and Palazzo dei Conservatori, housing the Capitoline Museums with their fine collections of sculpture and paintings. The absence of cars makes the hill a welcome retreat from the squeal of brakes below, but you should brave the traffic to visit Palazzo Venezia and its museum.

Victor Emmanuel Monument
This huge white marble monument to Italy's first king was completed in 1911 ❿

San Marco
The church of the Venetians in Rome has a fine 9th-century apse mosaic ⓬

Palazzo Venezia
The museum's finest exhibits, such as this 13th-century gilded angel decorated with enamel, date from the late Middle Ages ⓫

Roman Insula
This is a ruined apartment block dating from Imperial Rome ❺

Cordonata
Michelangelo's great staircase changed the orientation of the Capitol towards the west ❹

Aracoeli Staircase
When it was built in 1348, the staircase became a centre for political debate ❻

(see p106)

KEY

  Suggested route

0 metres   75

0 yards   75

★ **Palazzo dei Conservatori**
In this part of the Capitoline Museums a fine series of reliefs from the Temple of Hadrian (see p106) is displayed in the courtyard ❷

Santa Maria in Aracoeli
The treasures hidden behind the church's brick facade include this 15th-century fresco of the Funeral of St Bernardino *by Pinturicchio* ❼

LOCATOR MAP
See Central Rome Map pp12–13

★ **Palazzo Nuovo**
This bust of Augustus in the Hall of the Emperors is one of many fine Classical sculptures in the Capitoline Museums ❶

Palazzo Senatorio was used by the Roman Senate from about the 12th century. It now houses the offices of the mayor.

★ **Piazza del Campidoglio**
Michelangelo designed both the geometric paving and the facades of the buildings ❸

Temple of Jupiter
This artist's impression shows the gold and ivory statue of Jupiter that stood in the temple ❽

Tarpeian Rock
In ancient Rome traitors were thrown to their death from this cliff on the Capitol ❾

STAR SIGHTS

★ **Piazza del Campidoglio**

★ **Palazzo dei Conservatori**

★ **Palazzo Nuovo**

Capitoline Museums: Palazzo Nuovo ❶

See pp70–71.

Capitoline Museums: Palazzo dei Conservatori ❷

See pp72–3.

Piazza del Campidoglio ❸

Map 5 A5 & 12 F5. *See Getting There p65.*

WHEN EMPEROR Charles V visited Rome in 1536, Pope Paul III Farnese was so embarrassed by the muddy state of the Capitol that he asked Michelangelo to draw up plans for repaving the piazza, and for renovating the facades of the Palazzo dei Conservatori and Palazzo Senatorio.

Michelangelo came up with the idea of a third building, the Palazzo Nuovo, to form a piazza in the shape of a trapezium, embellished with Classical sculptures chosen for their relevance to Rome. Building started in 1546 but progressed so slowly that Michelangelo only lived to oversee the double flight of steps at the entrance of Palazzo Senatorio.

The piazza was completed in the 17th century, the design remaining largely faithful to the original. Pilasters two storeys high and balustrades interspersed by statues link the buildings thematically. The piazza faces west towards St Peter's, the Christian equivalent of the Capitol and site of other great commissions executed by Michelangelo for Pope Paul III.

Cordonata ❹

Map 5 A5 & 12 F5. *See Getting There p65.*

FROM PIAZZA VENEZIA, the Capitol is approached by a gently rising, subtly widening ramp – the Cordonata. At the foot is a pair of granite Egyptian lions, and on the left a 19th-century monument to Cola di Rienzo, close to where the dashing 14th-century tyrant was executed. The top of the ramp is guarded by restored Classical statues of the Dioscuri, Castor and Pollux.

Roman Insula ❺

Piazza d'Aracoeli. **Map** 5 A5 & 12 F4. *67 10 30 65.* *See Getting There p65. Open by appt only: apply to Ripartizione X (see p367).*

TWO THOUSAND YEARS ago the urban poor of Rome used to make their homes in *insulae* – apartment blocks.

One of the statues of the Dioscuri at the top of the Cordonata

These were often badly maintained by landlords, and expensive to rent in a city where land costs were high. This 2nd-century AD tenement block, of barrel-vault construction, is the only survivor in Rome from that era. The fourth, fifth and part of the sixth storey remain above current ground level.

In the Middle Ages, a section of these upper storeys was converted into a church; its bell tower and 14th-century Madonna in a niche are visible from the street.

During the Fascist years, the area was cleared, and three lower floors emerged. Some 380 people may have lived in the tenement, in the squalid conditions described by the 1st-century AD satirical writers Martial and Juvenal. The latter mentions that he had to climb 200 steps to reach his garret.

This *insula* may once have had more storeys. The higher you lived, the more dismal the conditions, as the poky spaces of the building's upper levels testify.

The Cordonata in an 18th-century painting by Antonio Canaletto

Aracoeli Staircase ❻

Piazza d'Aracoeli. **Map** 5 A5 & 12 F4.
🚌 *See **Getting There** p65.*

THE ARACOELI Staircase numbers 124 marble steps (122 if you start from the right) and was completed in 1348, some say in thanks for the passing of the Black Death, but probably in view of the 1350 Holy Year.

The 14th-century tribune-turned-tyrant Cola di Rienzo used to harangue the masses from the Aracoeli Staircase; in the 17th century foreigners used to sleep on the steps, until Prince Caffarelli, who lived on the hill, scared them off by rolling barrels filled with stones down them.

Popular belief has it that by climbing the steps on your knees you can win the national lottery. From the top there is a good view of Rome, with the domes of Sant' Andrea della Valle and St Peter's slightly to the right.

Aracoeli Staircase

Santa Maria in Aracoeli ❼

Piazza d'Aracoeli (entrances via Aracoeli Staircase and door behind Palazzo Nuovo). **Map** 5 A5 & 12 F4.
📞 679 81 55. 🚌 *See **Getting There** p65.* **Open** 7am–noon, 4pm–5.30pm (Jun–Sep: 6.30pm) daily.

DATING FROM AT LEAST the 6th century, the church of Santa Maria in Aracoeli, or St Mary of the Altar in the Sky, stands on the northern summit of the Capitoline, on

Ceiling commemorating Battle of Lepanto in nave of Santa Maria in Aracoeli

the site of the ancient temple to Juno. Its 22 columns were taken from various ancient buildings; the inscription on the third column to the left tells us that it comes *"a cubiculo Augustorum"* – from the bedroom of the emperors.

The church of the Roman senators and people, Santa Maria in Aracoeli has been used to celebrate many triumphs over adversity. Its ceiling, with naval motifs, commemorates the Battle of Lepanto (1571), and was built under Pope Gregory XIII Boncompagni, whose family crest, the dragon, can be seen towards the altar end.

Many other Roman families and individuals are honoured by memorials in the church. To the right of the entrance door, the tombstone of archdeacon Giovanni Crivelli, rather than being set into the floor of the church, stands eternally to attention, partly so that the signature "Donatelli" (by Donatello) can be read at eye-level.

The frescoes in the first chapel on the right, painted by Pinturicchio in the 1480s in the beautifully clear style of the early Renaissance, relate the life and death of St Bernardino of Siena. On the left-hand wall, the perspective of *The Burial of the Saint* slants to the right, taking into account the position of the viewer from just outside the chapel.

The church is most famous, however, for an icon with apparently miraculous powers, the *Santo Bambino*, a 15th-century olive-wood figure of the Christ child which was carved out of a tree from the garden of Gethsemane. Its powers are said to include resurrecting the dead, and it is sometimes summoned to the bedsides of the gravely ill. The original figure was stolen in 1994 but has been replaced by a replica.

At Christmas the Christ Child takes its place in the centre of a picturesque crib (second chapel to the left) but is usually to be found in the sacristy, as is the panel of the *Holy Family* from the workshop of Giulio Romano.

The miraculous olive-wood Christ Child at Santa Maria in Aracoeli

Capitoline Museums: Palazzo Nuovo ❶

A COLLECTION of Classical statues has been kept on the Capitoline hill since the Renaissance. The first group of bronze sculptures was given to the city by Pope Sixtus IV in 1471 and more additions were made by Pope Sixtus V in 1586. The Palazzo Nuovo was designed by Michelangelo as part of the renovation of the Piazza del Campidoglio, and after its completion in 1654, a number of the statues were transferred there. In 1734 Pope Clement XII Corsini decreed that the building be turned into the world's first public museum.

MUSEUM GUIDE

The two floors of the Palazzo Nuovo are devoted chiefly to sculpture. Most of the finest works, such as the Capitoline Venus, are Roman copies of Greek masterpieces. There are also two collections of busts assembled in the 18th century for visitors keen to identify all the philosophers and poets of ancient Greece and the rulers of ancient Rome. The price of entry includes admission to the Palazzo dei Conservatori, which is directly opposite.

Hall of the Philosophers
The hall contains a rich mix of portraits of Greek politicians, scientists and literary figures. They are Roman copies that decorated the libraries, villas and gardens of the wealthy in ancient times.

Portrait of a Flavian Lady
The woman wears the fanciful and elaborate hairstyle popular among the female aristocracy of the 1st century AD.

Capitoline Venus

3

4   **5**

First floor

Courtyard

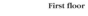

★ **Marcus Aurelius**
This bronze equestrian statue of the emperor dates from the 2nd century AD. It used to stand on a pedestal in the centre of the Campidoglio, but has now been restored and is housed in the Palazzo Nuovo.

4   **5**

Ground floor

The facade of Palazzo Nuovo was designed by Michelangelo, but the work was actually finished in 1654 by the brothers Carlo and Girolamo Rainaldi.

STAR SCULPTURES

★ **Marcus Aurelius**

★ **Discobolus**

★ **Dying Galatian**

KEY TO FLOORPLAN

■ Non-exhibition space

☐ Exhibition space

Mosaic of the Doves
This charming, naturalistic mosaic once decorated the floor of Hadrian's Villa at Tivoli (see p269). It shows doves drinking water from a vase.

★ **Discobolus**
The twisted torso was part of a Greek statue of a discus thrower. An 18th-century French sculptor, Monnot, made the additions that turned him into a wounded warrior.

VISITORS' CHECKLIST

Musei Capitolini, Piazza del Campidoglio. **Map** 5 A5 & 12 F5. ☏ 67 10 30 69. 🚌 44, 46, 64, 70, 81, 110 and many other routes to Piazza Venezia. **Open** 9am–7pm Tue–Sat, 9am–1.45pm Sun. Last adm: 30 mins before closing. **Closed** 1 Jan, 1 May, 25 Dec. **Adm charge** (free last Sun of month). Entrance ticket is also valid for Palazzo dei Conservatori. 📷

Red Faun
Found at Tivoli, the famous red marble satyr is a 2nd-century AD version of a Greek original – an example of Hadrian's fondness for all things Greek.

Stairs to ground floor

2

7   8

Stairs to first floor

2   3

1

★ **Dying Galatian**
Great compassion is conveyed in this Roman copy of an original Greek work of the 3rd century BC.

9   8   7

Alexander Severus as Hunter
In this marble of the 3rd century AD, the emperor's pose is a pastiche of Perseus, holding up the head of Medusa the Gorgon after he had killed her in her sleep.

Main entrance

Capitoline Museums: Palazzo dei Conservatori ❷

T HE PALAZZO DEI CONSERVATORI was the
seat of the city's magistrates during
the late Middle Ages. Its frescoed halls
are still used occasionally for political
meetings and the ground floor houses
the municipal registry office. The palazzo
was built by Giacomo della Porta who
carried out Michelangelo's designs for the
Piazza del Campidoglio in the mid-16th
century. While much of the
palazzo is given over to
sculpture, the art galleries
on the second floor hold
works by Veronese,
Guercino, Tintoretto,
Rubens, Caravaggio,
Van Dyck and Titian.

Facade of Palazzo dei Conservatori
*Work began on this Michelangelo design
in 1563, the year before his death.*

MUSEUM GUIDE
*The rooms on the first
floor are remarkable for
their original 16th-and
17th-century decoration
and for a number of the
Classical statues. The
second-floor art gallery
houses paintings and a
collection of porcelain in
room 6. Both the Museo
Nuovo and Braccio Nuovo
sections are now closed.*

**Burial and Glory
of St Petronilla**
*This huge Baroque altar-
piece was painted in
1622–3 by Guercino to
hang in St Peter's.*

Stairs to
second floor

★ **St John the Baptist**
*Painted in 1595–6,
Caravaggio's sensual
portrait of the young
saint presents a highly
unorthodox image of the
forerunner of Christ.*

Stairs to
first floor

Second-floor
art gallery

Courtya

**Main
entrance**

The Horatii and Curatii
*D'Arpino's fresco was painted
in 1613 and depicts a duel
taken from early Roman legend.*

KEY TO FLOORPLAN
- ☐ Garden
- ☐ Non-exhibition space
- ☐ Temporarily closed
- ☐ Exhibition space

Endymion
The youth doomed to sleep forever by the goddess Diana was painted by Pier Francesco Mola (1612–66) who studied under Cavalier d'Arpino.

VISITORS' CHECKLIST

See p71.

STAR EXHIBITS

★ **She-Wolf**

★ **St John the Baptist by Caravaggio**

★ **Spinario**

Braccio Nuovo

Esquiline Venus
The 1st-century BC figure was associated with the cult of Isis.

Museo Nuovo

Roman Garden

26

25

19

Constantine II
The head of a colossal 4th-century AD statue of the emperor has survived, along with a hand and other odd fragments.

First floor

16 17

8 18

7

6

★ **Spinario**
This is a charming bronze sculpture from the 1st century BC of a boy trying to remove a thorn from his foot.

★ **She-Wolf**
The Etruscan bronze of the wolf dates from the early 5th century BC. The legendary twins, Romulus and Remus (see pp16–17), were probably added in the 15th century.

Temple of Jupiter ⑧

Via del Tempio di Giove. **Map** 5 A5 & 12 F5. 🚌 See **Getting There** p65.

THE TEMPLE of Jupiter, the most important in ancient Rome, was founded in honour of the arch-god around 590 BC on the southern summit of the Capitoline hill. From the few traces that remain, archaeologists have been able to reconstruct the rectangular, Greek appearance of the temple as it once stood. In places you can see remnants of its particularly Roman feature, the podium. Most of this lies beneath the Museo Nuovo wing of the Capitoline Museums *(see pp72–3)*.

By walking around the site, from the podium's south-western corner in Via del Tempio di Giove to its south-eastern corner in Piazzale Caffarelli, you can see that the temple was about the same size as the Pantheon.

Ancient coin showing the Temple of Jupiter

Tarpeian Rock ⑨

Via di Monte Caprino and Via del Tempio di Giove. **Map** 5 A5 & 12 F5. 🚌 See **Getting There** p65.

THE SOUTHERN TIP of the Capitoline is called the Tarpeian Rock (Rupe Tarpea), after Tarpeia, the young daughter of Spurius Tarpeius, defender of the Capitol in the 8th-century BC Sabine War.

The Sabines, bent on vengeance for the rape of their women by Romulus and

Sabine soldiers crushing the treacherous Tarpeia with their shields

his men, bribed Tarpeia to let them up on to the Capitol. As the Augustan historian Livy records, the Sabines used to wear heavy gold bracelets and jewelled rings on their left hands, and Tarpeia's reward for her treachery was to be "what they wore on their shield-arms".

The Sabines kept to the letter of the bargain if not to its spirit – they repaid Tarpeia not with their jewellery but by crushing her to death between their shields. Tarpeia was possibly the only casualty of her act of treachery – as the invading warriors met the Roman defenders, the Sabine women leapt between the two opposing armies, forcing a reconciliation. Traitors and other condemned criminals were subsequently executed by being thrown over the sheer face of the rock.

The place is still considered dangerous, and at present is fenced off, while surveying work is carried out.

Victor Emmanuel Monument ⑩

Piazza Venezia. **Map** 5 A5 & 12 F4. 🚌 See **Getting There** p65. **Not open** to the public.

KNOWN AS Il Vittoriano, this monument was begun in 1885 and inaugurated in 1911 in honour of Victor Emmanuel II of Savoy, the first king of a unified Italy. The king is depicted here in a gilt bronze equestrian statue, over-sized like the monument itself – the statue is 12 m (39 ft) long.

The edifice contains a museum of the Risorgimento, the events that led to unification *(see pp36–7)*. It has, however, been closed since the early 1980s. Built in austere white Brescian marble, the "wedding cake" or "typewriter" (two of the many insulting nicknames given to this unloved white elephant) will never mellow into the ochre tones of surrounding buildings. It is widely held to be the epitome of self-important, insensitive architecture.

Victor Emmanuel Monument in Piazza Venezia

Palazzo Venezia and Museum ⓫

Via del Plebiscito 118. **Map** 5 A4 & 12 E4. 【 *679 88 65*. ▨ *See* **Getting There** *p65.* **Open** *9am–2pm Tue–Sat, 9am–1pm Sun (last adm: 30 mins before closing).* **Closed** *1 Jan, 1 May, 25 Dec.* **Adm charge.** 🄾 🕭 *Temporary exhibitions.*

O NE OF THE first Renaissance civic buildings in Rome, the palazzo's arched windows and doors are so harmonious that the facade was once attributed to the great Humanist architect Leon Battista Alberti (1404–72). It was more probably built by Giuliano da Maiano, who is

Pope Paul II

known to have carved the fine doorway on to the piazza.

Palazzo Venezia was built in 1455 for the Venetian cardinal Pietro Barbo, who later became Pope Paul II. It was at times a papal residence, at other times the Venetian Embassy to Rome, before passing into Austrian hands in 1797. Since 1916 it has belonged to the state, and in the Fascist era Mussolini used it as his headquarters, addressing crowds from the central balcony.

The interior is best seen on a visit to the Museo del Palazzo Venezia, Rome's most underrated museum, which holds first-class collections of early Renaissance painting; painted wood sculptures and Renaissance chests from all over Italy; tapestries from all over Europe; majolica; silver; Neapolitan ceramic figurines; Renaissance bronzes; arms and armour; Baroque terracotta sculptures by Bernini, Algardi and others; and 17th- and 18th-century Italian painting. There is a marble screen from the Aracoeli convent, which was destroyed to make way for the Victor Emmanuel Monument, and a bust of Paul II, showing him to rank with Martin V and Leo X among the fattest-ever popes. The building also houses the national art library (closed).

Palazzo Venezia with Mussolini's balcony in the centre

San Marco ⓬

Piazza San Marco 48. **Map** 5 A4 & 12 F4. 【 *679 52 05*. ▨ *See* **Getting There** *p65.* **Open** *8am–12.30pm, 4pm–7pm daily.* 🔽 🚫

T HE CHURCH of San Marco was founded in 336 by St Mark, the then pope, in honour of St Mark the Evangelist. The relics of Pope Mark lie under the altar. The church was restored by Pope Gregory IV in the 9th century – the magnificent apse mosaics date from this period.

Further major rebuilding took place in 1455–71, when Pope Paul II Barbo made San Marco the church of the Venetian commu-

Coat of arms of Pope Paul II

nity in Rome. The blue and gold coffered ceiling is decorated with Pope Paul's heraldic crest, the lion rampant, recalling the lion of St Mark, the patron saint of Venice. The appearance of the rest of the interior, with its colonnades of Sicilian jasper, was largely the creation of Filippo Barigioni in the 1740s. Complemented by an interesting array of funerary monuments in the aisles, the taste is typical of the late Roman Baroque.

Leon Battista Alberti, whose name is also mentioned tentatively in connection with Palazzo Venezia, may have been the architect of the elegant travertine arcade and loggia of the facade.

San Marco's apse mosaic of Christ, with Gregory IV on the far left

Forum

THE FORUM was the centre of political, commercial and judicial life in ancient Rome. The largest buildings were the basilicas, where legal cases were heard. According to the playwright Plautus, the area teemed with "lawyers and litigants, bankers and brokers, shopkeepers and strumpets, good-for-nothings waiting for a tip from the rich". As

Figure of barbarian on the Arch of Constantine

Rome's population boomed, the Forum became too small. In 46 BC Julius Caesar built a new one, setting a precedent that was followed by emperors from Augustus to Trajan. As well as the Imperial Fora, emperors also erected triumphal arches to themselves, and just to the east Vespasian built the Colosseum, centre of entertainment after the business of the day.

SIGHTS AT A GLANCE

Churches and Temples
Temple of Saturn **5**
Temple of Castor and Pollux **8**
Temple of Vesta **9**
Temple of Antoninus and Faustina **11**
Temple of Romulus and Santi Cosma e Damiano **12**
Santa Francesca Romana **14**
Temple of Venus and Rome **17**

Historic Buildings
Basilica Aemilia **1**
Curia **2**
Basilica Julia **7**

House of the Vestal Virgins **10**
Basilica of Constantine and Maxentius **13**
Trajan's Markets pp88–9 **18**
Torre delle Milizie **20**
Casa dei Cavalieri di Rodi **21**
Mamertine Prison **24**
Colosseum pp92–5 **27**

Museums
Antiquarium Forense **15**

KEY

▨ Tour of the Forum maps

Ⓜ Metro station

Arches and Columns
Arch of Septimius Severus **4**
Column of Phocas **6**
Arch of Titus **16**
Column of Trajan **19**
Arch of Constantine **26**

Ancient Sites
Rostra **3**
Forum of Augustus **22**
Forum of Caesar **23**
Forum of Nerva **25**

GETTING THERE

The simplest way to reach the area is by Metro to Colosseo on line B. The main entrance to the Forum is on Via dei Fori Imperiali, served by buses 11, 27, 81, 85, 87 and 186. Many more routes go to Piazza Venezia. For Trajan's Markets, the best buses are ones such as the 64, 65, 70 and 75 which stop in Via IV Novembre.

SEE ALSO

• *Street Finder*, maps 5, 8, 9, 12

• *Where to Stay* pp294–5

• *Triumphal Arches Walk* pp278–9

View of the Forum with the Colosseum rising behind the bell tower of Santa Francesca Romana

A Tour of the Roman Forum: West

To APPRECIATE THE LAYOUT of the Forum before visiting its confusing patchwork of ruined temples and basilicas, it is best to view the whole area from above, from the back of the Capitol. From there you can make out the Via Sacra (the Sacred Way), the route followed through the Forum by religious and triumphal processions towards the Capitol. Up until the 18th century when archaeological excavations began, the Arch of Septimius Severus and the columns of the Temple of Saturn lay half buried underground. Excavation of the Forum continues, and the ruins uncovered date from many different periods of Roman history.

The Temple of Vespasian was the point from where Piranesi made this 18th-century engraving of the Forum. Its three columns were then almost completely buried.

Temple of Saturn
The eight surviving columns of this temple stand close by the three columns of the Temple of Vespasian **5**

Temple of Concord

Portico of the Dii Consentes

Rostra
These are the ruins of the platform used for public oratory in the Forum **3**

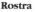

Basilica Julia
Named after Julius Caesar, who ordered its construction, the basilica housed important law courts **7**

Column of Phocas
One of the very last monuments erected in the Forum, this single column dates from AD 608 **6**

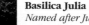

★ Arch of Septimius Severus
A 19th-century engraving shows the arch after the Forum was first excavated ❹

Santi Luca e Martina was an early medieval church, but was completely rebuilt in 1640 by Pietro da Cortona.

LOCATOR MAP
See Central Rome Map pp12–13

STAR SIGHTS

★ Arch of Septimius Severus

KEY

– – – Suggested route

| 0 metres | 75 |
| 0 yards | 75 |

Curia
A modern reconstruction has been built on the site of the chamber of the Roman Senate ❷

Basilica Aemilia
This large meeting hall was razed to the ground in the 5th century AD ❶

Entrance to Forum

The Temple of Julius Caesar was erected in his memory by Augustus on the spot where Caesar's body was cremated after his assassination in 44 BC.

Julius Caesar

To Roman Forum: East
See pp80–81

Temple of Castor and Pollux
A temple to the twin sons of Jupiter stood on this spot from the 5th century BC. This section of cornice and the columns supporting it date from the rebuilding of AD 6 ❽

A Tour of the Roman Forum: East

THE EASTERN END of the Roman Forum is dominated by the massive barrel-vaulted ruins of the Basilica of Constantine. To picture the building as it was in the 4th century AD, you must imagine marble columns, floors and statues, and glittering tiles of gilt bronze. The remains of the other important buildings are scanty, though the garden and ponds in the centre of the House of the Vestal Virgins make it a very attractive spot. The two churches in this part of the Forum cannot be reached from within the archaeological area, but are accessible from the road outside.

The Regia was the office of the Pontifex Maximus, the chief priest of ancient Rome.

To Forum entrance

Temple of Antoninus and Faustina
The portico of this temple, built in AD 141, has been incorporated in the church of San Lorenzo in Miranda ⓫

VIA SACRA

An early Iron Age necropolis was found here in 1902. Finds from it, such as this burial urn, are on view in the Antiquarium.

Temple of Vesta
Partly reconstructed, this tiny temple to the goddess of the hearth was one of ancient Rome's most sacred shrines ❾

Temple of Romulus
This domed building from the 4th century AD has survived as part of the church of Santi Cosma e Damiano ⓬

★ **House of the Vestal Virgins**
The priestesses who tended the sacred flame in the Temple of Vesta lived here. The house was a large rectangular building around a central garden ❿

★ **Basilica of Constantine**
The stark remains of the basilica's huge arches and ceilings give some idea of the original scale and grandeur of the Forum's public buildings ⑬

LOCATOR MAP
See Central Rome Map pp12–13

Santa Francesca Romana
The church takes its name from a saint who cared for the Roman poor in the 15th century ⑭

Antiquarium Forense
A small museum houses archaeological finds made in the Forum. They include this frieze of Aeneas and the Founding of Rome *from the Basilica Aemilia* ⑮

Colonnade surrounding Temple of Venus and Rome

Temple of Venus and Rome
These extensive ruins are of a magnificent temple, built here in AD 135 by the Emperor Hadrian, largely to his own design ⑰

VIA DEI FORI IMPERIALI

VIA SACRA

Ruined Baths

Arch of Titus
This 19th-century reconstruction shows how the arch may have looked when it spanned the flagstoned roadway of the Via Sacra ⑯

STAR SIGHTS

★ **Basilica of Constantine**

★ **House of the Vestal Virgins**

KEY

– – – Suggested route

0 metres 75

0 yards 75

Melted coins embedded in the floor of the Basilica Aemilia

Basilica Aemilia ❶

See Visitors' Checklist.

ORIGINALLY this building was a rectangular colonnaded hall, with a multicoloured marble floor and a bronze-tiled roof. It was built by the consuls Marcus Aemilius Lepidus and Marcus Fulvius Nobilor in 179 BC. The two consuls, who were elected annually, exercised supreme power over the Republic.

Basilicas in ancient Rome served no religious purpose; they were meeting halls for politicians, moneylenders and *publicani* (businessmen contracted by the state to collect taxes). A consortium agreed to hand over a specified sum to the state, but its members were allowed to collect as much as they could and keep the difference. This is why tax-collectors in the Bible were so loathed.

The basilica was rebuilt many times; it was finally burned down when the Goths sacked Rome in AD 410. Business seems to have carried on until the last moment, for the pavement is splashed with tiny lumps of coins that melted in the fire.

Curia ❷

See Visitors' Checklist.

A MODERN REPLICA has been built over the ruins of the hall where Rome's Senate (chief council of state) used to meet. The first Curia stood on the site now occupied by the church of Santi Luca e Martina, but after the building was destroyed by fire in 52 BC, Julius Caesar built a new Curia at the edge of the Forum. This was restored by Domitian in AD 94 and, after another fire, rebuilt by Diocletian in the 3rd century. The replica you see today is based on Diocletian's Curia. Inside are two relief panels commissioned by Trajan to decorate the Rostra. One shows Trajan destroying records of unpaid taxes to free citizens from debt; in the other he sits on a throne receiving a mother and child.

Replica of the Curia

Rostra ❸

See Visitors' Checklist.

Ruins of the Imperial Rostra

SPEECHES WERE delivered from this dais, the most famous – thanks to Shakespeare – being Mark Antony's "Friends, Romans, Countrymen" oration after the assassination of Julius Caesar in 44 BC. Caesar himself had just reorganized the Forum and this speech was made from the newly-sited Rostra, where the ruins now stand. In the following year the head and hands of Cicero were put on show here after he had been put to death by the second Triumvirate (Augustus, Mark Antony and Marcus Lepidus). Fulvia, Mark Antony's wife, stabbed the great orator's tongue with a hairpin. It was also here that Julia, Augustus's daughter, was said to have played the prostitute – one of many scandalous acts that led to her banishment.

The dais took its name from the ships' prows *(rostra)* with which it was decorated. Sheathed in iron (for ramming enemy ships), these had been captured at the Battle of Antium in the 4th century BC.

Honorary statue

Relief panel in balustrade, showing Trajan's acts of charity

Prows of ships *(rostra)*

ROSTRA
This reconstruction shows the platform for public speaking in the Forum, as it looked in Imperial times.

Arch of Septimius Severus ❹

See Visitors' Checklist.

THIS TRIUMPHAL ARCH, one of the most striking and best preserved monuments of the Forum, was erected in AD 203 to celebrate the tenth anniversary of the accession of Septimius Severus. The relief panels – largely eroded – celebrate the emperor's victories in Parthia (modern-day Iraq and Iran) and Arabia.

Barbarian captives, Arch of Severus

Originally, the inscription along the top of the arch was to Septimius and his two sons, Caracalla and Geta, but after Septimius died Caracalla murdered Geta, and had his brother's name removed. Even so the holes into which the letters of his name were pegged are still visible.

During the Middle Ages the central arch, half buried in earth and debris, was used to shelter a barber's shop.

Triumphal arch of the Emperor Septimius Severus

Temple of Saturn ❺

See Visitors' Checklist.

THE MOST PROMINENT of the ruins in the fenced-off area between the Forum and the Capitoline hill is the Temple of Saturn. It consists of a high platform, eight columns and a section of entablature. There was a temple dedicated to

Ionic capitals on the surviving columns of the Temple of Saturn

Saturn here as early as the 5th century BC, but it had to be rebuilt many times and the current remains date only from the 4th century AD.

Saturn was the mythical god-king of Italy, said to have presided over a prosperous and peaceful Golden Age from which slavery, private property, crime and war were absent. As such, he appealed particularly to the lower and slave classes. Every year, between 17 December and 23 December, Saturn's reign was remembered in a week of sacrifices and feasting, known as the Saturnalia.

As long as the revels lasted, the normal social order was turned upside down. Slaves were permitted to drink and dine with (and sometimes even be served by) their masters. Senators and other high-ranking Romans would abandon the aristocratic togas that they usually wore to distinguish them from the lower classes and put on more democratic, loose-fitting gowns. During the holidays all the law courts and schools in the city were closed. No prisoner could be punished, and no war could be declared.

People also celebrated the Saturnalia in their own homes: they exchanged gifts, in particular special wax dolls and wax tapers, and played light-hearted gambling games, the stakes usually being nuts, a symbol of fruitfulness. Much of the spirit and many of the rituals of the festival have been preserved in the Christian celebration of Christmas.

Column of Phocas ❻

See Visitors' Checklist.

THIS COLUMN, 13.5 m (44 ft) high, is one of the few to have remained upright since the day it was put up. Until 1816, when an inquisitive Englishwoman, Lady Elizabeth Foster, widow of the fifth Duke of Devonshire, decided to excavate its pedestal, nobody knew what it was. It turned out to be the youngest of the Forum's monuments, erected in AD 608 in honour of the Byzantine emperor, Phocas, who had just paid a visit to Rome. The column may have been placed here as a mark of gratitude to Phocas for giving the Pantheon to the pope *(see pp110–11).*

Slender, fluted Column of Phocas

Remains of the Basilica Julia, a Roman court of civil law

Basilica Julia ❼

See Visitors' Checklist, p82.

THIS IMMENSE basilica, which occupied the area between the Temple of Saturn and the Temple of Castor and Pollux, was begun by Julius Caesar in 54 BC and completed after his death by his great nephew Augustus. It was damaged by fire almost immediately afterwards in 9 BC, but was subsequently repaired and dedicated to the emperor's grandsons, Gaius and Lucius.

After numerous sackings and pilferings, only the steps, pavement and column stumps remain. Nevertheless the ground plan is fairly clear. The basilica had a central hall, measuring 82 m by 18 m

(260 ft by 59 ft), surrounded by a double portico. The hall was on three floors, while the outer portico had only two.

The Basilica Julia was the seat of the *centumviri*, a body of 180 magistrates who tried civil law cases. They were split into four chambers of 45 men, and unless a case was particularly complicated they would all sit separately.

The four courts were, however, divided only by screens or curtains, and the voices of lawyers and cheers and boos of spectators in the upper galleries echoed through the building. Lawyers used to hire crowds of spectators, who would applaud every time the lawyer who was paying them made a point and jeer at his opponents. The clappers and booers must have had a good deal of time on their hands: scratched into the steps are chequerboards where they played dice and other gambling games to while away the time between cases.

TEMPLE OF VESTA
The temple preserved the shape of an original primitive structure made of wooden posts with a thatched roof.

Cella (sacred inner chamber)

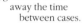

Ring of Corinthian columns   Sacred flame

Temple of Castor and Pollux ❽

See Visitors' Checklist, p82.

THE THREE SLENDER fluted columns of this temple form one of the Forum's most beautiful ruins. The first temple here was probably dedicated in 484 BC in honour of the mythical twins and patrons of horsemanship, Castor and Pollux. During the battle of Lake Regillus (496 BC) against the ousted Tarquin kings, the Roman dictator Postumius promised to build a temple to the twins if the Romans were victorious. Some said the twins appeared on the battlefield, helped the Romans to victory and then materialized in the Forum – the temple marks the spot – to announce the news.

The temple, like most buildings in the Forum, was rebuilt many times. The three surviving columns date from the last occasion on which it was rebuilt – by the future Emperor Tiberius after a fire in 12 BC. For a long period the temple housed the city's office of weights and measures, and it was also used at times by a number of bankers.

Corinthian columns of the Temple of Castor and Pollux

Temple of Vesta ❾

See Visitors' Checklist, p82.

THE FORUM's most elegant temple, a circular building originally surrounded by a ring of 20 fine fluted columns, dates from the 4th century AD, though there had been a temple on the site for far longer. It was partially reconstructed in 1930.

The cult of the Vestals was one of the oldest in Rome, and centred on six Vestal Virgins, who were required to keep alight the sacred flame of Vesta, the goddess of the hearth. This responsibility was originally entrusted to the daughters of the king, but it then passed to the Vestals, the only group of women priests in Rome. It was no easy task, as the flame was easily blown out by the wind. Any Vestal who allowed the flame to die was whipped by the high priest *(Pontifex Maximus)* and dismissed.

The girls, who had to belong to noble families, were selected when they were between six and ten years old. They served for 30 years: the first ten were spent learning their duties, the next ten performing them and the final ten teaching novices. They enjoyed high status and financial security, but were compelled to remain virgins. The penalty for transgressing was to be buried alive, although only ten Vestals are recorded as ever having suffered this fate. The men concerned were whipped to death. When Vestals retired, they were free to live the rest of their lives as ordinary citizens. If they wished they could marry, but few ever did.

Another of the Vestals' duties was to guard the Palladium, a sacred statue of the goddess Pallas Athenae. The irreverent Emperor Heliogabalus burgled the temple in the 3rd century AD. He thought he had succeeded in stealing the Palladium, but the Vestals had been warned of his intention and had replaced it with a replica.

Honorary statue of a Vestal Virgin

Restored section of Temple of Vesta

Central courtyard of the House of the Vestal Virgins

House of the Vestal Virgins ❿

See Visitors' Checklist, p82.

As soon as a girl became a Vestal she came to live in the House of the Vestal Virgins. Originally this was an enormous complex with about 50 rooms on three storeys. The only substantial remains today are some of the rooms around the central courtyard. This space is perhaps the most evocative part of the Forum. Overlooking ponds of water lilies and plump goldfish is a row of eroded, and mostly headless, statues of senior Vestals, dating from the 3rd and 4th centuries AD. The better-preserved examples were transferred to the Museo Nazionale Romano *(see p163)*. On one of the pedestals the inscription has been removed because the Vestal in question suffered some disgrace. It is thought she may have been a certain Claudia, known to have betrayed the cult by converting to Christianity.

Though many of the rooms surrounding the courtyard are well-preserved – some even retain flights of steps leading to an upper floor – you are not allowed inside them. If you peep into the series of rooms along the south side, however, you might be able to see the remains of a mill, used for grinding the grain with which the Vestals made a special sacrificial cake. The bakery was next door.

Temple of Antoninus and Faustina ⓫

See Visitors' Checklist, p82.

One of the forum's oddest sights is the Baroque facade of the church of San Lorenzo in Miranda rising above the porch of a Roman temple. First dedicated in AD 141 by the Emperor Antoninus Pius to his late wife Faustina, the temple was rededicated to them both on the death of the emperor. In the 11th century it was converted into a church because it was thought San Lorenzo (St Lawrence) had been condemned to death there. The current church, dating from the 17th century, is closed to the public.

Temple of Antoninus and Faustina

Temple of Romulus and Santi Cosma e Damiano ⓬

See Visitors' Checklist, p82. **Santi Cosma e Damiano** 🕿 699 15 40. **Open** 9am–12.30pm, 3pm–7pm daily. **Adm charge** for crib. 🛉 📷 ♿

NO-ONE IS SURE to whom the so-called Temple of Romulus was dedicated, but it wasn't to Romulus, the founder of Rome, or to the son of the Emperor Maxentius.

The temple is a circular brick building, topped by a cupola, with two rectangular side rooms and a concave porch. The heavy, dull bronze doors are original.

Since the 6th century the temple has acted as a vestibule to the church of Santi Cosma e Damiano, which itself occupies an ancient building – a hall in Vespasian's Forum of Peace. The entrance to the church is on Via dei Fori Imperiali. The beautiful carved figures of its 18th-century Neapolitan *presepio* (crib or Nativity scene) are back on view now, and the church has a vivid Byzantine apse mosaic with Christ pictured against orange clouds.

Roof of the Temple of Romulus

Basilica of Constantine and Maxentius ⓭

See Visitors' Checklist, p82.

THE BASILICA'S three vast, coffered barrel vaults are powerful relics of what was the largest building in the Forum. Work began in the early 4th century under the Emperor Maxentius. When he was deposed by Constantine after the Battle of the Milvian Bridge in AD 312, work on the massive project continued under the new regime. The building, which, like other Roman basilicas, was used for the administration of justice and for carrying on business, is often referred to simply as the Basilica of Constantine.

The area covered by the basilica was roughly 100 m by 65 m (330 ft by 215 ft). It was originally designed to have a long nave and aisles running from east to west, but Constantine switched the axis around to create three short broad aisles with the main entrance in the centre of the long south wall. The height of the building was 35 m (115 ft). In the apse at the western end, where it could be seen from all over the building, stood a 12-m (39-ft) statue of the emperor, made partly of wood and partly of marble. The giant head, hand and foot are on display in the courtyard of the Palazzo dei Conservatori *(see pp72–3)*. The roof of the basilica glittered with gilded tiles until the 7th century when they were stripped off to cover the roof of the old St Peter's.

The three barrel-vaulted aisles of the basilica were used as law courts.

The octagonal coffers in the vaulted ceiling were originally faced with marble.

The main entrance was added by Constantine in AD 313.

The roof was supported by eight massive Corinthian columns. One now stands in Piazza Santa Maria Maggiore *(see p173).*

Santa Francesca Romana

Piazza di Santa Francesca Romana. **Map** 5 B5. 📞 679 55 28. 🚌 11, 27, 81, 85, 87, 186. Ⓜ Colosseo. **Open** 9.30am–12.30pm, 3.30pm–7pm daily. 🚹 📷 🔊

Dedication to Titus and Vespasian on the Arch of Titus

EVERY YEAR on 9 March devout Roman drivers try to park as close as possible to this Baroque church with a pleasant Romanesque bell tower. The aim of their strange pilgrimage is to have their vehicles blessed by Santa Francesca Romana, the patron saint of motorists. Francesca was a 15th-century wife and mother from Trastevere who founded a society of pious women devoted to helping the poor and sick. After she had been canonized in 1608 the church, which was originally called Santa Maria Nova, was rededicated to Francesca.

Bell tower of Santa Francesca

The most curious sight inside the church is a flagstone with what are reputed to be the imprints of the knees of St Peter and St Paul. The story goes that a magician, Simon Magus, decided to prove that his powers were superior to those of the Apostles by levitating himself above the Forum. As Simon was in mid-air, Peter and Paul fell to their knees and prayed fervently that God would show who was boss. Simon immediately plummeted to his death.

Antiquarium Forense ⓯

See Visitors' Checklist, p82.

THE FORMER CONVENT of Santa Francesca Romana is now occupied by the offices in charge of the excavations of the Forum and a small museum. The latter is currently being reorganized, and only a couple of rooms are open. They contain Iron Age burial urns, graves and their skeletal occupants along with some ancient bric-a-brac exhumed from the Forum's drains. When the reorganization is complete you should be able to see fragments of statues, capitals, friezes and other architectural decoration taken from the Forum's buildings.

Frieze of Aeneas in the Antiquarium Forense

Arch of Titus ⓰

See Visitors' Checklist, p82.

THIS TRIUMPHAL ARCH was erected in AD 81 by the Emperor Domitian in honour of the victories of his brother, Titus, and his father, Vespasian, in Judaea. In AD 68 the Jews, weary of being exploited by unscrupulous Roman officials, rebelled. A bitter war broke out which ended two years later in the fall of Jerusalem and the Jewish Diaspora.

Although the reliefs inside the arch are badly eroded, you can make out a triumphant procession of Roman soldiers carrying off spoils from the Temple of Jerusalem. The booty includes the altar, silver trumpets and a golden seven-branched candelabrum.

Temple of Venus and Rome ⓱

See Visitors' Checklist, p82.

THE EMPEROR Hadrian designed this temple to occupy what had been the vestibule to Nero's Golden House. Many of the columns have been re-erected, and though there is no access, there is a good view as you leave the Forum and from the upper tiers of the Colosseum. The temple, the largest in Rome, was dedicated to Roma, the personification of the city, and to Venus because she was the mother of Aeneas, father of Romulus and Remus. Each goddess had her own *cella* (shrine). When the architect Apollodorus pointed out that the seated statues in the niches were too big (had they tried to "stand" their heads would have hit the vaults), Hadrian had him put to death.

Statue of goddess　　**Porphyry column**

Cross-section of Temple of Venus and Rome

Trajan's Markets ⑱

ORIGINALLY CONSIDERED among the wonders of the Classical world, Trajan's Markets now show only a hint of their former splendour. Emperor Trajan and his architect, Apollodorus of Damascus, built this visionary new complex of 150 shops and offices (probably used for administering the corn dole) in the early 2nd century AD. It was the ancient Roman equivalent of the modern shopping centre, selling everything from silks and spices imported from the Middle East to fresh fish, fruit and flowers.

Trajan
The emperor was a benevolent ruler and a successful general.

The Markets Today
Above the facade stands the 13th-century Torre delle Milizie, built for defensive purposes.

Cross vaulting

Main Hall
Twelve shops were built on two floors, and the corn dole was shared out on the upper storey. This was a free corn ration given to Roman men to prevent hunger.

Via Biberatica
The main street which runs through the market may have been lined with inns and shops selling pepper and spices.

Small semicircle of shops

Staircase

TIMELINE

AD 100	AD 500	1000	1300	1800	1950
AD 100–112 Building of Trajan's Markets	**472** Invasion by Ricimer the Suevian. Some of his Germanic troops stationed here	**1200s** Torre delle Milizie built on top of the markets	**1572** Convent of Santa Caterina da Siena built over part of markets	**1924** Many medieval houses demolished	
AD 117 Death of Trajan	**552** Byzantine takeover of Rome. Markets occupied and fortified by the army	**1300s** Annibaldi and Caetani families vie for control of the area	**1828** First tentative excavations, but value of site not recognized	**1911–14** Convent demolished	
AD 98 Trajan succeeds Nerva as emperor				**1930–33** Markets finally excavated	

VISITORS' CHECKLIST

Mercati Traianei, Via IV Novembre.
Map 5 B4. ☎ *67 10 36 13.*
*57, 64, 65, 70, 75, 170 to Via IV
Novembre and many routes to
Piazza Venezia.* **Open** *9am–7pm
Tue–Sat, 9am–1pm Sun (last
adm: 30 mins before closing).*
Closed *Mon, public hols.*
Adm charge, *except for last
Sunday of each month.* 📷 ♿

The Markets in the 16th Century
*This fanciful fresco depicts a gladiatorial
combat taking place in front of the partly-buried
remains of Trajan's Markets.*

A Market Shop
*Shops were built with
arched entrances, with
jambs and lintels
creating rectangular
portals and windows.
A wooden mezzanine
was used for storage.*

Upper Corridor
*Shops on this upper level
were thought to have sold
wine and oil as a number
of storage jars were
discovered here.*

**Large hall with
semidomed
ceiling**

**Wall dividing
market area from
Forum of Trajan**

The terrace
over the archway
spanning Via
Biberatica has
a good view of
the Forum of
Trajan below.

Shops on the ground floor of
the large curving semicircle
were smaller than those on
the upper storeys. They were
also cooler and probably sold
vegetables, fruit and flowers.

MARKET SHOPPING

Shops opened early and closed about
noon. The best ones were decorated
with mosaics of the goods they sold.
Almost all the shopping was done
by men, though women visited the
dressmaker and cobbler. The
tradesmen were almost all male.
In employment records for the
period AD 117–193, the only
female shopkeepers mentioned
are three wool-sellers, two
jewellers, a greengrocer
and a fishwife.

Fish mosaic

Trajan's Markets ⑱

See pp88–9.

Column of Trajan ⑲

Via dei Fori Imperiali. **Map** 5 A4 &
12 F4. *See Visitors' Checklist for
Trajan's Markets, p89.*

Detail of Trajan's Column

THIS ELEGANT marble column
was inaugurated by Trajan
in AD 113, and celebrates his
two campaigns in Dacia
(Romania) in AD 101–2 and
AD 105–6. The column, base
and pedestal are 40 m (131 ft)
tall – precisely the same height
as the spur of the Quirinal hill
which was excavated to make
room for Trajan's Forum.
Spiralling up the column are
minutely detailed scenes from
the campaigns, beginning with
the Romans preparing for war
and ending with the Dacians
being ousted from their
homeland. The column is
pierced with small windows
to illuminate its internal spiral
staircase (closed to the public).
If you wish to see the reliefs
in detail there is a complete
set of casts in the Museo
della Civiltà Romana at EUR
(see p267).

When Trajan died in AD 117
his ashes, along with those of
his wife, Plotina, were placed
in a golden urn in the column's
hollow base. The column's
survival was largely thanks to
the intervention of Pope
Gregory the Great (reigned
590–604). He was so moved
by a relief showing Trajan
helping a woman whose son
had been killed that he
begged God to release the
emperor's soul from hell. God

duly appeared to the pope to
say that Trajan had been
rescued, but requested him
not to pray for the souls of
any more pagans.

According to legend, when
Trajan's ashes were exhumed
his skull and tongue were not
only intact, but his tongue
told of his release from hell.
The land around the column
was then declared sacred and
the column itself was spared.
The statue of Trajan remained
on top of the column until
1587, when it was replaced
with one of St Peter.

Torre delle Milizie ⑳

Mercati Traianei, Via IV Novembre.
Map 5 B4. *Closed for restoration.*

FOR CENTURIES this massive
brick tower was thought to
have been the one in which
Nero stood watching Rome
burn, after he had set it alight
in order to clear the city's
slums. It is uncertain whether
arson was among Nero's
crimes, but it is certain that he
did not watch the fire from
this tower – it was built in the
13th century.

Casa dei Cavalieri di Rodi ㉑

Piazza del Grillo 1. **Map** 5 B5.
📞 67 10 20 70. 🚌 11, 27, 81, 85,
87, 186. **Open** by appt only.

Loggia, Casa dei Cavalieri di Rodi

SINCE THE 12TH CENTURY the
crusading order, the Knights
of St John, also known as the
Knights of Rhodes (Rodi) or
Malta, have had their priorate
in this medieval house above
the Forum of Augustus. If you
are lucky enough to get
inside, ask to see the beautiful
Cappella di San Giovanni
(Chapel of St John).

Forum of Augustus ㉒

Piazza del Grillo 1. **Map** 5 B5 & 12 F5.
📞 69 94 10 20. 🚌 11, 27, 81, 85,
87, 186. **Open** by appt only.

**Podium of the Temple of Mars in
the Forum of Augustus**

THE FORUM of Augustus
was built to celebrate
Augustus's victory over Julius
Caesar's assassins, Brutus and
Cassius, at the Battle of
Philippi in 41 BC. The temple
in its centre was dedicated to
Mars the Avenger. The forum
stretched from a high wall at
the foot of the sleazy Suburra
quarter to the edge of the
Forum of Caesar. At least half
of it is now concealed below
Mussolini's Via dei Fori
Imperiali. The temple is easily
identified, with its cracked
steps and four Corinthian
columns. Originally it had a
statue of Mars which looked
very like Augustus. In case
anyone failed to notice the
resemblance, a giant statue of
Augustus himself was placed
against the Suburra wall.

Forum of Caesar ㉓

Via del Carcere Tulliano. **Map** 5 A5.
📞 69 94 10 20. 🚌 11, 27, 81, 85,
87, 186. **Open** by appt only.

THE FIRST of Rome's Imperial
fora was built by Julius
Caesar. He spent a fortune –
most of it booty from his
conquest of Gaul – buying up
and demolishing houses on
the site. Pride of place went
to a temple dedicated in 46
BC to the goddess Venus
Genetrix, from whom Caesar
claimed descent. The temple
contained statues of Caesar
and Cleopatra as well as of
Venus. All that remains of this
temple to vanity is a platform
and three Corinthian columns.

The forum was enclosed by a double colonnade which sheltered a row of shops, but this burnt down in AD 80 and was rebuilt by Domitian and Trajan. Trajan also added the Basilica Argentaria (an important financial exchange) and a heated public lavatory. The forum is not open to the public, but parts of it are visible from above in Via dei Fori Imperiali.

Mamertine Prison 24

Clivo Argentario 1. **Map** 5 A5.
679 29 02. 81, 85, 87, 186.
Open Apr–Sep: 9am–noon, 2.30pm–6pm; Oct–Mar: 9am–noon, 2pm–5pm. **Donation** expected.

19th-century engraving of guards visiting prisoners in the Mamertine

BELOW THE 16th-century church of San Giuseppe dei Falegnami (St Joseph of the Carpenters) is a dank dungeon in which, according to Christian legend, St Peter was imprisoned. He is said to have caused a spring to bubble up into the cell, and used the water to baptize the two prison guards.

The prison was in an old cistern with access to the city's main sewer (the Cloaca Maxima). The lower cell, the Tullianum, was used for executions and bodies were thrown into the sewer. Among the enemies of Rome to be executed here was the Gaulish leader Vercingetorix, defeated by Julius Caesar in 52 BC.

17th-century view of the ruined Forum of Nerva

Forum of Nerva 25

Piazza del Grillo 1 (reached through Forum of Augustus). **Map** 5 B5.
69 94 10 20. 11, 27, 81, 85, 87, 186. **Closed** for excavations.

THE FORUM of Nerva was begun by his predecessor, Domitian, and completed in AD 97. Little more than a long corridor with a colonnade along the sides and a Temple of Minerva at one end, it was also known as the Forum Transitorium because it lay between the Forum of Peace built by the Emperor Vespasian in AD 70 and the Forum of Augustus. Vespasian's forum is almost completely covered by Via dei Fori Imperiali, as is much of the Forum of Nerva itself. Excavations have unearthed Renaissance shops and

taverns, but only part of the forum can be seen, including the base of the temple and two columns that were part of the original colonnade. These support a relief of Minerva above a frieze of young girls learning to sew and weave.

Arch of Constantine 26

Between Via di San Gregorio and Piazza del Colosseo. **Map** 8 F1.
11, 15, 27, 81, 85, 87, 186, 673.
13, 30b. Colosseo.

THIS TRIUMPHAL ARCH was dedicated in AD 315 to celebrate Constantine's victory three years before over his co-emperor, Maxentius. Constantine claimed he owed his victory to a vision of Christ, but there is nothing Christian about the arch – in fact, most of the medallions, reliefs and statues were scavenged from earlier monuments.

Medallion on the Arch of Constantine

There are statues of Dacian prisoners taken from Trajan's Forum and reliefs of Marcus Aurelius, including one where he distributes bread to the poor. Inside the arch are reliefs of Trajan's victory over the Dacians. These were probably by the artist who worked on the Column of Trajan.

Colosseum 27

See pp92–5.

North side of the Arch of Constantine, facing the Colosseum

Colosseum ㉗

Rome's greatest amphitheatre
was commissioned by the
Emperor Vespasian in AD 72 on
the marshy site of a lake in the
grounds of Nero's palace, the
Domus Aurea *(see p175)*. Deadly
gladiatorial combats and wild
animal fights were staged free
of charge by the emperor and
wealthy citizens for public viewing.
The Colosseum was built to a practical design,
with its 80 arched entrances allowing easy
access to 55,000 spectators, but it is also a
building of great beauty. The drawing
here shows how it looked in AD 80.
It was one of several similar amphi-
theatres built in the Roman Empire,
and some survive at El Djem in
North Africa, Nîmes and Arles in
France and Verona in northern Italy.
Despite being
damaged over
the years by
neglect and
theft, it remains
a majestic
sight to
this day.

**Outer Wall of the
Colosseum**
*Stone plundered
from the facade in
the Renaissance
was used to build
several palaces,
bridges and parts
of St Peter's.*

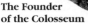

**The Founder
of the Colosseum**
*Vespasian was a professional
soldier who became emperor
in AD 69, founding the
Flavian dynasty.*

The outer walls are
made of travertine.

FLORA OF THE COLOSSEUM

By the 19th century the
Colosseum was heavily
overgrown.
Different micro-
climates in
various parts
of the ruin had
created an im-
pressive variety
of herbs, grasses
and wild flowers.
Several botanists
were inspired to
study and catalogue
them and two books
were published,
one listing 420
different species.

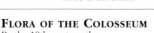

Borage, a herb

The bollards
anchored the
velarium.

The velarium was a
huge awning which
shaded spectators from
the sun. Supported on
poles fixed to the
upper storey of the
building, it was then
hoisted into position
with ropes anchored
to bollards outside
the stadium.

TIMELINE

	80 Vespasian's son, Titus, stages inaugural festival in the amphitheatre. It lasts 100 days
AD 70	**100**
72 Emperor Vespasian begins work on the Colosseum	**81–96** Amphitheatre completed in reign of Domitian

Internal Corridors

These were designed to allow the large and often unruly crowd to move freely and to be seated within ten minutes of arriving at the Colosseum.

The vomitorium was the exit used from each numbered section.

Brick formed the inner walls.

Corinthian columns

Ionic columns

Doric columns

The podium was a large terrace where the emperor and the wealthy upper classes had their seats.

Entry routes to take the spectators to their seats were reached by means of staircases to the various levels of the amphitheatre.

Arched entrances, 80 in total, were all numbered to let in the vast crowds that attended the fights.

Colossus of Nero

The Colosseum may have acquired its name from this huge gilt bronze statue that stood near the amphitheatre.

A gladiator's shield

230 Colosseum restored by Severus	**404** Gladiatorial combats banned		**1200s** Frangipane family turn Colosseum into a fortress			**1870** All vegetation removed
				15th–16th centuries Ruins used as quarry. Travertine blocks recycled by popes		
200	**400**	**1300**	**1500**		**1700**	**1900**
48 Thousandth anniversary celebration of founding of Rome by Romulus and Remus	**442** Building damaged in an earthquake	**523** Wild animal fights banned	**1312** Emperor Henry VII gives Colosseum to the Senate and people of Rome		**1749** Colosseum dedicated to Passion of Jesus	**1893–6** Structure below arena revealed

How Fights were Staged in the Arena

THE EMPERORS HELD shows here which often began with animals performing circus tricks. Then on came the gladiators, who fought each other to the death. When one was killed, attendants dressed as Charon, the mythical ferryman of the dead, carried his body off on a stretcher, and sand was raked over the blood ready for the next bout. A badly-wounded gladiator would surrender his fate to the crowd. The "thumbs up" sign from the emperor meant he could live, "thumbs down" that he die, and the victor became an instant hero. Animals were brought here from as far away as North Africa and the Middle East. The games held in AD 248 to mark the 1,000th anniversary of the founding of Rome saw the death of a host of lions, elephants, hippos, zebras and elks.

Beneath the Arena
Late 19th-century excavations exposed the network of underground rooms where the animals were kept.

Interior of the Colosseum
The stadium was built in the form of an ellipse, with tiers of seats around a vast central arena.

Emperor's entrance

Emperor's box

Layout of underground passages

Tiers of seats

Consul's box

Consul's entrance

Gladiators' entrance

A complex of rooms, passages and lifts lie underneath the arena.

Dramatic Entrances
Below the sand was a wooden floor through which animals, men and scenery appeared in the arena.

Roman Gladiators
These were usually slaves, prisoners of war or condemned criminals. Most were men, but there were a few female gladiators.

The Colosseum by Antonio Canaletto
This 18th-century view of the Colosseum shows the Meta Sudans fountain (now demolished). Water "sweated" from a metal ball on top of its brick cone.

Metal fencing kept animals penned in, while archers stood by just in case any escaped.

Seating was tiered, and different social classes were segregated.

A winch brought the animal cages up to arena level when they were due to fight.

A ramp and trap door enabled the animal to reach the arena after walking along a corridor.

Cages were like three-sided lifts which went up to the next level where the animals were released.

SEA BATTLES IN THE ARENA

The historian Dion Cassius, writing in the 4th century AD, relates how, 150 years earlier, the Colosseum's arena was flooded to stage a mock sea battle. Scholars now believe that he was mistaken. The spectacle probably took place in the Naumachia of Augustus, a water-filled arena situated across the Tiber in Trastevere.

PALATINE

ACCORDING TO LEGEND, Romulus and Remus were brought up here by a wolf in a cave. Traces of Iron Age huts, dating from the 9th century BC, have been found on the Palatine hill, providing archaeological support for the area's legendary links with the founding of Rome. The Palatine was a very desirable place to live, becoming home to some of the city's most famous inhabitants. The great orator Cicero had a house here, as did the lyric poet Catullus. Augustus was born on the hill and continued to live here in very modest

Fresco of mask in the House of Augustus

circumstances even when he became emperor. The two buildings identified as the House of Augustus and the House of Livia, his wife, are among the best preserved here. The first emperor's example of frugality was ignored by his successors, Tiberius, Caligula and Domitian, who all built extravagant palaces here. The ruins of Tiberius's palace lie beneath the 16th-century Farnese Gardens. The most extensive ruins are those of the Domus Augustana and Domus Flavia, the two wings of Domitian's palace, and the later extension built by Septimius Severus.

SIGHTS AT A GLANCE

Temples
Temple of Cybele ❻

Historic Buildings
Domus Flavia ❶
Domus Augustana ❸
House of Livia ❺

Ancient Sites
Cryptoporticus ❷
Stadium ❹
Huts of Romulus ❼

Parks and Gardens
Farnese Gardens ❽

SEE ALSO

• **Street Finder**, map 8

GETTING THERE

There are two ways of getting on to the Palatine hill; either through the Roman Forum (from Via dei Fori Imperiali) or through the entrance in Via di San Gregorio. One ticket is valid for both Forum and Palatine. The best buses are the 11, 27, 81, 85, 87, 186; all stop in Via dei Fori Imperiali near the main entrance. Colosseo Metro station *(see p77)* is also handy.

KEY

Tour of the Palatine map

0 metres 200
0 yards 200

Towering ruins of the Palace of Septimius Severus on the Palatine hill

A Tour of the Palatine

SHADED ON ITS LOWER SLOPES with pines, and scattered in spring with wild flowers, the Palatine is the most pleasant and relaxing of the city's ancient sites. You can reach the hill by walking up from the Roman Forum *(see pp76–7)*. The area is dominated by the ruins of the Domus Flavia and the Domus Augustana, two parts of Domitian's huge palace built at the end of the 1st century AD. What you are able to see depends on where excavations are taking place at the time.

Huts of Romulus
These are traces of a 9th-century BC village on the Palatine ❼

To Farnese Gardens
See p101

House of Augustus

Temple of Cybele
Also known as the Temple of the Magna Mater, this was the centre of an important fertility cult ❻

★ House of Livia
Many of the wall paintings have survived in the house where Augustus lived with his wife Livia ❺

STAR SIGHTS

★ Domus Flavia

★ House of Livia

KEY

— — — Suggested route

0 metres	75
0 yards	75

★ Domus Flavia
This oval fountain was designed to be seen from the dining hall of the palace ❶

Domus Augustana
The Roman emperors lived in this part of the palace, wh… the Domus Flavia was used f… public functions ❸

Cryptoporticus
In this long underground gallery, built by Nero, the stuccoes that decorated the walls and vault have been replaced with copies **2**

LOCATOR MAP
See Central Rome Map pp12–13

The Palatine Museum is housed in a former convent, but has been closed for many years.

Octagonal fountain of the Domus Flavia

Stadium
Part of the Imperial palace, this enclosure may have been used by the emperors as a private garden **4**

To Forum entrance

The exedra of the Stadium may have housed a balcony for emperors to view races.

Baths of Septimius Severus

The Palace of Septimius Severus (reigned AD 193–211) was an extension of the Domus Augustana. It projected beyond the hillside, requiring enormous arched supports.

Substructure of palace

Domus Flavia ❶

See Visitors' Checklist.

Marble pavement in the courtyard of the Domus Flavia

IN AD 81 DOMITIAN, the third of the Flavian dynasty of emperors, decided to build a splendid new palace on the Palatine hill. But the western peak, the Germalus, was covered with houses and temples, while the eastern peak, the Palatium, was very steep. So the emperor's architect, Rabirius, flattened the Palatium and used the soil to fill in the cleft between the two peaks, burying (and preserving) a number of Republican-era houses.

The palace had two wings – one official (the Domus Flavia), the other private (the Domus Augustana). It was the main Imperial palace for 300 years. At the front of the Domus Flavia, the surviving stubs of columns and fragments of walls trace the shapes of three adjoining rooms. In the first of these, the Basilica, Domitian dispensed his personal brand of justice.

The central Aula Regia was a throne room decorated with 12 black basalt statues. The third room (now covered with corrugated plastic) was the Lararium, a shrine for the household gods known as Lares (usually the owner's ancestors). It may have been used for official ceremonies or by the palace guards.

Fearing assassination, Domitian had the walls of the courtyard covered with shiny marble slabs designed to act as mirrors so that he could see anyone lurking behind him. In the event, he was assassinated in his bedroom, possibly on the orders of his wife, Domitia. The courtyard is now a pleasant place to pause; the flower beds in the centre follow the maze pattern of a sunken fountain pool.

Cryptoporticus ❷

See Visitors' Checklist.

THE CRYPTOPORTICUS, a series of underground corridors, was built by Nero to connect his Golden House *(see p175)* with the palaces of earlier emperors on the Palatine. A further branch leading to the Palace of Domitian was added later. Its vaults are decorated with delicate stucco reliefs – copies of originals now kept in the Palatine's closed museum.

Domus Augustana ❸

See Visitors' Checklist.

THIS PART of Domitian's palace was called the Domus Augustana because it was the private residence of the "august" emperors. On the upper level a high brick

wall remains, and you can make out the shape of its two courtyards. The far better preserved lower level is closed to the public, though you can look down on its sunken courtyard with the geometric foundations of a fountain in its centre. Sadly, you can't see the stairs linking the two levels (once lit by sunlight falling on a mirror-paved pool), nor the surrounding rooms, paved with coloured marble.

Stadium ❹

See Visitors' Checklist.

Stadium viewed from the south

THE STADIUM on the Palatine was laid out at the same time as the Palace of Domitian. It is not clear whether it was a public stadium, a private track for exercising horses, or simply a large garden. The alcove in the eastern wall looks as though it may have held a box from which the emperor could have watched races. It is, however, known that the Stadium was used for foot races by the Ostrogothic king, Theodoric, in the 6th century – he added the small oval-shaped enclosure at the southern end of the site.

Remains of the Domus Augustana and the Palace of Septimius Severus

House of Livia ❺

See Visitors' Checklist. If closed, apply to custodian.

Fresco in the House of Livia

THIS HOUSE dating from the 1st century BC is one of the best preserved on the Palatine. It was probably part of the house in which the Emperor Augustus and his wife Livia lived. Compared with later Imperial palaces, it is a relatively modest home. According to Suetonius, the biographer of Rome's early emperors, Augustus slept in the same small bedroom for 40 years on a low bed which had "a very ordinary coverlet". He wore home-made clothes

Detail of floor mosaic (woven by Livia, his sister Octavia and daughter Julia), but he was vain enough to wear shoes with extremely thick soles to conceal the fact that he was rather short.

The ground level of the Palatine is now above the house, so you walk down a flight of steps and along a mosaic-paved corridor into a courtyard. Its imitation marble wall frescoes have been detached in order to preserve them, but they still hang in situ. Though they are very faded, you can still make out the veining patterns. Leading off the courtyard are three small reception rooms. The frescoes in the central one include a faded scene of Hermes coming to the rescue of Zeus's beloved Io, who is guarded by the 100-eyed Argos. In the left-hand room you can make out frescoed figures of griffins and other beasts, while the decor in the right-hand room includes landscapes and cityscapes.

Temple of Cybele ❻

See Visitors' Checklist.

OTHER THAN a platform with a few column stumps and capitals, there is little to see of the Temple of Cybele, a popular fertility goddess imported to Rome from Asia. The priests of the cult castrated themselves in the belief that if they sacrificed their own fertility it would guarantee that of the natural world. The annual festival of Cybele, from March 22–4, culminated with frenzied eunuch-priests slashing their bodies to offer blood to the goddess, and the ceremonial castration of novice priests.

Statue of the goddess Cybele

Huts of Romulus ❼

See Visitors' Checklist.

ACCORDING TO LEGEND, after killing his brother Remus, Romulus founded a village on the Palatine. In the 1940s a series of holes was found filled with earth lighter in colour than the surrounding soil. Archaeologists deduced that these holes must originally have held the supporting poles of three Iron Age huts – the first foundations of Rome *(see pp16–17)*.

Farnese Gardens ❽

See Visitors' Checklist.

IN THE MID-16TH century Cardinal Alessandro Farnese, grandson of Pope Paul III, bought the ruins of Tiberius's palace on the Palatine. He filled in the ruined building and had Vignola, architect of the interior of the Gesù church, design a garden for him. The result was one of the first botanical gardens in Europe, its terraces linked by steps stretching from the House of Vestal Virgins in the Forum to the Palatine's Germalus peak. The gardeners introduced a number of plants to Italy and Europe, among them *Acacia farnesiana*. Farnese was at the centre of a glittering set which included a number of courtesans, so the parties here are likely to have been somewhat unholy.

The area was dug up during the excavation of the Palatine and re-landscaped afterwards. Nevertheless the tree-lined avenues, rose gardens and glorious views still make it an ideal place to unwind.

Farnese pavilions, relics of the age when the Palatine was a private garden

PIAZZA DELLA ROTONDA

THE PANTHEON, one of the great buildings in the history of European architecture, has stood at the heart of Rome for nearly 2,000 years. The historic area around it has seen uninterrupted economic and political activity throughout that time. Palazzo di Montecitorio, built for Pope Innocent X as a papal tribunal in 1697, is now the Italian parliament and many nearby buildings are government offices. This is also the main financial district of Rome with banking headquarters and the stock exchange. Not many people live here, but in the evenings, Romans stroll in the narrow streets and fill the lively restaurants and cafés that make this a focus for the city's social life.

Bitter-style apéritif, popular in Roman cafés

SIGHTS AT A GLANCE

Churches and Temples
Temple of Hadrian ❶
Sant'Ignazio di Loyola ❸
Gesù pp114–15 ❾
Santa Maria sopra Minerva ⓫
Pantheon pp110–11 ⓭
Sant'Eustachio ⓮
La Maddalena ⓯
Santa Maria in Campo Marzio ⓲
San Lorenzo in Lucina ⓴

Historic Streets and Piazzas
Piazza di Sant'Ignazio ❷
Via della Gatta ❼

Historic Buildings
Palazzo del Collegio Romano ❹
Palazzo Doria Pamphilj ❻
Palazzo Altieri ❽
Palazzo Baldassini ⓱
Palazzo Borghese ⓳
Palazzo di Montecitorio ㉑
Palazzo Capranica ㉔

Columns, Obelisks and Statues
Pie' di Marmo ❿
Obelisk of Santa Maria sopra Minerva ⓬
Obelisk of Montecitorio ㉒
Column of Marcus Aurelius ㉓

Fountains
Fontanella del Facchino ❺

Cafés and Restaurants
Caffè Giolitti ⓰

KEY
Street-by-Street map
Ⓟ Parking

GETTING THERE
The area has no Metro station, but is about 15 minutes' walk from Spagna or Barberini Metro stops. There are some convenient bus stops in Via del Plebiscito, served by the 56, 64, 70, 90, 492 and many other routes. Piazza Colonna is served by the 56, 60, 85 and all buses that go up Via del Corso. The only bus that passes through the narrow streets of the area is the 119 electric minibus, which stops right outside the Pantheon.

0 metres 200
0 yards 200

SEE ALSO

• **Street Finder**, maps 4, 5, 12
• **Where to Stay** pp294–5
• **Restaurants** pp310–11

The immense granite columns of the Pantheon

Street-by-Street: Piazza della Rotonda

I F YOU WANDER THROUGH this area, sooner or later you will emerge into Piazza della Rotonda with its jumble of open-air café tables in front of the Pantheon. The refreshing splash of the fountain makes it a welcome resting place. In this warren of narrow streets, it can be hard to realize just how close you are to some of Rome's finest sights. The magnificent art collection of Palazzo Doria Pamphilj and the Baroque splendour of the Gesù are just a few minutes' walk from the Pantheon. At night there is always a lively buzz of activity, as people dine in style or enjoy the coffee and ice creams for which the area is famous.

Temple of Hadrian
The columns of this Roman temple now form the facade of the stock exchange ❶

Piazza di Sant'Ignazio
The square is a rare example of stylish domestic architecture from the early 18th century ❷

La Tazza d'Oro enjoys a reputation for the wonderful coffee consumed on its premises as well as for its freshly-ground coffee to take away. *(See p319.)*

Santa Maria sopra Minerva
The rich decoration of Rome's only Gothic church was added in the 19th century ⓫

★ **Pantheon**
The awe-inspiring interior of Rome's best-preserved ancient temple is only hinted at from the outside ⓭

PIAZZA DI SANT'IGNAZIO

VIA DI SANT' IGNAZIO

VIA DEL SEMINARIO

PIAZZA DELLA ROTONDA

PIAZZA DELLA MINERVA

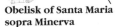

Obelisk of Santa Maria sopra Minerva
In 1667 Bernini dreamed up the idea of mounting a recently discovered obelisk on the back of a marble elephant ⓬

★ Sant'Ignazio di Loyola
Andrea Pozzo painted this glorious Baroque ceiling (1685) to celebrate St Ignatius and the Jesuit order ❸

LOCATOR MAP
See Central Rome Map pp12–13

Fontanella del Facchino
The water in this small 16th-century fountain spurts from a barrel held by a porter ❺

Palazzo del Collegio Romano
Up until 1870, the college educated many leading figures in the Catholic Church ❹

★ Palazzo Doria Pamphilj
Among the masterpieces in the art gallery of this magnificent family palazzo is this portrait of Pope Innocent X by Velázquez (1650) ❻

Via della Gatta
The street is named after the statue of a cat ❼

Palazzo Altieri
This enormous 17th-century palazzo is decorated with the arms of Pope Clement X ❽

★ Gesù
The design of the first-ever Jesuit church had a great impact on religious architecture ❾

Pie' di Marmo
This marble foot is a stray fragment from a gigantic Roman statue ❿

KEY

– – – Suggested route

| 0 metres | 75 |
| 0 yards | 75 |

STAR SIGHTS

★ **Pantheon**

★ **Palazzo Doria Pamphilj**

★ **Gesù**

★ **Sant'Ignazio di Loyola**

Temple of Hadrian ❶

La Borsa, Piazza di Pietra. **Map** 4 F3 & 12 E2. 🚌 56, 60, 71, 81, 85, 90, 119, 492. **Not open** to the public.

THIS TEMPLE, built to honour the Emperor Hadrian as a god, was dedicated by his successor Antoninus Pius in AD 145. The remains of the temple are visible on the southern side of Piazza di Pietra, incorporated in a 17th-century building. This was originally a papal customs house, completed by Carlo Fontana and his son in the 1690s. Today the building houses the Roman stock exchange (La Borsa).

Eleven marble Corinthian columns 15 m (49 ft) high stand on a base of *peperino*, a volcanic rock quarried from the Alban hills to the south of Rome. The columns decorated the northern flank of the temple enclosing its inner shrine, the *cella*. The *peperino* wall of the *cella* is still visible behind the columns, as is part of the coffered portico ceiling.

A number of reliefs from the temple, representing conquered Roman provinces, are now in the courtyard of the Palazzo dei Conservatori *(see pp72–3)*. They reflect the mostly peaceful foreign policy of Hadrian's reign.

Remains of Hadrian's Temple

Piazza di Sant'Ignazio ❷

Map 4 F4 & 12 E3. 🚌 56, 60, 71, 81, 85, 90, 119, 492.

ONE OF THE MAJOR works of the Roman Rococo, the piazza (1727–8) is Filippo Raguzzini's masterpiece. It offsets the imposing facade of the church of Sant'Ignazio with the intimacy of the

Illusionistic ceiling in the crossing of Sant'Ignazio

houses of the bourgeoisie. The theatrical setting, the curvilinear design and the playful forms of its windows, balconies and balusters mark the piazza as one of a highly distinctive group of structures. Along with Palazzo Doria Pamphilj (1731), the facade of La Maddalena (1735) and the aristocratic Spanish Steps (1723), it belongs to that happy moment when Rome's bubbly Rococo triumphed over conservative Classicism.

Sant'Ignazio di Loyola ❸

Piazza di Sant'Ignazio. **Map** 4 F4 & 12 E3. 📞 679 44 06. 🚌 56, 60, 71, 81, 85, 90, 119, 492. **Open** 7.30am–12.30pm, 4pm–7.15pm daily. 📷 ⛪

THE CHURCH was built by Cardinal Ludovisi in 1626 in honour of St Ignatius of Loyola, founder of the Society of Jesus and the man who most embodied the zeal of the Counter Reformation.

Together with the Gesù *(see pp114–15)*, Sant'Ignazio forms the nucleus of the Jesuit area in Rome. Its vast interior, lined with precious stones, marble, stucco and gilt, creates a thrilling sense of theatre. The church has a Latin-cross plan, with an apse and many side chapels. A cupola was planned

but never built, so the space it would have filled was covered by a fake perspective painting. The piers built to bear the weight of the cupola help support the observatory of the Collegio Romano.

Palazzo del Collegio Romano ❹

Piazza del Collegio Romano. **Map** 5 A4 & 12 E3. 🚌 56, 60, 62, 85, 90, 95, 160, 492. **Not open** to the public.

SHARING THE SAME BLOCK as the church of Sant'Ignazio, the palazzo used to house a college run by the Jesuits; many future bishops, cardinals and popes studied here. The college was confiscated in 1870 and was turned into an ordinary school. The portals bear the coat of arms of its founder, Pope Gregory XIII Boncompagni (reigned 1572–85). The facade is also decorated with a bell, two sundials and a clock. On the right is a tower built in 1787 as an observatory. Up until 1925 its time signal regulated all the clocks throughout the city.

Portal of the Collegio Romano

Fontanella del Facchino ❺

Via Lata. **Map** 5 A4 & 12 E3. 🚌 *56, 60, 62, 85, 90, 95, 160, 492.*

IL FACCHINO (the Porter), once in the Corso, now set into the wall of the Banco di Roma, was one of Rome's "talking statues" like Pasquino *(see p124).* Created around 1590, the fountain may have been based on a drawing by Florentine painter Jacopino del Conte. The statue of a man holding a barrel probably represents a member of the Università degli Acquaroli (Fraternity of Watercarriers), though it is also claimed to be of Martin Luther, or of Abbondio Rizzio, a porter who died carrying a barrel.

The Facchino drinking fountain

Palazzo Doria Pamphilj ❻

Piazza del Collegio Romano 1A. **Map** 5 A4 & 12 E3. 📞 679 43 65. 🚌 *56, 60, 62, 85, 90, 95, 160, 492.* **Open** 10am–5pm Mon–Wed, Fri–Sun. **Closed** public hols. **Adm charge.** ♿ limited. 📷 compulsory for private apartments, otherwise ask. 📱

PALAZZO DORIA PAMPHILJ is a great island of stone in the heart of Rome, the oldest parts dating from 1435. Through the Corso entrance you can glimpse the 16th-century porticoed courtyard with the coat of arms of the della Rovere family. The next owners were the Aldobrandini family. Between 1601 and 1647 the mansion acquired a second courtyard and flanking wings at the expense of a public bath that stood nearby.

When the Pamphilj family took over, they completed the Piazza del Collegio Romano facade and the Via della Gatta wing, a splendid chapel and a theatre inaugurated by Queen Christina of Sweden in 1684.

In the first half of the 18th century, Gabriele Valvassori created the gallery above the courtyard and a new facade along the Corso, using the highly decorative style of the period known as the *barocchetto*, which now dominates the building. The stairways and salons, the Mirror Gallery and the picture gallery all radiate a joyous sense of light and space.

The family collection in the Doria Pamphilj gallery has over 400 paintings dating from the 15th to the 18th century, including the famous portrait of Pope Innocent X Pamphilj by Velázquez. There are also important works by Titian, Caravaggio, Lorenzo Lotto, Guercino and Claude Lorrain. The rooms in the private apartment have many of their original furnishings on display, including splendid Brussels and Gobelins tapestries.

Via della Gatta ❼

Map 5 A4 & 12 E3. 🚌 *56, 60, 62, 85, 90, 95, 160, 492.*

THIS NARROW STREET runs between the great Palazzo Doria Pamphilj and the smaller Palazzo Grazioli. The ancient marble sculpture of a cat *(gatta)* that gives the street its name can be seen on the first cornice on the corner of Palazzo Grazioli.

Via della Gatta's marble cat

Palazzo Altieri ❽

Via del Gesù 93. **Map** 4 F4 & 12 E3. 🚌 *56, 64, 70, 81, 90 and many other routes. See **Shops** p333.*

THE ALTIERI FAMILY is first mentioned in Rome's history in the 9th century. This palazzo was built by the last male heirs, the brothers Cardinal Giambattista di Lorenzo Altieri and Cardinal Emilio Altieri, later Pope Clement X (reigned 1670–76). Many surrounding houses had to be demolished, but an old woman called Berta refused to leave, so her hovel was incorporated in the palazzo. Its windows are still visible on the west end of the building. Most of Palazzo Altieri is now occupied by the enormous material and clothing business, Bises.

Gesù ❾

See pp114–15.

Caravaggio's *Rest during the Flight into Egypt* in Palazzo Doria Pamphilj

Marble foot from a Roman statue

Pie' di Marmo ⑩

Via di Santo Stefano del Cacco.
Map 4 F4 & 12 E3. 🚌 56, 64, 70,
81, 90, 90b, 119.

IT WAS POPULARLY believed in
the Middle Ages that half
the population of ancient
Rome must have been made
up of bronze, golden and
marble statues. Fragments of
these giants, usually gods or
emperors, are scattered over
the city. This piece, a marble
foot (pie' di marmo), comes
from an area dedicated to the
Egyptian gods Isis and Serapis
and was probably part of a
statue in one of the temples.
These statues were painted
and covered with jewels and
clothes given by the faithful –
a great fire hazard with
unattended burning tapers.

Santa Maria sopra Minerva ⑪

Piazza della Minerva 42. **Map** 4 F4 &
12 E3. 📞 679 39 26. 🚌 56, 64, 70,
81, 90, 119. **Open** 7am–noon, 4pm–
7pm daily, but phone to check.
Cloister open 8.30am–1pm, 4pm–
7.30pm daily. 🚻 🔊 **Concerts**.

FEW OTHER CHURCHES can
display such a complete
and impressive record of
Italian art. Dating from the
13th century, the Minerva is
one of the very few examples
of Gothic architecture in
Rome. It was the traditional
stronghold of the Dominicans,
whose anti-heretical zeal
earned them the punning
nickname of *Domini Canes*
(the hounds of the Lord).
Built on ancient ruins,
supposed to have been the
Temple of Minerva, the
simple T-shaped vaulted
building acquired rich chapels
and works of art by which its

many patrons wished to be
remembered. Note the
Cosmatesque 13th-century
tombs and the exquisite
works of 15th-century Tuscan
and Venetian artists. Native
Roman talent of the period
can be admired in Antoniazzo
Romano's *Annunciation*,
featuring Cardinal Juan de
Torquemada, uncle of the
infamous Spanish Inquisitor.
The more monumental style
of the Roman Renaissance is
well represented in the tombs
of the 16th-century Medici
popes, Leo X and his cousin
Clement VII, and in the richly
decorated Aldobrandini
Chapel. Near the steps of
the choir is the celebrated
sculpture of the *Risen Christ*,
started by Michelangelo but
completed by Raffaele da
Montelupo in 1521.
There are also splendid
works of art from the
Baroque period, including
a tomb and a bust by
Bernini. The church is
visited not only for its
art, but also because it
contains the tombs of
many famous Italians:
St Catherine of Siena,
who died here in 1380;
the Venetian sculptor
Andrea Bregno (died
1506); the Humanist
Cardinal Pietro Bembo
(died 1547); and Fra
Angelico, the Dominican
friar and painter, who
died in Rome in 1455.

Obelisk of Santa Maria sopra Minerva ⑫

Piazza della Minerva. **Map** 4 F4 &
12 D3. 🚌 56, 64, 70, 81, 90, 119.

ORIGINALLY MEANT to decorate
Palazzo Barberini as a kind
of joke, this exotic elephant
and obelisk sculpture is typical
of Bernini's inexhaustible
imagination. (The elephant
was actually sculpted by Ercole
Ferrata to Bernini's design.)
The old obelisk was found
in the garden of the
monastery of Santa Maria
sopra Minerva, and the friars
wanted the monument
erected in their piazza. The
elephant was provided with
its enormous saddle-cloth
because of a friar's
insistence that the gap
under the animal's
abdomen would
undermine its stability.
Bernini knew better: you
need only look at
the Fontana dei
Fiumi (*see p120*)
in Piazza Navona
to appreciate his
use of empty space.
The elephant, an
ancient symbol of
intelligence and piety,
was chosen as the
embodiment of the
virtues on which
Christians should
build true wisdom.

Bernini's Egyptian obelisk and marble elephant

Nave of Santa Maria sopra Minerva

Pantheon ⑬

See pp110–11.

Sant'Eustachio ⑭

Piazza Sant'Eustachio. **Map** 4 F4 & 12 D3. ☎ 686 53 34. 🚌 70, 81, 87, 90, 90b, 119, 186, 492. **Open** 4.30pm–8pm Mon–Sat, 9.30am– 12.30pm Sun. 🚹 📷

THE ORIGINS of this church go back to early Christian times, when it offered succour to the poor. In medieval times many charitable brotherhoods elected Sant'Eustachio as their patron and had chapels here.

The dumpy Romanesque bell tower is one of the few surviving parts of the medieval church, which was totally redecorated in the 17th and 18th centuries.

Bell tower of Sant'Eustachio

La Maddalena ⑮

Piazza della Maddalena. **Map** 4 F3 & 12 D2. ☎ 679 77 96. 🚌 70, 81, 87, 90, 90b, 492. **Open** 7.30am– noon, 5pm–7.45pm daily. 🚹 📷

SITUATED IN a small piazza near the Pantheon, the Maddalena's Rococo facade, built in 1735, epitomizes the love of light and movement of the late Baroque. Its curves are reminiscent of Borromini's San Carlo alle Quattro Fontane *(see p161)*. The facade has been lovingly restored, despite the protests of diehard Neo-Classicists who dismiss its painted stucco as icing sugar.

The small size of the Maddalena did not deter the 17th- and 18th-century

The old-fashioned *salone* of the Caffè Giolitti

decorators who filled the interior with ornament from the floor to the top of the elegant cupola. The organ loft and choir are particularly powerful examples of the Baroque's desire to fire the imagination of the faithful.

Many of the paintings and sculptures employ the new Christian imagery of the Counter Reformation. In the niches of the nave, for example, the statues are personifications of virtues such as Humility and Simplicity. There are also scenes from the life of San Camillo, who died in the adjacent convent in 1614. The church belonged to his followers, the Camillians, a preaching order active in Rome's hospitals. Like the Jesuits, they commissioned powerful works of art to convey the force of their religious message.

La Maddalena's stuccoed facade

Caffè Giolitti ⑯

Via degli Uffici del Vicario 40. **Map** 4 F3 & 12 D2. ☎ 699 12 43. 🚌 56, 60, 90, 119, 492. **Open** Apr–Oct, Dec: daily; Nov, Jan–Mar: 7am–2am Tue–Sun, 7am–3am Sat.

FOUNDED IN 1900, the Caffè Giolitti is the heir to the *Belle Époque* cafés that lined the nearby Corso in Rome's first days as capital of the new Italian state. Its *salone* holds tourists in summer, Roman families at weekends, and on weekdays a varied crowd of office workers, construction workers and officials from the nearby parliament in Palazzo di Montecitorio.

Palazzo Baldassini ⑰

Via delle Coppelle 35. **Map** 4 F3 & 12 D2. 🚌 70, 81, 90, 90b, 119. **Not open** to the public.

MELCHIORRE BALDASSINI built his home in the style of the Florentine Renaissance, skilfully adapted to the more austere surroundings of Rome. With its cornices marking the different floors and wrought-iron window grilles, this is one of the best examples of a Roman palazzo of the early 16th century. It stands in the part of Rome still known as the Renaissance Quarter, which grew up around the long straight streets such as Via di Ripetta and Via della Scrofa built at the time of Pope Leo X (reigned 1513–21).

Pantheon ⓭

IN THE MIDDLE AGES the Pantheon, the Roman "temple of all the gods", became a church; in time this magnificent building with its awe-inspiring domed interior became a symbol of Rome itself. The rectangular portico screens the vast hemispherical dome: only from inside can its true scale and beauty be appreciated. The rotunda's height and diameter are equal: 43.3 m (140 ft). The hole at the top of the dome, the *oculus*, provides the only light. We owe this marvel of Roman engineering to the Emperor Hadrian (AD 118–125), who designed it to replace an earlier temple built by Marcus Agrippa, son-in-law of Augustus. The shrines that now line the wall of the Pantheon range from the Tomb of Raphael to those of the kings of modern Italy.

★ **Interior of Dome**
The dome was cast by pouring concrete mixed with tufa and pumice over a temporary wooden framework.

The walls of the drum supporting the dome are 6 m (19 ft) thick.

The immense portico is built on the foundations of Agrippa's temple.

The portico, enclosed by granite columns

STAR FEATURES

★ **Interior of Dome**

★ **Tomb of Raphael**

Bell Towers
This 18th-century view by Bernardo Bellotto shows Bernini's much-ridiculed turrets, which were removed in 1883.

Floor Patterning
The marble floor, restored in 1873, preserves the original Roman design.

RAPHAEL AND LA FORNARINA

Raphael, at his own request, was buried here when he died in 1520. He had lived for years with his model, La Fornarina *(see p210)*, seen here in a painting by Giulio Romano, but she was excluded from the ceremony of his burial. On the right of his tomb is a memorial to his fiancée, Maria Bibbiena, niece of the artist's patron, Cardinal Dovizi di Bibbiena.

VISITORS' CHECKLIST

Piazza della Rotonda. **Map** 4 F4 & 12 D3. 68 30 02 30.
64, 70, 75, 119.
Open 9am–6.30pm Mon–Sat, 9am–1pm Sun & public hols. **Closed** 1 Jan, 1 May, 25 Dec.
Concerts.

Oculus

Coffering
Constructing the dome from hollow decorative coffers reduced its weight.

Relieving Arches
Brick arches embedded in the structure of the wall act as internal buttresses, distributing the weight of the dome.

★ **Tomb of Raphael**
The artist's body rests below a Madonna by Lorenzetto (1524).

TIMELINE

27–25 BC Marcus Agrippa builds first Pantheon	*Inscription on pediment*	**735** Gregory III roofs the Pantheon in lead	**1305–77** While papal seat is in Avignon, Pantheon is used as fortress and poultry market	**1888** Tomb of King Vittorio Emanuele II completed
30 BC	**AD 100**	**600**	**1100**	**1600**
AD 118 Hadrian builds new Pantheon	**609** Pope Boniface IV consecrates Pantheon as church of Santa Maria ad Martyres	**663** Byzantine Emperor Constans II strips gilded tiles from the roof	**1632** Urban VIII melts down bronze from portico for Bernini's baldacchino in St Peter's	

Bernini's curving southern facade of Palazzo di Montecitorio

Santa Maria in Campo Marzio ⑱

Piazza in Campo Marzio 45. **Map** 4 F3 & 12 D2. 📞 678 70 21. 🚌 56, 60, 90, 90b, 119, 492. **Closed for renovation.**

Around the courtyard through which you enter the church, there are fascinating remnants of medieval houses, once the property of the original monastery. The church itself was rebuilt in 1685 by Antonio de Rossi, using a square Greek-cross plan with a cupola. Above the altar is a 12th-century painting of the Madonna, which gives the church its name.

Palazzo Borghese ⑲

Largo della Fontanella di Borghese. **Map** 4 F3 & 12 D1. 🚌 70, 81, 90, 90b, 119. **Not open** to the public.

The palazzo was acquired in about 1605 by Cardinal Camillo Borghese, just before he became Pope Paul V. Flaminio Ponzio was hired to enlarge the building and give it the grandeur appropriate to the residence of the pope's family. He added a wing overlooking Piazza Borghese and the delightful porticoed courtyard inside. Subsequent enlargements included the building and decoration of a great *nympheum* known as the Bath of Venus. For more than two centuries this palazzo housed the Borghese family's renowned collection of paintings, which was bought

by the Italian state in 1902 and transferred to the Villa Borghese *(see pp260–61).*

Pope Paul V, who commissioned Palazzo Borghese for his family

San Lorenzo in Lucina ⑳

Via in Lucina 16A. **Map** 4 F3 & 12 E1. 📞 687 14 94. 🚌 70, 81, 90, 90b, 119. **Open** 8.30am–noon, 4.30pm–7.30pm daily. ♿ 📷

The church is one of Rome's oldest Christian places of worship, and was probably built on a well sacred to Juno, protectress of women. It was rebuilt in the 12th century, and today's external appearance is typical of the period: a portico

with re-used Roman columns, crowned by medieval capitals, a plain triangular pediment and a Romanesque bell tower with coloured marble inlay.

In contrast, the interior of the church was totally rebuilt in the 17th century. The old basilical plan was destroyed and the two side naves were replaced by richly-decorated Baroque chapels. Don't miss the fine busts in the Fonseca Chapel, designed by Bernini, or the *Crucifixion* by Guido Reni above the main altar. There is also a 19th-century monument honouring French painter Nicolas Poussin, who died in Rome in 1655 and was buried in the church.

Palazzo di Montecitorio ㉑

Piazza di Montecitorio. **Map** 4 F3 & 12 E2. 🚌 56, 60, 85, 90, 90b, 119, 492. **Not open** to the public.

The palazzo's first architect, Bernini, got the job after he presented a silver model of his design to the wife of his patron, Prince Ludovisi. The building was completed in 1697 by Carlo Fontana and became the Papal Tribunal of Justice. In 1871 it was chosen to be Italy's new Chamber of Deputies and by 1918 it had doubled in size with a second grand facade. The 630 members of parliament are elected by a system of proportional representation that ensures that no single party ever gains an overall majority.

The church of San Lorenzo in Lucina

Emperor Augustus's obelisk

Obelisk of Montecitorio ②

Piazza di Montecitorio. **Map** 4 F3 & 12 E2. *56, 60, 85, 90, 119, 492.*

T HE MEASUREMENT of time in ancient Rome was always a rather hit-and-miss affair: for many years the Romans relied on an imported (and therefore inaccurate) sundial, a trophy from the conquest of Sicily. In 10 BC the Emperor Augustus laid out an enormous sundial in the Campus Martius. Its centre was roughly in today's Piazza di San Lorenzo in Lucina. The shadow was cast by an enormous granite obelisk that he had brought back from Heliopolis in Egypt. Unfortunately this sundial too became inaccurate after only 50 years, possibly as a result of subsidence.

The obelisk was still in the piazza in the 9th century, but then disappeared until it was rediscovered lying under medieval houses in the reign of Pope Julius II (1503–13). The pope was intrigued, because Egyptian hieroglyphs were thought to hold the key to the wisdom of Adam before the Fall, but it was only under Pope Benedict XIV (reigned 1740–58) that the obelisk was finally unearthed. It was erected in its present location in 1787 by Pope Pius VI.

Column of Marcus Aurelius ㉓

Piazza Colonna. **Map** 5 A3 & 12 E2. *56, 60, 85, 90, 90b, 119, 492.*

C LEARLY AN IMITATION of the Column of Trajan (see p90), this monument was erected after the death of Marcus Aurelius in AD 180 to commemorate his victories over the barbarian tribes of the Danube. The 80-year lapse between the two works produced a great artistic change: the wars of Marcus Aurelius are rendered with simplified pictures in stronger relief, sacrificing Classical proportions for the sake of clarity and immediacy. The spirit of the work is more akin to the 4th-century Arch of Constantine (see p91) than to Trajan's monument. Gone are the heroic qualities of the Roman soldiers, by now mostly barbarian mercenaries, and a sense of respect for the vanquished. A new emphasis on the supernatural points to the end of the Hellenistic tradition and the beginning of the Christian culture.

Composed of 28 drums of marble, the column was restored in 1588 by Domenico Fontana on the orders of Pope Sixtus V. The emperor's statue on the summit was replaced by a bronze of St Paul. The 20 spirals of the low relief chronicle the German war of AD 171–3, and (above) the Sarmatic war of AD 174–5. The column is almost 30 m (100 ft) high and 3.7 m (12 ft) in diameter. An internal spiral staircase leads to the top. The easiest way to appreciate the sculptural work, however, is to visit the Museo della Civiltà Romana at EUR (see p267) and study the casts of the reliefs.

Palazzo Capranica ㉔

Piazza Capranica. **Map** 4 F3 & 12 D2. *56, 60, 85, 90, 90b, 119, 492.*

Windows of Palazzo Capranica

O NE OF ROME'S small number of surviving 15th-century buildings, the palazzo was commissioned by Cardinal Domenico Capranica both as his family residence and as a college for higher education. Its fortress-like appearance is a patchwork of subsequent additions, not unusual in the late 15th century, when Rome was still hovering between medieval and Renaissance taste. The Gothic-looking windows on the right of the building show the cardinal's coat of arms and the date 1451 is inscribed on the doorway underneath. The palazzo is now a shell housing a popular cinema.

Relief of the emperor's campaigns on the Column of Marcus Aurelius

Gesù ⑨

DATING FROM BETWEEN 1568 and 1584, the Gesù was the first Jesuit church to be built in Rome. Its design epitomizes Counter Reformation Baroque architecture and has been much imitated throughout the Catholic world. The layout proclaims the church's two major functions: a large nave with side pulpits for preaching to great crowds, and a main altar as the centrepiece for the celebration of the mass. The illusionistic decoration in the nave and dome was added a century later. Its message is clear and confident: faithful, Catholic worshippers will be joyfully uplifted into the heavens while Protestants and other heretics are flung into hell's fires.

★ Chapel of Sant'Ignazio
Above its altar is a statue of the saint, framed by gilded lapis lazuli columns. The chapel was built in 1696–1700 by Andrea Pozzo, a Jesuit artist.

Triumph of Faith Over Heresy
This vivid Baroque allegory sculpted by Théudon illustrates the great ambition of Jesuit theology.

ST IGNATIUS AND THE JESUIT ORDER

Spanish soldier Ignatius Loyola (1491–1556) joined the Church after being wounded in battle in 1521. He came to Rome in 1537 and founded the Jesuits, sending missionaries and teachers all over the world to win souls for Catholicism.

Main entrance

STAR FEATURES

★ **Nave Ceiling Decorations**

★ **Chapel of Sant'Ignazio**

★ **San Roberto Bellarmino**

Allegorical Figures
Antonio Raggi made these stuccoes, which were designed by Il Baciccia to complement the figures on his own nave frescoes.

Madonna della Strada
This 15th-century image, called the Madonna of the Road, was originally displayed on the outer facade of a nearby church of the same name.

VISITORS' CHECKLIST

Piazza del Gesù. **Map** 4 F4 & 12 E4. 678 63 41. 44, 46, 56, 60, 62, 64, 65, 70, 81, 90 and many other routes to Largo di Torre Argentina or Piazza Venezia. **Open** 7am–12.30pm, 4pm–7.15pm daily.

★ **San Roberto Bellarmino**
Bernini captured the forceful personality of this anti-Protestant theologian, who died in 1621.

The Chapel of St Francis Xavier is a memorial to the great missionary who died alone on an island off China in 1552.

★ **Nave Ceiling Decorations**
The figures in Il Baciccia's astonishing fresco of the Triumph of the Name of Jesus *spill out on to the coffered vaulting of the nave.*

Cupola Frescoes
The cupola was completed by della Porta to Vignola's design. The frescoes, by Il Baciccia, feature Old Testament figures.

TIMELINE

1500	1600	1700
1540 Founding of the Society of Jesus (the Jesuits)	**1571** Giacomo della Porta's design chosen for the facade	**1696–1700** The Chapel of Sant' Ignazio is designed by Andrea Pozzo, a Jesuit artist
	1584 Church's consecration	**1773** Pope Clement XIV orders the suppression of the Jesuit order
1545–63 Council of Trent defines the new Catholic orthodoxy	**1568–71** Vignola builds the church up to the crossing under the patronage of Cardinal Alessandro Farnese	**1670–83** Giovanni Battista Gaulli (Il Baciccia) paints the nave vault, dome and apse
1556 Death of Ignatius	**1622** Ignatius Loyola is canonized	

Piazza Navona

THE FOUNDATIONS of the buildings surrounding the elongated oval of Piazza Navona were the ruined grandstands of the vast Stadium of Domitian. The piazza today still provides a dramatic spectacle with the obelisk of the Fontana dei Fiumi in front of the church of Sant' Agnese in Agone as its focal point.

Lion on Fontana dei Fiumi

The predominant style of the area is Baroque, many of its finest buildings dating from the reign of Innocent X Pamphilj (1644–55), patron of Bernini and Borromini. Of special interest is the complex of the Chiesa Nuova, headquarters of the Filippini, the order founded by San Filippo Neri, the 16th-century "Apostle of Rome".

SIGHTS AT A GLANCE

Churches and Temples
Sant'Agnese in Agone ❹
Santa Maria dell'Anima ❺
Santa Maria della Pace ❻
San Luigi dei Francesi ❼
Sant'Ivo alla Sapienza ❾
Sant'Andrea della Valle ❿
Chiesa Nuova ⓯
Oratorio dei Filippini ⓰
San Salvatore in Lauro ㉑
Sant'Apollinare ㉕

Museums
Palazzo Braschi ⓬
Museo Napoleonico ㉒

Historic Buildings
Palazzo Pamphilj ❸
Palazzo Madama ❽
Palazzo Massimo alle Colonne ⓫
Torre dell'Orologio ⓱
Palazzo del Banco di Santo Spirito ⓲
Palazzo Gaddi ⓳
Palazzo Altemps ㉓

Fountains and Statues
Fontana dei Fiumi ❶
Pasquino ⓭

Historic Streets and Piazzas
Piazza Navona ❷
Via del Governo Vecchio ⓮
Via dei Coronari ⓴

Restaurants
Hostaria dell'Orso ㉔

SEE ALSO

• *Street Finder*, maps 4, 11, 12

• *Where to Stay* pp294–5

• *Restaurants* pp310–11

GETTING THERE
This central area is within walking distance of many parts of the city. Much of the area itself is closed to traffic, but it is easily reached by bus. The principal routes along Corso Vittorio Emanuele II are the 64 from Termini station to St Peter's and the 46. Corso del Rinascimento, which runs parallel to Piazza Navona, is served by several useful routes, including the 70, 81, 90 and 492.

KEY
Street-by-Street map
P Parking

0 metres   200
0 yards   200

Piazza Navona, with the Fontana del Moro and church of Sant'Agnese in Agone

Street-by-Street: Piazza Navona

No OTHER PIAZZA in Rome can rival the theatricality of Piazza Navona. Day and night there is always something going on in the pedestrian area around its three flamboyant fountains. The Baroque is also represented in many of the area's churches. To discover an older Rome, walk along Via del Governo Vecchio to admire the facades of its Renaissance buildings and browse in the fascinating antiques shops.

Oratorio dei Filippini
The musical term oratorio comes from this place of informal worship 16

Torre dell' Orologio
This clock tower by Borromini (1648) is part of the Convent of the Filippini 17

VIA DEL CORALLO

VIA DEL GOVERNO VECCHIO

VIA DI PARIONE

Chiesa Nuova
This church was rebuilt in the late 16th century for the order founded by San Filippo Neri 15

To Corso Vittorio Emanuele II

Via del Governo Vecchio
This street preserves a large number of fine Renaissance houses 14

Santa Maria della Pace
The medallion shows Pope Alexander VII, who had the church restored by Pietro da Cortona in 1656 6

Pasquino
Romans hung satirical verses and dialogues on this weatherbeaten statue 13

Palazzo Pamphilj
This grand town house was built for Pope Innocent X and his family in the mid-17th century 3

CORSO VITTORIO EMANUELE II

PIAZZA DI PASQUINO

PIAZZA DI SAN PANTALEO

STAR SIGHTS

* ★ Sant'Andrea della Valle
* ★ San Luigi dei Francesi
* ★ Piazza Navona

KEY

– – – Suggested route

0 metres   75

0 yards   75

Palazzo Braschi
A late 18th-century building with a splendid balcony, the palazzo houses the Museo di Roma 12

Palazzo Massimo alle Colonne
The magnificent curving colonnade (1536) is by Baldassarre Peruzzi 11

Sant'Agnese in Agone
Borromini's startling concave facade (1657) dominates one side of Piazza Navona ④

Santa Maria dell'Anima
For four centuries this has been the German church in Rome ⑤

Fontana dei Fiumi
Bernini designed this fountain supporting an obelisk ①

Palazzo Madama
A spread-eagled stone lionskin decorates the central doorway of the palazzo, now the Italian Senate ⑧

LOCATOR MAP
See Central Rome Map pp12–13

★ San Luigi dei Francesi
An 18th-century statue of St Louis stands in a niche in the facade ⑦

★ Piazza Navona
This unique piazza owes its shape to a Roman race track and its stunning decor to the genius of the Roman Baroque ②

The Fontana del Moro was remodelled in 1653 by Bernini, who designed the central sea god.

Sant'Ivo alla Sapienza
This tiny domed church is one of Borromini's most original creations. He worked on it between 1642 and 1660 ⑨

To Campo de' Fiori

★ Sant'Andrea della Valle
The church, with its grandiose facade by Carlo Rainaldi (1665), has gained fame outside Rome as the setting of the first act of Puccini's Tosca ⑩

Fontana dei Fiumi ❶

Piazza Navona. **Map** 4 E4 & 11 C3.
🚌 70, 81, 87, 90, 90b, 186, 492.

BUILT FOR POPE Innocent X
Pamphilj, this magnificent
fountain in the centre of
Piazza Navona was unveiled
in 1651. The pope's coat of
arms, the dove and the olive
branch, decorate the bold
pyramid rock formation
supporting the Egyptian
obelisk, which once stood in
the Circus of Maxentius on
the Appian Way. Bernini
designed the fountain, which
was paid for by means of
highly unpopular taxes on
bread and other staples. The
great rivers then known – the
Ganges, the Danube, the Nile
and the River Plate – are
represented by four giants.

The Nile's veiled head
symbolizes the river's
unknown source, but there is
also a legend that the veil
conveys Bernini's dislike for
the nearby Sant'Agnese in
Agone, designed by his rival
Borromini. Similarly, the

View of Palazzo Pamphilj across Piazza Navona

athletic figure of the River
Plate, cringing with arm
upraised, is supposed to
express Bernini's fear that the
church will collapse. Sadly
these widely-believed stories
can have no basis in fact:
Bernini had completed the
fountain before Borromini
started work on the church.

Piazza Navona ❷

Map 4 E3 & 11 C2. 🚌 46, 62, 64,
70, 81, 87, 90, 90b, 186, 492.

ROME'S MOST beautiful
Baroque piazza follows
the shape of Domitian's
Stadium, which once stood on
this site – some of its arches
are still visible below the
church of Sant'Agnese in
Agone. The *agones* were
athletic contests held in the
1st-century stadium, which
could seat 33,000. The word
"Navona" is thought to
be a corruption of *in
agone*. The piazza's
unique appearance and
atmosphere were
created in the 17th
century with the
addition of the Fontana
dei Fiumi. The other

fountains, the Fontana di
Nettuno and the Fontana del
Moro, date from the previous
century but have been altered
several times since. The figure
known as Il Moro is a late
work by Bernini.

Up until the 19th century,
Piazza Navona was flooded
during August by stopping
the fountain outlets. The rich
would splash around in
carriages, while street urchins
paddled after them. Today the
piazza is a favourite in all
seasons, especially in winter
when it fills with colourful
stalls selling toys and sweets
for the feast of the Befana.

Palazzo Pamphilj ❸

Piazza Navona. **Map** 4 E4 & 11 C3.
🚌 46, 62, 64, 70, 81, 87, 90, 90b,
186, 492. **Not open** to the public.

**Family dove and olive branch on
facade of Palazzo Pamphilj**

IN 1644 Giovanni Battista
Pamphilj became pope,
assuming the name of
Innocent X. During his 10-
year reign, he heaped riches
on his own family, especially
his domineering sister-in-law,
Olimpia Maidalchini. The
"talking statue" Pasquino *(see
p124)* gave her the nickname
"Olim-Pia", Latin for "formerly
virtuous". She lived in the
grand Palazzo Pamphilj,
which has frescoes by Pietro
da Cortona and a gallery by
Borromini. The building is
now the Brazilian embassy.

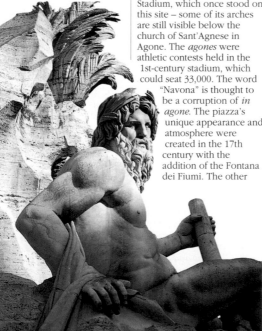

Symbolic figure of the River Ganges in Bernini's Fontana dei Fiumi

Sant'Agnese in Agone ❹

Piazza Navona. **Map** 4 E4 & 11 C3.
📞 679 44 35. 🚌 70, 81, 87, 90,
90b, 492. **Open** 5pm–6.30pm
Mon–Sat, 10am–1pm Sun & public
hols. 🚹 📷 ♿

Tᴴᴱ ᴄʜᴜʀᴄʜ ɪѕ believed to
have been founded on the
site of the brothel where, in
AD 304, the young St Agnes
was exposed naked to force
her to renounce her faith. A
marble relief in the crypt
shows the miraculous growth
of her hair, which fell around
her body to protect her
modesty. She was martyred
on this site and is buried in
the catacombs that bear her
name along the Via
Nomentana *(see p264)*.

Today's church was
commissioned by Pope
Innocent X in 1652. The first
architects were father and son,
Girolamo and Carlo Rainaldi,
but they were replaced by
Borromini who worked
on the church from
1653 to 1657. He
stuck more or less to
the Rainaldi
scheme except
for the concave
facade designed
to emphasize
the dome. A statue
of St Agnes on the
facade is said to
be reassuring the
Fontana dei Fiumi's
statue of the River
Plate that the
church is stable.

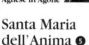

**Statue of St Agnes
on facade of Sant'
Agnese in Agone**

Carlo Saraceni's *Miracle of St Benno and the Keys of Meissen Cathedral*

Santa Maria dell'Anima ❺

Via della Pace 20. **Map** 4 E4 & 11 C2.
📞 683 37 29. 🚌 70, 81, 87, 90,
90b, 492. **Open** 7.30am– 7pm Mon–
Sat, 8am–1pm, 3pm–7pm Sun.
🚹 📷 ♿

Pᴏᴘᴇ ᴀᴅʀɪᴀɴ ᴠɪ (reigned
1522–3), son of a ship-
builder from Utrecht, was the
last non-Italian pope before
John Paul II. He would have
disapproved of his superb

tomb by Baldassarre Peruzzi
in Santa Maria dell'Anima. It
stands to the right of
Giulio Romano's
damaged altarpiece and
is redolent of the
pagan Renaissance
spirit the pope had so
condemned during
his brief, rather
gloomy reign, when
patronage of the arts
ground to a halt. Santa
Maria dell'Anima is
the German church in
Rome and some of its
paintings, such as the
Miracle of St Benno by
Carlo Saraceni (1618),
illustrate events connected
with the history of Germany.

Santa Maria della Pace ❻

Vicolo del Arco della Pace 5. **Map**
4 E3 & 11 C2. 📞 686 11 56. 🚌 70,
81, 87, 90, 90b, 186, 492. **Closed** for
restoration. 🚹 📷 ♿ 2 steps.

A ᴅʀᴜɴᴋᴇɴ ѕᴏʟᴅɪᴇʀ allegedly
pierced the breast of a
painted Madonna on this site,
causing it to bleed. Pope
Sixtus IV della Rovere

(reigned 1471–84) placated
the Virgin by ordering Baccio
Pontelli to build her a church
if she would bring the war
with Turkey to an end. Peace
was restored and the church
was named Santa Maria della
Pace (St Mary of Peace).

The cloister was added by
Bramante in 1504. As in his
famous Tempietto *(see p219)*
he scrupulously followed
Classical rules of proportion
to produce a thoroughly
original result, achieving a
monumental effect in a
relatively small space.

Pietro da Cortona may have
had Bramante's Tempietto in
mind when he added the
church's charming semi-
circular portico in 1656. The
interior, a short nave ending
under an octagonal cupola,
houses Raphael's famous
frescoes of four *Sybils*, and
four *Prophets* by his pupil
Timoteo Viti, painted for the
banker Agostino Chigi in
1514. Baldassarre Peruzzi also
did some work in the church
(fresco in the first chapel on
the left), as did the architect
Antonio da Sangallo the
Younger, who designed the
second chapel on the right.

San Luigi dei Francesi ❼

Via Santa Giovanna d'Arco.
Map 4 F4 & 12 D2. 688 27 1.
70, 81, 87, 90, 90b, 492.
Open 8am–12.30pm, 3.30pm–7pm
daily. **Closed** Thu pm.

THE FRENCH national church was founded in 1518, but it took until 1589 to be finished, with contributions by Giacomo della Porta and Domenico Fontana. Visitors are drawn to the church by the many well-known Frenchmen buried here and by the three Caravaggios in the fifth chapel on the left, dedicated to St Matthew.

Painted between 1597 and 1602, these were Caravaggio's first great religious works: the *Calling of St Matthew*, the *Martyrdom of St Matthew* and *St Matthew and the Angel*. The first version of this last painting was rejected because of its vivid realism: never before had a saint been shown as a tired old man with dirty feet, and a second version had to be painted. All three works display very disquieting realism and highly dramatic use of light.

Caravaggio, whose paintings of St Matthew hang in San Luigi dei Francesi

Shield linking symbols of France and Rome on facade of San Luigi

Palazzo Madama ❽

Corso del Rinascimento. **Map** 4 F4 & 12 D3. 70, 81, 87, 90, 90b, 492.
Open first Sat of month.

THIS 16TH-CENTURY palazzo was built for the Medici family, who had owned a bank here in the previous century. It was the residence of the Medici cardinals, the cousins Giovanni and Giuliano. Both later became pope, Giovanni as Leo X and Giuliano as Clement VII. Caterina de' Medici, Clement VII's niece, also lived here before she was married to Henry, son of King Francis I of France in 1533.

The palazzo takes its name from Madama Margherita of Austria, illegitimate daughter of Emperor Charles V, who married Alessandro de' Medici and, after his death, Ottavio Farnese. This caused the fabulous art collection of the Florentine Medici family to be broken up; part was inherited by the Roman Farnese family.

The spectacular facade was built in the 17th century by Paolo Maruccelli. He gave it an ornate cornice and whimsical decorative details on the roof. Since 1871 the palazzo has been the seat of the Senate, the upper house of the Italian parliament.

Cornice of Palazzo Madama

Sant'Ivo alla Sapienza ❾

Corso del Rinascimento 40.
Map 4 F4 & 12 D3. 70, 81, 87, 90, 90b, 492. **Open** for mass 9am–noon Sun. **Closed** Jul, Aug.

THE CHURCH'S lantern is crowned with a cross on top of a dramatic twisted spiral – a highly distinctive landmark from Rome's roof terraces. Seen from close by, this Borromini church is even more striking. No other Baroque church is quite like it. Based on a ground design of astonishing geometrical complexity, the walls are a breathtaking combination of concave and convex surfaces. The church stands in the small courtyard of the Palazzo della Sapienza, seat of the old University of Rome from the 15th century until 1935.

Lantern and spire of Sant'Ivo

Sant'Andrea della Valle ⓾

Piazza Sant'Andrea della Valle.
Map 4 E4 & 12 D4. 686 13 39.
46, 62, 64, 70, 81, 87, 90, 90b, 492. **Open** 7.30am–noon, 4.30pm–7.30pm.

Dome of Sant'Andrea della Valle

THE CHURCH is the scene of the first act of Puccini's opera *Tosca*, though opera fans will not find the Attavanti chapel, a poetic invention. The real church has much to recommend it – the recently restored facade shows the flamboyant Baroque style at its best. Inside, a golden light filters through high windows, showing off the gilded interior. Here lie the two popes of the Sienese Piccolomini family: on the left of the central nave is the tomb of Pius II, the first Humanist pope (reigned 1458–64); Pope Pius III lies opposite – he reigned for less than a month in 1503.

The church is famous for its beautiful dome, the largest in Rome after St Peter's. It was built by Carlo Maderno in 1622–5 and was painted with splendid frescoes by Domenichino and Giovanni Lanfranco. The latter's extravagant style, to be seen in the dome fresco *Glory of Paradise*, won him most of the commission, and the jealous Domenichino is said to have tried to kill his colleague. He failed, but Domenichino's jealousy was unnecessary, as shown by his two beautiful paintings of scenes from the life of St Andrew around the apse and altar. In the Strozzi Chapel, built in the style of Michelangelo, the altar has copies of the *Leah* and *Rachel* by Michelangelo in San Pietro in Vincoli *(see p170)*.

Palazzo Massimo alle Colonne ⓫

Corso Vittorio Emanuele II 141.
Map 4 F4 & 11 C3. 46, 62, 64, 70, 81, 87, 90, 186, 492. **Open** 7am–1pm 16 Mar every year.

Roman column, Palazzo Massimo

DURING THE LAST two years of his life, Baldassarre Peruzzi built this palazzo for the Massimo family, whose home had been destroyed in the Sack of Rome in 1527. Peruzzi displayed great ingenuity in dealing with an awkwardly shaped site. The previous building had stood on the ruined Theatre of Domitian, which created a curve in the great processional Via Papalis. Peruzzi's convex colonnaded facade follows the line of the street. His originality is also evident in the small square upper windows, the courtyard and the stuccoed vestibule. The Piazza de' Massimi entrance has a Renaissance-style, frescoed facade. A single column from the theatre has been set up in the piazza.

The Massimo family traced its origins to Quintus Fabius Maximus, conqueror of Hannibal in the 3rd century BC, and their proud coat of arms is borne by an infant Hercules. Over the years the family produced many great Humanists, and in the 19th century, it was a Massimo who negotiated peace with Napoleon. On 16 March each year the palazzo opens to the public to commemorate young Paolo Massimo's resurrection from the dead by San Filippo Neri in 1538.

Palazzo Braschi ⓬

Piazza San Pantaleo 10. **Map** 4 E4 & 11 C3. 687 53 45. 46, 62, 64, 70, 81, 87, 90, 186, 492. **Open** 9am–7pm Tue–Sat, 9am–1pm Sun (phone to check for the Museodi Roma).

ON ONE SIDE of Piazza San Pantaleo is the last Roman palazzo to be built for the family of a pope. Palazzo Braschi was built in the late 18th century for Pope Pius VI Braschi's nephews by the architect Cosimo Morelli. He gave the building its imposing facade which looks out on to the piazza.

The palazzo now houses the municipal Museo di Roma. It holds collections of pictures, drawings and everyday objects illustrating life in the city from medieval times until the last century.

Angel with raised wing by Ercole Ferrata, flanking the facade of Sant'Andrea della Valle

Pasquino ⑬

Piazza di Pasquino. **Map** 4 E4 & 11 C3. 🚌 46, 62, 64, 70, 81, 87, 90, 492.

Pasquino, the most famous of Rome's satirical "talking statues"

THIS ROUGH CHUNK of marble is all that remains of a Hellenistic group, probably representing the incident in Homer's *Iliad* in which Menelaus shields the body of the slain Patroclus. For years it lay as a stepping stone in a muddy medieval street until it was erected on this corner in 1501, near the shop of an outspoken cobbler named Pasquino. Freedom of speech was not encouraged in papal Rome, so the cobbler wrote out his satirical comments on current events and attached them to the statue.

Other Romans were quick to follow suit, hanging their maxims and verses on the statue by night to escape punishment. Despite the wrath of the authorities, the sayings of the "talking statue" (renamed Pasquino) were part of popular culture right up until the 19th century. Other statues started to "talk" in the same satirical vein; Pasquino used to conduct dialogues with another statue known as Marforio that stood in Via del Campidoglio and is now in the courtyard of Palazzo Nuovo *(see pp70–71)*. Rome's only English-language cinema, which is in Trastevere, is called the Pasquino *(see p347)*.

Via del Governo Vecchio ⑭

Map 4 E4 & 11 B3. 🚌 46, 62, 64.

THE STREET TAKES its name from Palazzo del Governo Vecchio, the seat of papal government in the 17th and 18th centuries. Once part of the Via Papalis, which led from the Lateran to St Peter's, the street is lined with 15th- and 16th-century houses and small workshops. Particularly interesting are the 15th-century houses at No. 104 and No. 106. The small palazzo at No. 123 was once thought to have been the home of Bramante. Opposite is Palazzo del Governo Vecchio. It is also known as Palazzo Nardini, from the name of its founder, which is inscribed on the first-floor windows along with the date 1477.

Via del Governo Vecchio

Chiesa Nuova ⑮

Piazza della Chiesa Nuova. **Map** 4 E4 & 11 B3. 📞 687 52 89. 🚌 46, 62, 64. **Open** 8am–noon, 4.30pm–7pm daily. ✝ 📷

Facade of the Chiesa Nuova

SAN FILIPPO NERI (St Philip Neri) is the most appealing of the Counter Reformation saints. A highly unconventional reformer, he required his noble Roman followers to humble themselves in public. He made aristocratic young men parade through the streets of Rome in rags or even with a fox's tail tied behind them, and set noblemen to work as labourers building his church. With the help of Pope Gregory XIII, his church was built in place of an old medieval church, Santa Maria in Vallicella, and it has been known ever since as the Chiesa Nuova (new church).

Begun in 1575 by Matteo da Città di Castello and continued by Martino Longhi the Elder, it was consecrated in 1599 (although the facade, by Fausto Rughesi, was only finished in 1606). Against San Filippo's wishes, the interior was decorated after his death; Pietro da Cortona frescoed the nave, dome and apse, taking nearly 20 years. There are also three paintings by Rubens: *Madonna and Angels* above the altar, *Saints Domitilla, Nereus and Achilleus* on the right of the altar, and *Saints Gregory, Maurus and Papias* on the left. San Filippo is buried in his own chapel, to the left of the altar.

Borromini's facade of the Oratorio

Oratorio dei Filippini ⓖ

Piazza della Chiesa Nuova. **Map** 4 E4 & 11 B3. 686 93 74. 46, 62, 64. **Admission** on request to caretaker. **Concerts**.

WITH THE ADJOINING church and convent, the oratory formed the centre of Filippo Neri's religious order, founded in 1575. Its members are commonly known as Filippini. The musical term "oratorio" (a religious text sung by solo voices and chorus) derives from the services held here.

Filippo Neri came to Rome aged 18 to work as a tutor. The city was undergoing a period of religious strife and an economic slump after the Sack of Rome in 1527. There was also an outbreak of the plague. It was left to newcomers like Neri and Ignazio di Loyola to revive the spiritual life of the city.

Neri formed a brotherhood of laymen who worshipped together and helped pilgrims and the sick *(see Santissima Trinità dei Pellegrini p146)*. He founded the Oratory as a centre for religious discourse. Its conspicuous curving brick facade was built by Borromini in 1637–43.

Torre dell' Orologio ⓗ

Piazza dell'Orologio. **Map** 4 E4 & 11 B3. 46, 62, 64.

BORROMINI BUILT this clock tower to decorate one corner of the Convent of the Oratorians of San Filippo Neri in 1647–8. It is typical of Borromini in that the front and rear are concave and the sides convex. The mosaic of the Madonna beneath the clock is by Pietro da Cortona, while on the corner of the building is a small tabernacle to the Madonna flanked by angels in the style of Bernini.

Pietro da Cortona (1596–1669)

Palazzo del Banco di Santo Spirito ⓘ

Via del Banco di Santo Spirito. **Map** 4 D4 & 11 A2. 41, 46, 62, 64, 982. **Open** normal banking hours.

FORMERLY THE MINT of papal Rome, this palazzo is often referred to as the Antica Zecca (old mint). The upper storeys of the facade, built by Antonio da Sangallo the Younger in the 1520s, are in the shape of a Roman triumphal arch. Above it stand two Baroque statues symbolizing Charity and Thrift, and in the centre of the arch above the main entrance an inscription records the founding of the Banco di Santo Spirito by Pope Paul V Borghese in 1605.

Pope Paul was a very shrewd financier and he encouraged Romans to deposit their money at the bank by offering the vast estates of the Hospital of Santo Spirito *(see p226)* as security. The system catered only for the rudimentary banking requirements of the population, but business was brisk as people deposited money here safe in the knowledge that they could get it out simply by presenting a chit. The hospital coffers also gained from the system. The Banco di Santo Spirito still exists, but is now part of the Banco di Roma.

Facade of the Banco di Santo Spirito, built to resemble a Roman arch

Palazzo Gaddi ⑲

Via del Banco di Santo Spirito 42.
Map 4 D3 & 11 A2. ▦ *41, 46, 62, 64, 280.* **Not open** to the public.

Portrait of Michelangelo in his old age by Jacopino del Conte

Traditionally attributed to the Florentine Jacopo Sansovino, Palazzo Gaddi was owned by Florentine families for many generations. Cardinal Gaddi, himself born into a famous Florentine family, the Altoviti, built the palazzo in the 16th century during the reign of Pope Clement VII de' Medici, when the Tuscan colony in Rome flourished. Michelangelo is known to have lived at the palazzo; close by is the place where the Sienese banker Agostino Chigi set up his first bank in Rome. For years Chigi kept the papal tiara in safe keeping as security against a loan made to Pope Julius II.

Via dei Coronari ⑳

Map 4 D3 & 11 B2. ▦ *46, 62, 64, 70, 81, 87, 90, 90b, 186, 492.*

Large numbers of medieval pilgrims making their way to St Peter's walked along this street to cross over the Tiber at Ponte Sant'Angelo. Of the businesses that sprang up to try to part the pilgrims from their money, the most enduring was the selling of rosaries, and the street is still named after the rosary sellers *(coronari)*.

The street followed the course of the ancient Roman Via Recta (straight street), which originally ran from today's Piazza Colonna to the Tiber.

Making one's way through the vast throng of people in Via dei Coronari could be extremely hazardous. In the Holy Year of 1450, some 200 pilgrims died, crushed by the crowds or drowned in the Tiber. Following the tragedy, Pope Nicholas V demolished the Roman triumphal arch that stood at the entrance to Ponte Sant'Angelo. In the late 15th century, Pope Sixtus IV encouraged the building of private houses and palaces along the street.

Although the rosary sellers have been replaced by antiques dealers, the street still has many original buildings from the 15th and 16th centuries. One of the earliest, at Nos. 156–7, is known as the House of Fiammetta, the mistress of Cesare Borgia.

Antiques shop, Via dei Coronari

San Salvatore in Lauro ㉑

Piazza San Salvatore in Lauro 15.
Map 4 E3 & 11 B2. 📞 *687 51 87.*
▦ *46, 62, 64, 280.* **Open** *8.30am– noon Mon, Wed, Sat, Sun, 4.30pm– 7pm daily.* ✝

The church is named "in Lauro" after the laurel grove that grew here in ancient times. Today's church was built at the end of the 16th century by

Cloister, San Salvatore in Lauro

Ottaviano Mascherino. The bell tower and sacristy were 18th-century additions by Nicola Salvi, famous for the Trevi Fountain *(see p159)*. The church contains the first great altarpiece by the 17th-century artist Pietro da Cortona, *The Birth of Jesus*, in the first chapel to the right.

The adjacent San Giorgio convent, to the left, has a pretty Renaissance cloister, a frescoed refectory and the monument to Pope Eugenius IV (reigned 1431–47), moved here when old St Peter's was pulled down. An extravagant Venetian, he spent thousands of ducats on his gold tiara, but requested a "simple, lowly burial place" near his predecessor Pope Eugenius III. His portrait, by Salviati, is in the refectory.

In 1669 the church became the seat of a pious association, the Confraternity of the Piceni, inhabitants of the Marche region. Fanatically loyal to the pope, the Piceni were traditionally employed as papal soldiers and tax-collectors.

Facade of San Salvatore in Lauro

Museo Napoleonico ㉒

Piazza di Ponte Umberto 1.
Map 4 E3 & 11 C1. 📞 *68 80 62 86.*
🚌 *70, 81, 87, 90, 90b, 280, 492.*
***Open** 9am–7pm Tue–Sat, 9am–1pm
Sun.* **Adm charge.** 🚫 ♿ 📷 *only.*

Entrance to Museo Napoleonico

THIS MUSEUM contains memorabilia and portraits of Napoleon Bonaparte and his family. Personal relics of Napoleon himself include an Indian shawl he wore during his exile on St Helena.

After his death in 1821, the pope allowed many of the Bonaparte family to settle in Rome, including his formidable mother Letizia, who lived in Palazzo Misciattelli on Via del Corso, and died there in 1836. Of her other children, the most intriguing is the flighty Pauline, who married the Roman Prince Camillo Borghese. The museum has a cast of her right breast, made by Canova in 1805 as a preparatory study for his statue of her as a reclining Venus, now in the Museo Borghese *(see p260–61).* Portraits and personal effects of

many other members of the family are on display, including court dresses, uniforms, and even a penny-farthing bicycle that belonged to Prince Eugène, the son of Emperor Napoleon III.

The last male of the Roman branch of the family was Napoleon Charles, portrayed in a late 19th-century painting by Guglielmo de Sanctis. The collection was assembled in 1927 by the Counts Primoli, the sons of Charles's sister, Carlotta Bonaparte.

Palazzo Altemps ㉓

Via Sant'Apollinare 8. **Map** 4 E3 &
11 C2. 🚌 *70, 81, 87, 90, 90b, 280,
492.* **Not open** to the public.

THE PALAZZO was built for Girolamo Riario, nephew of Pope Sixtus IV, and the Riario coat of arms can still be seen in the janitor's room. In the popular uprising that followed the pope's death in 1484, the building was sacked and Girolamo fled the city.

In 1568 the palazzo was bought by Cardinal Marco Sittico Altemps. His family was of German origin – the name is an Italianization of Hohenems – and extremely influential in the church. In 1565, when the cardinal's brother married San Carlo Borromeo's sister, Ortensia, Pope Pius IV marked the day with the last great tournament to be held in the Vatican's Belvedere Courtyard *(see pp234–5).* The palazzo was renovated in

Belvedere of Palazzo Altemps

the 1570s by Martino Longhi the Elder, who added the great belvedere, crowned with obelisks and a marble unicorn. The Altemps were ostentatious collectors; the courtyard and the staircase leading from it are lined with ancient sculptures. The palazzo is now a seminary.

Hostaria dell' Orso ㉔

Via dei Soldati 25. **Map** 4 E3 & 11 C2.
📞 *686 42 50.* 🚌 *70, 81, 87, 90,
90b, 280, 492.* **Open** 8pm–midnight
Mon–Sat.

NOW A RESTAURANT, this ancient inn has a 15th-century portico and loggia built with columns taken from Roman ruins. Legend has it that Dante once stayed here. Later visitors to Rome known to have used the inn include the 16th-century French writers Rabelais and Montaigne.

Dante Alighieri (1265–1321)

Sant'Apollinare ㉕

Piazza Sant'Apollinare 49. **Map** 4 E3 &
11 C2. 📞 *68 30 80 37.* 🚌 *70, 81,
87, 90, 90b, 492.* **Open** 7.30–10am
Mon–Sat, 7.30–11.30am Sun. 🔲 📷

FOUNDED IN medieval times, the church was rebuilt by Ferdinando Fuga in the 18th century. It is dedicated to the saint said to have accompanied St Peter from Antioch to Rome, who later became the first Bishop of Ravenna. At a special service held every Sunday, Gregorian chants are sung by the priests.

Piazza di Spagna

By the 16th century, the increase in numbers of visiting pilgrims and ecclesiastics was making life in Rome's already congested medieval centre unbearable. A new triangle of roads was built, still in place today, to help channel pilgrims as quickly as possible from the city's north gate, the Porta del Popolo, to the Vatican. By the 18th century hotels had sprung up all over

Lion fountain in Piazza del Popolo

the district. Today this attractive area offers much more: the superb works of Renaissance and Baroque art in Santa Maria del Popolo and Sant' Andrea delle Fratte, the magnificent reliefs of the restored Ara Pacis, art exhibitions in the Villa Medici, fine views of the city from the Spanish Steps and the Pincio Gardens and Rome's most famous shopping streets, centred around Via Condotti.

Sights at a Glance

Churches
Sant'Andrea delle Fratte ❶
Trinità dei Monti ❿
All Saints ⓬
Santa Maria dei Miracoli and
Santa Maria in Montesanto ⓮
*Santa Maria del
Popolo pp138–9* ⓱
San Rocco ㉑
Santi Ambrogio e Carlo
al Corso ㉒

Museums and Galleries
Keats-Shelley
Memorial House ❼
Casa di Goethe ⓭

Historic Buildings
Collegio di Propaganda
Fide ❷
Villa Medici ⓫

Arches, Gates and Columns
Colonna dell'Immacolata ❸
Porta del Popolo ⓲

Historic Streets and Piazzas
Via Condotti ❹
Piazza di Spagna ❻

Spanish Steps ❾
Piazza del Popolo ⓰

Monuments and Tombs
Ara Pacis ⓳
Mausoleum of Augustus ⓴

Parks and Gardens
Pincio Gardens ⓯

Cafés and Restaurants
Caffè Greco ❺
Babington's Tea Rooms ❽

0 metres   300
0 yards   300

Getting There

For Piazza di Spagna and the shops around Via Condotti, Spagna Metro station on line A is more convenient than the main bus routes along Via del Corso and Via del Tritone. Stay on until Flaminio Metro if you wish to visit Piazza del Popolo. For getting around locally, the 119 minibus, which goes up Via del Babuino, is very handy.

Key

▦	Street-by-Street map
Ⓜ	Metro station
Ⓟ	Parking
—	City Wall

See Also

• **Street Finder**, maps 4, 5
• **Where to Stay** pp294–5
• **Restaurants** pp310–11
• **Shops** pp322–37

The Spanish Steps leading up to the church of Trinità dei Monti

Street-by-Street: Piazza di Spagna

T HE NETWORK of narrow
streets between Piazza di
Spagna and Via del Corso is
one of the liveliest areas in
Rome, drawing throngs of
tourists and Romans to its
discreet and elegant shops.
In the 18th century the area
was full of hotels for
frivolous English aristocrats
doing the Grand Tour, but
there were also artists,
writers and composers, who
took the city's history and
culture more seriously.

Caffè Greco
*Busts and portraits
recall the café's former
artistic patrons* ❺

★ Piazza di Spagna
*For almost three centuries
the square with its curious
Barcaccia fountain in the
centre has been the chief
meeting place for
visitors to Rome* ❻

**Via delle
Carrozze** took
its name from the
carriages of wealthy
tourists that used to
queue up there
for repairs.

Via Condotti
*This shadowy,
narrow street
has the smartest
shops in one of
the smartest
shopping areas in
the world* ❹

Bulgari sells
very expensive
jewellery behind
an austere
shopfront in
Via Condotti.

| 0 metres | | 75 |
| 0 yards | | 75 |

KEY

– – – Suggested route

Ⓜ Metro station

Trinità dei Monti
This 16th-century church has a spectacular setting and some of the finest views in Rome ⑩

Babington's Tea Rooms
English tourists are catered for in the style of the 1890s ⑧

LOCATOR MAP
See Central Rome Map pp12–13

Colonna dell'Immacolata
A Roman column supports a statue of the Virgin Mary ③

Collegio di Propaganda Fide
This facade (1665) was one of the last works of the great Francesco Borromini ②

Sant'Andrea delle Fratte
Pasquale Marini painted The Redemption *to decorate the interior of Borromini's high dome in 1691* ①

★ Keats-Shelley Memorial House
The library is part of the small museum established in the house where the English poet Keats died in 1821 ⑦

★ Spanish Steps
Even obscured by crowds, the steps are one of the glories of late Baroque Rome ⑨

STAR SIGHTS

★ Piazza di Spagna

★ Keats-Shelley Memorial House

★ Spanish Steps

Sant'Andrea delle Fratte ❶

Via Sant'Andrea delle Fratte 1.
Map 5 A3. 🛈 *679 31 91*. 🚌 *119*.
Ⓜ *Spagna*. **Open** *6.30am–12.30pm,
4pm–7pm daily*. 🕇 📷 ♿

WHEN SANT'ANDREA delle Fratte was built in the 12th century, this was the northernmost edge of Rome. Though the church is now firmly embedded in the city, its name (*fratte* means thickets) recalls its original setting.

The church was completely rebuilt in the 17th century, partly by Borromini. His bell tower and dome, best viewed from the higher ground further up Via Capo le Case, are remarkable for the complex arrangement of concave and convex surfaces. The bell tower is particularly fanciful, with angel caryatids, flaming torches resembling ice cream cones, and exaggerated scrolls like semi-folded hearts supporting a spiky crown.

In 1842, the Virgin Mary appeared in the church to a Jewish banker, who promptly converted to Christianity and became a missionary. Inside, the chapel of the Miraculous Madonna is the first thing you notice. The church is better known, however, for the angels that Borromini's rival, Bernini, carved for the Ponte Sant'Angelo. Pope Clement IX declared they were too lovely to be exposed to the weather, so they remained with Bernini's family until 1729, when they were moved to the church.

Collegio di Propaganda Fide ❷

Via di Propaganda 1. **Map** 5 A2.
🛈 *69 88 01 01*. 🚌 *119*. Ⓜ *Spagna*.
Open *to individuals on written request*.

BUILT FOR the Jesuits in 1662 when they were at the height of their power, the Collegio di Propaganda Fide (College for the Propagation of the Faith) was Borromini's last work. The headquarters of the Jesuits had to be a remarkable building, but the extraordinary facade (now thickly coated with grime) must have outstripped even their expectations. It is striped with broad pilasters, between which the first-floor windows bend in, and the central bay bulges out. A rigid band divides ground and first floors, and the cornice above the convex central bay swerves inwards. The more you look at it, the more restless it seems. The unhappy architect committed suicide shortly after completing it.

Entrance to the Jesuit College

Colonna dell'Immacolata ❸

Piazza Mignanelli. **Map** 5 A2.
🚌 *119*. Ⓜ *Spagna*.

INAUGURATED IN 1857, the column commemorates Pope Pius IX's proclamation of the doctrine of the Immaculate Conception, holding that the Virgin Mary was the only human being ever to have been born "without the stain of original sin". The column itself dates from ancient Rome. Now crowned with a statue of the Virgin Mary, it is one of the many pagan monuments in the city to have been converted to Christian use.

**Portrait of Pope Pius IX
(reigned 1846–78)**

**Angel by Bernini,
Sant'Andrea delle Fratte**

Via Condotti ❹

Map 5 A2. 🚌 81, 90, 90b, 119.
Ⓜ *Spagna. See* **Shops and Markets**
pp322–33.

Named after the conduits that carried water to the Baths of Agrippa near the Pantheon, Via Condotti is now home to the most traditional of Rome's designer clothes shops. It is also extremely popular for early evening strolls, when elegant, perfumed ladies and men in immaculate suits and flowing trench coats mingle with tourists in shorts and trainers. The most famous shops here are Beltrami (for leather), Ferragamo (for exquisitely crafted and often fantastical shoes), Hermès and Gucci.

Slightly younger designers such as Laura Biagiotti, Gianfranco Ferrè, Gianni Versace and the Fendi sisters have shops on parallel Via Borgognona. Valentino's shops are on Via Maria dei Fiori and Via Bocca di Leone, which cross Via Condotti just below Piazza di Spagna, and Giorgio Armani and Emporio Armani are on nearby Via del Babuino, among the discreet art galleries, exclusive antique shops and furnishing stores.

View along Via Condotti towards the Spanish Steps

Caffè Greco ❺

Via Condotti 86. **Map** 5 A2.
☎ 679 17 00. 🚌 81, 90, 90b, 119.
Ⓜ *Spagna.* **Open** 8am–8.45pm Mon–Sat. **Closed** 1 Jan, two weeks in August, 25–26 Dec. ♿

This café was opened by a Greek (hence *greco*) in 1760, and throughout the 18th

The 230-year-old Caffè Greco

century it was a favourite meeting place for foreign artists. Writers such as Keats, Byron and Goethe and composers like Liszt, Wagner and Bizet all breakfasted and drank here. So too did Casanova, and mad King Ludwig of Bavaria. Today, Italians stand in the crowded foyer to sip espresso coffee, and foreigners sit at tables in a cosy back room, against walls studded with the portraits of the café's famous customers.

Piazza di Spagna ❻

Map 5 A2. 🚌 119. Ⓜ *Spagna.*

Shaped like a crooked bow tie and surrounded by tall shuttered houses painted in muted shades of ochre, cream and russet, Piazza di Spagna (Spanish square) is crowded all day and (in summer) most of the night. It is the most famous square in Rome, and has long been the haunt of foreign visitors and expatriates.

In the 17th century Spain's ambassador to the Holy See had his headquarters on the square, and the area around it was deemed to be Spanish territory. Foreigners who unwittingly trespassed were liable to be dragooned into the Spanish army. In the 18th and 19th centuries Rome was almost as popular with visitors as it is today, and the

square stood at the heart of the city's main hotel district. Some of the travellers came in search of knowledge and artistic inspiration, but most were more interested in gambling, collecting ancient statues to adorn their family homes, and conducting love affairs with Italian women.

Not surprisingly, the wealthy travellers attracted hordes of beggars, who were usually supplied with tear-jerking letters by scribes who worked in the square.

The Fontana della Barcaccia in the square is the least showy of Rome's Baroque fountains, and it is often completely screened from view by people resting on its rim. It was designed either by the famous Gian Lorenzo Bernini or by his father Pietro. Because the pressure from the aqueduct that feeds the fountain is extremely low there are no spectacular cascades or spurts of water. Instead, Bernini constructed a leaking boat – *barcaccia* means useless, old boat – which lies half submerged in a shallow pool.

The bees and suns that decorate the Fontana della Barcaccia are taken from the family coat of arms of Pope Urban VIII Barberini, who commissioned the fountain.

Pope Urban VIII's arms, with the Barberini bees

The Fontana della Barcaccia at the foot of the Spanish Steps

Bust of Shelley by Moses Ezekiel

Keats-Shelley Memorial House **❼**

Piazza di Spagna 26. **Map** 5 A2.
[678 42 35. **▦** 119. **M** Spagna.
Open 9am–1pm, 3pm–6pm (Oct–Mar:
2.30pm–5.30pm) Mon–Fri. **Closed**
public hols, 10 days in Aug. **Adm
charge**. **Ø** **✎** book in advance. **📷**

I N NOVEMBER 1820 the English
poet John Keats came to
stay with his friend, the
painter Joseph Severn, in a
dusty pink house, the Casina
Rossa, on the corner of the
Spanish Steps. Suffering from
consumption, Keats had been
sent to Rome by his doctor, in
the hope that the mild, dry
climate would help the young
man's recovery. Depressed
because of scathing criticism
of his work and tormented by
his unrequited love for a
young girl named Fanny
Brawne, Keats died the
following February aged 25.

His death inspired his friend
and fellow poet, Percy Bysshe
Shelley, to write the poem
Mourn not for Adonais. In
July 1822 Shelley himself was
drowned in a boating accident
in the Gulf of La Spezia off
the coast of Tuscany. Keats,
Shelley and Severn are all
buried in Rome's Protestant
Cemetery *(see p205)*.

In 1906 the house was
bought by an Anglo-American
association and preserved as
a memorial and library in
honour of English Romantic
poets. The relics include a
lock of Keats's hair, some
fragments of Shelley's bones
in a tiny urn and a garish
carnival mask picked up by
Lord Byron as a souvenir of a
trip to Venice. You can visit
the room where Keats died,
though all the original
furniture was burnt after his
death, on papal orders.

Babington's Tea Rooms **❽**

Piazza di Spagna 23. **Map** 5 A2.
[678 60 27. **▦** 119.
M Spagna. **Open** 9am–11.30pm
Wed–Mon. **Closed** public hols.
♿

T HESE AUGUST, old-fashioned
tea rooms were opened in
1896 by two Englishwomen,
Anna Maria and Isabel Cargill
Babington, to serve homesick
British tourists with scones,
jam and pots of Earl Grey tea.
The food remains homely –
shepherd's pie and chicken
supreme for lunch, muffins
and cinnamon toast for tea –
though these days the menu
offers pancakes with maple
syrup for breakfast as well as
the traditional bacon and egg.

**Purveyors of English breakfasts to
homesick exiles since 1896**

Spanish Steps **❾**

Scalinata della Trinità dei Monti,
Piazza di Spagna. **Map** 5 A2. **▦** 119.
M Spagna.

I N THE 17TH century the
French owners of Trinità dei
Monti decided to link the
church with Piazza di Spagna
by building a magnificent
new flight of steps. They also
planned to place an equestrian
statue of King Louis XIV at the
top. Pope Alexander VII Chigi
was not too happy at the

The Spanish Steps in spring with azaleas in full bloom

prospect of erecting a statue of a French monarch in the papal city, and the arguments continued until the 1720s when an Italian architect, Francesco de Sanctis, produced a design that satisfied both the French and the papacy. The steps, completed in 1726, combine straight sections, curves and terraces to create one of the city's most dramatic and distinctive landmarks.

When the Victorian novelist Charles Dickens visited Rome, he reported that the Spanish Steps were the meeting place for artists' models, who would dress in colourful traditional costumes, hoping to catch the attention of a wealthy artist. The steps are now a popular place to sit, write postcards, take photos, flirt, busk or just watch the passers-by.

Trinità dei Monti ⑩

Piazza della Trinità dei Monti.
Map 5 A2. [679 41 79. ▦ 119.
Ⓜ Spagna. **Open** 10am–12.30pm,
4pm–6pm daily. 🛈 📷

Trinità dei Monti's bell towers

THE VIEWS of Rome from the platform in front of the twin bell towered facade of Trinità dei Monti are so beautiful that the church itself is often ignored. It is, however, unusual for Rome, for it was founded by the French in 1495, and although it was later badly damaged, there are still traces of attractive late Gothic latticework in the vaults of the transept. The interconnecting side chapels are decorated with Mannerist paintings, including two fine works by Daniele da Volterra.

19th-century engraving of the inner facade of the Villa Medici

A pupil of Michelangelo, Volterra had to paint clothes on the nudes in the *Last Judgment* in the Sistine Chapel, in response to the objections of Pope Pius IV.

Michelangelo's influence is obvious in the powerfully muscled bodies shown in the *Deposition* (second chapel on the left). The circles of gesturing figures and dancing angels surrounding the Virgin Mary in the *Assumption* (third chapel on the right), have more in common with the graceful style of Raphael.

Villa Medici ⑪

Accademia di Francia a Roma, Viale della Trinità dei Monti 1. **Map** 5 A2.
[676 11. ▦ 119. Ⓜ Spagna.
Accademia and gardens open spring
& autumn: Sun am. Otherwise
variable, so phone first. **Exhibitions,
concerts. Adm charge.** 🛈

SUPERBLY POSITIONED on the Pincio hill above Piazza di Spagna, this 16th-century villa has kept the name it assumed when Cardinal Ferdinando de' Medici bought it in 1576. From the terrace you can look across the city to Castel Sant'Angelo, from where Queen Christina of Sweden is said to have fired the large cannon ball which now sits in the basin of the fountain.

The villa is now home to the French Academy. This

The 17th-century French painter Nicolas Poussin

was founded by Louis XIV in 1666 to give a few select painters the chance to study in Rome. Nicolas Poussin was one of the first advisers to the Academy, Ingres was a director and ex-students include Fragonard and Boucher.

After 1803 when the French Academy moved to the Villa Medici, musicians were also admitted; both Berlioz and Debussy came to Rome as students of the Academy.

All Saints ⑫

Via del Babuino 153B. **Map** 4 F2.
[360 01 881. ▦ 90, 90b, 119.
Open 9am–noon, 5.30pm–6.30pm
daily. 🛈

IN 1816 THE POPE gave English residents and visitors the right to hold Anglican services in Rome, but it wasn't until the early 1880s that they acquired a site to build their own church. The architect chosen for the job was G E Street, best known in Britain for his Neo-Gothic churches and the London Law Courts. All Saints is also built in Victorian Neo-Gothic, and the interior, though splendidly decorated with different coloured Italian marbles, has an unmistakably English air. It even has an organ originally from Huddersfield. Street also designed St-Paul's-within-the-walls in Via Nazionale. Its interior is a jewel of British Pre-Raphaelite art.

Casa di Goethe ⓫

18–20 Via del Corso. **Map** 4 F1.
🚌 90, 90b, 119, 926. **Not open** to
the public.

THE GERMAN POET, dramatist
and novelist Johann
Wolfgang von Goethe (1749–
1832) lived in this house from
1786 until 1788, working on
the journal that eventually
formed part of his travel book
The Italian Journey. Rome's
noisy street life irritated him,
especially during Carnival
time, and he was a little
perturbed by the number of
murders in his neighbourhood,
but Rome rejuvenated him
and his book became one of
the most influential ever to be
written about Italy.

Santa Maria dei Miracoli and Santa Maria in Montesanto ⓬

Piazza del Popolo. **Map** 4 F1. 🚌 90,
90b, 95, 119, 926. Ⓜ Flaminio. **Santa
Maria dei Miracoli** ☎ 361 02 50.
Open 6am–1pm, 5pm–7pm
Mon–Sat, 8am–1pm, 5pm–7pm Sun,
public hols. 🚻 📷 ♿ **Santa Maria
in Montesanto** ☎ 361 05 94. **Open**
5pm–8pm (Nov–Mar: 4pm–7pm)
daily, **closed in August.** 🚻 📷

THE TWO CHURCHES at the
south end of Piazza del
Popolo were designed by the
architect Carlo Rainaldi
(1611–91), proof that he could
be as ingenious as his
contemporaries Bernini and
Borromini.
To provide a focal point for
the piazza, the churches had
to look symmetrical, but
the site on the

Portrait of Goethe in the Roman countryside by Tischbein (1751–1821)

left was narrower than that on
the right. Rainaldi solved the
problem by giving Santa Maria
dei Miracoli (on the right) a
circular dome and Santa Maria
in Montesanto an oval one,
cleverly squeezing it into the
narrower site, while the sides
of the supporting drums that
face the piazza are identical.

Pincio Gardens ⓭

Il Pincio. **Map** 4 F1. 🚌 90, 90b, 95,
119, 926. Ⓜ Flaminio. ♿

THE PINCIO GARDENS lie
above Piazza del Popolo,
on a hillside that has been so
skilfully terraced and richly
planted with trees that, from
below, the zig-zagging road
climbing to the gardens is
virtually invisible.
There were magnificent
gardens on the Pincio hill
in ancient Roman times,
but the present gardens
were designed in the early
19th century by Giuseppe
Valadier (who also re-
designed the
Piazza del
Popolo).

The Pincio Gardens water clock

The broad avenues, lined
with umbrella pines, palm
trees and evergreen oaks
soon became a fashionable
place to stroll, and even this
century such diverse characters
as Gandhi and Mussolini,
Richard Strauss and King
Farouk of Egypt patronized
the Casina Valadier, an
exclusive café and restaurant
in the grounds.
From the Pincio's main
square, Piazzale Napoleone I,
the panoramic views of Rome
stretch from the Monte Mario
to the Janiculum. For full
effect, approach the gardens
from the grounds of Villa
Borghese *(see pp258–9)*
above the Pincio, or along
Viale della Trinità dei Monti.

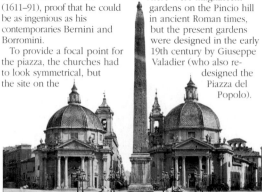
**The twin churches of Santa Maria di Montesanto (left) and Santa Maria
dei Miracoli in a 19th-century view of Piazza del Popolo**

The panorama is particularly beautiful at sunset, the traditional time for tourists to take a stroll in the gardens.

One of the most striking features of the park itself is an Egyptian-style obelisk which Emperor Hadrian erected on the tomb of his favourite, the beautiful male slave Antinous. After the slave's premature death (according to some accounts he died saving the emperor's life), Hadrian deified him.

The 19th-century water clock on Via dell'Orologio was designed by a Dominican monk. It was displayed at the Paris Exhibition of 1889.

Traditional carnival band in Piazza del Popolo

The Casina Valadier restaurant in the Pincio Gardens

Piazza del Popolo **16**

Map 4 F1. 🚍 *90, 90b, 95, 119, 926.* Ⓜ *Flaminio.*

A VAST COBBLED OVAL standing at the apex of the triangle of roads known as the Trident, Piazza del Popolo forms a grand symmetrical antechamber to the heart of Rome. Twin Neo-Classical facades stand on either side of the Porta del Popolo; an Egyptian obelisk rises in the centre; and the matching domes and porticoes of Santa Maria dei Miracoli and Santa Maria di Montesanto flank the beginning of Via del Corso.

Although it is now one of the most unified squares in Rome, Piazza del Popolo evolved gradually over the centuries. In 1589 the great town-planning pope, Sixtus V, had the obelisk erected in the centre by Domenico Fontana.

Over 3,000 years old, the obelisk was originally brought to Rome by Augustus to adorn the Circus Maximus after the conquest of Egypt. Almost a century later Pope Alexander VII commissioned Carlo Rainaldi to build the twin Santa Marias.

In the 19th century the piazza was turned into a grandiose oval by Giuseppe Valadier, the designer of the Pincio Gardens. He also encased Santa Maria del Popolo in a Neo-Classical shell to make its south facade fit in better with the overall appearance of the piazza.

In contrast to the piazza's air of ordered rationalism, many of the events staged here were barbaric. In the 18th and 19th centuries, public executions were held in Piazza del Popolo, often as part of the celebration of Carnival. Condemned men were sometimes hammered to death by repeated blows to the temples. The last time a criminal was executed in this way was in 1826, even though the guillotine had by then been adopted as a more scientific means of execution.

The riderless horse races from the piazza down Via del Corso were scarcely more humane: the performance of the runners was enhanced by feeding the horses stimulants, wrapping them in nail-studded ropes, and letting off fireworks at their heels.

Santa Maria del Popolo **17**

See pp138–9.

Porta del Popolo **18**

Between Piazzale Flaminio and Piazza del Popolo. **Map** 4 F1. 🚍 *90, 90b, 95, 119, 926.* Ⓜ *Flaminio.*

T HE VIA FLAMINIA, built in 220 BC to connect Rome with Italy's Adriatic coast, enters the city at Porta del Popolo, a grand 16th-century gate built on the orders of Pope Pius IV Medici. The architect, Nanni di Baccio Bigio, modelled it on a Roman triumphal arch. The outer face has statues of St Peter and St Paul on either side of the arch and a huge Medici coat of arms above.

A century later, Pope Alexander VII commissioned Bernini to decorate the inner face to celebrate the arrival in Rome of Queen Christina of Sweden. Lesser visitors were often held up while customs officers rifled their luggage. The only way to speed things up was with a bribe.

Porta del Popolo's central arch

Santa Maria del Popolo ⑰

ONE OF ROME'S greatest stores of artistic treasures, this early Renaissance church was commissioned by Pope Sixtus IV della Rovere in 1472. Among the artists who worked on the building were Andrea Bregno and Pinturicchio. Later additions were made by Bramante and Bernini. Many illustrious families have chapels here, all decorated with appropriate splendour. The Della Rovere Chapel has delightful Pinturicchio frescoes, the Cerasi Chapel has two Caravaggio masterpieces, the *Conversion of St Paul* and the *Crucifixion of St Peter*, but the finest of all is the Chigi Chapel designed by Raphael for his patron, the banker Agostino Chigi. The most striking of the church's many Renaissance tombs are the two by Andrea Sansovino behind the main altar.

★ Chigi Chapel
Raphael designed this chapel, which has an altarpiece by Sebastiano del Piombo. Niches on either side of the altar house sculptures by Bernini and Lorenzetto. Mosaics in the dome show God as creator of the seven heavenly bodies.

Kneeling Skeleton
This floor mosaic of the figure of death was added to the Chigi Chapel in the 17th century.

MORS·AD·CÆLOS

NERO'S GHOST

Nero lived on in the imagination of the people long after the fall of the Roman Empire. In the Middle Ages a legend arose that a walnut tree growing here on the spot where his ashes were buried was haunted by the emperor. Ravens roosting in the tree were thought to be demons tormenting him for his hideous crimes. When the first church was built here in 1099 by Pope Paschal II, the tree was cut down, supposedly putting an end to the supernatural events that had terrified local people.

Entrance

Cybo Chapel

Della Rovere Chapel
Pinturicchio painted the frescoes in the lunettes and the Adoration *above the altar in 1485–9.*

STAR FEATURES

★ Chigi Chapel

★ Caravaggio Paintings in Cerasi Chapel

★ Delphic Sibyl

The altarpiece of *The Assumption* is by Annibale Carracci (1540–1609).

★ **Caravaggio Paintings in Cerasi Chapel**
One of two Caravaggios in the Cerasi Chapel, The Crucifixion of St Peter *uses dramatic fore-shortening to highlight the sheer effort involved in turning the saint's crucifix upside down.*

Stained Glass
In 1509 French artist Guillaume de Marcillat was invited to provide Rome's first two stained-glass windows.

The Tomb of Ascanio Sforza, who died in 1505, is by Andrea Sansovino.

★ **Delphic Sibyl**
This is one of a series of frescoes by Pinturicchio, some Classical and others Biblical, painted in 1508–9 to decorate the ceiling of the apse.

The altar houses the 13th-century painting known as the *Madonna del Popolo.*

The Tomb of Giovanni della Rovere (1483) is by pupils of Andrea Bregno.

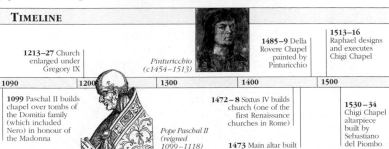

TIMELINE

			1485–9 Della Rovere Chapel painted by Pinturicchio	**1513–16** Raphael designs and executes Chigi Chapel
1213–27 Church enlarged under Gregory IX	*Pinturicchio (c1454–1513)*			
1090	**1200**	**1300**	**1400**	**1500**
1099 Paschal II builds chapel over tombs of the Domitia family (which included Nero) in honour of the Madonna	*Pope Paschal II (reigned 1099–1118)*	**1472–8** Sixtus IV builds church (one of the first Renaissance churches in Rome) **1473** Main altar built		**1530–34** Chigi Chapel altarpiece built by Sebastiano del Piombo

Ara Pacis ⑲

Via di Ripetta. **Map** 4 F2.
📞 68 80 68 48. **🚌** 81, 90, 90b,
119, 926. **Open** 9am–4pm Tue–Sat,
9am–1pm Sun (last adm: 30 mins
before closing). **Adm charge.** **📷**

R ECONSTRUCTED at great
expense over a period of
many years, the Ara Pacis
(Altar of Peace) is one of the
most significant monuments
of ancient Rome. It celebrates
the peace created throughout
the Mediterranean area by the
Emperor Augustus after

Marcus Agrippa (right)

victorious campaigns in Gaul
and Spain. The monument
was commissioned by the
Senate in 13 BC and completed
four years later. It is a square
enclosure on a low platform
with the altar in the centre.
All the surfaces are decorated
with magnificent friezes and
reliefs carved in Carrara
marble. Their high quality
indicates that the craftsmen must have been
Greek. The reliefs on the
north and south walls
depict a procession that
took place on 4 July 13
BC, in which the
members of the

Frieze on south wall showing procession with the family of Augustus

emperor's family can be
identified, ranked by their
position in the succession. Heir
apparent at the time was
Marcus Agrippa, husband of
Augustus's daughter Julia. All
the portraits in the relief are
carved with extraordinarily
effective realism, even the
innocent toddler clinging to
his mother's skirts.

The tale of the rediscovery
of the Ara Pacis dates back to
the 16th century, when the
first panels were unearthed.
One section ended up in
Paris, another in Florence.
Further finds were made in
the late 19th century, when
archaeologists finally realized

just what they had discovered.
What we see today has all
been pieced together since
1938. The reconstruction, in
part original, in part facsimile,
is enshrined in a large glass
hangar creating a wonderful
spectacle when lit up at night.

**Livia (right), Augustus's wife and
the mother of Tiberius, with an
unidentified member of the family**

South wall

East wall

The altar was used
once a year for a
sacrifice on the
anniversary of the
monument's
inauguration.

West wall

North wall

An acanthus frieze
runs around the
lower half of the
outside wall.

**Augustus's young
grandson, Lucius**

Mausoleum of Augustus ⑳

Piazza Augusto Imperatore. **Map** 4 F2.
🚇 *81, 90, 90b, 119, 926.* **Adm** *by written permission only: apply to Ripartizione X, Piazza Campitelli 7.*
📞 *67 10 20 70.*

NOW JUST a weedy mound, ringed with cypresses and sadly strewn with litter, this was once the most prestigious burial place in Rome. Augustus had the mausoleum built in 28 BC, the year he became sole ruler, as a tomb for himself and his descendants. The circular building was 87 m (270 ft) in diameter with two obelisks (now in Piazza del Quirinale and Piazza dell' Esquilino) at the entrance.

Inside were four concentric passageways (linked by corridors) where the urns containing the ashes of the Imperial family were placed. The first to be buried there was Augustus's favourite nephew, Marcellus, who had married Julia, the emperor's daughter. He died in 23 BC, possibly poisoned by Augustus's second wife Livia, who felt that her son, Tiberius, would make a more reliable emperor. When Augustus died in AD 14, his ashes were placed in the mausoleum, Tiberius duly became emperor, and dynastic poisonings continued to fill the family vault with urns.

This sinister monument was later used as a medieval fortress, a vineyard, a private garden, and even, in the 18th century, as a bullring.

Augustus, the first Roman emperor

Madonna, San Rocco and Sant'Antonio with Victims of the Plague by Il Baciccia (1639–1709)

San Rocco ㉑

Largo San Rocco 1. **Map** 4 F2.
📞 *689 64 16.* 🚇 *81, 90, 90b, 119.* **Open** *7.30am–9am, 5pm–7.45pm Mon–Sat, 9am–1pm, 5pm–7.45pm Sun.* **Closed** *17–31 Aug.* ✝ 📷

THIS CHURCH, with a restrained Neo-Classical facade by Giuseppe Valadier, the designer of Piazza del Popolo, began life as the chapel of a 16th-century hospital with beds for 50 men – San Rocco was a healer of the plague-stricken. A maternity wing was added for the wives of Tiber bargees to save them from having to give birth in the insanitary conditions of a boat. The hospital came to be used by unmarried mothers, and one section of the hospital was set aside for women who did not wish to give their names. They were even permitted to wear a veil for the duration of their stay. Unwanted children were sent to an orphanage, and if any mothers or children died they were buried in anonymous graves.

The hospital was abandoned at the turn of the century, and demolished in the 1930s during the excavation of the Mausoleum of Augustus. The church has an interesting Baroque altarpiece by Il Baciccia, the artist who decorated the ceiling of the Gesù *(see pp114–15).*

Santi Ambrogio e Carlo al Corso ㉒

Via del Corso 437. **Map** 4 F2.
📞 *687 83 32.* 🚇 *81, 90, 90b, 119.* **Open** *7.30am–12.30pm, 5pm–7pm (Oct–Mar: 7.30pm) daily. Ring porter's door to left of church if closed.* 🚫

THIS CHURCH belonged to the Lombard community in Rome, and is dedicated to two canonized bishops of Milan, Lombardy's capital. In 1471, Pope Sixtus IV gave the Lombards a church which they dedicated to Sant'Ambrogio, who died in 397. Then in 1610, when Carlo Borromeo was canonized, the church was rebuilt in his honour. Most of the new church was the work of father and son, Onorio and Martino Longhi, but the fine dome is by Pietro da Cortona. The altarpiece by Carlo Maratta (1625–1713) is the *Gloria dei Santi Ambrogio e Carlo.* An ambulatory leads behind the altar to a chapel housing the the heart of San Carlo in a richly decorated reliquary.

Statue of San Carlo by Attilio Selva (1888–1970) behind the apse of Santi Ambrogio e Carlo

CAMPO DE' FIORI

BETWEEN Corso Vittorio Emanuele II and the Tiber, the city displays many distinct personalities. The open-air market of Campo de' Fiori preserves the lively, bohemian atmosphere of the medieval inns that once flourished here, while the area also contains Renaissance palazzi, such as Palazzo Farnese and Palazzo Spada, where powerful Roman families built

18th-century Madonna in Campo de' Fiori

their fortress-like houses near the route of papal processions. Close by, overlooking the picturesque Tiber Island, lies the old Jewish Ghetto, where many traces of daily life from past centuries can still be seen. The Portico of Octavia and the Theatre of Marcellus are spectacular examples of the city's many-layered history, built up over the half-ruined remains of ancient Rome.

SIGHTS AT A GLANCE

Churches and Temples
Santissima Trinità
dei Pellegrini ④
Santa Maria dell'Orazione
e Morte ⑥
San Girolamo della Carità ⑧
Sant'Eligio degli Orefici ⑨
Santa Maria di Monserrato ⑩
San Carlo ai Catinari ⑰
Santa Maria in Campitelli ⑲
San Nicola in Carcere ㉒
San Giovanni dei Fiorentini ㉘

Museums and Galleries
Palazzo Spada ⑤

Piccola Farnesina ⑬
Burcardo Theatre Museum ⑭

Historic Buildings
Palazzo Pio Righetti ②
Palazzo del Monte di Pietà ③
Palazzo Farnese ⑦
Palazzo Ricci ⑪
Palazzo della Cancelleria ⑫
Palazzo Cenci ㉕
Casa di Lorenzo Manilio ㉖

Fountains
Fontana delle Tartarughe ⑱

Historic Streets and Piazzas
Campo de' Fiori ①
Tiber Island ㉓
Ghetto and Synagogue ㉔
Via Giulia ㉗

Ancient Sites
Area Sacra ⑯
Theatre of Marcellus ⑳
Portico of Octavia ㉑

Famous Theatres
Teatro Argentina ⑮

GETTING THERE
Most of the streets around Campo de' Fiori are too narrow for buses, but many routes converge on Largo Argentina, a useful starting point for exploring. The 90 and 90b will also take you to Via del Teatro di Marcello. Only three buses, the 46, 62 and 64, go the full length of Corso Vittorio Emanuele II.

SEE ALSO

- **Street Finder**, maps 4, 8, 11, 12
- **Where to Stay** pp294–5
- **Restaurants** pp310–11
- **Via Giulia Walk** pp276–7

KEY

▢ Street-by-Street map

🅿 Parking

Fruit stalls beneath the statue of Giordano Bruno in the Campo de' Fiori market

Street-by-Street: Campo de' Fiori

THIS FASCINATING PART of Renaissance Rome is
also an exciting area for shopping and night
life, centred on the market square of Campo de'
Fiori. Its stalls supply many nearby restaurants
and young people shop for clothes in Via dei
Giubbonari. Popular reasonably-priced
restaurants and pizzerias keep the area
alive late into the night. By day there
are great buildings to admire, though few
are open to the public. Two exceptions are
the Piccola Farnesina with its collection of
Classical statues and Palazzo Spada,
home to many important paintings.

**Sant'Eligio
degli Orefici**
*A small Renaissance
church designed by
Raphael is concealed
behind a later facade* 9

Palazzo Ricci
*Painted Classical scenes
were a favourite form of
decoration for the facades
of Renaissance houses* 11

**San Girolamo
della Carità**
*The chief attraction
of this church is
Borromini's fabulous
Spada Chapel* 8

**Santa Maria di
Monserrato**
*This church, which has
strong connections with
Spain, houses a Bernini
bust of Cardinal Pedro
Foix de Montoya* 10

**Santa Maria
dell'Orazione
e Morte**
*A pair of
dramatic winged
skulls flank the
doorway to this
church dedicated to
the burial of the dead* 6

Palazzo Farnese
*Michelangelo and other
great artists helped create
this monumental
Renaissance palazzo* 7

KEY

– – – Suggested route

0 metres   75

0 yards   75

Palazzo della Cancelleria
The papal administration ran the affairs of the church from this vast building ⑫

Piccola Farnesina
This plaque honours Giovanni Barracco. His sculpture collection is housed in the palazzo ⑬

LOCATOR MAP
See Central Rome Map pp12–13

★ **Campo de' Fiori**
The colourful market makes this one of the city's most entertaining squares ❶

Palazzo Pio Righetti
Heraldic eagles stare down from the pediments of the palazzo's windows ❷

Palazzo del Monte di Pietà
This was a papal institution, where the poor pawned their possessions in order to borrow small sums of money ❸

Santissima Trinità dei Pellegrini
The principal role of this church was one of charity, looking after poor pilgrims arriving in Rome ❹

★ **Palazzo Spada**
The picture gallery houses a collection started by two wonderfully eccentric 17th-century cardinals ❺

STAR SIGHTS

★ Campo de' Fiori

★ Palazzo Spada

Campo de' Fiori ❶

Piazza Campo de' Fiori. **Map** 4 E4 & 11 C4. ▥ 46, 62, 64, 70, 81, 87, 90, 90b, 492, 926. See **Markets** p338.

THE CAMPO DE' FIORI (field of Flora), once a meadow, occupies the site of the open space facing the Theatre of Pompey. Cardinals and noblemen used to rub shoulders with fishmongers and foreigners in the piazza's market, making it one of the liveliest areas of medieval and Renaissance Rome. Today's market retains much of the traditional lively atmosphere.

In the centre of the square is a statue of a hooded figure. This is the philosopher Giordano Bruno, who was burnt at the stake for heresy on this spot in 1600 – a grim reminder of the executions that were held here.

The piazza was surrounded by inns for pilgrims and other travellers. Many of these were once owned by the successful 15th-century courtesan, Vannozza Catanei, mistress of Pope Alexander VI Borgia. On the corner between the piazza and Via del Pellegrino you can see Catanei's shield, which she had decorated with her own coat of arms and those of her husband and her lover, the Borgia pope.

Market stalls in Campo de' Fiori

Window pediment with heraldic lion and pine cones, Palazzo Pio Righetti

Palazzo Pio Righetti ❷

Piazza del Biscione 89. **Map** 4 E5 & 11 C4. ▥ 46, 62, 64, 70, 81, 87, 90, 186, 492. **Not open** to the public.

THE VAST 17th-century Palazzo Pio Righetti was built over the ruined Theatre of Pompey. The windows of the palazzo are decorated with lions and pine cones from the coat of arms of the Pio da Carpi family who lived here.

The curve of the Theatre of Pompey, completed in 55 BC, is followed by Via di Grotta Pinta. This was Rome's first permanent theatre built of stone and concrete. In places, for example the basement of the Pancrazio restaurant, you can see early examples of *opus reticulatum* – small square blocks of tufa (porous rock) set diagonally as a facing for a concrete wall.

Palazzo del Monte di Pietà ❸

Piazza del Monte di Pietà 33. **Map** 4 E5 & 11 C4. ▐ 51 72 66 10. ▥ 44, 56, 60, 65, 75, 170, 710. **Chapel open** 7.40am–2pm Tue–Fri. **Closed** public hols. **Adm** by appt or on request to porter.

THE MONTE, as it is known, is a public institution, founded in 1539 by Pope Paul III Farnese as a pawnshop to staunch the usury then rampant in the city. The building still has offices and auction rooms for the sale of unredeemed goods.

The stars with diagonal bands on the huge central plaque decorating the facade are the coat of arms of Pope Clement VIII Aldobrandini,

added when Carlo Maderno enlarged the palace in the 17th century. The clock on the left was added later.

Within, the chapel is a jewel of Baroque architecture, adorned with gilded stucco, marble panelling and reliefs. The decoration makes a perfect setting for the sculptures by Domenico Guidi – a bust of San Carlo Borromeo and a relief of the *Pietà*. There are also splendid reliefs by Giovanni Battista Théudon and Pierre Legros of Biblical scenes illustrating the charitable nature of the institution.

Relief by Théudon of *Joseph Lending Grain to the Egyptians* in Palazzo del Monte di Pietà

Santissima Trinità dei Pellegrini ❹

Piazza della Trinità dei Pellegrini. **Map** 4 E5 & 11 C5. ▐ 686 84 51. ▥ 44, 56, 60, 65, 75, 170, 710 and many other routes. **Closed** for restoration.

THE CHURCH WAS donated in the 16th century to a charitable organization founded by San Filippo Neri to care for the poor and the sick, in particular the

Guido Reni's *Holy Trinity*

thousands of paupers who flocked in pilgrimage to Rome during the special holy years known as Jubilees.

The 18th-century facade has niches with statues of the Evangelists by Bernardino Ludovisi. The interior, with Corinthian columns, ends in a horseshoe vault and apse, dominated by Guido Reni's striking altarpiece of the *Holy Trinity* (1625). The frescoes in the lantern are also by Reni.

Other interesting paintings include *St Gregory the Great Freeing Souls from Purgatory*, by Baldassarre Croce (third chapel to the left); Cavalier d'Arpino's *Virgin and Saints* (second chapel to the left); and a painting by Borgognone (1677), showing the Virgin and recently canonized saints, including San Carlo Borromeo and San Filippo Neri. In the sacristy are depictions of the nobility washing the feet of pilgrims, a custom started by San Filippo.

Fresco in the dome of Santissima Trinità

Palazzo Spada ❺

Piazza Capo di Ferro 13. **Map** 4 E5 & 11 C4. **(** 686 11 58. **▦** 44, 46, 62 64, 65, 70, 87, 90, 492 and many other routes. **Gallery open** 9am–7pm Tue–Sat, 9am–1pm Sun. **Adm charge**. **▢ ▢ ▢ Adm** to other rooms by request to Ufficio Personale, Consiglio di Stato **(** 682 71. **Ø**

Tʜɪs ᴍᴀᴊᴇsᴛɪᴄ ᴘᴀʟᴀᴢᴢo, built around 1540 for Cardinal Capo di Ferro, has an elegant stuccoed courtyard and facade decorated with reliefs evoking Rome's glorious past.

Cardinal Bernardino Spada, who lived here in the 17th century with his brother Virginio (also a cardinal), hired Bernini and Borromini to work on the building. The brothers' whimsical delight in false perspectives resulted in a colonnaded gallery by Borromini that appears four times longer than it really is.

The cardinals also amassed a superb private collection of paintings. These are now displayed in the Galleria Spada together with some Classical statues and 18th-century furniture. The wide range of artists represented includes Rubens, Dürer and Guido Reni. Works to look out for by lesser artists include *The Visitation* by Andrea del Sarto (1486–1530), *Cain and Abel* by Giovanni Lanfranco (1582–1647) and *The Death of Dido* by Guercino (1591–1666).

Santa Maria dell'Orazione e Morte ❻

Via Giulia. **Map** 4 E5 & 11 B4. **▦** 23, 65, 280. **Open** for mass 6pm Sun, public hols. **✝**

A ᴘɪous ᴄᴏɴꜰʀᴀᴛᴇʀɴɪᴛʏ was formed here in the 16th century to collect the bodies of the unknown dead and give them a Christian burial. The theme of death is stressed in this church, dedicated to St Mary of Prayer and Death. The doors and windows of Ferdinando Fuga's dramatic Baroque facade are decorated with winged skulls. Above the central entrance there is a *clepsydra* (an ancient hourglass) – symbolic of death.

Offertory box in Santa Maria dell'Orazione e Morte

Palazzo Farnese ❼

Piazza Farnese. **Map** 4 E5 & 11 B4. **▦** 46, 62, 64, 70, 71, 87, 90, 492, 926. **Not open** to the public.

Aɴ ɪᴍᴘᴏsɪɴɢ building that became the prototype for many princely palaces, Palazzo Farnese was originally built for Cardinal Alessandro Farnese, who commissioned the greatest artists of the time to work on its design.

After the cardinal became Pope Paul III in 1534, the building was redesigned by Antonio da Sangallo the Younger. He was assisted in this by Michelangelo, who contributed the great cornice and central window of the main facade, and the third level of the courtyard.

Michelangelo had a plan for the Farnese gardens to be connected by a bridge to the Farnese home in Trastevere, Villa Farnesina *(see pp220–21)*. The elegant arch spanning Via Giulia belongs to this sadly unrealized scheme. The palazzo was finally completed in 1589, on a less ambitious scale, by Giacomo della Porta. It is now the home of the French Embassy.

Majestic facade of Palazzo Farnese

Spada Chapel in San Girolamo

San Girolamo della Carità ⑧

Via di Monserrato 62A. **Map** 4 E5 & 11 B4. 🕿 687 97 86. 🚌 23, 46, 62, 64, 65, 280. **Open** 10am–noon Wed, 10.30am–11.30am Sun. 🕇 📷

THE CHURCH was built on the site of the home of San Filippo Neri, the 16th-century saint from Tuscany. This warm, patient character renewed Rome's spiritual and cultural life by his friendly, open approach to religion. He would have loved the frolicking putti shown surrounding his statue, in his chapel, reminding him of the Roman urchins he had cared for during his lifetime.

The breathtaking Spada Chapel was designed by Borromini, and is unique both as a work of art and as an illustration of the spirit of the Baroque age. All architectural elements are concealed so that the space of the chapel's interior is defined solely by decorative marblework and statues. Veined jasper and precious multicoloured marbles are sculpted to imitate flowery damask and velvet hangings. Even the altar rail is a long swag of jasper drapery held up by a pair of kneeling angels with wooden wings.

Although there are memorials to former members of the Spada family, oddly there is no indication as to which of the Spadas was responsible for endowing the chapel. It was probably art-lover Cardinal Virginio Spada, a follower of San Filippo Neri.

Sant'Eligio degli Orefici ⑨

Via di Sant'Eligio 8A. **Map** 4 D4 & 11 B4. 🕿 686 82 60. 🚌 23, 41, 46, 62, 64, 65, 280. **Open** 10.30am–12.30pm Mon, Tue, Thu & Sat (Fri by request only). When closed ring at No. 9 Via di Sant'Eligio. **Closed** Aug & Sep. 🕇 📷

THE NAME of the church still records the fact that it was commissioned by a rich corporation of goldsmiths (orefici) in the early 16th century. The original design was by Raphael, who, like his master Bramante, had acquired a sense of the grandiose from the remains of Roman antiquity. The influence of some of Bramante's works, such as the choir of Santa Maria del Popolo (see p138–9), is evident in the simple way the arches and pilasters define the structure of the walls.

The cupola of Sant' Eligio is attributed to Baldassarre Peruzzi, while the facade was added in the early 17th century by Flaminio Ponzio. Among the various 16th-century painters who decorated the interior was Taddeo Zuccari, who worked on Palazzo Farnese (see p147).

Santa Maria di Monserrato ⑩

Via di Monserrato. **Map** 4 E4 & 11 B3. 🕿 686 58 61. 🚌 23, 41, 46, 62, 64, 65, 280. **Closed** to the public except by special permission: apply to the rector at the address above. 🕇 📷

An early bust by Bernini of Cardinal Pedro Foix de Montoya

THE ORIGINS of this, the Spanish national church in Rome, go back to 1506, when a hospice for Spanish pilgrims was begun by a brotherhood dedicated to the Virgin of Montserrat in Catalonia. Don't miss Bernini's bust of Pedro Foix de Montoya, the church's benefactor, and Annibale Carracci's painting of *San Diego de Alcalà*. There is also a copy of a Sansovino statue of St James in the third chapel on the left and some beautiful 15th-century tombs by Andrea Bregno and Luigi Capponi in the courtyard and side chapels.

San Diego **by Annibale Carracci**

Statue of San Filippo Neri by Pierre Legros

Palazzo Ricci ⓫

Piazza de' Ricci. **Map** 4 D4 & 11 B4.
🚌 23, 46, 62, 64, 65, 280.
Not open to the public.

PALAZZO RICCI was famous for its frescoed facade – now rather faded – originally painted in the 16th century by Polidoro da Caravaggio, a follower of Raphael.

In Renaissance Rome it was common to commission artists to decorate the outsides of their houses with heroes of Classical antiquity. A fresco by a leading artist such as Polidoro, reputedly the inventor of this style of painting, was a conspicuous status symbol. Decorative schemes like this required inventiveness to outshine the other palazzi, a mastery of perspective and, above all, great dexterity as the painting on wet plaster had to be completed before it dried.

Palazzo della Cancelleria ⓬

Piazza della Cancelleria. **Map** 4 E4 & 11 C3. 📞 69 88 48 16. 🚌 44, 46, 62, 64, 70, 81, 87, 90, 90b, 492, 926. **Open** with permit from Vatican only.

THE PALAZZO, a supreme example of the confident architecture of the Early Renaissance, was begun in 1485. It was financed partly with the gambling winnings of Cardinal Raffaele Riario. Roses, the emblem of the Riario family, adorn the vaults and capitals of the beautiful Doric courtyard. The palazzo's interior was decorated after the Sack of Rome in 1527. Giorgio Vasari boasted that he had completed work on one enormous room in just 100 days; Michelangelo allegedly retorted: "It looks like it." Other Mannerist artists, Perin del Vaga and Francesco Salviati, frescoed the rooms of the cardinal in charge of the Papal Chancellery, the office that gave the palazzo its name when it was installed here by Pope Leo X. On the right of

Part of the frescoed facade of Palazzo Ricci

the main entrance is the unobtrusive and rather quaint church of San Lorenzo in Damaso, founded by Pope Damasus (reigned 366–384). Its surrounding porticoes housed libraries which held the first Papal Archives.

Piccola Farnesina ⓭

Corso Vittorio Emanuele II 166. **Map** 4 E4 & 11 C3. 📞 68 80 68 48. 🚌 46, 62, 64, 70, 81, 87, 90, 90b, 492, 926. **Open** 9am–7pm Tue–Sat, 9am–1pm Sun & public hols. **Adm charge.** 🚫

THIS DELIGHTFUL miniature palazzo acquired its name from the lilies decorating its cornices. These were mistakenly identified as part of the Farnese family crest. In fact they were part of the coat of arms of a French clergyman, Thomas Leroy, for whom the palazzo was built in 1523.

The entrance is in a new facade built to overlook Corso Vittorio Emanuele II when the road was constructed at the turn of the century. The original facade on the left of today's entrance is attributed to Antonio da Sangallo the Younger. Note the asymmetrical arrangement of its windows and ledges. The elegant central courtyard also retains its original appearance. The Piccola Farnesina now houses the Museo Barracco, a collection of ancient sculpture assembled during the last century by the politician Baron Giovanni Barracco. A bust of the baron

Lily on facade of the Piccola Farnesina

can be seen in the courtyard. The collection includes Assyrian, Egyptian, Greek and Etruscan works as well as Roman ones. Some of the exhibits are rather fragmentary, but in the setting of this fine Renaissance building they make an attractive display.

Inner courtyard, Piccola Farnesina

Burcardo Theatre Museum ⓮

Via del Sudario 44. **Map** 4 F4 & 12 D4. 📞 68 80 67 55. 🚌 44, 46, 56, 60, 62, 64, 70, 81, 90, 90b, 492, 926. **Closed** for restoration until further notice. **Library open** 9am–1.30pm Mon–Wed & Fri, 9am–5.30pm Thu.

THIS LATE 15th-century house belonged to Johannes Burckhardt, chamberlain to Pope Alexander VI Borgia and author of a diary of Rome under the Borgias. His house now holds Rome's most complete collection of theatre literature, plus Chinese puppets and comic masks from the various regions of Italy.

Teatro Argentina **⑮**

Via di Torre Argentina. **Map** 4 F4 &
12 D4. ☎ 68 80 46 01. 🚌 44, 46,
56, 60, 62, 64, 70, 81, 90, 90b, 94,
492, 926. **Plays** performed Oct–Jun.
See **Entertainment** pp346–7.

O NE OF ROME'S most
important theatres was
founded by the powerful
Sforza Cesarini family in 1730,
though the facade dates from
a century later. Many famous
operas were first performed
here. In 1816, for example,
the theatre saw the ill-fated
début of Rossini's *Barber of
Seville*, during which the
composer insulted the
unappreciative audience, who
then pursued him, enraged,
through the streets of Rome.
Many of Verdi's masterpieces
were first produced here.

Detail of facade, Teatro Argentina

Area Sacra **⑯**

Largo di Torre Argentina. **Map** 4 F4 &
12 D4. 🚌 44, 46, 56, 60, 62, 64, 70,
81, 90, 90b, 94, 492, 926. Apply for
permit to: Ripartizione X (see p367).

T HE REMAINS of four temples
were discovered here
during rebuilding in the 1920s.
They date from the era of the
Republic, and are among the
oldest to have been found in
Rome. For the purpose of
identification, they are known
as A, B, C and D. The oldest
(temple C) dates back to the
4th century BC. It was placed
on a high platform preceded
by an altar and is typical of
Italic temple plans as opposed
to the Greek model. Temple A
is from the 3rd century BC. In
medieval times the small
church of San Nicola was built
over its podium. The remains
of its two apses are still visible.
The column stumps to the
north belonged to a great

San Carlo at Prayer by Guido Reni

portico, known as the
Hecatostylum (portico of 100
columns). In Imperial times
two marble lavatories were
built here – the remains of
one are visible behind temple
A. Behind temples B and C
are remains of a great
platform of tufa blocks. These
have been identified as part
of the Curia of Pompey, a
rectangular building housing a
statue of Pompey, where the
Senate met and where Julius
Caesar was assassinated on
15 March 44 BC.

**Area Sacra, with circular ruins of
temple B in the foreground**

San Carlo ai
Catinari **⑰**

Piazza B Cairoli. **Map** 4 F5 & 12 D4.
☎ 689 38 74. 🚌 44, 56, 60, 65, 75,
170, 710, 926. **Open** 7.30am–noon,
4.30pm–7pm Mon–Sat, 8.30am–
12.30pm, 4.30pm–7.30pm Sun. 🕇 📷

I N 1620 ROME'S Milanese
congregation decided to
honour Cardinal Carlo

Borromeo, with this great
church. It is called "ai
Catinari" on account of the
bowl-makers' *(catinari)*
shops in the area. The
solemn travertine facade
was completed in 1638 by
the Roman architect Soria.
The 16th-century basilical
plan is flanked by chapels.
The St Cecilia chapel was
designed and decorated by
Antonio Gherardi, who
added a family portrait.
The church's paintings and
frescoes by Pietro da Cortona
and Guido Reni are confident,
mature works of the Counter
Reformation, depicting the
life and acts of the recently
canonized San Carlo. Make
sure you also see the ornate
crucifix, inlaid with marble,
glass and mother-of-pearl, by
the 16th-century sculptor
Algardi on the sacristy altar.

Sacristy altar, San Carlo ai Catinari

Fontana delle
Tartarughe **⑱**

Piazza Mattei. **Map** 4 F5 & 12 D4.
🚌 44, 56, 60, 65, 75, 170, 710, 926.

T HE DELIGHTFUL Fontana
delle Tartarughe –
tartarughe are tortoises – was
commissioned by the Mattei
family to decorate "their"
piazza between 1581 and
1588. The design was by
Giacomo della Porta, but the
fountain owes much of its
grace and charm to the four
slender bronze youths each
resting one foot on the head
of a dolphin, sculpted by
Taddeo Landini. Nearly a
century later an unknown

sculptor was inspired to add the struggling tortoises to complete the composition.

Della Porta's graceful Fontana delle Tartarughe

Santa Maria in Campitelli ⑲

Piazza di Campitelli. **Map** 4 F5 & 12 E5. **[** 68 80 39 78. **🚌** 57, 90, 90b, 92, 94, 95, 716. **Open** 7am–noon, 4pm–7pm daily. **🚹 📷 ♿**

Cherubs, Santa Maria in Campitelli

IN 17TH-CENTURY ROME the plague could still strike fiercely and there were no reliable, effective remedies. Many Romans simply prayed for a cure to a sacred medieval icon of the Virgin, the Madonna del Portico. When a particularly lethal outbreak of plague abated in 1656, popular gratitude was so strong that a new church was built to house the icon in appropriate splendour.

The church, designed by Bernini's pupil, Carlo Rainaldi, was completed in 1667. The main elements of the lively Baroque facade are the graceful columns, symbolizing the supporters of the true faith.

Inside the church a fabulous gilded altar tabernacle with spiral columns was designed by Giovanni Antonio de Rossi to contain the image of the Virgin. The side chapels are decorated by some of Rome's

finest Baroque painters: Sebastiano Conca, Giovanni Battista Gaulli (known as Il Baciccia) and Luca Giordano.

Theatre of Marcellus ⑳

Via del Teatro di Marcello. **Map** 4 A5 & 12 E5. **[** 481 48 00. **🚌** 57, 90, 90b, 92, 94, 95, 716. **Closed** except for **concerts**. See **Entertainment** p343.

THE CURVED OUTER WALL of this vast amphitheatre has supported generations of Roman buildings. It was built by the Emperor Augustus, who dedicated it to Marcellus, his nephew and son-in-law, who had died aged 19 in 23 BC. By the 13th century the theatre had been converted into the fortress of the Savelli family. In the 16th century Baldassarre Peruzzi built a great palace on the theatre ruins for the Orsini family, including a garden facing the Tiber. The lower arches were later occupied by humble dwellings and workshops.

Close to the theatre stand three beautiful Corinthian columns and a section of frieze. These belonged to the Temple of Apollo, which housed many works of art plundered by the Romans from Greece in the 2nd century BC.

The Theatre of Marcellus by Thomas Hartley Cromek (1809–73)

Portico of Octavia ㉑

Via del Portico d'Ottavia. **Map** 4 F5 & 12 E5. **🚌** 57, 90, 90b, 92, 94, 95, 716.

BUILT IN HONOUR of Augustus's sister Octavia (the abandoned wife of Mark Antony), this is the only surviving portico of what used to be the monumental piazza of Circus Flaminius.

The rectangular portico enclosed temples dedicated to Jupiter and Juno, decorated with bronze statues. The part we see today is the great central atrium originally covered by marble facings.

In the Middle Ages a great fish market and a church, Sant'Angelo in Pescheria, were built in the ruins of the portico. As the church was associated with the fishing activities of the nearby river port, aquatic flora and fauna feature in many of its inlays. Links with the Tiber are also apparent in the stucco facade on the adjacent Fishmonger's Oratory, built in 1689. The church has a detached fresco of the Madonna and angels painted by the school of Benozzo Gozzoli.

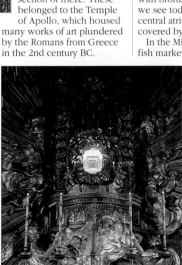

Lavish altar tabernacle in Santa Maria in Campitelli

San Nicola in Carcere ㉒

Via del Teatro di Marcello 46. **Map** 5 A5
& 12 E5. **[** 68 30 71 98. **[** 57, 90,
90b, 92, 94, 95, 716. **Open** 7.30am–
noon, 4pm–7pm Mon–Sat, 10am–
1pm Sun. **Closed** Aug–mid-Sep. **[**] [☉]

Tiber Island, with Ponte Cestio linking it to Trastevere

THE MEDIEVAL CHURCH of San
Nicola in Carcere stands
on the site of three Roman
temples of the Republican era
which were converted into
a prison in the Middle Ages
(*carcere* means prison). The
temples of Juno, Spes and
Janus faced a city gate leading
from the Forum Holitorium,
the city's vegetable and oil
market, to the road down to
the port on the Tiber. The
columns embedded in the
walls of the church belonged
to two flanking temples
whose platforms are now
marked by grass lawns.

The church was rebuilt in
1599 and restored in the 19th
century, but the bell tower
and Roman columns are part
of the original
design.

**Facade and medieval bell tower
of San Nicola in Carcere**

Tiber Island ㉓

Isola Tiberina. **Map** 8 D1 & 12 D5.
[15, 23, 97, 774, 780.

IN ANCIENT TIMES the island,
which lay opposite the city's
port, had large structures of
white travertine at either end
built to resemble the stern and
prow of a ship.

Since 293 BC, when a
temple was dedicated here to
Aesculapius, the god of
healing and protector against
the plague, the island has
been associated with the sick.
There is still a hospital on the

island. San Bartolomeo, the
church in the island's central
piazza, was built on the ruins
of the Temple of Aesculapius
in the 10th century. Its
Romanesque bell tower is a
useful landmark, clearly visible
from the banks of the Tiber.

From the Ghetto area you
can reach the island by a
footbridge, the Ponte Fabricio.
The oldest original bridge
over the Tiber still in use, it
was built in 62 BC. In
medieval times the Pierleoni,
and then the Caetani, two
powerful families, controlled
this strategic point by means
of a tower, still in situ. The
other bridge to the island, the
Ponte Cestio, is inscribed with
the names of the Byzantine
emperors associated with its
restoration in AD 370.

Ghetto and Synagogue ㉔

Synagogue, Lungotevere dei Cenci.
Map 4 F5 & 12 E5. **[** 684 00 61 .
[23, 44, 56, 60, 65, 75, 170, 710,
774. **Open** 9.30am–5pm (6pm in
summer) Mon–Thu, 9.30am–1.30pm
(5pm in summer) Fri, 9.30am–12.30pm
Sun. **Closed** Sat. **[**] [**] [**] Ghetto,
main street is Via del Portico d'Ottavia.

EVEN THOUGH they were first
brought to Rome as slaves
by Pompey the Great, Jews
were much appreciated for
their financial and medical
skills during the time of the
Roman Empire. In the Middle
Ages their relative freedom
continued; in fact, the anti-
Pope Anacletus came from a
converted Jewish family.

Systematic persecution
began in the 16th century.
From 25 July 1556 all the Jews
of Rome were forced to live
inside a high-walled enclosure

erected on the orders of Pope
Paul IV. The Ghetto was in a
particularly unhealthy part of
Rome. Inhabitants were
allowed out only during the
day. On Sundays they were
driven into the church of
Sant'Angelo in Pescheria to
listen to Christian sermons –
a practice abolished only in
1848. Persecution started
again under Fascism, when
hundreds were sent to
German concentration camps.

Today many Jews still live
here and the medieval streets,
with shops selling typical
Roman kosher food, retain
much of their old character.
The imposing Synagogue on
Lungotevere was built in 1874.

Synagogue overlooking the Tiber

Palazzo Cenci ㉕

Vicolo dei Cenci. **Map** 4 F5 & 12 D5.
[44, 56, 60, 65, 75, 170, 710. **Not
open** to the public.

PALAZZO CENCI belonged to
the family of Beatrice
Cenci, who was accused,
together with her brothers and
stepmother, of witchcraft and
the murder of her tyrannical
father. She was condemned to
death and beheaded at Ponte
Sant'Angelo in 1599.

Most of the original medieval
palazzo has been demolished,
and the building you see
today dates back to the 1570s,
though its rather forbidding
appearance seems medieval.

Heraldic half-moons decorate the main facade on Via del Progresso while pretty balconies open on the opposite side where a medieval arch joins the palace to Palazzetto Cenci, designed by Martino Longhi the Elder. Inside is a traditional courtyard with an Ionic-style loggia; many of the rooms retain the original 16th-century decoration that the unfortunate Beatrice would have known as a child.

Balcony of Palazzo Cenci

Casa di Lorenzo Manilio ㊱

Via del Portico d'Ottavia 1D. **Map** 4 F5 & 12 D5. 🚌 44, 56, 60, 65, 75, 170, 710. **Not open** to the public.

BEFORE THE RENAISSANCE, most Romans had only vague, confused ideas of their city's glorious past, but after the 15th-century revival of interest in the philosophy and arts of antiquity, some were even encouraged to build houses recalling the splendour of ancient Rome. In 1468 a certain Lorenzo Manilio built a great house for his family, decorating it with an elegant Classical plaque. The Latin inscription dates the building according to the ancient Roman method – 2,221 years

after the foundation of the city – and mentions the owner's name. Original reliefs are embedded in the facades as well as a fragment of an ancient sarcophagus. The Piazza Costaguti facade features windows patriotically inscribed with the legend *Ave Roma* (Hail Rome).

Row of Roman busts decorating the Casa di Lorenzo Manilio

Via Giulia ㊲

Map 4 D4 & 11 A3. 🚌 23, 65, 280.

THIS PICTURESQUE 16th-century street was built by Bramante for Pope Julius II della Rovere. Lined with aristocratic palazzi dating from the 16th–18th centuries as well as churches and antique shops, Via Giulia makes a fascinating walk *(see pp276–7)*.

Mask fountain in Via Giulia

San Giovanni dei Fiorentini ㊳

Via Acciaioli 2. **Map** 4 D4 & 11 A2. 📞 68 80 24 01. 🚌 23, 46, 62, 64, 65, 280. **Open** 7am–noon (1.30pm Sun), 5pm–7.30pm (Oct–Mar: 4.30pm–7pm) daily. ✝

THE CHURCH of St John of the Florentines was built for the large Florentine community living in this area. Pope Leo X wanted it to be an expression of the cultural superiority of Florence over Rome. Started in the early 16th century, the church took over a century to build. The principal architect was Antonio da Sangallo the Younger, but many others contributed before Carlo Maderno's elongated cupola was finally completed in 1614. The present facade, recently cleaned and restored, was added in the 18th century.

The church was decorated mainly by Tuscan artists. One interesting exception is the 15th-century statue of San Giovannino by the Sicilian Mino del Reame in a niche above the sacristy. The spectacular high altar houses a marble group by Antonio Raggi, the *Baptism of Christ*. The altar itself is by Borromini, who is buried in the church along with Carlo Maderno.

This is the only church in Rome which admits animals: the faithful can bring their pets, and an Easter lamb-blessing takes place here.

Antonio Raggi's *Baptism of Christ* in San Giovanni dei Fiorentini

QUIRINAL

ONE OF THE original seven hills of Rome, the Quirinal was a largely residential area in Imperial times. To the east of the hill were the vast Baths of Diocletian, still standing today in front of what is now the main rail station. Abandoned during the Middle Ages, the district returned to favour in the late 16th century. The

1st-century BC stucco in the
Museo Nazionale Romano

prime site was taken by the popes for the Palazzo del Quirinale. Great families such as the Colonna and the Aldobrandini had their palazzi lower down the hill. With the end of papal rule in 1870, the Quirinal became the residence of the kings of Italy, and the surrounding area, especially along Via Nazionale, was redeveloped.

SIGHTS AT A GLANCE

Churches
Santi Apostoli ❹
San Marcello al Corso ❻
Santa Maria in Trivio ❽
Santi Vincenzo e Anastasio ❿
Sant'Andrea al Quirinale ⓫
San Carlo alle Quattro Fontane ⓬
San Bernardo alle Terme ⓮
Santa Maria degli Angeli ⓱
Santa Maria dei Monti ㉑
Sant'Agata dei Goti ㉒
Santi Domenico e Sisto ㉔

Museums and Galleries
Museo delle Cere ❺
Accademia Nazionale di San Luca ❾

Museo Nazionale Romano ⓲
Palazzo delle Esposizioni ⓴

Historic Piazzas
Piazza della Repubblica ⓳

Historic Buildings
Palazzo del Quirinale ❷
Palazzo Colonna ❸
Baths of Diocletian ⓰

Fountains and Statues
Castor and Pollux ❶
Trevi Fountain ❼
Le Quattro Fontane ⓭
Moses Fountain ⓯

Parks and Gardens
Villa Aldobrandini ㉓

GETTING THERE
The area has Metro stops at Repubblica and Cavour. Useful buses include the 64, 65, 70 and 75 along Via Nazionale and the 71 and 81, which go under the Quirinal through the Traforo Umberto I tunnel. There is no bus to the top of the Quirinal, however. You have to walk up Via XXIV Maggio.

KEY

▢	Street-by-Street map
M	Metro station
P	Parking

0 metres   300
0 yards   300

SEE ALSO
• *Street Finder*, maps 5, 6, 12
• *Where to Stay* pp294–5
• *Restaurants* pp310–11
• *Bernini Walk* pp282–3

Fontana delle Naiadi in Piazza della Repubblica

Street-by-Street: The Quirinal Hill

EVEN THOUGH Palazzo del Quirinale is closed to the public, it is well worth walking up the hill to the palace to see the giant Roman statues of Castor and Pollux in the piazza and enjoy fine views of the city below. Come down the hill by way of the narrow streets and stairways that lead to one of Rome's unforgettable sights, the Trevi Fountain. Many small churches lie hidden away in the back streets. Towards Piazza Venezia there are grand palazzi, including that of the Colonna, one of Rome's most ancient and powerful families.

Santa Maria in Via is famous for its medieval well and miraculous 13th-century icon of the Madonna.

Santa Maria in Trivio
The attractive facade of this tiny church conceals a rich Baroque interior ⑧

Accademia Nazionale di San Luca
The art academy has works by famous former members, such as Canova and Angelica Kauffmann ⑨

★ Trevi Fountain
Rome's grandest and best-known fountain almost fills the tiny Piazza di Trevi ⑦

Santi Vincenzo e Anastasio
The grand facade of this small Baroque church is on a corner facing the Trevi Fountain ⑩

San Marcello al Corso
This stark Crucifixion by Van Dyck hangs in the sacristy of the church ⑥

Palazzo Odescalchi has a Bernini facade from 1664, with a balustrade and richly decorated cornice. The building faces Santi Apostoli.

Museo delle Cere
The emphasis of this wax museum, opened in 1953, is on horror ⑤

To Piazza Venezia

Palazzo del Quirinale
The old papal palace is now the home of the president of Italy **2**

PIAZZA DI SPAGNA
VIA VENETO
QUIRINAL
CAPITOL
FORUM
ESQUILINE

LOCATOR MAP
See Central Rome Map pp12–13

In Piazza del Quirinale, by the president's palace, security is always very strict. Palace guards can often be seen in colourful dress uniform.

Castor and Pollux
The statues are grouped with an obelisk and a fountain **1**

Piazza della Pilotta is dominated by the imposing facade of the Gregorian University.

Santi Apostoli
The figures of Christ and the Apostles on the balustrade were added by Carlo Rainaldi in 1681 **4**

Palazzo Colonna
One of the art gallery's finest old masters is Annibale Carracci's The Bean Eater **3**

STAR SIGHTS

★ **Trevi Fountain**

KEY

 Suggested route

0 metres   75

0 yards   75

Castor and Pollux ❶

Piazza del Quirinale. **Map** 5 B4.
🚌 *52, 53, 56, 60, 61, 62, 71, 81, 95, 119, 492 and many other routes.*

Quirinal fountain and obelisk with Roman statues of Castor and Pollux

Castor and pollux – the patrons of horsemanship – and their prancing horses stand in splendour in the Piazza del Quirinale. Over 5.5 m (18 ft) high, these statues are huge Roman copies of 5th-century BC Greek originals. They once stood at the entrance to the nearby Baths of Constantine. Pope Sixtus V had them restored and placed here in 1588. Formerly known as the "horse tamers", they gave the square its familiar name of Monte Cavallo (horse hill).

The obelisk which stands between them was brought here in 1786 from the Mausoleum of Augustus. In 1818 the composition was completed by the addition of a massive granite basin, once a cattle trough in the Forum.

Palazzo del Quirinale ❷

Piazza del Quirinale. **Map** 5 B3. 🚌 *52, 53, 56, 60, 61, 62, 71, 81, 95, 119, 492 and many other routes.* **Open** *on the 2nd and 4th Sunday of each month.*

By the 1500s, the Vatican had a reputation as an unhealthy location because of the high incidence of malaria, so Pope Gregory XIII chose this superb site on the highest of Rome's seven hills as a summer residence for the popes. Work began in 1574. The Piazza del Quirinale has buildings on three sides while the fourth is open, giving a splendid view of the city to the great dome of St Peter's in the distance.

Many great architects worked on the palace, before it assumed its present form in the 1730s. Domenico Fontana designed the main façade, Carlo Maderno the huge chapel and Bernini the narrow wing that runs the length of Via del Quirinale.

Following the unification of Italy in 1870, it became the official residence of the king, then in 1947 of the president of the republic. For security reasons, the palace and gardens have been closed to the public since 1979.

Palazzo del Quirinale, official residence of the president of Italy

Palazzo Colonna ❸

Via della Pilotta 17. **Map** 5 A4 & 12 F3. 📞 *679 43 62.* 🚌 *57, 64, 65, 70, 75, 81, 170, 492, 710 and many other routes.* **Open** *9am–1pm Sat only (last adm: noon).* **Closed** *Aug.* **Adm charge.** ⌀

Pope martin v Colonna (reigned 1417–31) began building the palazzo, but most of the structure dates from the 18th century. The art gallery, built by Antonio del Grande between 1654 and 1665, is the only part open to the public. The pictures are numbered but unlabelled, so pick up a guide on the way in. Go up the stairs and through the antechamber

Canova's monument to Pope Clement XIV in Santi Apostoli, with figures of Humility and Modesty

leading to a series of three gleaming marble rooms with prominent yellow columns, the Colonna family emblem (*colonna* means column).

The ceiling frescoes celebrate Marcantonio Colonna's victory over the Turks at the Battle of Lepanto (1571). On the walls are 16th- to 18th-century paintings, including Annibale Carracci's *Bean Eater (see p157)*. The room of landscape paintings, many by Poussin's brother-in-law Gaspare Dughet, reflects the 18th-century taste of Cardinal Girolamo Colonna. Beyond is a room with a ceiling fresco of the *Apotheosis of Martin V*. The throne room has a chair reserved for visiting popes and a copy of Pisanello's portrait of the portly Martin V.

The gallery also offers a fine view of the private palace garden, site of the ruined Temple of Serapis.

Santi Apostoli ❹

Piazza dei Santi Apostoli. **Map** 5 A4 & 12 F3. 📞 *69 92 19 51.* 🚌 *56, 60, 64, 65, 70, 75, 85, 90, 170, 492 and many other routes.* **Open** *6.30am–noon, 4pm–7.15pm daily.* ✝ 📷

The original 6th-century church on this site was rebuilt in the 15th century by Popes Martin V Colonna and

Sixtus IV della Rovere, whose oak tree crest decorates the capitals of the late 15th-century portico. Inside the portico on the left is Canova's 1807 memorial to the engraver Giovanni Volpato. The church itself contains a much larger monument by Canova, his Tomb of Clement XIV (1789).

The Baroque interior by Francesco and Carlo Fontana was completed in 1714. Note the 3-D effect of Giovanni Odazzi's painted *Rebel Angels*, who really look as though they are falling from the sky. A huge 18th-century altarpiece by Domenico Muratori shows the martyrdom of the Apostles James and Philip, whose tombs are in the crypt.

Museo delle Cere ❺

Piazza dei Santi Apostoli 67.
Map 5 A4 & 12 F3. 679 64 82.
56, 60, 64, 65, 70, 75, 85, 90,
170, 492 and many other routes.
Open 9am–8pm daily. **Adm charge**.

Facade of Rome's wax museum

EXHIBITS in Rome's wax museum include politicians and a recreation of Mussolini's last cabinet meeting. For the ghoulishly inclined, it also boasts a vintage electric chair.

San Marcello al Corso ❻

Piazza San Marcello 5. **Map** 5 A4 &
12 F3. 678 08 88. 56, 60, 62,
70, 85, 90, 95, 492. **Open** 7am–noon,
4pm–7pm Mon–Sat, 8.30am–noon,
4pm–7pm Sun.

THIS CHURCH was originally one of the first places of Christian worship in Rome, which were known as *tituli*.

A later Romanesque building burned down in 1519, and was rebuilt by Jacopo Sansovino with a single nave and many richly-decorated private chapels on either side.

The third chapel on the right has fine frescoes of the Virgin Mary by Francesco Salviati. The decoration of the next chapel was interrupted by the Sack of Rome in 1527. Raphael's follower Perin del Vaga fled, leaving the ceiling frescoes to be completed by Daniele da Volterra and Pellegrino Tibaldi when peace returned to the city.

In the nave stands a splendid Venetian-style double tomb by Sansovino, a memorial to Cardinal Giovanni Michiel (victim of a Borgia poisoning in 1503) and his nephew, Bishop Antonio Orso.

Trevi Fountain ❼

Fontana di Trevi. **Map** 5 A3 & 12 F2.
52, 53, 58, 60, 61, 62, 71, 95,
492 and many other routes.

MOST VISITORS assume that it has always been there, but by the standards of the Eternal City, the Trevi Fountain is a fairly recent creation.

Rome's grandest fountain, the Trevi

Nicola Salvi's theatrical design for Rome's largest and most famous fountain was completed only in 1762. The central figures are Neptune, flanked by two Tritons. One struggles to master a very unruly "sea-horse", the other leads a far more docile animal. These symbolize the two contrasting moods of the sea.

The site originally marked the terminal of the Aqua Virgo aqueduct built in 19 BC. One of the first-storey reliefs shows a young girl (the legendary virgin after whom the aqueduct was named) pointing to the spring from which the water flows.

Chapel in San Marcello al Corso, decorated by Francesco Salviati

Santa Maria in Trivio 8

Piazza dei Crociferi 49. **Map** 5 A3 & 12 F2. 678 96 45. 52, 53, 58, 60, 61, 62, 71, 95, 492 and many other routes. **Open** 8.10am–noon, 4pm–7.30pm daily.

Facade of Santa Maria in Trivio at the turn of the century

IT HAS BEEN SAID that Italian architecture is one of facades, and nowhere is this clearer than in the 1570s facade of Santa Maria in Trivio, delightfully stuck on to the building behind it. Note the false windows. There is illusion inside too, particularly in the ceiling frescoes, which show scenes from the New Testament by Antonio Gherardi (1644–1702).

The name of the tiny church probably means "St Mary-at-the-meeting-of-three-roads". The word Trivio has been corrupted to Trevi, hence the name of the famous fountain.

Accademia Nazionale di San Luca 9

Piazza dell'Accademia di San Luca 77. **Map** 5 A3 & 12 F2. 679 88 50. 52, 53, 56, 58, 60, 61, 62, 71, 81, 95, 119, 492. **Open** 10am–1pm Mon, Wed, Fri and last Sun of month (last adm: 12.15pm). **Closed** Jul, Aug, public hols & Mon after last Sun of month. apply to custodian.

ST LUKE IS supposed to have been a painter, hence the name of Rome's academy of fine arts. Appropriately, the gallery contains a painting of

St Luke Painting a Portrait of the Virgin by Raphael and his followers. The academy's heyday was in the 17th and 18th centuries, when many members made gifts of their work to the collection. Canova, for example, donated a model for his famous marble group, the *Three Graces*.

Of particular interest are three fascinating self-portraits by women: the 17th-century Italian Lavinia Fontana; the 18th-century Swiss Angelica Kauffmann, whose painting is copied from a portrait of her by Joshua Reynolds; and Elisabeth Vigée-Lebrun, the French painter of the years before the 1789 Revolution.

Santi Vincenzo e Anastasio 10

Vicolo dei Modelli 73. **Map** 5 A3 & 12 F2. 678 30 98. 52, 53, 58, 60, 61, 62, 71, 95, 492 and many other routes. **Open** 7am–noon, 4pm–7.30pm daily.

OVERLOOKING the Trevi Fountain is one of the most over-the-top Baroque facades in Rome. Its thickets of columns are crowned by

the huge coat of arms of Cardinal Raimondo Mazzarino, who commissioned Martino Longhi the Younger to build the church in 1650. The female bust above the door is of one of the cardinal's famous nieces, either Louis XIV's first love, Maria Mancini (1639–1715), or her younger sister, Ortensia. In the apse, memorial plaques record the popes whose *praecordia* (a part of the heart) are enshrined behind the wall. This gruesome tradition was started at the end of the 16th century by Pope Sixtus V. It continued until Pius X put a stop to it in the early years of this century.

Facade of Santi Vincenzo e Anastasio by Martino Longhi

Self-portrait by Lavinia Fontana in the Accademia Nazionale di San Luca

Interior of Bernini's oval Sant'Andrea al Quirinale

Sant'Andrea al Quirinale ⓫

Via del Quirinale 29. **Map** 5 B3.
489 031 87. 56, 64, 65, 70, 75, 94, 170. **Open** 10am–noon, 4pm–7pm Wed–Mon (closed in the afternoon in August). **Gratuity** expected by sacristan for showing St Stanislas's rooms.

KNOWN AS the "Pearl of the Baroque" because of its beautiful roseate marble interior, Sant'Andrea was designed by Bernini and executed by his assistants between 1658 and 1670. It was built for the Jesuits, hence the many IHS emblems (*Jesus Hominum Salvator* – Jesus Saviour of Mankind).

The site for the church was wide but shallow, so Bernini pointed the long axis of his oval plan not towards the altar, but towards the sides; he then leads the eye round to the altar end. Here he ordered works of art in various media which function not in isolation, but together. The

crucified St Andrew (Sant' Andrea) of the altarpiece looks up at a stucco version of himself, who in turn ascends towards the lantern and the Holy Spirit.

Do not miss the rooms of St Stanislas Kostka. The quarters of the Jesuit novice, who died in 1568 aged 19, reflect not his own spartan taste, but the richer style of the 17th-century Jesuits. The Polish saint has been brilliantly immortalized in marble by Pierre Legros (1666–1719).

San Carlo alle Quattro Fontane ⓬

Via del Quirinale 23. **Map** 5 B3.
488 32 61. 52, 53, 56, 60, 61, 62, 95, 492. **Open** 9.30am–12.30pm Mon–Sat; 4pm–6pm Mon–Fri.

IN 1634, the Spanish Trinitarians, an order whose role was to pay the ransom of Christian hostages to the Arabs, commissioned Borromini to design a church and convent at the Quattro Fontane crossroads. The church, so small it would fit inside one of the piers of St Peter's, is also known as "San Carlino".

Although dedicated to Carlo Borromeo, the 16th-century Milanese cardinal canonized in 1620, San Carlo is as much a monument to Borromini. Both the facade and the interior employ bold, fluid curves that give light and life to a small, cramped site. The oval dome and tiny lantern are particularly ingenious. The undulating lines of the facade are decorated with angels and a statue of San Carlo. Finished in 1667, the facade is one of Borromini's very last works.

There are further delights in the playful inverted shapes in the cloister and the stucco work in the refectory (now the sacristy), which houses a painting of San Carlo by Orazio Borgianni (1611).

In a small room off the sacristy hangs a portrait of Borromini himself wearing the Trinitarian cross. Borromini committed suicide in 1667, and in the crypt (which may soon be opened to the public) a small curved chapel reserved for him remains empty.

Dome of San Carlo alle Quattro Fontane, lit by concealed windows

Le Quattro Fontane ⑬

Intersection of Via delle Quattro Fontane and Via del Quirinale.
Map 5 B3. ▩ *56, 60, 61, 64, 65, 70, 75, 95, 119, 492.* Ⓜ *Barberini.*

Fountain of Strength (or Juno)

THESE FOUR small fountains are attached to the corners of the buildings at the intersection of two narrow, busy streets. They date from the great redevelopment of Rome in the reign of Sixtus V (1585–90). Each fountain has a statue of a reclining deity. The river god accompanied by the she-wolf is clearly the Tiber; the other male figure may be the Nile or the Aniene. The female figures represent Strength and Fidelity or the goddesses, Juno and Diana.

The crossroads is at the highest point of the Quirinal hill and commands splendid views of three distant landmark obelisks: those placed by Sixtus V in front of Santa Maria Maggiore and Trinità dei Monti, and the one that stands in Piazza del Quirinale.

San Bernardo alle Terme ⑭

Via Torino 94. **Map** 5 C3.
▤ *488 21 22.* ▩ *60, 61, 62, 65, 492.*
Ⓜ *Repubblica.* **Open** *6.30am–noon, 1pm–7pm daily.* ▮ ▣ ▮

THE CHURCH is on the southern side of the piazza of the same name. It was once one of four round

towers which stood at the corners of the ruined Baths of Diocletian (Terme di Diocleziano). Like a miniature Pantheon, the church has a dome with octagonal coffering and a small opening at the top to light the interior. In the great circular wall supporting the dome there are eight niches, housing huge plaster statues of saints by Camillo Mariani (1567–1611).

It was only in 1598 that Countess Caterina Nobili Sforza had the idea of transforming this tower into a church. She lies buried beneath one of the fine 18th-century marble altars.

Moses Fountain ⑮

Fontana dell'Acqua Felice, Piazza San Bernardo. **Map** 5 C2. ▩ *60, 61, 62, 65, 492.* Ⓜ *Repubblica.*

Fontana's Moses Fountain

OFFICIALLY KNOWN as the Fontana dell'Acqua Felice, this fountain owes its popular name to the grotesque

statue of Moses in the central niche. The massive structure with its three elegant arches was designed by Domenico Fontana to mark the terminal of the Acqua Felice aqueduct, so-called because it was one of the many great improvements commissioned by Felice Peretti, Pope Sixtus V. Completed in 1586, it brought clean piped water to this quarter of Rome for the first time.

Pope Sixtus V, the great town-planner

The notorious statue of Moses striking water from the rock is larger than life and the proportions of the body are obviously wrong. Sculpted either by Prospero Bresciano or Leonardo Sormani, it is a clumsy attempt at recreating the awesome appearance of Michelangelo's Moses in the church of San Pietro in Vincoli *(see p170).* As soon as it was unveiled, it was said to be frowning at having been brought into the world by such an inept sculptor.

The side reliefs also illustrate water stories from the Old Testament: Aaron leading the Israelites to water and Joshua pointing the army towards the Red Sea. The fountain's four lions are copies of Egyptian originals (now in the Vatican Museums), which Sixtus V had put there for public "convenience" and "delight".

Fidelity (or Diana) with her attendant dog, one of the Quattro Fontane

of ground between the present Piazza dei Cinquecento and Piazza della Repubblica. The baths, the most extensive in Rome, could accommodate up to 3,000 bathers at a time. The best-preserved areas have been adapted to house the church of Santa Maria degli Angeli and the Museo Nazionale Romano.

Santa Maria degli Angeli ⑰

Piazza della Repubblica. **Map** 5 C3.
📞 488 08 12. 🚌 57, 65, 75, 170, 492, 910 and many other routes. Ⓜ Repubblica, Termini. **Open** 8am–12.30pm, 4pm–7pm (6.30pm in winter). 🚻 📷 ♿ 🚮

INCORPORATED into the ruined Baths of Diocletian by Michelangelo in 1563, the church was so altered in the 18th century by Luigi Vanvitelli it has lost most of its original character. The most striking works of art are a fresco of the *Martyrdom of St Sebastian* by Domenichino and a gigantic statue of St Bruno by Jean-Antoine Houdon. An exhibition in the sacristy gives a detailed account of Michelangelo's original design.

Museo Nazionale Romano ⑱

Viale Enrico de Nicola 79. **Map** 6 D2.
📞 48 90 35 07. 🚌 57, 65, 75, 170, 492, 910 and many other routes. Ⓜ Repubblica, Termini. **Open** 9am–2pm Tue–Sat, 9am–1pm Sun & public hols (last adm: 30 min before closing). **Adm charge**. 📷 ♿

FOUNDED IN 1889, the Museo Nazionale holds most of the antiquities found in Rome since 1870. It has also absorbed pre-existing collections, notably that of the Ludovisi family, to become one of the world's leading museums of Classical art. It occupies the part of the Baths of Diocletian not taken up by the church of Santa Maria degli Angeli, including the former Carthusian monastery, which

Part of the Museo Nazionale Romano in the Baths of Diocletian

Baths of Diocletian ⑯

Terme di Diocleziano, Piazza della Repubblica. **Map** 6 D3. 🚌 57, 65, 75, 170, 492, 910 and many other routes. Ⓜ Repubblica, Termini.

BUILT IN AD 298–306 under the infamous Emperor Diocletian, who murdered thousands of Christians, the baths *(see pp22–3)* occupied well over a hectare (2.5 acres)

Gold coin with head of the Emperor Diocletian (AD 285–305)

Egyptian relief showing head crowned with symbolic cobra in the Museo Nazionale Romano

has a cloister designed by Michelangelo when he was working on Santa Maria.

Unfortunately, the museum is an extreme example of the malaise afflicting many Roman museums. The majority of its rooms, which contain many first-class sarcophagi, mosaics and detached frescoes, are closed to the public. As an end in itself, a visit to the museum therefore gives more frustration than pleasure. However, if you have an hour to kill while waiting for a train from Termini station, it is well worth popping across Piazza dei Cinquecento to see the disorderly but evocative array of sculptural fragments on display around the central Renaissance courtyard.

Plans for the future include the opening of a whole new section of the museum in the former Palazzo Massimo in Piazza dei Cinquecento.

Piazza della Repubblica ⑲

Map 5 C3. 🚌 4, 16, 36, 38, 60, 61, 62, 65, 75, 192, 492 and many other routes. Ⓜ Repubblica.

Romans often refer to the piazza by its old name, Piazza Esedra, so-called because it follows the shape of an *exedra* (a semicircular recess) that was part of the Baths of Diocletian. The piazza was part of the great redevelopment undertaken when Rome became capital of a unified Italy. Under its sweeping 19th-century colonnades there were once elegant shops, but they have been ousted by banks, travel agencies and cafés.

In the middle of the piazza stands the Fontana delle Naiadi. Mario Rutelli's four naked bronze nymphs caused something of a scandal when they were unveiled in 1901. Each reclines on an aquatic creature symbolizing water in its various forms: a seahorse for the oceans, a water snake for rivers, a swan for lakes, and a curious frilled lizard for subterranean streams. The figure in the middle, added in 1911, is of the sea god Glaucus, who represents man victorious over the hostile forces of nature.

Piazza della Repubblica and the Fontana delle Naiadi

Palazzo delle Esposizioni ⑳

Via Nazionale 194 (second entrance in Via Milano). **Map** 5 B4. 📞 474 59 03. 🚌 56, 64, 65, 70, 75, 94, 170. **Open** 10am–9pm Wed–Mon (last adm: 8.30pm). **Closed** public hols. **Adm charge**. ⌀ ♿ from Via del Quirinale entrance only. **Concerts, lectures, films**. See **Entertainment** pp346–7. 🍴 ▯ 🛍

Facade of the Palazzo delle Esposizioni

This somewhat grandiose building, with wide steps, Corinthian columns and statues, was designed as an exhibition-centre by the architect Pio Piacentini and built by the city of Rome in 1882 during the reign of Umberto I. The main entrance looks like a triumphal arch.

The exhibition space has recently been modernized. Exhibitions change every three months, with paintings, sculpture, live performances and films on offer. Foreign films are usually shown in the original language. The palazzo also houses the Galleria Comunale d'Arte Moderna, closed to the public since the early 1980s.

Santa Maria dei Monti ㉑

Via Madonna dei Monti 41. **Map** 5 B4. 📞 48 55 31. 🚌 11, 27, 81. Ⓜ Cavour. **Open** 7am–noon, 5pm– daily. ✝ 🛍 ♿

Designed by Giacomo della Porta, this church, dating from 1580, has a particularly splendid dome. Over the high altar is a medieval stunning painting of the Madonna, patroness of this quarter of Rome. The altar in the left transept houses the tomb and effigy of the unworldly French saint Benoit-Joseph Labre, who died here in 1783, having spent his life as a solitary pilgrim. He slept rough in the ruins of the Colosseum, gave away any charitable gifts he received, and came regularly to Santa Maria dei Monti to worship. His faith could not sustain his body: still in his mid-thirties, he collapsed and died outside the church. The foul rags he wore are preserved.

One of the bronze nymphs of the fountain in Piazza della Repubblica

Sant'Agata dei Goti ㉒

Via Mazzarino 16 and Via Panisperna.
Map 5 B4. 📞 *488 80 61.* 🚌 *57, 64, 65, 70, 81, 170.* **Open** *7am–9pm, 5.30pm–7pm Mon–Sat, 9.30am–10am Sun.* 🚻 📷 ♿

THE GOTHS who gave their name to this church (*Goti* are Goths) occupied Rome in the 6th century AD. They were Arian heretics who denied the divinity of Christ. The church was founded shortly before the main Gothic invasions, between AD 462 and 470, and the beautiful granite columns date from this period. The main altar has a well-preserved 12th-century Cosmatesque tabernacle, but the most delightful part of the church is the charming 18th-century courtyard built around an ivy-draped well.

Villa Aldobrandini ㉓

Via Panisperna. Entrance to gardens:
Via Mazzarino 1. **Map** 5 B4.
🚌 *57, 64, 65, 70, 75, 170.*
Gardens open *dawn–dusk daily.*
Villa not open *to the public.*

BUILT IN the 16th century for the Dukes of Urbino and acquired for his family by Pope Clement VIII Aldobrandini (reigned 1592–1605), the villa is now government property and houses an international law library.

The villa itself, decorated with the family's six-starred coat of arms, is closed to the public, but the gardens and terraces, hidden behind a high wall that runs along Via Nazionale, can be reached through an iron gate in Via Mazzarino. Steps lead up past 2nd-century AD ruins into the recently renovated gardens, highly recommended as an oasis of tranquillity in the centre of the city. Gravel paths lead between formal lawns and clearly marked specimen trees, and benches are provided for the weary. Since the garden is raised some 10 m (30 ft) above street level, the views are excellent.

18th-century courtyard of Sant'Agata dei Goti

Santi Domenico e Sisto ㉔

Largo Angelicum 1. **Map** 5 B4.
📞 *670 21.* 🚌 *57, 64, 65, 70, 75, 170.* **Open** *by appt only.* **Closed** *Jul–Sep.* 📷

Chapel in Santi Domenico e Sisto

THE CHURCH has a tall, slender Baroque facade rising above a steep flight of steps. This divides into two curving flights that sweep up to the terrace in front of the entrance. The pediment of the facade is crowned by eight flaming candlesticks.

The interior has a vaulted ceiling with a large fresco of the *Apotheosis of St Dominic* by Domenico Canuti (1620–84). The first chapel on the right was decorated by Bernini, who may also have designed the sculpture of Mary Magdalene meeting the risen Christ in the Garden of Gethsemane. This fine marble group was executed by Antonio Raggi (1649). Above the altar is a 15th-century terracotta plaque of the Madonna and Child. On the left over a side altar is a large painting of the Madonna from the same period, attributed to Benozzo Gozzoli (1420–97), a pupil of Fra Angelico.

Facade of Santi Domenico e Sisto

ESQUILINE

THE ESQUILINE is the largest and highest of Rome's seven hills. In Imperial Rome the western slopes overlooking the Forum housed the crowded slums of the Suburra. On the eastern side there were a few villas belonging to wealthy citizens like Maecenas, patron of the arts and adviser to Augustus. The essential character of the place has persisted through two millennia; it is still one of the poorer quarters

Michelangelo's *Rachel* **in San Pietro in Vincoli**

of the city. The area is now heavily built up, except for a rather seedy park on the Colle Oppio, a smaller hill to the south of the Esquiline, where you can see the remains of the Baths of Titus, the Baths of Trajan and Nero's Golden House. The area's main interest, however, lies in its churches. Many of these were founded on the sites of private houses where Christians met to worship secretly in the days when the religion was banned.

SIGHTS AT A GLANCE

Churches
San Martino ai Monti **1**
San Pietro in Vincoli **2**
Santa Pudenziana **3**
Santa Maria Maggiore
pp172–3 **4**
Santa Prassede **5**
Santa Bibiana **7**

Museums
Museo Nazionale d'Arte
Orientale **9**

Historic Piazzas
Piazza Vittorio Emanuele II **8**

Ancient Sites
Auditorium of Maecenas **10**
Nero's Golden House **11**

Arches
Arch of Gallienus **6**

GETTING THERE
This area is close to Termini station and has several other Metro stops: Vittorio Emanuele and Manzoni on line A, Cavour and Colosseo on line B. Bus routes here are a little confusing. Among the most useful are the 93 and 93b from Termini to Santa Maria Maggiore and then along Via Merulana.

SEE ALSO

• *Street Finder*, maps 5, 6

• *Restaurants* pp310–11

• *Mosaics Walk* pp280–81

KEY

	Street-by-Street map
FS	Railway station
M	Metro station
P	Parking

0 metres   300
0 yards   300

Southern facade of Santa Maria Maggiore by night

Street-by-Street: The Esquiline Hill

T HE SIGHT that draws most people to this rather scruffy part of Rome is the great basilica of Santa Maria Maggiore. But it is also well worth searching out some of the smaller churches on the Esquiline: Santa Pudenziana and Santa Prassede with their celebrated mosaics, and San Pietro in Vincoli, home to one of Michelangelo's most famous sculptures. To the south, in the Colle Oppio park, are the scattered remains of the Baths of Trajan.

Santa Pudenziana
The apse of this ancient church has a magnificent 4th-century mosaic of Christ surrounded by the Apostles ❸

Piazza dell'Esquilino
was furnished with an obelisk in 1587 by Pope Sixtus V. This helped to guide pilgrims coming from the north to the important church of Santa Maria Maggiore.

To the Colosseum

★ **San Pietro in Vincoli**
The church's treasures include Michelangelo's Moses *and the chains that bound St Peter* ❷

The Baths of Trajan (AD 109) were the first to be built on the massive scale later used in the Baths of Diocletian and of Caracalla

★ Santa Maria Maggiore
This imposing rear facade was added by Baroque architect Carlo Rainaldi in 1673. Santa Maria's interior is one of the most richly decorated in Rome ❹

LOCATOR MAP
See Central Rome Map pp12–13

The Tomb of Pius V (died 1572) by Domenico Fontana stands in this less well-known Sistine Chapel, under the northeast dome of Santa Maria Maggiore.

Arch of Gallienus
This was built in the 3rd century AD to replace an entrance in the old Servian Wall ❻

To Vittorio Emanuele Metro

★ Santa Prassede
The 9th-century mosaics in the Chapel of San Zeno are among the finest in Rome ❺

The Torre dei Capocci, a restored medieval tower, is one of the area's most distinctive landmarks.

San Martino ai Monti
The frescoes include 17th-century Roman landscapes and scenes from the life of Elijah by Gaspare Dughet ❶

KEY

‒ ‒ ‒ Suggested route

| 0 metres | 75 |
| 0 yards | 75 |

STAR SIGHTS

★ Santa Maria Maggiore

★ San Pietro in Vincoli

★ Santa Prassede

San Martino ai Monti ●

Viale del Monte Oppio 28. **Map** 6 D5.
⬛ 487 31 26. 🚍 11, 16, 27, 70, 71, 81, 93, 93b, 613. Ⓜ Cavour, Vittorio Emanuele. **Open** 7am–noon, 4.30pm–7pm (Oct–Mar: 4.30pm–6.30pm) daily. 🚻 📷 ♿

Fresco of old San Giovanni in Laterano in San Martino ai Monti

Christians have been worshipping on the site of this church since the 3rd century, when they used to meet in the house of a man named Equitius. In the 4th century, after Constantine had legalized Christianity, Pope Sylvester I built a church, one of very few things he did during his pontificate. In fact he was so insignificant that in the 5th century a more exciting life was fabricated for him – which included tales of him converting Constantine, curing him of leprosy and forcing him to close all pagan temples. Pope Sylvester's fictional life was further enhanced in the 8th century, with the forgery of a document in which Constantine offered him the Imperial crown.

Pope Sylvester's church was replaced in about AD 500 by St Symmachus, rebuilt in the 9th century and then transformed completely in the 1650s. Consequently, the only immediate signs of its age are the ancient Corinthian columns dividing the nave and aisles. The most interesting features of the interior are a series of frescoed landscapes of the Campagna (the countryside

around Rome) by the 17th-century French artist Gaspare Dughet, Poussin's brother-in-law, in the right aisle. The frescoes by Filippo Gagliardi, at either end of the left aisle, show old St Peter's and the interior of San Giovanni in Laterano before Borromini's redesign. If you can find the sacristan, you can go beneath the church to see the remains of Equitius's house.

San Pietro in Vincoli ●

Piazza di San Pietro in Vincoli 4A.
Map 5 C5. ⬛ 488 28 65. 🚍 11, 27, 81. Ⓜ Colosseo. **Open** 7am–12.30pm, 3.30pm–7pm (Oct–Mar: 6pm) daily. 🚻 📷 ♿ 🚹

According to tradition, the two chains (vincoli) used to shackle St Peter while he was being held in the depths

Reliquary with St Peter's chains

of the Mamertine Prison (see p91) were subsequently taken to Constantinople. In the 5th century, Empress Eudoxia deposited one in a church in Constantinople and sent the other to her daughter Eudoxia in Rome. She in turn gave hers to Pope Leo I, who had this church built to house it. Some years later the second chain was brought to Rome, where it linked miraculously with its partner.

The chains are still here, displayed below the high altar, but the church is now best known for Michelangelo's Tomb of Pope Julius II. When it was commissioned in 1505, Michelangelo spent eight months searching for perfect blocks of marble at Carrara in Tuscany, but Pope Julius became more interested in the building of a new St Peter's and the project was laid aside. After the pope's death in 1513, Michelangelo resumed work on the tomb, but had only finished the statues of Moses and the Dying Slaves when Pope Paul III persuaded him to start work on the Sistine Chapel's Last Judgment. Michelangelo had planned a vast monument with over 40 statues, but the tomb that was built – mainly by his pupils – is simply a facade with six niches for statues. The Dying Slaves are in Paris and Florence, but the tremendous bearded Moses is here. The horns on Moses' head should really be beams of light – they are the result of the Hebrew original from the Old Testament being wrongly translated.

Michelangelo's Moses in San Pietro

Apse mosaics in Santa Prassede, showing the saint with St Paul

Santa Pudenziana ❸

Via Urbana 160. **Map** 5 C4.
(481 46 22. **🚌** 16, 70, 71, 93, 93b, 613. **M** Cavour.
Open 8am–noon, 3pm–6pm daily.
🏛 📷

IN THE NORMAL COURSE of events, churches tend to be dedicated to existing saints. In this case, the church, through a linguistic accident, created a brand new saint. In the 1st century AD a Roman senator called Pudens lived on this site, and, according to legend, allowed St Peter to lodge with him. In the 2nd

century a bath house was built on this site and in the 4th century a church was established inside the baths. This was known as the *Ecclesia Pudentiana* (the church of Pudens). In time it was assumed that "Pudentiana" was a woman's name and a life was created for her – she became the sister of Prassede and was credited with caring for Christian victims of persecution. In 1969 both saints were declared invalid, though their churches both kept their names.

The 19th-century facade of the church retains an 11th-century frieze depicting both Prassede and Pudenziana

dressed as crowned Byzantine empresses – the Church's way of asserting that it was as important as the temporal authority of Byzantium.

The apse has a remarkable 4th-century mosaic, clearly influenced by Classical pagan art in its use of subtle colours. The Apostles are represented as Roman senators in togas. Unfortunately, a clumsy attempt at restoration in the 16th century destroyed two of the Apostles and left other figures without their legs.

Santa Maria Maggiore ❹

See pp172–3.

Santa Prassede ❺

Via Santa Prassede 9A. **Map** 6 D4.
(488 24 56. **🚌** 16, 93, 93b, 613.
M Vittorio Emanuele. **Open** 7.30am–noon, 4pm–6.30pm daily. **🏛 📷 ♿**

9th-century mosaics, Santa Prassede

THE CHURCH was founded by Pope Paschal II in the 9th century on the site of a 2nd-century oratory. Artists from Byzantium decorated the church with glittering, jewel-coloured mosaics. Those in the apse and choir depict stylized white-robed elders, the haloed elect looking down from the gold and blue walls of heaven, spindly-legged lambs, feather-mop palm trees and bright red poppies. In the apse, Santa Prassede and Santa Pudenziana stand on either side of Christ, with the fatherly arms of St Paul and St Peter on their shoulders. There are also beautiful mosaics in the Chapel of St Zeno, built as a mausoleum for Pope Paschal's mother, Theodora.

11th-century frieze and medallions on the facade of Santa Pudenziana

Santa Maria Maggiore ❹

O F ALL THE GREAT Roman basilicas, Santa
Maria has the most successful blend
of different architectural styles. Its colonnaded triple nave is part of the original
5th-century building. The Cosmatesque
marble floor and delightful Romanesque
bell tower, with its blue ceramic roundels,
are medieval. The Renaissance saw a new
coffered ceiling, and the Baroque gave
the church twin domes and its imposing
front and rear facades. The mosaics are
Santa Maria's most
famous feature. From
the 5th century come
the Biblical scenes
in the nave and the
spectacular mosaics
on the triumphal
arch. Medieval high-
lights include a 13th-
century enthroned
Christ in the loggia.

★ Cappella Paolina
*Flaminio Ponzio designed this
richly decorated chapel (1611)
for Pope Paul V Borghese.*

**Obelisk in Piazza
dell'Esquilino**
*The Egyptian obelisk
was erected by Pope
Sixtus V in 1587
as a landmark
for pilgrims.*

LEGEND OF THE SNOW

In 352, Pope Liberius had a
dream in which the Virgin
told him to build a church
on the spot where he found
snow. When it fell on the
Esquiline, on the morning of
5 August in the middle of a
baking Roman summer, he
naturally obeyed. The miracle
of the snow is commemorated
each year by a service during
which thousands of white
petals float down from the
ceiling of Santa Maria.
Originally roses
were used, but
nowadays the
petals are more
usually taken
from dahlias.

Coffered Ceiling
*The gilded ceiling, possibly
by Giuliano da Sangallo,
was a gift of Alexander VI
Borgia at the end of the 15th
century. The gold is said
to be the first brought from
America by Columbus.*

TIMELINE

352 Virgin appears to
Pope Liberius

432–40 Sixtus III
completes church

1347 Cola di Rienzo
crowned Tribune of
Rome in Santa Maria

*Pope Gregory
VII*

1673 Carlo
Rainaldi
rebuilds apse

300 AD	600	900	1200	1500	1800

420 Probable
founding date

1075 Pope Gregory
VII kidnapped by
opponents while
reading Christmas
mass in Santa Maria

*Coat of arms
of Gregory VII*

1288–92
Nicholas IV
adds apse
and transepts

1743 Ferdinando
Fuga adds main
facade on orders
of Benedict XIV

★ Coronation of the Virgin Mosaic
This is the central image of a series of wonderful apse mosaics of the Virgin by Jacopo Torriti (1295).

Baldacchino *(1740s)*
Its columns of red porphyry and bronze were the work of Ferdinando Fuga.

VISITORS' CHECKLIST

Piazza di Santa Maria Maggiore.
Map 6 D4. 48 31 95.
16, 27, 70, 71, 93, 93b to
Piazza di Santa Maria Maggiore
& many routes to Piazza dei
Cinquecento. 14. Termini,
Cavour. **Open** 7am–7pm daily
(last adm: 15 mins before
closing).

★ Tomb of Cardinal Rodriguez
The Gothic tomb (1299) contains magnificent Cosmatesque marblework.

★ Cappella Sistina
The chapel was built for Pope Sixtus V (1585–90) by Domenico Fontana and houses the pope's tomb.

Column in Piazza Santa Maria Maggiore
A bronze of the Virgin and Child was added to this ancient marble column in 1615. The column came from the Basilica of Constantine in the Forum.

STAR FEATURES

★ Cappella Sistina

★ Coronation of the Virgin Mosaic

★ Cappella Paolina

★ Tomb of Cardinal Rodriguez

Arch erected in memory of Emperor Gallienus

Arch of Gallienus ❻

Via Carlo Alberto. **Map** 6 D4. 🚌 4, 9, 16, 70, 71. **M** *Vittorio Emanuele.*

SQUASHED between two buildings just off Via Carlo Alberto is the central arch of an originally three-arched gate erected in memory of Emperor Gallienus, who was assassinated by his Illyrian officers in AD 262. It was built on the site of the old Esquiline Gate in the Servian Wall, parts of which are visible nearby.

Santa Bibiana ❼

Via Giovanni Giolitti 154.
Map 6 F4. ☎ 446 10 21. 🚌 11, 70, 71. **M** *Vittorio Emanuele.* **Open** *7am–10am, 4.30pm–7.30pm daily (phone first).* 🚹 📷 ♿

THE DECEPTIVELY simple facade of Santa Bibiana was Bernini's first foray into architecture. It is a clean, economic design with superimposed pilasters and deeply shadowed archways. The church itself was built on the site of the palace belonging to Bibiana's family. This is where the saint was buried

after being flogged to death with leaded cords during the brief persecution of the Christians that took place in the reign of Julian the Apostate (361–3). Just inside the church is a small column against which Bibiana is said to have been whipped. Her remains, along with those of her mother Dafrosa and her sister Demetria, who also suffered martyrdom, are preserved in an alabaster urn below the altar. In a niche above the altar stands a statue of Santa Bibiana by Bernini – the first fully-clothed figure he ever sculpted. He depicts her standing beside a column, holding the cords with which she was whipped, apparently on the verge of a deadly swoon.

Early sculpture by Bernini of the martyr Santa Bibiana (1626)

Piazza Vittorio Emanuele II ❽

Map 6 E5. 🚌 4, 9, 11, 70, 71, 105. 🚊 14, 516, 517. **M** *Vittorio Emanuele. See **Markets** p338.*

PIAZZA VITTORIO, as it is called for short, is one of the city's main open-air food markets. The arcaded square was built in the urban development undertaken after the unification of Italy in 1870. It was named after Italy's first king, but there is nothing regal about its appearance today. The shabby arcades shelter shops and stalls selling all sorts of cheap shoes and clothes.

The equally neglected garden area in the centre of the square contains a number of mysterious ruins, including a large mound, the remains of a Roman fountain from the 3rd century AD and the Porta Magica, a curious 17th-century doorway inscribed with alchemical signs and formulae.

Museo Nazionale d'Arte Orientale ❾

Via Merulana 248. **Map** 6 D5. ☎ 487 50 77. 🚌 4, 9, 16, 70, 71, 93, 93b, 613. **M** *Vittorio Emanuele.* **Open** *9am–7pm Tue & Thu, 9am–2pm Wed, Fri & Sat, 9am–1pm Sun.* **Adm charge.**

THE MUSEUM occupies part of the late 19th-century Palazzo Brancaccio, which became the home of the Italian Institute of the Middle and Far East in 1957. The collection ranges from prehistoric Iranian ceramics, sculpture from Afghanistan, Nepal, Kashmir and India to 18th-century Tibetan paintings on vellum. From the Far East there are collections of Japanese screen paintings and Chinese jade.

The most unusual exhibits are the finds from the Italian excavation of the ancient civilization of Swat in

4th-century relief from Kashmir

Nepalese Bodhisattva in the Museo Nazionale d'Arte Orientale

northeast Pakistan. This fascinating culture lasted from the 3rd century BC to about the 10th century AD. Its wonderfully exotic, sensual reliefs show an unusual combination of Hellenistic, Buddhist and Hindu influences.

Auditorium of Maecenas ❿

Largo Leopardi. **Map** 6 D5.
🚌 4, 9, 16, 70, 71, 81, 93, 93b, 613. Ⓜ *Vittorio Emanuele.*
Open *9am–1.30pm Sun.*
🚫 &

MAECENAS, fop, gourmet and patron of the arts, was also an astute adviser and colleague of the Emperor Augustus. He was fabulously rich, and spent some of his wealth creating a fantastic villa and gardens on the Esquiline hill, most of which has long disappeared beneath the modern city. The partially reconstructed auditorium, isolated on a traffic island, is all that remains.

Inside, a semicircle of tiered seats suggests that it may have been a place for readings and performances. If it was, then Maecenas would have been entertained here by his protégés, the lyric poet Horace and Virgil, author of the *Aeneid,* reading their latest works. However, water ducts have also been discovered and it may well have been a *nympheum* – a kind of summerhouse – with

fountains. Traces of frescoes remain on the walls: you can make out garden scenes and a procession of miniature figures – including one of a characteristically drunken Dionysus being propped upright by a satyr.

Nero's Golden House ⓫

Domus Aurea, Via Labicana 136. **Map** 5 C5. 📞 699 01 10. 🚌 15, 81, 85, 87, 186. **Closed** *for restoration; phone the Soprintendenza Archeologica at the above number (8am–1.30pm) to arrange a visit.*

Frescoed room in the ruins of Nero's Golden House

AFTER ALLEGEDLY setting fire to Rome in AD 64, Nero decided to build himself an outrageous new palace. It occupied part of the Palatine, and most of the Celian and Esquiline hills – an area approximately 25 times the

size of the Colosseum. The vestibule on the Palatine side of the complex contained a colossal gilded statue of Nero. There was an artificial lake, with gardens and woods where imported wild beasts were allowed to roam. According to Suetonius in his life of Nero, the palace walls were adorned with gold and mother-of-pearl, rooms were designed with ceilings that showered guests with flowers or perfumes, the dining hall rotated and the baths were fed with both sulphurous water and sea-water.

Tacitus described Nero's debauched garden parties, with banquets served on barges and lakeside brothels serviced by aristocratic women, though as Nero killed himself in AD 68, he did not have long to enjoy his new home.

Nero's successors, anxious to distance themselves from the monster-emperor, did their utmost to erase all traces of the palace. Vespasian drained the lake and built the Colosseum *(see pp92–5)* in its place, Titus and Trajan each erected a complex of baths over the palace, and Hadrian placed the Temple of Venus and Rome *(see p87)* over the vestibule.

Rooms from one wing of the palace have survived, buried beneath the ruins of the Baths of Trajan on the Oppian hill. A number of wall-paintings can still be seen, but the underground chambers are damp and dangerous. They have been closed to the public since a landslide in 1984.

18th-century artist's impression of Nero's Golden House

LATERAN

IN THE MIDDLE AGES the Lateran Palace was the residence of the popes, and the basilica of San Giovanni beside it rivalled St Peter's in splendour. After the return of the popes from Avignon at the end of the 14th century, the area declined in importance. Pilgrims still continued to visit San Giovanni and Santa

Cherub from San Giovanni in Laterano

Croce in Gerusalemme, but the area remained sparsely inhabited. Ancient convents slumbered amid gardens and vineyards until Rome became capital of Italy in 1870 and a network of residential streets was laid out here to house the influx of newcomers. Archaeological interest lies chiefly in the Aurelian Wall and the ruins of the Aqueduct of Nero.

SIGHTS AT A GLANCE

Churches
San Giovanni in Laterano pp182–3 ❶
Santa Croce in Gerusalemme ❺
Santi Quattro Coronati ⓫
San Clemente pp186–7 ⓬
Santo Stefano Rotondo ⓭

Shrines
Scala Santa and Sancta Sanctorum ❷

Arches and Gates
Porta Asinaria ❸
Porta Maggiore ❼

Ancient Sites
Amphiteatrum Castrense ❹
Baker's Tomb ❽
Aqueduct of Nero and the Freedmen's Tombs ❾

Museums
Museum of Musical Instruments ❻

Historic Buildings
Villa Wolkonsky ❿

SEE ALSO

• **Street Finder**, maps 6, 9, 10

• **Restaurants** pp310–11

• **Mosaics Walk** pp280–81

GETTING THERE
San Giovanni Metro station on line A is just outside the city wall, but handy for many of the sights in the area. The 16, 85, 87, 93 and 93b are among the many buses to Piazza di San Giovanni in Laterano. This can also be reached by the 13 and 30b trams. These are slow, but their routes make them useful for exploring this part of Rome.

| 0 metres | 300 |
| 0 yards | 300 |

KEY

	Street-by-Street map
—	City Wall
M	Metro station
P	Parking

15th-century apse fresco in Santa Croce in Gerusalemme

Street-by-Street: Piazza di San Giovanni

Both the basilica of San Giovanni and the Lateran Palace look out over a huge open area, the Piazza di San Giovanni, laid out at the end of the 16th century with an Egyptian obelisk, the oldest in Rome, in the centre. Sadly the traffic streaming in and out of the city through Porta San Giovanni tends to detract from its grandeur. Across the square is the building housing the Scala Santa (the Holy Staircase), one of the most revered relics in Rome and the goal for many pilgrims. The area is also a venue for political rallies, and the feast of St John on 23 June is celebrated with a fair at which Romans consume vast quantities of snails.

The Chapel of Santa Rufina, originally the portico of the baptistry, has a 5th-century mosaic of spiralling foliage in the apse.

The Cloister of San Giovanni fortunately survived the two fires that destroyed the early basilica. A 13th-century masterpiece of mosaic work, the cloister now houses fragments from the medieval basilica.

Piazza di San Giovanni in Laterano boasts an ancient obelisk and parts of Nero's Aqueduct. This 18th-century painting by Canaletto shows how the piazza once looked.

STAR SIGHTS

★ San Giovanni in Laterano

KEY

— — — Suggested route

0 metres 75
0 yards 75

The Chapel of San Venanzio is decorated with a series of 7th-century mosaics on a gold background. This detail from the apse shows one of the angels flanking the central figure of Christ. San Venanzio was an accomplished 6th-century Latin poet.

LOCATOR MAP
See Central Rome Map pp12–13

The Lateran Palace, residence of the popes until 1309, was rebuilt by Domenico Fontana in 1586.

★ **San Giovanni in Laterano**
Borromini's interior dates from the 17th century, but the grand facade by Alessandro Galilei, with its giant statues of Christ and the Apostles, was added in 1735 ❶

Scala Santa
This door at the top of the stair-case leads to the Sancta Sanctorum, the pope's private chapel ❷

Porta Asinaria
This minor gateway, no longer in use, is as old as the Aurelian Wall, dating back to the 3rd century AD ❸

The Triclinio Leoniano is a piece of wall and a mosaic from the dining hall of 8th-century Pope Leo III.

San Giovanni in Laterano ❶

See pp182–3.

Scala Santa and Sancta Sanctorum ❷

Piazza di San Giovanni in Laterano 14. **Map** 9 C1. 🛈 70 49 44 89. 🚌 4, 15, 16, 81, 85, 87, 186 and many other routes. 🚃 13, 30b. Ⓜ San Giovanni. **Open** 6.30am–11.50am, 3.30pm–6.45pm (Oct–Mar: 3pm– 6.45pm) daily. ✝ ◎

Devout Christians climbing the Scala Santa on their knees

O N THE EAST SIDE of Piazza di San Giovanni in Laterano, a building designed by Domenico Fontana (1589) houses two surviving parts of the old Lateran Palace. One is the pope's private chapel, the Sancta Sanctorum, the other the holy staircase, the Scala Santa. The 28 steps, said to be those that Christ ascended in Pontius Pilate's house during his trial, are supposed to have been brought from Jerusalem by St Helena, mother of the Emperor Constantine. This belief, however, cannot be traced back any earlier than the 7th century.

The steps were moved to their present site by Pope Sixtus V (reigned 1585–90) when the old Lateran Palace was destroyed. No foot may touch the holy steps, so they are covered by wooden boards. They may only be climbed by the faithful on their knees, a penance that is performed especially on

Good Friday. In the vestibule there are various 19th-century sculptures including an *Ecce Homo* by Giosuè Meli (1874).

The Scala Santa and two side stairways lead to the Chapel of St Lawrence or Sancta Sanctorum (Holy of Holies), built by Pope Nicholas III in 1278. Decorated with fine Cosmatesque marble-work, the chapel contains many important relics, the most precious being an image of Jesus – the *Acheiropoeton* or "picture painted without hands", said to be the work of St Luke, assisted by an angel. The image was taken on procession in medieval times to ward off plagues.

Porta Asinaria ❸

Between Piazza di Porta San Giovanni and Piazzale Appio. **Map** 10 D2. 🚌 4, 15, 16, 81, 85, 87. 🚃 13, 30b. Ⓜ San Giovanni. See **Markets** p339.

T HE PORTA ASINARIA (Gate of the Donkeys) is one of the minor gateways in the Aurelian Wall *(see p196).* Twin circular towers were added and a small enclosure built around the entrance; the remains are still visible today. From outside the walls you can see the gate's white travertine facade and two rows of small windows, giving light to two corridors built into the wall above the gateway. In

Porta Asinaria from inside the wall

AD 546 treacherous barbarian soldiers serving in the Roman army opened this gate to the hordes of the Goth Totila, who mercilessly looted the city. In 1084 the Holy Roman Emperor Henry IV entered Rome via Porta Asinaria with the antipope Guibert to oust Pope Gregory VII. The gateway was badly damaged later that year by the pope's rescuer, the Norman Robert Guiscard, who set the whole area around San Giovanni in Laterano on fire.

The area close to the gate, especially in the Via Sannio, is the home of a popular flea-market. During the week, the streets fill with stalls selling cheap clothes, both new and second-hand, shoes and camping equipment, and bargains can often be found.

Amphiteatrum Castrense ❹

Between Piazza di Santa Croce in Gerusalemme and Viale Castrense. **Map** 10 E1. 🚌 9. 🚃 13, 30b. **Not open** to the public.

Columns and bricked-up arches of the Amphiteatrum Castrense

T HIS SMALL 3rd-century amphitheatre was used for games and baiting animals. It owes its preservation to the fact that it was incorporated in the Aurelian Wall *(see p196),* which included several existing high buildings in its fortifications. The graceful arches framed by brick semicolumns were blocked up. The amphitheatre is best seen from outside the walls, from where there is also a good view of the bell tower of Santa Croce in Gerusalemme.

Discovery and Triumph of the Cross, attributed to Antoniazzo Romano, in Santa Croce in Gerusalemme

Santa Croce in Gerusalemme ❺

Piazza di Santa Croce in Gerusalemme
12. **Map** 10 E1. 🕻 *701 47 69.*
🚌 *9.* 🚃 *13, 30b.* **Open** *6am–12.30pm, 3.30pm–7pm daily.*
🕆 📷 🔲

Emperor Constantine's mother St Helena founded this church in AD 320 in the grounds of her private palace. Although the church stood at the edge of the city, the relics of the Crucifixion that St Helena had brought back from Jerusalem made it a centre of pilgrimage. Most important were the pieces of Christ's Cross (*croce* means cross) and part of Pontius Pilate's inscription in Latin, Hebrew and Greek: "Jesus of Nazareth King of the Jews".

In the crypt is a Roman statue of Juno, found at Ostia (*see pp270–71*), transformed into a statue of St Helena by replacing the head and arms and adding a cross. The 15th-century apse fresco shows the medieval legends that arose around the Cross. Helena is shown holding it over a dead youth and restoring him to life. Another episode shows its recovery from the Persians by the Byzantine Emperor Heraclitus after a bloody battle. In the centre of the apse is a magnificent tomb by Jacopo Sansovino made for Cardinal Quiñones, Emperor Charles V's confessor (died 1540).

Museum of Musical Instruments ❻

Museo degli Strumenti Musicali, Piazza di Santa Croce in Gerusalemme.
Map 10 E1. 🕻 *701 47 96.* 🚌 *9.*
🚃 *13, 30b.* **Open** *9am–7pm Tue & Thu, 9am–1.30pm Wed, Fri–Sun.*
Closed *public hols.* **Adm charge.** 📷

One of Rome's lesser-known museums, the building stands on the site of the Sessorianum, the great Imperial villa belonging to Empress St Helena, later included in the Aurelian Wall. Opened in 1974, the museum has a collection of over 3,000 instruments from all over the world. It includes instruments typical of the various regions of Italy, and wind, string and percussion instruments of all ages (including Egyptian, Greek and Roman). There are also sections dedicated to church and military music.

The greater part of the collection is composed of Baroque instruments: don't miss the gorgeous Barberini harp, remarkably well-preserved, on the first floor in Room 13. There are spinets, harpsichords and clavichords of many different kinds, and one of the first pianos ever made, dating from 1722.

18th-century statue of St Helena on the facade of Santa Croce

Art Nouveau entrance to the Museum of Musical Instruments

San Giovanni in Laterano ①

EARLY IN THE 4th century, the Laterani family were disgraced and their land taken by Emperor Constantine to build Rome's first Christian basilica. Today's church retains the original shape, but has been destroyed by fire twice and rebuilt several times. Borromini undertook the last major rebuild of the interior in 1646, and the main facade is an 18th-century addition. Before the pope's move to Avignon in 1309, the adjoining Lateran Palace was the official papal residence, and until 1870 all popes were crowned in the church. The pope is the Bishop of Rome and here in the city's main cathedral he celebrates Maundy Thursday mass and attends the annual blessing of the people.

Cappella di San Venanzio
This chapel is attached to the baptistry and is decorated with 7th-century mosaics.

Entrance to museum

Apse

Papal Altar
Only the pope can celebrate mass at this altar. The Gothic baldacchino, decorated with frescoes, dates from the 14th century.

★ **Cloisters**
Built by the Vassalletto family in about 1220, the cloisters are remarkable for their twisted twin columns and inlaid marble mosaics.

TIMELINE

AD 313 Constantine gives Laterani site to Pope Melchiades for a church		**896** Church damaged in earthquake	**1144** Church dedicated to San Giovanni in Laterano	**1377** Return of popes from Avignon	**1646** Borromini rebuilds interior
314–18 Five-aisled basilical church is built			**1309** Papacy moves to Avignon		
AD 300	800		1000	1400	
324 Basilica consecrated by Pope Sylvester I and dedicated to the Redeemer	**904–911** Church rebuilt under Pope Sergius III		**1300** First Holy Year proclaimed	**1360** Church burnt down for second time	**1586** Domenico Fontana builds north facade
			1308 Church destroyed by fire	**1730–40** Alessandro Galilei constructs main facade	

★ Baptistry
*Though much restored,
the domed baptistry dates
back to Constantine's
time. It assumed its
present octagonal shape
in AD 432 and the design
has served as the model
for baptistries throughout
the Christian world.*

VISITORS' CHECKLIST

Piazza di San Giovanni in
Laterano 4. **Map** 9 C2. **[** 77
20 79 91. **━** 4, 15, 16, 85, 87,
93, 93b and other routes to
Piazza San Giovanni. **M** San
Giovanni. **━** 13, 30b. **Church
and Cloister open** 7am–7pm
(Oct–Mar: 6pm) daily. **Museum
closed** for restoration. **Adm
charge** for cloister. **🔲 🔲 🔲**

STAR FEATURES

★ Baptistry

★ Cloisters

North Facade
*This was added
by Domenico
Fontana in 1586.
The pope gives his
blessing from the
upper loggia.*

**The original Lateran
Palace** was almost
destroyed by the fire of
1308 which devastated San
Giovanni. Pope Sixtus V
commissioned Fontana to
replace it in 1586.

**Statues of
Christ and
the Apostles**

Boniface VIII Fresco
*This fragment showing
the pope proclaiming
the Holy Year of 1300
is attributed to Giotto.*

A side door is
opened once
every 25 years
for Holy Year.

**Main entrance
on east facade**

TRIAL OF A CORPSE
Fear of rival factions led
the early popes to extra-
ordinary lengths. An absurd
case took place at the
Lateran Palace in 897
when Pope Stephen VI
tried the corpse of his
predecessor, Formosus,
for disloyalty to
the Church. The
corpse was
found guilty, its
right hand was
mutilated and it
was thrown in-
to the Tiber.

**Pope
Formosus**

Corsini Chapel
*This chapel was built in the
1730s for Pope Clement XII.
The altarpiece is a mosaic
copy of Guido Reni's painting
of Sant'Andrea Corsini.*

Porta Maggiore ➐

Piazza di Porta Maggiore. **Map** 6 F5.
🚋 *105*. 🚎 *13, 14, 19, 19b, 516, 517*.

ORIGINALLY the two arches of Porta Maggiore were not part of the city wall, but part of an aqueduct built by the Emperor Claudius in AD 52. They carried the water of the Aqua Claudia over the Via Labicana and Via Prenestina, two of ancient Rome's main southbound roads. You can still see the original roadway beneath the gate. In the large slabs of basalt – a hard volcanic rock used in all old Roman roads – note the great ruts created by generations of cartwheels. On top of the arches separate conduits carried the water of two aqueducts: the Aqua Claudia, and its offshoot, the Aqueduct of Nero. They bear inscriptions from the time of the Emperors Vespasian and Titus, who restored them in AD 71 and AD 81. In all, six aqueducts from different water sources entered the city at Porta Maggiore.

The Aqua Claudia was 68 km (43 miles) long, with more than 15 km (9 miles) above ground. Its majestic arches are a distinctive feature of the Roman countryside, and a popular brand of mineral water still bears its name. One stretch of the Aqua Claudia had its arches bricked up when it was incorporated into the 3rd-century Aurelian Wall *(see p196)*.

Relief showing breadmaking on the tomb of the baker Eurysaces

Baker's Tomb ➑

Piazzale Labicano. **Map** 6 F5. 🚋 *105*.
🚎 *13, 14, 19, 19b, 516, 517*.

IN THE MIDDLE of the tram junction near Porta Maggiore stands the tomb of the rich baker Eurysaces and his wife Atistia, built in 30 BC. Roman custom forbade burials within city walls, and the roads leading out of cities became lined with tombs and monuments for the middle and upper classes. This tomb is shaped like a baking oven: a low-relief frieze at the top shows Eurysaces presiding over his slaves in the various phases of breadmaking. The inscription proudly asserts his origins and reveals him as a freed slave, probably of Greek origin. Many men like him saved money from their meagre slave salaries to earn their freedom and set up businesses, becoming the backbone of Rome's economy.

Relief on the Tomb of the Statilii freedmen

Aqueduct of Nero and the Freedmen's Tombs ➒

Intersection of Via Statilia and Via di Santa Croce in Gerusalemme.
Map 10 D1. 🚋 *9, 105*. 🚎 *13, 14, 19, 19b, 30b*. **Apply** for permit: *Ripartizione X, (see p367)*.

THE AQUEDUCT was built by Nero in the 1st century AD as an extension of the Aqua Claudia. It was later extended to supply the Imperial residences on the Palatine. Partly incorporated into later buildings, the imposing arches make their way via the Lateran to the Celian hill. Along the first section of the aqueduct, in Via Statilia, is a small tomb in the shape of a house, dating from the 1st century BC, bearing the names and likenesses of a small group of freed slaves. Their name, Statilii, indicates that they had been freed by the noble Statilii, the family of Claudius's notorious wife Messalina. Servants of families often pooled funds in this way to pay for a dignified burial in a common resting place.

Porta Maggiore, a city gate formed by the arches of an aqueduct

Well-preserved section of Nero's Aqueduct near San Giovanni

Villa Wolkonsky ⑩

Via Conte Rosso. **Map** 10 D1.
🚌 *4, 81.* 🚊 *13, 30b.* **Not open** *to the public.*

NOW THE RESIDENCE of the British ambassador, the villa has a beautiful garden strewn with Roman remains, including arches of the Aqua Claudia and a columbarium, or collective grave, of the 2nd century AD. Sadly, garden parties for British residents are no longer given here on the Queen's official birthday.

Santi Quattro Coronati ⑪

Via dei Santi Quattro Coronati 20. **Map** 9 B1. 📞 *70 47 54 27.* 🚌 *15, 81, 85, 87, 118.* 🚊 *13, 30b.* **Open** *9.30am– noon, 3.30pm–6pm (Oct–Mar: 9.30am–noon) daily.* ⛪ 📷 ♿

Cloister of Santi Quattro Coronati

THE NAME of this fortified convent (Four Crowned Saints) refers to four Christian soldiers martyred after they refused to worship a pagan god. For centuries it was the bastion of the pope's residence, the Lateran Palace. Its high apse still looms over the houses below, while a Carolingian tower dominates the entrance. Erected in the 4th century AD, it was rebuilt after the invading Normans set fire to the neighbourhood in 1084. Hidden within is the garden of the delightful inner cloister (admission on request), one of the earliest of its kind, built around 1220.

The remains of medieval frescoes can be seen in the Chapel of Santa Barbara, but the convent's main feature is the Chapel of St Sylvester – its remarkable frescoes (1246) recount the legend of the conversion to Christianity of

the Emperor Constantine by Pope Sylvester I (reigned 314– 35), then living as a hermit on Monte Soratte, north of Rome.

Stricken by the plague, Constantine is prescribed a bath in children's blood, to the horror of the matrons of Rome. Unable to bring himself to obey, Constantine is visited in a dream by St Peter and St Paul. They advise him to find Sylvester, who cures him and baptizes him. The final scene shows the emperor kneeling before the pope. The implied idea of the pope as heir to the Roman Empire would affect the whole course of medieval European history.

San Clemente ⑫

See pp186–7.

Santo Stefano Rotondo ⑬

Via di Santo Stefano 7. **Map** 9 B2. 📞 *70 49 37 17.* 🚌 *15, 118, 673.* **Open** *9am–1pm, 3.30pm–6pm (summer), 9am–noon, 3pm–4.30pm (winter).* 🚫

ONE OF ROME'S earliest Christian churches, Santo Stefano Rotondo was built between 468 and 483. It has an unusual circular plan with four chapels in a cruciform. The

Distinctive circular outline of Santo Stefano Rotondo

round inner area was surrounded by concentric corridors with 22 Ionic supporting columns. The high drum in the centre is 22 m (72 ft) high and just as wide. It is lit by 22 high windows, a few of them restored or blocked by restorations carried out under Pope Nicholas V (reigned 1447–55), who consulted the Florentine architect Leon Battista Alberti. The archway in the centre of the church may have been added during this period, when the outer corridor was eliminated.

In the 16th century the church walls were frescoed by Niccolò Pomarancio, with particularly gruesome illustrations of the martyrdom of innumerable saints. Some of the medieval decor remains in the chapels: in the first chapel to the left of the entrance is a 7th-century mosaic of Christ with San Primo and San Feliciano.

Fresco of St Sylvester and Constantine in Santi Quattro Coronati

San Clemente ⑫

SAN CLEMENTE PROVIDES an opportunity to travel back through three layers of history. At street level, there is a 12th-century church; underneath this lies a 4th-century church; and below that are ancient Roman buildings, including a Temple of Mithras. Mithraism, an all-male fertility cult imported from Persia in the 1st century BC, was a rival to Christianity during the age of Imperial Rome.

The upper levels are dedicated to St Clement, the fourth pope, who was exiled to the Crimea and martyred by being tied to an anchor and drowned. His life is illustrated in some of the frescoes in the 4th-century church. The site was taken over in the 17th century by Irish Dominicans, who still continue the excavating work begun by Father Mullooly in 1857.

Entrance to the church is through a door in Via di San Giovanni in Laterano.

Paschal Candlestick
This 12th-century spiralling candlestick, striped with glittering mosaic, is a magnificent example of Cosmati work.

18th-Century Facade
Twelfth-century columns were used in the arcade.

★ **Cappella di Santa Caterina**
The restored frescoes by the 15th-century Florentine artist, Masolino, show scenes from the life of the martyred St Catherine of Alexandria.

12th-century church

4th-century church

Piscina
This deep pit was discovered in 1967. It could have been used as a font or fountain.

1st–3rd-century temple and buildings

TIMELINE

2nd century Site possibly used for secret Christian worship

Late 2nd century Temple of Mithras built

867 Reputed transfer of remains of San Clemente to Rome

1108 New church built over 4th-century church

1857 Original 4th-century church rediscovered by Father Mullooly

AD 10	500	1000	1500	1900

90–99 Papacy of St Clement

4th century First church built over courtyard of earlier Roman building

1084 Church destroyed during Norman invasion led by Robert Guiscard

1667 Church and convent given to Irish Dominicans

AD 64 Nero's fire destroys area

1861 Church is excavated. Roman ruins discovered

★ Apse Mosaic
The 12th-century
Triumph of the
Cross *includes*
beautifully detailed
animals and
acanthus leaves.

Schola Cantorum
The 6th-century
enclosure for the
choir was retained
for the new church,
built in 1108.

★ Triclinium and
Altar of Mithras
The altar, with a
relief of Mithras
slaying the bull,
stands in the
triclinium, *a room*
used for ritual
banquets.

Temple of
Mithras

★ 11th-
Century
Frescoes
Commissioned by
the de Rapiza family,
one shows the story of a boy
found alive in St Clement's
tomb beneath the Black Sea.

Catacomb
Discovered in
1938 and dating
from the 5th or 6th
century, it contains
16 wall tombs
known as loculi.

VISITORS' CHECKLIST

Via di San Giovanni in Laterano.
Map 9 B1. **☎** 70 45 10 18.
81, 85, 87, 93. **M** Colosseo.
13, 30b. **Open** 9am–12.30pm,
3.30pm–6.30pm (Oct–Mar: 6pm)
Mon–Sat, 10am–12.30pm,
3.30pm–6.30pm Sun. **Adm**
charge to excavations. **⛪ ⓞ**

STAR FEATURES

★ Apse Mosaic

★ Cappella di Santa
Caterina

★ 11th-Century
Frescoes

★ Triclinium and Altar
of Mithras

IOVINVSALVMNVS

CARACALLA

THE CELIAN HILL overlooks the Colosseum, and takes its name from Caelius Vibenna, the legendary hero of Rome's struggle against the Tarquins *(see pp16–17)*. In Imperial Rome this was a fashionable place to live, and some of its vanished splendour is still apparent in the vast ruins of the Baths of Caracalla. Today, thanks to

Capital from ruins of Baths of Caracalla

the Archaeological Zone established at the turn of the century, it is a delightfully peaceful area, a green wedge from the Aurelian Wall to the heart of the city. Through it runs the cobbled Via di Porta San Sebastiano, part of the old Via Appia. This road leads to Porta San Sebastiano, one of the best-preserved gates in the ancient city wall.

SIGHTS AT A GLANCE

Churches
Santi Giovanni e Paolo ❶
San Gregorio Magno ❷
Santa Maria in Domnica ❹
San Sisto Vecchio ❻
Santi Nereo e Achilleo ❼
San Cesareo ❽
San Giovanni a Porta Latina ❾
San Giovanni in Oleo ❿
Santa Balbina ⓰

Arches and Gates
Arch of Dolabella ❸
Arch of Drusus ⓭
Porta San Sebastiano and the Aurelian Wall ⓮
Sangallo Bastion ⓯

Historic Buildings
UN Food and Agriculture Organization ⓱
Baths of Caracalla ⓲

Tombs
Columbarium of Pomponius Hylas ⓫
Tomb of the Scipios ⓬

Parks and Gardens
Villa Celimontana ❺

GETTING THERE
Circo Massimo Metro station is handy if you are visiting the churches and parks on the Celian hill. For the Baths of Caracalla and other sights closer to Porta San Sebastiano, take the 90 or 118 along Viale delle Terme di Caracalla. Other buses, such as the 93, 97 and 613, go to Piazzale Numa Pompilio, a useful central starting point for exploring the area.

SEE ALSO

• *Street Finder*, maps 8, 9

• *Where to Stay* pp294–5

• *Restaurants* pp310–11

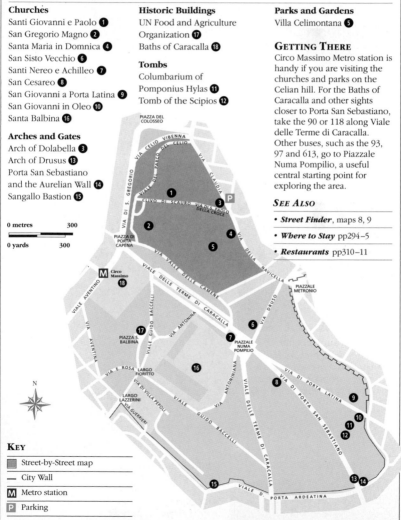

KEY

- ▦ Street-by-Street map
- — City Wall
- Ⓜ Metro station
- Ⓟ Parking

Mosaic of an athlete from the Baths of Caracalla

Street-by-Street: The Celian Hill

In the course of a morning exploring the green slopes of the Celian hill, you will see a fascinating assortment of archaeological remains and beautiful churches. A good starting point is the church of San Gregorio Magno, from where the Clivo di Scauro leads up to the top of the hill. The steep narrow street passes the ancient porticoed church of Santi Giovanni e Paolo with its beautiful Romanesque bell tower soaring above the surrounding medieval monastery buildings. Of the parks on the hill, the best kept and most peaceful is the Villa Celimontana with its formal walks and avenues. It is a good place for a picnic, as there are few bars or restaurants in the area.

Clivo di Scauro, the Roman *Clivus Scauri*, leads up to Santi Giovanni e Paolo, passing under the flying buttresses that support the church.

VIA DI SAN GREGORIO

CLIVO DI SCAURO

La Vignola is a delightful Renaissance pavilion, reconstructed here in 1911 after it had been demolished during the creation of the Archaeological Zone around the Baths of Caracalla.

To Circo Massimo Metro

San Gregorio Magno
A monastery and chapel were founded here by Pope Gregory the Great at the end of the 6th century **2**

★ **Santi Giovanni e Paolo**
The nave of the church, lit by a blaze of chandeliers, has been restored many times, assuming its present appearance in the 18th century **1**

★ **Villa Celimontana**
The delightful 16th-century villa built for the Mattei family is now the centre of a public park **5**

Trams passing over the Celian hill from the Colosseum rumble up a picturesque narrow track through the Parco del Celio.

LOCATOR MAP
See Central Rome Map pp12–13

Ruins of the Temple of Claudius are visible over a large area of the Celian hill. These travertine blocks have been incorporated in the base of the bell tower of Santi Giovanni e Paolo.

The gateway of San Tommaso in Formis is decorated with a wonderful 13th-century mosaic showing Christ with two freed slaves, one white, one black.

Arch of Dolabella
Built in the 1st century AD, probably as an entrance to the city, this archway was later incorporated in Nero's aqueduct to the Palatine ❸

STAR SIGHTS

★ **Santi Giovanni e Paolo**

★ **Santa Maria in Domnica**

★ **Villa Celimontana**

KEY

– – – Suggested route

0 metres 75

0 yards 75

★ **Santa Maria in Domnica**
This church is famed for its 9th-century mosaics. These Apostles appear on the triumphal arch above the apse, flanking a medallion containing the figure of Christ ❹

Santi Giovanni e Paolo ❶

Piazza Santi Giovanni e Paolo 13.
Map 9 A1. 〖 *700 57 45*. 🚌 *11,
15, 27, 90, 673*. 🚃 *13, 30b*.
Ⓜ *Colosseo or Circo Massimo*.
Open *8.30am–noon, 3.30pm–7pm
(Oct–Mar: 6.30pm) daily.* 🚻 📷 ♿
church only (not Roman house).

Sʌɴᴛɪ ɢɪovᴀɴɴɪ ᴇ ᴘᴀoʟo is
dedicated to two martyred
Roman officers whose house
stood on this site. Giovanni
(John) and Paolo (Paul) had
served the first Christian
emperor, Constantine. When
they were later called to arms
by the pagan emperor, Julian
the Apostate, they refused
and were beheaded in their
own house in AD 362.

Built towards the end of the
4th century, the church
retains many elements of its
original structure. The Ionic
portico dates from the 12th
century, and the apse and bell
tower were added by
Nicholas Breakspeare, the
only English pope, who
reigned as Adrian IV (1154–9).
The base of the superb 13th-
century bell tower was part of
the Temple of Claudius
that stood on this site. In
common with many
Romanesque bell
towers, it has inlaid
marble and ceramic
roundels decorating
the brickwork.

The interior,
remodelled in 1718,
has granite piers and
columns. A tomb slab in the
nave marks the burial place of
the martyrs, whose relics are
preserved in an urn under the
high altar. In a tiny room near
the altar, a magnificent 13th-
century fresco depicts the
figure of Christ flanked by his
Apostles (ask the sacristan to
unlock the door for you).

Excavations beneath the
church have revealed two
Roman houses, of the 2nd and
3rd centuries, united and used
as a Christian burial place. The
two-storeyed construction,
with 20 rooms and a labyrinth
of corridors, has well-preserved
pagan and Christian paintings.
The arches to the left of the
church were part of a 3rd-
century street of shops.

Fresco of Christ and the Apostles in Santi Giovanni e Paolo

San Gregorio Magno ❷

Piazza di San Gregorio. **Map** 8 F2.
〖 *700 82 27*. 🚌 *11, 15, 27, 673*.
🚃 *13, 30b*. Ⓜ *Circo Massimo*.
Open *9am–noon, 3.30pm–6pm daily.*
🚻 📷

Facade of San Gregorio Magno

Tᴏ ᴛʜᴇ ᴇɴɢʟɪsʜ, this is one
of the most important
churches in Rome, for it was
from here that St Augustine
was sent on his mission to
convert England to Christianity.
The church was founded in
AD 575 by San Gregorio
Magno (St Gregory the Great),
who turned his family home
on this site into a monastery.
It was rebuilt in medieval
times and restored in 1629–33
by Giovanni Battista Soria. To
reach the church you ascend a
flight of steps from the street.

The forecourt contains some
interesting tombs. To the left
is that of Sir Edward Carne,
who came to Rome several
times between 1529 and 1533
as King Henry VIII's envoy to
gain the pope's consent to the
annulment of Henry's marriage
to Catherine of Aragon.

The interior, remodelled by
Francesco Ferrari in the mid-
18th century, is typically
Baroque, except for the fine
mosaic floor and some ancient
columns. At the end of the
right aisle is the chapel of St
Gregory. Leading off it, another
small chapel, believed to have
been the saint's own cell,
houses his episcopal throne –
a Roman chair of sculpted
marble. The Salviati Chapel
on the left contains a picture
of the Virgin said to have
spoken to St Gregory.

Outside, amid the cypresses
to the left of the church,
stand three small chapels,
dedicated to St Andrew,
St Sylvia (Gregory the Great's
mother) and St Barbara.

**Marble throne of Gregory the Great
from the 1st century BC**

Arch of Dolabella ❸

Via di San Paolo della Croce.
Map 9 A2. 🚌 15, 673.

THE ARCH was built in AD 10 by the consuls Cornelius Dolabella and Caius Junius Silanus, possibly on the site of one of the gateways of the old Servian Wall. Made of solid travertine blocks, it was subsequently used to support Nero's extension of the Claudian aqueduct, built to supply the Imperial palace on the Palatine hill.

The restored Arch of Dolabella

Santa Maria in Domnica ❹

Piazza della Navicella 12. **Map** 9 A2.
📞 700 15 19. 🚌 15, 673.
Open 9am–noon, 3.30pm–7pm
(Oct–Mar: 6pm) daily. 🚻 📷 ♿

THE CHURCH overlooks the Piazza della Navicella (little boat), which takes its name from the 16th-century fountain there. It was made from an ancient stone galley, probably a temple offering made by a Roman traveller on his safe return to the city. The church dates from the 9th century; in the 16th century Pope Leo X added the portico and the coffered ceiling.

In the apse behind the slightly incongruous modern altar is a superb 9th-century mosaic commissioned by Pope Paschal I. Wearing the square halo of the living, the pope appears at the feet of the Virgin and Child. The Virgin, surrounded by a throng of angels, holds a handkerchief in the manner of a fashionable lady at a Byzantine court.

Villa Celimontana ❺

Piazza della Navicella. **Map** 9 A2.
🚌 15, 81, 85, 87, 90, 673.
Park open 7am–dusk daily.

THE DUKES OF MATTEI bought this land in 1553 and transformed the vineyards that covered the hillside into a formal garden. As well as palms and other exotic trees, the garden even has its own Egyptian obelisk. Villa Mattei, built in the 1580s, is now known as Villa Celimontana and houses the Italian Geographical Society.

The Mattei family used to open the park to the public on the day of the Visit of the Seven Churches, an annual event instituted by San Filippo Neri in 1552. Starting from the Chiesa Nuova (see p124), Romans went on foot to the city's seven major churches. When they reached Villa Mattei, they were given a meal of bread, wine, salami, cheese, an egg and two apples. The garden, now owned by the city of Rome, still makes an ideal place for a picnic.

Park of Villa Celimontana

San Sisto Vecchio ❻

Piazzale Numa Pompilio 8. **Map** 9 A3.
📞 77 20 51 74. 🚌 90, 93, 97, 613,
671. **Open** 9am–11am, 3.30pm–
5.30pm daily. **Closed** Aug. 🚫

THIS SMALL CHURCH is of great historical interest as it was granted to St Dominic in 1219 by Pope Honorius III. The founder of the Dominican order soon moved his own headquarters to Santa Sabina (see p204), San Sisto becoming the first home of the order of Dominican nuns. The best feature of the church itself is the 13th-century bell tower.

Apse mosaic of the Virgin and Child in Santa Maria in Domnica

Santi Nereo e Achilleo ❼

Via di Porta San Sebastiano 4.
Map 9 A3. ☎ 575 79 96. 🚌 *90, 93, 613, 671.* **Open** *10am–noon, 4pm–6pm Sat–Thu.* 📷 ♿

A CCORDING to legend, St Peter, after escaping from prison, was fleeing the city when he lost a bandage from his wounds. The original church was founded here in the 4th century on the spot where the bandage fell, but later on it was rededicated to the 1st-century AD martyrs St Nereus and St Achilleus.

Detail of mosaic, Santi Nereo e Achilleo

Restored at the end of the 16th century, the church has retained many medieval features, including some fine 9th-century mosaics on the triumphal arch. A magnificent pulpit rests on an enormous porphyry pedestal which was found nearby in the Baths of Caracalla. The walls of the side naves are decorated with a series of rather grisly 16th-century frescoes by Niccolò Pomarancio, showing in clinical detail how each of the Apostles was martyred.

Fresco by Niccolò Pomarancio of the *Martyrdom of St Simon* in Santi Nereo e Achilleo

San Cesareo ❽

Via di Porta San Sebastiano.
Map 9 A3. ☎ 58 23 01 40. **Closed** *for restoration.*

T HIS SPLENDID old church, built over Roman ruins of the 2nd century AD, has been closed since 1988. You can still admire Giacomo della Porta's fine Renaissance facade, but if the workmen will let you in, you can also see Cosmatesque mosaic work and carving to rival that of any church in Rome. The episcopal throne, altar and pulpit are decorated with delightful birds and beasts. The church was restored in the 16th century by Pope Clement VIII, whose coat of arms decorates the ceiling.

San Giovanni a Porta Latina ❾

Via di San Giovanni a Porta Latina.
Map 9 B3. ☎ 70 49 17 77. 🚌 *4, 90.* **Open** *7am–12.15pm, 3pm–6pm daily.* **Donation** *expected.*
✝ 📷 ♿

T HE CHURCH of "St John at the Latin Gate" was founded in the 5th century, rebuilt in 720 and restored in 1191. This is one of the most picturesque of the old Roman churches. Classical columns support the medieval portico, and the 12th-century bell tower is superb. A tall cedar tree shades an ancient well standing in the forecourt. The interior has recently been restored, but it preserves the rare simplicity of its early origins with ancient columns of varying styles lining the aisles. Traces remain of early medieval frescoes. There are

12th-century frescoes showing 46 different scenes from both the Old and New Testaments, which are among the finest of their kind in Rome.

Fresco, San Giovanni a Porta Latina

San Giovanni in Oleo ❿

Via di Porta Latina. **Map** 9 C4. 🚌 *4, 90.* **Closed** *for restoration.*

Frieze of San Giovanni in Oleo

T HE NAME of this charming octagonal Renaissance chapel means "St John in Oil". The tiny building marks the spot where, according to legend, St John was boiled in oil – and came out unscathed, or even refreshed. An earlier chapel is said to have existed on the site; the present one was built in the early 16th century. The design has been attributed to Bramante or Antonio da Sangallo the Younger. It was restored by Borromini, who altered the roof, crowning it with a cross supported by a sphere decorated with roses. He also added a terracotta frieze of roses and palm leaves. The wall paintings inside the chapel include one of St John in a cauldron of boiling oil.

Niches for funerary urns in the Columbarium of Pomponius Hylas

Columbarium of Pomponius Hylas ⓫

Via di Porta Latina 10. **Map** 9 B4.
🚌 4, 90. **Open** by appt only: apply
to Ripartizione X, Via del Portico
d'Ottavia 29 or phone
67 10 20 70.

KNOWN AS a columbarium because it resembles a dovecote (*columba* is the Latin word for dove), this kind of vaulted tomb was normally built by rich Romans to house the cremated remains of their freedmen. Many similar tombs have been uncovered in this part of Rome, which up until the 3rd century AD lay outside the city wall. This one, excavated in 1831, dates from the 1st century AD. An

Mosaic inscription in the Columbarium of Pomponius Hylas

inscription informs us that it is the Tomb of Pomponius Hylas and his wife, Pomponia Vitalinis. Above her name is a "V" which indicates that she was still living when the inscription was made. The tomb was probably a commercial venture. Niches in the interior walls of the columbarium were sold to people who could not afford to build vaults of their own.

Tomb of the Scipios ⓬

Via di Porta San Sebastiano 9.
Map 9 B4. 📞 70 49 00 53. 🚌 4, 90. **Closed** for restoration.

THE SCIPIOS were a family of conquering generals. Southern Italy, Corsica, Algeria, Spain and Asia Minor all fell to their victorious Roman armies. The most famous of all was Publius Cornelius Scipio Africanus, who defeated the great Carthaginian general Hannibal at the Battle of Zama in 202 BC. Scipio Africanus himself was not buried here in the family tomb, but at Liternum near Naples, where he owned a favourite villa. The Tomb of the Scipios was discovered in 1780. It contained various sarcophagi,

statues and niches with terracotta burial urns. Many of the originals have now been moved to the Vatican Museums and copies stand in their place.

The earliest sarcophagus was that of Cornelius Scipio Barbatus, consul in 298 BC, for whom the tomb was built. Members of his illustrious family continued to be buried here up to the middle of the 2nd century BC. Excavations in the area have revealed many other archaeological finds: a columbarium similar to that of Pomponius Hylas, a Christian catacomb and a three-storey house dating from the 3rd century AD, which was built over the Tomb of the Scipios.

Arch of Drusus ⓭

Via di Porta San Sebastiano.
Map 9 B4.

Arch of Drusus, part of the Aqua Antoniniana aqueduct

ONCE MISTAKENLY identified as a triumphal arch, the so-called Arch of Drusus merely supported the branch aqueduct that supplied the Baths of Caracalla. It was built in the 3rd century AD, so had no connection with Drusus, a stepson of the Emperor Augustus. Its monumental appearance was due to the fact that it carried the aqueduct across the important route, Via Appia. The arch still spans the old cobbled road, just 50 m (160 ft) short of the gateway Porta San Sebastiano.

Fortified gateway of Porta San Sebastiano

Porta San Sebastiano and the Aurelian Wall ⑭

Museo delle Mura, Via di Porta San Sebastiano 18. **Map** 9 B4. **⚏** 70 47 52 84. **Open** 9am–7pm Tue–Sat, 9am–1.30pm Sun (last adm: 30 mins before closing). **Closed** public hols. **Adm charge.** ⌀

Mᴏꜱᴛ ᴏꜰ the Aurelian Wall, begun by the Emperor Aurelian (AD 270–75) and completed by his successor Probus (AD 276–82), has survived. Aurelian ordered its construction as a defence against marauding Germanic tribes, whose raids were penetrating deeper and deeper into Italy. Some 18 km (11 miles) round, with 18 gates and 381 towers, the wall took in all the seven hills of Rome. It was raised to almost twice its original height by Maxentius (AD 306–12).

Porta San Sebastiano, the gate that leads to the Via Appia Antica *(see p284)* is the largest and best-preserved gateway in the wall. It was rebuilt by the Emperor Honorius in the 5th century AD. Originally the Porta Appia, in Christian times it gradually became known as the Porta San Sebastiano, because the Via Appia led to the Basilica and Catacombs of San Sebastiano, which were popular places of pilgrimage.

It was at this gate that the last triumphal procession to enter the city by the Appian Way was received in state – that of Marcantonio Colonna

after the victory of Lepanto over the Turkish fleet in 1571. Today the gate's towers house a museum containing prints and models illustrating the history of the walls. The views are spectacular, especially out over the unchanging landscape of the Via Appia.

The wall continued to be Rome's main defence until 1870, when it was breached by Italian artillery just by Porta Pia, close to today's British Embassy. Many of the gates are still in use, and although the city has spread, most of its noteworthy historical and cultural sights still lie within the walls.

Sangallo Bastion ⑮

Viale di Porta Ardeatina. **Map** 9 A4. **⚏** 93, 94, 160, 613, 671. **Closed** for restoration.

Pope Paul III Farnese

Hᴀᴜɴᴛᴇᴅ ʙʏ the memory of the Sack of Rome in 1527 and fearing attack by the Turks, Pope Paul III asked Antonio

da Sangallo the Younger to reinforce the Aurelian Wall. Work on the huge projecting bastion began in 1537. For the moment its massive bulk can be admired from outside.

Santa Balbina ⑯

Piazza di Santa Balbina 8. **Map** 8 F3. **⚏** 578 02 07. **⚏** 160. **M** Circo Massimo. **Open** 8am–6pm daily. ☗

Oᴠᴇʀʟᴏᴏᴋɪɴɢ the Baths of Caracalla, this isolated church framed by cypresses is dedicated to Santa Balbina, a 2nd-century virgin martyr. Dating back to the 4th century, this is one of the oldest churches in the city. Inside stands the magnificent sculpted and inlaid tomb of Cardinal Stefanus de Surdis, signed by Giovanni di Cosma and dated 1303.

UN Food and Agriculture Organization ⑰

Viale delle Terme di Caracalla. **Map** 8 F2. **⚏** 11, 15, 27, 90, 118, 673. **⚏** 13, 30b. **M** Circo Massimo. **Closed** to public.

Obelisk of Axum (4th century AD)

Tʜᴇ ꜰᴏᴏᴅ and Agriculture Organization of the United Nations is based here in a modern building completed in 1951. Before it stands the obelisk of Axum, looted from Ethiopia by Mussolini, who commissioned the building originally to house the Ministry of Italian Africa.

Baths of Caracalla ⑱

Viale delle Terme di Caracalla 52.
Map 9 A3. 575 86 26.
🚌 90, 93, 160. **Open** 9am– dusk
Tue–Sat, 9am–1pm, Sun, Mon.
Closed public hols. **Adm charge.**
📷 ♿

COMPLETED by the Emperor
Caracalla in AD 217, the
baths functioned for about
300 years, until the plumbing
was destroyed by invading
Goths. Over 1,500 bathers at a
time could enjoy the facilities.
A Roman bath was a long and
complicated business,
beginning with a sort of
Turkish bath, followed by a
spell in the *calidarium*, a
large hot room
with pools of
water to
moisten the
atmosphere.
Then came the
lukewarm
tepidarium, a
visit to the
large central
meeting place,
known as the
frigidarium,
and finally a plunge
into the *natatio*, an
open-air swimming

Part of one of the gymnasia in the Baths of Caracalla

pool. For the rich, this was
followed by a rub-down with
scented woollen cloth. As
well as the baths, there were
spaces for exercise, libraries,
art galleries and gardens –
a true leisure centre. Most
of the rich marble
decorations of the baths
were removed by the
Farnese family in the 16th
century to adorn the
interior of Palazzo
Farnese *(see p147).*

Until recently, open-air operas
were staged here – the vocal
exertions of the performers
are now thought to pose a
threat to the structure of this
ancient monument.

**Fragment of
mosaic pavement**

KEY

☐	Calidarium (very hot)
☐	Tepidarium (lukewarm)
☐	Frigidarium (cold)
☐	Natatio (pool)
☐	Garden

Greek and
Latin libraries

Water tanks

Stadium

Conference and
meeting rooms

Gymnasium

Conference and
meeting room

Front
entrance

Changing
rooms

Gymnasia

Storage room for
oils and perfumes

AVENTINE

T HIS IS ONE of the most peaceful areas within the walls of the city. Although it is largely residential, there are some unique historic sights. From the top of the Aventine hill, crowned by the magnificent basilica of Santa Sabina, there are fine views across the river to Trastevere and St Peter's. At the

Mask fountain in courtyard of Santa Sabina

foot of the hill, ancient Rome is preserved in the two tiny Temples of the Forum Boarium and the Circus Maximus. The liveliest streets are in Testaccio, which has shops, restaurants and clubs, while to the south, beside Rome's solitary pyramid, the Protestant Cemetery is another oasis of calm.

SIGHTS AT A GLANCE

Churches and Temples
Santa Maria in Cosmedin ❶
San Giorgio in Velabro ❸
San Teodoro ❹
Santa Maria della
Consolazione ❺
San Giovanni Decollato ❻
Temples of the
Forum Boarium ❽
Santa Sabina ❾
Santi Bonifacio e Alessio ❿
San Saba ⓯

Historic Buildings
Casa dei Crescenzi ❼

Arches
Arch of Janus ❷

Historic Streets and Piazzas
Piazza dei Cavalieri di Malta ⓫

Ancient Sites
Monte Testaccio ⓬
Circus Maximus ⓰

Monuments and Tombs
Protestant Cemetery ⓭
Pyramid of Caius Cestius ⓮

GETTING THERE
The quickest way is by Metro line B to Piramide or Circo Massimo. For a more interesting trip, take a tram – the 13 or 30b. Several buses go down Viale Aventino to Piramide, but the only bus to the top of the Aventine hill is the 94.

KEY
◼ Street-by-Street map
— City Wall
Ⓜ Metro station
🅿 Parking

SEE ALSO
- **Street Finder**, maps 7, 8, 12
- **Where to Stay** pp294–5
- **Restaurants** pp310–11

Pines and orange trees on the Aventine hill with dome of St Peter's in the distance

Street-by-Street: Piazza della Bocca della Verità

T HE AREA ATTRACTS VISITORS eager to place their hands inside the
Bocca della Verità (the Mouth of Truth) in the portico of
Santa Maria in Cosmedin. There are many other sights to see in
this quiet corner of the city beside the Tiber, which was the site
of ancient Rome's first port and its busy
cattle market. Substantial Classical
remains include two small temples from
the Republican age and the Arch of
Janus from the later Empire. In the 6th
century the area became home to a
Greek community from Byzantium, who
founded the churches of San Giorgio in
Velabro and Santa Maria in Cosmedin.

Sant'Omobono,
a late 16th-century
church, now stands
in isolation in the
middle of an
important
archaeological site.
The remains of
sacrificial altars and
two temples from the
6th century BC have
been discovered.

Casa dei Crescenzi
*This 11th-century building
used columns and capitals
from ancient Roman
temples* ❼

Ponte Rotto, as this forlorn ruined
arch in the Tiber is called, means
simply "broken bridge". Built in the
2nd century BC, its original name
was the Pons Aemilius.

★ **Temples of the
Forum Boarium**
*The tiny round
Temple of Hercules
and its neighbour,
the Temple of
Portunus, are the
best preserved
of Rome's
Republican
temples* ❽

LUNGOTEVERE DEI PIERLEONI

TEVERE

PONTE PALATINO

STAR SIGHTS

★ **Santa Maria in
Cosmedin**

★ **Temples of the
Forum Boarium**

★ **Santa Maria
in Cosmedin**
*This medieval church has a
fine marble mosaic floor and
a Gothic baldacchino* ❶

Santa Maria della Consolazione
This 16th-century church used to serve a hospital nearby **5**

San Teodoro
The 15th-century portal of this ancient round church is decorated with the arms of Pope Nicholas V **4**

LOCATOR MAP
See Central Rome Map pp12–13

San Giovanni Decollato
The plain Renaissance facade was completed in about 1504 **6**

VIA DEI FIENILI

San Giorgio in Velabro
The simple 12th-century portico of Ionic columns was destroyed by a bomb in 1993 **3**

VIA DI SAN TEODORO

...LLATO

...ZA DELLA
...CA DELLA
...ERITÀ

Arch of Janus
This square structure with arches on each side dates from the 4th century AD **2**

The Arco degli Argentari, dedicated to the Emperor Septimius Severus in AD 204, is decorated with scenes of religion and war.

VIA DEI CERCHI

The Fontana dei Tritoni by Carlo Bizzaccheri was built here in 1715. The style shows the powerful influence of Bernini.

...LA GRECA

Bocca della Verità

Santa Maria in Cosmedin ❶

Piazza della Bocca della Verità 18.
Map 8 E1. 678 14 19. 15, 23, 57, 90, 92, 94, 95, 160, 716. **Open** 9am–1pm, 2.30pm–6pm daily (5pm winter). Phone first.

THIS BEAUTIFUL unadorned church was built in the 6th century on the site of the ancient city's food market. The elegant Romanesque bell tower and portico were added during the 12th century. In the 19th century a Baroque facade was removed and the church restored to its original simplicity. It contains many fine examples of Cosmati work, in particular the mosaic pavement, the raised choir, the bishop's throne and the canopy over the main altar.

Set into the wall of the portico is the Bocca della Verità (Mouth of Truth). This may have been a drain cover, dating back to before the 4th century BC. Medieval tradition had it that the formidable jaws would snap shut over the hand of those who told lies – a useful trick for testing the faithfulness of spouses.

Arch of Janus ❷

Via del Velabro. **Map** 8 E1. 15, 57, 90, 92, 95, 160, 716.

PROBABLY DATING from the reign of Constantine, this imposing four-faced marble arch stood at the bustling crossroads on the edge of the Forum Boarium, near the ancient docks. It was an ideal place for merchants and customers to do business in the shade. On the keystones above the four arches you can see small figures of the goddesses Roma, Juno, Ceres and Minerva. In medieval times the arch used to form the base of a tower fortress. It was restored to its original shape in 1827.

San Giorgio in Velabro ❸

Via del Velabro 19. **Map** 8 E1. 679 33 35. 15, 57, 90, 90b, 92, 94, 95, 160, 716, 774, 780. **Closed** for restoration.

San Giorgio in Velabro before the 1993 bombing

IN THE HOLLOW of the street named after the Velabrum, the swamp where Romulus and Remus are said to have been found by the she-wolf, is a small church dedicated to St George, whose bones lie under the altar. The 7th-century basilica has suffered over the centuries from periodic floods, but has been restored to its original appearance, with a double row of assorted granite and marble columns (taken from ancient Roman temples) dividing the triple nave. The austerity of the cool grey interior is relieved by golden frescoes in the apse (attributed to Pietro Cavallini, 1295). The facade and the bell tower date from the 12th century.

Recent testimony to the church's low-lying location is given by the high water-level mark of 1870 in the portico.

San Teodoro ❹

Via di San Teodoro. **Map** 8 E1. 678 66 24. 15, 57, 90, 92, 95, 160, 716. **Open** 10am–6pm daily.

IF YOU HAPPEN to be in the area on a Sunday morning, you will find this small round 6th-century church at the foot of the Palatine a truly delightful place to visit for a weekly mass. It is well worth going inside – the 6th-century mosaics in the apse are breathtaking, as is the Florentine cupola (1454). The very fetching outer courtyard was designed by Carlo Fontana in 1705.

The church of San Teodoro, one of Rome's hidden treasures

The Arch of Janus, where cattle dealers sheltered from the midday sun

Facade of Santa Maria della Consolazione

Santa Maria della Consolazione ⑤

Piazza della Consolazione 84.
Map 5 A5. [678 46 54. ☐ 57, 64, 90, 92, 94, 95, 160, 716.
Open 7am–noon, 3.30pm–6.30pm daily (6pm winter). [☐ ☐

THE CHURCH STANDS near the foot of the Tarpeian Rock, the site of public execution of traitors since the time of the Sabine War.

In 1385, Giordanello degli Alberini, a condemned nobleman, paid two gold florins for an image of the Virgin Mary to be placed here, to provide some small consolation to prisoners in their final moments. Hence the name of the church that was built here in 1470. It was reconstructed between 1583 and 1606 by Martino Longhi who provided the early Baroque facade.

The church's 11 side-chapels are owned by noble families and local crafts guild members. In the presbytery is the famed image of Mary, attributed to Antoniazzo Romano.

San Giovanni Decollato ⑥

Via di San Giovanni Decollato 22.
Map 8 E1. [699 07 28.
☐ 15, 57, 90, 92, 95, 160, 716.
Closed for restoration.

THE MAIN ALTAR is dominated by Giorgio Vasari's *Beheading of St John* (1553) from which the church takes its name, San Giovanni

Decollato. In 1490 Pope Innocent VIII gave this site to build a church for a very specialized Florentine confraternity. Ghoulishly attired in black robes and hoods, their task was to encourage condemned prisoners to repent and to give them a decent burial after they had been hanged. In the cloisters there are seven manholes (one of them reserved for women), which received the bodies.

The oratory contains a cycle of frescoes describing the life of St John the Baptist by the leading Florentine Mannerists, Jacopino del Conte and Francesco Salviati. In style the figures resemble some of those in the Sistine Chapel.

Casa dei Crescenzi ⑦

Via Luigi Petroselli. **Map** 8 E1. ☐ 15, 23, 57, 90, 92, 94, 95, 160, 716.

STUDDED WITH archaeological fragments, the house is what remains of a 12th-century tower fortress. It was built by the powerful Crescenzi family in order to keep an eye on the old docks of Rome (today the site of the Anagrafe or Public Records Office) and on the bridge where the family collected a toll.

Ancient Roman fragments in the Casa dei Crescenzi

Temples of the Forum Boarium ⑧

Piazza della Bocca della Verità.
Map 8 E1. ☐ 15, 23, 57, 90, 92, 94, 95, 160, 716.

Temple of Portunus

THESE MIRACULOUSLY well-preserved Republican temples are particularly appealing by moonlight, in their grassy enclave under the umbrella pines beside the Tiber. They date from the 2nd century BC and were saved for posterity when they were reconsecrated as Christian churches in the Middle Ages. They offer rare examples of combined elements from Greek and Roman architecture.

The rectangular temple (formerly known as the Temple of Fortuna Virilis) was in fact dedicated to Portunus, the god of rivers and ports – a reference to the nearby port of ancient Rome. Set on a podium, it has four Ionic travertine columns fluted at the front and 12 half-columns, embedded in the tufa wall of the *cella* – the room that housed the image of the god. Nearby is the small circular Temple of Hercules. It is often referred to as the Temple of Vesta because of its similarity to the one in the Forum.

Luminous interior of Santa Sabina

Santa Sabina ❾

Piazza Pietro d'Illiria 1. **Map** 8 E2.
📞 574 35 73. 🚌 94. **Open** 7am–
12.45pm, 3.30pm–6pm daily. 📷 ♿

H IGH ON the Aventine stands
a perfect early Christian
basilica, founded by Peter of
Illyria in AD 422 and restored
to its original simplicity early
this century. Light filters
through high 9th-century
windows on to a wide nave
framed by white Corinthian
columns supporting an arcade
decorated with a marble frieze.
Over the main door is a 5th-
century blue and gold mosaic
dedicatory inscription; the
pulpit, carved choir and
bishop's throne are from the
9th century.

The church was given to
the Dominicans in the 13th
century and in the nave is
the magnificent mosaic
tombstone of one of the first
leaders of the order, Muñoz
de Zamora (died 1300). The
side portico has 5th-century
panelled doors carved from
cypress wood, representing
scenes from the Bible,
including one of the earliest
Crucifixions in existence.

Santi Bonifacio e
Alessio ❿

Piazza di Sant'Alessio 23. **Map** 8 D2.
📞 574 34 46. 🚌 94. **Open**
8.30am–noon, 3.30 pm–6.30pm
(Oct–Mar: 6pm) daily. 📷 ♿

T HE CHURCH is dedicated to
two early Christian martyrs,
whose remains lie under the
main altar. Legend has it that

Alessio, son of a rich senator
living on the site, fled to the
East to become a pilgrim and
avoid an impending marriage.
Returning home after many
years, he died as a servant,
unrecognized, under the stairs
of the family entrance hall,
clutching the manuscript of
his story for posterity.

The original 5th-century
church has undergone
substantial changes over the
centuries. Noteworthy are the
18th-century facade with its
five arches, the restored
Cosmati doorway and
pavement, and the magnificent
Romanesque five-storey bell
tower (1217). An 18th-century
Baroque chapel by Andrea
Bergondi houses part of the
famous staircase. Other relics
include the well from Alessio's
family home and the glowing
Byzantine Madonna of the
Intercession brought to Rome
from Damascus at the end of
the 10th century.

Piazza dei Cavalieri
di Malta ⓫

Map 8 D2. 🚌 23, 57, 94, 95, 716.

S URROUNDED BY cypress
trees, this ornate walled
piazza decorated with obelisks
and military trophies was
designed by Piranesi in 1765.
It is named after the Order of
the Knights of Malta
(Cavalieri di Malta)
whose priory (at
No. 3) is famous
for the bronze
keyhole through
which there is a
miniature view of
St Peter's, framed
by a tree-lined
avenue. The priory
church, Santa
Maria del Priorato,
restored and
decorated in Neo-
Classical style by
Piranesi in the 18th
century, can be
visited with
permission from
the headquarters of
the Order. At the
southwest corner
of the square is the
international
Benedictine church

of Sant'Anselmo, where the
strains of Gregorian chant
may be heard on Sunday
mornings at 9.30am.

**Doorway of the Priory of the
Knights of Malta**

Monte Testaccio ⓬

Via Galvani. **Map** 8 D4. 🚌 27, 92.
Closed to public.

F ROM ABOUT 140 BC to AD
250 this hill was created
by the dumping of millions of
testae (hence Testaccio) –
fragments of the amphorae
used to carry goods to the
nearby warehouses. The
artificial hill is 36 m (120 ft)
high, but its full archaeological
significance was not realized
until the late 18th century.

Facade of Santi Bonifacio e Alessio

Protestant Cemetery ⑬

Via Caio Cestio 6. **Map** 8 D4.
⊠ 574 19 00. ⬚ 11, 23, 27, 57, 94,
95, 716. ⬚ 13, 30b. Ⓜ Piramide.
Open 9am–6pm (Oct–Mar: 5pm) Tue–
Sun (last adm 30 mins before closing).
Donation expected. ⬚ ⬚

T HE PEACE of this well-tended
cemetery beneath the
Aurelian Wall is profoundly
moving. Non-Catholics, mainly
English and German, have
been buried here since 1738.
In the oldest part are
the graves of John
Keats (died 1821),
whose epitaph reads:
"Here lies One
Whose Name was
writ in Water", and
his friend Joseph
Severn (died 1879);
not far away are the
ashes of Percy
Bysshe Shelley
(died 1822).
Goethe's son
Julius is also
buried here.

Tombstone of John Keats

Pyramid of Caius Cestius ⑭

Piazzale Ostiense. **Map** 8 E4. ⬚ 11, 23,
57, 94, 95. ⬚ 13, 30b. Ⓜ Piramide.

Memorial pyramid of Caius Cestius

C AIUS CESTIUS, a wealthy
praetor (senior Roman
magistrate), died in 12 BC.
His one claim to fame is his
tomb, an imposing pyramid
faced in white marble set in
the Aurelian Wall near Porta
San Paolo. It stands 27 m
(89 ft) high and, according to
an inscription, took 330 days
to build. Unmistakable as a
landmark, it must have looked
almost as incongruous when
it was built as it does today.

Detail of carving on sarcophagus in the portico of San Saba

San Saba ⑮

Via di San Saba. **Map** 8 F3.
⊠ 574 33 52. ⬚ 11, 27, 94, 673.
⬚ 13, 30b. **Open** 7am–noon,
4pm–7pm daily. ⬚ ⬚

T UCKED AWAY in a residential
street on the Little Aventine
hill, San Saba began life as an
oratory for Palestinian monks
fleeing from Arab invasions in
the 7th century. The existing
church dates from the 10th
century and has undergone
much restoration. The portico
houses a fascinating collection
of archaeological remains.
The church has three naves
in the Greek style and a short
fourth 11th-century nave to
the left with vestiges of 13th-
century frescoes of the life of
St Nicholas of Bari. Particularly
intriguing is a scene of three
naked young ladies lying in
bed, who are saved from

penury by the gift of a bag of
gold from St Nicholas, the
future Santa Claus. The
beautiful marble inlay in the
main door, the floor and the
remains of the choir are all
13th-century Cosmati work.

Circus Maximus ⑯

Via del Circo Massimo. **Map** 8 F2.
⬚ 11, 15, 27, 90, 94, 673.
⬚ 13, 30b. Ⓜ Circo Massimo.

W HAT WAS ONCE ancient
Rome's largest stadium is
today little more than a long
grassy esplanade. Set in the
valley between the Palatine
and Aventine hills, the Circus
Maximus was continually
embellished and expanded
from the 4th century BC until
AD 549 when the last races
were held. The grandstands
held some 250,000 spectators,
cheering wildly at the horse
and chariot races, athletic
contests and wild animal fights,
betting furiously throughout.
The Circus had a central
dividing barrier *(spina)* with
seven large egg-shaped objects
on it used for counting the
laps of a race. These were
joined in 33 BC by seven
bronze dolphins that served a
similar purpose. In 10 BC
Augustus built the Imperial
box under the Palatine and
decorated the *spina* with the
obelisk that now stands in the
centre of Piazza del Popolo
(see p137). A second obelisk,
which was added in the 4th
century by Constantius II, is
now in Piazza di San Giovanni
in Laterano *(see pp178–9)*.

Reconstruction of the Circus Maximus in its heyday

TRASTEVERE

THE PROUD and aggressively independent inhabitants of Trastevere, the area "across the Tiber", consider themselves the most authentic Romans. In one of the most picturesque old quarters of the city, it is still possible to glimpse scenes of everyday life that seem to belong to bygone centuries. There are, however, signs that much of the earthy, proletarian character of the place may soon be destroyed by the proliferation of fashionable restaurants, clubs and

Romanesque bell tower

boutiques. Some of Rome's most fascinating medieval churches lie hidden away in the patchwork of narrow, cobbled backstreets, the only clue to their location an occasional glimpse of a Romanesque bell tower. Santa Cecilia was built on the site of the martyrdom of the patron saint of music, San Francesco a Ripa commemorates St Francis of Assisi's visit to Rome, and Santa Maria in Trastevere is the traditional centre of the spiritual and social life of the area.

SIGHTS AT A GLANCE

Churches
Santa Maria della Scala **3**
Santa Maria dei
Sette Dolori **4**
Santa Maria in Trastevere
pp212–13 **6**
San Crisogono **7**
Santa Cecilia in Trastevere **8**
San Francesco a Ripa **9**

Museums and Galleries
Sant'Egidio and Museo
del Folklore **5**

Historic Buildings
Casa della Fornarina **1**

Bridges
Ponte Sisto **2**

Parks and Gardens
Villa Sciarra **10**

SEE ALSO

- *Street Finder*, maps 4, 7, 8, 11
- *Where to Stay* pp294–5
- *Restaurants* pp310–11
- *Tiber Walk* pp274–5

KEY

▨	Street-by-Street map
—	City Wall
P	Parking

GETTING THERE

Nearly all the bus routes that serve this area go along the broad, central Viale di Trastevere. The 75 and 170 are convenient if you are coming from Termini station or Piazza Venezia. From the Via Veneto area, take the 56 or 60, both of which have their terminus *(capolinea)* in Piazza Sonnino. From the Vatican it is best to take a 23 or 280 along Lungotevere.

0 metres   300
0 yards   300

A typical *vicolo* (narrow alleyway) between the densely-packed buildings of Trastevere

Street-by-Street: Trastevere

Aʟʟ ʏᴇᴀʀ ʀᴏᴜɴᴅ ᴛʀᴀsᴛᴇᴠᴇʀᴇ is a major attraction both for its restaurants, clubs and cinemas, and for its picturesque maze of narrow cobbled alleyways. On summer evenings the streets are packed with jostling groups of pleasure-seekers, especially during the noisy local festival, the Festa de Noantri (see p59). Everywhere café and restaurant tables spill out over pavements, especially around Piazza di Santa Maria in Trastevere and outside the pizzerias along Viale di Trastevere. There are also kiosks selling slices of watermelon and *grattachecca*, a mixture of syrup and grated ice. It is usually easier to appreciate the antique charm of Trastevere's narrow streets in the more tranquil atmosphere of the early morning.

Casa della Fornarina
Raphael's beautiful mistress is said to have lived here. There is now a flourishing restaurant in the back garden ❶

Santa Maria dei Sette Dolori
This church (1643) is a minor work by Borromini ❹

Santa Maria della Scala
The church's unassuming facade conceals a rich Baroque interior ❸

Sant'Egidio and Museo del Folklore
This 17th-century fresco of Sant' Egidio by Pomarancio decorates the left-hand chapel in the church. The convent next door is a museum of Roman life and customs ❺

★ **Santa Maria in Trastevere**
The church is famous for its 12th-century mosaics by Pietro Cavallini. This detail is from a mosaic of the prophet Isaiah to the left of the apse ❻

The fountain of Piazza di Santa Maria in Trastevere by Carlo Fontana (1692) is a popular meeting place. At night it is floodlit and dozens of young people sit on the steps around its octagonal base.

Sᴛᴀʀ Sɪɢʜᴛs

★ **Santa Maria in Trastevere**

Kᴇʏ

– – – Suggested route

0 metres	75
0 yards	75

Ponte Sisto
This bridge was built on the orders of Sixtus IV in 1474 to link Trastevere to central Rome ②

LOCATOR MAP
See Central Rome Map pp12–13

Piazza Belli is named after Giuseppe Gioacchino Belli (1791–1863), who wrote satirical sonnets in Roman dialect rather than academic Italian. At the centre of the piazza stands a statue of the poet (1913).

Vicolo del Piede is one of the picturesque narrow streets lined with restaurant tables leading off Piazza di Santa Maria in Trastevere.

The Torre degli Anguillara (13th century) is the only survivor of the many medieval towers that once dominated the Trastevere skyline. The building is home to a society devoted to the study of Dante.

San Crisogono
The Romanesque bell tower dates from the early 12th century. The plain portico is a later addition (1626), but is in keeping with the spirit of this ancient church ⑦

Restaurant at the rear of La Fornarina's house

Casa della Fornarina ❶

Via di Santa Dorotea 20. **Map** 4 D5 & 11 B5. 🏛 *581 82 84.* 🚌 *23, 65, 280.* See **Restaurants** p316.

NOTHING IS REALLY known about Raphael's model and lover, La Fornarina, yet over the centuries she has acquired a name and even a brief biography. She was called Margherita, her father was a Sienese baker (*La Fornarina* means the baker's girl) and his shop was here in Trastevere conveniently near Raphael's frescoes in the Villa Farnesina (*see pp220–21*). Behind the house there is now a successful restaurant, Da Romolo.

Margherita's longstanding liaison with Raphael earned her a reputation as a "fallen woman". Worse, Raphael, wishing to be absolved before dying, turned her away from his deathbed. Four months after his death she supposedly took refuge in the convent of Santa Apollonia in Trastevere.

She is generally assumed to have been the model for Raphael's famous portrait of *La Donna Velata* (woman with a veil) in the Palazzo Pitti in Florence.

Ponte Sisto ❷

Map 4 E5 & 11 B5. 🚌 *23, 65, 280.*

NAMED AFTER Pope Sixtus IV della Rovere (reigned 1471–84), who commissioned it, this bridge was built by his architect, Baccio Pontelli, to replace an ancient Roman

bridge. Pope Sixtus IV also built the Sistine Chapel (*see pp244–7*) and the Hospital of Santo Spirito (*see p226*), and restored many churches and monuments. The pope's enterprising spirit had to contend with great financial difficulties: his predecessor's collection of precious gems and his own silver plate had to be sold or mortgaged in order to finance his projects.

Pope Sixtus IV probably raised the money he needed to build the bridge by levying a tax on the city's prostitutes. Several popes are known to have resorted to this very unpopular form of taxation.

Pope Sixtus IV

Santa Maria della Scala ❸

Via della Scala. **Map** 4 D5 & 11 B5. 🏛 *58 06 23 30.* 🚌 *23, 65, 280.* **Church open** for mass only. 🕆 *7.30am, 5.30pm Sun & public hols.*

Santa Maria della Scala's altar

THIS CHURCH belongs to a time of great building activity that lasted about 30 years from the end of the 16th to the early 17th century. Its rather simple facade contrasts with a rich interior decorated with multicoloured marbles and a number of spirited Baroque altars and reliefs.

Santa Maria dei Sette Dolori ❹

Via Garibaldi 27. **Map** 7 B1. 🏛 *589 73 27.* 🚌 *23, 65, 280.* **Closed** to public.

BORROMINI DESIGNED this church, begun in the early 1640s and, like many of his projects, left incomplete. The rough brick facade and the convex and concave surfaces are typical of his work. Rounded corners and the impressive columns accentuate the church's small proportions.

Sant'Egidio and Museo del Folklore ❺

Piazza Sant'Egidio 1. **Map** 7 C1. 🚌 *23, 56, 60, 65, 280.* **Museo del Folklore** 🏛 *581 37 17.* **Open** *9am–6.30pm Tue–Sat, 9am–1.30pm Sun (last adm: 30 mins before closing).* **Adm charge.** **Church open** for services only. 🕆 *8.30pm daily.*

BUILT IN 1630, Sant'Egidio was the church of the adjoining Carmelite convent, one of many founded in the area to shelter the poor and destitute. The convent is now a folklore museum, containing a wealth of material relating to the festivals, pastimes, superstitions and customs of the Romans when they lived under papal rule. There are old paintings and prints of the city and tableaux showing scenes of everyday life in 18th- and 19th-century Rome, including reconstructions of shops and a tavern. The museum also has manuscripts by the much-loved local dialect poets Belli and Trilussa.

Watercolour of public scribe (1880) in the Museo del Folklore

Santa Maria in Trastevere ❻

See pp212–13.

San Crisogono ❼

Piazza Sonnino 44. **Map** 7 C1. 581 82 25. 56, 60, 75, 170, 710. **Open** 7am–11am, 4pm–7pm Mon–Sat, 8am–1pm Sun. **Adm charge** for excavations.

THIS CHURCH was built on the site of one of the city's oldest *tituli* (private houses used for Christian worship). An 8th-century church with 11th-century frescoes can still be seen beneath the present church. This dates from the early 12th century, a period of intense building activity in the popular quarters of Rome. San Crisogono was decorated by Pietro Cavallini – the apse mosaic by his school remains.

Most of the columns were taken from previous buildings, including the great porphyry ones of the triumphal arch. The mosaic floor is the result of recycling precious marble from various Roman ruins.

Apse mosaic in San Crisogono

Santa Cecilia in Trastevere ❽

Piazza di Santa Cecilia. **Map** 8 D1. 589 92 89. 56, 60, 75, 710. **Open** 10am–noon, 4pm–6pm (winter: 10am–noon, 3pm–5pm) daily. **Adm charge** for excavations. **Cavallini fresco** can be seen 10am–11.30am Tue & Thu, 11am–noon Sun.

ST CECILIA, ARISTOCRAT and patron saint of music, was martyred here in AD 230. After an attempt at scalding her to death, she was beheaded. A church was founded – perhaps in the 4th century – on the site of her house (still to be seen beneath the church, with the remains of a Roman tannery). For a long time her body went missing, but it turned up in the Catacombs of San Callisto *(see p265)*. In the 9th century it was reburied here by Pope Paschal I, who rebuilt the church. A fine apse mosaic survives from this period.

The altar canopy by Arnolfo di Cambio and the fresco of *The Last Judgment* by Pietro Cavallini, reached through the adjoining convent, date from the 13th century, one of the few periods when Rome had a distinctive artistic style of its own. In front of the altar is a statue of St Cecilia by Stefano Maderno, who used her miraculously preserved remains as a model when she was briefly disinterred in 1599.

San Francesco a Ripa ❾

Piazza San Francesco d'Assisi 88. **Map** 7 C2. 581 90 20. 44, 75, 170, 710. **Open** 7am–11.30am, 4pm–7pm daily.

ST FRANCIS OF ASSISI lived here in a hospice when he visited Rome in 1219 and his stone pillow and crucifix are preserved in his cell. The church was rebuilt by his follower, the nobleman Rodolfo Anguillara, who is portrayed on his tombstone wearing the Franciscan habit.

Entirely rebuilt in the 1680s by Cardinal Pallavicini, the church is rich in sculptures. Particularly flamboyant are the 18th-century Rospigliosi and Pallavicini monuments in the transept chapel. Not to be missed in the Altieri chapel (fourth on the left, along the nave) is Bernini's breathtaking sculpture, the *Ecstasy of Beata Ludovica Albertoni.*

Detail of 13th-century fresco by Pietro Cavallini in Santa Cecilia

Villa Sciarra ❿

Via Calandrelli 35. **Map** 7 B2. 44, 75, 710. **Park open** 9am–sunset daily. **House closed** for restoration.

IN ROMAN TIMES the site of this small, attractive public park was a nymph's sanctuary. It is especially picturesque in spring, when its cherry trees and wisterias are in full bloom. The paths through the park are decorated with Romantic follies, fountains and statues, and there are splendid views of the city over the Janiculum bastions.

Bernini's *Ecstasy of Beata Ludovica Albertoni* (1674) in San Francesco a Ripa

Santa Maria in Trastevere ❻

Pᴿᴼᴮᴬᴮᴸʸ ᴛʜᴱ ꜰɪᴿˢᵀ official Christian place of worship to be built in Rome, this basilica became the focus of devotion to the Virgin Mary. According to legend, the church was founded by Pope Callixtus I in the 3rd century, when Christianity was still a minority cult. Today's church is largely a 12th-century building, remarkable for its mosaics, in particular those by Pietro Cavallini. The 22 granite columns in the nave were taken from the ruins of ancient Roman buildings. Despite some 18th-century Baroque additions, Santa Maria has retained its medieval character. This friendly church has strong links with the local community.

Piazza Santa Maria in Trastevere
The piazza in front of the church is the traditional heart of Trastevere. Today it is surrounded by lively bars and restaurants. Carlo Fontana built the octagonal fountain in the late 17th century.

The floor, relaid in the 1870s, is a recreation of the Cosmatesque mosaic floor of the 13th century.

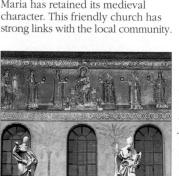

The bell tower was built in the 12th century. At the top is a small mosaic of the Virgin.

★ **Facade Mosaics**
The 12th-century mosaic shows Mary feeding the baby Jesus and ten women holding lamps. Eight of the lamps are lit, symbolizing virginity; the veiled women whose lamps have gone out are probably widows.

Sᴛᴀʀ Fᴇᴀᴛᴜʀᴇs

★ **Cavallini Mosaics**

★ **Facade Mosaics**

Mᴏᴅᴇsᴛ Dᴏɴᴏʀs
Many of Rome's mosaics include a portrait of the pope or cardinal responsible for the building of the church. Often the portrait is dwarfed by the rest of the picture, which glorifies the saint to whom the church is dedicated. On the facade of Santa Maria, two tiny unidentified figures kneel at the Virgin's feet. Were they to stand up, the men would barely reach her knees.

Facade mosaic, detail

The portico was remodelled in 1702 by Carlo Fontana. Statues of four popes decorate the balustrade above.

Front entrance

15th-century wall tabernacle by Mino del Reame

Apse Mosaic
The 12th-century mosaic in the basin of the apse shows the Coronation of the Virgin. She sits on Christ's right hand, surrounded by saints.

VISITORS' CHECKLIST

Piazza Santa Maria in Trastevere.
Map 7 C1. 581 94 43.
44, 56, 60, 75, 97, 170, 280, 710, 718, 719, 774, 780 to Viale di Trastevere (Piazza Sidney Sonnino); 23, 65 to Lungotevere Raffaello Sanzio. **Open** 7.30am–1pm, 4pm–7pm daily. 6pm daily.

★Cavallini Mosaics
The details in the six mosaics of the Life of the Virgin (1291) display a touching realism.

Madonna della Clemenza
The life-size icon probably dates from the 7th century. A replica is displayed above the altar of the Cappella Altemps.

Tomb of Cardinal Pietro Stefaneschi
The last of his line, Pietro Stefaneschi died in 1417. His tomb is by an otherwise unknown sculptor called Paolo.

TIMELINE

30 BC	AD 200	1150	1400	1650	1900

AD 217–22 Church founded by Pope Callixtus I

Pope Innocent II

1291 Pietro Cavallini adds mosaics of scenes from the life of the Virgin for his patron, Bertoldo Stefaneschi

1617 Domenichino designs coffered ceiling with octagonal panel of the Assumption of the Virgin

38 BC Jet of mineral oil spouts from the ground on this site. Later interpreted as a portent of the coming of Christ

c1138 Pope Innocent II starts rebuilding the church

1580 Martino Longhi the Elder restores church and builds family chapel for Cardinal Marco Sittico Altemps

1702 Pope Clement XI has portico rebuilt

1866–77 Church restored by Virginio Vespignani

JANICULUM

OVERLOOKING THE TIBER on the Trastevere side of the river, the Janiculum hill has often played its part in the defence of the city. The last occasion was in 1849 when Garibaldi held off the attacking French troops. The park at the top of the hill is filled with monuments to Garibaldi and his men. A popular place for walks, the park provides a welcome escape from the densely-packed streets of Trastevere.

Puppets in the park at the top of the Janiculum hill

You will often find puppet shows and other kinds of amusements for children. In medieval times most of the hill was occupied by monasteries and convents. Bramante built his miniature masterpiece, the Tempietto, in the convent of San Pietro in Montorio. The Renaissance also saw the development of the riverside area along Via della Lungara, where the rich and powerful built beautiful houses such as the Villa Farnesina.

SIGHTS AT A GLANCE

Churches and Temples
Sant'Onofrio **6**
San Pietro in Montorio **7**
Tempietto **8**

Museums and Galleries
Palazzo Corsini and Galleria Nazionale d'Arte Antica **2**

Historic Buildings
Villa Farnesina pp220–21 **1**

Fountains
Fontana Paola **9**

Monuments
Garibaldi Monument **5**

Arches and Gates
Porta Settimiana **3**

Parks and Gardens
Botanical Gardens **4**

SEE ALSO

• *Street Finder*, maps 3, 4, 7, 11
• *Where to Stay* pp294–5
• *Restaurants* pp310–11

GETTING THERE

The Janiculum (Il Gianicolo) is not the easiest part of Rome to reach by public transport. It can be approached either from the Vatican area *(see p223)* or from Trastevere *(see p207)*. There is only one bus, the 41, that goes up to the top of the hill, but the 44, 75 or 710 will take you from Piazza Venezia to a convenient point to start your walk. For sights along Via della Lungara, take the 23, 65 or 280, which go along Lungotevere.

0 metres   300
0 yards   300

KEY

▨ Tour of the Janiculum map

— City Wall

The staircase fountain in the Botanical Gardens

A Tour of the Janiculum

THE LONG HIKE to the top of the Janiculum is rewarded by wonderful views over the city. The park's monuments include a lighthouse and statues of Garibaldi and his wife Anita. There is also a cannon which is fired off at noon each day. In Via della Lungara, between the Janiculum and the Tiber, stand Palazzo Corsini with its national art collection and the Villa Farnesina, decorated by Raphael for his friend and patron, the fabulously wealthy banker Agostino Chigi.

Tasso's Oak is a memorial to the poet Torquato Tasso, who liked to sit here in the days before he died in 1595. The tree was struck by lightning in 1843.

The Manfredi Lighthouse, built in 1911, was a gift to the city of Rome from Italians in Argentina.

The Monument to Anita Garibaldi by Mario Rutelli was erected in 1932. The great patriot's Brazilian wife lies buried beneath the statue.

The view from Villa Lante, a beautiful Renaissance summer residence, gives a magnificent panorama of the whole city.

ROMA O MORTE

Garibaldi Monument
The inscription on the base of the equestrian statue means "Rome or Death" ❺

Botanical Gardens
*These were established in
1883 when part of the
grounds of Palazzo
Corsini was given
to the University
of Rome* 4

★ **Palazzo Corsini**
*This 15th-century triptych by
Fra Angelico hangs in the
Galleria Nazionale
d'Arte Antica* 2

LOCATOR MAP
See Central Rome Map pp12–13

★ **Villa Farnesina**
*The suburban villa of the
banker Agostino Chigi is
celebrated for its frescoes
by Raphael, Baldassarre
Peruzzi and other
Renaissance masters* 1

Porta Settimiana
*Looking through this
Renaissance gateway from
Via della Lungara, you catch
a glimpse of Trastevere's
warren of narrow streets* 3

KEY

– – – Suggested route

0 metres   75
0 yards   75

STAR SIGHTS

★ Villa Farnesina

★ Palazzo Corsini and
Galleria Nazionale
d'Arte Antica

Villa Farnesina ❶

See pp220–21.

Palazzo Corsini and Galleria Nazionale d'Arte Antica ❷

Via della Lungara 10. **Map** 4 D5 & 11 A5. [C] *68 80 23 23.* 🚌 *23, 41, 65, 280.* **Open** *9am–7pm Tue–Fri, 9am–2pm Sat, 9am–1pm Sun & public hols (last adm: 30 mins before closing).* **Closed** *1 May, 15 Aug, 25 Dec & 1 Jan.* **Adm charge.** 🚫 ♿ 🛈

Queen Christina's bedroom in the Palazzo Corsini

THE HISTORY of Palazzo Corsini is intimately entwined with that of Rome. Built for Cardinal Domenico Riario in the late 15th century, it has boasted among its many distinguished guests Bramante, the young Michelangelo, Erasmus and Queen Christina of Sweden, who died here in 1689. The old palazzo was completely rebuilt for Cardinal Neri Corsini by Ferdinando Fuga in 1736. As Via della Lungara is too narrow for a good frontal view, Fuga designed the facade so it could be viewed from an angle.

Palazzo Corsini now houses the Galleria Nazionale d'Arte Antica. This outstanding collection includes paintings by Rubens, Van Dyck, Murillo, Caravaggio and Guido Reni, together with 17th- and 18th-century Italian regional art. The palazzo is also home to the Accademia dei Lincei, a learned society founded in

1603, which once included Galileo among its members.

In 1797 Palazzo Corsini was the backdrop to momentous events: French General Duphot (the fiancé of Napoleon's sister Pauline) was killed here in a skirmish between papal troops and Republicans. The consequent French occupation of the city and the deportation of Pope Pius VI led to the proclamation of a short-lived Roman Republic (1798–9).

Porta Settimiana ❸

Between Via della Scala and Via della Lungara. **Map** 4 D5 & 11 B5. 🚌 *23, 65, 280.*

THIS GATE was built in 1498 by Pope Alexander VI Borgia to replace a minor passageway in the Aurelian Wall. The Porta Settimiana marks the start of Via della Lungara, a long straight road built in the early 16th century.

Botanical Gardens ❹

Largo Cristina di Svezia 24, off Via Corsini. **Map** 4 D5. [C] *686 41 93.* 🚌 *23, 65, 280.* **Open** *9am–6.30pm (Oct-Mar: 5.30pm) Mon–Sat.* **Closed** *Sun, public hols & Aug.*

SEQUOIAS, PALM TREES and splendid collections of orchids and bromeliads are housed in Rome's Botanical Gardens *(Orto Botanico).* The gardens contain more than 7,000 plant species from all over the world. Indigenous and exotic species are grouped

to illustrate their botanical families and their adaptation to different climates and eco-systems. There are also several interesting examples of plants like the gingko that have survived virtually unchanged from earlier eras. The gardens were originally part of the Palazzo Corsini, but since 1883 have belonged to the University of Rome.

Garibaldi Monument ❺

Piazzale Giuseppe Garibaldi. **Map** 3 C5. 🚌 *41, 44, 75, 710.*

Base of the Garibaldi Monument

THIS HUGE equestrian statue is part of a commemorative park, recalling the heroic events witnessed on the Janiculum when the French army attacked the city in 1849. Garibaldi's Republicans fended off the greatly superior French forces for weeks, until the Italians were overwhelmed. Garibaldi and his men escaped. The monument, erected in 1895, was the work of Emilio Gallori. Around the pedestal are four smaller sculptures in bronze showing battle scenes and allegorical figures.

Steps and tiered fountains at the Botanical Gardens

Courtyard of Sant'Onofrio

Sant'Onofrio ●

Piazza di Sant'Onofrio 2. **Map** 3 C4.
686 44 98. 41. **Open** 10am–
1.30pm Sun for mass; otherwise adm
by appt only. **Closed** Aug, except
saint's feast day on 12 Aug.
Museum open by appt only.

B EATO NICOLA da Forca
Palena, whose tombstone
guards the entrance, founded
this church in 1419 in honour
of the hermit Sant'Onofrio. It
retains the flavour of the 15th
century in the simple shapes
of the portico and the cloister.
In the early 17th century the
portico was decorated with
frescoes by Domenichino.

The monastery next to the
church houses a small museum
dedicated to the 16th-century
poet Torquato Tasso, who
died here in one of the cells.

San Pietro in Montorio ●

Piazza San Pietro in Montorio 2.
Map 7 B1. 581 39 40. 41,
44, 75, 710. **Open** 9am–noon,
4pm–6.30pm daily. If closed, ring bell
at door to right of church.

S AN PIETRO IN MONTORIO – the
church of St Peter on the
Golden Hill – was founded in
the Middle Ages near the spot
where St Peter was presumed
to have been crucified. It was
rebuilt by order of Ferdinand
and Isabella of Spain at the
end of the 15th century, and
decorated by outstanding
artists of the Renaissance.

The facade is typical of a
time when clean, geometric
shapes derived from Classical
architecture were in vogue.
The single nave ends in a
deep apse that once contained

Raphael's *Transfiguration*,
now in the Vatican. Two wide
chapels, one on either side of
the nave, were decorated by
some of Michelangelo's most
famous pupils. The left-hand
chapel was designed by one
of the few artists Michelangelo
openly admired, Daniele da
Volterra, also responsible for
the altar painting, the *Baptism
of Christ*. The chapel on the
right was the work of Giorgio
Vasari, who included a self-
portrait (in black, on the left)
in his altar painting, the
Conversion of St Paul.

The first chapel to the right
of the entrance contains a
powerful *Flagellation*, by the
Venetian artist Sebastiano del
Piombo (1518); Michelangelo
is said to have provided the
original drawings. Work by
Bernini and his followers can
be seen in the second chapel
on the left and in the flanking
De Raymondi tombs.

Tempietto ●

Via Garibaldi 33 (in courtyard of San
Pietro in Montorio). **Map** 7 B1.
581 39 40. 41, 44, 75, 710.
Open 9am–noon, 4pm–6.30pm daily.
See **The History of Rome** pp30–31.

I N 1502 BRAMANTE completed
what many consider to be
the first true Renaissance
building in Rome – the
Tempietto. The name means
simply "little temple". Its
circular shape echoes early
Christian *martyria*,
chapels built on
the site of a saint's
martyrdom. This
was believed to be
the place where St
Peter was crucified.

Bramante chose
the Doric order for
the 16 columns
surrounding the
domed chapel.
Above the columns
is a Classical frieze
and a delicate
balustrade. Though
the scale of the
Tempietto is tiny,
Bramante's masterly
use of Classical
proportions creates
a satisfyingly
harmonious whole.

The Tempietto illustrates the
great Renaissance dream that
the city of Rome would once
again relive its ancient glory.

Fontana Paola ●

Via Garibaldi. **Map** 7 B1. 41, 44,
75, 710.

Fontana Paola, built for Pope Paul V

T HIS MONUMENTAL FOUNTAIN
commemorates the
reopening in 1612 of an
aqueduct originally built by
Emperor Trajan in AD 109.
The aqueduct was renamed
the Acqua Paola after Paul V,
the Borghese pope who
ordered its restoration. When
it was first built, the fountain
had five small basins, but in
1690 Carlo Fontana altered the
design, adding the huge basin
you can see today. Despite
many laws intended to deter
them, generations of Romans
used this convenient pool of
fresh water for bathing and
washing their vegetables.

Bramante's round chapel, the Tempietto

Villa Farnesina ➊

THE WEALTHY SIENESE BANKER Agostino Chigi, who had established the headquarters of his far-flung financial empire in Rome, commissioned the villa in 1508 from his compatriot Baldassarre Peruzzi. The simple, harmonious design, with a central block and projecting wings, made this one of the earliest true Renaissance villas. The decoration was carried out between 1510 and 1519 and this has recently been restored. Peruzzi frescoed some of the interiors himself. Later, Sebastiano del Piombo, Raphael and his pupils added more elaborate works. The frescoes illustrate Classical myths, and the vault of the main hall, the Sala di Galatea, is adorned with astrological scenes showing the position of the stars at the time of Chigi's birth. Artists, poets, cardinals, princes and the pope himself were entertained here in magnificent style by their wealthy and influential host. In 1577 the villa was bought by Cardinal Alessandro Farnese. Since then, it has been known as the Villa Farnesina.

North Facade
The Loggia of Cupid and Psyche looks out on formal gardens that were used for parties and putting on plays.

Entrance

The Wedding of Alexander and Roxanne by Sodoma
Cherubs are shown helping the bride Roxanne to prepare for her marriage.

★ Triumph of Galatea by Raphael
The beautiful sea nymph Galatea was one of the 50 daughters of the god Nereus.

The Gabinetto delle Stampe sometimes holds exhibitions of rare prints.

Frescoes in the Room of Galatea
Perseus beheads Medusa in a scene from one of Peruzzi's series of mythological frescoes.

THE ARCHITECT

Baldassarre Peruzzi, painter and architect, arrived in Rome from Siena in 1503 aged 20 and became Bramante's chief assistant. Although his architectural designs were typical of Classicism, his painting owes more to Gothic influences, as his figurework is very highly stylized. On Raphael's death, he became Head of Works at St Peter's, but was captured in the Sack of Rome *(see p31)*, exiled to Siena until 1535, and died in 1536.

Baldassarre Peruzzi

★ Salone delle Prospettive

Peruzzi's frescoes create the illusion of looking out at views of 16th-century Rome through a marble colonnade.

VISITORS' CHECKLIST

Via della Lungara 230.
Map 4 D5 & 11 A5. 🚌 *23, 65, 280 to Lungotevere Farnesina.*
📞 *68 80 17 67.* **Open** *9am–1pm Mon–Sat.* 🚫 📷
Gabinetto delle Stampe *(rare print collection)* 📞 *68 98 02 30.* **Open** *9am–1pm Tue–Sat for occasional exhibitions.* 🚫

Fresco from the Salone delle Prospettive
This scene shows the Torre delle Milizie (see p90) as it looked in the 1500s.

★ Loggia of Cupid and Psyche
The model for the figure on the left in Raphael's painting of The Three Graces *was Agostino Chigi's mistress, the courtesan Imperia.*

Lunette in the Room of Galatea
This giant monochrome head by Peruzzi was once attributed to Michelangelo.

STAR FEATURES

★ **Triumph of Galatea by Raphael**

★ **Loggia of Cupid and Psyche**

★ **Salone delle Prospettive**

VATICAN

AS THE SITE where St Peter was martyred and buried, the Vatican became the residence of the popes who succeeded him. Decisions taken here have shaped the destiny of Europe, and the great basilica of St Peter's draws pilgrims from all over the Christian world. The papal palaces beside St Peter's house the Vatican Museums. With the added attractions of Michelangelo's Sistine Chapel and the Raphael Rooms, their wonderful

Nuns in St Peter's Square

collections of Classical sculpture make them the finest museums in Rome. The Vatican's position as a state within a state was guaranteed by the Lateran Treaty of 1929, marked by the building of a new road, the Via della Conciliazione. This leads from St Peter's to Castel Sant' Angelo, a monument to a far grimmer past. Built originally as the Emperor Hadrian's mausoleum, this papal fortress and prison has witnessed many fierce battles for control of the city.

SIGHTS AT A GLANCE

Churches and Temples
St Peter's pp230–33 **①**
Santo Spirito in Sassia **④**
Santa Maria in Traspontina **⑨**

Museums and Galleries
Vatican Museums pp234–47 **②**

Historic Buildings
Hospital of Santo Spirito **⑤**
Palazzo del Commendatore **⑥**
Palazzo dei Convertendi **⑦**
Palazzo dei Penitenzieri **⑧**

Palazzo Torlonia **⑫**
Castel Sant'Angelo pp248–9 **⑬**
Palazzo di Giustizia **⑭**

Gates
Porta Santo Spirito **③**

Historic Streets and Piazzas
The Borgo **⑩**
Vatican Corridor **⑪**

GETTING THERE
The quickest way to reach the area is by Metro line A to Ottaviano. This is especially convenient when visiting the Vatican Museums. The 64 bus runs regularly from Piazza dei Cinquecento, in front of Termini station. Other routes that serve the area include the 23, 81 and 492, which stop in Piazza del Risorgimento. There is a regular shuttle bus between St Peter's and the Vatican Museums.

| 0 metres | 400 |
| 0 yards | 400 |

KEY
- ▆ Tour of the Vatican map
- — City Wall
- P Parking

SEE ALSO
- **Street Finder**, maps 3, 4
- **Where to Stay** pp294–5
- **Restaurants** pp310–11

Dome of St Peter's dominating the Vatican skyline

A Tour of the Vatican

THE VATICAN, a centre of power for Catholics all over the world and a sovereign state since February 1929, is ruled by the pope. About 1,000 people live here, staffing the Vatican's facilities. There is a post office and shops, Vatican radio, broadcasting to the world in over 20 languages, a daily newspaper (*l'Osservatore Romano*), Vatican offices and a publishing house.

The Madonna of Guadalupe shows the miraculous image of the Madonna which appeared on the cloak of a Mexican Indian in 1531.

Papal heliport

The Grotto of Lourdes is a replica of the grotto in the southwest of France, where in 1858 the Virgin appeared to St Bernadette.

The Vatican Railway Station, opened in 1930, connects with the line from Rome to Viterbo, but is now used only for freight.

Radio Vatican is broadcast from this tower, part of the Leonine Wall built in 847.

The Papal Audience Chamber, by Pier Luigi Nervi, was opened in 1971. It seats up to 12,000.

The information office gives details of tours of the Vatican Gardens.

★ **St Peter's**
The Chapel of St Peter is in the Grottoes under the basilica. The rich marble decoration was added by Clement VIII at the end of the 16th century ❶

Piazza San Pietro was laid out by Bernini between 1656 and 1667. The narrow space in front of the church opens out into an enormous ellipse flanked by colonnades.

The obelisk was erected here in 1586 with the help of 150 horses and 47 winches.

STAR SIGHTS

★ **St Peter's**

★ **Vatican Museums**

The Eagle Fountain was built to celebrate the arrival of water from the Acqua Paola aqueduct at the Vatican. The eagle is the Borghese crest.

LOCATOR MAP
See Central Rome Map pp12–13

The Casina of Pius IV is a delightful summerhouse in the Vatican Gardens built by Pirro Ligorio in the mid-16th century.

Entrance to Vatican Museums

★ **Vatican Museums**
Raphael's Madonna of Foligno *(1513) is just one of the Vatican's many Renaissance masterpieces* ❷

The Galleon Fountain is a perfect scale model of a 17th-century ship in lead, brass and copper. It was made by a Flemish artist for Pope Paul V.

The Cortile della Pigna is mostly the work of Bramante. The niche for the pine cone, once a Roman fountain, was added by Pirro Ligorio in 1562.

KEY

— — — Suggested route

0 metres 75
0 yards 75

To Via della Conciliazione

St Peter's ❶

See pp230–33.

Vatican Museums ❷

See pp234–47.

Porta Santo Spirito ❸

Via dei Penitenzieri. **Map** 3 C3.
🚌 23, 34, 49, 64, 81, 492.

THIS GATE stands at what was the southern limit of the "Leonine City", the area enclosed within walls by Pope Leo IV as a defence against the Saracens who had sacked Rome in AD 845. The walls measure 3 km (2 miles) in circumference.

Work on the walls started in AD 846. Pope Leo supervised the huge army of labourers personally, and thanks to his encouragement, the job was completed in four years. He then led a solemn procession to consecrate his massive feat of construction.

Since the time of Pope Leo the walls have needed much reinforcement and repair. The gateway visible today at Porta Santo Spirito was built by the architect Antonio da Sangallo the Younger in 1543–4. It is framed by two huge bastions that were added in 1564 by

Pope Pius IV Medici. Sadly, Sangallo's design for a monumental entrance to the Vatican was never completed; the principal columns come to an end somewhat abruptly in a modern covering of cement.

Santo Spirito in Sassia ❹

Borgo Santo Spirito 4. **Map** 3 C3.
📞 687 93 10. 🚌 23, 34, 41, 46, 64.
Open 7am–12.30pm, 4pm–8pm daily. 🚹 📷 ♿

Nave of Santo Spirito in Sassia

BUILT ON THE SITE of a church erected by King Ine of Wessex, who died in Rome in the 8th century, the church is the work of Antonio da Sangallo the Younger. It was rebuilt (1538–44) after the

Sack of Rome had left it in ruins in 1527. The facade was added under Pope Sixtus V (1585–90). The nave and side chapels are decorated with a series of light, lively frescoes. The pretty bell tower is earlier, dating from the reign of Sixtus IV (1471–84). It was probably the work of the pope's architect Baccio Pontelli, who also built the nearby Hospital of Santo Spirito, and the Ponte Sisto (see p210) further down the River Tiber.

Sixtus V's arms over door of Santo Spirito

Hospital of Santo Spirito ❺

Borgo Santo Spirito 2. **Map** 3 C3.
🚌 23, 34, 41, 46, 64. **Octagonal chapel open** 8.30am–2pm daily.

THE HOSPITAL is said to have been founded as a result of a nightmare experienced by Pope Innocent III (reigned 1198–1216). In the dream, an angel showed him the bodies of Rome's unwanted babies dredged up from the Tiber in fishing nets. The pope hastened to build a hospice for sick paupers.

In 1475 the hospital was reorganized by Pope Sixtus IV

Fresco of an angel in the octagonal chapel of the Hospital of Santo Spirito

to care for the influx of poor pilgrims expected for the Holy Year. For its day, Sixtus's hospital was a revolutionary building. Cloisters separated the different categories of patient. One is still reserved for orphans and their nurses.

Unwanted infants were passed through a revolving barrel-like contraption known as the *rota,* still visible to the left of the central entrance in Borgo Santo Spirito. This was to guarantee anonymity. Martin Luther, who came here in 1511, was scandalized by the number of abandoned children he saw, believing them to be "the sons of the pope himself".

In the centre, under the hospital's conspicuous drum, is an octagonal chapel, where mass was said for patients. This room can be visited; the rest of the building still functions as a hospital.

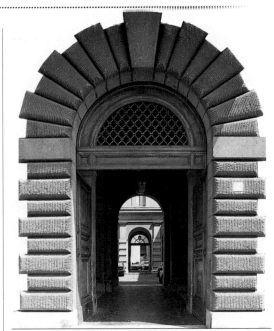

Rusticated doorway of the Palazzo dei Convertendi

The *rota* of Santo Spirito, where mothers left unwanted babies

Palazzo del Commendatore ❻

Borgo Santo Spirito 3. **Map** 3 C3.
🚌 23, 34, 41, 46, 64. **Courtyard only open** to the public.

As DIRECTOR of the Hospital of Santo Spirito, the Commendatore not only ran the hospital, he was also responsible for its estates and revenues. This important post was originally given to members of the pope's family.

The palazzo, built next door to the hospital, has a spacious 16th-century frescoed loggia appropriate to the dignity and sobriety of its owners. The frescoes represent the story of the founding of the Hospital of Santo Spirito. To the left of the entrance is the Spezieria, or Pharmacy. This still has the wheel used for grinding the bark of the cinchona tree to produce the drug quinine, first introduced here in 1632 by Jesuits from Peru as a cure for malaria.

Above the courtyard is a splendid clock (1827). The dial is divided into six; it was not until 1846 that the familiar division of the day into two periods of 12 hours was introduced in Rome by Pope Pius IX.

Palazzo dei Convertendi ❼

Via della Conciliazione 43.
Map 3 C3. 🚌 23, 34, 41, 46, 64.
Not open to the public.

With the building of Via della Conciliazione in the 1930s, Palazzo dei Convertendi was taken down and later moved to this new site nearby. The house, which is partly attributed to the architect Bramante, is where the artist Raphael died in 1520.

Palazzo dei Penitenzieri ❽

Via della Conciliazione 33. **Map** 3 C3.
📞 686 54 35. 🚌 23, 34, 41, 46, 64. *See* **Where to Stay** *p295.*

The palazzo owes its name to the fact that the place was once home to the confessors *(penitenzieri)* of St Peter's. Their place has now been taken by tourists, as the building has been converted into the Hotel Columbus. Originally built by Cardinal Domenico della Rovere in 1480, the palazzo still bears the family's coat of arms, the oak tree *(rovere* means oak), on its graceful courtyard well-head. On the cardinal's death, the palazzo was acquired by Pope Julius II della Rovere's favourite, Cardinal Francesco Alidosi. Suspected of treason, the cardinal was murdered in 1511 by the pope's nephew, the Duke of Urbino, who also took possession of his palazzo. A few of the rooms still contain beautiful frescoes.

Della Rovere arms

View of the Tiber and the Borgo between Castel Sant'Angelo and St Peter's by Gaspare Vanvitelli (1653–1736)

Santa Maria in Traspontina ❾

Via della Conciliazione 14.
Map 3 C3. 68 30 00 63.
23, 34, 41, 46, 64. **Open**
6.30am–noon, 4pm–7.30pm
daily.

The facade of the Carmelite church of Santa Maria in Traspontina

THE CHURCH occupies the site of an ancient Roman pyramid, believed in the Middle Ages to have been the Tomb of Romulus. The pyramid was destroyed by Pope Alexander VI Borgia, but representations of it survive in the bronze doors at the entrance to St Peter's and in a Giotto triptych in the Vatican Pinacoteca *(see p240)*.

The present church was begun in 1566 to replace an earlier one which had been in the line of fire of the cannons defending Castel Sant'Angelo during the Sack of Rome in 1527. The papal artillery officers insisted that the dome of the new church should be as low as possible, so it was built without a supporting drum. The first chapel to the right is dedicated to the gunners' patron saint, Santa Barbara, and is decorated with warlike motifs. In the third chapel on the left are two columns, said to be those to which St Peter and Paul were bound before martyrdom.

The Borgo ❿

Map 3 C3. 23, 34, 41, 46, 64.

THE WORD BORGO derives from the German *burg*, meaning town. Rome's Borgo is where the first pilgrims to St Peter's were housed in hostels and hospices, often for quite lengthy periods. The first of these foreign colonies, called "schools", was founded in AD 725 by a Saxon, King Ine of Wessex, who wished to live a life of penance and to be buried near the Tomb of St Peter. These days hotels and

hostels have made the Borgo a colony of international pilgrims once again. Much of the area's character was destroyed by redevelopment in the 1930s, but it is still enjoyable to explore the old narrow streets on either side of Via della Conciliazione.

Vatican Corridor ⓫

Castel Sant'Angelo to the Vatican.
Map 3 C3. 23, 34, 41, 46, 64.

Clement VII, who used the Vatican Corridor to evade capture in 1527

LOCALLY KNOWN as the Passetto (small corridor), this long passageway was built into the fortifications during medieval times. Meant to link the Vatican with the fortress of Castel Sant'Angelo, it constituted a fortified escape route which could also be used to control the strategic Borgo area. Arrows and other missiles could be fired from its bastions on to the streets and houses below. The corridor was used in 1494 by Pope Alexander VI Borgia when Rome was invaded by King Charles VIII of France. In 1527 it enabled Pope Clement VII to take refuge in Castel Sant'Angelo, as the troops commanded by the Constable of Bourbon began the Sack of Rome.

Palazzo Torlonia ⓬

Via della Conciliazione 30. **Map** 3 C3.
🚌 *23, 34, 41, 46, 64.* **Not open to** *the public.*

Palazzo Torlonia (1496), unaffected by changes to the surrounding area

THE PALAZZO was built in the late 15th century by the wealthy Cardinal Adriano Castellesi, in a style closely resembling Palazzo della Cancelleria (*see p149*). The cardinal was a much-travelled rogue, who collected vast revenues from the bishopric of Bath and Wells which he was given

Pope Leo X

by his friend King Henry VII of England. In return he gave Henry his palazzo for use as the seat of the English ambassador to the Holy See. Castellesi was finally stripped of his cardinalate by Pope Leo X Medici and disappeared from history.

Since then the palazzo has had many owners and tenants. In the 17th century it was rented for a time by Queen Christina of Sweden. The Torlonia family, who acquired the building in 1820, owed its fortune to the financial genius of shopkeeper-turned-banker Giovanni Torlonia. He lent money to the impoverished Roman nobility and bought up their property during the Napoleonic Wars.

Castel Sant'Angelo ⓭

See pp248–9.

Palazzo di Giustizia ⓮

Piazza Cavour. **Map** 4 E3. 🚌 *34, 49, 70, 87, 186, 280, 492, 990.* **Not open** *to the public.*

THE MONUMENTAL Palazzo di Giustizia (Palace of Justice) was built between 1889 and 1910 to house the national law courts. Its riverside facade is crowned with a bronze chariot and fronted by giant statues of the great men of Italian law.

The building was supposed to embody the new order replacing the injustices of papal rule, but it has never endeared itself to the Romans. It was soon dubbed the Palazzaccio (roughly, "the ugly old palazzo") both for its appearance and for the nature of its business. By the 1970s the building was collapsing under its own weight and may prove impossible to repair.

The ornate travertine facade of the Palazzo di Giustizia

St Peter's ❶

THE CENTRE of the Roman Catholic faith, St Peter's draws pilgrims from all over the world. Few are disappointed when they enter the sumptuously decorated basilica beneath Michelangelo's vast dome.

A shrine was erected on the site of St Peter's tomb in the 2nd century and the first great basilica, ordered by the Emperor Constantine, was completed around AD 349. By the 15th century it was falling down, so in 1506 Pope Julius II laid the first stone of a new church. It took more than a century to build and all the great architects of the Roman Renaissance and Baroque had a hand in its design.

★ Dome of St Peter's
Designed by Michelangelo, though not finished in his lifetime, the spectacular cupola, 132.5 m (435 ft) high, gives unity to the majestic interior of the basilica.

The nave is 211.5 m (690 ft) long.

Papal Altar
The present altar dates from the reign of Clement VIII (1592–1605). The plain slab of marble found in the Forum of Nerva stands under Bernini's baldacchino, overlooking the well of the confessio, the crypt where St Peter's body is reputedly buried.

Baldacchino
This magnificent canopy of gilded bronze, supported on spiral columns 20 m (66 ft) high, was designed by Bernini in the 17th century.

TIMELINE

AD 61 Burial of St Peter		1506 Julius II lays first stone	1547 Michelangelo named as chief architect of St Peter's		1626 New basilica of St Peter's consecrated
	324 Constantine builds basilica	1452 Nicholas V plans restoration		1593 Dome completed	

AD 60	800	1500	1550	1600	
200 Altar built marking grave of St Peter	1503 Pope Julius II chooses Bramante as architect for new basilica	1538 Antonio da Sangallo the Younger made director of works	1606 Carlo Maderno extends basilica	1614 Maderno finishes the facade	
800 Charlemagne crowned Holy Roman Emperor in St Peter's		1514 Raphael director of works	1564 Death of Michelangelo		

★ View from the Dome
The superb symmetry of Bernini's colonnade can be appreciated from the dome.

The two minor cupolas at the corners of the transept are by Vignola.

Pope Urban VIII's Keys
At the base of the columns of the baldacchino, the coat of arms of Pope Urban VIII features the keys to the Kingdom of Heaven.

VISITORS' CHECKLIST

Piazza San Pietro. **Map** 3 B3.
69 88 44 66, 69 88 48 66.
64 to Piazza San Pietro or 23, 32, 49, 81, 492, 991 to Piazza del Risorgimento. Connecting bus from Vatican Museums.
19 to Piazza del Risorgimento.
Ottaviano. **Basilica open** 7am–7pm (Oct–Mar: 6pm).
Treasury open 9am–6.30pm (Oct–Mar: 5.30pm). **Vatican Grottoes open** 7am–6pm (Oct–Mar: 5pm). **Dome open** 8am–6pm (Oct–Mar: 5pm). **Adm charge** to Treasury and Dome. **Papal audiences:** Regular public audiences, usually at 11am on Wed in Papal Audience Chamber, but sometimes in Piazza San Pietro. Tickets (free) from Prefecture of Pontifical Household (north side of piazza). **Open** 9am–1pm Mon –Sat, or write to: Prefettura della Casa Pontificia, 00120 Città del Vaticano. Appearances also at noon on Sundays at the library window to bless the crowd in Piazza San Pietro below.

Facade by Carlo Maderno (1614)

Stairs to the dome

Filarete Door
Finished in 1445, Antonio Averulino's bronze door came from the original basilica.

Entrances

Piazza San Pietro
On special religious occasions the pope appears on a balcony above the square to bless the crowds.

A Guided Tour of St Peter's

THE BASILICA is 187 m (615 ft) long and its vast marble-encrusted interior contains 11 chapels and 45 altars in addition to a wealth of precious works of art. Some were salvaged from the original basilica and others commissioned from late Renaissance and Baroque artists, but much of the elaborate decoration is owed to Bernini's work in the mid-17th century. The two side aisles are 76 m (250 ft) long and converge under Michelangelo's enormous dome. The central focus of the building is the Papal Altar beneath Bernini's great baldacchino, filling the space between four massive piers which support the dome. From the basilica you can visit the Grottoes, the Treasury and St Peter's Sacristy, or climb up to the terrace for panoramic views.

⑤ Baldacchino by Bernini
Commissioned by Pope Urban VIII in 1624, the extravagant Baroque canopy dominates the nave and crowns the Papal Altar, at which only the pope may celebrate mass.

Bernini's Monument to Urban VIII

④ Throne of St Peter in Glory
In the domed apse, look up to the window above Bernini's Baroque sculpture of 1666. It lights the image of the Holy Spirit, shown as a dove amid clouds, rays of sunlight and flights of angels.

Entrance to Treasury and Sacristy

HISTORICAL PLAN OF THE BASILICA OF ST PETER'S

St Peter was buried in AD 64 in a necropolis near his crucifixion site at the Circus of Nero. Constantine built a basilica on the burial site in AD 324. In the 15th century the old church was found to be unsafe and had to be demolished. It was rebuilt in the 16th and 17th centuries. By 1614 the facade was ready, and in 1626 the new church was consecrated.

KEY

■	Circus of Nero
■	Constantinian
■	Renaissance
■	Baroque

Entrance to Necropolis

③ Monument to Pope Alexander VII
Bernini's last work was finished in 1678 and is in an alcove on the left of the transept. The pope sits among the figures of Truth, Justice, Charity and Prudence.

② Monument to Leo XI
On the left beneath the aisle arch is Alessandro Algardi's white marble 1650 monument to Leo XI, whose reign as pope lasted only 27 days.

KEY

– – – Tour route

⑥ Angelo della Navicella
A fragment of Giotto's beautiful 13th-century mosaic, salvaged from the old basilica, is now in the Grottoes. A later copy of the entire mosaic of Jesus and St Peter fishing on Lake Tiberias decorates the atrium.

⑦ St Peter
Until recently this famous 13th-century statue, now attributed to Arnolfo di Cambio, was thought to be a late Roman work. Situated at the end of the nave, it is sculpted in bronze with a delicate filigree halo.

Entrance to Grottoes

The Tabernacle by Bernini is made of gilt bronze in the shape of a temple.

Chapel of St Sebastian

Stuart Monument by Canova

The Porta Santa (Holy Door) is opened only in Holy Years.

⑧ Pietà
This famous marble sculpture was finished in 1499 when Michelangelo was only 25. It stands in a chapel to one side of the nave, protected by glass since being damaged in 1972.

Filarete Door

Navicella Mosaic

Atrium by Carlo Maderno

① Tomb of Maria Sobieski
The first impressions of the interior of the basilica are of the vast scale and perfect symmetry. Near the entrance is Filippo Barigioni's 18th-century monument to the wife of James Stuart, the Old Pretender.

Vatican Museums ❷

THE BUILDINGS that house one of the world's most important art collections were originally papal palaces built for Renaissance popes such as Sixtus IV, Innocent VIII and Julius II. The long courtyards and galleries, linking Innocent VIII's Belvedere Palace to the other buildings, are by Donato Bramante and were commissioned for Julius II in 1503. Most of the later additions to the buildings were made in the 18th century, when priceless works of art accumulated by earlier popes were first put on show. This complex of museums also houses the Sistine Chapel and the Raphael Rooms, and should not be missed.

★ Atrium of the Four Gates
Built by Camporese in 1792–3, this vast domed edifice was the original entrance to the Vatican Museums.

The Belvedere Palace was commissioned in the late 15th century by Pope Innocent VIII.

★ Cortile della Pigna
This huge bronze pine cone, part of an ancient Roman fountain, once stood in the courtyard of old St Peter's. Its niche was designed by Pirro Ligorio.

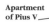

Cortile della Biblioteca

Cortile del Belvedere

Apartment of Pius V

Sistine Chapel

Borgia Tower

Borgia Apartment

Raphael Loggia

Cortile di San Damaso

STAR FEATURES

★ Cortile della Pigna

★ Atrium of the Four Gates

★ Bramante Stairway

Spiral Ramp
The spectacular stairway up to the museums from the street was designed by Giuseppe Momo in 1932.

Entrance

Simonetti Stairway
Built in the 1780s with a vaulted ceiling, the stairs were part of the conversion of the Belvedere Palace into the Pio-Clementine Museum.

Cortile Ottagonale
The inner court of the Belvedere Palace was given its octagonal shape in 1773.

★ Bramante Stairway
Pope Julius II built the spiral staircase within a square tower as an entrance to the palace. The staircase could be ridden up on horseback in case of emergency.

Braccio Nuovo

TIMELINE

1000	1500	1600	1700	1800
1198 Innocent III creates papal palace	**1503** Bramante lays out Belvedere Courtyard **1509** Raphael begins work on Rooms	**1655** Bernini designs Scala Regia	**1756** Foundation of Christian Museum	**1800–23** Chiaramonti Museum founded **1837** Etruscan Museum founded
1473 Pope Sixtus IV builds Sistine Chapel	**1503–13** Pope Julius II starts Classical sculpture collection	*Bramante (1444–1514)*	**1758** Museum of Pagan Antiquities founded **1776–84** Pius VI enlarges museum	**1822** Braccio Nuovo is opened **1970** Pope Paul VI opens Gregorian Museum of Pagan Antiquities

Exploring the Vatican Museums

Four centuries of papal patronage and connoisseurship have resulted in one of the world's great collections of Classical and Renaissance art. The Vatican houses many of the great archaeological finds of central Italy including the *Laocoön* group, discovered in 1506 on the Esquiline, the *Apollo del Belvedere* and the Etruscan bronze known as the *Mars of Todi*. During the Renaissance, parts of the museums were decorated with wonderful frescoes commissioned for the Sistine Chapel, the Raphael Rooms and the Borgia Apartment.

Mars of Todi

Gallery of the Candelabra
Once an open loggia, this gallery of Greek and Roman sculpture has a fine view of the Vatican Gardens.

Room the Big

Gallery of Tapestries

Etruscan Museum

Siege of Malta
The Gallery of Maps is an important record of 16th-century history and cartography.

Upper floor

Raphael Loggia

Modern Religious Art

Sistine Chapel

Raphael Rooms

GALLERY GUIDE
Visitors have to follow a one-way system. It is best to concentrate on a single collection or to choose one of the suggested itineraries. These are colour-coded so that you can follow them throughout the museums. They vary in length from 90 minutes to five hours. If you are planning a long visit, make sure you allow plenty of time for resting. Conserve your stamina for the Sistine Chapel and the Raphael Rooms; they are 20–30 minutes' walk from the entrance, without allowing for any viewing time along the way.

Sala dei Misteri
This is one of the rooms of the Borgia Apartment, richly decorated with Pinturicchio frescoes.

Gregorian Profane Museum

Pio-Christian Museum

Pinacoteca

St Jerome
Leonardo da Vinci's unfinished work, lost then rediscovered in the 19th century, shows the artist's mastery of anatomy.

Entrance

Round Room

Pio-Clementine Museum

Greek Cross Room

Stairs up

Egyptian Museum

Stairs down

Braccio Nuovo

Room of the Busts
This contains portraits of emperors and other notable Romans.

Chiaramonti Museum

Vatican Library

Lapidary Gallery

Lower floor

Laocoön
This 1st-century AD marble group depicts the Trojan priest Laocoön and his sons struggling with two snakes.

Room of the Animals
Roman mosaics, like these delightful ducks, decorate the walls and floor of this room of animal sculptures.

Apollo del Belvedere
This Roman copy of a Greek statue of the sun god Apollo perfectly embodies the ideals of Classical beauty.

KEY TO FLOORPLAN

- Egyptian and Assyrian art
- Greek and Roman art
- Etruscan and Italic art
- Early Christian and medieval art
- 15th- to 19th-century art
- Modern Religious art
- Non-exhibition space
- Temporarily closed

Exploring the Vatican's Collections

THE VATICAN'S GREATEST TREASURES are its Greek and
Roman antiquities. These have been on display
since the 18th century. The 19th century saw the
addition of exciting discoveries from Etruscan tombs
and excavations in Egypt. In the Pinacoteca (art gallery)
there is a small, choice collection of paintings, including
works by Raphael, Titian and Leonardo. Works by great
painters and sculptors are also on view throughout the
older parts of the museums in the form of sumptuous
decorations commissioned by the Renaissance popes.

Coloured bas-relief from an Egyptian tomb (c2400 BC)

EGYPTIAN AND ASSYRIAN ART

THE EGYPTIAN COLLECTION
contains finds from 19th-
and 20th-century excavations
in Egypt and statues which
were brought to Rome in
Imperial times. There are also
Roman imitations of Egyptian
art from Hadrian's Villa *(see
p269)* and from the Campus
Martius district of ancient
Rome. Egyptian-style statuary
from Hadrian's Villa was used
to decorate the Greek Cross
Room, the entrance to the
new wing built in 1780 by
Michelangelo Simonetti.

The genuine Egyptian works,
exhibited on the lower floor of
the Belvedere Palace, include
statues, mummies, mummy
cases and funerary artefacts.
There is also a large collection
of documents written on
papyrus, the paper the ancient
Egyptians made from reeds.
Among the main treasures is a
colossal granite statue of
Queen Tuia, the mother of
Rameses II, found on the site
of the Horti Sallustiani gardens

(see p251) in 1714. The statue,
which dates from the 13th
century BC, may have been
brought to Rome by the
Emperor Caligula (reigned
AD 37–41), who had an
unhealthy interest in
pharaohs and in his own
mother, Agrippina.

Also noteworthy are
the head of a statue of
Mentuhotep IV (21st
century BC), the
beautiful mummy
case of Queen
Hetep-heret-es,
and the tomb of
Iri, the guardian
of the Pyramid of
Cheops (22nd
century BC).

The Assyrian
Stairway is
decorated with
fragments of
reliefs from
the palaces of
the Kings of
Nineveh (8th century BC).
These depict the military
exploits of King Sennacherib
and his son Sargon II, and
show scenes from Assyrian
and Chaldean mythology.

ETRUSCAN AND OTHER PRE-ROMAN ART

THIS COLLECTION comprises
artefacts from pre-Roman
civilizations in Etruria and
Latium, from Neolithic times
to the 1st century BC, when
these ancient populations were
assimilated into the Roman
state. Pride of place in the
Gregorian Etruscan Museum
goes to the objects found in
the Regolini-Galassi tomb,
excavated in 1836 at the
necropolis of Cerveteri *(see
p271)*. The tomb was found
intact and yielded numerous
everyday household objects,
plus a throne, a bed and a
funeral cart, all cast in bronze,
dating from the 7th century
BC. Beautiful black vases,
delightful terracotta figurines
and bronze statues such as
the famous *Mars of Todi*,
displayed in the Room of the
Bronzes, show the Etruscans
to have been a highly civilized,
sophisticated people.

A number of Greek vases
that were found in Etruscan
tombs are on display in the
Vase Collection. The Room of
the Italiot Vases contains only
vases produced locally in the
Greek cities of Southern Italy
and in Etruria itself. These
date from the 3rd to the 1st
century BC.

**Etruscan
gold clasp
(fibula)
from the 7th
century BC**

Head of an athlete in mosaic from the Baths of Caracalla

GREEK AND ROMAN ART

THE GREATER PART of the Vatican Museums is dedicated to Greek and Roman art. Exhibits line connecting corridors and vestibules; walls and floors display fine mosaics; and famous sculptures decorate the main courtyards.

The first serious organization of the collection took place in the reign of Julius II (1503–13) around Bramante's Belvedere Courtyard. The prize pieces form the nucleus of the 18th-century Pio-Clementine Museum. In the pavilions of the Octagonal Courtyard and in the surrounding rooms are sculptures considered among the greatest achievements of Western art. The *Apoxyomenos* (an athlete wiping his body after a race) and the *Apollo del Belvedere* are high-quality Roman copies of Greek originals of about 320 BC. The magnificent *Laocoön*, sculpted by three artists from Rhodes, had long been known to exist from a description by Pliny the Elder. It was rediscovered near the ruins of Nero's Golden House *(see p175)* in 1506. Classical works such as these had a profound influence on Michelangelo and other Renaissance artists.

The much smaller Chiaramonti Museum, named after Pope Pius

VII Chiaramonti, was laid out by Canova in the early 19th century. It includes a striking colossal head of the goddess Athene. The Braccio Nuovo, an extension of the Chiaramonti, decorated with Roman floor mosaics, contains a statue of Augustus from the villa of his wife Livia at Prima Porta. Its pose is based on the famous *Doryphoros* by the Greek sculptor Polyclitus, of which there is a Roman copy on display opposite.

Exhibits in the Vase Rooms range from the Greek geometric style (8th century BC) to black-figure vases from Corinth, such as the famous vase by Exekias, with Achilles and Ajax playing a game similar to draughts (530 BC), and the later red-figure type, such as the *kylix* (a wide shallow cup) with Oedipus and the Sphinx from the 5th century BC. A stairway links this section to the Gallery of the Candelabra and the Room of the Biga (a two-horse chariot). The horses and harness were added in the 18th century.

The Gregorian Profane Museum, housed in a new wing, charts the evolution of Roman art from dependence upon Greek models to a recognizably Roman style.

The *Doryphoros* or spear-carrier, a Roman copy in marble of an original Greek bronze

Original Greek works include large marble fragments from the Parthenon in Athens. There is also a Roman copy of *Athene and Marsyas* by Myron, which was part of the decoration of the Parthenon. Totally Roman in character are two reliefs known as the Rilievi della Cancelleria,

Marble relief of the Emperor Vespasian

because they were discovered beneath the Palazzo della Cancelleria *(see p149)* in the 1930s. They show military parades of the Emperor Vespasian and his son Domitian. This section also has fine Roman floor mosaics. There are two from the Baths of Caracalla *(see p197)*, depicting athletes and referees. They date from the 3rd century AD. Most striking of all is a mosaic that creates the impression of an unswept floor, covered with debris after a meal. Away from the main Classical collections, in one of the rooms of the Vatican Library, is the *Aldobrandini Wedding*, a beautiful Roman fresco of a bride being prepared for her marriage, dating from the 1st century AD.

Floor mosaic from the Baths of Otricoli in Umbria, in the Round Room

Detail from Giotto's *Stefaneschi Triptych*

EARLY CHRISTIAN AND MEDIEVAL ART

THE MAIN COLLECTION of early Christian antiquities is in the Pio-Christian Museum, founded in the last century by Pope Pius IX and formerly housed in the Lateran Palace. It contains inscriptions and sculpture from catacombs and early Christian basilicas. The sculpture consists chiefly of reliefs decorating sarcophagi, though the most striking work is a free-standing 4th-century statue of the *Good Shepherd*. The sculpture's chief interest lies in the way it blends Biblical episodes with pagan mythology. Christianity adopted Classical images so that its doctrines could be understood in clear visual terms. The idealized pastoral figure of the shepherd, for example, became Christ himself, while bearded philosophers turned into the Apostles. At the same time, Christianity laid claim to be the spiritual and cultural heir of the Roman Empire.

The first two rooms of the Pinacoteca are dedicated to late medieval art, mostly wooden panels painted in tempera which served as altarpieces. The outstanding work is Giotto's altarpiece dating from about 1300, known as the *Stefaneschi Triptych*. It expresses much the same theme as the early Christian works: the continuity between the Classical world of the Roman Empire and the new order of Christian Europe. The crucifixion of St Peter takes place between two landmarks of ancient Rome, the Pyramid of Caius Cestius *(see p205)*, and the pyramid known in the Middle Ages as the Tomb of Romulus, which stood near the Vatican. The triptych, which decorated the main altar of old St Peter's, includes portraits of Pope St Celestine V (reigned 1294–6), and of the donor, Cardinal Jacopo Stefaneschi, shown offering the triptych to St Peter.

The Vatican Library has a number of medieval treasures exhibited rather haphazardly in showcases; these include woven and embroidered cloths, reliquaries, enamels and icons. One of the aims of the 18th-century reorganization of the Vatican collections was to glorify Christian works by contrasting them with earlier pagan creations. In the long Lapidary Gallery over 3,000 stone tablets with Christian and pagan inscriptions are displayed on opposite walls. The world's greatest collection of its kind, it may be visited only with special permission.

15TH- TO 19TH- CENTURY ART

THE RENAISSANCE POPES, many of whom were cultured connoisseurs of the arts, considered it their duty to sponsor the leading painters, sculptors and goldsmiths of

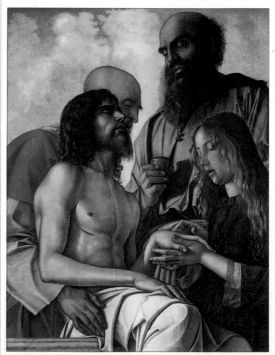

***Pietà* by the Venetian artist Giovanni Bellini (1430–1516)**

RAPHAEL'S LAST PAINTING

When Raphael died in 1520, the *Transfiguration* was found in his studio, almost complete. The wonderful luminous work was placed at the head of the bier where the great artist's body lay. It depicts the episode in the Gospels in which Christ took three of the Apostles to the top of a mountain, where He appeared to them in divine glory. In the detail shown here Christ floats above the ground in a halo of ethereal light.

the age. The galleries around the Cortile del Belvedere were all decorated by great artists between the 16th and the 19th centuries. The Gallery of Tapestries is hung with tapestries woven in Brussels to designs by students of Raphael; the Apartment of Pope Pius V has beautiful 15th-century Flemish tapestries; and the Gallery of Maps is frescoed with 16th-century maps of ancient and contemporary Italy. When you go to visit the Raphael Rooms *(see pp242–3)*, you should not overlook the nearby Room of the Chiaroscuri and Pope Nicholas V's tiny private chapel, frescoed by Fra Angelico between 1447 and 1451. Similarly, before reaching the Sistine Chapel *(see pp244–7)*, visit the Borgia Apartment, frescoed in a decorative, flowery style by Pinturicchio and his students in the 1490s. The contrast with Michelangelo's Sistine Chapel ceiling, begun in 1508, could hardly be greater. Another set of fascinating frescoes decorates the Loggia of Raphael, but this requires special permission to visit.

Many important works by Renaissance masters are on show in the Pinacoteca (art gallery). Highlights among the works by 15th-century painters are a fine *Pietà* by the Venetian Giovanni Bellini and Leonardo da Vinci's unfinished *St Jerome*. Of the

great 16th-century works, do not miss the fine altarpiece by Titian, the *Crucifixion of St Peter* by Guido Reni, the *Deposition* by Caravaggio and the *Communion of St Jerome* by Domenichino. Raphael has a whole room dedicated to his work. It contains the beautiful *Madonna of Foligno* and the *Transfiguration* as well as eight tapestries made to his designs.

Lunette of the *Adoration of the Magi* by Pinturicchio in the Room of the Mysteries in the Borgia Apartment

MODERN RELIGIOUS ART

MODERN ARTISTS exhibited in the Vatican Museums face daunting competition from the great works of the past. Few modern works are displayed conspicuously, the exceptions being Momo's spiral staircase of 1932, which greets visitors as they enter the museums, and Giò Pomodoro's abstract sculpture in the centre of the Cortile della Pigna.

In 1973 a contemporary art collection was inaugurated by Pope Paul VI. Housed in the Borgia Apartment, it includes over 800 exhibits by modern artists from all over the world, donated by collectors or the artists themselves. Works in a great variety of media show many contrasting approaches to religious subjects. There are paintings, drawings, engravings and sculpture by 19th- and 20th-century artists, as well as mosaics, stained glass, ceramics and tapestries. Well-known modern painters such as Georges Braque, Paul Klee, Edvard Munch and Graham Sutherland are all represented. There are also drawings by Henry Moore, ceramics by Picasso and stained glass by Fernand Léger. Projects for modern church ornaments include Matisse's decorations for the church of St Paul de Vence, Luigi Fontana's models for the bronze doors of Milan cathedral, and Emilio Greco's panels for the doors of Orvieto cathedral.

***Town with Gothic Cathedral* by Paul Klee (1879–1940)**

Raphael Rooms

POPE JULIUS II'S PRIVATE APARTMENTS were built above those of his hated predecessor, Alexander VI, one of the Borgias, who died in 1503. Julius was impressed with Raphael's work and chose him to redecorate the four

rooms *(stanze)*. Raphael and his pupils began the task in 1508, replacing existing works by several better-known artists, including Raphael's own teacher, Perugino. The work took over 16 years and Raphael himself died before its completion. The frescoes express the religious and philosophical ideals of the Renaissance. They quickly established Raphael's reputation as an artist in Rome, putting him on a par with Michelangelo, then working on the ceiling of the Sistine Chapel.

Detail from *The Expulsion of Heliodorus from the Temple*, showing Pope Julius II watching the scene from his litter

KEY TO FLOORPLAN

① Hall of Constantine

② Room of Heliodorus

③ Room of the Segnatura

④ Room of the Fire in the Borgo

HALL OF CONSTANTINE ①

THE FRESCOES in this room were started in 1517, three years before Raphael's death, but Raphael himself probably had little hand in their execution. As a result they are not held in the same high regard as those in the other rooms. The work was completed in 1525 in the reign of Pope Clement VII by Giulio Romano and two other former pupils of Raphael, Giovanni Francesco Penni and Raffaellino del Colle.

The theme of the decoration is the triumph of Christianity over paganism. The four major frescoes show scenes from the life of Constantine and include his *Vision of the Cross* and his victory over his rival Maxentius at *The Battle of the Milvian Bridge*, for which Raphael had provided a preparatory sketch. In both *The Baptism of Constantine* and *The Donation of Constantine*, the figure of Pope Sylvester *(see p170)* was given the features of Clement VII.

ROOM OF HELIODORUS ②

THIS PRIVATE antechamber was decorated by Raphael between 1512 and 1514. The main frescoes show the miraculous protection granted to all the Church's ministers, doctrines and property. The room's name refers to the fresco on the right, *The Expulsion of Heliodorus from the Temple*. This shows a story from Jewish history, in which a thief called Heliodorus is felled

Swiss guards waiting with papal chair in *The Mass at Bolsena*

by a horseman as he tries to make off with the treasure from the Temple of Jerusalem. The scene is witnessed by the pope, borne on a litter by courtiers. The incident is also a thinly-veiled reference to Julius II's success in driving foreign armies out of Italy. In *The Meeting of Leo I and Attila* Raphael pays a similar compliment to the pope's political skill. Pope Leo was originally given the face of Julius II, but after his death, Raphael substituted the features of Julius's successor, Leo X.

The Mass at Bolsena depicts a miracle that occurred in 1263. A priest

***The Battle of the Milvian Bridge*, completed by one of Raphael's assistants**

The Liberation of St Peter, a three-part composition, shows the saint asleep in his cell in the middle section, led out of prison by an angel on the right, while, on the left, the prison guards cower in terror

who doubted that the bread and wine really were the body and blood of Christ suddenly saw the host bleed while he was celebrating mass. Julius II appears in this fresco, accompanied by a colourful group of Swiss guards.

Julius appears yet again as St Peter in *The Liberation of St Peter*. This fresco is remarkable for its dramatic lighting effects, achieved despite the painting's awkward shape and its position above a window.

ROOM OF THE SEGNATURA ③

THE NAME is derived from a special council which met in this room to sign official documents. The frescoes here were completed between 1508 and 1511. The scheme Raphael followed was dictated by Pope Julius II. It reflects the Humanist belief that there could be perfect harmony between Classical culture and Christianity in their mutual search for truth.

The Dispute over the Holy Sacrament, the first fresco completed by Raphael for Pope Julius, represents the triumph of religion and spiritual truth. The consecrated host is shown at the centre of the painting. This links the group of learned scholars, who discuss its significance, to the Holy Trinity and the saints floating on clouds up above.

On the opposite wall, *The School of Athens (see p30)* is a bustling scene

centred around the debate on the search for truth between Greek philosophers Plato and Aristotle. It also features portraits of many of Raphael's contemporaries, including Leonardo da Vinci, Bramante and Michelangelo. The other works include a portrait of the bearded Pope Julius II, who in 1511 vowed not to shave until he managed to rid Italy of all usurpers.

ROOM OF THE FIRE IN THE BORGO ④

THIS WAS ORIGINALLY the dining room, but when the decoration was completed under Pope Leo X, it became a music room. All the frescoes exalt the reigning pope by depicting events in the lives of his namesakes, the 9th-century popes Leo III and IV. The main frescoes were finished by two of Raphael's assistants between 1514 and 1517,

following their master's own plans. The most famous, *The Fire in the Borgo*, was painted from Raphael's designs and reflects his maturity as an artist. It celebrates the miracle that took place in 847, when Pope Leo IV extinguished a fire raging in the Borgo *(see p228)* by making the sign of the cross. The incident is likened to the flight of Aeneas from Troy described by Virgil. The figure of Aeneas appears in the foreground carrying his father on his back. This borrowing of an event from Classical legend shows a new willingness to experiment on the part of Raphael. Sadly, his pupils did not always follow his designs faithfully and this, combined with some poor restoration, has spoilt the work.

Detail from *The Fire in the Borgo*, showing Aeneas, the Trojan hero, with his father on his back, fleeing from the fire

The Dispute over the Holy Sacrament, the first fresco completed in the Rooms

Sistine Chapel: The Walls

THIS IS the main chapel in the Vatican Palace, named Cappella Sistina after its founder, Pope Sixtus IV. Its massive walls were frescoed by some of the finest artists of the 15th and 16th centuries, including Michelangelo, Perugino and Botticelli. The 12 paintings on the side walls show parallel episodes from the lives of Moses and of Christ. The decoration of the chapel walls was completed by Michelangelo, who added the great altar wall fresco, *The Last Judgment*.

KEY TO THE FRESCOES: ARTISTS AND SUBJECTS

The Last Judgment

☐ Perugino   ☐ Botticelli   ☐ Ghirlandaio

☐ Rosselli   ☐ Signorelli   ☐ Michelangelo

1 Baptism of Christ in the Jordan
2 Temptations of Christ
3 Calling of St Peter and St Andrew
4 Sermon on the Mount
5 Handing over the Keys to St Peter
6 Last Supper
7 Moses's Journey into Egypt
8 Moses Receiving the Call
9 Crossing of the Red Sea
10 Adoration of the Golden Calf
11 Punishment of the Rebels
12 Last Days of Moses

THE LAST JUDGMENT BY MICHELANGELO

Detail showing figure of Christ

AMONG MICHELANGELO's last works in the refurbished Sistine Chapel, *The Last Judgment* was completed in 1541 and is considered the masterpiece of his mature years. Commissioned by Pope Paul III Farnese, the work required the destruction of some earlier frescoes and the removal of two windows above the altar. A new wall was erected which slanted inwards to stop the dust settling on it. Michelangelo worked unassisted on the fresco for seven years.

The painting depicts the souls of the dead rising up to face the wrath of God, a subject rarely used for an altar decoration. It was chosen by the pope as a warning to Catholics to adhere to their faith in the turmoil of the Reformation. In fact the work conveys the artist's own tormented attitude to his faith.

The huge fresco offers none of the soothing certainties of Christian orthodoxy, nor the ordered world view of Classicism. In a dynamic, emotional composition, the figures are caught up in a swirling vortex of motion. The dead are torn from their graves and hauled up to face Christ the Judge, whose athletic, muscular figure is the focus of all the painting's movement.

Christ shows little sympathy for the agitated saints who surround him, clutching the instruments of their martyrdom. Neither is any pity shown towards the damned, hurled downwards to the demons in hell. Here Charon, pushing people off his boat into the depths of Hades, and the infernal judge Minos, are taken

Looking towards *The Last Judgment*

from Dante's *Inferno*. Minos is given a pair of ass's ears, and is actually a portrait of courtier Biagio da Cesena, who had objected to the nude figures in the fresco. Michelangelo's self-portrait can be spotted on the skin held by the martyr St Bartholomew. The painting illustrates the artist's belief that suffering is vital in finding faith in God.

St Bartholomew with his skin, bearing the face of Michelangelo

WALL FRESCOES

**Detail from Botticelli's fresco
*Temptations of Christ***

WHEN THE Sistine Chapel was built, the papacy was a strong political power with vast accumulated wealth. In 1475 Pope Sixtus IV was able to summon some of the greatest painters of his day to decorate the chapel. Among the artists employed were Perugino, who was Raphael's master and is often credited with overseeing the project, Sandro Botticelli, Domenico Ghirlandaio, Cosimo Rosselli and Luca Signorelli. Their work on the chapel's frescoes took from 1481 to 1483.

Although frequently overlooked by visitors who concentrate on Michelangelo's work, the frescoes along the side walls of the chapel include some of the finest works of 15th-century Italian art. The two cycles of frescoes represent scenes from the lives of Moses and Christ. Above them in the spaces between the windows are portraits of the earliest popes, painted by various artists, including Botticelli.

The fresco cycles start at the altar end of the chapel, with the story of Christ on the right-hand wall and that of Moses on the left. Originally there were two paintings, *The Birth of Christ* and *The Finding of Moses*, on the wall behind the altar, but these were both destroyed to make way for Michelangelo's *The Last Judgment*.

The final paintings of the two cycles are also lost. They were on the entrance wall, which collapsed during the 16th century. When the wall was restored, they were replaced with poor substitutes.

As was customary at the time, each fresco contains a series of scenes, linked thematically to the central episode. Hidden meanings and symbols connect each painting with its counterpart on the opposite wall, and there are also many allusions to contemporary events.

The elaborate architectural details in the frescoes include familiar Roman monuments. The Arch of Constantine *(see p91)* provides the backdrop for the *Punishment of the Rebels* by Botticelli, the fifth panel in the cycle of Moses, in which the artist himself appears as the last figure but one on the right. Two similar arches appear in the painting opposite, Perugino's *Handing over the Keys to St Peter*.

Moses was both spiritual and temporal leader of his people. He called down the wrath of God on those who challenged his decisions, thus

The crowd of onlookers in the *Calling of St Peter and St Andrew* by Ghirlandaio

setting a precedent for the power exercised by the pope. In *Handing over the Keys to St Peter*, Christ confers spiritual

and temporal authority on St Peter by giving him the keys to the Kingdoms of Heaven and Earth. The golden-domed building in the centre of the vast piazza represents both the Temple of Jerusalem and the Church, as founded by Peter, the first pope. The fifth figure on the right is thought to be a self-portrait by Perugino.

Botticelli's *Temptations of Christ* includes a view of the

**The central episode in Botticelli's
*Punishment of the Rebels***

Hospital of Santo Spirito, rebuilt in 1475 by Sixtus IV *(see p226)*. Here the devil is disguised in the habit of a Franciscan monk. Portraits of both Botticelli and Filippino Lippi are visible in the left hand corner. A portrait of the pope's nephew, Girolamo Riario, appears in the painting of the *Crossing of the Red Sea* by Rosselli, in which the sea is literally red. This painting also commemorates the papal victory at Campomorto in 1482.

Perugino's *Handing over the Keys to St Peter*

Sistine Chapel: The Ceiling

MICHELANGELO FRESCOED the chapel ceiling for Pope Julius II between 1508 and 1512. Refusing assistance, he worked alone on specially designed scaffolding. The subjects are from the Old Testament – except for the Classical Sibyls, who appear because they were said to have prophesied the birth of Christ. The main picture here shows the ceiling before its recent restoration; the smaller details show the colours revealed after cleaning.

The Creation of Adam
A powerful but tender study of hands shows Adam receiving spiritual grace and intellectual strength from God.

Creation of the Sun and Moon
On the third day the dynamic figure of God the Creator commands the sun to shed its light on the earth.

```
10  15  26  17  28  19  30  21  32  23  12
14   1   2   3   4   5   6   7   8   9  25
11  16  27  18  29  20  31  22  33  24  13
```

KEY

☐ **GENESIS 1** God Dividing Light from Darkness; **2** Creation of the Sun and Moon; **3** Separating Waters from Land; **4** Creation of Adam; **5** Creation of Eve; **6** Original Sin; **7** Sacrifice of Noah; **8** The Deluge; **9** Drunkenness of Noah.

☐ **ANCESTORS OF CHRIST 26** Solomon with his Mother; **27** Parents of Jesse; **28** Rehoboam with Mother; **29** Asa with Parents; **30** Uzziah with Parents; **31** Hezekiah with Parents; **32** Zerubbabel with Parents; **33** Josiah with Parents.

☐ **PROPHETS 14** Jonah; **15** Jeremiah; **18** Daniel; **19** Ezekiel; **22** Isaiah; **23** Joel; **25** Zechariah.

☐ **SIBYLS 16** Libyan Sibyl; **17** Persian Sibyl; **20** Cumaean Sibyl; **21** Erythrean Sibyl; **24** Delphic Sibyl.

☐ **OLD TESTAMENT SCENES OF SALVATION 10** Punishment of Haman; **11** Moses and the Brazen Serpent; **12** David and Goliath; **13** Judith and Holofernes.

The Creation of Eve
God has just created Eve from one of the sleeping Adam's ribs. The shape of the tree suggests Christ's Cross.

Original Sin shows the tasting of the Tree of Knowledge and the expulsion of Adam and Eve from the Garden of Eden.

The Ignudi are athletic male nudes that frame the main scenes on the ceiling.

The Deluge concentrates on the figures of the people stranded by the flood.

Delphic Sibyl
The beautiful prophetess of the Greek Oracle of Delphi is portrayed in a moment of intense inspiration.

Castel Sant'Angelo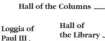

T HE MASSIVE FORTRESS of Castel Sant'Angelo takes
its name from the statue of the Archangel
Michael on its summit. It began
life in AD 139 as the Emperor
Hadrian's mausoleum. Since
then it has had many roles: as
part of the Emperor Aurelian's
city wall, as a medieval citadel and prison, and as
the residence of the popes in times of political unrest.
From the dank cells in the lower levels to the fine
apartments of the Renaissance popes above, a 58-
room museum covers all aspects of the castle's history.

Mausoleum of Hadrian
*This artist's impression shows
the tomb before Aurelian
fortified its walls in AD 270–75.*

Courtyard of Honour
*Heaps of stone cannonballs
decorate the courtyard, once
the castle's ammunition store.*

The Treasury was probably
the original site of Hadrian's
burial chamber.

Hall of the Columns

**Loggia of
Paul III**

**Hall of
the Library**

PROTECTING THE POPE
The Vatican Corridor leads from
the Vatican Palace to Castel
Sant'Angelo. It was built in 1277
to provide an escape route
when the pope was in danger.
The pentagonal ramparts built
around the castle during the
17th century improved its
defences in times of siege.

**The Rooms of
Clement VIII**
are inscribed with
the family crest of
the Aldobrandini
pope (1592–1605).

The spiral ramp
was the entrance
to the mausoleum.

The Hall of Justice is
decorated with a fresco
of *The Angel of Justice* by
Domenico Zaga (1545).

■ Walls and fortifications

□ Vatican Corridor

★ **View from Terrace**
*The castle's terrace, scene of the
last act of Puccini's* Tosca, *offers
splendid views in every direction.*

**The Chamber of
the Urns** housed the
ashes of members of
Hadrian's family.

STAR FEATURES

★ **Sala Paolina**

★ **View from Terrace**

★ **Staircase of Alexander VI**

VISITORS' CHECKLIST

Lungotevere Castello. **Map** 4 D3 & 11 A1. 687 50 36. 23, 64, 87, 280 to Lungotevere Castello; 34, 49, 64, 70, 81, 186, 926, 990 to Piazza Cavour. Lepanto. **Open** 9am–7pm daily (last adm: 1 hr before closing). **Closed** public hols, 2nd & 4th Tue of month. **Adm charge.** 10.30am Sun only. **Exhibitions.**

Bronze Angel
The gigantic statue of the Archangel Michael is by the 18th-century Flemish sculptor Pieter Verschaffelt.

The Round Hall houses the original model from which Verschaffelt's angel was cast.

★ Sala Paolina
The illusionistic frescoes by Perin del Vaga and Pellegrino Tibaldi (1544–7) include one of a courtier entering the room through a painted door.

Hall of Apollo
The room is frescoed with scenes from mythology attributed to the pupils of Perin del Vaga (1548).

Ventilation shaft

★ Staircase of Alexander VI
This staircase cuts right through the heart of the building.

Bridge

TIMELINE

AD 139 Mausoleum completed by Antoninus Pius	**590** Legendary date of appearance of Archangel Michael above the castle	**1493** Pope Alexander VI restores Vatican Corridor	*Facade of Castel Sant'Angelo*
		1390 Pope Boniface IX remodels the castle	
AD 100	**500**	**1000**	**1500**
271 Tomb is incorporated into Aurelian Wall and fortified		**1527** Castle withstands siege during Sack of Rome	**1557** Ramparts built to protect the castle
AD 130 Hadrian begins family mausoleum	*Cannonballs in the Courtyard of Honour*	**1542–9** Sala Paolina and apartments built for Pope Paul III	**1870** Castle used as barracks and military prison

VIA VENETO

IN IMPERIAL ROME, this was a suburb where rich families owned luxurious villas and gardens. Ruins from this era can be seen in the excavations in Piazza Sallustio, named after the most extensive gardens in the area, the Horti Sallustiani.

Film director Federico Fellini

After the Sack of Rome in the 5th century, the area reverted to open countryside. Not until the 17th century did it recover its lost splendour, with the building of Palazzo Barberini and the now-vanished Villa Ludovisi.

When Rome became capital of Italy in 1870, the Ludovisi sold their land for development. They kept a plot for a new house, but tax on the profits from the sale was so high, they had to sell that too. By 1900, Via Veneto had become a street of smart modern hotels and cafés. It featured prominently in Fellini's 1960 film *La Dolce Vita*, a scathing satire on the lives of film stars and idle rich, but since then has lost its position as the meeting place of the famous.

SIGHTS AT A GLANCE

Churches and Temples
Santa Maria della Concezione ❸
Santa Susanna ❼
Santa Maria della Vittoria ❽

Historic Buildings
Casino dell'Aurora ❷
Palazzo Barberini ❻

Famous Streets
Via Veneto ❶

Fountains
Fontana delle Api ❹
Fontana del Tritone ❺

SEE ALSO

- *Street Finder*, map 5
- *Where to Stay* pp294–5
- *Restaurants* pp310–11

0 metres 200

0 yards 200

N

GETTING THERE

This is one of the easiest parts of Rome to reach by public transport. Barberini and Repubblica Metro stations on line A are very handy, and Stazione Termini is only 10–15 minutes' walk away. The Via Veneto itself starts at Piazza Barberini, well served by buses from all parts of the city. The 95 goes the whole length of Via Veneto to Porta Pinciana. Other useful routes include the 52, 53, 56, 58 and 60 along Via del Tritone.

KEY

▨	Street-by-Street map
—	City Wall
Ⓜ	Metro station
Ⓟ	Parking

The onset of autumn in Via Veneto

Street-by-Street: Via Veneto

T HE STREETS AROUND VIA VENETO, though within the
walls of ancient Rome, contain little dating from
before the unification of Italy in 1870. With its hotels,
restaurants, bars and travel agencies, the area is the
centre of 20th-century tourism in the way that Piazza di
Spagna was the hub of the tourist trade in the Rome of
the 18th-century Grand Tour. However, glimpses of the
old city can be seen among the modern streets. These
include Santa Maria della Concezione, the church of the
Capuchin friars, whose convent once stood in its own
gardens. In the 17th century Palazzo Barberini was built
here for the powerful papal family. Bernini's Fontana
del Tritone and Fontana delle Api have stood in Piazza
Barberini since it was the meeting place of cart tracks
entering the city from
surrounding vineyards.

Casino dell'Aurora
*A pavilion is all that
remains of the great
Ludovisi estate that
once occupied most of
this quarter of Rome* ❷

**Santa Maria della
Concezione**
*This church is best
known for the
macabre collection of
bones in its crypt* ❸

Fontana delle Api
*Bernini's drinking
fountain is decorated
with bees, emblem
of his Barberini
patrons* ❹

Fontana del Tritone
*Bernini's muscular sea god
has been spouting water
skywards for 350 years* ❺

VIA VENETO

PIAZZA BARBERINI

VIA DI SAN NICOLA DA TOLENTI

Ⓜ

VIA DI SAN BASILIO

VIA BARBERINI

★ **Palazzo
Barberini**
*Pietro da Cortona
worked on his spectacular
ceiling fresco* The Triumph of Divine
Providence *between 1633 and 1639* ❻

VIA XX SETTEMBRE

The Porta Pinciana was built in AD 403. Only the central arch of white travertine is original.

Villa Borghese

VIA VENETO

QUIRINAL

LOCATOR MAP
See Central Rome Map pp12–13

Via Veneto
Built during the redevelopment of Rome at the end of the 19th century, this street of smart hotels and spacious pavement cafés enjoyed its heyday during the 1950s and 1960s ❶

STAR SIGHTS

★ **Santa Maria della Vittoria**

★ **Palazzo Barberini**

Santa Susanna
This church is dedicated to a martyr executed during Diocletian's persecution of Christians in the 3rd century AD ❼

KEY

– – – Suggested route

0 metres   75

0 yards   75

★ **Santa Maria della Vittoria**
The highlight of this Baroque church is the Cornaro Chapel, designed to resemble a theatre. The centre of the stage is occupied by Bernini's thrilling sculpture of the Ecstasy of St Teresa ❽

Pavement café in Via Veneto

Via Veneto ❶

Map 5 B1. 🚌 *52, 53, 56, 58, 58b, 95, 490, 495 and many other routes.* Ⓜ *Barberini.*

Via Veneto descends in a lazy curve from the Porta Pinciana to Piazza Barberini, lined in its upper reaches with exuberant turn-of-the-century hotels and canopied pavement cafés. It was laid out in 1879 over a large estate sold by the Ludovisi family in the great building boom of Rome's first years as capital of Italy. Palazzo Margherita, intended to be the new Ludovisi family palazzo, was completed in 1890. It now houses the American embassy.

In the 1960s this was the most glamorous street in Rome, its cafés patronized by film stars and plagued by the *paparazzi*. Most of the people drinking in the cafés today are tourists, as film stars now seem to prefer the livelier bohemian atmosphere of Trastevere.

Palazzo Margherita, the US embassy

Casino dell'Aurora ❷

Via Lombardia 46. **Map** 5 B2. 🗧 *48 39 42.* 🚌 *52, 53, 56, 58.* **Open** by appt only.

The casino (a stately country residence) was a summerhouse in the grounds of the Ludovisi palace. It was built by Cardinal Ludovisi in

the 17th century, and frescoed by Guercino. The subject of the ceiling fresco is Aurora, the goddess of dawn. It is a dizzying work creating the impression that the Casino has no roof, but lies open to a cloudy sky, across which horses pull Aurora's carriage away from the darkness of night towards the light of day.

Santa Maria della Concezione ❸

Via Veneto 27. **Map** 5 B2. 🗧 *487 11 85.* 🚌 *52, 53, 56, 58, 58b, 490, 495 and many other routes.* Ⓜ *Barberini.* **Open** *7am–noon, 3.45pm–7.30pm daily.* **Crypt open** *9am–noon, 3pm–6pm Fri–Wed.* **Donation** *expected.* ✝ 📷

Pope Urban VIII's brother, Antonio Barberini was a cardinal and a Capuchin friar. In 1626 he founded this plain, unassuming church at what is now the foot of the Via Veneto. When he died he was buried not, like most cardinals, in a grand marble sarcophagus, but below a simple flagstone close to the altar, where you can read the bleak epitaph in Latin: "Here lies dust, ashes, nothing".

The grim reality of death is illustrated even more graphically in the crypt beneath the church, where generations of Capuchin friars have decorated the walls of the five vaulted chapels with the bones and skulls of their departed brethren. In all, some 4,000 skeletons were used to create this macabre *memento mori*. Some of the bones are wired together to form Christian symbols such as crowns of thorns, sacred hearts and crucifixes. There are also a number of complete skeletons, including one of a Barberini princess who died as a child. At the exit, an inscription in Latin reads: "What you are, we used to be. What we are, you will be."

Pope Urban VIII

Fontana delle Api ❹

Piazza Barberini. **Map** 5 B2. 🚌 *52, 53, 56, 58, 58b, 490, 495 and many other routes.* Ⓜ *Barberini.*

The fountain of the bees – *api* are bees, symbol of the Barberini family – is one of Bernini's more modest works. Tucked away in a corner of Piazza Barberini, it is quite easy to miss. Dating from 1644, it pays homage to Pope Urban VIII Barberini, and features rather crab-like bees which appear to be sipping the water as it dribbles down into the basin. A Latin inscription informs us that the water is for the use of the public and their animals.

Bernini's Fontana delle Api

Fontana del Tritone ❺

Piazza Barberini. **Map** 5 B3. 🚌 *52, 53, 56, 58, 58b, 490, 495 and many other routes.* Ⓜ *Barberini.*

In the centre of busy Piazza Barberini is one of Bernini's liveliest fountains, the Triton Fountain. It was created for Pope Urban VIII Barberini in 1642, shortly after the completion of his palace on the ridge above. Acrobatic dolphins stand on their heads, twisting their tails together to support a huge scallop shell on which the sea god Triton kneels, blowing a spindly column of water up into the air through a conch shell. Entwined artistically among the dolphins' tails are the papal tiara, the keys of St Peter and the Barberini coat of arms.

The Triton and his conch shell in Bernini's Fontana del Tritone

Palazzo Barberini ❻

Via delle Quattro Fontane 13. **Map** 5 B3.
🕻 481 45 91. 🚌 52, 53, 56, 58, 58b, 490, 495 and many other routes. Ⓜ Barberini. **Open** 9am–7pm Tue–Sat, 9am–1pm Sun and public hols (last adm: 30 mins before closing). **Adm charge**. 📷

WHEN MAFFEI BARBERINI became Pope Urban VIII in 1623 he decided to build a grand palace for his family. The site he chose was then on the fringes of the city, over-looking a ruined temple. The architect, Carlo Maderno, designed it as a typical rural villa, with wings extending into the surrounding gardens. Maderno died in 1629, shortly after the foundations had been laid, and Bernini took over, assisted by Borromini. The peculiar pediments on some of the top floor windows, and the oval staircase inside, are almost certainly by Borromini.

Of the many sumptuously decorated rooms, the most striking is the Gran Salone, with a dazzling illusionistic ceiling fresco by Pietro da Cortona. The palazzo also houses paintings from the 13th to the 16th centuries, part of the Galleria Nazionale d'Arte Antica, with important works by Filippo Lippi, El Greco and Caravaggio. There is also a Holbein portrait of King Henry VIII of England dressed for his wedding to Anne of Cleves. Of greater local significance are Guido Reni's *Beatrice Cenci*, the young woman executed for planning her father's murder *(see p150)*, and *La Fornarina*, traditionally identified as a portrait of Raphael's mistress, although not painted by him.

Santa Susanna ❼

Piazza San Bernardo. **Map** 5 C2. 🕻 482 75 10. 🚌 16, 36, 37, 60, 61, 62, 910 and many other routes. Ⓜ Repubblica. **Open** 9.30am–noon, 4pm–7pm Mon–Sat, 10am–noon Sun.

Facade of Santa Susanna

SANTA SUSANNA'S most striking feature is its vigorous Baroque facade by Carlo Maderno, finished in 1603. Christians have worshipped on the site since at least the 4th century. In the nave, there are four huge frescoes by Baldassarre Croce (1558–1628), painted to resemble tapestries. These depict scenes from the life of Susanna, an obscure Roman saint who was martyred here, and the rather better-known life of the Old Testament Susanna, who was spotted bathing in her husband's garden by two lecherous judges.

When it has been restored, Santa Susanna will resume its function as the Catholic church for Americans in Rome.

Santa Maria della Vittoria ❽

Via XX Settembre 17. **Map** 5 C2.
🕻 482 61 90. 🚌 16, 36, 37, 60, 61, 62, 910 and many other routes.
Ⓜ Repubblica. **Open** 6.30am–noon, 4.30pm–7pm daily. 🕇 🚫

SANTA MARIA della Vittoria is an intimate Baroque church with a lavishly decorated candlelit interior. It contains one of Bernini's most ambitious sculptural works, the *Ecstasy of St Teresa* (1646), centrepiece of the Cornaro Chapel, built to resemble a miniature theatre. It even has an audience: sculptures of the chapel's benefactor, Cardinal Federico Cornaro, and his ancestors sit in boxes, as if watching and discussing the scene played out in front of them.

Visitors may be shocked or thrilled by the apparently physical nature of St Teresa's ecstasy. She lies on a cloud, her mouth half open and her eyelids closed, with rippling drapery covering her body. Looking over her with a smile, which from different angles can appear either tender or cruel, is a curly-haired angel holding an arrow with which he is about to pierce the saint's body for a second time. The marble figures are framed and illuminated by rays of divine light materialized in bronze.

Bernini's astonishing *Ecstasy of St Teresa*

FURTHER AFIELD

THE MORE INQUISITIVE visitor to Rome may wish to try a few excursions to the large parks and some of the more isolated churches on the outskirts of the city. With a day to spare, you can explore the villas of Tivoli and the ruins of the ancient Roman port of Ostia. Traditional haunts of the

Dish (3rd century BC) in Villa Giulia

Grand Tour *(see p130)*, such as the catacombs and the ruined aqueducts of Parco Appio Claudio, still offer glimpses of the rapidly vanishing Campagna, the country-side around Rome. More modern sights include the suburb of EUR, built in the Fascist era, and the memorial at the Fosse Ardeatine.

SIGHTS AT A GLANCE

Towns and Areas
EUR ⑭
Tivoli ⑰

Historic Roads
Via Appia Antica ➐

Churches
Santa Costanza ➍
Sant'Agnese fuori le Mura ➎
San Lorenzo fuori le Mura ➏
San Paolo fuori le Mura ⑮

Museums and Galleries
Museo Borghese pp260–61 ➋
Villa Giulia pp262–3 ➌

Parks and Gardens
Villa Borghese ➊
Parco Appio Claudio ⑬
Villa Doria Pamphilj ⑯
Villa d'Este ⑱
Villa Gregoriana ⑲

Ancient Sites
Hadrian's Villa ⑳
Ostia Antica ㉑

Tombs and Catacombs
Catacombs of San Callisto ➑
Catacombs of San Sebastiano ➒
Catacombs of Domitilla ➓
Fosse Ardeatine ⑪
Tomb of Cecilia Metella ⑫

KEY

███ Main sightseeing areas

══ Motorway

0 kilometres 2

0 miles 1

SIGHTS OUTSIDE ROME

SIGHTS OUTSIDE THE CENTRE

Caryatids beside the canal of the Canopus at Hadrian's Villa

Villa Borghese ●

Map 2 E5. 🚌 *3, 4, 52, 53, 57, 95, 490, 495, 910.* 🚊 *19, 19b, 30b.*
Park open *dawn to sunset.* **Zoo** *Viale del Giardino Zoologico.* **Map** *2 E4.*
📞 *321 65 64.* 🚌 *3, 52, 910.* 🚊 *19, 19b, 30b.* **Open** *8.30am–4.30pm (last adm: 3.30pm) daily.* **Closed** *1 May.*
📷 ♿ 🍴 🛍 📕

Galleria Nazionale d'Arte Moderna
Viale delle Belle Arti 131. **Map** *2 D4.*
📞 *322 981.* 🚊 *19, 19b, 30b.* **Open** *9am–7pm Tue–Sat; 9am–1pm Sun & public hols.*
🚫 ♿ 🛍 📕 📕

British School at Rome, designed by Edwin Lutyens in 1911

T HE VILLA and its park were designed in 1605 for Cardinal Scipione Borghese, nephew of Pope Paul V. The park was the first of its kind in Rome. It contained 400 newly-planted pine trees, garden sculpture by Bernini's father, Pietro, and dramatic waterworks built by Giovanni Fontana. The layout of the formal gardens was imitated by other prominent Roman families at Villa Ludovisi and Villa Doria Pamphilj, but the cardinal's 18th-century successors preferred a more natural-looking park.

In the early 19th century Prince Camillo Borghese assembled the family's magnificent art collection in the Casino Borghese, now the home of the Galleria and Museo Borghese.

In 1902 the park became the property of the Italian state. Within its 6-km (4-mile) circumference there are now museums and galleries, foreign academies and schools of archaeology, a zoo, a riding school, a grassy amphitheatre, an artificial lake, an aviary and an array of summer houses, fountains, Neo-Classical statuary and exotic follies.

There are several ways into the park, including a monumental entrance on Piazzale Flaminio, built for Prince Camillo Borghese in 1825 by Luigi Canina. Other conveniently-sited entrances are at Porta Pinciana at the end of Via Veneto and from the Pincio Gardens *(see p136)*. The main attraction of Italian gardens in hot weather is shade, so the long avenues are lined with hedges and trees. Piazza di Siena, a pleasantly open, grass-covered amphitheatre surrounded by tall umbrella pines, was the inspiration for Ottorino Respighi's famous symphonic poem *The Pines of Rome,* written in 1924. Near Piazza di Siena are the so-called Casina di Raffaello, said to have been owned by Raphael, and the

18th-century Palazzetto dell'Orologio. These were summerhouses from which people enjoyed the beautiful vistas across the park. Many buildings in the park were originally surrounded by formal gardens: the Casino Borghese and the nearby 17th-century Casino della Meridiana and its aviary (the Uccelliera) have both kept their geometrical flowerbeds. Throughout the park the intersections of paths and avenues are marked by fountains and statues. West of Piazza di Siena is the Fontana dei Cavalli Marini (the Fountain of the Seahorses) added during the villa's 18th-century remodelling. Walking through the park you will encounter statues of Byron, Goethe and Victor Hugo, and a gloomy equestrian King Umberto I.

Dotted about the park are picturesque temples made to look like ruins, including a circular Temple of Diana between Piazza di Siena and Porta Pinciana, and a Temple of Faustina, wife of Emperor Antoninus Pius, on the hill north of Piazza di Siena. The nearby medieval-looking Fortezzuola by Canina contains the works of the sculptor Pietro Canonica, who lived in the building and died there in 1959. In the garden stands Canonica's *Monument to the Alpino and his Mule,* which honours the humblest

Statue of the English poet Byron by Thorvaldsen

Neo-Classical Temple of Diana

Ionic temple dedicated to Aesculapius, built on the lake island

protagonists in Italy's alpine battles against Austria in World War I.

In the centre of the park is the Giardino del Lago, its main entrance marked by an 18th-century copy of the Arch of Septimius Severus.

The garden has an artificial lake complete with an Ionic Temple to Aesculapius, the god of health, by the 18th-century architect Antonio Asprucci. Rowing boats and ducks make the lake a favourite with children, banana trees and bamboo grow around the shore, and clearings are studded with sculptures.

Surrounded by flowerbeds south of the lake is the Art Nouveau Fontana dei Fauni, one of the garden's prettiest sculptures. In a clearing close to the entrance on Viale Pietro Canonica are the original Tritons of the Fontana del Moro in Piazza Navona *(see p120)* – they were moved here and replaced by copies in the 19th century.

From the northwest the park is entered by the Viale delle Belle Arti, where the Galleria Nazionale d'Arte Moderna houses a fairly uninspiring collection of 19th- and 20th-century paintings. The Art Nouveau character of the area dates from the International Exhibition held here in 1911, for which pavilions were built by many nations, the most impressive being the British School at Rome, by Edwin Lutyens,

with a facade adapted from the upper west portico of St Paul's Cathedral in London. Originally a School of Archaeology, the school now offers the chance to study literature, fine arts and history. The statues close by are equally international: they include Simon Bolivar and other liberators of Latin America, and the great Persian poet Firdusi.

Beyond the art gallery, in the northeastern corner of the park, lie a rather depressing Zoo and the Museo Zoologico. A far greater attraction is the pretty 16th-century Villa Giulia with its world-famous collection of Etruscan and other pre-Roman remains.

Zoo entrance

Another Renaissance building of importance is the Palazzina of Pius IV, close to the Via Flaminia entrance. It was designed by the architect Vignola in 1552 and then transformed into an elegant apartment for Pius IV's nephew Carlo Borromeo. It is now the home of the Italian Embassy to the Holy See.

Museo Borghese ❷

See pp260–61.

Villa Giulia ❸

See pp262–3.

A stone lion guarding the ornate entrance to the Zoo

Museo Borghese ②

THE VILLA AND PARK were laid out by Cardinal Scipione Borghese, favourite nephew of Paul V, who had the house designed for pleasure and entertainment. The hedonistic cardinal was also an extravagant patron of the arts and he commissioned sculptures from the young Bernini which now rank among his most famous works. Scipione also opened his pleasure park to the public. Today the villa houses the superb private Borghese collection of sculptures and paintings in the Museo and Galleria Borghese.

Facade of the Villa Borghese
This painting (1613) by the villa's Flemish architect Jan van Santen shows the highly ornate facade of the original design.

MUSEUM GUIDE

The museum is divided into two sections: the sculpture collection (Museo Borghese) occupies the entire ground floor and the picture gallery (Galleria Borghese) is on the upper floor. The Galleria Borghese has reopened to the public after extensive restoration work.

★ Pluto and Persephone
One of Bernini's finest works, the sculpture shows Pluto carrying off his bride. The sculptor's astonishing skill with marble can be clearly seen in the twisting figures.

Sleeping Hermaphrodite

Dated around 150 BC, this is a bronze Roman copy of the Greek original by Polycles. The head and mattress were added by Andrea Bergondi in the 17th century.

The Egyptian Room
Frescoes show episodes in Egyptian history and Egyptian motifs.

TIMELINE

1613 15-year-old Bernini sculpts *Aeneas and Anchises*	**Early 1800s** Statues and reliefs are considered too ornate and stripped from the villa's facade	**1809** Much of the collection is sold by Prince Camillo Borghese to France and goes to Louvre	**1902** Villa, grounds and collection bought by the state
1621–5 Bernini sculpts *Pluto and Persephone*			
1625	**1725**	**1825**	
1622–5 Bernini sculpts *Apollo and Daphne*		**1805** Canova sculpts the semi-nude, reclining Pauline Borghese	**Early 1900s** Balustrade round the forecourt is bought by Lord Astor for the Cliveden estate in England
1613–15 The Flemish architect Jan van Santen designs and builds Villa Borghese	*Daphne's fingers turning into leaves*		

Rear entrance

★ **Apollo and Daphne**
Bernini's most famous masterpiece depicts the nymph Daphne fleeing the sun god Apollo at the moment of Daphne's dramatic transformation into a tree.

★ **David**
Modelling David's face on his own, the 25-year-old Bernini captured the moment before David threw the stone that slew Goliath.

★ **Pauline Borghese**
Napoleon's sister Pauline posed as Venus for the sculptor Canova. Once the statue was completed, Pauline's husband Camillo Borghese kept it locked away, even denying Canova access.

Front entrance

Gladiator Mosaic
The floor is decorated with the fragments of a 4th-century AD mosaic from a villa in Torrenova.

KEY TO FLOORPLAN

☐ Exhibition space

▨ Non-exhibition space

STAR SCULPTURES

★ **Pauline Borghese by Canova**

★ **Apollo and Daphne by Bernini**

★ **David by Bernini**

★ **Pluto and Persephone by Bernini**

Villa Giulia ⊙

THIS VILLA was built as a country retreat for Pope Julius III, and was designed for entertaining rather than as a permanent home. It once housed an impressive collection of statues – 160 boatloads were sent to the Vatican after the pope died in 1555. The villa, gardens, pavilions and fountains were designed by exceptional architects: Vignola (designer of the Gesù), Vasari and the sculptor Ammannati. Michelangelo also contributed. The villa's main features are its facade, the courtyard and garden and the *nympheum*. Since 1889 Villa Giulia has housed the Museo Nazionale Etrusco, with its outstanding collection of pre-Roman antiquities from central Italy.

Faliscan Crater of the Dawn
This ornate vase, painted in the free style of the 4th century BC, shows Dawn rising in a chariot.

First floor

Chigi Vase
Battle and hunting scenes adorn this Corinthian vase from the 6th century BC.

★ **Husband and Wife Sarcophagus**
This 6th-century BC masterpiece, from Cerveteri, shows a dead couple at the eternal banquet.

Museum Guide
*This is the most important Etruscan museum in Italy, housing artefacts from most of the major excavations in Tuscany and Lazio. Rooms **1–10** and **23–34** are arranged by site and include Vulci, Todi, Veio and Cerveteri, while private collections are in rooms **11–22**.*

Votive Offering
The religious Etruscans made artefacts, such as this model of a boy feeding a bird, in their gods' honour.

TIMELINE

1550 Work begins on Villa Giulia under Pope Julius III	**1655** Queen Christina of Sweden stays in villa as Vatican guest	**1889** Etruscan museum founded **Late 1700s** First large-scale studies of Etruscan artefacts	**1919** Castellani private collection donated to museum	
1550	**1650**	**1750**	**1850**	**1950**
Late 1500s First, chance finds of Etruscan artefacts raise some scholastic interest			**1908** Barberini private collection bought by the state	**1972** Pesciotti private collection bought by the state
1555 Villa completed	*Corner decoration of bronze chariot used to burn incense*			

Facade
The villa's facade dates from 1552–3. The entrance is designed in the form of a triumphal arch.

★ Reconstruction of an Etruscan Temple
Count Adolfo Cozza built the Temple of Alatri here in 1891. He based his design on the accounts of Vitruvius and 19th-century excavations.

Nympheum
Literally, the "area dedicated to the nymphs", this is a sunken courtyard decorated with Classical mosaics, statues and fountains.

STAR EXHIBITS

★ Husband and Wife Sarcophagus

★ Ficoroni Cist

★ Reconstruction of an Etruscan Temple

Main entrance

Ground floor

★ Ficoroni Cist
Engraved and beautifully illustrated, this fine bronze marriage coffer dates from the 4th century BC.

KEY TO FLOORPLAN

▢ Ground floor

▢ First floor

▢ Non-exhibition space

Santa Costanza ❹

Via Nomentana 349. **℡** *861 08 40.*
▥ *36, 36b, 37, 60, 136, 137.* **Open**
*9am–noon Mon–Sat, 4pm–6pm Tue–
Sat, 4pm–6pm Sun and public hols.*
Adm charge. 📷 ⛐ 🎫

**Circular interior of 4th-century
church of Santa Costanza**

THE ROUND CHURCH of Santa
Costanza was originally
built in the early 4th century
as a mausoleum for Emperor
Constantine's daughters
Constantia and Helena. The
dome and its drum are
supported by a circular arcade
which rests on 12 magnificent
pairs of granite columns. The
ambulatory that runs around
the outside of the central
arcade has a barrel-vaulted
ceiling decorated with
wonderful 4th-century mosaics
of fruit, flowers, animals and
birds and even charming
scenes of a Roman grape
harvest. In a niche on the far
side of the church from the
entrance is a replica of
Constantia's ornately carved
porphyry sarcophagus. The
original was moved to the
Vatican Museums in 1790.

Constantia's sanctity is
somewhat debatable – she
was described by the historian Marcellinus as a fury
incarnate, constantly goading
her equally unpleasant
husband Hannibalianus to
violence. Her canonization
was probably the result of
some confusion with a saintly
nun of the same name.

Part of the 4th-century mosaic in the ambulatory of Santa Costanza

Sant'Agnese fuori le Mura ❺

Via Nomentana 349. **℡** *861 08 40.*
▥ *36, 36b, 37, 60, 136, 137.* **Open**
*9am–noon Mon–Sat, 4pm–6pm Tue,
Sat, Sun and public hols.* **Adm charge**
to catacombs. 📷 ⛐ 🎫

THE CHURCH OF Sant'Agnese
stands among a group of
early Christian buildings which
includes the ruins of a covered
cemetery, some extensive
catacombs and the crypt where
the 13-year-old martyr St Agnes
was buried in AD 304. Agnes
was exposed naked by order
of Emperor Diocletian, furious
that she should have rejected
the advances of a young man
at his court, but her hair
miraculously grew to protect
her modesty. The church is
said to have been built at the
request of the Emperor
Constantine's daughter,
Constantia, after she had
prayed at the Tomb of St Agnes
for delivery from leprosy.

Though much altered over
the centuries, the form and
much of the structure of the
4th-century basilica remain
intact. In the 7th-century apse
mosaic St Agnes appears as a
bejewelled Byzantine empress
in a stole of gold and a violet
robe. According to tradition
she appeared like this eight
days after her death holding a
white lamb. Every year on 21
January two lambs are blessed
on the church altar and a
vestment called the *pallium* is
woven from their wool. Every
newly-appointed archbishop
is sent a *pallium* by the pope.

Steps leading down to Sant'Agnese

San Lorenzo fuori le Mura ❻

Piazzale del Verano 3. **℡** *49 15 11.*
▥ *11, 71, 492.* **▤** *19, 19b, 30b.*
Open *7am–noon, 4pm–5.30pm daily.*
📷 ⛐

JUST OUTSIDE the eastern wall
of the city, set off by the
cypresses of the Campo
Verano cemetery, stands the

Apse mosaic in Sant'Agnese, showing the saint flanked by two popes

church of San Lorenzo.
Roasted slowly to death in
AD 258, San Lorenzo was one
of the most revered of Rome's
early Christian martyrs. The
first basilica erected over his
burial place by Constantine
was largely rebuilt in 576 by
Pope Pelagius II. Close by
stood a 5th-century church
dedicated to the Virgin Mary.
The intriguing two-levelled
church we see today is the
result of these two churches
being knocked into one. This
process, started in the 8th
century, was completed in
the 13th century by Pope
Honorius III, when the nave,
the portico and much of the
decoration were added. The
remains of San Lorenzo are in
the choir of the 6th-century
church (beneath
the 13th-century
high altar).
   The church
was restored
after it was
badly damaged
by Allied
bombers in an
air raid during
World War II.

**Romanesque
bell tower of
San Lorenzo**

**12th-century cloister of
San Lorenzo fuori le Mura**

either side lies a vast maze of
catacombs. Today the road
starts at Porta San Sebastiano
(see p196). Major Christian
sights include the church of
Domine Quo Vadis?, built on
the spot where St Peter is
said to have met Christ while
fleeing from Rome, and the
Catacombs of San Callisto
and San Sebastiano. Among
the tombs lining the road
are those of Cecilia Metella
(see p266) and of Romulus,
son of the Emperor Maxentius,
who died in AD 309.

Via Appia Antica ❼

*218. See **Walks** pp284–5.*

THE FIRST PART of the Via
Appia was built in 312 BC
by the Censor Appius Claudius
Caecus. When it was extended
to the ports of Benevento,
Taranto and Brindisi in 190
BC, the road became Rome's
link with its expanding
empire in the East. It was the
route taken by the funeral
processions of the dictator
Sulla (78 BC) and Emperor
Augustus (AD 14) and it was
along this road that St Paul
was led a prisoner to Rome
in AD 56.
   Gradually abandoned
during the Middle Ages, the
road was restored in the mid-
16th century by Pope Pius IV.
It is lined with ruined family
tombs and the collective burial
places known as columbaria,
while beneath the fields on

Catacombs of San Callisto ❽

*Via Appia Antica 110. 513 67 25.
218, 660. **Open** 8.30am–noon,
2.30pm–5.30pm (Oct–Mar: 5pm)
Thu–Tue. **Closed** February and public
hols. **Adm charge.***

IN BURYING their dead in
underground cemeteries
outside the city walls, the
early Christians were simply
obeying the laws of the time.
They were not forced to use
them because of persecution.
Because so many saints were
buried there, the catacombs
later became shrines and
places of pilgrimage.
   The vast Catacombs of San
Callisto are on four different
levels and only partly explored.
The rooms and connecting
passageways are hewn out of
volcanic tufa. The dead were

placed in niches, known as
loculi, which held two or three
bodies. The most important
rooms were decorated with
stucco and frescoes. The area
that can be visited includes
the Crypt of the Popes, where
many of the early popes were
buried, and the Crypt of Santa
Cecilia, where the saint's body
was discovered in 820 before
being moved to her church in
Trastevere (see p211).

Catacombs of San Sebastiano ❾

*Via Appia Antica 136. 788 70 35.
218, 660. **Open** 8.30am–noon,
2.30pm–5.30pm Fri–Wed. **Closed**
14 Nov–12 Dec, public hols. **Adm
charge.***

THE 17TH-CENTURY church of
San Sebastiano, above the
catacombs, occupies the site
of a basilica from the age of
Constantine. Preserved at the
entrance to the catacombs is
the *triclia*, a building that
once stood above ground
and was used by parties of
mourners for taking funeral
refreshments. Its walls are
covered with graffiti invoking
St Peter and St Paul, whose
remains may have been
moved here during one of the
periods when the Christians
were persecuted by the
Roman authorities.

Cypresses lining the Via Appia

Catacombs of Domitilla ❿

Via delle Sette Chiese 282.
📞 511 03 42. 🚌 94, 218, 613.
Open 8.30am–noon, 2.30pm–
5.30pm (Oct–Mar: 5pm) Wed–Mon.
Closed Jan. **Adm charge.** 🚫 📷

THIS NETWORK of catacombs
is the largest in Rome.
Many of the tombs from the
1st and 2nd centuries AD
have no Christian connection.
In the burial chambers that
can be visited there are
frescoes of both Classical and
Christian scenes, including
one of the earliest depictions
of Christ as the *Good Shepherd*.
Above the catacombs stands
the basilica of Santi Nereo e
Achilleo. After rebuilding and
restoration, little remains of
the original 4th-century church.

Fosse Ardeatine ⓫

Via Ardeatina 174. 📞 513 67 42.
🚌 218. **Open** 8.30am–5pm daily
(last adm: 30 mins before closing).
📷

ON THE EVENING of 24 March
1944, Nazi forces took 335
prisoners to this abandoned
quarry south of Rome and shot
them at point blank range.
The execution was in reprisal
for a bomb attack that had
killed 32 German soldiers.
The victims included various
political prisoners, 73 Jews
and ten other civilians, among
them a priest and a 14-year-
old boy. The Germans blew
up the tunnels where the
massacre had taken place, but
a local peasant had witnessed
the scene and later helped

find the corpses. The site is
now a memorial to the values
of the Resistance against the
Germans, which gave birth to
the modern Italian Republic.
A forbidding bunker-like
monument houses the rows
of identical tombs containing
the victims. Beside it is a
museum of the Resistance.
Interesting works of modern
sculpture include *The Martyrs*,
by Francesco Coccia, and the
gates shaped like a wall of
thorns by Mirko Basaldella.

**Bronze entrance gates to the Fosse
Ardeatine by Mirko Basaldella**

Tomb of Cecilia Metella ⓬

Via Appia Antica, III Miglio.
📞 780 24 65. **Open** 9am–
1 hr before sunset (7pm latest)
Tue–Sat, 9am–1pm Mon & Sun.
Closed public hols. 📷

ONE OF THE most famous
landmarks on the Via
Appia Antica is the huge drum-
shaped tomb built for the noble
Cecilia Metella. Her father and
husband were rich patricians
and successful generals of late
Republican Rome, but hardly
anything is known about the

**Fragments of marble relief on the
Tomb of Cecilia Metella**

woman herself. Byron muses
over her unknown destiny in
his poem *Childe Harold*. In
1302 Pope Boniface VIII gave
the tomb to his family, the
Caetani, who incorporated it
in a fortified castle that blocked
the Via Appia, allowing them
to control the traffic on the
road and exact high tolls. The
marble facing of the tomb
was pillaged by Pope Sixtus V
at the end of the 16th century.

Parco Appio Claudio ⓭

Via Lemonia. 🚌 557, 558, 650,
663, 664, 765. **Open** 24 hrs daily.

THE PARK covers a large
expanse of land between
the Via Appia Nuova and the
Via Tuscolana. One day it
may become part of one vast
archaeological park stretching
from here to the Colosseum
and the Forum. Its main
features are the remains of
three aqueducts, the Aqua
Marcia dating from 140 BC,
the Aqua Claudia, completed
in AD 52 by the Emperor
Claudius, and the Felice

Ruins of the Aqua Claudia aqueduct (1st century AD) in the Parco Appio Claudio

Aqueduct built by Sixtus V in the 16th century. The arches of Roman aqueducts carried water in separate conduits from two or three different sources *(see pp20–21)*. The area is an excellent place to enjoy uninterrupted views of the Roman Campagna and the Alban hills to the south.

EUR ⑭

🚌 93, 97, 197, 293, 493, 765, 771, 791. Ⓜ EUR Fermi, EUR Palasport.
Museo della Civiltà Romana
Piazza G. Agnelli. 📞 592 61 35.
Open 9am–7pm Tue–Sat, 9am–1pm Sun and public hols.
Adm charge.

EUR's Palazzo della Civiltà del Lavoro, the "Square Colosseum"

THE ESPOSIZIONE Universale di Roma (EUR), a suburb to the south of the city, was built originally for an international exhibition, a kind of "Work Olympics", that was planned for 1942, but never took place because of the war. The architecture was intended to glorify Fascism and to modern eyes the style of the public buildings is very overblown and rhetorical. The Palazzo della Civiltà del Lavoro (the Palace of the Civilization of Work) is an unmistakable landmark for people arriving from Fiumicino airport.

The scheme was completed in the 1950s. In terms of town planning, EUR has been quite successful and people are still keen to live here. The great marble halls house a number

19th-century mosaic on facade of San Paolo fuori le Mura

of government offices and museums. The Museo della Civiltà Romana has a vast scale model of Rome at the time of Constantine and casts of the reliefs on the Column of Trajan. To the south is a lake and park, and the huge domed Palazzo dello Sport built for the 1960 Olympics.

San Paolo fuori le Mura ⑮

Via Ostiense 186. 📞 541 03 41.
🚌 23, 93b, 170, 223, 673. Ⓜ San Paolo. **Open** 7.30am–6.40pm daily (last adm: 15 mins before closing).
🚻 📷 ♿ 🏛

TODAY'S CHURCH IS a faithful if somewhat soulless reconstruction of the great 4th-century basilica destroyed by fire on the night of 15 July 1823. A few fragments of the original church survived. The triumphal arch over the nave is decorated on one side with much-restored 5th-century mosaics. On the other side are mosaics by Pietro Cavallini, originally on the facade. The splendid Venetian apse mosaics (1220) represent the figures of Christ with St Peter, St Andrew, St Paul and St Luke.

The fine marble canopy over the high altar is signed by the sculptor Arnolfo di Cambio (1285) "together with his partner Pietro", who may have been Pietro Cavallini. Below the altar is the *confessio*, the tomb of St Paul, whose body was

supposed to have been buried here. To the right is an impressive Paschal candlestick by Nicolò di Angelo and Pietro Vassalletto.

The one part of San Paolo spared completely by the fire was the cloister with its pairs of colourful inlaid columns, some octagonal, some spiral, supporting the arcade. Built largely by the Vassalletto family and completed around 1214, it is considered one of the most beautiful in Rome.

Villa Doria Pamphilj ⑯

Via di San Pancrazio. 🚌 41, 75, 144.
Park open dawn–dusk daily.

ROME'S LARGEST public park, the Villa Doria Pamphilj, was laid out in the mid-17th century for Prince Camillo Pamphilj. His uncle Pope Innocent X paid for the magnificent summer residence, the Casino del Bel Respiro, and numerous fountains and summerhouses, some of which still survive. Today the park is a popular meeting place for joggers and dog lovers.

Casino del Bel Respiro, Villa Doria Pamphilj

Day Trips around Rome

Tivoli, a favourite place to escape the heat of the Roman summer

Tivoli ⑰

Town is 31 km (20 miles) northeast of Rome. **FS** *from Roma Termini or Tiburtina.* COTRAL from Rebibbia (on Metro line B).

TIVOLI HAS BEEN a popular summer resort since the days of the Roman Republic. Among the famous men who owned villas here were the poets Catullus and Horace, Caesar's assassins Brutus and Cassius, and the Emperors Trajan and Hadrian. Tivoli's main attractions were its clean air and beautiful situation on the slopes of the Tiburtini hills, its healthy sulphur springs and the waterfalls of the Aniene – the Emperor Augustus said these had cured him of insomnia. The Romans' luxurious lifestyle was revived in Renaissance times by the owners of the Villa d'Este,

Detail of Fontana dell'Organo at Villa d'Este

the town's most famous sight.

In the Middle Ages Tivoli suffered frequent invasions as its position made it an ideal base for an advance on Rome. In 1461 Pope Pius II built a fortress here, the Rocca Pia, declaring: "It is easier to regain Rome while possessing Tivoli, than to regain Tivoli while possessing Rome."

After suffering heavy bomb-damage in 1944, Tivoli's main buildings and churches were speedily restored. The town's cobbled streets are still lined with medieval houses. The Duomo (cathedral) houses a beautiful 13th-century life-size wooden group representing the *Deposition from the Cross.*

Villa d'Este ⑱

Piazza Trento, Tivoli. **C** 0774-31 20 70. **M** COTRAL from Rebibbia (on line B). **Open** 9am–1 hr before sunset Mon–Sat. **Closed** 1 Jan, 1 May, 25 Dec. **Adm charge.**

THE VILLA OCCUPIES the site of an old Benedictine convent. In the 16th century the estate was developed by Cardinal Ippolito d'Este, son of Lucrezia Borgia. A palace was designed by Pirro Ligorio to make the most of its hilltop situation, but the villa's fame rests more on the terraced gardens and fountains laid out by Ligorio and Giacomo della Porta.

Though the gardens have suffered over the centuries from neglect, the grottoes and fountains still give a vivid impression of the frivolous luxury enjoyed by the princes of the church. From the great loggia of the palace you descend through the privet-lined paths to the Grotto of Diana and Bernini's Fontana del Bicchierone. Below to the right is the Rometta (little Rome), a model of Tiber Island with allegorical figures and the legendary she-wolf.

The Rometta is at one end of the Viale delle Cento Fontane. Its 100 fountains are in the shape of grotesques, obelisks, ships and the eagles of the d'Este coat of arms, now overgrown with moss. Other fountains have also lost much of their former glory. The Fontana dell'Organo was a water-organ, in which the force of the water pumped air through the pipes, but it has long been silent. The garden's lowest level has flower beds, fountains and splendid views out over the plain below.

Terrace of 100 Fountains in the gardens of Villa d'Este

Villa Gregoriana ⑲

Largo Massimo, Tivoli. **FS** *Tivoli, then short walk.* **Open** 9.30am–1 hr before sunset daily. **Adm charge.**

THE MAIN ATTRACTIONS of this steeply sloping wooded park are the beautiful waterfalls and grottoes created over the centuries by the River Aniene. The park is named after Pope Gregory XVI, who in the 1830s ordered the building of a tunnel as a way of eradicating the danger of flooding. This created a new waterfall, the Grande Cascata, which plunges a full 108 m (350 ft) into the valley behind the town.

The Canopus, extensively restored, with replicas of its original caryatids lining the bank of the canal

Hadrian's Villa ⑳

Villa Adriana, Via Tiburtina. Site is 6 km (4 miles) southwest of Tivoli. ☎ 0774-53 02 03. 🚆 Tivoli, then local bus No. 4. 🚌 COTRAL from Rebibbia (on Metro line B). **Open** 9am–90 mins before sunset daily (last adm: 1 hr before closing). **Closed** 1 Jan, 1 May, 25 Dec. **Adm charge**. 📱 🚻

BUILT AS a private summer retreat between AD 118 and 134, Hadrian's Villa was a vast open-air museum of the finest architecture of the Roman world. The grounds of the Imperial palace covered an area of 120 hectares (300 acres) and were filled with full-scale reproductions of the emperor's favourite buildings from Greece and Egypt. Although excavations began in the 16th century, many of the ruins lying scattered in the surrounding fields have yet to be identified with any certainty. The grounds of the villa make a very picturesque site for a picnic, with scattered fragments of columns lying among olive trees and cypresses.

For an idea of how the whole complex would have looked in its heyday, study the scale model in the building beside the car park. The most important buildings are signposted and several have been partially restored or reconstructed. One of the most impressive is the so-called Maritime Theatre. This is a round pool with an island in the middle, surrounded by columns. The island, reached by means of a swing bridge, was probably Hadrian's private studio, where he withdrew from the cares of the Empire to indulge in his two favourite pastimes, painting and architecture. There were also theatres, Greek and Latin libraries, two bath houses, extensive housing for guests and the palace staff, and formal gardens with fountains, statues, pools.

Hadrian was a lover of Greek philosophy as well as architecture. One part of the gardens is thought to have been Hadrian's reproduction of the Grove of Academe, where Plato lectured to his

Fragment of marble mosaic pavement in the Imperial palace

students. He also had a replica made of the Stoà Poikile, a beautiful painted colonnade in Athens, from which the Stoic philosophers took their name. Hadrian's copy of the Poikile enclosed a great piazza with a central pool. The so-called Hall of the Philosophers close to the Poikile was probably a library.

The most ambitious of Hadrian's replicas was the Canopus, a sanctuary of the god Serapis near Alexandria. For this a canal 185 metres (200 yards) long was dug and Egyptian statues were imported to decorate the temple and its grounds. This impressive piece of engineering has been restored and the banks of the canal are lined with caryatids.

Another picturesque spot in the grounds is the Vale of Tempe, the legendary haunt of the goddess Diana with a stream representing the river

Pair of Ionic columns in the vaulted baths of Hadrian's Villa

Peneios. Below ground the emperor even built a fanciful recreation of the underworld, Hades, reached through underground tunnels, of which there were many linking the various parts of the villa.

Plundered by barbarians who camped here in the 6th and 8th centuries, the villa fell into disrepair. Its marble was burnt to make lime for cement and Renaissance antiquarians contributed further to its destruction. Statues unearthed in the grounds are on show in museums around Europe. The Vatican's Egyptian Collection (see p238) has many fine works that were found here.

Ostia Antica ㉑

Viale dei Romagnoli 717. Site is 25 km
(16 miles) southwest of Rome. 🔲 563
50 009. Ⓜ Magliana on line B, then
train to Ostia Antica. **Excavations
open** winter: 9am–4.30pm daily;
summer: 9am–6pm daily. **Closed** 1
Jan, 1 May, 25 Dec. **Museum open**
9am–1pm daily. **Closed** public hols.
Adm charge.

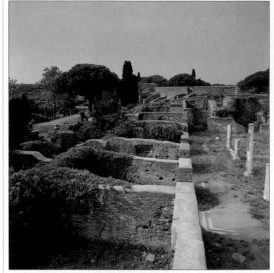

Ruins of shops, offices and houses near Ostia's theatre

IN REPUBLICAN TIMES Ostia was
Rome's main commercial
port and a military base
defending the coastline and
the mouth of the Tiber. The
port continued to flourish
under the Empire, despite the
development of Portus, a new
port slightly to the northwest,
in the 2nd century AD. Ostia's
decline began in the 4th
century, when a reduction in
trade was followed by the
gradual silting up of the
harbour. Worse was to come
when malaria became endemic
in the area and the city, whose
population is reckoned to
have been nearly 100,000 at its
peak, was totally abandoned.

Buried for centuries by
sand, the city is remarkably
well preserved. The site is
less spectacular than Pompei
or Herculaneum because
Ostia died a gradual death,
but it gives a more complete
picture of life under the
Roman Empire. People of all
social classes and from all
over the Mediterranean lived
and worked here.

Visitors can understand the
layout of Ostia's streets almost
at a glance. The main road
through the town, the
Decumanus Maximus, would
have been filled with hurrying
slaves and citizens, avoiding
the jostling carriages and
carts, while tradesmen

pursued their business under
the porticoes lining the street.
The floorplans of the public
buildings along the road are
very clear. Many were bath
houses, such as the Baths of
the Cisiarii (carters) and the
grander Baths of Neptune,
named after their fine black-
and-white floor mosaics.
Beside the restored theatre,
three large masks, originally
part of the decoration of the
stage, have been mounted
on large blocks of tufa.
Beneath the great brick
arches that supported the
semicircular tiers of seats
were taverns and shops.
Classical plays are put on
here in the summer.

The Tiber's course has
changed considerably since
Ostia was the port of Rome. It
once flowed past just to the
north of Piazzale delle

**Mask decorating
the theatre·**

Corporazioni, the square
behind the theatre. The
corporations were the guilds
of the various trades involved
in fitting out and
supplying ships:
tanners and rope-
makers, ship
builders and
timber merchants,
ships' chandlers
and corn weighers.
There were some
60 or 70 offices
around the square.
Mosaics showing
scenes of everyday
life in the port and
the names and
symbols of the
corporations can
still be seen.

There were also offices used
by ship-owners and their
agents from places as far apart
as Tunisia and the south of
France, Sardinia and Egypt. In
one office, belonging to a
merchant from the town of
Sabratha in North Africa,
there is a delightful mosaic
of an elephant.

The main cargo coming into
Rome was grain from Africa.
Much of this was distributed
free to prevent social unrest.
Although only men received
this *annona* or corn dole, at
times over 300,000 were
eligible. In the centre of the
square was a temple, probably

Mural from Ostia of merchant ship being loaded with grain

dedicated to Ceres, goddess of the harvest. Among the buildings excavated are many large warehouses in which grain was stored before it was shipped on to Rome.

The Decumanus leads to the Forum and the city's principal temple, erected by Hadrian in the 2nd century AD and dedicated to Jove, Juno and Minerva. In this rather romantic, lonely spot, it is hard to imagine the Forum as a bustling centre, where justice was dispensed and officials

Floor mosaic of Nereid and sea monster in the House of the Dioscuri

Detail of floor mosaic in the Piazzale delle Corporazioni

met to discuss the city's affairs. In the 18th century it was used as a sheepfold.

Away from the main street are the buildings where Ostia's inhabitants lived. The great majority were housed in rented apartments in blocks three or four storeys high known as *insulae*. These varied considerably in their comfort and decoration. The House of Diana was one of the smarter ones, with a balcony around the second floor, a private bath house and a central courtyard with a cistern where tenants came to collect their water. Around the ground floor of the block were shops, taverns and bars selling snacks and drinks. In the bar at the House of Diana you can see the marble counter used by customers buying their sausages and hot wine sweetened with honey.

For the wealthy there were detached houses *(domus)* such as the House of the Dioscuri, which has fine coloured mosaics, and the House of Cupid and Psyche, named after a charming statue found there. This is now in the site's small museum, along with other sculptures and reliefs found in Ostia.

Among the houses and shops there are other fascinating buildings including a laundry and the firemen's barracks. The religions practised in Ostia reflect the cosmopolitan nature of the port. There are also no fewer than 18 temples dedicated to the Persian god Mithras, as well as a Jewish Synagogue dating from the 1st century AD and a Christian basilica. A plaque records the death of St Augustine's mother in a hotel here in AD 387.

ALSO WORTH SEEING

Anagni FS *from Termini (c50 min).* Picturesque hill-town with papal palace and famous Romanesque cathedral.

Bracciano FS *from Termini or Tiburtina (c90 min).* 🚌 *from Lepanto, on Metro line A (bus c90 min).* Volcanic lake with villages and wooded hills. Nice for walks or a visit to Orsini Castle. Swimming in summer.

Cerveteri FS *from Termini, Tiburtina or Ostiense to Cerveteri-Ladispoli, then local bus (c70 min).* 🚌 *from Via Lepanto, on Metro line A (bus c80 min).* One of the greatest Etruscan cities. Necropolis with complete streets and houses.

Nemi FS *from Anagnina, on Metro line A (bus c60 min).* Charming village at volcanic lake in the Castelli Romani. Famous for its wine and strawberries.

Palestrina FS *from Rebibbia, on Metro line B (bus c70 min).* Impressive Roman sanctuary to goddess Fortuna. Museum and the Mosaic of the Nile.

Pompei FS *from Termini. Express train to Pompei (c160 min) or any train to Naples, then change to local train (c170 min).* 🚌 *Special bus tours from tourist agents.* Excavations of the wealthy Roman city where the busy daily life was put to an end by the eruption of Vesuvius in AD 79.

Subiaco 🚌 *from Rebibbia, on Metro line B (bus c120 min).* Birthplace of St Benedict. Two monasteries to visit.

Tarquinia FS *from Termini or Ostiense (c180 min).* 🚌 *from Via Lepanto, on Metro line A. Change at Civitavecchia (c150 min).* Outstanding collection of Etruscan objects and frescoes from Tarquinia's necropolis.

Viterbo FS *from Termini (c150 min) or COTRAL train from Roma Nord, Piazzale Flaminio, on Metro line A (c120 min).* 🚌 *from Saxa Rubra reached by the COTRAL train above (bus c90 min).* Medieval quarter, papal palace and archaeological museum within 13th-century walls.

SIX GUIDED WALKS

Bernini angel on Ponte Sant'Angelo

ROME IS an excellent city for walking. The distances between major sights in the historic centre are easily covered on foot and many streets are pedestrianized. When you get tired, there are plenty of pavement cafés in wonderful settings, such as Piazza Navona and Campo de' Fiori. If you are interested in archaeology, then a walk across the Forum *(see pp76–87)* and over the Palatine *(see pp96–101)* takes you away from the roaring traffic of modern Rome to a different world of scattered ruins and shady pine trees.

The first of the six suggested walks takes in picturesque quarters on either side of the Tiber, the river that has played such an important part in the city's development. The second walk, along the perfectly straight Via

Giulia, gives a vivid impression of the Renaissance city. The next three walks each follow a particular theme. For visitors who wish to savour the glory of ancient Rome, there is a walk taking in the surviving triumphal arches of the emperors. For those who prefer the Middle Ages, there is a tour of early Christian churches with well-preserved mosaics, and for those who enjoy the Roman Baroque there is a walk concentrating on the great contribution of Bernini to the appearance of the city.

The Romans were famous for the straightness of their roads. The final walk is outside the central sightseeing area along the best-known of all Roman roads, the Via Appia Antica, parts of which are still intact after more than 2,000 years of use.

CHOOSING A WALK

Bernini
(pp282–3)

Via Giulia
(pp276–7)

The Six Walks
The routes of the first five walks are marked on the larger map, which also shows the main sightseeing areas of Rome. The smaller inset map shows the location of the Via Appia walk in relation to the central area.

Mosaics
(pp280–81)

Tiber
(pp274–5)

Triumphal Arches
(pp278–9)

Via Appia Antica
(pp284–5)

KEY

··· Walk routes

— City Wall

| 0 kilometres | 1 |
| 0 miles | 0.5 |

Pedestrians strolling across Ponte Sant'Angelo

A Two-Hour Walk by the River Tiber

ROME OWES ITS VERY EXISTENCE to the Tiber; the city grew up around an easy fording point where a market place developed. The river could also be a hazard; shallow and torrent-like, it flooded the city every winter up to 1870, when work began on the massive Lungotevere embankments that run along both sides of the river. These provide many fine views from points along their avenues of plane trees. The walk also explores the neighbourhoods along the riverside, in particular the Jewish Ghetto and Trastevere, which have preserved much of their character from earlier periods in the colourful history of Rome.

From the old port of Rome to Via dei Funari

Starting from the church of Santa Maria in Cosmedin ① (see p202), cross the piazza to the Temples of the Forum Boarium ② (see p203). This was the cattle market that stood near the city's river port. The river here has preserved two less obvious structures from ancient Rome: the mouth of the Cloaca Maxima ③, the city's great sewer, and one arch of a ruined bridge, known as the Ponte Rotto ④. In Via di Ponte Rotto stands the extraordinary medieval Casa dei Crescenzi ⑤ (see p203), decorated with fragments of Roman temples. Passing the modern Anagrafe (public records office) ⑥, built on the site of the old Roman port, you come to San Nicola in Carcere ⑦ (see p152).

You are now in the Foro Olitorio, Rome's ancient vegetable market. To the east stand the ruins of a Roman portico and the medieval house of the Pierleoni family. Head for the massive Theatre

Santa Maria in Cosmedin ①

of Marcellus ⑧ (see p151), and look for the three Corinthian columns of the Temple of Apollo beside it. Turn into Piazza Campitelli and walk up to Santa Maria in Campitelli ⑨ (see p151). The church honours a miraculous image of the Virgin credited with halting the plague in 1656. The 16th-century piazza was the home of Flaminio Ponzio, its architect, who lived at No. 6. Take Via dei Delfini to Piazza Margana where you should look up at the 14th-century tower of the Margani family ⑩. Retrace your steps, then go up Via dei Funari (Street of the Ropemakers) to the 16th-century facade of Santa Caterina dei Funari ⑪.

The Ghetto

From Piazza Lovatelli take Via Sant'Angelo in Pescheria, which

leads to the ruined Portico of Octavia ⑫ (see p151) in the Jewish Ghetto (see p152). The Roman portico, once Rome's fish market, houses the church of Sant'Angelo in Pescheria. Find the marble plaque on the facade: fish longer than this slab were given to the city's *conservatori* (governors). Turn into the Ghetto: two column stumps belonging to the Portico stand in front of a patched-up doorway made of fragments of Roman sculpture. The cramped buildings and streets around Via del Portico

Arch of the Ponte Rotto ④

Main altar of Santa Maria in Campitelli ⑨

d'Ottavia are typical of old Rome: see the Casa di Lorenzo Manilio ⑬ *(see p153)*, and turn down Via delle Cinque Scole, past Palazzo Cenci ⑭ *(see p152)*, towards the river. On Lungotevere walk past the Synagogue ⑮ *(see p152)* to the small church of San Gregorio ⑯. Here stood the gates of the Ghetto, which were locked at sundown.

Across the river to Trastevere

Crossing to Tiber Island *(see p152)* by Ponte Fabricio, with its two ancient

Classical relief of Medusa above the doorway of Palazzo Cenci ⑭

much of the spirit of old Trastevere. Walk up to the start of Viale di Trastevere at Piazza Belli. After crossing the road look back

Santa Maria in Trastevere, don't miss the old-fashioned chemist's shop at No. 7. The piazza itself, in front of the magnificent church of Santa Maria in Trastevere ㉒ *(see pp212–13)*, has a cheerful atmosphere, and the fountain steps are a favourite meeting place. Go back a little way to Via del Moro. This leads to Piazza Trilussa, dominated by the fountain of the Acqua Paola ㉓, where you emerge on to the bank of the river again. Note the life-like statue, near the fountain, of Roman poet Trilussa, who wrote in the local dialect. From Ponte Sisto ㉔ *(see p210)*, look back to Tiber Island and, beyond it, to the medieval bell tower of Santa Maria in Cosmedin, set against the pine trees on the summit of the Palatine.

The western tip of Tiber Island

0 metres 250

0 yards 250

stone heads on the parapet, you can enjoy a good view of the river in both directions. On the island itself, you should not miss the Pierleoni Tower ⑰ or the church of San Bartolomeo all'Isola ⑱.

Trastevere

As you cross into Trastevere, you can see the medieval house of the powerful Mattei family ⑲, with its fragments of ancient sculpture. Beyond it, Piazza in Piscinula and the surrounding streets retain

KEY

— Walk route

🔆 Good viewing point

at the medieval tower of the Anguillara ⑳ and the statue honouring the poet Gioacchino Belli ㉑ *(see p209)*. As you go down Via della Lungaretta to Piazza

Piazza in Piscinula, old Trastevere

TIPS FOR WALKERS

Starting point: *Piazza della Bocca della Verità.*

Length: *3.5 km (2 miles).*

Getting there: *The 15, 23, 57, 90, 90b, 92 and 95 buses all stop near Santa Maria in Cosmedin.*

Best time for walk: *This walk can be very romantic in the evenings, but is enjoyable at any time.*

Stopping-off points: *Piazza Campitelli and Piazza Margana have typical Roman restaurants, and Via del Portico d'Ottavia has two kosher restaurants and a bakery. Tiber Island has a bar and the famous Sora Lella restaurant (see p314). In Viale Trastevere, there are bars and pizzerias of all kinds. Piazza Santa Maria in Trastevere has lively bars and restaurants with outdoor tables.*

A One-Hour Walk along Via Giulia

LAID OUT BY BRAMANTE for Pope Julius II in the early 16th century, Via Giulia was the first Renaissance street to slice through Rome's jumble of medieval alleys. The original plan included new law courts in a central piazza, but this project was abandoned for lack of cash. The street is now occupied mainly by antiques shops and furniture restorers. On summer evenings the street is lit with hundreds of oil lamps, and cloisters and courtyards provide romantic settings for a special season of concerts.

Baroque capital on the facade of Sant'Eligio degli Orefici ⑦

From Lungotevere to Largo della Moretta

Starting from Lungotevere dei Tebaldi ① at the eastern end of Via Giulia, you will see ahead of you an archway ② spanning the road. This was the start of Michelangelo's unrealized project linking Palazzo Farnese and its gardens *(see p147)* with the Villa Farnesina *(see pp220–21)* on the other side of the river.

Just before you reach the archway, you will see to your left the curious Fontana del Mascherone ③, in which an ancient grotesque mask and granite basin were combined to create a Baroque fountain.

Beyond the Farnese archway on the left is the lively Baroque facade of the church of Santa Maria dell'Orazione e Morte ④ *(see p147)*. A bit further along on the same side of the road stands Palazzo Falconieri ⑤, enlarged by Borromini in 1650. Note its two stone falcons glowering at each other across the width of the facade. On the other side of the road you pass the yellow-ish facade of Santa Caterina da Siena ⑥, church of the Sienese colony in Rome, which has pretty 18th-century reliefs. The figures of Romulus and Remus symbolize Rome

Relief of Romulus and Remus on Santa Caterina da Siena ⑥

and Siena – there is a legend that the city of Siena was founded by the less fortunate of the twins. After passing the short street that leads down to Sant'Eligio degli Orefici ⑦ *(see p148)* and the facade of Palazzo Ricci ⑧ *(see p149)*, you come to an area of half-demolished buildings around the ruined church of San Filippo Neri ⑨, called Largo della Moretta. If you look to the left down to the river, you can see

Fontana del Mascherone ③

Ponte Mazzini and the huge prison of Regina Coeli on the other side of the Tiber. At this point you may like to make a small detour to the right to the beginning of Via del Pellegrino, where there is an inscription ⑩, defining the *pomerium*, or boundary, of the city in the time of the Emperor Claudius.

From Largo della Moretta to the Sofas of Via Giulia

Further on, facing the narrow Vicolo del Malpasso are the imposing prisons, the Carceri

Nuove ⑪, built by Pope Innocent X Pamphilj in 1655. When first opened, they were a model of humane treatment of prisoners, but were replaced by the Regina Coeli prison across the river at the end of the 19th century. The buildings now house offices of the Ministry of Justice and a small Museum of Crime.

At the corner of Via del Gonfalone, a small side street running down to the river,

KEY

—   Walk route

࿊   Good viewing point

0 metres		250
0 yards		250

Farnese archway across Via Giulia, built to a design by Michelangelo ②

the traditional distribution of bread to the poor that took place on the saint's feast day.

On the corner there are more travertine blocks belonging to the foundations of Julius II's projected law courts, known because of their curious shape as the "Sofas of Via Giulia".

The Florentine Quarter

Your next stop should be the imposing Palazzo Sacchetti at No. 66 ⑮. Originally this was the house of Antonio da Sangallo the Younger, the architect of Palazzo Farnese, but it was greatly enlarged by later owners. The porticoed courtyard houses a 15th-century Madonna and a striking Roman relief of the 3rd century AD. Just opposite Palazzo Sacchetti, note the beautiful late Renaissance portal of Palazzo Donarelli ⑯. The 16th-century house at No. 93 is richly decorated with stuccoes and coats of arms ⑰. No. 85 is another typical Renaissance palazzo with a heavily rusticated ground floor ⑱. There is a tradition

Plaque honouring Antonio da Sangallo on Palazzo Sacchetti ⑮

that, like many houses of the period, it once belonged to Raphael. Palazzo Clarelli ⑲ was built by Antonio da Sangallo the Younger as his own house. The inscription above the doorway bears the name of Duke Cosimo II de' Medici, whose family later bought the palazzo.

This whole area used to be inhabited by a flourishing Florentine colony, which had its own water-mills built on pontoons along the Tiber. Their national church is San Giovanni dei Fiorentini ⑳ (see p153), the final great landmark at the end of Via Giulia. Many Florentine artists and architects had a hand in its design, including Sangallo and Jacopo Sansovino.

Coat of arms of Pope Paul III Farnese on the facade of Via Giulia No. 93 ⑰

you can see part of the foundations of Julius II's planned law courts. Just down the street stands the small Oratorio di Santa Lucia del Gonfalone ⑫, which is often used for concerts.

The next interesting facade is Carlo Rainaldi's 17th-century Santa Maria del Suffragio ⑬ on the left. On the same side is San Biagio degli Armeni ⑭, the Armenian church in Rome. It is often referred to by local people as San Biagio della Pagnotta (of the loaf of bread). The nickname originates from

Detail on the side of the door of Santa Maria del Suffragio ⑬

TIPS FOR WALKERS

Starting point: Lungotevere dei Tebaldi, by Ponte Sisto.
Length: 1 km (1,100 yds).
Getting there: Take either a 46, 62 or 64 to Corso Vittorio Emanuele II, then walk down Via dei Pettinari or a 23, 65 or 280 along Lungotevere.
Best time for walk: On summer evenings the street is lit by oil lamps. At Christmas, there are cribs on display in shop windows.
Stopping-off points: There are bars in Via Giulia, at Nos. 21 and 84. Campo de' Fiori has better bars, with outdoor tables, and a wide choice of places to eat. These include a Chinese restaurant in Via dei Giubbonari and a fried fish restaurant in Piazza Santa Barbara dei Librai (closed Sun).

A 90-Minute Tour of Rome's Triumphal Arches

R OME'S GREATEST GIFT to architecture was the arch and the Roman people's highest tribute to its victorious generals was the triumphal arch. In Imperial times, arches were erected to honour an emperor's campaign victories almost as a matter of course, promoting his personal cult and ensuring his subsequent deification. Spectacular processions passed through these arches. Conquering generals, cheered by rapturous crowds, rode in their chariots to the Capitol, accompanied by their legions bearing spoils from their campaigns.

Part of the Via Sacra, once spanned by the Arch of Augustus ③

Arches of the Forum

This walk through the Forum and around the base of the Palatine takes in Rome's three great surviving triumphal arches and two arches of more

Relief of barbarian captives on the Arch of Septimius Severus ①

humble design that were used simply as places of business. It starts from the Arch of

TIPS FOR WALKERS

Starting point: The Roman Forum, entrance Largo Romolo e Remo, on Via dei Fori Imperiali.
Length: 2.5 km (1½ miles).
Getting there: The nearest Metro stations is Colosseo on line B. Buses 11, 27, 81, 85, 87, 186 stop in Via dei Fori Imperiali, near the Forum entrance.
Best time for walk: Any time of day during Forum opening hours (see p82) is suitable.
Stopping-off points: Several bars and restaurants overlook the Colosseum. There is a small bar in Via dei Cerchi and a smarter one behind San Giorgio in Velabro, in Piazza San Giovanni Decollato (closed Sun). For a meal, try Alvaro al Circo Massimo (closed Mon) in Via di San Teodoro.

Emperor Septimius Severus ① and his sons Geta and Caracalla (*see p83*) in the Forum. Erected in AD 203, it celebrates a successful campaign in the Middle East. Eight years later when Caracalla had his brother killed, all mention of Geta was removed from the inscription.

Look up at the reliefs showing phases of the campaigns. Set in tiers, they are probably the sculptural counterparts of the paintings illustrating the general's feats that were borne aloft in the triumphal procession. On the right, the inhabitants of a fortified city surrender to the Romans' siege machines. Below are smaller friezes showing the triumphal procession itself.

Heading east, make your way through the Forum to the ruins of the Temple of Julius Caesar ②. The temple was built by Augustus in 42 BC, on the site where Caesar's body was cremated after Mark Antony's famous funerary oration. A nearby sign marks the ruins of the Arch of Augustus ③, spanning the Via Sacra between the Temple of Castor and Pollux ④ (*see p84*) and the Temple of Caesar. This arch, erected after Augustus had defeated Mark Antony and Cleopatra, was demolished in 1545, and its materials were used in the

Capital from Temple of Castor and Pollux ④

new St Peter's. From here, proceed uphill towards the elegant Arch of Titus ⑤ (*see p87*). Compared with Septimius Severus's arch, it shows an earlier, simpler style. Look up at the beautiful lettering of the inscription before you examine the inner bas-reliefs. These show

KEY

—   Walk route

☼   Good viewing point

Ⓜ   Metro station

0 metres   250

0 yards   250

Arch of Titus in a 19th-century watercolour by the English artist Thomas Hartley Cromek ⑤

through the arch would have been carrying building materials quarried from the Forum's various ruins.

Arch of Constantine

Leave the Forum by heading down the hill towards the Colosseum ⑥ *(see pp92–5)* and the nearby Arch of Constantine ⑦ *(see p91)*. This arch, hastily built to commemorate the emperor's victory over his rival Maxentius in AD 312, is a patchwork of reliefs from different periods. Stand on the Via di San Gregorio side and compare the earlier panels at the top (AD 180–193) with the hectic battle scenes just above the

Arches of Domitian's extension to the Claudian Aqueduct ⑨

smaller arches, sculpted in AD 315. In the curious dwarf-like soldiers, you can see the transition from Classicism to a cruder medieval style of sculpture.

Now take Via di San Gregorio, which runs along the valley between the Palatine and Celian hills. This was the ancient route taken by most triumphal processions. Passing the entrance to the Palatine ⑧ and

the well-preserved arches of the Claudian Aqueduct ⑨ on the right, you come to Piazza di Porta Capena ⑩, named after the gate that stood here to mark the beginning of the Via Appia *(see p284)*. After rounding the back of the Palatine, follow Via dei Cerchi, which runs alongside the grassy area that preserves the oval outline of the Circus Maximus ⑪ *(see p205)*.

Arches of the Forum Boarium

When you reach the church of Sant'Anastasia ⑫, turn right up Via di San Teodoro, then first left down Via del Velabro. Straddling the street is the four-sided Arch of Janus ⑬ *(see p202)*, erected in the 3rd century AD. This is not a triumphal arch but a covered area where merchants could take shelter from the sun or rain when discussing business. Like the Arch of Titus, it became part of a fortress built by the Frangipane family during the Middle Ages.

Tucked away beside the nearby church of San Giorgio in Velabro ⑭ *(see p202)* is what looks like a large rectangular doorway. This is the Arco degli Argentari, or Moneychangers' Arch ⑮. Look up at the inscription, which says that it was erected by local silversmiths in honour of Septimius Severus and his family in AD 204. As in the emperor's triumphal arch, the name of Geta has been obliterated by his brother and murderer, Caracalla. Geta's figure has also been removed from among the portraits on the panels inside the arch. Triumph in Imperial Rome could be very short-lived.

Roman legionaries carrying the spoils looted from the conquest of Jerusalem, heralds holding plaques with the names of vanquished peoples and cities, and Titus riding in triumph in his chariot.

The medieval Frangipane family turned the Colosseum into a vast impregnable stronghold and incorporated the Arch of Titus into their fortifications. Notice the wheelmarks scratched on the inside walls of the arch by generations of carts; they indicate the steady rise in the level of the Forum before it was eventually excavated in the 18th and 19th centuries. Many of the carts that passed

Four-sided Arch of Janus ⑬

A Three-Hour Tour of Rome's Best Mosaics

IN IMITATION of the audience chambers of Imperial palaces, Rome's early Christian churches were decorated with colourful mosaics. These were pieced together from cubes of marble, coloured stone and fragments of glass. To create a golden background, gold leaf was placed between pieces of glass. These were then heated so that they fused. The glorious colours and subjects portrayed gave the faithful a glimpse of the heavenly court of the King of Kings. This walk concentrates on a few of the churches decorated in this wonderful medium.

Apse mosaic in the Chapel of Santa Rufina ③

San Giovanni

Start from Piazza di Porta San Giovanni, where you can visit the heavily-restored mosaic which was originally in the banqueting hall of Pope Leo III (reigned 795–816) ①, showing Christ among the Apostles. On the left are Pope Sylvester and the Emperor Constantine, on the right, Pope Leo and Charlemagne just before he was crowned

Obelisk and side facade of San Giovanni in Laterano ②

Holy Roman Emperor in AD 800. Inside the church of San Giovanni in Laterano ② *(see pp182–3)*, the 13th-century apse mosaic shows Christ as he appeared miraculously during the consecration of the church. In the panels by the windows, look for the small figures of two Franciscan friars; these are the artists Jacopo Torriti (left) and Jacopo de Camerino (right). Leave by

the exit on the right near the splendid 16th-century organ and head for the octagonal Baptistry of San Giovanni ③, where the Chapel of Santa Rufina has a beautiful apse mosaic in green, azure and gold, dating from the 5th century. In the neighbouring Chapel of San Venanzio, there are golden 7th-century mosaics, showing the strong influence of the Eastern Church at this time.

Santo Stefano Rotondo to San Clemente

Leave the piazza by the narrow road that leads to the round church of Santo Stefano Rotondo ④ *(see p185)*. One of its chapels contains a 7th-century Byzantine mosaic honouring two martyrs buried here. Further on, in Piazza della Navicella, is the church of Santa Maria in Domnica ⑤ *(see p193)*. It houses the superb mosaics commissioned by Pope Paschal I, who gave new impetus to Rome's mosaic production in the 9th century. He is represented kneeling beside the Virgin. On leaving the church, notice the facade of San Tommaso in Formis ⑥, which has a charming mosaic of Christ flanked by two freed slaves, one black and one white, dating from the 13th

Ceiling mosaic, Baptistry of San Giovanni ③

Interior of Baptistry of San Giovanni ③

century. From here, head up the steep hill, past the forbidding apse of Santi Quattro Coronati ⑦ *(see p185)*, to the fascinating church of San Clemente ⑧ *(see pp186–7)*. Its 12th-century apse mosaic shows the cross set in a swirling pattern of

acanthus leaves. San Clemente also has a fine 12th-century Cosmatesque mosaic floor.

The Colle Oppio
Passing the old entrance to the church, cross Via Labicana and walk up the hill to the small Colle Oppio park ⑨. This has fine views of the Colosseum and contains the ruins of Nero's Golden House ⑩ *(see p175)* and the Baths of Trajan ⑪. Across the park lie San Martino ai Monti ⑫ *(see p170)*, which has a 6th-century mosaic portrait of Pope St Sylvester in the crypt, and Santa Prassede ⑬ *(see p171)*. Here the Chapel of St Zeno contains the most important Byzantine mosaics in Rome, reminiscent of the fabulous mosaics of Ravenna. Pope Paschal I erected the chapel as a mausoleum for his

14th-century facade mosaics by Filippo Rusuti. Inside, the 5th-century mosaics in the nave depict Old Testament stories, while the triumphal arch has scenes relating to the birth of Christ, including one of the Magi wearing striped stockings. In the apse there is a Coronation of the Virgin by Jacopo Torriti (1295).

On leaving Santa Maria, pass the obelisk ⑮ in the piazza behind the church and go downhill to Via Urbana and Santa Pudenziana ⑯ *(see p171)*. The figures in the apse mosaic, one of the oldest in Rome (AD 390), are remarkable for their naturalism. The two women with crowns are traditionally identified as Santa Prassede and Santa Pudenziana.

Mosaic saint in Santa Prassede ⑬

When you leave the church, you can either retrace your steps to Santa Maria Maggiore or walk down Via Urbana to Via Cavour Metro station.

11th-century frieze above the doorway of Santa Pudenziana ⑯

mother Theodora. The apse and triumphal arch of the church itself also have fine mosaics. When you move on to Santa Maria Maggiore ⑭ *(see pp172–3)*, go to the column in the centre of the piazza in front of the church to see the beautiful

KEY

— Walk route

— City Wall

☆ Good viewing point

Ⓜ Metro station

0 metres   250
0 yards   250

TIPS FOR WALKERS

Starting point: Piazza di Porta San Giovanni.
Length: 3.5 km (2 miles).
Getting there: The nearest Metro station is San Giovanni, on line A, in Piazzale Appio, just outside Porta San Giovanni. The 81, 85, 87 buses and the 13 and 30b trams stop in front of San Giovanni in Laterano.
Best time for walk: It is advisable to go in the morning, in order to to appreciate the mosaics in the best possible light.
Stopping-off points: The bars and restaurants in Piazza del Colosseo are popular with artists, who like to draw the Colosseum on the paper tablecloths. In the Parco del Colle Oppio there is a small café kiosk with tables. There are several bars around Santa Maria Maggiore, some with outdoor tables.

A Two-Hour Walk around Bernini's Rome

GIAN LORENZO BERNINI (1598–1680) is the artist who probably left the strongest personal mark on the appearance of the city of Rome. Favourite architect, sculptor and town-planner to three successive popes, he turned Rome into a uniquely Baroque city. This walk traces his enormous influence on the development and appearance of the centre of Rome. It starts from the busy Largo di Santa Susanna just north of Termini station, at the church of Santa Maria della Vittoria.

Facade of Santa Maria in Via ⑬

Bernini's Fontana del Tritone ②

Quirinale. The long wing of the Palazzo del Quirinale ⑦ *(see p158)*, nicknamed the Manica Lunga (long sleeve), is by Bernini. On the other side of the road is the facade of Sant'Andrea al Quirinale ⑧ *(see p161)*, one of Bernini's greatest churches. When you reach the Piazza del Quirinale ⑨, note the doorway of the palazzo, attributed to Bernini. From the piazza, go up the

composer Donizetti lived at No. 77 and turn into Via Santa Maria in Via, where the church ⑬ has a fine Baroque

Through Piazza Barberini

Santa Maria della Vittoria ① *(see p255)* houses the Cornaro Chapel, the setting for one of Bernini's most revolutionary and controversial sculptures, the *Ecstasy of St Teresa* (1646). From here take Via Barberini to Piazza Barberini. In its centre is Bernini's dramatic Fontana del Tritone ② *(see p254)* and at one side stands the more modest Fontana delle Api ③ *(see p254)*. As you go up Via delle Quattro Fontane, you catch a glimpse of Palazzo Barberini ④ *(see p255)* built by Bernini and several other artists for Pope Urban VIII. The gateway and cornices are decorated with the bees that made up part of the Barberini family crest. Next make your way to the crossroads, decorated by Le Quattro Fontane ⑤ *(see p162)*, to enjoy the splendid views in all four directions.

Passing the diminutive San Carlo alle Quattro Fontane ⑥ *(see p161)*, built by Bernini's rival Borromini, take Via del

stairs to Via della Dataria, and into Vicolo Scanderbeg which leads to a small piazza with the same name ⑩. Scanderbeg was the nickname of the Albanian prince Giorgio Castriota (1403–68), the "Terror of the Turks". His portrait is preserved on the house where he lived.

The Trevi Fountain

Go along the narrow Vicolo dei Modelli ⑪, where male models waited to be chosen by artists, then turn towards the Trevi Fountain ⑫ *(see p159)*. Its energy is clearly inspired by Bernini's work, a tribute to his lasting influence on Roman taste. Leave the piazza along Via delle Muratte where the

Neptune Fountain at the north end of Piazza Navona ⑱

facade by Bernini's follower Carlo Rainaldi. At the top of this street, turn left down to Via del Corso. On the other side of the road, you will see the towering Column of Marcus Aurelius ⑭ *(see p113)* in Piazza Colonna. Beyond this is Palazzo Montecitorio ⑮, begun in 1650 by Bernini and now the home of the Italian parliament *(see p112)*.

Pantheon to Piazza Navona
Via in Aquiro leads you to the Pantheon ⑯ *(see pp110–11)*. Refusing Pope Urban VIII's request for him to redecorate

Collegio Innocenziano by Bernini's rival Borromini in Piazza Navona ⑱

the dome, Bernini said that although St Peter's had a hundred defects, the Pantheon did not have any. From the Pantheon, make a small detour to Piazza della Minerva where you can see the bizarre Bernini obelisk, supported by a small elephant, by the church of Santa Maria sopra Minerva ⑰ *(see p108)*. Then retrace your steps and take Salita dei Crescenzi to

KEY

— Walk route

❉ Good viewing point

Ⓜ Metro station

0 metres	250
0 yards	250

Angel on Ponte Sant'Angelo

reach the fabulous Piazza Navona ⑱ *(see p120)* which was remodelled by Bernini for Pope Innocent X Pamphilj. The design for the central fountain, the Fontana dei

Fiumi *(see p120)*, was by Bernini, though the figures symbolic of the four rivers were sculpted by other artists. The central figure in the Fontana del Moro, however, is by Bernini himself. Bernini's contemporaries were fascinated by the innovative use of shells, rocks and other natural forms in his fountains, and his expert handling of water to create constant movement.

An extended walk
More energetic walkers may like to head towards the river to see the Ponte Sant'Angelo and its Bernini angels; and then on to St Peter's *(see pp230–33)* where they can admire Bernini's great colonnaded piazza in front of the church, the papal tombs, his altar decorations and the bronze baldacchino.

TIPS FOR WALKERS

Starting point: Largo di Santa Susanna.
Length: 3.5 km (2 miles).
Getting there: Take Metro line A to Repubblica or any bus to Termini, then walk. Buses 60, 61, 62 and 137 stop in Via Barberini.
Best time for walk: Go either between 9am and noon for good lighting conditions in the churches, or between 4pm and 7pm.
Stopping-off points: The Piazza Barberini and Fontana di Trevi areas have lots of bars and pizzerias for tourists. The many elegant cafés en route include the famous Caffè Giolitti (see p109) and there is a vast choice of outdoor cafés and restaurants around Piazza della Rotonda and Piazza Navona.

A 90-Minute Walk along the Via Appia Antica

LINED WITH CYPRESSES AND PINES as it was when the ancient Romans came here by torchlight to bury their dead, the Via Appia is wonderfully atmospheric. The fields are strewn with ruined tombs set against the picturesque background of the Alban hills to the south. Although the marble or travertine stone facings of most tombs have been plundered, a few statues and reliefs survive or have been replaced by copies.

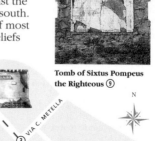

Tomb of Sixtus Pompeus the Righteous ⑨

Capo di Bove
Start from the Tomb of Cecilia Metella ① *(see p266)*. In the Middle Ages this area acquired the name Capo di Bove (ox head) from the frieze of festoons and ox heads still visible on the tomb. On the other side of

Gothic windows in the church of San Nicola ②

the road you can see the ruined Gothic church of San Nicola ②, which, like the Tomb of Cecilia Metella, was part of the medieval fortress of the Caetani family.

Proceed to the crossroads ③, where many original Roman paving slabs, huge blocks of extremely durable volcanic basalt, are still in place. Just

The ruined church of San Nicola ②

past the next turning (Via Capo di Bove), you will see on your left the nucleus of a great mausoleum overgrown with ivy, known as the Torre di Capo di Bove ④. Beyond it,

on both sides of the Appia, are other tombs, some still capped with the remains of the medieval towers that were built over them. On the right after passing some private villas, you come to a military zone around the Forte Appio ⑤, one of a series of forts built around the city in the 19th century. On the left, a little further on, stand the ruins of the Tomb of Marcus Servilius ⑥, showing fragments of reliefs excavated in 1808 by the Neo-Classical sculptor Antonio Canova. He was one of the first to work on the principle that excavated tombs and their inscriptions and reliefs should be allowed to remain in situ. On the other side of the road stands a tomb with a relief of a man, naked except for a short cape, known as the

"Heroic Relief" ⑦. On the left of the road are the ruins of the so-called Tomb of Seneca ⑧. The great moralist Seneca owned a villa near here, where he committed suicide in AD 65 on the orders of Nero.

The next major tomb is that of the family of Sixtus Pompeus the Righteous, a freed slave of the 1st century AD ⑨. The verse inscription records the father's sadness at having to bury his own children, who died young.

Artist's impression of how the mausoleums and tombs lining the Via Appia looked in the 2nd century AD

Section of the Via Appia Antica, showing original Roman paving

From Via dei Lugari to Via di Tor Carbone

Just past Via dei Lugari on the right, screened by trees, is the Tomb of Pope St Urban (reigned 222–230) ⑩. Set back from the road on the left stands a large ruined podium, probably part of a Temple of Jupiter ⑪. The next stretch was excavated by the architect Luigi Canina early in the 19th century. On the right is the Tomb of Caius Licinius ⑫, followed by a smaller Doric tomb ⑬ and the imposing Tomb of Hilarius

Fuscus ⑭, with five portrait busts in relief of members of his family. Next comes the Tomb of Tiberius Claudius Secondinus ⑮, where a group of freedmen of the Imperial household were buried in the 2nd century AD.

Passing a large ruined columbarium, you reach the Tomb of Quintus Apuleius ⑯ and the reconstructed Tomb of the Rabirii freed slaves (1st century BC) ⑰. This has a frieze of three half-length figures above an inscription.

The figure on the right is a priestess of Isis. Behind her you can see the outline of a *sistrum*, the metal rattle used at ceremonies of the cult.

The majority of the tombs are little more than shapeless stacks of eroded brickwork. Two exceptions in the last stretch of this walk are the Tomb of the Festoons ⑱, with its reconstructed frieze of festive putti, and the Tomb of the Frontispiece ⑲, which has a copy of a relief with four portraits. The two central figures are holding hands.

When you reach Via di Tor Carbone, the Via Appia still stretches out ahead of you in a straight line and, if you wish to extend your walk, there are many more tombs and ruined villas to visit along the way.

KEY

— Walk route

☆ Good viewing point

| 0 metres | 250 |
| 0 yards | 250 |

Figure on the Tomb of the Heroic Relief ⑦

TIPS FOR WALKERS

Starting point: Tomb of Cecilia Metella.

Length: 3 km (2 miles).

Getting there: Take the 118 bus from San Giovanni in Laterano or the Colosseum. On the way back, the 118 goes along the Via Appia Pignatelli. Allow plenty of time for waiting for the bus.

Best time for walk: Go fairly early, before it gets too hot.

Stopping-off points: There is a bar near the church of Domine Quo Vadis?, before the start of the walk, but it is best to bring your own refreshment. There are also several well-established restaurants on the first stretch of the Appia, including the Cecilia Metella, Via Appia Antica 125/127, tel 513 67 43 (closed Mon).

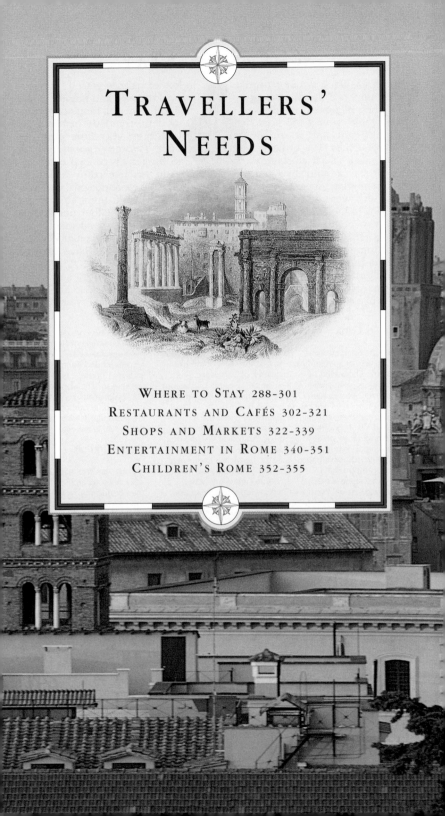

TRAVELLERS'
NEEDS

WHERE TO STAY 288-301
RESTAURANTS AND CAFÉS 302-321
SHOPS AND MARKETS 322-339
ENTERTAINMENT IN ROME 340-351
CHILDREN'S ROME 352-355

WHERE TO STAY

ROME HAS BEEN a major tourist centre since the Middle Ages, when pilgrims from all over Europe came to visit the home of Catholicism and its relic-packed churches. The nostalgic can still sleep in a 15th-century hotel, or stay around the Campo de' Fiori market, where visiting ecclesiastics were entertained by courtesans in the Renaissance era. Those who prefer their history a little less raffish could opt for an ex-monastery or convent, or stay in a still-functioning religious house. Romantics could sleep in the house once occupied by Keats, while stargazers could stay

Porter at the Majestic Hotel

in former palaces graced by celebrities of the past and present. Rome can offer the full range of accommodation, mostly in historical buildings, very little purpose-built. *Pensione* (guesthouse) is no longer an official category, but in practice many retain the name and more personal character that has made them so popular with travellers. Other possibilities include hostels, residential hotels and self-catering accommodation.

The 72 hotels we have selected are organized in the *Choosing a Hotel* chart *(pp294–5)* and in the listings *(pp296–301)* according to their price category and area.

WHERE TO LOOK

AROUND the Spanish Steps and Piazza di Spagna lies the traditional heartland of foreign visitors, with some of the most exclusive smaller hotels. Similar places can be found all over the centre, to the west of Via del Corso.

While moderately priced accommodation is rare in central Rome, the advantages of staying right on the doorstep of the city's many ancient sights cannot be over-estimated; you can walk to the major areas of interest and easily return at midday for a shower and siesta. If the

less expensive hotels we have recommended in the centre are full, try the Borgo – close to the Vatican – or the lively quarter of Trastevere.

Those in search of glamour should head for Via Veneto, which has many grand and luxurious hotels.

If you're looking for a peaceful retreat, try the area around the Aventine, or one of the high-class hotels next to the Villa Borghese park.

Although many of the streets immediately around Termini station are rather seedy, the area is nonetheless a convenient stopover for travellers and there's a

concentration of cheap hotels, with some decent (if basic) ones among them. The hotels recommended lie in a fairly safe area on the east side of the station. The approach to the centre from Termini has a number of good hotels that are particularly suitable for the business traveller.

HOTEL PRICES

ROME MAY STILL have more cheap accommodation than London or New York, but rates for comparable establishments have caught up. Prices are set by the state, and hotels are supposed to display the official rate on the door of each room. VAT is usually included, and has been taken into account in the price categories on p291.

It is rare, but not unheard-of, for Roman hotels to have low and high season rates, so it can be worth bargaining as you will inevitably be quoted the official rate, even in the winter months before and after Christmas, when competition is less strong. Discounts for long-stay visitors and groups are often negotiable.

Rooms without a bathroom can cost about 30% less. Single travellers are badly catered for, and though it is possible to find a single room for 60% of the price of a double, on average you'll

The Verdi Room in Via Veneto's Majestic Hotel *(see p301)*

The Plaza Minerva *(see p296)*

pay 70%, and occasionally 90%. Where breakfast is included in the quoted price, you can ask for the relevant amount to be deducted from your bill if you don't want it.

HIDDEN EXTRAS

Even if the room price includes service, you are still expected to tip at least L1,000 for room service and around L2,000 for bellboys.

Hotels will often add hefty surcharges to international phone calls, and may charge extra for parking and air conditioning. The cost of drinks in minibars can be high – you can buy a cheaper supply from local shops.

FACILITIES

Hotel standards have improved of late – you can expect air conditioning and some bathrooms with hair dryers in middle-range establishments and direct-dial phones in middle to lower price rooms, although budget travellers staying in cheaper hotels shouldn't expect much more than a clean room.

Because most hotels occupy historic buildings, room sizes can vary dramatically even within the same establishment (and this is often reflected in the

pricing), so don't be afraid to ask to see your room before you check in. For the same reason, swimming pools are few and far between, but roof terraces or gardens are common across the range.

Top-class hotels will usually have some soundproofing; otherwise noise levels can be dreadful, in which case ask for a room facing away from the road. The chart on pages 294–5 indicates which hotels have a quiet location – this covers both peaceful neighbourhoods and certain quiet streets in busy areas which don't have a constant stream of traffic.

Parking in central Rome is a problem, though a few hotels have a limited number of parking spaces of their own.

Business visitors to the capital are well catered for, with hotel facilities ranging from fax machines to meeting rooms *(see pp294–5)*.

HOW TO BOOK

The italian postal service tends to be unreliable, so it is safer to book by phone or fax. You should do this at least two months in advance if you want a particular hotel in May, June, September or October; Easter and Christmas are also busy.

If a deposit is required you can pay by credit card or international money order. Under Italian law a booking is valid as soon as the deposit is paid, so you're likely to lose money if you pull out. If you arrive by train, touts may descend on you at the station with offers of accommodation.

They can be of some use if you are looking for a budget hotel, but you should exercise the usual caution. A better bet if you haven't booked anywhere in advance is to head for one of the tourist board offices. Here, staff will reserve you a room within the price range you specify.

The Portoghesi Hotel *(see p296)*

Villa San Pio garden *(see p299)*

CHECKING IN AND OUT

Italian hoteliers are legally obliged to register you with the police, which is the reason they always ask for your passport. They usually hold on to it for a few hours, but you need it if you're going to change money. Everyone in Italy is supposed to carry with them some sort of identification.

In some of Rome's cheaper *pensioni*, don't be surprised if you are asked to pay in advance. To speed up the checking out process, mention in advance if you intend to pay by credit card.

The Locarno *(see p297)*

TOURIST BOARDS

The provincial and state tourist boards can provide advice on accommodation and reserve rooms.

Rome Provincial Tourist Board (EPT)
Via Parigi 5, 00185.
📞 48 89 92 55.

EPT Leonardo da Vinci Airport, Fiumicino, 00054.
📞 65 95 44 71.

EPT Termini Station,
Piazza dei Cinquecento, 00185.
📞 482 40 78 or 487 12 70.

Italian State Tourist Board (ENIT)
Via Marghera 2, 00185.
📞 497 11.

The reception area of the Regina Hotel Baglioni *(see p301)*

DISABLED TRAVELLERS

Provision for disabled travellers is very poor. Small hotels that occupy parts of buildings sometimes only start their rooms up several flights of stairs, whereas certain establishments can accommodate disabled guests on the ground floor, or only have a couple of rooms which are appropriate. Ramps, wide doorways and bathroom handrails are rare.

Our entries for wheelchair access in the listings below rely on the establishments' own assessments; any specific requirements should be checked before booking.

There is a private organization, Associazione Nazionale dei Andicappati at via Tommaso Fortifiocca 100, which gives advice to disabled travellers. They can be contacted on 781 07 72.

TRAVELLING WITH CHILDREN

Italians love children and they are usually welcome across the range of hotels. Facilities, however, tend to be unimpressive on paper. Most hotels can provide cots or small beds, but high chairs, children's meals and baby-sitting services are rare. In practice, though, many establishments – especially smaller, family-run ones – go out of their way to be helpful.

Many hotels do not have any special rates for children, especially in high season, and charge a standard rate if you require an extra bed in a

room, whether it's for a baby or an adult, which can add anything from a few thousand *lire* to 40% on to the price of a double room. For a family with older children, two-room suites are sometimes to be found. For hotels providing children's facilities, see Choosing a Hotel *(pp294–5)*.

SELF-CATERING

Anyone staying in the city for more than a couple of weeks should consider renting an apartment, which can be arranged by a couple of agencies. **International Services** has a list of studios and flats; the **Landmark Trust** leases a flat (booked three years in advance) in the house where Keats died, near the Spanish Steps.

SELF-CATERING AGENCIES

International Services
Via del Babuino 79, 00187.
[36 00 00 18. **FAX** 36 00 00 37.

Landmark Trust
Shottesbrooke, Maidenhead SL6 3SW, Great Britain. **[** 01628-82 59 25.
FAX 01628-82 54 17.

RESIDENTIAL HOTELS

If you want the comfort and privacy of your own apartment coupled with the services of a hotel, you could opt to stay in a *residenza*. Prices range from around L500,000 to over L3 million for a week in a two-bedded room, though some *residenze* are only available for fort-nightly or monthly lets. A full

list is available from tourist board offices *(see p289)*; the following are some of the most central:

Residence Babuino
Via del Babuino 172, 00187.
[361 16 63.

Di Ripetta
Via di Ripetta 231, 00186.
[323 11 44. **FAX** 320 39 59.

In Trastevere
Vicolo Moroni 35, 00153.
[581 27 68.

Ripa
Via Orti di Trastevere 1, 00153.
[586 11.

Vittoria
Via Vittoria 60, 00187.
[679 75 33.

RELIGIOUS INSTITUTIONS

If you don't mind an early curfew when the rest of Rome is still swinging, quite a few religious institutions take in paying guests. You do not have to be a practising Catholic to stay in one of these, but be sure to book well in advance as all of the following places cater for groups of students and pilgrims. **Domus Mariae** and **Istituto Madri Pie** are near the Vatican; **Congregazione Suore dello Spirito Santo** is further out of town, 6 km (4 miles) west of the centre. Prices are in the same range as the cheapest hotels.

Domus Mariae
Via Aurelia 481, 00165.
[663 88 23.

The Gregoriana *(see p297)*

Istituto Madri Pie
Via A. de Gasperi 4, 00165.
C 63 19 67.

Congregazione Suore dello Spirito Santo
Via della Pineta Sacchetti 227, 00168.
C 305 31 01.

Facade of the Excelsior *(see p301)*

BUDGET ACCOMMODATION

EVEN IF YOU'RE TRAVELLING on a shoestring, it's possible to find a clean, decent room in Rome. Dormitory accommodation can be found at rock-bottom prices in simple establishments, such as the **Ottaviano.** Youth hostels are a good option – and not just for the young. At the **Ostello del Foro Italico** bed, breakfast and shower can all be had at a very reasonable price.

Women can get single, double or triple rooms at the **Young Women's Christian Association** (YWCA). Its location near Termini is convenient but insalubrious, so those arriving at night should take care. The **Protezione della Giovane** organization has a useful

information office for women under 25; they will try to find you somewhere to stay.

HOSTEL AND DORMITORY ADDRESSES

Ottaviano
Via Ottaviano 6, 00192.
C 39 73 72 53,
or 39 73 81 38.

Associazione Italiana Alberghi per la Gioventù
(Youth Hostel Association)
Via Cavour 44, 00184.
C 487 11 52.

Ostello del Foro Italico
Viale delle Olimpiadi 61, 00194.
C 323 62 79.

Residenza Universitaria de Lollis
Via Cesare de Lollis 20, 00185.
Rooms in August only. Details from Youth Hostel Association, above.

YWCA
Via C. Balbo 4, 00184.
C 488 39 17.

Protezione della Giovane
Via Urbana 158.
C 488 14 89.

CAMPING

MOST CAMPSITES are well out of town – suitable for an occasional excursion into Rome – with the exception of **Flaminio**, which is near the Olympic Village, 6 km (4 miles) north of the centre.

Flaminio
Via Flaminia Nuova 821, 00191.
C 333 26 04.

USING THE LISTINGS

The hotels on pages 296–301 are organized according to area and price. The symbols after the hotel's address show the facilities it offers.

⊟ rooms with bath and/or shower available
1 single rate rooms available
⊞ rooms for more than two people available, or an extra bed can be put in a double room
24 24-hour room service available
TV television in all rooms
Y minibar in all rooms
⚡ non-smoking rooms available
※ rooms with good view
▤ air conditioning in all rooms
▩ swimming pool in hotel
⊟ business facilities: message-taking service, fax machine for guests, desk and telephone in each room and a meeting room within the hotel
⊹ child cots and babysitting service
⅗ wheelchair access (phone for details)
⬛ lift
⬛ pets allowed in bedrooms (confirm that you are bringing a pet). The majority of hotels accept guide dogs
P hotel parking available
⬤ garden/terrace open to guests
Y bar
⁋ restaurant
⌸ tourist information
⬛ credit cards accepted
AE American Express
DC Diners Club
MC Mastercard/Access
V Visa
JCB Japanese Credit Bureau

Price categories for a double room with bath or shower including breakfast, tax and service:
Ⓛ under L100,000
ⓁⓁ L100,000–L199,000
ⓁⓁⓁ L200,000–L299,000
ⓁⓁⓁⓁ L300,000–L399,000
ⓁⓁⓁⓁⓁ over L400,000

Rome's Best: Hotels

ROMAN HOTELS RANGE from frescoed palaces and *fin-de-siècle* bastions of faded glamour, to family-run guesthouses. Most are within easy reach of restaurants, shops and transport. Whatever the price level, all the hotels shown on this map have something special to offer, whether it's a chic location, or a roof terrace with soaring views across the city. The only drawback is that these places and the others listed on pages 294–301 are exceptions to the many unremarkable hotels in the city, so you should book well in advance. The hotels shown here are the best in their particular style or price range.

Hotel Raphaël

Sole al Pantheon

The writers Jean Paul Sartre and Simone de Beauvoir stayed in this superbly located – and recently refurbished – 15th-century palazzo. (See p296.)

N

0 metres 500

0 yards 500

Raphael
Full of antiques and art, the Raphael offers a central location. (See p297.)

Piaz Spag

Pia de Roto

Vatican

Piazza Navona

Campo de' Fiori

Janiculum

Trastevere

Campo de' Fiori
Central Rome's best bargain offers small, well-furnished rooms and terrific views from the sixth-floor roof terrace. (See p298.)

Teatro di Pompeo
This guesthouse-style hotel was built on the ruins of an ancient theatre. (See p299.)

Sant'Anselmo
To be sure of getting a room you need to book well in advance at this peacefully located Roman villa. An added bonus is the lovely secluded garden. (See p299.)

Hassler
Luxurious suites and an air of faded grandeur remind visitors of the Hassler's heyday. The roof-top restaurant is Rome's most famous. (See p298.)

Villa Borghese
Welcoming public rooms and a cool, shaded courtyard, with a leafy canopy above, create an unpretentious and relaxed atmosphere in this pleasantly informal hotel. (See p301.)

Carriage
The serene atmosphere makes this city-centre hotel a special haven. (See p297.)

Via Veneto

Quirinal

Esquiline

pitol

Forum

Palatine

Caracalla

Lateran

tine

Grand
Good service and extensive facilities are the main features of this old-fashioned, luxury hotel. (See p299.)

Scalinata di Spagna
The prized location at the top of the Spanish Steps, and a large private terrace, make this hotel a popular choice with visitors. (See p298.)

Inghilterra
Sip a cocktail in the Inghilterra's club-like bar, once frequented by Ernest Hemingway. (See p298.)

Choosing a Hotel

THE 71 HOTELS listed in the following pages have all been inspected and assessed. This choosing chart shows some of the features which may affect your hotel choice. The hotels are listed alphabetically within their price category. For more detailed information, see pages 296–301.

	Price	NUMBER OF ROOMS	LARGE ROOMS	BUSINESS FACILITIES	HOTEL PARKING	RECOMMENDED RESTAURANT	CLOSE TO SHOPS AND RESTAURANTS	QUIET LOCATION	24-HOUR ROOM SERVICE
FORUM *(see p296)*									
Forum	ⓛⓛⓛⓛ	76		■					●
PIAZZA DELLA ROTONDA *(see p296)*									
Mimosa	ⓛ	11					●	■	
Abruzzi	ⓛⓛ	25					●		
Santa Chiara	ⓛⓛⓛ	97					●		
Colonna Palace	ⓛⓛⓛⓛ	110	●				●		
Holiday Inn Crowne Plaza Minerva	ⓛⓛⓛⓛ	134	●	■			●	■	
Nazionale	ⓛⓛⓛⓛ	87	●	■			●		●
Sole al Pantheon	ⓛⓛⓛⓛ	30					●		
PIAZZA NAVONA *(see p296)*									
Navona	ⓛ	26					●	■	
Due Torri	ⓛⓛⓛ	26					●	■	
Genio	ⓛⓛⓛ	60					●		
Portoghesi	ⓛⓛⓛ	27				●	●	■	
Raphael	ⓛⓛⓛⓛ	63					●	■	
PIAZZA DI SPAGNA *(see p297)*									
Jonella	ⓛ	9					●		
Firenze	ⓛⓛ	25	●				●		●
Lydia	ⓛⓛ	17					●		
Margutta	ⓛⓛ	21					●	■	
Suisse	ⓛⓛ	13	●				●	■	
Homs	ⓛⓛⓛ	50					●	■	
Locarno	ⓛⓛⓛ	38		■	●		●		
Mozart	ⓛⓛⓛ	31					●	■	
Piazza di Spagna	ⓛⓛⓛ	16					●		
Carriage	ⓛⓛⓛ	27	●				●		
Condotti	ⓛⓛⓛ	17	●				●		
Gregoriana	ⓛⓛⓛ	19				●	●	■	●
Manfredi	ⓛⓛⓛ	15		■			●	■	
dei Borgognoni	ⓛⓛⓛⓛ	50		■	●		●	■	
Hassler	ⓛⓛⓛⓛ	100	●	■	●	■	●	■	
d' Inghilterra	ⓛⓛⓛⓛ	105		■			●	■	●
Scalinata di Spagna	ⓛⓛⓛⓛ	15			●		●		●
Valadier	ⓛⓛⓛⓛ	38		■			●	■	●
CAMPO DE' FIORI *(see p298)*									
Campo de' Fiori	ⓛⓛ	27					●	■	
Della Lunetta	ⓛⓛ	36					●	■	
Piccolo	ⓛⓛ	15					●		
Pomezia	ⓛⓛ	22					●		
Smeraldo	ⓛⓛ	35					●		
Sole	ⓛⓛ	58		■	●		●	■	
Rinascimento	ⓛⓛⓛ	19					●	■	
Teatro di Pompeo	ⓛⓛⓛ	12		■	●		●	■	

Price categories for a double room per night, including breakfast, tax and service:
Ⓛ under L100,000
ⓁⓁ L100,000–L199,000
ⓁⓁⓁ L200,000–L299,000
ⓁⓁⓁⓁ L300,000–L399,000
ⓁⓁⓁⓁⓁ over L400,000.

HOTEL PARKING
Car parking facilities attached to the hotel or in the hotel complex.

CLOSE TO SHOPS AND RESTAURANTS
Within a 5-minute walk of a good area for shops, bars, cafés and restaurants.

BUSINESS FACILITIES
Message-taking service, fax machine for guest use, desk and telephone in each room and a meeting room which is available within the hotel.

	Price	Number of Rooms	Large Rooms	Business Facilities	Hotel Parking	Recommended Restaurant	Close to Shops and Restaurants	Quiet Location	24-Hour Room Service
QUIRINAL *(see p299)*									
Grand	ⓁⓁⓁⓁⓁ	171	●	■		■			●
TERMINI *(see p299)*									
Cervia	Ⓛ	26							
Gexim	Ⓛ	9						■	
Katty	Ⓛ	11							
Mari	Ⓛ	13	●						
Restivo	Ⓛ	6							
Hotel Giuliana	ⓁⓁ	20			●		●		
Canada	ⓁⓁⓁ	70	●	■	●				
AVENTINE *(see p299)*									
Aventino	ⓁⓁ	23	●	■				■	●
Domus Aventina	ⓁⓁⓁ	26	●	■				■	●
Sant'Anselmo	ⓁⓁⓁ	46		■				■	●
Villa San Pio	ⓁⓁⓁ	59	●	■	●			■	●
TRASTEVERE *(see p300)*									
Carmel	Ⓛ	10							
VATICAN *(see p300)*									
Alimandi	ⓁⓁ	30						■	
Amalia	ⓁⓁ	30					●		
Columbus	ⓁⓁⓁ	92		●	●				●
Atlante Star	ⓁⓁⓁⓁ	70	●	■	●		●		●
VIA VENETO *(see p300)*									
Merano	ⓁⓁ	32					●		
Oxford	ⓁⓁⓁ	58		■	●				
Residenza	ⓁⓁⓁ	29	●				●		
Alexandra	ⓁⓁⓁⓁ	45			●		●		
Romantik Barocco	ⓁⓁⓁⓁ	28		■			●		
Victoria	ⓁⓁⓁⓁ	120		■			●	■	●
Bernini Bristol	ⓁⓁⓁⓁⓁ	126	●	■			●		●
Excelsior	ⓁⓁⓁⓁⓁ	327	●	■	●		●		●
Imperiale	ⓁⓁⓁⓁⓁ	95		■			●		●
Majestic	ⓁⓁⓁⓁⓁ	96			●		●		
Regina Hotel Baglioni	ⓁⓁⓁⓁⓁ	130	●	■	●		●		
Sofitel Roma	ⓁⓁⓁⓁⓁ	124	●	■			●	■	
VILLA BORGHESE *(see p301)*									
Villa Borghese	ⓁⓁⓁ	31			●				●
Aldrovandi Palace	ⓁⓁⓁⓁⓁ	140		■	●				
Lord Byron	ⓁⓁⓁⓁⓁ	37		■		■		■	●

FORUM

Forum

Via Tor de' Conti 25, 00184. **Map** 5 B5.
[C] 679 24 46. **FAX** 678 64 79.
[TX] 62 25 49. **Rooms**: 76.
AE, DC, MC, V.

Occupying a palace built out of materials from the ruins of the nearby Imperial Fora, the Forum is an old-fashioned hotel, with mellow, wood-panelled public rooms, and a sunny roof-terrace restaurant giving wonderful views over the archaeological centre.

PIAZZA DELLA ROTONDA

Mimosa

Via di Santa Chiara 61, 00186. **Map** 4 F4 & 12 D3. [C] 68 80 17 53. **FAX** 083 35 57. **Rooms**: 11. 1.

The Mimosa is a clean, if slightly scruffy, family-run hotel close to the Pantheon. Rooms are cool and the five communal bathrooms and showers are immaculate. As the hotel is popular with groups of visiting students, book well ahead.

Abruzzi

Piazza della Rotonda 69, 00186.
Map 4 F4 & 12 D3. [C] 679 20 21.
Rooms: 25.

The Abruzzi provides clean, basic rooms with terracotta-tiled floors in an ochre-coloured palazzo overlooking the Pantheon. The rooms at the back are not the best, but quiet. No breakfast is served.

Santa Chiara

Via di Santa Chiara 21, 00186.
Map 4 F4 & 12 D3. [C] 687 29 79.
FAX 687 31 44. **Rooms**: 97.
AE, DC, MC, V, JCB.

Conveniently located in the historic centre, the Santa Chiara occupies an apricot-washed palazzo. Public rooms are cool, particularly the marble reception area and the lounge. Bedrooms are carpeted, and have good-quality furnishings.

Colonna Palace

Piazza di Montecitorio 12, 00186.
Map 4 F3 & 12 E2. [C] 678 13 41.
FAX 679 44 96. **TX** 62 14 67 CIFCOL.
Rooms: 110.
AE, DC, MC, V.

The Colonna Palace stands on the same piazza as Italy's Chamber of Deputies, and so attracts politicians as well as tourists. Bedrooms are spacious, though the bathrooms are small. Breakfast is served in a basement room livened up by frescoes. There are lovely views from the impressive roof garden where a jacuzzi has recently been installed.

Holiday Inn Crowne Plaza Minerva

Piazza della Minerva 69, 00186.
Map 4 F4 & 12 D3. [C] 69 94 18 88.
FAX 679 41 65. **TX** 62 00 91 HINMIN.
Rooms: 134.
AE, DC, MC, V, JCB.

Occupying Palazzo Fonseca behind the Pantheon, this is Rome's newest luxury hotel. The interior was designed by Post-Modern architect Portoghesi, and its centrepiece is the lounge, canopied in semi-translucent Venetian glass, and presided over by a statue of Minerva. The large bedrooms are decorated in shades of beige and coral. Views from the roof terrace are magnificent, stretching over the Pantheon, St Peter's and the Janiculum hill.

Nazionale

Piazza di Montecitorio 131, 00186.
Map 4 F3 & 12 E2. [C] 69 50 01.
FAX 678 66 77. **Rooms**: 87.
AE, DC, MC, V, JCB.

Home to Robert de Niro while he was making *Godfather II*, the Nazionale is usually frequented by visiting tourists, businessmen and politicians – it stands right on the corner of the Chamber of Deputies. Public rooms are comfortable, particularly the lounge, with its brocade sofas and flower arrangements. Some of the rooms are huge, and most are also partially furnished with British and Italian antiques.

Sole al Pantheon

Piazza della Rotonda 63, 00186.
Map 4 F4 & 12 D3. [C] 678 04 41. **FAX** 699 406 89. **Rooms**: 30.
AE, DC, MC, V.

A hotel since 1467, the Sole's illustrious list of former guests ranges from Renaissance writer Ariosto to Jean-Paul Sartre and Simone de Beauvoir. It is easy to explain it attraction: its location opposite the Pantheon is unbeatable, and though it has been modernized (60% of the rooms now have jacuzzis) there are still bedrooms with painted, panelled ceilings.

PIAZZA NAVONA

Navona

Via dei Sediari 8, 00186. **Map** 4 F4 & 12 D3. [C] 686 42 03. **Rooms**: 21.
18.

A superb location – across the road from Piazza Navona and five minutes' stroll from the Pantheon – means that it's hard to find a room here unless you book well in advance. The hotel is run largely by the owners' Australian son-in-law, who is extremely helpful. Bedrooms are basic, but some of them have bathrooms. The restaurant opens for groups of 15 or more.

Due Torri

Vicolo del Leonetto 23–25, 00186.
Map 4 E3 & 11 C1. [C] 687 69 83.
FAX 686 54 42. **Rooms**: 26. AE, DC, MC, V.

This amiable hotel is a short walk from both Piazza Navona and the Spanish Steps, tucked into an alleyway in the artisans' district of the old town. Bedrooms vary: some are stylish, others plain and rather small. The lounge is both elegant and homely, with swept back drapes, statuettes, an immense gilt-framed mirror and pink velvet sofas.

Genio

Via Zanardelli 28, 00186. **Map** 4 E3 & 11 C2. [C] 683 37 81. **FAX** 68 30 72 46.
Rooms: 64.
AE, DC, MC, V, JCB.

On a fairly busy road just behind Piazza Navona, the Genio's bedrooms are ordinary, though quite comfortable. The location, however, and a roof terrace where you can picnic with your own food, make it worth considering.

Portoghesi

Via dei Portoghesi 1, 00186.
Map 4 E3 & 11 C2. [C] 686 42 31.
FAX 687 69 76. **Rooms**: 27.
MC, V.

Ideally located on a cobbled street a couple of minutes' walk from Piazza Navona, the Portoghesi is a fairly simple hotel, with slightly dated bedrooms. The public rooms, however, are elegant and there's a roof terrace looking on to the dome of the Portuguese community's church next door.

Raphael

Largo Febo 2, 00186. **Map** 4 E3 &
11 C2. **[** 68 28 31. **FAX** 687 89 93.
TX 62 23 96 RHOTEL. **Rooms**: 63. [icons]
[icons] AE, DC, MC, V, JCB. ⓁⓁⓁⓁⓁ

The Raphael is curtained with ivy
and situated on a cobbled street
just off Piazza Navona. The big
reception lounge has the air of
an exhibition hall, being full of
antique statues, modern sculpture
and even a painted sled. There is
a restaurant in the basement
where pride of place goes to an
ornate wine cabinet. Bedrooms are
decorated with parquet floors,
marbled walls and 18th-century-
style furniture as well as paisley
curtains. The rooms on the top
floor have terrific views.

PIAZZA DI SPAGNA

Jonella

Via della Croce 41, 00187. **Map** 4 F2.
[679 79 66. **Rooms**: 5. 1 [icon] Ⓛ

The Jonella occupies an orange-
coloured palazzo on one of the
most attractive shopping streets in
the Piazza di Spagna area. The
décor is somewhat down-at-heel,
but the location and low prices
make it worth considering. The
owner occasionally pops out to
shop, so if you arrive when no-
one's there, be patient and wait
for their return.

Firenze

Via Due Macelli 106, 00187. **Map** 5 A2
& 12 F1. **[** 679 72 40. **FAX** 678 56 36.
Rooms: 25. [icons] TV [icon]
[icons] AE, MC, V. ⓁⓁ

The Firenze lies a short distance
from Piazza di Spagna on a busy
main road. The owner has set her
elegant stamp on the hotel:
Chinese urns and gilt-framed
mirrors greet you in the entrance
hall, and the bedrooms are large
and beautifully decorated. There
is also a leafy terrace where you
can take breakfast.

Lydia

Via Sistina 42, 00187. **Map** 5 B2.
[679 38 15. **FAX** 679 72 63.
TX 62 33 13. **Rooms**: 28. [icons] 6. 1
[icons] AE, DC, MC, V. ⓁⓁ

The Lydia is a pleasant hotel,
popular with students, on a busy
road a few minutes' walk from the
Spanish Steps. Rooms have pale
blue walls and pastel bedcovers,
and two retain their old ceiling
frescoes. If you're not fortunate
enough to get one of these,
content yourself with breakfasting

in the chandelier-lit dining room,
which is also decorated with
beautiful frescoes. Some of the
street-facing rooms can be noisy.

Margutta

Via Laurina 34, 00187. **Map** 4 F1.
[322 36 74. **FAX** 320 03 95. **Rooms**:
21. [icons] AE, DC, MC, V. ⓁⓁ

The Margutta sits on a quiet
cobbled street just below the
Piazza del Popolo. The scruffy
facade and slightly grubby seats in
the lobby are forgotten as soon as
you get into your room, which
has white walls and green
wrought-iron bedsteads and
candle-holders. If you wish to stay
in one of the three attic rooms
that share a pretty roof terrace, be
sure to book well in advance.

Suisse

Via Gregoriana 54–56, 00187.
Map 5 A2 & 12 F1. **[** 678 36 49.
FAX 678 12 58. **Rooms**: 13. [icon] 8.
1 [icons] ⓁⓁ

Occupying the third floor of a
dusty palazzo (the entrance is at
No. 54), the Suisse is a small,
pleasant hotel with friendly staff.
Chinese prints hang along the
corridors and in the rooms. These
also have polished floors, moulded
ceilings and marble-topped
dressers and tables. Breakfast is
served in the bedrooms.

Homs

Via della Vite 71–72, 00187.
Map 5 A3 & 12 F1. **[** 679 29 76.
FAX 678 04 82. **Rooms**: 50. [icons] 1
[icons] TV [icons]
AE, DC, MC, V. ⓁⓁⓁ

On one of the quieter, less
pretentious shopping streets in the
Piazza di Spagna area, the Homs
has clean, pleasant rooms with
dark-green carpets, white walls
and white bathrooms. The
breakfast room opens out on to a
pleasant terrace.

Locarno

Via della Penna 22, 00186. **Map** 4 F1.
[361 08 41, 361 08 42, 361 08 43.
FAX 321 52 49. **Rooms**: 38. [icons]
TV [icons] P [icon]
[icons] AE, DC, MC, V, JCB. ⓁⓁⓁ

Situated on a small, busy side-
street near the Tiber, a brief walk
from Piazza del Popolo, the
Locarno is an attractive 1920s
hotel with an Art Nouveau door
and swags of lilac growing across
its facade. Old-fashioned touches
remain, with a grandfather clock
and Tiffany lamp in the reception,
and a marble-topped bar of
polished wood. Outside, there's a
patio packed with greenery and
kept cool by a tiny fountain.

Mozart

Via dei Greci 23, 00187. **Map** 4 F2.
[36 00 19 15. **FAX** 36 00 17 35.
Rooms: 31. [icons] 1 TV [icons]
[icons] AE, DC, MC, V, JCB.
ⓁⓁⓁ

Located in a cobbled street
between Piazza del Popolo and
Piazza di Spagna, the Mozart is
immediately appealing. Decor is
attractively worn and includes a
Venetian mirror. There's a breakfast room, as well as a bar-café,
which opens off the stone-lagged
reception. Rooms have ceramic-
tiled or parquet floors, and bathrooms tend to be small, most
having only a shower.

Piazza di Spagna

Via Mario de' Fiori 61, 00187.
Map 5 A2 & 12 F1. **[** 679 30 61,
679 64 12. **FAX** 679 06 54. **Rooms**: 16.
[icons] 1 TV [icons]
[icons] AE, MC, V, JCB. ⓁⓁⓁ

Close to the designer boutiques of
Via Condotti, this attractive, small
hotel has simple, but good-sized
rooms, with tiled floors and a
couple of bathrooms with jacuzzis.
The breakfast room and bar are
tiny, so most residents decide to
take breakfast in their own rooms.

Carriage

Via delle Carrozze 36, 00187.
Map 5 A2. **[** 699 01 24.
FAX 678 82 79. **TX** 62 62 46.
Rooms: 27. [icons] 1 TV [icons]
[icons] AE, DC, MC, V, JCB. ⓁⓁⓁⓁ

Situated in a street where
noblemen used to park their
carriages, this hotel's elegance is
immediately evident in the
reception area, with its panelling,
candelabra and gilt-framed mirrors.
The rooms live up to expectations,
decorated in a serene shade of
blue, with some antique furniture.
Two rooms open on to the leafy,
terracotta tiled terrace for all
residents while two have their
own private terraces.

Condotti

Via Mario de' Fiori 37, 00187.
Map 5 A2 & 12 F1. **[** 679 47 69.
FAX 679 04 52. **Rooms**: 17. [icons] 1
TV [icons] [icons]
AE, DC, MC, V, JCB. ⓁⓁⓁⓁ

Close to Piazza di Spagna and in
the heart of the designer shopping
district, the Condotti is a
comfortable, welcoming hotel with
an ambience and style all of its
own. Rooms are medium to large
and well decorated. One room has
its own small terrace and three
others share one.

For key to symbols *see p291*

Gregoriana

Via Gregoriana 18, 00187. **Map** 5 A2 & 12 F1. 679 42 69. **FAX** 678 42 58. *Rooms*: 19.

The Gregoriana is a stylish, congenial hotel, situated close to the Spanish Steps in a tree-lined, quiet street of elegant palazzi. The first- and third-floor corridors are papered with a leopard-spotted print, while that of the second floor is in the style of William Morris. The rooms are all the same: black lacquer doors, terracotta-coloured carpets, flowery wallpaper and 1920s drawings on the walls. Rather peculiarly, there are no public rooms, so breakfast and drinks are served in the bedrooms.

Manfredi

Via Margutta 61, 00187. **Map** 5 A2. 320 76 76, 320 76 95. **FAX** 320 77 36. *Rooms*: 15.

This pretty hotel is excellently located, just off Piazza di Spagna, in a cobbled street of art galleries and antique shops. The reception area and bar-breakfast room are paved with marble and decorated in soft pastels. The comfortable bedrooms are all soundproofed, with pale fabric wall coverings and co-ordinated furnishings.

Dei Borgognoni

Via del Bufalo 126, 00187. **Map** 5 A3 & 12 F1. 69 94 15 05. **FAX** 69 94 15 01. **TX** 62 30 74 BUFALO. *Rooms*: 50.

This elegant hotel is just off Piazza San Silvestro, five minutes from the Spanish Steps. In the public rooms, modern style is coupled with traditional oil paintings. The bedrooms – some of which have terraces – are exquisite and beautifully understated.

Hassler

Piazza Trinità dei Monti 6, 00187. **Map** 5 A2. 69 93 40. **FAX** 678 99 91. **TX** 61 02 08. *Rooms*: 100.

Standing at the top of the Spanish Steps, with magnificent views of Rome from its roof terrace, restaurant (*see p313*) and suites, the Hassler was once host to royalty and the glitterati of Europe and America. Its *dolce vita* days are over, but the lounges and

bedrooms lit by Venetian glass chandeliers, the wood-panelled bar and marble bathrooms retain the air of a more extravagant era.

D' Inghilterra

Via Bocca di Leone 14, 00187. **Map** 5 A2. 69 98 1. **FAX** 69 92 22 43. **TX** 61 45 52. *Rooms*: 105.

Liszt and Hemingway are among the writers, artists and musicians who have stayed here. In the heart of Rome's designer shopping area and close to the Spanish Steps, it's still a desirable place to stay. The bedrooms are all individually decorated and furnished. The bar could have been lifted straight from a London gentlemen's club, and the restaurant walls, painted with views of gardens and the sky-frescoed ceiling create the illusion of dining in the open.

Scalinata di Spagna

Piazza Trinità dei Monti 17, 00187. **Map** 5 A2. 67 93 006. **FAX** 69 94 05 98. *Rooms*: 15.

This hotel occupies a small 18th-century villa at the top of the Spanish Steps. Breakfast is at a communal table under the gaze of a parrot. Some rooms retain their panelled ceilings. Book well ahead if you want to stay in one of the rooms that open out on to the large terrace.

Valadier

Via della Fontanella 15, 00187. **Map** 4 F1. 361 19 98. **FAX** 320 15 58. **TX** 62 08 73. *Rooms*: 38.

Slickly decorated with shiny wood and marble, the Valadier styles itself as an intimate hideaway for those on a romantic visit to Rome. Public rooms are tailor-made for seduction, with low sofas, marble floors and oriental rugs. If you believe the hotel's publicity, the bizarre art selection is there to provide shy Casanovas with conversation openers.

CAMPO DE' FIORI

Campo de' Fiori

Via del Biscione 6, 00186. **Map** 4 E4 & 11 C4. 687 48 86. **FAX** 687 60 03. *Rooms*: 27. 13.

This very good value, mid-range hotel occupies a well-kept house,

just off the Campo de' Fiori market square. You enter the tiny reception area along a passage-way, in which mirrors intriguingly repeat a series of columns into an illusory optical suggestion of infinity. The small bedrooms have beams and paisley furnishings, or sky-painted ceilings, lacy walls and frilly bedcovers. On the sixth floor a split-level roof garden gives vertiginous but aesthetically rewarding views over the Pantheon, the Victor Emmanuel monument and St Peter's.

Della Lunetta

Piazza del Paradiso 68, 00186. **Map** 4 E4 & 11 C4. 686 10 80, 687 76 30. **FAX** 689 20 28. *Rooms*: 36.

On a tiny, crumbling piazza, midway between Corso Vittorio Emanuele and Piazza Campo de' Fiori, the Lunetta is a popular, well-maintained little hotel with neat, clean rooms and a courtyard. More bathrooms are gradually being installed and a rooftop garden is being renovated. No breakfast is served.

Piccolo

Via dei Chiavari 32, 00186. **Map** 4 E4 & 11 C4. 68 80 25 60. *Rooms*: 15. 4.

Close to Piazza Campo de' Fiori, the Piccolo is a family-run hotel at the cheap end of its price band. There is, however, nothing cheap about the atmosphere. Cool and serene, with clean, simple rooms in a variety of sizes. The Piccolo also has a separate bar-breakfast room.

Pomezia

Via dei Chiavari 12, 00186. **Map** 4 E4 & 12 D4. 686 13 71. **FAX** 686 13 71. *Rooms*: 22. 11.

In the heart of the lively Campo de' Fiori district, the Pomezia was renovated recently and now has spotless, simply decorated rooms and a bar in the reception area to welcome weary arrivals.

Smeraldo

Vicolo dei Chiodaroli 9, 00186. **Map** 4 F5 & 12 D4. 687 59 29. **FAX** 68 80 54 95. *Rooms*: 35. 23.

Situated in the heart of the bustling Campo de' Fiori quarter, the Smeraldo offers an oasis of serenity, with clean, simple rooms in an ochre-washed building with shutters over the windows.

Sole

Via del Biscione 76, 00186. **Map** 4 E4 & 11 C4. 68 80 68 73, 68 80 52 58. FAX 689 37 87. **Rooms**: 58. 31. 1

Possibly the oldest hotel in Rome, this appealing establishment occupies a palazzo just off the central market square of Campo de' Fiori. Rooms are furnished in a slightly haphazard way, but with some character. There are small sitting areas and a leafy, sunny terrace with a drink and snack machine. No breakfast is served.

Rinascimento

Via del Pellegrino 122, 00186. **Map** 4 E4 & 11 B3. 687 48 13. FAX 683 35 18. TX 62 02 07 HTLRIN. **Rooms**: 19. 1 TV AE, MC, V.

With an appealing location in the Campo de' Fiori district, close to artisans' workshops and a variety of trattorias, the Rinascimento is housed in an old palazzo with stone arched windows. The bedrooms, however, tend to be slightly worn and have rather cramped bathrooms.

Teatro di Pompeo

Largo del Pallaro 8, 00186. **Map** 4 E4 & 11 C4. 68 30 01 70, 687 25 66. FAX 68 80 55 31. **Rooms**: 12. 1 TV AE, DC, MC, V.

This small, courteously run hotel sits over the ruins of the first permanent theatre in the city, which was completed in 55 BC by Pompey the Great. You can eat breakfast among the original theatre arches, and the bar has a terracotta floor and marble tables.

QUIRINAL

Grand

Via V. E. Orlando 3, 00185. **Map** 5 C2. 47 09. FAX 482 38 67. TX 61 02 10. **Rooms**: 170. 24 TV AE, DC, MC, V, JCB.

To step into the Grand is to enter another world. Cherubs cavort over the reception area; flowers and fruit are carved on the walls of the lounge and rich pastel rugs lie on the parquet floor. Facilities include a sauna, beauty salon, hairdresser and a restaurant renowned as one of the most beautiful in the country. The standard of bedrooms varies, but you might find yourself sleeping in an antique bed, reading by the light of a genuine Venetian lamp.

TERMINI

Cervia

Via Palestro 55, 00185. **Map** 6 E2. 49 10 57. FAX 49 10 56. **Rooms**: 27. 7. MC, V.

The Cervia is a 20-room hotel housed in the same palazzo as the Mari and the Restivo. Some of the rooms have been refurbished with sponge-painted walls and private bathrooms, and these give excellent value. The rest, however, tend to be a bit more basic. The public areas are immaculate, and there is also a pleasant up-to-date bar-breakfast room.

Gexim

Via Palestro 34, 00185. **Map** 6 E2. 446 02 11, 444 13 11. FAX 444 13 11. **Closed** last 2 wks in Aug. **Rooms**: 9. 5.

Don't be put off by the shabby exterior of the palazzo – the Gexim, which occupies part of the third floor, is a cut above most cheap hotels. Pastel-painted walls are hung with prints of Impressionist paintings and all the bedrooms, bathrooms and public areas are spotless. The hotel has recently been renovated.

Katty

Via Palestro 35, 00185. **Map** 6 E2. 444 12 16. FAX 444 12 16 **Rooms**: 11. 2.

The Katty has clean, basic rooms, some of which have an occasional piece of antique furniture. It's extremely popular with British and American students, so either book in advance or turn up early, ideally between 8am and 9am. No breakfast is served.

Mari

Via Palestro 55, 00185. **Map** 6 E2. 446 21 37. FAX 482 83 13. **Rooms**: 21. 10. 1 MC, V.

This friendly hotel run by three women has clean, pleasant rooms with no frills. If it's full, Mari 2 nearby at Via Calatafimi 38 (tel 474 03 71) has more rooms (half with bathrooms) and is also good value. There is a 5% surcharge for paying with credit cards.

Restivo

Via Palestro 55, 00185. **Map** 6 E2. 446 21 72. **Rooms**: 6. 1

In the same building as the Mari, the Restivo has six immaculately maintained bedrooms. The elderly lady owner has a hall full of gifts and postcards from grateful guests who often return again and again.

Hotel Giuliana

Via Palermo 36, 00184. **Map** 5 C4. 488 07 95. FAX 482 42 87. **Rooms**: 20. 1 TV AE, DC, V, JCB.

Within walking distance of many major sights, and 10 minutes from Termini station, this small hotel offers bright, clean accommodation at very reasonable prices. Helpful, English-speaking staff are happy to offer advice on any aspect of your visit, from transport tips to restaurant recommendations. Many guests return time and again, so do book in advance to be sure of a room.

Canada

Via Vicenza 58, 00185. **Map** 6 E2. 445 77 70. FAX 445 07 49. **Rooms**: 70. 1 TV AE, DC, MC, V.

Outside the centre, behind Termini station, the Canada is an above-average, mid-range hotel. Rooms are very comfortable, and there's a pleasant lounge-bar with attractive cane seats and squashy sofas. The service is courteous.

AVENTINE

Aventino

Via San Domenico 10, 00153. **Map** 8 D2. 574 51 74, 578 32 14. FAX 578 36 04. **Rooms**: 23. 1 DC, MC, V.

Run by the owners of Villa San Pio and Sant'Anselmo, the Aventino is more modest, with large but fairly simple rooms. However, its lush, garden location is gorgeous, and the breakfast room, with a magnificent armoire and stained glass, a reminder of headier days.

Domus Aventina

Via di Santa Prisca 11B, 00153. **Map** 8 E2. 574 61 35. FAX 57 30 00 44. **Rooms**: 26. 1 24 TV AE, DC, MC, V, JCB.

This immaculate hotel occupies a 14th-century convent situated at the foot of the Aventine hill. Rooms are large, and simply decorated in pastel tones, and there are wonderful views of the Celian hill from many of the balconies – 18 rooms have them – and from the huge terrace.

Sant'Anselmo

Piazza di Sant'Anselmo 2, 00153. **Map** 8 D2. 574 51 74. FAX 578 36 04. **Rooms**: 46. 1 DC, MC, V.

This pretty villa, among the gardens of the peaceful Aventine, is within walking distance of the Colosseum. The entrance hall ceiling is stencilled with flowers; there are chandeliers and corridors with floors of inlaid marble. The lounge looks on to the hotel's secluded garden. Some rooms have antique, hand-painted furniture. Book well in advance.

Villa San Pio

Via Sant'Anselmo 19, 00153. **Map** 8 E3. 578 32 14, 574 35 47. **FAX** 578 36 04. **Rooms**: 59.

DC, MC, V.

The Villa San Pio occupies a yellow and ochre villa set in a garden graced with statues. The elegant entrance hall is furnished with velvet and brocade chairs, a painted grandfather clock and an 18th-century Venetian tapestry. While some of the rooms are simple, others have embroidered bedspreads and flower-stencilled furniture; others open on to the garden. There are two bars. Breakfast or drinks can also be taken in the bedrooms or garden.

TRASTEVERE

Carmel

Via Mameli 11, 00153. **Map** 7 C2. 580 99 21. **Rooms**: 10. 9.

The Carmel's most appealing feature is a terrace with a leafy canopy, potted plants and garden furniture. A couple of rooms open off the terrace. All ten rooms are spotless, and most have bathrooms. The owner is not keen on having children to stay and you must be sure to book in advance as she closes the hotel when she thinks trade will be slack.

VATICAN

Alimandi

Via Tunisi 8, 00192. **Map** 3 B2. 39 72 39 48. **FAX** 39 72 39 43. **Rooms**: 32. 26.

AE, DC, MC, V.

On a quietish street just below the entrance to the Vatican Museums, the Alimandi is a simple *pensione* at the cheap end of its price band – hence its popularity with young travellers. Rooms are clean and adequate. The outstanding feature of this guesthouse is a lovely large roof terrace, where you can arrange to sit out and have a barbecue, if you ask in advance.

Amalia

Via Germanico 66, 00192. **Map** 3 C2. 39 72 33 54, 39 72 33 56. **FAX** 39 72 33 65. **Rooms**: 30. 20.

AE, DC, MC, V, JCB.

Situated between the Ottaviano Metro station and the Vatican, the Amalia attracts mainly Italian visitors. It has spotless rooms ranged on three floors, a lounge with a bar and a coffee machine off the reception area.

Columbus

Via della Conciliazione 33, 00193. **Map** 3 C3. 686 54 35. **FAX** 686 48 74. **Rooms**: 92.

AE, DC, MC, V.

Perfect for anyone wishing to stay near the Vatican, the Columbus occupies an austere former monastery. Heavy wrought-iron light fittings hang in the reception hall; the magnificent upper lounge has a beamed ceiling and terra-cotta floor; the function room – housed in the old refectory – has kept its frescoes, and there is a walled terrace garden. The bedrooms are well-equipped, though the beds are narrow.

Atlante Star

Via Vitelleschi 34, 00193. **Map** 3 C2. 687 32 33. **FAX** 687 23 00. **TX** 62 23 55. **Rooms**: 70.

AE, DC, MC, V, JCB.

This hotel is a good option if you're in Rome on business and need on-site office facilities. The rooftop restaurant has panoramic views of St Peter's, but both service and atmosphere leave much to be desired. Double rooms are modest in size and singles can be cramped, some of them with only a shower. Avoid street-facing rooms as they can be noisy.

VIA VENETO

Merano

Via Veneto 155, 00187. **Map** 5 B2. 482 17 96. **FAX** 482 18 10. **Rooms**: 30.

AE, DC, MC, V.

The Merano is a small, friendly *pensione* in a 19th-century palazzo which also houses a piano bar and hairdresser. The décor is a little dated and relatively high prices, for what is essentially a guesthouse, reflect the up-market location. The hotel's best feature is its sunny, parquet-floored breakfast room.

Oxford

Via Boncompagni 89, 00187. **Map** 5 C1. 42 82 89 52. **FAX** 42 81 53 49. **TX** 63 03 92. **Rooms**: 58.

AE, DC, MC, V, JCB.

On a quiet road off Piazza Fiume, about ten minutes' walk from Via Veneto, the Oxford has stylish public rooms: squashy sofas of shocking-pink and modern pictures in the reception area; striped sofas and abstract art in the bar. The bedrooms are more dated, with hessian-covered walls and candlewick bedspreads.

Residenza

Via Emilia 22–24, 00187. **Map** 5 B2. 488 07 89. **FAX** 48 57 21. **Rooms**: 29.

AE, MC, V.

The Residenza is an elegant hotel that occupies a villa in a quiet road off the Via Veneto. Kilim rugs decorate the lounges. There is a canopied terrace with pine furniture, and a terracotta-tiled roof garden, edged with potted plants. The bedrooms are less stylish than the public rooms, but are comfortable, large and well-equipped.

Alexandra

Via Veneto 18, 00187. **Map** 5 B2. 488 19 43. **FAX** 487 18 04. **TX** 62 26 55. **Rooms**: 45.

AE, DC, MC, V, JCB.

One of the less expensive hotels on the up-market Via Veneto, the Alexandra has a pleasant conservatory-style breakfast room and a lounge decorated with chintz and brocade. All the bedrooms are different and you could just as easily end up in a room furnished with antiques as one with splash-painted walls. If you are a light sleeper ask for an internal room, as the windows do not block out all the traffic noise.

Romantik Barocco Hotel

Piazza Barberini 9 (entrance on Via della Purificazione 4), 00187. **Map** 5 B3. 487 20 01. **FAX** 48 59 94. **Rooms**: 28.

AE, DC, MC, V, JCB.

Occupying a restored palazzo at the bottom of Via Veneto, the Barocco is ideal for anyone who prefers a small hotel. Bedrooms are pleasant with unobtrusive décor, and some have a working area. There are two small lounges (one with a bar) and a restaurant.

Victoria

Via Campania 41, 00187. **Map** 5 B1.
[47 39 31. FAX 487 18 90.
TX 61 02 12. **Rooms:** 120.
AE, DC, MC, V.

Situated on a quiet road at the top
of Via Veneto and overlooking the
walls abutting the Porta Pinciana,
the Victoria prides itself on being
a "hotel for individuals", keeping
its personal touch by refusing large
group bookings. It is renowned for
good service. There are stylish
public rooms and an attractive roof
terrace, but the bedrooms are
rather small and uninspired.

Bernini Bristol

Piazza Barberini 23, 00187. **Map** 5 B3.
[488 30 51. FAX 482 42 66.
TX 61 05 54. **Rooms:** 126.
AE, DC, MC, V, JCB.

This unprepossessing brick
building overlooks a busy piazza
that has Bernini's Triton fountain
as its centrepiece. The marble-
laden hotel is comfortable, with
a roof garden, but the décor is
uninspiring and the atmosphere
more conducive to work than
pleasure. The central location
and secretarial facilities ensure a
steady stream of business visitors.

Excelsior

Via Veneto 125, 00187. **Map** 5 B1.
[47 08. FAX 482 62 05. TX 61 02 32.
Rooms: 327.
AE, DC, MC, V, JCB.

Exotically sculpted balconies
supported by statues set the tone
for this extravagant hotel, which
houses boutiques, saunas, a
restaurant and a famous piano bar.
Public rooms are sumptuous, with
marble walls and floors, rich
carpets and brocade furnishings,
and the corridors are panelled
with silk or imitation marble. The
bedrooms are elegant and spacious
with chandeliers, painted and
gilded wooden panelling and
ornate, marble bathrooms.

Imperiale

Via Veneto 24, 00187. **Map** 5 B2.
[482 63 51. FAX 482 63 51.
TX 62 10 71. **Rooms:** 95.
AE, DC, MC, V.

One of the more reasonably priced
Via Veneto hotels, the Imperiale
lacks the panache of its more
glamorous neighbours, but the
friendly staff make for a quiet but

relaxed atmosphere. The lounge
is more of a place to wait than to
spend an evening, but the bar is
quite pleasant and the bedrooms
are well decorated, with pretty
co-ordinating furnishings and
small marble bathrooms.

Majestic

Via Veneto 50, 00187. **Map** 5 B2.
[48 68 41, 482 80 14. FAX 488 09 84,
488 56 57. TX 62 22 62. **Rooms:** 96.
AE, DC, MC, V, JCB.

Founded in 1889, the Majestic is
the oldest of Via Veneto's hotels.
Since its five-year refurbishment it
has played host to international
stars such as Madonna, Pavarotti
and Stallone. Most of the furniture
and much of the décor in the
public rooms are original, down
to the startling lime-green and gilt
lounge. Bedrooms and corridors
are decorated in a bold, bright
style, particularly on the fifth floor,
where carpets with a zig-zag
pattern provide the background to
chintz and brocade.

Regina Hotel Baglioni

Via Veneto 72, 00187. **Map** 5 B2.
[47 68 51. FAX 48 54 83. TX 62 08 63.
Rooms: 130.
AE, DC, MC, V.

The exuberance of the Baglioni's
exterior – it is painted vanilla and
strawberry pink and decorated
with grimacing masks – continues
in the reception area where a
wrought-iron staircase is guarded
by the statue of a sea god. The
bedrooms are painted in vivid
shades of coral, aqua and blue,
and many are very spacious.
Double glazing in the rooms
overlooking Via Veneto cuts down
on some of the traffic noise but
light sleepers might still prefer to
ask for a room at the back of the
hotel when booking.

Sofitel Roma

Via Lombardia 47, 00187. **Map** 5 B2.
[47 80 21. FAX 482 10 19.
TX 62 22 47. **Rooms:** 124.
AE, DC, MC, V, JCB.

Overlooking the beautifully-kept
grounds of the Villas Medici and
Ludovisi, the Boston is a quiet,
old-fashioned hotel, convenient
for both the Via Veneto and the
Spanish Steps. The rooms are
decorated in pastel shades, and
some are very large. Views from
the roof terrace stretch from the
Villa Borghese right up to St
Peter's and the Vatican City.

Villa Borghese

Via Pinciana 31, 00198. **Map** 2 F5.
[841 41 00. FAX 844 26 36.
Rooms: 31.
AE, DC, MC, V, JCB.

This immediately likeable hotel
occupies a villa close to Villa
Borghese. Although the hotel is on
a rather busy main road, the
atmosphere is pleasant: more that
of a private home than a hotel.
Public rooms include an intimate,
old-fashioned bar, a lounge with
comfortable sofas and floral soft
furnishings, and there is a
courtyard sheltered by a pretty
ivy-covered pergola. The rooms
are on the small side but they are
tastefully decorated.

Aldrovandi Palace

Via Aldrovandi 15, 00197. **Map** 2 E4.
[322 39 93. FAX 322 14 35.
TX 61 61 41 ALDROV. **Rooms:** 140.
AE, DC, MC, V, JCB.

Among the most restful luxury
hotels in the city, the Aldrovandi is
just outside the centre of Rome on
a fairly busy road overlooking
Villa Borghese. The reception
lounge is elegant, decorated with
rich soft furnishings, carpets,
chandeliers and lots of vases of
fresh flowers. The real highlight of
the hotel, however, is the sunny
garden with its attractive
swimming pool, which is overlooked by an airy restaurant.

Lord Byron

Via de Notaris 5, 00197. **Map** 2 D4.
[361 30 41. FAX 322 04 05.
TX 61 12 17 HBYRON. **Rooms:** 37.
AE, DC, MC, V, JCB.

This small, refined hotel is housed
in a dazzling white building in the
residential district of Parioli. It was
originally a monastery, but there
is nothing ascetic about its rooms
today. The lounge is lavishly
furnished with antiques and
tapestry-seated chairs and the tiny
sitting room has capacious sofas
and old-fashioned portraits. The
restaurant is decorated with plenty
of chintz and fresh flowers and
serves some of the best food in
Rome. All the bedrooms have
tapestry and floral soft furnishings
with marble coffee tables and are
provided with a full decanter of
port, which comes with the
compliments of the management.

RESTAURANTS AND CAFÉS

IN ROME, eating out can be both a joy and an entertainment. On warm summer evenings tables flow out into every conceivable open space and diners dedicate long hours to the popular social activity of people watching (and of being noticed and admired themselves) in a confusion of passers-by, buskers, rose sellers and traffic. Although Romans have always loved to linger at the table, the lavish feasts of ancient Rome have slimmed down and today's cooking is based on simplicity, freshness and good quality local raw ingredients in

Waiter at Alberto Ciarla (see p316)

what is essentially a seasonal cuisine. Fast food is gradually arriving, but it is fundamentally alien to the Roman temperament and way of life.

The 66 restaurants reviewed in this chapter have been selected from the best that Rome can offer across all price ranges. The chart on pages 310–11 will help narrow down your selection, and the map on page 308 shows the highlights of the list. The section on *Light Meals and Snacks* featured on pages 318–21 has details of recommended cafés, pizzerias, wine bars and other places for more casual eating.

WHERE TO FIND GOOD RESTAURANTS

EVERY AREA of the city has its own culinary delights. True Roman cooking can be found in the old slaughterhouse area of Testaccio and in the Jewish quarter (the Ghetto) near Campo de' Fiori. Around the university, in San Lorenzo, northeast of the city centre, you will find lots of cheap pizzerias and trattorias.

Near Termini station there's a good selection of African – particularly Ethiopian and Eritrean – restaurants. For dining outdoors, which often means in beautifully secluded piazzas, or in impressively ancient parts of the city, try the restaurants in the narrow streets of Trastevere (the old

artists' quarter), around Campo de' Fiori, or along the old Via Appia Antica.

TYPES OF RESTAURANTS

IN GENERAL, a *trattoria* is an unassuming, family-run establishment with good home cooking, while a *ristorante* is more up-market, more elegant and thus more expensive.

Many eating places – where paper tablecloths give a clue to low prices – simply have no name. They offer an open doorway and, more often than not, excellent, basic home cooking. Some of them offer a great deal more than that, and your chances of finding authentic Roman cooking are higher in the best of these establishments than in expensive restaurants.

There will probably be times when you don't want a full-blown restaurant meal, and Rome offers a huge variety of places for more casual eating *(see pp318–21)*. One type of place offering snacks or more

Fresh artichokes, a Roman speciality

substantial dishes is the *enoteca*, which doubles as a well-stocked wine shop for browsers and connoisseurs.

The sign *vino e cucina* (wine and food), sadly fast disappearing, holds the same promise. Other places for a sit-down, informal lunch or dinner are *birrerie*, which are not only for beer drinkers, but which also offer pizzas or even four-course meals.

There's plenty of interesting takeaway food on sale throughout the day – *pizza al taglio* (pizza by the slice) is available all over the city. For full-size pizzas, choose places with wood stoves *(forno a legna)* for better results than from electric ovens. Other takeaways such as whole roast chicken, potatoes or *supplì* (fried rice croquettes) can be had from *rosticcerie*. A self-service *tavola calda* will serve an impressive array of hot food and is ideal for lunchtimes.

VEGETARIAN FOOD

PURELY VEGETARIAN restaurants are largely unknown in Rome, but everywhere you'll find pasta or rice dishes (risotto) using interesting combinations of vegetables, salads, artichokes cooked in different ways, or vegetables stuffed and then baked in the oven. Most menus are very adaptable.

The interior of Relais le Jardin (see p317)

THE PRICE OF A MEAL

WHAT YOU PAY will clearly depend on your choice of establishment. In a *tavola calda* or Roman pizzeria, for example, you can often eat for as little as L15,000 a head. A local trattoria costs perhaps L25,000, whereas in a full-blown restaurant reckon on around L50,000 and up. Bottled wine, as opposed to a jug or carafe of house wine *(vino della casa)*, commands higher prices but should offer a more interesting range of tastes *(see p306)*. House wine is usually acceptable, though.

READING THE MENU

NOT EVERY restaurant automatically provides a menu – the waiter will often tell you the day's specialities *(piatti del giorno)*, usually not mentioned on the standard menu but almost always worth ordering. If you are not sure about these, you can always ask for *la lista* (the menu) and then allow yourself to be guided.

A meal could begin with *antipasti* (appetizers) or *primi piatti* – the latter consisting of *pasta asciutta* (pasta with some kind of sauce), *pasta in brodo* (clear broth with pasta in it), *pasta al forno* (baked pasta), risotto or a substantial soup. You then move on to the *secondi*, the main meat or fish course, for which you'll need to order vegetables *(contorni)* separately if you would like them. Afterwards you have *formaggi* (cheeses), *frutta* (fruit) or *dolci* (desserts). Romans don't usually eat

One of many Trastevere cafés

Outdoor café life in the piazza outside Santa Maria in Trastevere

cheese as well as a sweet dish, but cheese often comes with fruit such as pears, figs or melon. Strong espresso coffee, and perhaps a liqueur *(amaro* or *digestivo)* rounds off the meal *(see p306)*. You may want to skip the first course, or you may prefer to choose a salad or vegetable dish. Pasta alone tends not to be seen as a full meal.

OPENING TIMES

RESTAURANTS are generally open from about noon to 3pm and from 8pm to 11pm or much later. The busiest times tend to be 9pm–9.30pm for dinner and 1pm–1.30pm at lunchtime. Dinner is generally the preferred time for dedicated, relaxed eating, particularly in summer, when it will begin and end late as the heat of the day subsides. Bars are open all day, often from the early hours, serving all kinds of drinks (alcohol can be sold at any time of day) and snacks. The quietest month is August, when many restaurant owners take their annual holiday (shown by *chiuso per ferie* signs).

BOOKING A TABLE

BOOKING *(prenotazione)* is generally advisable. Sunday is the main lunch date of the week when you should definitely book; the same usually goes for Saturday evening. Check the weekly closing day if you don't book. Many places are closed on Mondays, and Sunday evening can also be difficult.

In summer try to book a shady table outside, since air conditioning is not universal.

WHEELCHAIR ACCESS

ROME is becoming more solicitous towards those in wheelchairs, but a call to the restaurant in advance will help secure the right table.

TAKING CHILDREN ALONG

CHILDREN are made very welcome, particularly in family-run places. You can usually order half-portions (but expect to pay more than half), or just ask for an extra plate. High chairs *(seggioline)* may also be available in some of the establishments.

USING THE LISTINGS

Key to symbols in the listings on pp312–17.

|O| fixed price menus
🚭 non-smoking area
V vegetarian dishes
🚼 child portions and sometimes high chairs
🔥 wheelchair access
T jacket and tie required
🎵 live music
🌂 tables outside
🍷 exceptional wine list
★ highly recommended
💳 credit cards accepted
AE American Express
DC Diners Club
MC Mastercard/Access
V Visa
JCB Japanese Credit Bureau

Price categories for a three-course meal for one, including a half bottle of house wine, cover charge, tax and service:
Ⓛ up to L35,000
ⓁⓁ L35,000–L55,000
ⓁⓁⓁ L55,000–L75,000
ⓁⓁⓁⓁ L75,000–L100,000
ⓁⓁⓁⓁⓁ over L100,000

What to Eat in Rome

Bulb of fresh garlic

THE TRADITIONAL *cucina romanesca* has always relied on local markets full of fresh seasonal vegetables, fruit, cheese and meat from the nearby countryside plus seafood from the Mediterranean. As in the rest of Italy, pasta is an important part of the menu; one popular dish is the famous *spaghetti alla carbonara,* which was devised in Rome. Many genuinely Roman meat dishes are based on the so-called *quinto quarto* (fifth quarter) – head, innards, tail, trotters and so on. Highly flavoured with olive oil, herbs, lard, bacon *(pancetta)* or pig's cheek *(guanciale)* they become a culinary delight. Fish from the Mediterranean is excellent. In season, mushrooms and artichokes may be served in dozens of different ways. *Misticanza* is also good in season; it's a fresh mix of salad leaves including the peppery *rughetta* (rocket) and *puntarelle* (curly endive shoots, often served with anchovy dressing). For dessert you should not miss out on ice cream, or puddings like the classic *tiramisù.*

Maritozzi alla Panna
These soft buns with raisins and candied peel are filled with whipped cream.

Bruschetta
Toasted bread is rubbed with garlic and olive oil; tomato can be added.

Fresh basil

Anchovies

Artichoke hearts

Baby octopus

Roasted peppers

Antipasto
Italian appetizers may include olives, cured meats, seafood and grilled or preserved vegetables.

Supplì
Fried rice croquettes are stuffed with mozzarella and make a tasty snack.

Olive Oil and Vinegar
Always on the table, these are for dressing salads and flavouring antipasto.

Filetti di Baccalà
A Jewish speciality, deep-fried cod fillets are a typical Roman snack or first course.

Risotto alla Romana
Liver, sweetbreads, Marsala and pecorino cheese are used to make this risotto.

TYPICAL ITALIAN PASTA

Penne rigate (quills)

Farfalle (butterflies)

Fusilli (spirals)

Conchigliette (shells)

Cappelletti (small hats)

Bucatini all'Amatriciana
Pasta tubes are served with bacon, tomatoes and onion, with grated pecorino on top.

Spaghetti alla Carbonara
Chopped bacon, eggs and cheese are used to prepare this famous local dish.

Gnocchi alla Romana
Small potato or semolina dumplings are served with tomato or just with butter.

Fiori di Zucca e Carciofi Fritti
Courgette flowers in batter and whole artichokes deep-fried are popular antipasti.

Coda alla Vaccinara
A traditional Roman dish, this is made from braised oxtail with tomatoes.

Saltimbocca alla Romana
Veal with Parma ham and sage, this tasty dish is also served rolled and skewered.

Fave al Guanciale
Fresh springtime broad beans are simmered with bacon and onion.

Parmesan

Italian Cheeses
Parmesan is the best-known Italian cheese but Rome's classic is pecorino romano, made from ewe's milk. The mature, hard version is often used grated, but fresh pecorino can be eaten as a dessert cheese. Mild buffalo-milk mozzarella is the classic one for pizza.

Mozzarella

Crostata di Ricotta
This Roman cheesecake is filled with ricotta, Marsala and lemon.

Tiramisù
Mascarpone cheese, coffee and chocolate are combined for this wonderful dessert.

What to Drink in Rome

Roman mosaic showing bird and vines

ITALY IS ONE OF Europe's most significant wine-producing countries, keeping up a tradition started in the hills around Rome over 2,000 years ago. Today, wine is usually drunk with meals as a matter of course, and knowing the difference between *rosso* (red) and *bianco* (white) may be all the vocabulary you need to get by. Beer is widely available too, as well as good ranges of apéritifs and digestifs. Rome's drinking water, another debt to the ancient Romans, is particularly good, fresh and sweet, and in abundant supply.

The vineyards of Frascati, southeast of Rome

WHITE WINE

Orvieto **Frascati**

VINES THRIVE in the warm climate of Lazio, the region around Rome, producing abundant supplies of inexpensive dry white wine for the city's cafés and restaurants. It is usually sold by the carafe. Of local bottled wines, Frascati is the best-known, but Castelli Romani, Marino, Colli Albani and Velletri are very similar in style. All are made from one grape variety, the Trebbiano, though better quality versions contain a dash of Malvasia for perfume and flavour. Other central Italian whites worth trying are Orvieto and Verdicchio. Quality white wines from all over Italy, including fine whites from Friuli in the northeast, are widely available in Rome.

Calcaia comes from Barberani, a reliable producer of Orvieto.

Bigi produce good quality Orvieto, especially the single-vineyard Torricella.

Casal Pilozzo is an easy-drinking white wine from Frascati producers, Colli di Catone. Choose the youngest vintage.

Colle Gaio, with its rich, fruity flavour, stands out among the dry white Frascatis.

WINE TYPE	GOOD VINTAGES	GOOD PRODUCERS
WHITE WINE		
Friuli (Pinot Bianco, Chardonnay, Pinot Grigio, Sauvignon)	The most recent	Gravner, Jermann, Puiatti, Schiopetto, Volpe Pasini
Orvieto/ Orvieto Classico	The most recent	Antinori, Barberani, Bigi, Il Palazzone
RED WINE		
Chianti/ Chianti Classico/ Chianti Rufina	90, 88, 85	Antinori, Castello di Ama, Castello di Cacchiano, Castello di Volpaia, Felsina Berardenga, Fontodi, Frescobaldi, Isole e Olena, Il Palazzino, Riecine, Rocca delle Macie, Ruffino, Vecchie Terre di Montefili, Villa Cafaggio
Brunello di Montalcino/ Vino Nobile di Montepulciano	90, 88, 85	Altesino, Avignonesi, Biondi Santi, Caparzo, Case Basse, Lisini, Il Poggione, Poliziano, Villa Banfi
Barolo/ Barbaresco	90, 89, 88, 85, 82, 78	Aldo Conterno, Altare, Ceretto, Clerico, Gaja, Giacomo Conterno, Giacosa, Mascarello, Ratti, Voerzio

RED WINE

THOUGH SOME local red wine is made, most of the bottled red wine in Rome comes from other parts of Italy. Regions like Tuscany and Piedmont produce very good everyday drinking as well as top-class wines like Barolo. Price should reflect quality – try Dolcetto, Rosso di Montalcino or Montepulciano for good value reds.

Tuscan table wine   **Barolo**

Montepulciano d'Abruzzo, a rich and juicy red wine, is always good value. It is produced in the Abruzzi region east of Rome.

Chianti Classico Riserva is older and stronger than a normal Chianti Classico.

Torre Ercolana is produced in small quantities and is generally regarded as one of Lazio's best red wines. It is made from Cesanese and Cabernet grapes and requires at least five years' ageing.

READING THE LABEL

ITALY has a two-tier system for labelling quality wine. DOC *(denominazione di origine controllata)* means you can be sure the wine is from the region declared on the label and is made from designated grape varieties. A higher classification – DOCG *(denominazione di origine controllata e garantita)* – is given to top wines such as the reds Barolo, Barbaresco, Chianti Classico and Brunello di Montalcino.

Chianti Classico

APÉRITIFS AND OTHER DRINKS

BITTER, herb-flavoured drinks like Martini, Campari or Aperol are the most popular apéritifs. (Ask for an *analcolico* if you prefer a non-alcoholic one.) Italians drink their apéritifs neat or with ice and soda. Strong, herby after-dinner drinks, known as *digestivi* or *amari*, are worth trying if you need to settle your stomach. Italian brandy and grappa can be very fiery. Italian beer, popular with pizza, is made in lager style.

Campari

Refrigerated storage for wine and beer

SOFT DRINKS

ITALIAN FRUIT juices are good and most bars squeeze fresh orange juice *(spremuta)* on the spot. Iced tea and coffee are refreshing in summer, and fruit-flavoured tea, such as peach, is very popular.

DRINKING WATER

Unlike many Mediterranean cities, Rome benefits from a constant supply of fresh drinking water, piped down from the hills through a system of pipes and aqueducts which has changed little from ancient Roman times. Only if there is a sign saying *acqua non potabile* is the water not safe to drink.

One of Rome's many fresh water drinking fountains

Coffee is almost more important to Roman life than wine. Take espresso for neat strong black coffee at any time of day, milky cappuccino for breakfast or mid-afternoon, caffelatte for extra milk.

Espresso

Cappuccino

Caffelatte

Rome's Best: Restaurants and Cafés

ROME IS NOT particularly known for luxury restaurants, but more for atmospheric places where the focus is on the social side of dining and on regional cooking. An amazing variety can be found. Many places specialize, often priding themselves on being the best of their kind – whether they offer superb espresso, or traditional foods like deep-fried salted cod *(baccalà)*. Other restaurants can offer especially beautiful settings or are known as the best places to see and be seen. The selection here shows some of the many highlights of a city where eating is taken very seriously.

Caffè Giolitti
This historic ice cream shop serves a variety of flavours, to eat in or take away. (See p320.)

Romolo nel Giardino della Fornarina
For romantic Roman eating, Romolo is best in the summer, with its walled garden, candlelit tables and guitar music.
(See p316.)

Vatican

Piazza Navona

Campo de' Fiori

Janiculum

Il Delfino
This snack bar at Largo Argentina sells everything from whole chickens on the spit, to salads, sandwiches and supplì *(rice croquettes): a feast for the eye.*
(See p320.)

Trastevere

Filetti di Baccalà
This small, crowded place serves tasty fried fillets of cod – one of Rome's most traditional dishes – and offers a truly Roman experience. (See p320.)

Piperno
For over a century, traditional Roman Jewish cooking has been the speciality of Piperno, in the heart of the Jewish Ghetto. (See p314.)

Babington's Tea Rooms
This old-fashioned, genteel establishment at the foot of the Spanish Steps serves English tea and cakes. (See p320.)

Caffè Greco
Famous as the haunt of writers, artists and intellectuals in the 19th century, this café still retains the faded grandeur shown in this painting. (See p320.)

Tazza d'Oro
This figure graces the wall on the outside of Tazza d'Oro, where you will find some of the best coffee in Rome – its espresso is rated highly by connoisseurs. (See p320.)

Piazza di Spagna

Via Veneto

za della onda

Quirinal

Capitol

Esquiline

Forum

Palatine

Lateran

Aventine

Caracalla

| 0 metres | 500 |
| 0 yards | 500 |

Sora Lella
This Roman trattoria is famous for its setting on the Isola Tiberina and for the fashionable crowd which it attracts. (See p314.)

Vecchia Roma
Summer is the best time to eat here and make the most of the quiet and pretty Baroque piazza. (See p314.)

Choosing a Restaurant

THE RESTAURANTS in this guide have been selected for their good value or exceptional food. This chart highlights some of the factors which may influence your choice. Entries are alphabetical within price category. For more details on the restaurants, see pages 312–17. Information on cafés and wine bars is on pages 318–21.

Restaurant	Price	Fixed Price Menu	Vegetarian Dishes	Tables Outside	Seafood Specialities	Late Opening	Air Conditioning	Attractive Setting
PIAZZA DELLA ROTONDA (see p312)								
Da Gino	Ⓛ							
Il Buco	ⓁⓁ	●		●			■	
Sangallo	ⓁⓁ	●					■	
Vecchia Locanda	ⓁⓁⓁ		■	●	■	●	■	●
La Rosetta ★	ⓁⓁⓁⓁⓁ				■		■	
El Toulà	ⓁⓁⓁⓁ	●	■		■		■	
PIAZZA NAVONA (see p312)								
La Taverna	ⓁⓁ	●		●			■	●
Nel Regno del Re Ferdinando	ⓁⓁⓁ		■		■	●	■	
Osteria dell'Antiquario	ⓁⓁⓁ	●		●			■	●
Il Convivio ★	ⓁⓁⓁⓁ	●			■		■	
Papà Giovanni	ⓁⓁⓁ		■				■	
PIAZZA DI SPAGNA (see p313)								
Al 34	ⓁⓁ		■	●	■		■	
Birreria Viennese	ⓁⓁ	●				●	■	
Fiaschetteria Beltramme	ⓁⓁ				■			
Mario alle Vite	ⓁⓁ			●			■	
Porto di Ripetta	ⓁⓁⓁ	●			■	●	■	
Sogo-Asahi	ⓁⓁⓁⓁ	●			■		■	
Hassler Roof Restaurant	ⓁⓁⓁⓁⓁ						■	●
CAMPO DE' FIORI (see p313)								
Bella Shanghai	Ⓛ	●	■				■	
Le Maschere	ⓁⓁ		■	●		●	■	
Al Pompiere	ⓁⓁ							
Il Cardinale	ⓁⓁⓁ		■		■		■	
Il Drappo	ⓁⓁⓁ	●		●		●	■	
Vecchia Roma	ⓁⓁⓁ		■	●	■		■	●
Piperno	ⓁⓁⓁⓁ			●	■			
Sora Lella	ⓁⓁⓁⓁ						■	
Camponeschi	ⓁⓁⓁⓁⓁ			●	■	●		●
QUIRINAL (see p314)								
Colline Emiliane	ⓁⓁ						■	
Al Moro	ⓁⓁⓁ				■		■	
Il Posto Accanto	ⓁⓁⓁ		■		■		■	
Quadrifoglio	ⓁⓁⓁ					●	■	
TERMINI (see p314)								
Gemma alla Lupa	Ⓛ	●	■	●			■	
Coriolano	ⓁⓁⓁⓁ		■		■		■	
ESQUILINE (see p314)								
Trattoria Monti	ⓁⓁ	●	■					
Cicilardone	ⓁⓁⓁ							
La Tana del Grillo	ⓁⓁⓁ							
Agata e Romeo	ⓁⓁⓁⓁ	●				●	■	

Price categories for a three-course meal for one, half a bottle of house wine, and all unavoidable extra charges such as cover, service, tax:
Ⓛ up to L35,000
ⓁⓁ L35–55,000
ⓁⓁⓁ L55–75,000
ⓁⓁⓁⓁ L75–100,000
ⓁⓁⓁⓁⓁ over L100,000.

★ Means highly recommended.

FIXED PRICE MENU
Restaurant offering *menu turistico* (tourist menu): usually three or four courses without wine or coffee, for a set price.

VEGETARIAN DISHES
Restaurant with a good selection of vegetarian dishes.

LATE OPENING
Last orders on or after 11.30pm.

ATTRACTIVE SETTING
Restaurant set in a pretty piazza or with a garden terrace, or with a lovely view.

		Fixed Price Menu	Vegetarian Dishes	Tables Outside	Seafood Specialities	Late Opening	Air Conditioning	Attractive Setting
LATERAN *(see p315)*								
Alfredo a Via Gabi	ⓁⓁ						●	
Cannavota	ⓁⓁⓁ	●			●			
Charly's Saucière	ⓁⓁⓁ					●	●	
AVENTINE *(see p315)*								
Perilli a Testaccio	ⓁⓁ						●	
Checchino dal 1887 ★	ⓁⓁⓁ				●			
TRASTEVERE *(see p315)*								
Da Lucia	ⓁⓁ			●				
La Taverna di Bambù	ⓁⓁ		●			●	●	
La Cornucopia	ⓁⓁⓁ	●		●	●	●	●	●
Da Paris	ⓁⓁⓁ			●	●		●	●
Peccati di Gola	ⓁⓁⓁ			●	●			
Romolo nel Giardino della Fornarina	ⓁⓁⓁ			●		●	●	●
Tentativo ★	ⓁⓁⓁ	●				●	●	
Cul De Sac 2 ★	ⓁⓁⓁⓁ				●		●	
Alberto Ciarla ★	ⓁⓁⓁⓁ	●		●	●	●	●	
JANICULUM *(see p316)*								
Antico Arco	ⓁⓁ		●		●	●	●	
VATICAN *(see p316)*								
Macondo	ⓁⓁ		●	●			●	
San Luigi	ⓁⓁⓁ		●				●	
Les Etoiles	ⓁⓁⓁⓁ				●			
VIA VENETO *(see p317)*								
Cantina Cantarini	ⓁⓁ			●	●	●		
Tullio	ⓁⓁⓁ		●		●		●	
Andrea	ⓁⓁⓁ		●		●		●	
Giovanni	ⓁⓁⓁⓁ	●			●		●	
San Benedetto	ⓁⓁⓁⓁ	●			●		●	
George's ★	ⓁⓁⓁⓁⓁ		●	●		●	●	●
Le Sans Souci ★	ⓁⓁⓁⓁⓁ		●		●	●	●	
VILLA BORGHESE *(see p317)*								
Al Ceppo	ⓁⓁⓁ		●	●	●		●	
Relais la Piscine ★	ⓁⓁⓁⓁ	●		●	●		●	●
Relais le Jardin ★	ⓁⓁⓁⓁ				●		●	

PIAZZA DELLA ROTONDA

Da Gino

Vicolo Rosini 4 (Piazza del Parlamento). **Map** 4 F3 & 12 D1. 【 687 34 34. **Open** 12.45pm–3pm, 8pm–10.30pm Mon–Sat. **Closed** Aug. 🛗 Ⓛ

Journalists, politicians and the initiated scramble for a seat under the kitsch, frescoed pergola of this ancient, ultra-Roman trattoria to feast upon traditional daily dishes: *gnocchi* and *osso buco* (Thursdays), *baccalà* (Fridays), tripe (Saturdays), plus classic sturdy soups and delectable homemade *tiramisù*.

Il Buco

Via di Sant'Ignazio 8. **Map** 4 F4 & 12 E3. 【 678 32 98, 678 44 67. **Open** 12.30pm–4pm, 7pm–midnight Tue–Sun. **Closed** 10 Aug–1 Sep. 🍴🛗🔥 AE, DC, MC, V. Ⓛ Ⓛ

Much has happened since the tiny *buco* (hole) opened in 1891 – the small osteria has become a large restaurant, yet the calm atmosphere, unfailing courtesy and formidable Tuscan menu remain. From the traditional *crostini* (liver pâté canapés), robust *ribollita* (thick vegetable soup) and huge Florentine steaks, to the final *tozzetti* (almond biscuits) with vin santo (dessert wine), this is a truly Tuscan experience.

Sangallo

Vicolo della Vaccarella 11. **Map** 4 F3 & 12 D2. 【 686 55 49. **Open** 7pm–1am Mon–Sat. **Closed** Aug. 🍴🛗 🄴 AE, DC, MC, V. Ⓛ Ⓛ Ⓛ

This elegant fish restaurant has an interesting menu which is complemented by an impressive wine list. Antipasti include *crostini con calameretti al radicchio* (baby squid and redicchio served on toast). First courses such as *cannolicchi con peperoni e frutti di mare* (pasta with razor clams, peperoni and sea food) are prepared delicately and simply. Ask about the speciality of the day.

Vecchia Locanda

Vicolo Sinibaldi 2. **Map** 4 F4 & 12 D3. 【 68 80 28 31. **Open** 12.30pm–3pm, 7pm–midnight Mon–Sat. Ⓥ 🍴 🛗 🄴 AE, MC. Ⓛ Ⓛ Ⓛ

Visit this small, family-run Ligurian restaurant in summer, when tables line the secluded arched street. Everything shows extreme care –

including the impeccable service. An imaginative combination of herbs and vegetables characterizes the menu: risotto with courgette flowers, *porcini* mushroom crêpes, stuffed truffled rabbit and lots of fresh fish. There's a good selection of French and regional wines.

La Rosetta

Via della Rosetta 9. **Map** 4 F4 & 12 D2. 【 68 30 88 41. **Open** 1pm–3pm, 7.30pm–11.30pm Mon–Sat. **Closed** 3 wks Aug, Christmas. 🛗 🍴 ★ 🄴 AE, DC, MC, V. Ⓛ Ⓛ Ⓛ Ⓛ

Despite the exorbitant prices, people flock nightly (having booked in advance) for a seat in the elegant, tightly-packed rooms. Fresh fish and seafood arrive daily from Sicily and, cooked in the simplest ways, achieve culinary perfection. Enthusiastic waiters and quality French and Italian wines, particularly the Sicilian whites, do justice to the cuisine.

El Toulà

Via della Lupa 29B. **Map** 4 F3 & 12 D1. 【 687 34 98. **Open** 1pm–3pm, 8pm–11pm Tue–Fri, 8pm–11pm Mon, Sat. **Closed** Aug, Christmas. 🍴 Ⓥ 🍴 🄴 AE, DC, MC, V. Ⓛ Ⓛ Ⓛ Ⓛ

El Toulà is justly renowned as one of the most exclusive, traditional and luxurious restaurants in Rome. The Venetian-inspired cooking is serious and professional, with forays into the realms of the best classic international cuisine. In dignified, sober surroundings the service is exemplary and the selection of wines superb.

PIAZZA NAVONA

La Taverna

Via del Banco di Santo Spirito 58. **Map** 4 D3 & 11 A2. 【 686 41 16. **Open** noon–3pm, 7pm–11pm Tue–Sun. 🍴🛗🎵🛗🄴▤ AE, DC, MC, V, JCB. Ⓛ Ⓛ

Tourists and local residents mingle in Giovanni's crowded Roman trattoria to enjoy the family atmosphere and traditional regional cooking. Particularly appreciated are the *rigatoni all'amatriciana, coda alla vaccinara* and, on Thursday, Friday and Saturday respectively, *gnocchi, baccalà* and tripe.

Nel Regno del Re Ferdinando

Via dei Banchi Nuovi 8. **Map** 4 D4 & 11 B2. 【 68 80 11 67. **Open** 8pm–1am Mon–Sat. **Closed** Aug. 🎋 Ⓥ 🄴 AE, MC, V. Ⓛ Ⓛ Ⓛ

Reminiscent of a classic 19th-century taverna, Re Ferdinando is a rare representative in Rome of the southern Campania region. Delights include some colourful vegetable and fish antipasto, and *maccheroni*. Another speciality is *sartù di riso* (a savoury rice mould covered in tomato sauce, cheese and breadcrumbs and baked in the oven). The Neapolitan desserts are delicious. There is a separate non-smoking room. Good regional wines include many from Ischia.

Osteria dell'Antiquario

Piazzetta San Simeone 27. **Map** 4 E3 & 11 B2. 【 687 96 94. **Open** 8pm–11.30pm Mon–Sat. **Closed** 15 Aug, 20 Dec–7 Jan. 🍴🛗🍴🄴 AE, DC, MC, V, JCB. Ⓛ Ⓛ Ⓛ

In the comfort of the elegantly restructured rooms of an old antique shop, Giorgio Nisti offers an unusual menu dictated by the whims of the chef and the daily market, with traditional dishes creatively adapted to contemporary health-conscious tastes. There is an impressive choice of regional, French and Californian wines.

Il Convivio

Via dell'Orso 44. **Map** 4 E3 & 11 C2. 【 686 94 32. **Open** 1pm–2.30pm, 8pm–10.30pm Mon–Fri, 8pm–10.30pm Sun. **Closed** 2 weeks Aug–Sep. 🍴🛗🍴 ★ 🄴 AE, DC, MC, V. Ⓛ Ⓛ Ⓛ Ⓛ

An air of sophisticated tranquillity pervades this intimate restaurant, one of the very best specializing in modern creative cookery. Its young chef, one of the three brother-owners from the Marches, creates both subtle and unusual combinations of flavours, and the highly personalized menu evolves with the seasons. The wine list is extensive and service is discreet.

Papà Giovanni

Via dei Sediari 4. **Map** 4 F4 & 12 D3. 【 686 53 08. **Open** 1pm–3pm, 8pm–11.30pm Mon–Sat. **Closed** Aug, public hols. 🎋 Ⓥ 🍴 🄴 MC, V. Ⓛ Ⓛ Ⓛ

Nearly 60 years have passed since Papà Giovanni first sold his country wines in Rome; the bottles lining the walls are testimony to the past and to the superb cellar of Giovanni's son, Renato Sentuti. Here diners sample the best of the new lighter Roman cuisine. Classics such as *cacio e pepe*, salt cod and tripe live alongside exotic salads and truffled dishes. Desserts include ricotta soufflé with strawberry sauce, hot chocolate profiteroles and exquisite sorbets.

PIAZZA DI SPAGNA

Al 34

Via Mario de' Fiori 34. **Map** 5 A2.
(679 50 91. **Open** 12.30pm–3pm,
7.30pm–11pm Tue–Sun. **Closed** Aug
V ▦ **&** **Ꮛ** AE, DC, MC, V, JCB. **Ⓛ Ⓛ**

For a comfortable chat or a
romantic *tête-à-tête*, Al 34 provides
the perfect setting. Predominantly
featuring southern Italian cooking,
the extensive menu offers an
esoteric choice, particularly where
vegetables and herbs are allied
with pasta, meat and fish. Given
the atmosphere and its location,
the prices are affordable.

Birreria Viennese

Via della Croce 21. **Map** 5 A2.
(679 55 69. **Open** 11.30am–
midnight Thu–Tue. **Closed** 1–15 Aug.
❿ ▦ **Ꮛ** AE, DC, MC, V, JCB.
Ⓛ Ⓛ

The stained-glass entrance leads to
a long, crowded room where, for
more than 60 years, traditional
beers and Austrian specialities
have been sampled. Try sausages,
goulash, *Wienerschnitzel*,
sauerkraut, or the massive *piatto
di legno della Transilvania*
(wooden platter heaped with
delights, for two). Wine is
available, and the service is
extremely helpful and courteous.

Fiaschetteria Beltramme

Via della Croce 39. **Map** 4 F2. **Open**
12.10pm–3pm, 7.45pm–10.30pm
Mon–Sat. **Closed** 23 Dec–7 Jan. **🏃**
Ⓛ Ⓛ

This small Roman trattoria bears
witness to its glorious past; signed
photos and paintings line the long
walls, and the crowded tables
make sharing – and new
friendships – inevitable. The family
atmosphere is enhanced by
traditional basic fare – *pasta e ceci*,
minestra di fagioli, fresh fish and
typical meat dishes. Efficient,
speedy service means this is not a
place for lingering over dinner.

Mario alla Vite

Via della Vite 55. **Map** 5 A3 & 12 E1.
(678 38 18. **Open** 12.30pm–3pm,
7.30pm–11pm Mon–Sat. **Closed**
Aug. ▦ **Ꮛ** AE, DC, MC, V, JCB.
Ⓛ Ⓛ

Despite an exclusive address,
Mario has kept prices reasonable,
and his food is still simple, honest
Tuscan fare. Elbow-to-elbow
dining, haphazard service and
noisy confusion seem inevitable.
Nevertheless, the food is worth it –
traditional *fagioli al fiasco*

(cannellini beans in oil), *ribollita*
(thick vegetable soup), Florentine
steaks and delicious pastries are
the attractions, along with a wide
selection of wines.

Porto di Ripetta

Via di Ripetta 250. **Map** 4 F2.
(361 23 76. **Open** 1pm–3pm,
8pm–midnight Mon–Sat. **Closed**
Aug. **❿** **♈** **Ꮛ** AE, DC, MC, V,
JCB. **Ⓛ Ⓛ Ⓛ**

The fame of this restaurant
depends largely on the genius of
chef Maria Romani. With the fish
that arrives daily from her native
Marches she creates inspired
combinations such as fish and
broad bean soup or giant prawns
with artichokes. It is expensive,
but worth it; the business lunch
menu is much cheaper. There's a
selection of excellent wines.

Sogo-Asahi

Via di Propaganda 22. **Map** 5 A2.
(678 60 93. **Open** noon–2.30pm,
7.30pm–midnight Mon–Sat. **❿** **&**
Ꮛ AE, DC, MC, V, JCB. **Ⓛ Ⓛ Ⓛ**

This luxury, top-quality restaurant
is a find for lovers of Japanese
cooking. Traditional Japanese
specialities are elegantly served by
helpful and knowledgeable
waiters: *sashimi* (raw fish) and
melt-in-the-mouth tempura are
accompanied by saké, Japanese
beer or a good Italian wine. The
special set menus are particularly
inexpensive at lunchtime. Sogo-
Asahi opens in August, when most
of Rome's restaurants are closed.

Hassler Roof Restaurant

Piazza Trinità dei Monti 6. **Map** 5 A2.
(69 93 40. **Open** 7.30am–11.30am,
noon–2.30pm, 7.30pm–10pm Mon–
Sat, 7.30am–11.30am, 12.30pm–3pm,
7.30pm–10pm Sun. **♈** **♫** **&** **Ꮛ**
AE, DC, MC, V, JCB. **Ⓛ Ⓛ Ⓛ Ⓛ**

Perched on the sixth floor of the
Hotel Hassler, overlooking the
Spanish Steps, the roof restaurant
commands a breathtaking view of
Rome. Come for the gargantuan
and pricy Sunday brunch. The wine
list is excellent and the hovering
waiter service timely and discreet.
In the evening, when prices are
higher, there's piano music.

CAMPO DE' FIORI

Bella Shanghai

Corso Vittorio Emanuele II 333.
Map 4 E4 & 11 C3. **(** 686 16 84.
Open 11am–3pm, 6pm–midnight
daily. **❿** **V** **Ꮛ** AE, MC, V. **Ⓛ**

Centrally located and inexpensive,
this is the place to go for Chinese
food which is fairly standard, but
certainly not mundane. The menu
contains such unusual dishes as
strips of beef and bamboo cooked
in a curry sauce and served up in
a steaming pot, and aubergines
cooked with chopped carrots and
mincemeat. There are tables outside, the service is fast and
friendly, and there is a modest
selection of wines and beers.

Le Maschere

Via Monte della Farina 29.
Map 4 F5 & 12 D4. **(** 687 94 44.
Open 7pm–midnight Tue–Sun.
Closed Aug. **V** **♈** **Ꮛ** AE, DC,
MC, V, JCB. **Ⓛ Ⓛ**

There is an agreeable sensation of
being in the country as you cross
the spacious tiled hall and descend
to the rustic indoor terrace with its
high reed-lined ceiling, a roofed
grill and eerily-lit wall masks.
Candles on the tables, and a
subdued conversational hum, lull
you in preparation for the fiery
Calabrian food to come. Charming
service and good Calabrian house
wine (plus a short list) ensure an
enjoyable evening.

Al Pompiere

Via S. M. dei Calderari 38. **Map** 4 F5
& 12 D5. **(** 686 83 77. **Open**
noon–3pm, 7.30pm–11pm Mon–Sat.
Closed Aug. **♈** **Ꮛ** MC, V.
Ⓛ Ⓛ

In the heart of the Jewish Ghetto,
Al Pompiere occupies the first
floor of the 16th-century Palazzo
Cenci-Bolognetti. Under its
frescoed and open-beamed
ceilings, in a homely atmosphere,
all the classic dishes of the
substantial Roman cuisine are
expertly served: among them
fried courgette flowers with
anchovies, *rigatoni con la pajata*,
and baby lamb.

Il Cardinale

Via delle Carceri 6. **Map** 4 D4 & 11 B3.
(686 93 36. **Open** 12.45pm–3pm,
7.30pm–11.30pm Mon–Sat. **Closed**
Aug. **V** **&** **Ꮛ** AE, DC, MC, V.
Ⓛ Ⓛ Ⓛ

For genuine regional cooking,
using the best local ingredients
from the Castelli Romani, this
small, elegant yet comfortable
restaurant near Via Giulia is highly
recommended. Dishes range from
tasty robust soups, to specialities
such as *zucchine alla velletrana*
(baked courgettes) and *crema al
cocco* (coconut *crème brûlée*).
There are some particularly good
wines from Lazio.

For key to symbols *see p.303*

Il Drappo

Vicolo del Malpasso 9. **Map** 4 D4 & 11 B3. 687 73 65. **Open** 8pm–midnight Mon–Sat. **Closed** 1 Jan, 1–15 Aug, Easter, 25 Dec. 🎄 🛗 🍴 🖼 🖾 AE, DC, MC, V. ⓁⓁⓁ

A small, intimate restaurant, with ceiling drapes (hence the name), plants and candlelight, Il Drappo provides an authentic taste of Sardinia – traditional dishes imbued with flashes of culinary creativity. Everything is evocative of the island, including the wines, particularly the *seada* (sweet cheese-filled ravioli) for dessert. Try the *mirto* liqueur at the end.

Vecchia Roma

Piazza Campitelli 18. **Map** 4 F5 & 12 E5. 686 46 04. **Open** 1pm– 3pm, 8pm–11.30pm Thu–Tue. **Closed** 2 weeks Aug. 🔽 🛗 🖼 🍸 🖾 AE, DC. ⓁⓁⓁ

Set in a quiet, atmospheric piazza, this is one of the best places for a summer evening. Reliable Roman cooking is on offer, with tempting antipasto, simply-cooked fish and grilled meats, and a connoisseur's wine list. Specialities are summer salads and, in winter, numerous variations on polenta. Added pleasures are the 18th-century interior and the excellent service.

Piperno

Via Monte de' Cenci. **Map** 4 F5 & 12 D5. 68 80 66 29. **Open** 12.30pm–3pm, 8pm–11pm Tue–Sat, 12.30pm–3pm Sun. **Closed** Aug, Christmas, Easter. 🛗 🖼 🖾 AE, DC, MC, V. ⓁⓁⓁⓁ

Piperno, at the heart of the Jewish Ghetto, has been famed for over a century for its traditional Jewish/Roman dishes. Despite the competition, the restaurant is still unbeaten for lightly fried courgette flowers, vegetable *fritto misto*, *carciofi alla giudia*, tripe, and superb fish, served in plain surroundings. Service is familiarly attentive and timely. The house wine is excellent Frascati. Book well in advance.

Sora Lella

Via Ponte Quattro Capi 16, Isola Tiberina. **Map** 8 D1. 686 16 01. **Open** 1pm–2.30pm, 8pm–10.40pm Mon–Sat. **Closed** 30 days over Aug and Sep. 🛗 🖾 AE, MC, V. ⓁⓁⓁ

Founded by the exuberant Roman actress Sora Lella, this small, bright trattoria is a well-known place to people-watch. Sora Lella is now run by Lella's son Aldo. Dishes are based on traditional Roman

cuisine, but prices are very high for an essentially simple style of cooking. Go instead for the beautiful location on the Isola Tiberina, the often glamorous clientele, and the good service.

Camponeschi

Piazza Farnese 50. **Map** 4 E5 & 11 C4. 687 49 27. **Open** 8pm–12.30am Mon–Sat. **Closed** 10 days Aug. 🍴 🛗 🖼 🖾 AE, DC, MC, V. ⓁⓁⓁⓁ

Camponeschi is set in one of the most attractive piazzas in Rome, especially beautiful in summer. The extensive menu includes modern and regional Italian cooking, creative Mediterranean fish and meat dishes, soufflés and refined French specialities. There's a varied regional, French and Californian wine list.

QUIRINAL

Colline Emiliane

Via degli Avignonesi 22. **Map** 5 B3. 481 75 38. **Open** 12.45pm–2.45pm, 7.45pm–10.45pm Sat–Thu. **Closed** Aug. 🛗 🖾 MC, V. ⓁⓁ

Regional dishes are the hallmarks of this small family trattoria: one unpretentious room presenting a welcome haven from the nearby Via del Tritone. Enjoy food typical of the northern province of Emilia Romagna – salamis and cold meats, homemade pastas (tagliatelle, tortellini), boiled meats with *salsa verde* (spinach, onion and anchovy sauce) and strictly Emilian wines.

Al Moro

Vicolo delle Bollette 13. **Map** 5 A3 & 12 F2. 678 34 95. **Open** 1pm– 3.30pm, 8pm–11.30pm Mon–Sat. **Closed** Aug. ⓁⓁⓁ

Franco Romagnoli's trattoria is a reliable choice for traditional Roman cooking, using fresh local ingredients. Noisy and crowded, its closely packed tables do not encourage intimate dining. Classic dishes are served: *bucatini all'amatriciana*, *spaghetti alla Moro* (special *carbonara*), fried vegetables, excellent *baccalà alla Moro* (salt cod), tripe, *abbacchio*. There is a vast wine list.

Il Posto Accanto

Via del Boschetto 36A. **Map** 5 B4. 474 30 02. **Open** 12.30pm–3pm Mon–Fri, 8pm–10pm Mon–Sat. **Closed** Aug. 🔽 🎄 🛗 🖾 AE, DC, MC, V. ⓁⓁⓁ

Tiny, intimate and elegant, this family-run restaurant owes its success to a short, carefully chosen menu revolving around homemade pasta (excellent *tagliolini con asparagi* and *ravioli con zenzero* – ginger), simply prepared fish and meat, top-quality vegetables and familiar desserts (*tiramisù*), often prepared within sight of the lucky diners. There is a range of wines, as well as good grappas.

Quadrifoglio

Via del Boschetto 19. **Map** 5 B4. 482 60 96. **Open** 7pm–midnight Mon–Sat. **Closed** Aug. 🎄 🖾 AE, DC, MC, V. ⓁⓁ

Chef Pino Forlenza has researched diligently to reproduce authentic, skilfully prepared dishes from Naples, Campania and the tip of Africa. They are tailored to modern tastes by the carefully selected raw ingredients. These are delivered with southern hospitality and courteous service. Most of the wines are from Campania, too.

TERMINI

Gemma alla Lupa

Via Marghera 39. **Map** 6 E3. 49 12 30. **Open** noon–3.30pm, 7pm–11pm Mon–Sat. **Closed** 2 weeks Aug. 🍴 🔽 🛗 🖼 Ⓛ

Gemma's is a modest, family-run, typically Roman trattoria serving substantial portions of orthodox Roman cooking. The main features are its bustling atmosphere and speedy service. But it is a good choice where you eat well despite the low prices.

Coriolano

Via Ancona 14. **Map** 6 D1. 44 24 98 63. **Open** noon–3pm, 7pm–11pm Mon–Sat. **Closed** Aug. 🔽 🛗 🍸 🖾 AE, DC, MC, V. ⓁⓁⓁⓁ

This small restaurant aims at perfection with its lacy tablecloths and crystal glasses. The Italian menu changes with the seasons and uses only fresh raw materials, including fish. Specialities include home-made *ravioli di ricotta e spinaci*, *capretto* (kid) and creamy chocolate *zuppa del contadino*.

ESQUILINE

Trattoria Monti

Via di San Vito 13A. **Map** 6 D4. 446 65 73. **Open** 12.30pm–3pm, 7.30pm–11pm Wed–Mon. **Closed** Aug, 24 Dec–3 Jan. 🔽 🎄 🖾 DC, MC, V. ⓁⓁ

This small, unpretentious local trattoria serves delicate, creative regional dishes from the Marches. Franca Camerucci cooks, while husband Mario is attentive waiter and expert *sommelier*. Specialities include fried stuffed olives, artichokes and *ciauscolo* (salami); *tortello al rosso d'uova* (fresh pasta stuffed with ricotta, spinach and tomato); and *tacchino all'aceto balsamico* (lightly vinegared turkey slices). There's good Verdicchio house wine and a commendable wine list.

Cicilardone

Via Farini 12. **Map** 6 D4.
(48 35 49. **Open** noon–3pm Tue –Sat, 7.30pm–midnight Mon –Sat. **Closed** mid 2 wks Aug. AE, DC, MC, V, JBC. (L)(L)(L)

Ring at Cicilardone's door and your host – Domenico Lucia – will greet you like an old friend and converse about the gastronomic delights from the region of Basilicata. Try the *menu di assaggini* – a number of dishes to give you an idea of the regional taste, including traditional pastas and hot chocolate profiteroles. There are some unusual southern wines.

La Tana del Grillo

Via Alfieri 4. **Map** 6 E5.
(70 45 35 17. **Open** 12.30pm– 2.30pm, 7.30pm–11pm Tue –Sat, 7.30pm–11pm Mon. AE, DC, MC, V. (L)(L)(L)

Marisa Balboni runs an elegant and characteristically hospitable Emilian restaurant. Clients are pampered, from the cushioned chairs, restful prints and attractive tableware, to the wholesome food served with courtesy and care. Particularly recommended are the *polpettone all'emiliana* (meat loaf), *salame al sugo ferrarese* (Ferrarese salami), *cappellacci con la zucca* (pumpkin-stuffed pasta).

Agata e Romeo

Via Carlo Alberto 45. **Map** 6 D4.
(446 61 15. **Open** 1pm–2.30pm, 8pm–10.30pm Mon –Sat. **Closed** 2 wks Aug, Christmas. DC, MC, V. (L)(L)(L)(L)

One of the newer trattorie-turned-restaurants, its increasing prices sadly reflect recent popular acclaim. Nevertheless, Agata's skill in producing a changing menu of predominantly Roman and southern Italian dishes, and Romeo's impeccable service and range of carefully chosen wines, are hard to beat. Well-spaced, elegantly set tables are ideal for tranquil eating. The *menu degustazione* is recommended.

LATERAN

Alfredo a Via Gabi

Via Gabi 36. **Map** 10 D3.
(77 20 67 92. **Open** noon–3pm, 7.30pm–11pm Wed –Mon. **Closed** Aug. (L)(L)

This is a spacious local trattoria with a pavement pergola for outdoor eating. Specialities from Rome and the Marches – served in ample portions – include *tonnarelli ai sapori di bosco* (pasta with mushrooms), excellent *porcini* mushrooms (in season), *straccetti all'ortica* (meat in nettle sauce), and *panna cotta* (rich crème caramel) with fruit or chocolate. Service is cheerful and friendly.

Cannavota

Piazza San Giovanni in Laterano 20. **Map** 9 C1. **(** 77 20 50 07. **Open** 12.30pm–3pm, 7.45pm–11pm Thu –Tue. **Closed** 1–20 Aug. AE, DC, MC, V. (L)(L)(L)

Join the enthusiastic regulars who crowd this friendly restaurant if you are feeling especially hungry. Portions are generous, the cooking is traditional Italian and the service swift. Seafood – prawns, in particular – is excellent, but meat also features on the menu.

Charly's Saucière

Via San Giovanni in Laterano 270. **Map** 9 B1. **(** 70 49 47 00. **Open** 12.45pm–2.30pm, 8pm–11.15pm Tue –Fri, 8pm–midnight Mon & Sat. **Closed** 2 wks Aug. AE, MC, V, JCB. (L)(L)(L)

An old-style, unsurprising and well-established French restaurant, this has scarcely altered over the years and is especially warm and intimate on a winter evening. Diners choose from reassuring French and Swiss fare: pâtés, onion soup, cheese soufflé, fondues, *rösti*, steaks in a variety of sauces and crêpes, accompanied by a small but careful selection of wines. Service is professional and attentive.

AVENTINE

Perilli a Testaccio

Via Marmorata 39. **Map** 8 D3.
(574 24 15. **Open** 12.30pm–3pm, 7.30pm–11pm Thu –Tue. **Closed** Aug. (L)(L)

In the heart of Testaccio, this archetypal Roman trattoria is always packed with hungry regulars (and the occasional famous face). On offer are giant-

size quantities of robust traditional fare – *rigatoni alla pajata*, *spaghetti alla carbonara* (served in king-size bowls), *coda alla vaccinara*, *carciofi alla romana* – helpfully and efficiently served. Ignore the noise and hideous murals – tuck in and enjoy yourself.

Checchino dal 1887

Via di Monte Testaccio 30. **Map** 8 D4. **(** 574 38 16, 574 63 18. **Open** Oct–May: 12.30pm–3pm, 8pm–11pm Tue –Sat, 12.30pm–3pm Sun; Jun, Jul & Sep: 12.30pm–3pm, 8pm–11pm Tue –Sat. **Closed** Aug, 1 wk at Christmas. ★ AE, DC, MC, V. (L)(L)(L)(L)

Historic home of Roman cuisine for over 100 years, Checchino specializes in authentic dishes using the *quinto quarto* (offal, tripe, intestines and tail), originally discarded by the old slaughterhouse opposite. At the old convent tables under vaulted ceilings, with an open fire in winter, Ninetta Mariani and her two *sommelier* sons offer traditional *rigatoni alla pajata*, *coda alla vaccinara*, *crostata di ricotta*, a superb cheese tray and an extraordinary wine selection. Carved into the artificial Monte de' Cocci (made from broken amphoras), its cool, natural wine cellar deserves a special visit.

TRASTEVERE

Da Lucia

Vicolo del Mattonato 2. **Map** 7 B1. **(** 580 36 01. **Open** 1pm–4pm, 8pm– midnight Tue –Sun. **Closed** 2 wks Aug, 1 wk Christmas. (L)(L)

Head for this popular, well-worn trattoria off Via Garibaldi if you like genuine Roman cooking. You won't be disappointed by the *pasta e ceci, baccalà, pollo con i peperoni* (chicken with peppers), boiled meats and, incongruously, Milanese risotto. The service is take it or leave it, the wine basic. Outdoor tables make a more attractive dining area in summer.

La Taverna di Bambù

Via Santa Dorotea 2 (Piazza Trilussa). **Map** 4 E5. **(** 580 60 65. **Open** 7pm– midnight daily. MC, V. (L)(L)

An intimate Chinese restaurant, this is well known for its freshly prepared dishes served in abundant portions. A few Italianate specialities, such as pizza with onions, are offered as a concession to the host city, but the authentic Cantonese dishes such as crispy beef and spare ribs in orange sauce are excellent and well-complemented by a selective, extensive Italian wine list.

La Cornucopia

Piazza in Piscinula 18. **Map** 8 D1.
[580 03 80. **Open** 12.30pm–3pm, 8pm–11pm Mon–Sat. **† ◎ |** ▤ ▨
AE, MC, V. **Ⓛ Ⓛ Ⓛ**

One of the better fish restaurants in Trastevere, it is partly recommended for its candlelight, elegant place settings and, in summer, comfortable tables outside in the piazza. Dishes are mostly Mediterranean, with excellent antipasto, unusual pasta, simply cooked fish such as *spigola al vapore* (steamed sea bass) and selected meats. The Castelli house white will soften the bill.

Da Paris

Piazza San Calisto 7A. **Map** 7 C1.
[581 53 78. **Open** 12.30pm–3pm, 8pm–11pm Tue–Sat, 12.30pm–3pm Sun. **Closed** Aug. ▤ ▨ ▧ ▨ AE, DC, MC, V. **Ⓛ Ⓛ Ⓛ**

This classic Roman-Jewish restaurant is a firm favourite with choosy diners in Trastevere. Jole Cappellanti's homemade pasta and traditional dishes are a must and include *minestra di arzilla* (skate) and *trippa* (tripe) *alla romana*. The *fritto misto vegetale* is extraordinary, the fish fresh. There are good desserts and the owner's personal choice of wines.

Peccati di Gola

Piazza dei Ponziani 7A. **Map** 8 D1.
[581 45 29. **Open** 12.30pm–3pm, 8pm–11.30pm Tue–Sun. **Closed** 15 days Jan, 15 days Sep. ▤ ▧ ▩ ▨
▨ AE, DC, MC, V, JCB. **Ⓛ Ⓛ Ⓛ**

Situated in a quiet, ivy-clad piazza, Peccati di Gola (literally, "gluttony") is renowned for its Calabrian and Mediterranean fish cuisine successfully interpreted for modern tastes. There is delicious antipasto and a tantalizing choice of fresh seafood, risotti and fish.

Romolo nel Giardino della Fornarina

Via Porta Settimiana 8. **Map** 4 D5 & 11 B5. **[** 581 82 84. **Open** noon–3pm, 7.30pm–midnight Tue–Sun. **Closed** 3–26 Aug. ▤ ▨ ▨ AE, DC, MC, V. **Ⓛ Ⓛ Ⓛ** See p210.

A Roman institution, this was said to be the home of La Fornarina, Raphael's celebrated mistress and model, and is best enjoyed for its atmosphere on a summer evening. Eat out by candlelight in the walled courtyard, to the

accompaniment of a melancholy guitar. The food is Roman, including fried *mozzarella alla Fornarina* and *cervella e carciofi* (brains and artichokes).

Tentativo

Via della Luce 5. **Map** 8 D1. **[** 589 52 34. **Open** 8.30pm–11.30pm Mon–Sat. **Closed** Aug 15–1 Sep. **† ◎ |** ▨ ★ ▨ AE, MC,V. **Ⓛ Ⓛ Ⓛ**

Its full intriguing and ambitious name, *Tentativo di descrizione di un banchetto a Roma* ("an attempt to describe a Roman banquet") gives some clue as to the aspirations of this refined and intimate restaurant with its exclusive, ultra-modern decor. The creative nouvelle cuisine combines an adventurous but well-advised selection of flavours. Service is excellent.

Cul de Sac 2

Vicolo dell'Atleta 21. **Map** 8 D1.
[581 33 24. **Open** 8pm–11pm Tue–Fri, 8pm–11.30pm Sat, 12.30pm–2.30pm Sun. **Closed** Aug. ▨ ★ ▨ AE, DC, MC, V. **Ⓛ Ⓛ Ⓛ**

Cul de Sac 2 has emerged as both a wine lover's mecca and the most innovative and stylish restaurant in the capital. Guy, the chef, creates French-inspired flavours for pasta, fish, meat, extraordinary game and desserts. Trastevere's magical setting, the elegant white rooms with their antiques and the obliging service complete the exceptional appeal.

Alberto Ciarla

Piazza San Cosimato 40. **Map** 7 C1.
[581 86 68. **Open** 8pm–midnight Mon–Sat. **Closed** 15 days Aug, 15 days Jan. **† ◎ |** ▨ ▧ ▩ ▨ ★
▨ AE, DC, MC, V, JCB. **Ⓛ Ⓛ Ⓛ Ⓛ**

This is the quintessential restaurant for fish lovers – at least, those who are prepared to splash out. Elegant, dramatically dark decor is relieved by candlelight. Perfectly executed dishes fluctuate between the traditional and inventive, always with an eye to what's best in the market, ranging from simple to elaborately creative. A few innovatory meat dishes can be had. Ciarla, president of the Italian *sommeliers*, provides an exceptional wine list, with many French and Californian wines.

JANICULUM

Antico Arco

Via San Pancrazio 1, Piazzale Aurelio 7. **Map** 7 A1. **[** 581 52 74. **Open** noon–3pm, 8pm–midnight Tue–Sun. **Closed** 18–30 Aug. ▨ ▧ ▤ ▨ AE, DC, MC, V. **Ⓛ Ⓛ**

In this attractive 15th-century, ivy-clad restaurant, Danilo Albanesi has succeeded in creating the hospitable atmosphere of a tasteful private home, complete with faded photographs, old lace and laden sideboards. He brings alive ancient culinary traditions, with delicious results: rustic soups, fish, grills and simple, yet mouth-watering desserts. Try the carefully selected, mainly Tuscan, wines.

VATICAN

Macondo

Via Marianna Dionigi 37. **Map** 4 E2.
[321 26 01. **Open** 1pm–3pm, 7.30pm–11pm Mon–Sat. ▧ V ▩
Ⓛ Ⓛ

This brightly decorated, friendly little Caribbean restaurant is just the place to visit if you fancy a change from Italian cuisine. The food is fresh, light and plentiful and is always beautifully presented. The star dish is *pabellon criollo* (strips of beef, black beans, rice and fried plantain). Try such starters as *patacones y guacamole* (plantains and avocado dip), remembering to leave room for desserts such as the banana cake soaked in banana liquor. There is a good selection of wines at various prices as well as cocktails and Venezuelan rums.

San Luigi

Via Mocenigo 10. **Map** 3 B2.
[39 72 07 04. **Open** noon–3pm, 8pm–11pm Mon–Sat. **Closed** Aug.
V ▧ ▨ AE, MC, V.
Ⓛ Ⓛ Ⓛ

If you have just spent hours in the Vatican Museums, the pleasure of a relaxing restaurant with 19th-century decor and soft music will soothe your aching limbs. A set menu is on offer at lunchtime and a choice of traditional Neapolitan and creative dishes in the evening. Pastas and desserts are particularly successful. There's a choice of good French and Italian wines.

Les Etoiles

Via Vitelleschi 34. **Map** 3 C2. **[** 689 34 34. **Open** 12.30pm–2.30pm, 8.30pm–11pm daily. ▧ ▩ ▨ ▤
▨ AE, DC, MC, V, JCB.
Ⓛ Ⓛ Ⓛ Ⓛ

Located at the top of the Atlante Star hotel (*see p300*), this rooftop restaurant was completely renovated in 1992, and now includes free valet parking and a separate entrance with a lift leading directly to the restaurant levels. Taking up the top three floors of the hotel, the restaurant and its terraces offer panoramic views of the Rome skyline, including St Peter's. Speciality dishes include snails with truffles on pecorino cheese, quail's eggs on a bed of rocket with mustard dressing, and *tagliolini* (pasta) with clams and *finferli* (mushrooms).

VIA VENETO

Cantina Cantarini

Piazza Sallustio 12. **Map** 5 C2.
[48 55 28. **Open** 12.30pm–
3.30pm, 4.30pm–11pm Mon–Sat.
Closed Aug, 25 Dec–6 Jan.
AE, DC, MC, V, JCB.

Hidden away on a small square, this popular local trattoria is remarkable for the good nature of its waiters. Meat is on the menu from Monday to Wednesday, and fish the rest of the week. Typical dishes are *alla marchigiana* (from the Marches); the vegetable and veal *fritto misto* is amazingly light.

Tullio

Via San Nicola da Tolentino 26.
Map 5 B2. **[** 474 55 60. **Open**
12.30pm–3pm, 7.30pm–11pm
Mon–Sat. **Closed** Aug.
AE, DC, MC, V, JCB.

This genuine Tuscan restaurant is frequented by an enthusiastic clientele for its generous helpings and fair prices. Typical dishes include *porcini* mushrooms in every possible form, *pasta e fagioli*, grilled meat and fish and Florentine steaks – served in agreeable surroundings by courteous, speedy waiters.

Andrea

Via Sardegna 26. **Map** 5 C1.
[482 18 91, 474 05 57. **Open**
12.30pm–3pm, 7.45pm–11pm Mon–
Fri, 7.45pm–11pm Sat. **Closed** 2
weeks Aug. AE, DC,
MC, V, JCB.

This congenial, refined restaurant offers a superb array of antipasto, ranging from humble *suppli* (rice croquettes) to regal lobster (try it in *insalata catalana*). Leave room for the impressive seasonal first and second courses, and for desserts. There is an extensive choice of French and Italian wines.

Giovanni

Via Marche 64. **Map** 5 B1.
[482 18 34. **Open** 12.30pm–3pm,
7.30pm–11pm Sun–Thu, 12.30pm–
3pm Fri. **Closed** Aug. AE,
DC, MC, V.

A throng of satisfied regulars crowd this classic, well-established restaurant near Via Veneto. The efficient, reliable service is hard to beat. The place is run along traditional lines by the Sbrega family, with a strong regional influence from Lazio and the Marches. They serve fresh pasta dishes such as *tagliolini all'amatriciana*, vegetable soups, boned chicken with rice, unbeatable roast lamb, *osso buco*, fresh fish and *millefeuilles*. The house wines are good.

San Benedetto

Via Romagna 20–22. **Map** 5 C1.
[474 39 81, 488 28 20.
Open Oct–Mar: 12.30pm–4pm,
7.30pm–10.30pm Tue–Sat; Apr–Sep:
12.30pm–4pm, 7.30pm–10.30pm
Mon–Fri. **Closed** 10–22 Aug,
Christmas–New Year.
AE, DC, MC, V.

San Benedetto del Tronto in the Marches is the inspiration behind Pier Luigi Camiscioni's restaurant. Local fish is expertly cooked *alla marchigiana*. In addition, there are delicious antipasti (mussels, fresh sardines), soups and simple fried and grilled fish. Follow these with fruity desserts and excellent cheese and dessert wine from the Marches.

George's

Via Marche 7. **Map** 5 B2.
[42 08 45 75. **Open** 12.30pm–
3pm, 7.30pm–midnight (piano bar
2am) Mon–Sat. **Closed** Aug.
AE, DC, MC, V,
JCB.

Visit this slightly tarnished survivor from the *dolce vita* era for its nostalgic air of luxurious elegance. The softly illuminated rooms, garden terrace, tinkling piano music and impeccable service provide the perfect foil for George's tempting and expertly prepared international dishes. There is also a good selection of French and Italian wines.

Le Sans Souci

Via Sicilia 20. **Map** 5 C1.
[482 18 14. **Open** 8pm–midnight
Tue–Sun. **Closed** Aug.
AE, DC, MC, V, JCB.

This restaurant has overcome a glitzy fame to emerge as a sound exponent of elaborate French and Italian cuisine. The decor is black and gold throughout, with 17th-century gilt mirrors and chandeliers. In the sophisticated anteroom you can drink an apéritif at your leisure and consult the menu and magnificent wine list. As you might expect, the service is eagerly efficient.

VILLA BORGHESE

Al Ceppo

Via Panama 2. **Map** 2 F3.
[841 96 96. **Open** 12.30pm–3pm,
8pm–11pm Tue –Sun. **Closed** 3 wks
Aug. AE, DC,
MC, V, JCB.

In 20 years, two sisters from the Marches, Cristina and Marisella Milozzi, have won over an affectionate following of regulars in this exclusive, notoriously diffident area of Rome, attracted by the consistently reliable food and a hospitable yet refined family atmosphere. The strictly seasonal menu concentrates on traditional dishes with a touch of daily invention, as well as excellent grilled meats, homemade desserts and Italian wines.

Relais la Piscine dell'Aldrovandi Palace Hotel

Via G Mangili 6. **Map** 2 D4.
[321 61 26. **Open** 12.30pm–3pm,
7.30pm–11pm daily.
★ AE, DC, MC, V.

The autonomous restaurant of the Aldrovandi Palace Hotel is especially beautiful in summer when tables are set outside on the terrace by the pool. Jean Luc Frenat, the young Breton chef, produces an excellent, typically Mediterranean nouvelle cuisine, using prime meat and fish, vegetables and herbs. This is accompanied by meticulous service, wonderful desserts and a fully comprehensive wine list. Business lunches are a speciality.

Relais le Jardin dell'Hotel Lord Byron

Via Giuseppe de Notaris 5.
Map 2 D4. **[** 322 45 41. **Open**
12.30pm–2.30pm, 8pm–11pm
Mon–Sat. **Closed** Aug.
★ AE, DC, MC, V, JCB.

For many, this is Rome's greatest restaurant, located in the quiet, exclusive and green area of Parioli. Diners here are undaunted by absolutely top prices, high-class, impeccably correct service, and *haute cuisine* at its finest. The inspired chef draws predominantly on traditional Italian regional cooking, with exceptionally creative combinations of fruit, herbs and vegetables as partners to top-quality meats and fish. To finish, there are homemade desserts and pastries; the list of French, Italian and Californian wines is outstanding.

For key to symbols see p303

Light Meals and Snacks

W HERE SHOULD YOU GO for a casual bite to eat? Rome has the ability to satisfy the all-important stomach at most hours of the day and night. A sound network of *gelaterie, pasticcerie,* pizzerias, wine bars, *rosticcerie* and *tavole calde* mean that good food and drink are always just around the corner.

Start with a classic breakfast at your local stand-up bar: cappuccino and a hot *cornetto* (like a croissant). A heavy morning's sightseeing may leave you ready for an apéritif in one of Rome's elegant 19th-century bars, followed by lunch at a wine bar or Roman-style fast food. In the afternoon there are plenty of opportunities for coffee and cakes at a *pasticceria,* while the late-night bars, especially those with tables outside, are a source of endless entertainment, where you can sip a drink or linger over the final ice cream of the day.

PIZZERIAS

R OMAN PIZZERIAS are the natural choice for informal eating: they are noisy, convivial and fun. Most open only at night, when the wood ovens are lit and the embers glow reassuringly up until last orders. Look for the *forno a legna* (wood-burning oven) sign – electric ovens simply don't produce the same results. In the best pizzerias you sit in view of the vast marble slabs where the *pizzaioli* flatten the dough and whip the pizzas in and out of the oven on long-handled pallets. Turnaround is fast, so you may not be encouraged to linger.

The running order is straightforward: you might have a *bruschetta* (toasted tomato or garlic bread) to start, some *supplì* (fried rice croquettes), fried courgette flowers or *filetti di baccalà* (battered cod fillets), or perhaps a plate of *cannellini* beans in oil. Follow this with a *calzone* (folded-over pizza) or the classic Roman pizza – round, thin and crunchy – with various toppings: *napoletana* (tomato, anchovies, mozza-rella), *margherita* (without the anchovies), *capricciosa* (ham, artichokes, eggs, olives) and anything else the *pizzaiolo* fancies. Draught beer is the classic thing to drink, but wine is always available. You should expect to pay around L15,000 a head for a meal.

The most representative Roman pizzerias, from all points of view, are **Da Baffetto** (look for the queue outside) and its offspring, **La Montecarlo**; also **Remo** in Testaccio and **Ivo** in Trastevere, where tables line the road in summer. **Osteria Picchioni** and restaurant-cum-pizzeria **Manuia** prepare elaborate, up-market combinations. Another place not to be missed is **Panattoni**, where a huge variety of customers patiently queue for a pavement seat on Viale Trastevere in summer, or clamour for one of the marble-topped tables (hence its well-known nickname "the mortuary") inside.

ENOTECHE (WINE BARS)

E NOTECHE offer a fine selection of wines from Italy and around the world. They are usually run by experts, keen to share their knowledge and advise on the best combinations of wine and food. Some *enoteche* are simply shops for browsing. Others like **Achilli al Parlamento** and **Bevitoria Navona** offer the traditional *mescita* – wine and cham-pagne tasting by the glass, accompanied by snacks and canapés. Their prices are reasonable: about L1,500 for a glass on tap, L3,000 upwards for a quality wine, to about L8,000 for champagne. **Vineria Reggio** in Campo

de' Fiori is a typical spot for *mescita,* especially at night. Here business people, residents and tourists alike meet for an apéritif or to share a bottle at a table.

For more substantial food for as little as L20–25,000 a head, try the bistro- or restaurant-style *enoteche*, open at lunch and until late. Particularly recommended are the innovative **Cul de Sac 1**, **Trimani Wine Bar**, the tiny **Il Tajut** serving specialities from Friuli, and **Cavour 313**.

BIRRERIE (BEER HOUSES)

R OMAN BIRRERIE had their heyday in the early years of this century. The few that have survived the competition from subsequent pizzerias and *enoteche* are some of the best: German-style beer houses where you can still enjoy beer and substantial snacks in traditional wood-panelled rooms. The quiet **Premiata Fabbrica Birra Peroni**, serving classic beer-drinkers' fare, is worth a visit for its authentic, turn-of-the-century air of decadence, as is the permanently crowded **Fratelli Tempera**. Another place which attracts Italians and foreigners alike is the **Birreria Viennese/Wiener Bierhaus** with its excellent Transylvanian specialities, which come heaped generously on a wooden plate. If you eat here, or in the **Birreria Bavarese**, you'll spend around L30–50,000. Elsewhere will be cheaper if you want to concentrate more on drinking.

FAST FOOD

R OME HAS PLENTY of homespun fast food options for when you need something quick and inexpensive to eat. Slices of freshly baked pizza are available for a couple of thousand lire from *pizza al taglio* shops. Many of these places also sell spit-roasted chickens, *supplì* and other traditional pizzeria fare. *Rosticcerie* offer deliciously tasty roast chicken and potatoes as well as ready-made pasta dishes, cooked vegetables, salads and desserts – useful for picnics or for making a complete takeaway meal. For a similarly speedy but sit-down snack, bars with a *tavola calda* (hot table) have the same kind of selection, especially at lunchtime; one of the largest and most popular is **Il Delfino** at Largo Argentina. Vegetarians should seek out the **Centro Macrobiotico** near Piazza di Spagna. The **McDonald's** in Piazza di Spagna also offers a good range of fresh mixed salads.

Most *alimentari* (grocery shops) will make you up a *panino* (filled roll). Especially delicious are **Paladini's** hot plain pizza pockets stuffed with choices from the shop's counters, where you can also have a glass of wine. Try one of the region's specialities if you see the sign *porchetta*: whole aromatic roast pig with crackling, sliced into *rosette* (rolls) or thick country-bread sandwiches – there is a good stall selling these at the tram stop in Viale Carlo Felice opposite San Giovanni in Laterano. At the hole-in-the-wall **Er Buchetto** you can even sit down in relative comfort with a glass of wine. For a really typical Roman snack, make a late-afternoon detour to **Filetti di Baccalà** serving, as the name suggests, fried cod fillets and little else.

BARS, CAFÉS AND TEA ROOMS

R OMAN BARS are the city's lifeline: they are places to meet, eat, drink, pick up milk, buy coffee, make phone calls or find a toilet. Some of them are small, stand-up, basic one-counter bars for grabbing a quick *cornetto* and cappuccino and some may be more luxurious, grandiose affairs doubling as cake shop, ice cream parlour, tea room or *tavola calda*, or all of these in one. Most open early at around 7.30am and close late, particularly at weekends, at around midnight or 2am. In summer, tables cover all the

available outdoor space, and the fight for a place in the shade begins.

Traditionally elegant – and pricy – bars for people watching are the admirably located **Rosati** and **Doney**, as well as **Caffè Greco**, the 19th-century haunt of artists, writers and composers *(see p133)*, or the carefully restored **La Caffettiera** at the Pantheon. Another popular and well-established bar is the **Antico Caffè della Pace**. **Minim's de Paris**, **Caffè Flores** (with piano music) and **Selarum** in Trastevere are recommended for late-night drinks, as is **Zodiaco** on Monte Mario for its panoramic views.

Earlier in the day Rome's favoured meeting places are its tea rooms. **Babington's** *(see p134)* is the place to go for an expensive cup of tea and cakes in genteel surroundings, while **Dolci e Doni** is more relaxed. Try a *gran caffè speciale* at the counters of **Sant'Eustachio**, or one of Rome's best espressos at **Tazza d'Oro**. **Ciampini al Café du Jardin** with its garden setting and roof-top views is unbeatable in summer, particularly at the apéritif hour, as is the **Bar Parnaso** in Parioli.

Museum cafés are seldom open, or worth visiting. A welcome exception however is the café of the **Palazzo delle Esposizioni** which is open throughout the day *(see p164)*. If you're stuck for choice, try one of the grander, larger bars such as **Alemagna** – where you can stand, sit, eat and drink at any time of the day, well into the night.

PASTICCERIE (PASTRY SHOPS)

O N SUNDAY mornings you'll often see Romans emerging from the local *pasticceria* with a beautifully wrapped package. This can contain dainty individual pastries, whole cakes or tarts, traditional Easter *colombe* (doves) or Christmas *panettoni* – huge cakes with raisins and candied peel – all

for consumption by large gatherings of friends, relatives or family after lunch. The window displays of Rome's cake shops are often fantastic. These, and the aroma of brewing coffee, might tempt you in for a hot *cornetto* or a *brioche* in the early morning, a midday *pizzetta* or savoury tart, or choux pastry or fruit tart later in the afternoon.

GELATERIE (ICE CREAM PARLOURS)

I CE CREAM *(gelato)* is one of summer's particular delights, and nowhere more so than in Rome. Every well-equipped bar has its tubs of homemade ice cream, and in the *gelaterie* the choice is endless – water-ices made with a phenomenal variety of fruit; lemon and coffee *granite* (crushed ice); as well as more exotic ice cream specialities such as rice, *zuppa inglese* (English trifle), *zabaglione, tiramisù* and After Eight. Choose as many varieties as the size of your cone or cup will hold, topped with cream *(panna)* and then go for a stroll, or else take a break and be served with an ornate creation with all the trimmings at a table. *Gelaterie* are open all day until late at night, when they become evening entertainment.

Tre Scalini in Piazza Navona is a famous spot for enjoying the pricy yet so heavenly chocolate *tartufo,* while a summer evening in EUR, especially with children, nearly always ends in a trip to **Giolitti**, a historic ice cream name; try also the strategically placed, crowded original near the Pantheon *(see p109)*, also serving coffee and pastries. In the same area is the popular **Gelateria della Palma**.

Adults may prefer to pick their night-time treat at **Chalet del Lago**, again in EUR, while sitting beside the lake. If you come across a small kiosk bearing the sign *grattachecche* (most likely in Trastevere and Testaccio), try one of Rome's oldest traditions – ice grated on the spot and enlivened with a variety of classic flavourings.

DIRECTORY

FORUM

Pizzerias
Alle Carrette
Via della Madonna
dei Monti.
Map 5 B5.

PIAZZA DELLA ROTONDA

Pizzerias
Barroccio
Via dei Pastini 13.
Map 4 F4 & 12 D2.

Er Faciolaro
Via dei Pastini 123.
Map 4 F4 & 12 D2.

Wine Bars
Achilli al Parlamento
Via dei Prefetti 15.
Map 4 F3 & 12 D1.

Corsi
Via del Gesù 88.
Map 4 F4 & 12 E3.

Spiriti
Via di Sant'Eustachio 5.
Map 4 F4 & 12 D3.

Fast Food
Fiocco di Neve
Via del Pantheon 51.
Map 4 F4 & 12 D2.

**Bars, Cafés and
Tea Rooms**
La Caffettiera
Piazza di Pietra 65.
Map 4 F3 & 12 E2.

Camilloni
Piazza Sant'Eustachio 54.
Map 4 F4 & 12 D3.

Ciampini
Piazza S. Lorenzo in Lucina
29. **Map** 4 F3 & 12 D1.

Sant'Eustachio
Piazza Sant'Eustachio 82.
Map 4 F4 & 12 D3.

Tazza d'Oro
Via degli Orfani 82/84.
Map 4 F4 & 12 D2.

Teichner
Piazza S. Lorenzo in Lucina
17. **Map** 4 F3 & 12 E1.

Ice Cream Parlours
Gelateria della Palma
Via della Maddalena 20.
Map 4 F3 & 12 D2.

Giolitti
Via Uffici del Vicario 40.
Map 4 F3 & 12 D2.

PIAZZA NAVONA

Pizzerias
Da Baffetto (Volpetti)
Via del Governo Vecchio
114. **Map** 4 E4 & 11 B3.

Corallo
Via del Corallo 10.
Map 4 E4 & 11 B3.

La Montecarlo
Vicolo Savelli 12/13.
Map 4 E4 & 11 C3.

Wine Bars
Bevitoria Navona
Piazza Navona 72.
Map 4 E4 & 11 C2.

Cul de Sac 1
Piazza Pasquino 73.
Map 4 E4 & 11 C3.

Fast Food
Paladini
Via del Governo Vecchio
28/29. **Map** 4 E4 & 11 B3.

**Bars, Cafés and
Tea Rooms**
Antico Caffè della Pace
Via della Pace 5.
Map 4 E4 & 11 C3.

Pastry Shops
A Bella Napoli
Corso Vittorio Emanuele II
246. **Map** 4 E4 & 11 B3.

Ice Cream Parlours
Tre Scalini
Piazza Navona 28.
Map 4 E4 & 11 C3.

PIAZZA DI SPAGNA

Pizzerias
La Capricciosa
Largo dei Lombardi 8.
Map 4 F2.

Il Leoncino
Via del Leoncino 28.
Map 4 F2.

Wine Bars
Buccone
Via di Ripetta 19.
Map 4 F1.

Roffi Isabelli
Via della Croce 76 A.
Map 5 A2.

Beer Houses
Birreria Bavarese
Via Vittoria 47. **Map** 5 A2.

Birreria Viennese/
Wiener Bierhaus
Via della Croce 21.
Map 5 A2.

Fast Food
Centro Macrobiotico
Via della Vite 14.
Map 5 A3.

Fior Fiore
Via della Croce 17/18.
Map 5 A2.

McDonald's
Piazza di Spagna 46.
Map 5 A2.

**Bars, Cafés and
Tea Rooms**
Alemagna
Via del Corso 181.
Map 5 A3.

Babington's Tea Rooms
Piazza di Spagna 23.
Map 5 A2.

Caffè Greco
Via Condotti 86.
Map 5 A2.

Ciampini al Café
du Jardin
Piazza Trinità dei Monti.
Map 5 A2.

Dolci e Doni
Via delle Carrozze 85 B.
Map 4 F2.

Rosati
Piazza del Popolo 5.
Map 4 F1.

CAMPO DE' FIORI

Wine Bars
Bottega del Vino
da Beve
Via Santa Maria del Pianto
9 A/11.
Map 4 F5 & 12 D5.

Il Goccetto
Via dei Banchi Vecchi 14.
Map 4 D4 & 11 B3.

Vineria Reggio
Piazza Campo de' Fiori 15.
Map 4 E4 & 11 C4.

Fast Food
Il Delfino
Corso Vittorio Emanuele II
67. **Map** 4 F4 & 12 D4.

Filetti di Baccalà
Largo dei Librari 88.
Map 4 E5 & 11 C4.

Da Giovanni
Piazza Campo de' Fiori 39.
Map 4 E4 & 11 C4.

**Bars, Cafés and
Tea Rooms**
Alberto Pica
Via della Seggiola 12.
Map 4 F5 & 12 D5.

Caffè Flores
Lungotevere dei Vallati
25/27. **Map** 4 E5 & 11 C5.

Pastry Shops
Bernasconi
Largo di Torre Argentina 1.
Map 4 F4 & 12 D4.

La Dolceroma
Via del Portico d'Ottavia
20B. **Map** 4 F5 & 12 E5.

Il Forno del Ghetto
Via del Portico d'Ottavia 2.
Map 4 F5 & 12 E5.

QUIRINAL

Pizzerias
Est! Est! Est!
Via Principe Amedeo 4A.
Map 6 D3.

I Rioni
Via dei SS. Quattro
Coronati 24. **Map** 9 B1.

Wine Bars
Cavour 313
Via Cavour 313.
Map 5 B5.

Beer Houses
Albrecht
Via Rasella 52. **Map** 5 B3.

Fratelli Tempera
Via San Marcello 19.
Map 5 A4 & 12 F3.

Fast Food
Bar del Palazzo del
Yogobar
Via Mazzarino 8–10.
Map 5 B4.

Er Buchetto
Via del Viminale 2.
Map 5 C3.

McDonald's
Piazza della
Repubblica 40.
Map 5 C3.

Nadia e Davide
Via Milano 33.
Map 5 B4.

Bars, Cafés and Tea Rooms
Palazzo delle Esposizioni
Via Milano 9.
Map 5 B4.

TERMINI

Pizzerias
La Bruschetta
Via Ancona 35.
Map 6 D1.

Formula 1
Via degli Equi 13.
Map 6 F4.

Le Maschere
Via degli Umbri 8/14.
Map 6 F4.

Wine Bars
Trimani Wine Bar
Via Cernaia 37B.
Map 6 D2.

Beer Houses
Premiata Fabbrica Birra Peroni
Via Brescia 24/32.
Map 6 D1.

Pastry Shops
La Partenopea
Via Appia Nuova 198.
Map 10 E3.

ESQUILINE

Pizzerias
Osteria Picchioni
Via del Boschetto 16.
Map 5 B4.

Beer Houses
Marconi
Via di Santa
Prassede 9C.
Map 6 D4.

Fast Food
Cottini
Via Merulana 286.
Map 6 D4.

Palazzo del Freddo di Giovanni Fassi
Via Principe Eugenio
65/67.
Map 6 E5.

Bars, Cafés and Tea Rooms
Ristoro della Salute
Piazza del Colosseo 2.
Map 9 A1.

LATERAN

Fast Food
Viale Carlo Felice Porchetta Stall
Viale Carlo Felice.
Map 10 D1.

Ice Cream Parlours
Premiate Gelaterie Fantasia
Via La Spezia 100/102.
Map 10 E1.

AVENTINE

Pizzerias
Remo
Piazza Santa Maria
Liberatrice 44.
Map 8 D3.

Taverna Cestia
Via della Piramide
Cestia 67. **Map** 8 E3

Wine Bars
Palombi
Piazza Testaccio 38/41.
Map 8 D3.

TRASTEVERE

Pizzerias
Almacrì
Via F. Benaglia 3.
Map 7 B4.

Da Gildo
Via della Scala 31A.
Map 4 D5 & 11 B5.

Ivo
Via di San Francesco a
Ripa 158. **Map** 7 C1.

Panattoni
Viale Trastevere 53.
Map 7 C1.

Ar Popi Popi
Via delle Fratte di
Trastevere 45. **Map** 7 C1.

Da Vittorio
Via di San Cosimato 14A.
Map 7 C1.

Wine Bars
Il Cantiniere di Santa Dorotea
Via di S. Dorotea 9.
Map 4 D5 & 11 B5.

Ferrara
Via dell'Arco di San
Calisto 36. **Map** 7 C1.

Fast Food
McDonald's
Piazza Sonnino 39/40.
Map 8 D1.

Bars, Cafés and Tea Rooms
Selarum
Via dei Fienaroli 12.
Map 7 C1.

Pastry Shops
Valzani
Via del Moro 37B.
Map 7 C1.

Ice Cream Parlours
La Fonte della Salute
Via Cardinale Marmaggi
2/4/6. **Map** 7 C1.

Sacchetti
Piazza San Cosimato 62.
Map 7 C1.

VATICAN

Pizzerias
Pizzeria San Marco
Via Tacito 29.
Map 4 D2.

Il Tempio della Pizza
Viale Giulio Cesare 91.
Map 3 C1.

Wine Bars
Il Simposio di Piero Costantini
Piazza Cavour 16.
Map 4 E2.

Beer Houses
Tiroler Keller
Via G. Vitelleschi 23.
Map 3 C2.

VIA VENETO

Wine Bars
Marchetti
Via Sicilia 144.
Map 5 C1.

Bars, Cafés and Tea Rooms
Doney
Via Veneto 145.
Map 5 B2.

EUR

Fast Food
McDonald's
Piazzale Don Luigi Sturzo
21/22.

Bars, Cafés and Tea Rooms
Chalet del Lago
Lake, EUR.

Ice Cream Parlours
Giolitti
Casina dei Tre Laghi, Viale
Oceania 90.

FURTHER AFIELD

Wine Bars
Guerrini
Viale Regina Margherita
205/207.

Semidivino
Via Alessandria 230.

Il Tajut
Via Albenga 44.
Map 10 E3.

Fast Food
Svizzera Siciliana
Piazza Pio XI 10/11.

Bars, Cafés and Tea Rooms
Bar Parnaso
Piazza delle Muse 22.
Map 2 E2.

Il Cigno
Viale Parioli 16.
Map 2 E3.

Duse
Via Eleonora Duse 1E.
Map 2 F2.

Pannocchi
Via Bergamo 56.
Map 6 D1.

San Filippo
Via di Villa San Filippo
8/10. **Map** 2 F2.

Zodiaco
Viale Parco Mellini 90.

Pastry Shops
Euclide
Via F. Civinini 119.
Map 2 D3.

SHOPS AND MARKETS

ROME HAS BEEN a thriving centre for design and cosmopolitan shopping since ancient times. In the heyday of the Empire the finest craftsmen were drawn to Rome, and artefacts and produce of all kinds, including gold, furs, wine and slaves, were imported from far-flung corners of the Empire to service the needs of the wealthy Roman population.

Shopping in Rome today in many ways reflects this diverse tradition. Italian designers have

Window shopping in Rome, an absorbing pastime

an international reputation for their luxuriously chic style in fashion, knitwear and leather goods (especially shoes and handbags) as well as in interior design, fabrics, ceramics and glass. The artisan-craftsman tradition is strong and the love of good design filters through into the smallest items. It is not a city for bargains (though often better value than Florence or Milan), but the joys of window shopping here will offer plenty of compensation.

BEST BUYS

LEATHER GOODS of all kinds, including shoes and bags, are a strong point. Ready-to-wear Italian designer clothes are not cheap, but they are certainly less expensive than in other countries. Armani jeans are a good example *(see p327)*. You are also likely to find designer lighting fixtures, for example, at lower prices here. Both modern and traditional Italian ceramics and handicrafts can be very beautifully made and, if you have time to wander around the back streets, really unusual and individual gifts can often be found.

SALES

SALE TIME *(saldi)* is from mid-July to mid-September and the period from just before Christmas to the first week in March. Top designers

(see p326) slash prices by half, but their clothes are still very expensive even then. Good bargains can be found in the young designer wear shops *(see p327)* and good-quality large shoe sizes are sold off very cheaply (most Italians have small feet). Both of the Cesari shops *(see p327 and p333)* are well-known for their sales. In general, though, sales in Rome do not offer huge discounts.

Both the original and the sale price should be quoted on each reduced item. *Liquidazioni* (closing down sales) are usually genuine and can sometimes be worth investigating. However, other signs in shop windows such as *vendite promozionali* (special introductory prices) and *sconti* (discounts) are often only lures to get you into the shop. The sign on the door saying *entrata libera* means "browsers welcome".

Antiques at Acanto *(see p336)*

WHEN TO SHOP

SHOPS ARE GENERALLY open from 9am to 1pm and from 3.30pm to 7.30pm (4pm to 8pm in the summer months). Some of the shops in the centre stay open all day from 10.30am to 7.30pm. Most shops are closed on Sunday (except immediately before Christmas). Shops are also closed on Monday morning, apart from food and technical supply stores, which close on Thursday afternoons in winter and Saturday afternoons in summer.

August brings the city to a virtual standstill as Roman families escape the heat to the sea or the mountains. Signs saying *chiuso per ferie* (closed for vacation) appear everywhere in the shops. Most shops close for at least two weeks around 15 August, the national holiday.

Flower stalls in Piazza Campo de' Fiori *(see p338)*

SHOPPING ETIQUETTE

APART FROM a few department stores, most Roman shops are small, specializing in just one field. Browsing at leisure may at first seem daunting if you are used to large shopping centres. Customers will almost always receive better attention if they dress smartly – the emphasis on *fare la bella figura* (making a good impression) is taken seriously.

Stylish leather gloves on display

Sizes are not always uniform, so it's wise to try clothes on if possible before buying, since refunds and exchanges are not usually given.

HOW TO PAY

MOST SHOPS now accept all the major credit cards, whose signs are displayed on the shop window. Some will also accept foreign currency, though the exchange rate may not be good. When you make a purchase you are bound by Italian law to leave the shop with a *ricevuta fiscale* (receipt). You can try asking for a discount if paying cash and you may be lucky, though many shops have a *prezzi fissi* (fixed prices) sign.

VAT EXEMPTION

VALUE ADDED TAX – VAT (IVA in Italy) – ranges from 12% on clothing to 35% on luxury items such as jewellery and furs. Marked or advertised prices normally include the IVA. It is possible for non-European Community citizens

Craftsmen near Piazza Navona

to obtain an IVA refund for individual purchases that exceed L650,000, but be prepared for a long and bureaucratic process. The simplest method is to shop at a place displaying the "Euro Free Tax" sign. Present your passport when you make your purchase, and fill in a form from the shop; the shop then deducts the IVA, gives you a copy of the form, and sends their copy to the Euro Free Tax Organization in Milan which will then deal with the paperwork.

If you wish to buy something from a shop which is not part of the "Euro Free Tax" scheme, you must get the Italian customs to stamp the vendor's receipt at your departure, showing them the purchased article, and then post the stamped receipt back to the shop, who should then send you a refund.

Mercato delle Stampe *(see p338)*

DEPARTMENT STORES AND SHOPPING CENTRES

DEPARTMENT STORES, known as *grandi magazzini,* are few and far between in Rome. **La Rinascente** and **Coin** are good for ready-to-wear clothes, household linens and haberdashery, and have well-stocked perfume counters. La Rinascente give 10% discount to tourists on perfumes and cosmetics if you show your passport. The **Standa** and **Upim** chain stores offer moderately-priced medium-quality clothes and household goods.

Another alternative for the zealous shopper is to head for one of Rome's two shopping centres. **Cinecittà Due Centro Commerciale**, built in 1988, offers around a 100 shops plus bars, banks

Bargains in Via Sannio *(see p339)*

and restaurants within easy reach of the centre by Metro (line A to Cinecittà). An even bigger centre, called **I Granai**, has now opened in Via Laurentina, reachable by Metro (line B to Laurentina).

Cinecittà Due Centro Commerciale
Via Tuscolana. **Map** 10 E2.
722 09 10.

Coin
Piazzale Appio 7. **Map** 10 D2.
708 00 20.

I Granai
Via del Tintoretto.
51 95 57 77.

La Rinascente
Via del Corso 189. **Map** 5 A3 & 12 E2.
679 76 91.

Piazza Fiume. **Map** 6 D1.
884 12 31.

Standa
Via Cola di Rienzo 173. **Map** 4 D2.
324 32 83.

Viale Trastevere 60. **Map** 7 C2.
589 53 42.

Via Appia Nuova 181–3. **Map** 10 D2.
702 48 96.

Upim
Via del Tritone 172. **Map** 5 A3.
678 33 36.

Via Nazionale 211. **Map** 5 C3.
48 45 02.

Piazza S. Maria Maggiore. **Map** 6 D4.
446 55 79.

Rome's Best: Shopping Streets and Markets

T HE MOST INTERESTING shops in Rome are in the old centre, so shopping is easy to combine with sightseeing. The shops are often housed in medieval or Renaissance buildings and their window displays can be exquisite. Just like shopkeepers in past centuries, traders tend to specialize in one type of merchandise. Street names often refer to the old tradesmen: locksmiths in Via dei Chiavari, leather jerkin makers in Via dei Giubbonari and chairs in Via dei Sediari. Today, antique merchants have taken over from the rosary sellers on Via dei Coronari. The top names in fashion and modern design dominate the Via Condotti area, and the artisan-craftsman tradition is still strong around Campo de' Fiori and Piazza Navona.

Via dei Coronari
Art Nouveau and antiques enthusiasts will love browsing in the shops that line this charming street just northwest of Piazza Navona. But be prepared for high prices as most of the items are imported.

Via Cola di Rienzo
Situated close to the Vatican Museums, this long wide street has the finest food shops and is also good for clothes, books and gifts.

Via del Pellegrino
Book and art shops abound here next to working artisans in the historic centre. Don't miss the mirror-lined alley near Campo de' Fiori.

Via dei Cappellari
This narrow, medieval street is a great place for watching furniture restorers and other artisans plying their crafts in the open air.

Porta Portese
You can buy anything from antiques to a tin whistle at Trastevere's Sunday morning flea market. (See p339.)

Vatican

Piazza Navona

Janiculum

Cam de' Fi

Trasteve

Via Margutta
Up-market antique shops mix with genteel restaurants on this peaceful, cobbled street.

Via del Babuino
This street is renowned for designer furniture, lighting and glass, as well as interesting antique and fashion shops.

DESIGNER SHOPPING
All the well-known stars of the Italian fashion scene, plus exclusive jewellers, gift shops, shoe designers and tailors, are concentrated in this cluster of chic and stylish shopping streets by the Spanish Steps *(see pp326–31)*. Romans love to stroll here in the early evening.

Via Borgognona
Crowds flock here to buy, or just gaze at, high-fashion clothes, shoes, leather bags and other accessories.

0 metres   500
0 yards   500

Testaccio Market
A visual feast of fruit and vegetables greets the eye in this lively market. (See p338.)

Men's and Women's Fashion

ITALY IS ONE of the leading lights in high-class fashion, or *alta moda*. Many of the most famous designers are based in Milan, but Rome is home to a cluster of sophisticated and internationally distinguished fashion houses. There is also a wonderful selection of *alta moda* shops. Boutiques displaying an eclectic mix of designer goods rub shoulders with showrooms devoted to single collections. But even for those of us unable to splash out on genuine designer-wear, much fun can be gained from a stroll down the exclusive streets that radiate out from the Piazza di Spagna, as some of the window displays are truly spectacular.

The "atelier" made-to-measure fashions are beyond most pockets, but the designers also offer ready-to-wear alternatives in their boutiques. These are not cheap, but cost far less than a tailor-made garment.

If you're looking for clothes from unconventional designers, **Gente** is the place to go – its Roman showrooms have exclusive rights to the original couture collections of avant-garde stylists such as Dolce & Gabbana and Moschino, plus Europeans such as Jean-Paul Gaultier. **MaxMara** also has a number of branches here. Chic suits and separates are the mainstays of this popular label. The quality of fabric and finish is superb and, with suits available for around L1,000,000, its prices are much lower than other *alta moda* couture designers' ready-to-wear lines.

WOMEN'S HIGH FASHION

ROME'S MOST famous designer internationally is probably **Valentino**. However, one of the first houses to make a name for Roman fashion was **Sorelle Fontana**. This was *the* salon to be dressed by during the 1950s heyday of Rome's *dolce vita*. Sorelle Fontana has been dressing high society since the 1930s, and stocks a wide selection of ready-to-wear clothes and accessories.

Fendi occupies a large tract of the fashion street, Via Borgognona. Fendi made its name with high-fashion furs, then branched out into leather goods, accessories and ready-to-wear, collaborating with Karl Lagerfeld who designed the coveted double-F logo which emblazons its very collectable products. Third-generation family members design the younger, less expensive Fendissime line.

For well over a decade, **Laura Biagiotti** has reigned as Rome's queen of discreet, conservative couture. From her headquarters in a castle just outside Rome, she designs a range of timelessly elegant knitwear and silk separates for women who don't want to sacrifice style for comfort. She is famous for her use of cashmere and white as well as her creative use of fabrics and quality of finish. Her flagship showroom in Via Borgognona stocks her complete collection, which now includes hosiery,

perfumes, swimwear and leather goods. Her scarves make wonderful presents, and are often reduced in price during sales; other items from previous collections are available in the shop all year round at very good discounts.

Other internationally known Rome-based designers include **Renato Balestra** for tailored suits and glamorous evening wear and **Roberto Capucci**, who uses wonderful textures and fabrics in classy suits. **Raniero Gattinoni** produces elegant suits and blouses for both his made-to-measure and off-the-peg showrooms. **Mila Schön**'s speciality is dramatic evening wear.

Other luminaries of Italian fashion with shops in Rome include **Giorgio Armani**, **Gianfranco Ferrè, Gianni Versace** and **Trussardi**. A rising star in ready-to-wear is **Genny**. Based in Ancona, the Genny design team produces some really classic, elegant and stylish collections.

MEN'S TAILORS AND DESIGNER WEAR

ITALIAN MEN are every bit as fashion conscious as the women, and there is no shortage of choice in Rome for the well-dressed man. Suits generally begin at around L1,000,000, jackets L750,000 and trousers L250,000.

Most of the "star" designers of women's *alta moda* have a shop for men, like **Valentino Uomo** and **Versace Uomo**. The designs are less dramatic than the women's, with the accent on understated sophistication and casual sportiness. Valentino's distinctive monogrammed accessories are relatively affordable.

Battistoni is probably the most prestigious designer concentrating on menswear. Giorgio Battistoni and family's fine custom-made shirts and suits have been in demand with film stars and top society

VALENTINO

One of the high priests of Italian fashion, **Valentino Garavani** opened the doors of his Roman studio in 1959 to a distinguished clientele which included Sophia Loren, Audrey Hepburn and Jackie Kennedy, and has never looked back. He has created some of the most dramatic and flattering evening dresses of the last three decades. In the 1970s he began designing ready-to-wear lines for both men and women alongside his *alta moda* collections, and you can now find his very distinctive "V" logo on a wide range of accessories. Valentino's salon is in a huge palazzo in Piazza Mignanelli, and he also has a separate ready-to-wear boutique nearby (see p330).

for 50 years. **Etro** sells classically cut clothes and accessories for men and women in exotic Italian-designed printed fabrics.

Carlo Palazzi's Baroque palazzo setting offers elegant ready-to-wear, and the master tailor Peppino Scarapazzi will also make to measure. **Davide Cenci** has been a mecca for those in search of the English country gentleman look since 1926. **Brioni** offers traditional tailor-made and own-label ready-to-wear men's clothing. **Trussardi** sells beautifully tailored classics, and **Polidori Uomo** offers sober classics made-to-measure or ready-to-wear from its own gorgeous tweeds and wools. **Testa** has impeccably tailored suits that appeal to younger Romans, and **Enzo Ceci** is popular for ready-to-wear *alta moda* designs. **Degli Effetti** stocks more avant-garde designers such as Romeo Gigli and Jean-Paul Gaultier.

YOUNG DESIGNER WEAR

THERE IS A HUGE choice for the young. Top designers Valentino and Armani offer their particular style translated into more affordable lines at **Oliver** and **Emporio Armani** (Armani jeans are very good value at about L100,000). Fendi has its Fendissime line, and MaxMara's Penny Black label can be found in its **Max & Co** branches. Targeted at the younger set, these are good places to pick up stylish, sporty numbers. **Timberland** is another very popular casual label. Average prices are in the region of L100,000 for a shirt, L400,000 for raincoats, L800,000 for suits.

Energie is a big hit and has two shops with some of the best window displays in Rome. Teenagers flock here for jeans or T-shirts. **Aria**, **Diesel**, and **Box 233** are also very popular.

Bacillario and **Eventi** represent the more avant-garde styles – *dark*, as they call it here – fusing Gothic, New Age and punk influences which can result in some outrageous window creations. **Luna e L'altra** offers some

unconventional designer clothes in a pleasant, friendly atmosphere.

HIGH STREET FASHION

ROME IS NOT a good place to look for everyday wear, since there is a distinct lack of mid-price shops bridging the huge gap between the dazzlingly priced *alta moda* designer exclusives and the ultra-cheap goods sold in markets *(see pp338–9)*. Lower-budget shops do exist, but quality is often poor. If you have the stamina, you may find a bargain along Via del Corso, Via del Tritone, Via Nazionale, Via Cavour, Via Cola di Rienzo, Via Ottaviano or the Via dei Giubbonari.

The most convenient places to shop are department stores like La Rinascente, Standa and Upim *(see p323)*. They may not sound exciting, but you can browse at leisure and find nice things. It's also worth trying shops mentioned under Young Designer Wear – particularly the *alta moda* designers' cheaper lines such as **Emporio Armani** and **Max & Co**. At **Discount dell'Alta Moda** and **Discount System** you can find end-of-season designer labels at 50% less than the boutique prices. **Scala Quattordici** is a good place to buy simple linen dresses made by the owner. And while you don't need to come to Rome to shop at **Benetton**, there are many shops here, which sell the authentic garments in their universal colours.

KNITWEAR

KNITWEAR is a particular strength in Italian design, and in Rome there are plenty of specialist shops. **Laura Biagiotti** is celebrated for her luxurious cashmere separates, and **Missoni** for spectacular kaleidoscopic patterns and colours. Krizia no longer has a shop in Rome but its sophisticated knitwear is available from **Liz**. **Choses de Cachemire** has cashmere cardigans, pullovers and knitted suits. **Miranda** offers beautiful handmade

items, from wool scarves for less than L100,000 to coats for around L500,000. Other shops, such as the **Luisa Spagnoli** outlets, offer a wider selection, including lower-priced items.

LINGERIE

THIS IS ANOTHER Italian speciality excelling in both style and quality, with lines like La Perla exported world-wide. Lingerie is traditionally sold in top household linen shops *(see p333)* – **Cesari**, for example, is La Perla's main outlet in Rome. There are also boutiques specializing in lingerie and swimwear.

Liberti has a range of swim-wear that's ideal for Italian beaches, as well as lingerie and women's night attire. **Brighenti** is said to be where film stars go for their lingerie. **Tomassini** has original designs by Luisa Romagnoli. **Schostal** has more traditional underwear with a very good men's section.

SECOND-HAND CLOTHES

THOSE WHO are willing to browse will find a wide variety of second-hand clothes, whether inspired by a collector's interest in vintage clothes or a low budget. Apart from Via Sannio and Porta Portese markets *(see p339)*, which have many second-hand clothes stalls, the mecca is Via del Governo Vecchio. Among the best shops in this ancient street off Campo de' Fiori are **Mai Visto**, with a range of leather jackets in every colour, as well as clothes from the 1970s onwards, and **Moon**, which has mostly 1920s dresses and some hats and jewellery.

Le Gallinelle offers a marvellous selection of period hats and sells both second-hand and vintage clothes. At **Via dei Chiavari 40** you can find smart clothes from the 1920s onwards, and owner Solange also does some dressmaking on the spot and sells at reasonable prices. **Maga Morgana** will make reproductions of period dresses and costumes to order. Via del Pellegrino is also a good street for second-hand clothes.

Shoes and Accessories

ITALY'S LEATHER INDUSTRY is renowned all over the world, and shoes, bags and belts are a good buy in Rome. Accessories in general are not just an afterthought but an integral part of an outfit for the well-dressed Roman. The choice of stylish jewellery, scarves, ties and other accessories is excellent.

SHOES

ROME IS FULL of shoe shops, ranging from high-quality stores in the Via Condotti area (where prices tend to start at L250,000) to the more economical shops around the Trevi fountain, and every big market has its bargain shoe stalls on its fringes.

Probably the best-known shop is **Ferragamo** – one of the world's top shoe shops. It stocks classic yet fashion-conscious shoes, as well as women's clothing and leather goods – the silk signature scarves are quite a feature.

Fratelli Rossetti is a close contender for the number one position. Founded by brothers Renzo and Renato over 30 years ago, this company produces classic men's shoes and beautiful, dressy low-heeled shoes for women that reflect the most up-to-the minute trends. Along with **Campanile** in Via Condotti it represents the epitome of elegance. Its prices, of course, are sky-high but why not buy something small, and at least you'll have the bag! **Bruno Magli**, Bologna's well-known star, has dressy patent-leather pumps and other classic styles. **Beltrami** is an amazing shop boasting a spacious shopfront. It sells bags, as well as men's and women's shoes in classic and innova- tive styles. **De Bach** has colourful styles for women.

Rome's own **Raphael Salato** has three extremely elegant, high-priced shops: his shoes are genuine master- pieces of craftsmanship, and many are made of intricately embroidered leather. Nea- politan **Mario Valentino** is another Rome-based designer, with an impressive flagship shop on Via Frattina. He designs leather clothing, bags and accessories as well as

shoes – all beautifully tailored and expensive.

Via Frattina also has other, more moderately-priced shoe shops such as **Pollini** and **Ramirez**. Pollini makes boots and bags for men and women in trendy and imaginative styles. **Fausto Santini** stocks original, colourful designs for younger people at more reasonable prices. The same goes for **I Cervone**, which specializes in highly colourful women's shoes. **Borino** stocks simple and elegant, low-heeled designs. The **Mr Boots** shops stock a wide range of trendy boots and casual shoes for men and women, while **Dominici** sells witty, smart and affordable footware for women.

Guido Pasquali is a younger designer whose work combines an exciting freshness with a regard for the timeless dictates of good taste; his boots in particular are worth looking out for.

LEATHER BAGS AND ACCESSORIES

THE MOST FAMOUS of Rome's leather shops is trendy to- the-nth **Gucci**, a dandy's paradise selling shoes, suitcases, handbags, wallets, belts and other accessories. It has a fashion boutique for men and women and is well-known for its silk ties and scarves. **Fendi** also has exquisite leather goods as well as some lower-priced lines in synthetic materials and a range of gift items. Although their famous "stripe" line leather-finished synthetic handbags cost as much as L250,000 (and their all-leather ones start at L300,000), at least they are cheaper to buy here than abroad. **Valextra** has high-quality, fairly traditional briefcases, handbags, wallets and purses from Milan. **Skin,**

Ginocchi and the more economical suede and leather factory **Pappagallo** are all in the Via Sistina area. **Mandarina Duck**'s brightly coloured fabric bags and range of luggage are very much in fashion and make an attractive (and vegetarian) alternative to the more traditional leather styles.

There are also some great places to buy artisan leather- work. **Sirni** is at the top end of the scale with elegant bags and briefcases made in a workshop at the back. **Anna Maria Pirozzi** makes every- thing – belts and handbags etc – herself, and has a tiny workshop in Via Panisperna. Prices are very reasonable and she will even make special items to order. **Marco Marinucci** also has a work- shop, where bags, belts, wallets and shoes are made.

CLASSIC JEWELLERY

WHAT CARTIER is to Paris, Tiffany & Co is to New York and Asprey's is to London, **Bulgari** is to Rome. This internationally revered jeweller's has passers-by glued to the windows gazing at its large fat gemstones. These "windows" are rather curious small boxes inserted into a wall with one or two pieces of jewellery in each of them, which adds to the feeling of looking at precious items in a case at a museum. Bulgari's watches, especially the men's, are popular and very elegant, as are the famous mesh necklaces. It specializes in large, colourful stones in High Renaissance-style settings but also pro- duces contemporary designs. This was one of Andy Warhol's favourite shops, and it is the most palatial shop on Via Condotti. Inside, the shop's atmosphere is one of almost religious awe and contemplation.

Buccellati is an offshoot of the famous Florentine dynasty, which was begun by Mario Buccellati in the 1920s and patronized by the poet Gabriele D'Annunzio. Its delicately engraved designs are inspired by the Italian Renaissance, and are real classics, displaying superb craftsmanship.

Ansuini designs are fashionable yet classic with strong, imaginative themes being introduced for each new collection. **Massoni**, founded in 1790, is one of Rome's oldest jewellery houses. Its refined one-offs and brooches are quite outstanding. At **Moroni Gioielli** you will also find imaginative, unique pieces of the highest-quality workmanship. **Petocchi**, which was jeweller to the former Italian monarchy (1861–1946), the House of Savoy, has both traditional and contemporary styles on display.

Peroso is an old-fashioned shop which has been going since 1891 and specializes in antique jewellery and silverware. **Boncompagni Sturni** sells traditional designs with the emphasis on quality and craftsmanship. You have to ring the bell to be admitted to both of these shops, and they are extremely expensive.

Ouroboros is known for less expensive handmade gold and silver items. Traditional jewellery can be bought more cheaply in the Via dei Pettinari and Piazza del Monte di Pietà.

COSTUME JEWELLERY

For LESS conventional tastes, there are several shops selling innovative, avant-garde pieces, often using semi-precious metals and stones. **Via dei Coronari 193** is worth trying. **Via dei Pettinari 80** has an exciting mixture of Art Nouveau items and many other types of contemporary designs.

Delettré produces bold, unique designs influenced by Art Deco styles. You are as likely to find rock crystal here as diamonds. Their logo of a crescent moon and five stars was specially designed by Karl Lagerfeld.

Tempi Moderni has an interesting collection of Art Deco and Liberty period jewellery. You can also find some nice pieces from the 1920s and 1930s in Cose Così (see p336). **Bozart** is the place for trendy, flashy costume jewellery. **Siragusa** puts beautiful 3rd- and 4th-century BC beads and coins into handmade gold chains, in a museum-like shop just off the Piazza di Spagna.

TRADITIONAL GOLDSMITHS AND SILVERSMITHS

The MAINSTAY of Rome's jewellery industry is still the traditional artisan goldsmith and silversmith, working to order in tiny studio workshops. These are concentrated in the old Jewish Ghetto area, Campo de' Fiori, Ponte Sisto near Via Giulia, and Montepietà (where the pawnbrokers live). Artisan jewellery can also be found in Via dei Coronari, Via dell'Orso, Via del Pellegrino. The jewellers create individual pieces to their own designs and have often learned their profession from their parents and grandparents. They also do repair work, or take old gold jewellery, melt it down and make it into something to suit you. **Oddi e Seghetti** produces some traditional artisan jewellery and always works to customers' commissions.

GLOVES, HATS AND HOSIERY

If YOU'RE LOOKING for top quality, you will find an expensive line of gloves and scarves at **Merola**. **Di Cori** and **Sermoneta** stock every imaginable kind of glove. **Catello d'Auria** specializes in gloves and hosiery. The **Anticoli** gloves factory is one of the oldest in Rome and has a large selection at reasonable prices. It also sells belts, scarves, ties and handbags. **Borsalino** is the place for hats. **Calza e Calze** has the best range of hosiery in Rome – the friendly staff will serve you with almost any colour or pattern of tights and stockings that you could wish for.

SIZE CHART

For Australian sizes follow British and American convention.

Children's clothing

Italian	2-3	4-5	6-7	8-9	10-11	12	14	14+ (years)
British	2-3	4-5	6-7	8-9	10-11	12	14	14+ (years)
American	2-3	4-5	6-6x	7-8	10		12	14	16 (size)

Children's shoes

Italian	24	25½	27	28	29	30	32	33	34
British	7	8	9	10	11	12	13	1	2
American	7½	8½	9½	10½	11½	12½	13½	1½	2½

Women's dresses, coats and skirts

Italian	38	40	42	44	46	48	50
British	8	10	12	14	16	18	20
American	6	8	10	12	14	16	18

Women's blouses and sweaters

Italian	81	84	87	90	93	96	99 (cms)
British	31	32	34	36	38	40	42 (inches)
American	6	8	10	12	14	16	18 (size)

Women's shoes

Italian	36	37	38	39	40	41
British	3	4	5	6	7	8
American	5	6	7	8	9	10

Men's suits

Italian	44	46	48	50	52	54	56	58 (size)
British	34	36	38	40	42	44	46	48 (inches)
American	34	36	38	40	42	44	46	48 (inches)

Men's shirts (collar size)

Italian	36	38	39	41	42	43	44	45 (cms)
British	14	15	15½	16	16½	17	17½	18 (inches)
American	14	15	15½	16	16½	17	17½	18 (inches)

Men's shoes

Italian	39	40	41	42	43	44	45	46
British	6	7	7½	8	9	10	11	12
American	7	7½	8	8½	9½	10½	11	11½

DIRECTORY

WOMEN'S HIGH FASHION

Fendi
Via Borgognona 36A/39.
Map 5 A2. 679 76 41.

Genny
Piazza di Spagna 27.
Map 5 A2. 679 60 74.

Gente
Via del Babuino 82.
Map 4 F1. 320 76 71.
Also: Via Frattina 69.
Map 5 A2. 678 91 32.
Also: Via dei Due Macelli
62. **Map** 5 A3 & 12 F1.
679 27 27.

Gianfranco Ferrè
Via Borgognona 42C.
Map 5 A2. 679 00 50.

Gianni Versace
Via Bocca di Leone 26.
Map 5 A2.

Giorgio Armani
Via Condotti 77.
Map 5 A2. 699 14 61.
Also: Via del Babuino 140.
Map 4 F1. 322 15 81.

Laura Biagiotti
Via Borgognona 43–44.
Map 5 A2. 679 12 05.

Max & Co
Via Condotti 46.
Map 5 A2. 678 79 46.
Also: Via Frattina 28.
Map 5 A2. 679 36 38.

Mila Schön
Via Condotti 51-52.
Map 5 A2. 678 48 05.

Raniero Gattinoni
Piazza di Spagna 91.
Map 5 A2. 679 53 61.

Renato Balestra
Via Sistina 67. **Map** 5 A2.
679 55 37.

Roberto Capucci
Via Gregoriana 56.
Map 5 A2. 679 51 80.

Sorelle Fontana
Salita S. Sebastianello 4.
Map 5 A2. 679 86 52.

Trussardi
Via Condotti 49.
Map 5 A2. 679 21 51.

Valentino
Piazza Mignanelli 22.
Map 5 A2. 673 91.

Also: Via Bocca di Leone 15.
Map 5 A2. 679 58 62.

MEN'S TAILORS AND DESIGNER WEAR

Battistoni
Via Condotti 57 & 61A.
Map 5 A2. 678 62 41.

Brioni
Via Barberini 79.
Map 5 C2. 488 47 65.

Carlo Palazzi
Via Borgognona 7E.
Map 5 A2. 678 91 43.

Davide Cenci
Via Campo Marzio 1–7.
Map 4 F3 & 12 D2.
699 06 81.

Degli Effetti
Piazza Capranica 75–79.
Map 4 F3 & 12 D2.
679 02 02.

Enzo Ceci
Via della Vite 52.
Map 5 A3 & 12 E1.
679 88 82.

Etro
Via del Babuino 102.
Map 5 A2. 678 82 57.

Polidori Uomo
Via Borgognona 4C
Map 5 A2. 699 41 171.

Testa
Via Borgognona 13.
Map 5 A2. 679 61 74.
Also: Via Frattina 104.
Map 5 A2. 679 06 60.

Trussardi
See Women's High Fashion.

Valentino Uomo
Via Condotti 13.
Map 5 A2. 678 36 56.

Versus by Versace
Via Borgognona 34.
Map 5 A2.

YOUNG DESIGNER WEAR

Aria
Via Nazionale 239.
Map 5 C3. 48 44 21.

Bacillario
Via Laurina 43. **Map** 4 F1.

Box 233
Via Nazionale 233.
Map 5 C3. 481 45 18.

Diesel
Via del Corso 185.
Map 4 F3 & 12 E1.
678 66 41.

Emporio Armani
Via del Babuino 140.
Map 4 F1.
322 15 81.

Energie
Via del Corso 408–409.
Map 4 F2.
687 12 58, 687 10 04.
Also: Via del Corso
486–487. **Map** 4 F2.
322 70 46.

Eventi
Via dei Serpenti 134.
Map 5 B4.
48 49 60.

Luna e L'Altra
Via del Governo
Vecchio 105.
Map 4 E4 & 11 B3.
68 80 49 95.

Max & Co
Via Nazionale 56.
Map 5 C3.
48 90 31 10.
Also: Via Appia Nuova
201–203. **Map** 10 D2.
701 44 13.
Also: Via Salaria 59–61.
Map 6 D1.
854 67 15.

Oliver
Via del Babuino 61.
Map 4 F1.
360 01 906.

Timberland
Via del Babuino 75.
Map 4 F1.
679 08 36.

HIGH STREET FASHION

Benetton
Via Condotti 59.
Map 5 A2.
679 79 82.

Discount dell'Alta Moda
Via di Gesù e Maria 16A.
Map 4 F2.
361 37 96.

Discount System
Via del Viminale 35.
Map 5 C3. 482 39 17.

Emporio Armani
See Young Designer Wear.

Max & Co
See Young Designer Wear.

Scala Quattordici
Via della Scala 14.
Map 4 D5 & 11 B5.

KNITWEAR

Choses de Cachemire
Via del Babuino 105.
Map 4 F1. 679 84 88.

Laura Biagiotti
See Women's High Fashion.

Liz
Via Appia Nuova 90.
Map 10 D2.
700 36 09.

Luisa Spagnoli
Via del Corso 385.
Map 5 A4 & 12 F3.
679 39 83.
Also: Via Vittorio
Veneto 130. **Map** 5 B1.
488 58 81.
Also: Via Frattina 84B.
Map 5 A2.
679 55 17.
Also: Via Barberini 84.
Map 5 C2.
488 07 57.

Miranda
Via Francesco Crispi 44.
Map 5 B2.

Missoni Sport
Via del Babuino 96A–97.
Map 4 F1.
679 79 71.

Missoni Uomo
Piazza di Spagna 78.
Map 5 A2.
679 25 55.

LINGERIE

Brighenti
Via Frattina 7–8.
Map 5 A2. 679 14 84.

Cesari
Via del Babuino 195.
Map 5 B3. 361 34 51.

Liberti
Via del Tritone 101.
Map 12 F1.
488 22 46.

Schostal
Via del Corso 158.
Map 4 F3 & 12 E1.
679 12 40.

Tomassini
Via Sistina 119. **Map** 5 A2.
488 19 09.

SECOND-HAND CLOTHES

Le Gallinelle
Via del Boschetto 76.
Map 5 B4. 488 10 17.

Maga Morgana
Via del Governo Vecchio
27. **Map** 4 E4 & 11 C3.
687 99 95.

Mai Visto
Via del Governo Vecchio
85. **Map** 11 C3.
687 20 26.

Moon
Via del Governo Vecchio
89A. **Map** 4 E4 & 11 B3.

Via dei Chiavari 40
Via dei Chiavari 40.
Map 4 E4 & 11 C4.

SHOES

Beltrami
Via Condotti 84.
Map 5 A2. 679 13 30.

Borino
Via dei Pettinari 86.
Map 4 E5 & 11 C5.
687 56 70.

Bruno Magli
Via Vittorio Veneto 70A.
Map 5 B2. 488 43 55.

Campanile
Via Condotti 58.
Map 5 A2. 678 30 41.

De Bach
Via del Babuino 123.
Map 4 F1.

Dominici
Via del Corso 14.
Map 12 E1. 361 05 91.

Fausto Santini
Via Frattina 122.
Map 5 A2. 678 41 14.

Ferragamo
Via Condotti 73–74.
Map 5 A2. 679 15 65.
Also: Via Condotti 66.
Map 5 A2. 678 11 30.

Fratelli Rossetti
Via Borgognona 5A.
Map 5 A2. 678 26 76.

Guido Pasquali
Via Bocca di Leone 5.
Map 5 A2.
679 50 23.

I Cervone
Via del Corso 99.
Map 4 F2.
678 35 22.

Mario Valentino
Via Frattina 84.
Map 5 A2 & 12 E1.
679 12 46.

Mr Boots
Piazza Trilussa 33.
Map 4 E5.
580 38 20.
Also: Piazza Redi Roma 10.
Map 10 D3.
77 20 86 72.
Also: Via A Brunetti 2.
Map 4F1.
321 57 33.

Pollini
Via Frattina 22–24.
Map 5 A2 & 12 E1.
678 90 28.

Ramirez
Via del Corso 73.
Map 4 F3 & 12 E1.

Raphael Salato
Via Veneto 149.
Map 5 B1. 482 18 16.

LEATHER GOODS

Anna Maria Pirozzi
Via Panisperna 65.
Map 5 B4.

Fendi
See Women's High Fashion.

Ginocchi
Via Sistina 35. **Map** 5 B2.
488 39 25.

Gucci
Via Condotti 8. **Map** 5 A2.
678 93 40.

Mandarina Duck
Via di Propaganda 1.
Map 5 A2.
69 94 03 20.

Marco Marinucci
Via del Lungaretta 65A.
Map 7 C1.

Pappagallo
Via Francesco Crispi 115.
Map 5 B2.
678 30 11.

Sirni
Via della Stelletta 33.
Map 4 F3 & 12 D2.
68 80 52 46.

Skin
Via dei Due Macelli 59.
Map 5 A3 & 12 F1.
678 55 31.

Valextra
Via del Babuino 94.
Map 4 F1.
679 23 23.

CLASSIC JEWELLERY

Ansuini
Via del Babuino 150D.
Map 4 F1.
36 00 21 99.

Boncompagni
Via del Babuino 115.
Map 4 F1.
678 38 47.

Buccellati
Via Condotti 31.
Map 5 A2. 679 03 29.

Bulgari
Via Condotti 10.
Map 5 A2. 679 38 76.

Massoni
Largo Carlo Goldoni 48.
Map 4 F2 & 12 E1.
678 26 79.

Moroni Gioielli
Via Belsiana 32A.
Map 4 F2.
678 04 66.

Ouroboros
Via di Sant'Eustachio 14.
Map 4 F4 & 12 D3.

Peroso
Via Sistina 29. **Map** 5 B3.
474 79 52.

Petocchi
Piazza di Spagna 23.
Map 5 A2.
679 39 47.

COSTUME JEWELLERY

Bozart
Via Bocca di Leone 4.
Map 5 A2. 678 10 26.

Delettré
Via Fontanella Borghese.
Map 4 F2.

Siragusa
Via delle Carrozze 64.
Map 5 A2.
679 70 85.

Tempi Moderni
Via del Governo Vecchio
108. **Map** 4 E4 & 11 B3.
687 70 07.

Via dei Coronari 193
Via dei Coronari 193.
Map 4 E3 & 11 B2.
68 80 15 03.

Via dei Pettinari 80
Via dei Pettinari 80.
Map 4 E5 & 11 C5.

TRADITIONAL GOLDSMITHS AND SILVERSMITHS

Oddi e Seghetti
Via del Cancello 18.
Map 4 E3 & 11 C2.
68 80 26 43.

GLOVES, HATS AND HOSIERY

Anticoli
Via Lombardia 4.
Map 5 B2. 488 44 82.

Borsalino
Via IV Novembre 157B.
Map 5 A4 & 12 F3.
679 41 92.

Calza e Calze
Via della Croce 78.
Map 4 F2.

Catello d'Auria
Via dei Due Macelli 55.
Map 5 A2 & 12 F1.
679 33 64.

Di Cori
Piazza di Spagna 53.
Map 5 A2. 678 44 39.

Merola
Via del Corso 143.
Map 4 F3 & 12 E1.
679 19 61.

Sermoneta
Piazza di Spagna 61.
Map 5 A2.
679 19 60.

Interior Design

ITALIAN DESIGN belongs to a long-established tradition based on the skills of the master craftsman, and some firms have a history going back hundreds of years. Rome's stylish interior design shops are worth seeking out, even if it's only to look around and enjoy the ambience. You might well pick up some design ideas for your home, as well as finding some interesting or unusual things to buy.

FURNITURE

A WORLD-FAMOUS name in furniture design is **Cassina**: here its expensive hi-tech designs can be bought for far less than abroad. Its style features stark, clean-lined tables, armchairs and sofas in glass, tubular steel and leather in the tradition of architect-designed furniture by Le Corbusier, Eileen Gray, and Vico Magistretti. It can arrange for merchandise to be shipped abroad.

Stildomus, further down the same street, has a long, narrow showroom displaying mainly very fine modern wood furniture. **Fontana Arte** has some highly original furniture and lamps made almost entirely of glass.

Take a look at the nearby **Studio Punto Tre** if you want something different: it's packed with strangely painted chests of drawers, Egyptian-style artefacts and small bits and pieces that would make good presents.

Myricae dazzles with its sensible prices and its covetable Tuscan wrought iron and Venetian painted furniture in sun-drenched or delicate hues.

Spazio Sette, near Largo Argentina, has a spectacular showroom on three levels in the Palazzo Lazzaroni, a former cardinal's palace. It is one of Rome's premier home furnishing stores and, apart from furniture, it stocks items that would make interesting gifts. The furniture – modern, laminated, stack-up chairs and so forth, vases, glass, bowls, and kitchen equipment – is jumbled together in a fascinating display.

Magazzini Forma & Memoria is a design studio located in a cleverly converted old printing works on the edge of the Tiber, not far from St Peter's. It has four levels of display space for the latest in furniture and design items from Italy and elsewhere. In the basement there is a reading area, a health-food bar, and an exhibition space. All this and panoramic views at the top make it a fascinating place to visit.

LIGHTING FIXTURES

L IGHTING FIXTURES are one of the most popular and more easily transportable items, and there are a number of superb showrooms to visit. **Flos Arteluce** is a merger of two design houses whose Roman showroom displays its lights as if they were museum exhibits. The design style is chic and minimalist – plenty of black and white, chrome and steel.

Nearby **Artemide** is, like Flos Arteluce, a design house in its own right, and is similarly well-known abroad. Its Rome showroom is elegant, with expensive, hi-tech lighting design similar to Flos Arteluce. **Borghini** sells less famous names, and so is more economical.

Paolo Marj is a sculptor working in mixed media such as glass, wood and plastics to create lamps that are original works of art in themselves.

Italian lighting and other electrical equipment is designed for 220–240 volts. If you are going to use it in countries with lower voltages always ask the shop whether the product needs a transformer, as this can depend on the model. Lighting fixtures generally take screw-bulbs, although bayonet-bulbs of some designer models may be ordered.

KITCHENS AND BATHROOMS

A LTHOUGH YOU won't be able to take one home with you, you may like to look at a few of the ultra-modern hi-tech kitchens sold in Rome. For an overview of the latest designs, visit **La Residenza**, which has a selection of about 15 kitchen sets from about nine different Italian manufacturers. **Coas Tradizione Casa** in Piazza Cardelli has some interesting combinations in a centrally located showroom.

Italian bathroom shops concentrate almost entirely on modern design. **Odorisio** is the equivalent of La Residenza for bathrooms, and has some luxurious examples. **Ravasini**, nearby, has very decorative floral fixtures with some matching accessories. **Andreucci** also has a bathroom shop which sells all the latest styles.

TILES

T HE ITALIAN ceramic tile tradition is an ancient one. A great variety of tiles is displayed in kitchen and bathroom showrooms, but there are also specialist shops. The most beautiful and the most expensive is **Farnese**, looking ancient Roman in style with its mosaic tables. Di Donato uses old-fashioned methods to design and produce the tiles – hence the cost. He is influenced by Roman and Pompeian art but also produces modern one-off designs.

Ceramiche Musa specializes in modern tiles with decorative floral and ancient Roman motifs, which are popular with visitors. **Via Giulia** sells period tiles, in limited editions. You can become owner of an Art Nouveau tile for around L30,000–L60,000 but older or rarer examples can cost more.

GLASS

D ECORATIVE GLASS objects are a popular buy in Rome. **Navona Venetian Glass**, just behind Piazzo Navona, sells

Murano and other glass items at reasonable prices. This shop is open on Sundays – which can be useful for visitors on short trips to Rome. **Archimede Seguso** also specializes in Murano glass but includes smaller pieces and a range of gift-sized items.

Tupini, the Roman equivalent of the Harrods china department, has quality glass, china and silverware. **Arteque** is a very beautiful shop, with a more traditional flavour. For less expensive gifts, try **Stilvetro**. It is the ideal place for pasta bowls, glass and ceramics.

Shipment home can usually be arranged at any of these glass establishments so you may make your purchase without worrying about transporting it home.

FABRICS

Sumptuous furnishing fabrics are what **Cesari** in Via del Babuino is renowned for. It also has a linen and lingerie shop *(see p327)*. **Il Sigillo** offers fabrics and wallpapers to order from a rich assortment of samples. At **Galtrucco** you can choose material for a suit which they will make to measure so that your individual taste can be combined with their professional expertise.

If you are looking for worthwhile bargains, take a look round the old Jewish quarter that runs from Largo Argentina down to the Tiber; it is full of cheaper fabric shops such as **Paganini**. At sale time, remnants *(scampoli)* can be really good value, and you could find just the right fabric at just the right price.

HOUSEHOLD LINENS AND KITCHENWARE

A selection of lovely sheets can be found at **Frette**. If you enjoy designer kitchenware, don't miss **C.u.c.i.n.a.** in the cellars of No. 118 Via del Babuino. It stocks kitchen utensils from all over the world, as well as pots and pans in both rustic and hi-tech styles and countless space-saving accessories. **Single** specializes in stainless steel designs like Alessi, and also sells wooden bread-boards and a selection of assorted containers.

For the budget conscious, there is also **Salvoni**, whose basement is well stocked with cut-price gift ideas. You'll find and array of household and kitchenware, including silver, china and crystal items.

DIRECTORY

FURNITURE

Cassina
Via del Babuino 100–101.
Map 5 A2. **☎** 679 33 30.

Fontana Arte
Via Giulia 98.
Map 4 D4 & 11 A3.
☎ 686 75 43.

Magazzini Forma & Memoria
Vicolo di S. Onofrio 24.
Map 3 C4. **☎** 683 29 15.

Myricae
Via Frattina 36.
Map 5 A2. **☎** 67 95 335.

Spazio Sette
Via dei Barbieri 7.
Map 4 F5 & 12 D4.
☎ 68 80 42 61.

Stildomus
Via del Babuino 54.
Map 5 A2. **☎** 36 00 19 08.

Studio Punto Tre
Via Giulia 145.
Map 4 E4 & 11 B4.
☎ 686 43 21.

LIGHTING FIXTURES

Artemide
Via Margutta 107–108.
Map 4 F1. **☎** 36 00 18 02.

Borghini
Via Belsiana 87. **Map** 4 F2.
☎ 678 02 17.

Flos Arteluce
Via del Babuino 84.
Map 5 A2.
☎ 320 76 31.

Paolo Marj
Piazza del Fico 21a.
Map 11 B3.
☎ 66 37 627.

KITCHENS AND BATHROOMS

Andreucci
Via Po 39. **Map** 2 F5.
☎ 884 81 47.

Coas Tradizione Casa
Piazza Cardelli 5A.
Map 4 F3 & 12 D1.
☎ 686 75 79.

La Residenza
Via Cola di Rienzo 36.
Map 4 E1.
☎ 321 67 51.

Odorisio
Via Tomacelli 150.
Map 4 F2.
☎ 687 82 35.

Ravasini
Via di Ripetta 71.
Map 4 F2.
☎ 322 70 96.

TILES

Ceramiche Musa
Via Campo Marzio 39.
Map 4 F3 & 12 D1.
☎ 687 12 42.

Farnese
Piazza Farnese 52–53.
Map 4 E5 & 11 C4.
☎ 68 80 32 09.

"Via Giulia"
Via Giulia 22.
Map 4 D4 & 11 A3.
☎ 654 52 33.

GLASS

Archimede Seguso
Via dei Due Macelli 56.
Map 5 A2. **☎** 679 17 81.

Arteque
Via Giulia 13.
Map 4 D4 & 11 A3.
☎ 687 73 88.

Navona Venetian Glass
Corso Rinascimento 37–45.
Map 4 E3. **☎** 687 51 16.

Stilvetro
Via Frattina 56.
Map 5 A2. **☎** 679 02 58.

Tupini
Piazza S. Lorenzo in Lucina 8. **Map** 4 F3 & 12 E1.
☎ 687 14 58.

FABRICS

Cesari
Via del Babuino 16.
Map 5 A2. **☎** 361 14 41.
See p330.

Galtrucco
Via del Tritone 18–23.
Map 5 A3 & 12 F1.
☎ 678 90 22.

Paganini
Via delle Botteghe Oscure 50. **Map** 4 F5 & 12 E4.
☎ 678 68 31.

Il Sigillo
Via Laurina 15. **Map** 4 F1.
☎ 361 32 47.

HOUSEHOLD LINENS AND KITCHENWARE

C.u.c.i.n.a.
Via del Babuino 118 A.
Map 5 A2. **☎** 679 12 75.

Frette
Piazza di Spagna 10.
Map 5 A2. **☎** 679 06 73.

Salvoni
Via Arenula 36.
Map 4 F5. **☎** 68 80 67 70.

Single
Via Francesco Crispi 45–47.
Map 5 B2. **☎** 679 07 13.

Books and Gifts

Rome offers huge scope for gift buying. There are products from all over Italy as well as locally-produced artisan wares. Seeking out the smaller shops can be an adventure in itself, as many are in attractive parts of the city that you might not otherwise visit.

Some of the artisan ceramics are very unusual; there are beautiful books on Italian art and architecture, and there are wonderful paper products. Foodie gifts and drinks are always welcome – especially if it is something really special such as a 20-year-old balsamic vinegar. As well as the usual souvenirs, there is an abundance of religious artefacts – for obvious reasons – and Michelangelo masterpieces are the number one icon for T-shirts, statuettes and postcards.

Bookshops

Rome is rich in bookshops, from the encyclopedic to the very specialized. Italian books, both hardback and softback, are generally very attractive but also tend to be quite expensive.

Rizzoli, Rome's largest bookshop, has a wide selection on art and cookery among other subjects, and many books in English and other foreign languages. **Feltrinelli** has three shops in the capital. The most important is situated in Via del Babuino and offers a wide selection of contemporary literature. Milanese **Franco Maria Ricci** offers very beautiful art books, as well as its own glossy magazine *FMR*. **Libreria Godel** is also good for browsing – it has a lot of books on Rome, great postcards, art calendars and some second-hand art books. **Remainder** has half-price bargains and sells games for children too. There are lots of cut-price bargains as well as second-hand book stalls in Via delle Terme di Diocleziano and in Largo della Fontanella di Borghese.

Multimedia and Music

Rome's biggest music store is **Ricordi**. As well as records, cassettes and CDs, it sells musical instruments and musical scores in its four central outlets. By contrast, **Discoteca Frattina** is quite a small, handy music shop that also sells video cassettes. The multimedia shop **Mondadori** sells greetings cards, posters and videos, and has good map and music departments as well as stocking books.

Stationery and Paper Crafts

The delightful **Papirus** sells papercraft, boxes, obelisks, picture frames and other desk items. **Laboratorio Scatole** offers pretty marbled notebooks, writing paper, files and boxes in various sizes.

Pineider, stationery suppliers to the Roman gentry, will print exquisite visiting cards for you. They also sell handsome leather-bound desk diaries. Just as classy, though less traditional, **Vertecchi** is filled with original paper gifts: boxes of every size and shape, paper tablecloths and napkins, wrapping paper and dazzling Christmas decorations.

Artisan Handicrafts

Spacious and artistically rustic, **La Galleria** is filled with authentic artisan wares, including hand-woven textiles and beautiful ceramics that owner Clotilde Sambuco chooses from all parts of Italy. Domenico and Lavinia Sarti's **Bottega Artigiana** nearby is a small shop with ceramics made by the couple in their Anzio studio. You can buy vases and urns in unglazed terracotta and some attractive terracotta wall-light fittings. **Arti e Mestieri** is the workshop of a friendly mother and daughter who make original articles in wood and terracotta. For a really original gift, go to **Opificio Romano**, a workshop that reproduces ancient Roman and Pompeian mosaics, where they will recreate any design you choose to order.

Souvenirs and Religious Artefacts

Most of the tobacconists in central Rome sell postcards, stamps and a variety of souvenirs, and many cheap and sometimes appealingly kitsch souvenirs are sold by the mobile stalls around the major tourist attractions.

Bookshops near the main basilicas, such as **Libreria Belardetti**, sell souvenirs and religious mementos. Other shops specialize in religious articles for both the clergy and the layman. Facing the Vatican gates in Via di Porta Angelica there are several shops, such as **Al Pellegrino Cattolico**, selling mementos to visiting pilgrims.

Food

One of the unusual things about shopping in Rome is the absence of large-scale supermarkets in the centre. It has been local government policy to keep them out in order to protect the little *alimentari* or delicatessens. There are hundreds of these, not on the main shopping streets, but in small side streets running off them or in the "village" districts such as Monti, Trastevere, the Ghetto, Borgo and Campo de' Fiori. They are often crammed from floor to ceiling with all the irresistible delicacies that are typical of Italy.

Here you can buy, the day before your departure, your supply of parmesan and pecorino romano cheese *(see p305)*, Parma ham or prosciutto di montagna, attractive bottles of dark-green, extra-virgin unfiltered olive oil, dried porcini mushrooms and sun-dried tomatoes to take home (but check customs restrictions first). Food is by no means cheap, and most of the above are considered luxury items.

Pietro Franchi is without doubt the most exclusive delicatessen in the city, and its windows are a visual feast of seafood platters, pâtés, cheeses and cold meats. Next door is the famous coffee shop **Castroni**, which has Rome's largest selection of imported products from all over the world. It also stocks Italian olive oils, balsamic vinegars, honeys and preserves, and of course coffee.

Via della Croce deserves a special mention for its good selection of well-stocked *alimentari* like **Fratelli Fabbi**. Specialist food shops like **Fior Fiore** sell exquisite little almond and orange peel cakes, ricotta cheese, and piles of artichoke-, spinach- and tomato-flavoured pasta, as well as thin, crispy pizza straight from the oven.

The **Azienda Agricola** is a tiny shop selling specialist products. Enjoy the display of beautifully packaged bottles of olive oil flavoured with garlic or herbs, pâtés made of black or green olives, small jars of truffles, asparagus and artichokes, and their own preserves. They all make ideal and much-appreciated gifts.

Cheese-lovers can usually find lots of Italian varieties in any of the small *alimentari* in the city, but it's also worth trying the local cow, sheep and buffalo milk cheeses that are sold at the **Cisternino Cooperativa fra Produttori di Latte di Lazio** near Piazza Campo de' Fiori.

Boxes of chocolates and traditional confectionery and cakes such as *torrone* and *panettone* can be bought from good-quality bars. **L'Albero del Pane** sells wonderful wholemeal and rye flour breads and other health foods.

WINE

WINE IS GENERALLY sold in *alimentari* and also in supermarkets. There are, however, many specialist shops (look for the sign *Enoteca*) with a huge stock of wines and spirits. They invariably have a little bar where they serve wine and light snacks or canapés. Here you can find Italian wines, and usually local wines, mostly white, from the nearby Frascati, Colli Albani and Marino vineyards, on tap. One of the most select is **Enoteca Buccone**, which is housed in an old coach-house. Another well-known one is **Antica Enoteca** which has an old-world feeling to it. The **Enoteca del Corso** is more modern, with a good selection of Italian grappa and jars of marinated fruits. **Enoteca Corsi** in Via del Gesù is also worth a visit.

DIRECTORY

BOOKSHOPS

Feltrinelli
Via del Babuino 39–41.
Map 5 A2.
【 36 00 18 42.

Franco Maria Ricci
Via Borgognona 4D.
Map 5 A2. 【 679 34 66.

Libreria Godel
Via Poli 45. **Map** 5 A3 & 12 F2. 【 679 87 16.

Remainder
Piazza San Silvestro 28.
Map 5 A3 & 12 E1.
【 679 28 24.

Rizzoli
Largo Chigi 15. **Map** 5 A3 & 12 E2. 【 679 66 41.

MULTIMEDIA AND MUSIC

Discoteca Frattina
Via Frattina 50–51.
Map 5 A2. 【 679 14 93.

Mondadori
Piazza Cola di Rienzo 81–83.
Map 4 D2. 【 321 03 23.

Ricordi
Via Battisti 120. **Map** 5 A4 & 12 F3. 【 679 80 22.

STATIONERY AND PAPERCRAFT

Laboratorio Scatole
Via della Stelletta 27.
Map 4 F3 & 12 D2.
【 68 80 20 53.

Papirus
Via Capo Le Case 55A.
Map 5 A3 & 12 F1.
【 678 04 18.

Pineider
Via dei Due Macelli 68.
Map 5 A2 & 12 F1.
【 679 58 84;
Also: Via della Fontanella Borghese 22.
Map 4 F3 & 11 D1.
【 68 30 80 14.

Vertecchi
Via della Croce 70.
Map 4 F2. 【 678 31 10;

ARTISAN HANDICRAFTS

Bottega Artigiana
Via Santa Dorotea 21.
Map 4 D5 & 11 B5.
【 588 20 79.

La Galleria
Via della Pelliccia 29A–30.
Map 7 C1.
【 581 66 14.

Arti e Mestieri
Via dei Cappellari 57.
Map 4 E4 & 11 C4.
【 683 25 21.

Opificio Romano
Via dei Gigli d'Oro 9–10.
Map 4 E3 & 11 C2.
【 68 80 27 62.

SOUVENIRS AND RELIGIOUS ARTEFACTS

Al Pellegrino Cattolico
Via di Porta Angelica 83.
Map 3 C2. 【 68 80 23 51.

Libreria Belardetti
Via della Conciliazione 4.
Map 3 C3. 【 686 55 02.

FOOD

L'Albero del Pane
Via Santa Maria del Pianto 19–20. **Map** 4 F5 & 12 D5.
【 686 50 16.

Azienda Agricola
Vicolo della Torretta 3.
Map 4 F3 & 12 D1.
【 687 58 08.

Castroni
Via Cola di Rienzo 196.
Map 4 D2. 【 687 43 83.

Cisternino Cooperativa fra Produttori di Latte di Lazio
Vicolo del Gallo 19.
Map 4 E5 & 11 C4.
【 687 28 75.

Fior Fiore
Via della Croce 17–18.
Map 5 A2. 【 679 13 86.

Fratelli Fabbi
Via della Croce 27.
Map 5 A2. 【 679 06 12.

Pietro Franchi
Via Cola di Rienzo 204.
Map 4 D2. 【 683 26 69.

WINE

Antica Enoteca
Via della Croce 76B.
Map 5 A2. 【 679 08 96.

Enoteca Buccone
Via di Ripetta 19. **Map** 4 F1. 【 361 21 54.

Enoteca Corsi
Via del Gesù 88. **Map** 4 F4 & 12 E3. 【 679 08 21.

Enoteca del Corso
Corso Vittorio Emanuele II 293–295.
Map 4 D4 & 11 A3.
【 68 80 15 94.

Art and Antiques

ROME'S ART and antique shops range from exclusive establishments to contemporary art galleries. In response to a fashion for collecting early-20th-century artefacts, new dealers and galleries are springing up throughout Rome – Venini's Murano glass is popular, as are lighting and furniture. Many more sell general bric-a-brac and jewellery. Copies of antique prints can be picked up for a fraction of the originals' price. Rome is not good for antique bargains, but it's worth looking in shops along Via dei Cappellari and Via del Pellegrino or going to the Porta Portese Sunday market (see p339).

ANTIQUES AND OLD MASTER PAINTINGS

THERE ARE antique shops dotted all over the centre of Rome, though the cream tend to be concentrated in distinct areas. Discreet haggling in the shops is accepted practice, but even if you get a reduction in price, make sure the dealer provides you with the relevant export documents.

The famous Via del Babuino, and to a lesser extent Via Margutta, which is more famous for its art galleries, are home to around 30 of Rome's grandest showrooms for antique furniture, Old Master paintings and objets d'art.

W Apolloni is one of the city's most respected and prestigious shops, attracting museums and professional collectors, along with the interested browser, with fine 17th-century paintings, furniture and rare silver.

Cesare Lampronti, aided and complemented by his partner Carlo Peruzzi, is a top dealer in 16th- to 18th-century European paintings, with an emphasis on Roman and Italian works in general.

Amedeo di Castro, apparently no relation to the other four di Castros on this street, is a fourth-generation dealer in bas-relief sculptures and exquisite pieces from the 18th and early 19th centuries. **Claudio e Laura Moretti's** small, narrow shop is full of antique and later copies of marble busts and statues.

Via Giulia (see p153) has over 20 high-quality antique shops to choose from. Definitely worth a visit is **La Chimera**, which is a temple to owner Paola Cipriani's love of simply elegant Neo-Classical furniture and paintings. She also sells the occasional modern piece. Another shop not to miss on Via Giulia is **Antiquariato Valligiano**. It's the only place in Rome where you can find 19th-century Italian country furniture; a rustic antidote for those overpowered by the grandiose Baroque.

Via Monserrato, running parallel, is worth scouring for slightly lower-quality pieces at more attainable prices.

Via dei Coronari is almost exclusively devoted to antiques, with over 40 shops lining both sides of this picturesque street. Quality is very high – as are the prices. It is a good place for Baroque and Empire elaborate inlaid vases, secretaries and consoles.

L'Art Nouveau specializes in high-quality Art Nouveau (usually called Liberty here). The **Art Deco Gallery** sells furniture and sculpture from that period.

Piero Taloni has a superb collection of lighting fixtures from the Baroque through to Art Deco periods.

Slightly further away lies Via della Stelletta, which is home to a handful of unusual and fascinating shops.

Acanto is an inexpensively priced Aladdin's cave with an eclectic mix of objets d'art. It is the perfect place to search for religious memorabilia, Italian curiosities and prints.

Bilenchi is yet another specialist, this time in exquisite, turn-of-the-century lamps. Another relatively undiscovered area is Via del Boschetto and Via Panisperna. Shops around here tend to specialize in early-20th-century artefacts, with some English Victorian pieces thrown in.

Retrospettiva is strong on top designers and craftsmen selling furniture, Murano glass and Faenza pottery from 1900–50. **Tad** is a great place to come and browse, with a large collection of wierd and original design items from all around the world.

Of course there are many perennial favourites apart from these streets. The best way to discover them is through word of mouth or just by chance as you stroll along. **Cose Così** is a charming little shop full of small decorative pieces from 1800–1940 (watches, silver, glass, frames, vases and jewellery). **Manasse** is the best place to head for if you're after antique jewellery, icons and Fabergé eggs.

Anticaja e Petrella has an eccentric collection of used junk and printed ephemera stored under Sant'Andrea della Valle (see p123).

MODERN ART

ROME IS RICH in avant-garde galleries exhibiting paintings by recognized Modern Masters through to the up-and-coming generation of young, mainly Italian, artists.

Rome's art galleries are usually open 10am–1pm and 5pm–8pm Tue–Sat. Some open only in the afternoon; others also stay open on Monday afternoon. The best times to visit are afternoons and early evenings.

As with Rome's antique shops, the art galleries tend to be concentrated in a couple of distinct areas. The largest of these covers the triangle area between Via del Babuino and Via di Ripetta and adjoining streets, known locally as the Trident.

The pioneering **Agenzia d'Arte Moderna**, founded in 1913, promoted Futurism from the start and other modern art movements as well. There are works by Burri and Kounellis always on show.

Sperone, under the owner-directorship of Gian Enzo Sperone, shows works by American artists like Ray Smith, Julio Galan, and Jonathan Lasker. Also on view are Italian artists like Gallo, Bianchi, Dessi, Paladino and Merzi.

Apollodoro, which sells interesting design artifacts, has an entrance modelled on Borromini's illusionistic perspective in the garden gallery of Palazzo Spada *(see p147).*

One of this area's highlights is the Via Margutta art fair *(see p339),* which usually takes place around Christmas and in springtime. Via Giulia and its surroundings is the next area to investigate: **Galleria Giulia** is a gallery-cum-bookshop with work by artists such as Argeles, Boille, Cano, Cascella, Echaurren, Erba and Lionni, as well as by Bauhaus artists and German Expressionists.

Fabio Sargentini at **L'Attico** follows the latest trends in Italian art from Del Giudice to Corsini and Fabiani.

Trastevere is possibly better for more innovative ventures: The **Galleria Bondho** (previously Alessandro Bonomo) spotlights young Italian and foreign painters such as Schifano, Boetti, Twombly, Nunzio, Tremlett, LeWitt, Dokoupil. **De' Florio Arte** works with established and emerging contemporary artists from Italy and abroad in a gallery which has retained a real sense of history. In a stupendous villa a few miles outside Rome, **Mauro Vigneti** specializes in both Italian and international artists who are working in Rome.

ANTIQUE PRINTS AND PHOTOGRAPHS

THE JUSTIFIABLY celebrated **Nardecchia**, named after its cultivated owner Plinio, is the cream of Rome's print dealers. Look out for originals by the 18th-century engraver,

Piranesi, and views of the city and ancient Roman life.

Another Roman institution, **Casali**, has been trading for over 100 years. The family now runs two shops specializing in 16th- to 19th-century drawings and engravings of Roman scenes ranging from museum-standard Piranesi down to relatively inexpensive unknown and delightfully decorative floral scenes.

The Florence-based **Alinari** family is renowned for its old sepia photographs of Italy from 1890 onwards, including shots of Rome at the turn of the century. At its Roman outlet, prices of photographs from the original plates start at around L30,000 and mounted prints at L500,000. Larger sizes can be mounted on wood or card.

Another place definitely worth heading for in search of that perfect print of old Rome and some enjoyable, relaxing and maybe persuasive browsing is the **Mercato delle Stampe** *(see p338).*

DIRECTORY

ANTIQUES AND OLD MASTER PAINTINGS

Acanto
Via della Stelletta 10.
Map 4 F3 & 12 D2.
686 54 81.

Amedeo di Castro
Via del Babuino 77–78.
Map 4 F1. 320 76 50.

Anticaja e Petrella
Via Monte della Farina 62.
Map 4 F5 & 12D4.

Antiquariato Valligiano
Via Giulia 193.
Map 4 E5 & 11 B5.
686 95 05.

Art Deco Gallery
Via dei Coronari 14.
Map 4 E3 & 11 C2.
686 53 30.

L'Art Nouveau
Via dei Coronari 221.
Map 4 E3 & 11 C2.
68 80 52 30.

Bilenchi
Via della Stelletta 17.
Map 4 F3 & 12 D2.
687 52 22.

Cesare Lampronti
Via del Babuino 67.
Map 4 F1.
36 00 22 16.

La Chimera
Via Giulia 122.
Map 4 D4 & 11 A3.
68 30 83 44.

Claudio e Laura Moretti
Via dei Coronari 233A.
Map 4 E3.

Cose Così
Via del Governo
Vecchio 89.
Map 4 E4 & 11 C3.
68 80 53 63.

Manasse
Via Campo Marzio 44.
Map 4 F3 & 12 D2.
687 10 70.

Piero Taloni
Via dei Coronari 135.
Map 4 E3 & 11 B2.
687 54 50.

Retrospettiva
Via del Boschetto 77 A.
Map 5 B4. 481 42 12.

Tad
Via San Giacomo 5.
Map 4 F2.

W Apolloni
Via del Babuino 133–134.
Map 4 F1.
36 00 22 16.

MODERN ART

Agenzia d'Arte Moderna
Piazza del Popolo 3.
Map 4 F1.
361 09 75.

Galleria Bondho
Piazza Sant'Apollonia 3.
Map 7 C1.
581 05 79.

Apollodoro
Piazza Mignanelli 17.
Map 5 A2. 678 75 57.

L'Attico
Via del Paradiso 41.
Map 4 E4 & 11 C4.
686 98 46.

De' Florio Arte
Via della Scala 13.
Map 11B5. 589 47 41.

Galleria Giulia
Via Giulia 148.
Map 4 D4 & 11 B4.
68 80 20 61.

Mauro Vigneti
Via Bel Poggio 4,
Castelnuovo di Porto.
90 17 88 55.

Sperone
Via di Pallacorda 15.
Map 4 F3 & 12 D1.
689 35 25.

ANTIQUE PRINTS AND PHOTOGRAPHS

Alinari
Via Alibert 16 A. **Map** 5 A2.
679 29 23.

Casali
Piazza della Rotonda
81A/82.
Map 4 F4 & 12 D3.
678 35 15.

Nardecchia
Piazza Navona 25.
Map 4 E4 & 11 C3.
686 93 18.

Street Markets

Rome's open-air markets are essential to visit if you're interested in soaking up the bubbling exuberance and earthiness for which Romans are renowned. They are wonderfully vivid experiences too, as Italian stallholders have raised the display of even the humblest vegetable to an art form.

The city is dotted with popular, small local food markets, and there are several fascinating well-established markets near the centre, along with the famous flea market over in Trastevere.

It is important to keep your wits about you in markets because pickpockets work with lightning speed in the bustling crowds. But this said, Roman markets provide a vibrant source of entertainment and it would be a shame to let such caveats deter you from joining in the fun.

The street fairs that take place throughout the year are fun to go to, if they coincide with your visit, as they normally sell a good variety of local produce, handicrafts and clothes. Seasonal fairs also occur, especially around Christmas, when you can stock up on Italian specialities.

Campo de' Fiori

Piazza Campo de' Fiori. **Map** 4 E4 & 11 C4. ⓦ 44, 46, 62, 64, 70, 81, 90, 90b, 492. **Open** 7am–1.30pm Mon–Sat. See p146.

Right in the heart of the old city, Rome's most picturesque market is also its most historical. Its name, Campo de' Fiori, which translates as field of flowers, sometimes misleads people into expecting a flower market. In fact the name is said to derive from Campus Florae (Flora's square) – Flora being the lover of the great Roman general Pompey. A market has actually been held in this now rather shabby, but still beautiful, piazza for many centuries.

Every morning, except Sunday, the piazza is transformed by an array of stalls selling colourful fruit and vegetables, meat, poultry and fish. One or two stalls specialize in pulses, rice, dried fruit and nuts and there are also flower stalls situated near the fountain. But the huge open baskets of ready-stripped broccoli and spinach, chopped vegetables for minestrone and freshly prepared green salad mixes are the main attraction for visitors. They provide a real visual display as well as an edible feast.

The excellent delicatessen shops on the square, and bread shops nearby, complement the market. They make it a great place to stock up for an impromptu picnic if the weather turns out fine and you're tempted to do some *al fresco* dining in one of Rome's many attractive parks.

Mercato delle Stampe

Largo della Fontanella di Borghese. **Map** 4 F3 & 12 D1. ⓦ 119, also routes to Via Tomacelli. **Open** 7am–1pm Mon–Sat.

This market is a veritable haven for lovers of old prints, books (both genuine antiquarian and less-exalted second-hand), magazines and other printed ephemera. The quality varies, but it is a good deal more specialized than the *banche* or stalls near Termini station which are a more obvious tourist trap. Italian-speaking collectors can enjoy a field day leafing through back issues of specialist magazines. Other visitors might prefer the wonderful selection of illustrated art books and old prints of Rome. It is a good place to pick up that Piranesi print of your favourite Roman vista, ruin or church – but be prepared to bargain hard.

Mercato dei Fiori

Via Trionfale. **Map** 3 B1. Ⓜ Ottaviano. ⓦ 23, 70. **Open** 10.30am–1pm Tue.

Essentially a trade market, the Flower Market, just north of Via Andrea Doria, is open to the public only on Tuesdays. Housed in a covered hall, it has two floors brimming over with cut flowers upstairs and all kinds of pot plants on the lower floor. Anyone who has an interest in flowers will enjoy this wonderful array of Mediterranean blooms, which are on sale at giveaway prices.

Mercato Andrea Doria

Via Andrea Doria. **Map** 3 B1. Ⓜ Ottaviano. ⓦ 23, 70. **Open** 7am–1pm Mon–Sat.

The market used to stretch the whole length of this wide avenue. It has now been reorganized on to a huge square of open ground between Via Santamaura and Via Tunisi. Apart from the magnificent displays of fruit and vegetables, it has numerous stalls selling meat, poultry, fish and groceries, as well as an interesting clothes and shoe section. Situated northwest of the Vatican Museums, it is a little off the normal beaten track and has remained very much a Roman market that caters for the needs of the large local population.

Mercato di Piazza Vittorio

Piazza Vittorio Emanuele II. **Map** 6 E5. Ⓜ Vittorio Emanuele. ⓦ 4, 9. **Open** 7am–2pm Mon–Sat. See p174.

Bustling Piazza Vittorio was, until recently, perhaps the most Roman of the city's larger markets.

Organized as a cramped corridor of stalls around a central garden, it is the place where bargain-hunting *popolari*, Rome's bustling shoppers, buy their food. Stallholders offer cheap prices if you buy by the kilo, but watch out for bad fruit.

Lately it has become more international and now features African and Asian food stalls.

Sadly, the market's days are numbered, as the city council says that it defaces the 19th-century square. Some stalls have moved to the new site in Via Giolitti; others won't go. The battle is on, but make a visit before a splash of Roman colour is lost for ever.

Mercato di Testaccio

Piazza Testaccio. **Map** 8 D3. Ⓜ Piramide. ⓦ 11, 27. **Open** 7.30am–1.30pm Mon–Sat.

The covered market at Testaccio occupies the central area of its eponymous piazza. The few cheap clothing and shoe stalls skirting the outside are unremarkable, but the inside is well worth a visit. Lined with butchers, grocers and fishmongers, the whole central area is given over to fruit and vegetables – a theatre-set array of seductive colours and textures. Very popular with local residents, it offers super-fresh, high-quality produce and reasonable prices. Much of this market's charm for visitors lies in its compact size and relaxed, friendly atmosphere.

Porta Portese

Via Portuense & Via Ippolito Nievo.
Map 7 C3. 170, 280, 718, 719.
Open 6.30am–2pm Sun.

The *mercato delle pulci* or flea market is a relatively new market in Roman terms. Established shortly after the end of World War II, it is said to have grown out of the thriving black market that operated at Tor di Nona opposite Castel Sant'Angelo during those lean years. Stallholders come from as far away as Naples and set up shop in the early hours of the morning – if you are strolling in that direction after a late night in Trastevere, it's well worth pausing just to watch them.

Anything and everything seems to be for sale, piled high on stalls in carefully arranged disorder – clothes, shoes, bags, luggage, camping equipment, linen, towels, pots, pans, kitchen utensils, plants, pets, spare parts, cassettes and CDs, old LPs and 78s.

Furniture stalls tend to be concentrated around Piazza Ippolito Nievo along with what they call "antiques", though you may have to sort through an awful lot of junk before finding a real one. And then you will have to bargain for it. The technique is to offer them half the asked price and then walk away. A lot of people go just for the fun of it and always end up buying something.

There are also second-hand clothes – leather or sheepskin coats and jackets go for L10,000 – with many of the Via Sannio stall holders relocating here for the Sunday trade. The stretch along Via Ippolito Nievo is monopolized by "*i Russi di Porta Portese*", immigrant Russian stallholders selling caviar, icons (authenticity uncertain), lace, other ethnic handicrafts, old cameras and binoculars. A must if you have a Sunday morning to spare.

Mercato di Via Sannio

Via Sannio. **Map** 9 C2. San Giovanni. 16, 81, 87. **Open** 8am–1pm Mon–Fri, 8am–6pm Sat.

In the 1960s and 1970s this used to be Italy's answer to Carnaby Street. Today, at first glance, it doesn't seem to have anything very special to offer – random stalls selling inexpensive casual clothes, shoes, bags, belts, jewellery, toys, kitchen utensils and music cassettes. But towards the end of the street there is a large covered section which extends back to the Aurelian Wall *(see p196)* with many stalls piled high with second-hand clothes at very low prices for those who like to rummage. There is also a

section that sells military-style goods plus some camping and fishing equipment.

Some of these stalls move their wares to Porta Portese on a Sunday morning.

Local markets

Generally open 7am–1pm Mon–Sat.

Piazza delle Coppelle (map 4 F3 & 12 D2), near the Pantheon, is probably the most picturesque of the food markets sprinkled around the city. A tiny market devoted to food and fruit and flowers, it offers a charming splash of colour in the heart of the city.

Piazza San Cosimato (map 7 C1) in Trastevere hosts another lively local market with some tempting cheeses and salami.

There is a fairly big market on **Via Alessandria (map** 6 D1) in Nomentana, and other smaller ones in **Via della Pace (map** 4 E4 & 11 C3) near Piazza Navona, and in **Via Balbo (map** 5 C4) and **Via Milazzo (map** 6 E3) near Termini station. You can also visit the trade market, the **Mercato Generale (map** 8 D5), in Via Ostiense, which is open to the public after 10am.

STREET FAIRS

A special and interesting feature of shopping in Rome is the street fair:

The **Expo Tevere** exhibition starts each year between mid-June and mid-July on both sides of the river bank between the Sant'Angelo and Cavour bridges. Its stalls display Italian regional arts and crafts and also sell pasta, jam, olive oil, wines and liqueurs. Most items are cheaper than in the shops. The exhibition opens in the evening (6pm–1am). The entrance fee is minimal and also includes ferry transport across the Tiber.

There are two antiques fairs, both known as the **Fiera dell'Antiquariato**, that take place in Via dei Coronari. The first starts in the second half of May, 10am–1pm and 4pm–11pm daily. It makes a memorable event at night when lighted torches line the carpeted street. The second goes along Via dell'Orso as well and normally occurs in mid-October (but has also started in late September), Mon–Thu 3pm–11pm & Fri–Sun 10am–11pm. Stalls also sell leatherwork, jewellery and gifts.

The **Via Margutta Art Fair** usually takes place around Christmas and in springtime. Set in one of the most charming and exclusive streets of the city, it's an event not to be missed, although it's more for browsing as prices are very high.

The utterly glamorous **Spanish Steps Alta Moda Fashion Show** is a fairly new event and doesn't have a set date. The limited seating space is filled by invitation only. However, the public can squeeze in behind to enjoy this display of all-Italian designer fashion. So far it has been held mid- to late July.

Befana, the traditional Epiphany fair in Piazza Navona (mid-December until 6 January) is now rather down-at-heel, but still fascinating for those who have never seen it or for children. Stalls selling clay statues for nativities and sweets that look like pieces of coal are the main attraction.

Natale Oggi is a well-established event taking place near Christmas in the Fiera di Roma at EUR, and worth visiting to have a look at the special Italian Christmas treats.

Via Giulia hosts art fairs now and then, and open evenings when the antique and art galleries stay open late offering food and wine to all visitors.

Every year Trastevere hosts its very own carnival, known as the **Noantri** festival, around late July, when Viale Trastevere becomes overrun with the typical *porchetta* stalls *(see p341)*, party lights, gift stalls and people.

The details given here may change, so check the local listings or at the tourist office *(see p359)*.

ENTERTAINMENT IN ROME

THERE'S A PARTICULAR excitement attached to Roman entertainment. Football and opera, for example, are both worth experiencing for sheer atmosphere alone, whether or not you are a fan. The jazz scene is especially good with international stars appearing alongside local talent. And concerts and films take on an added dimension when performances take place beneath the stars in the many open-air arenas

Gregory Peck and Audrey Hepburn in *Roman Holiday*

spread across the city. Unexpectedly, given the general shutdown among shops, restaurants and museums, the summer remains Rome's liveliest time for live music and other cultural events. Rome's graceful Renaissance squares, vast parks, villa gardens, Classical ruins and other open spaces host various major arts festivals. If you prefer sport, or want to try out some Roman nightclubs, there's plenty on offer too.

PRACTICAL INFORMATION

THE HANDIEST source of information about what's on is *Trovaroma*, the weekly Thursday supplement to *La Repubblica* newspaper. It has a day-by-day rundown of what's on and where, and covers music, exhibitions,

Saxophonist at Alpheus (see p344)

theatre, cinemas, guided tours, restaurants and children's entertainment. Two weekly listings magazines, *Città Aperta* and *Romac'è*, have an English section covering the "Week in Rome". Daily newspapers like *Il Messaggero*, *Il Manifesto*, *Paese Sera* and *La Repubblica* usually list that evening's entertainment.

Two fortnightly magazines, *Wanted in Rome* and *Metropolitan*, provide less detailed listings in English. They can be found in Via Veneto newsagents or at English bookshops. Also worth getting hold of is *Carnet di Roma*, available at the beginning of each month from the EPT *(see p359)*, which gives details in English

of classical music, festivals, theatre and exhibitions in the city and surroundings.

Punctuality is not what Italians are renowned for, so don't be surprised if some events start slightly later than advertised in listings.

BOOKING TICKETS

BOOKING in advance is not part of Italian lifestyle. Two ticket agencies that will book theatre tickets for you (for a small fee) are **Gesman** and **Box Office**. As a rule, theatres themselves do not accept telephone bookings – you have to visit the box office in person. They will charge you a *prevendita* supplement (about 10% of the normal price) for any tickets sold in advance. The price of a theatre ticket can be anything between L10,000 and L70,000.

Tickets for classical concerts are usually sold on the spot, and are sometimes for that night only, an arrangement that favours the last-minute

decision to go. Opera is the exception. Tickets are sold months in advance, with just a few held back until two days before the performance.

Stage at Caffè Latino (see pp344-5)

It is usually easier (and also cheaper) to get tickets for the Caracalla Festival which takes place in the summer.

The **Teatro dell'Opera** box office *(see p343)* handles sales for both summer and winter seasons, and they have a high-tech booking system, with a computer which colour-codes unsold seats.

Tickets for most big rock and jazz events can be bought at **Orbis**, **Prontospettacolo** and at larger record shops such as **Rinascita**.

Remember that if you're trying to get hold of a ticket for a particular performance that has already sold out, you're extremely unlikely to be able to obtain one from

Member of contemporary dance group Momix (see p343)

unofficial sources – there are very few ticket touts in Rome, except at major football matches such as important finals.

REDUCED-PRICE TICKETS

THEATRES and concert venues tend not to offer discounts on tickets since performances are so often over-subscribed. Cinemas, however, offer people aged over 60 and disabled people a 30% reduction on weekdays. In recent years the Comune di Roma has sponsored reduced-price cinema tickets on one day per week (usually Wednesday) but this may be discontinued. Some clubs at the beach resorts such as Fregene offer reductions: look out for *due per uno* coupons in local bars that allow two people entrance for the price of one.

FACILITIES FOR THE DISABLED

FEW ROMAN venues provide easy access for people with restricted mobility, and any disabled visitors and their companions are likely to find the lack of provision for them very frustrating.

The situation does improve a little in summer, however, when a great many performances in the city are held at open-air venues. The Baths of Caracalla have wheelchair access, as do the classical concerts held in the beautiful gardens of Villa Giulia *(see pp262–3)*. For more general information on provision for the disabled, see page 359.

Performance in the Classical setting of the Baths of Caracalla *(see p342)*

OPEN-AIR ENTERTAINMENT

OPEN-AIR OPERA, cinema, classical music and jazz concerts fill the calendar from late June until the end of September. These performances outdoors can be wonderful, with spectacular settings and enthusiastic audiences. Some of them are grand affairs, but small events may be just as evocative – a guitar recital in the cloisters of Santa Maria della Pace *(see p342)*, for example, or jazz in the beautiful gardens of Villa Doria Pamphilj *(see p344)*.

Singers performing the *Barber of Seville*

Many cinemas roll back their ceilings in summer for open-air screenings, or else move to outdoor arenas, and there are also annual open-air cinema festivals. The Cineporto along the Tiber and the Festival di Massenzio offer films, food and small exhibitions in July and August. Theatre, too, moves outside in summer. Greek and Roman plays are staged at Ostia Antica *(see p270)* and other shows take place at the Anfiteatro del Tasso *(see p347)*.

Rome's most important, month-long summer festival is RomaEuropa, with main performances in the grounds of the Villa Medici. There are other, smaller festivals too, but times and venues change from year to year, so it's best to watch for posters around

the city for the most up-to-date information. More traditional is Trastevere's community festival, Festa de Noantri *(see p59)*, with music, fireworks and processions. This religious festival is on the Saturday after 16 July but celebrations continue well into August, so pace yourself for a long party! The Festa dell'Unità, run by the PDS (the former Communist Party), but not limited to politics, is generally held in September. The programme includes games, stalls, food and drink.

Finally, if you like your entertainment less structured, and somewhat more leisurely you can always do as the Romans do and take part in the *passeggiata* (early evening stroll) – the city's favourite spots are Piazza Navona *(see p120)* and along Via del Corso.

TICKET AGENCIES

Gesman
Via Angelo Emo 65. **Map** 3 A2.
Open 9am–1pm, 2pm–6pm Mon–Fri,
9am–1pm Sat. **(** 39 74 07 89.

Box Office
Viale Giulio Cesare 88. **Map** 3 C1.
*Box office tickets for classical music,
rock, pop and jazz concerts and
some sporting events.*
(372 02 16.

Orbis
Piazza dell'Esquilino 37. **Map** 6 D4.
(47 44 776.

Prontospettacolo
Telephone bookings only.
Open 10am–5pm Mon–Fri.
(39 38 72 97.

The Teatro dell'Opera *(see p342)*

Classical Music and Dance

CLASSICAL CONCERTS take place in a surprising number of venues: tickets for opera premières may be hard to get, but soloists, groups or orchestras playing in gardens, churches, villas or ancient ruins are more accessible. World-renowned soloists and orchestras make appearances throughout the year; past visitors have included Luciano Pavarotti and Placido Domingo, Catherine Malfitano and prima ballerina Sylvie Guillem.

Programmes are generally international in scope but sometimes you will find a festival dedicated to one of Italy's own, like Palestrina, the great 16th-century master of polyphonic church music, or Arcangelo Corelli, inventor of the Baroque *concerto grosso*.

MUSIC IN CHURCHES

ONE OF ROME'S main attractions for classical music lovers is the rich repertoire that can be heard in the city's churches. Always sacred in theme (by decree of Pope John Paul II), music is mainly performed as concerts rather than during services.

Programmes are posted around the city and outside the churches. You will often find very good musicians playing in the main churches, while the smaller, out-of-the-way churches frequently play host to young musicians and amateur choirs as well.

St Peter's *(see p230)* hosts one major RAI (national broadcasting company) concert on 5 December attended by the pope and free for the general public. It has two established choirs. The Coro della Cappella Giulia sing at the 10.30am mass and 5pm vespers on Sunday. The Coro della Cappella Sistina sing whenever the pope celebrates mass here, as on 29 June (St Peter and St Paul's day).

Important choral masses also take place on 25 January in **San Paolo fuori le Mura** *(see p267)*, when the pope attends, on 24 June in **San Giovanni in Laterano** *(p182)* and on 31 December at the **Gesù** *(pp114–5)* where the *Te Deum* is sung. The church of **Sant'Ignazio di Loyola** *(p106)* is another favourite venue for choral concerts.

Gregorian chant can be heard in **Sant'Apollinare** *(p127)* at 11am on Sundays and religious festivals.

Easter and the Christmas festivities are a great time for cheap and chilly concerts: there is usually neither entrance fee nor heating!

ORCHESTRAL, CHAMBER AND CHORAL MUSIC

THE **Auditorium di Santa Cecilia**, the national broadcasting company's **Foro Italico** and **Teatro dell' Opera** are Rome's three main auditoriums, with their own resident orchestras and choirs. The Orchestra e Coro dell' Accademia di Santa Cecilia is the top orchestra but the Orchestra e Coro di Roma della RAI is also good. All three offer interestingly varied seasons which include visiting groups and soloists from all over the world.

The season at the **Teatro Olimpico** usually offers very good chamber music, some orchestral concerts and ballet with at least one concert a week. They are advertised on large yellow posters with red borders, easily identifiable in the streets and a hallmark for high-level performances.

The Concerti del Tempietto concert series Festival Musicale delle Nazioni concentrates on the composers of a different country each month on Saturdays (9pm) and Sundays (5.45pm) between November and June at the **Sala Baldini**.

Ticket prices for classical concerts depend a lot on performers and venue. The **Auditorium del Foro Italico** sells tickets for most concerts for under L20,000; a ticket for the **Teatro Olimpico** costs between L25,000–L40,000, but seats for an important concert at **Teatro dell'Opera** may cost as much as L150,000.

The Associazione Musicale Romana organizes three annual festivals in the **Palazzo della Cancelleria** *(see p149)*: the Festival Internazionale di Cembalo (harpsichord festival) in March; Musica al Palazzo in May; and the Festival Internazionale di Organo in September.

It's always worth checking which musicians are playing at the **Teatro Ghione**, the **Oratorio del Gonfalone**, the **Aula La Sapienza**, or the **Sala Accademica di Via dei Greci**.

OPEN-AIR SUMMER CONCERTS

IN THE SUMMER music lovers can enjoy concerts in cloisters, palazzo courtyards and ancient ruins. Concerts can be one-offs or part of a festival programme, regular fixtures or impromptu. Do as the Romans do, don't plan until the last moment and keep an eye on the posters and listings pages *(see p340)* for the latest details.

Open-air opera and dance once had their home in the majestic Baths of Caracalla, but this venue is no longer used. Classical concerts are often part of festivals like RomaEuropa *(see p341)* but there are also open-air festivals and concert series dedicated to classical music. Among the more interesting is the Stagione Estiva dell'Orchestra dell'Accademia di Santa Cecilia held at the Ninfeo *(nympheum)* in the grounds of **Villa Giulia** *(see p263)*. Also listed as the Concerti a Villa Giulia, the concerts begin in July and tickets are under L20,000.

The Associazione Musicale Romana organizes Serenate in Chiostro – a lively and varied programme of concerts during July in the cloisters of **Santa Maria della Pace** *(see p121)* with tickets on sale for under L20,000. Estate al Tempietto (listed also as

Concerti del Tempietto) is the Tempietto orchestra's summer treat with concerts every evening from July to September in the **Area Archeologica del Teatro di Marcello** *(see p151)*. They're held in the adjacent basilica of San Nicola in Carcere if it rains.

Festival Villa Pamphilj in Musica, in July, is a series of concerts in the gardens of **Villa Doria Pamphilj** *(see p267)*. Programmes range from comic opera to jazz and 20th-century classical music.

Brass bands can be heard in the **Pincio Gardens** *(see p136)* on Sunday mornings from the end of April until mid-July – they usually strike up at around 10.30am.

CONTEMPORARY MUSIC

THE **Auditorium del Foro Italico**, the **Auditorium di Santa Cecilia** and the Accademia Filarmonica Romana (usually at the **Teatro Olimpico**) sometimes include modern pieces in their programmes but these are generally less popular than the classics and there is no set venue with a regular contemporary programme.

International names appear on festival programmes and at one-off concerts. The most interesting festivals are Nuovi Spazi Musicali (now part of RomaEuropa) in the summer, with free concerts transmitted on Italian radio, and the Festival Nuova Consonanza in the autumn. Modern Italian composers are performed in the Rassegna Nuova Musica Italiana concert series two or three times a year. It's also worth keeping an eye out for performances by scholars of the French Academy at **Villa Medici** *(see p135)*.

OPERA

I TALY AND OPERA are to many people synonymous. Critics will tell you (justifiably) that Rome's opera is nowhere near the standard of Milan's La Scala or Naples's San Carlo. But that doesn't mean it's not worth visiting – world-class singers do appear here *(see p38)*, mainly in premières or solo recitals. However you judge the quality of the performances, the surroundings in which they take place are often incomparable. In summertime the visual spectacle of *Aida*, say, performed in the open air, is simply magnificent.

The season starts late at **Teatro dell'Opera**, between November and January. In recent years programmes have concentrated on the great popular operas, rather than staging experimental productions or historical

recoveries. Tickets range from L25,000 to L250,000.

Until recently the Teatro dell' Opera would move outdoors in July and August to stage opera and ballet in the ancient Baths of Caracalla. This celebrated tradition has now stopped as the vibrations caused by the basso profundos and by nimble corps de ballet were deemed to pose a threat to the Baths' structure.

BALLET AND DANCE

O PPORTUNITIES to watch ballet or contemporary dance are fairly limited in Rome. The opera house's resident company Corpo di Ballo del Teatro dell'Opera di Roma performs the great classics as well as Roland Petit-style modern choreographies. Performances are staged at **Teatro dell'Opera**.

Contemporary dance is best served during the summer festivals but foreign companies often perform at **Teatro Olimpico** as well. American modern dance groups of the Moses Pendleton school – Pilobolus, Momix, ISO and Daniel Ezralow – are popular visitors. **Teatro Vascello** is another venue noted for experimental dance performances. In summer, entertaining outdoor performances are organized by **RomaEuropa Festival**.

DIRECTORY

For information about times or tickets for festivals and open-air concerts, see Trovaroma or similar listings.

ORCHESTRAL, CHAMBER AND CHORAL MUSIC

Auditorium del Foro Italico
Piazza Lauro de Bosis 5.
C 36 86 56 25.

Auditorium di Santa Cecilia
Via della Conciliazione 4.
Map 3 C3.
C 68 80 10 44.

Aula La Sapienza
Piazzale Aldo Moro 5.
C 361 00 52.

Oratorio del Gonfalone
Via del Gonfalone 32A.
Map 4 D4 & 11 A3.
C 687 59 52.

Sala Accademica di Via dei Greci
Via dei Greci 18.
Map 4 F2.
C 678 45 52.

Sala Baldini
Piazza Campitelli 9.
Map 4 F5 & 12 E5.
C 511 85 00, 501 87 69.

Teatro Olimpico
Piazza Gentile da Fabriano 17.
C 323 48 90, 323 49 36.

Teatro dell'Opera
See below.

Teatro Ghione
Via delle Fornaci 37.
Map 3 B4.
C 637 22 94.

OPERA

Teatro dell'Opera
Via Firenze 62 & Piazza Beniamino Gigli 8.
Map 5 C3.
C 481 70 03, 48 16 01.

BALLET AND DANCE

RomaEuropa Festival
Via xx Settembre 3.
C 4890 4024

Teatro Brancaccio
Via Merulana 244.
Map 6 D5.
C 487 45 63.

Teatro dell'Opera
See above.

Teatro Olimpico
See above.

Teatro Vascello
Via G Carini 72.
Map 7 A2.
C 588 10 21.

Rock, Jazz, Folk and World Music

ROME'S NON-CLASSICAL MUSIC SCENE is unpredictable, but if you have the patience, you'll come across a huge variety of music at the many clubs, as well as open-air events with foreign stars such as Madonna, Michael Jackson and Dire Straits. Publicity is often disorganized, but the "Music Box" section of *Trovaroma (see p340)* gives an idea of what's on.

It's not possible to book tickets in advance at the smaller venues – just turn up with everyone else. You will need to buy a *tessera* (membership card) though, costing anything from L1,000 to L20,000. Well-known musicians may mean a further entrance fee, but local groups are generally included in the membership.

ROCK MUSIC

BIG ROCK CONCERTS are held at EUR in the **Palazzo dello Sport**, or in a stadium: the **Stadio Flaminio**, the **Stadio Olimpico**, or in out-of-the-way **Ippodromo Capannelle**. Get there at least an hour before the gates open for a good seat. Testaccio's **Villaggio Globale Il Mattatoio** (a converted abattoir) is a large-scale, stand-up venue for concerts and other events. The facilities are basic, and again, over-crowding means you should turn up early.

Rome also has several lively clubs and discos which play rock music. Loyal devotees head for the good clubs in large numbers. Some are unpretentious and friendly and some, which are rather sumptuous and stylish, are frequented by the rich and famous. Entrance for the top spots can cost up to L40,000. A venue to be aware of is **Osiris**, near Campo de' Fiori, which puts on rock, mainstream pop and world music. Check what's on, too, at the **Antica Carboneria**, **Black Out**, with concerts held on Thursdays, or at the **Piper '90**, and, in the Vatican area, **Il Castello**, a converted cinema housing rock and jazz festivals and a club.

Forte Prenestino is an interesting venue – a former prison, it was taken over by squatters a few years ago, and turned into a social centre housing rock concerts, debates and art exhibitions. Nearer the centre are more traditional establishments. **Big Mama**, the trendy **Palladium** and **Caffè Caruso** are well-known, popular venues for a great variety of live bands.

JAZZ

ROME'S TASTE for jazz has developed over the years as a result of visits from American and other foreign musicians. Miles Davis played one of his last concerts at the Roma Jazz Festival, for instance, and guitarist Pat Metheny, Sonny Rollins, Gil Evans' Band, the Lounge Lizards, Spyrogyra, and Joe Zawinul's Syndicate are frequent visitors. Roma Jazz takes place every year, generally in July, with performances at the **Foro Italico** *(see p351)*, sometimes listed as the Stadio del Tennis in *Trovaroma*. Tickets, which cost around L35,000–40,000, are obtainable from Orbis *(see p341)* and other agents.

Outside festival times, the best jazz musicians play at **Palladium**, near San Paolo fuori le Mura, or at **Airport Café** and **Alpheus**. **Alpheus** is unique in offering separate concert halls and interesting festivals featuring high-quality jazz ensembles every night. Other, smaller venues, some of which encourage budding talent, include **Vicolo 49** where you are welcome to join in. Some of Rome's music schools also double as show-cases for new performers – these include **Mississippi Blues**, **Saint Louis Music City**, **Ciac Musica** and **Alexanderplatz**.

In summer, many of the music festivals take place outdoors at night. Jazz has featured in the Festival Villa Pamphilj in Musica in recent years, held every July and organized by I Concerti nel Parco. Tickets, costing around L15,000, are available from the Villa Pamphilj itself.

In winter, try two pub-style venues open until late: **La Finestra sul Cortile** and **Stardust** – the latter offers jazz on Tuesdays, and a pianist on other nights. Or check what's on at **Caffè Latino**, **Caffè Caruso**, **Fonclea** and **Melvyn's**.

There's a wide range of artists to look out for. Pianist Antonello Salis plays a mix of jazz and Caribbean rhythms. The quaintly named Crystal White and the Supernaturals are a resident Roman jazz funk formation. Guitar lovers may enjoy Eddie Palermo's fusion, and the major names to be aware of in jazz groups are Roberto Gatto, Maurizio Gianmarco, Massimo Moriconi and Massimo Urbani. Rome's other well-known bands include Orizzonte degli Eventi (fusion), Sestetto Swing di Roma (swing) and Area 2 (not strictly Roman) who play jazz-rock.

FOLK MUSIC

AT THE FOREFRONT of folk music in Rome for 30 years, **Folkstudio** in Trastevere is well worth a visit. Founded back in the 1960s, its cramped rooms have an informal, friendly, participatory atmosphere which welcomed up-and-coming stars such as Bob Dylan – a fact which is remembered here with fondness and pride. Irish folk music, and American country and western are much in demand, as well as the regional strains of Italian folk music. No drinks are sold, so bring your own. You'll need to buy a membership card to enter, costing around L10,000.

A recent arrival on Rome's folk music scene is the **Shamrock** in the Colosseum area offering country and blue-grass music. If you want to eat too, head for **Fonclea** near St Peter's, but check in *Trovaroma* to see who's playing – country music only features on some nights.

Visit some of Rome's Irish pubs and you may be lucky to find some spontaneous music-making going on. Places to try are the **Fiddler's Elbow** and **Druid's Den**, both in the Santa Maria Maggiore area. Also look out for where the Kay McCarthy Ensemble, or Square Dance are performing.

WORLD MUSIC

A STRONG Latin American colony has made its home in Rome since the 1970s. Latin American music is no passing fad here; Romans dance the night away together with the many Brazilian, Argentinian and Peruvian residents and merengue, salsa and soca are all very popular. For the last few years an open-air summer Caribe festival has taken place in Villa Borghese with live music and other attractions. It's by no means a certain annual event, but worth keeping an eye out for.

Many venues offer similar opportunities to enjoy Latin American music throughout the year: **El Charango** offers South American food as well as music and a small dance area. At **Yes Brazil** the owner and beautiful long-legged waitresses sway with the clientele to the bossa nova, offering a double delight of music and movement, all in the name of Terpsichore.

Various musicians alternate way into the night: watch out for the guitarist Giovanna Marinuzzi, who plays Brazilian music, and take care to book front tables ahead of time. Also look out for resident Brazilian musicians Brenazil, Carlos de Lima and Alvinho, and local salsa band Xenaya, or check what's on at the **Caffè Latino** and **K.K.** in the Ghetto, at **Caffè Caruso** in Testaccio and the **Bossa Nova** or **Melvyn's** in Trastevere.

Other regional musical styles have less of a presence, but exist nevertheless. Lovers of African music should look out for performances by Sanganà or Akwaba. African and Italian musicians play together with Pietro dall'Oglio's group at various venues in the city.

DIRECTORY

Airport Café
Via di Porta Castello 44.
Map 4 D3.
[686 83 28.

Akab
Via di Monte Testaccio 69.
Map 8 D4.
[574 41 54.

Alexanderplatz
Via Ostia 9. **Map** 3 B1.
[39 74 21 71.

Alpheus
Via del Commercio 36–8.
Map 8 D5.
[574 78 26.

Big Mama
Vicolo S. Francesco a Ripa
18. **Map** 7 C2.
[581 25 51.

Black Out
Via Saturnia 18.
Map 9 C3.
[70 49 67 91.

Bossa Nova
Via degli Orti di Trastevere
43. **Map** 7 C2.
[581 61 21.

Caffè Caruso
Via di Monte Testaccio 36.
Map 8 D4.
[574 50 19.

Caffè Latino
Via di Monte Testaccio 96.
Map 8 D4.
[574 40 20.

El Charango
Via di Sant'Onofrio 28.
Map 3 C4.
[687 99 08.

Ciac Musica
Via Tripoli 60.
[86 21 76 82.

Druid's Den
Via S. Martino ai Monti 28.
Map 6 D4.

Fiddler's Elbow
Via dell'Olmata 43.
Map 6 D4.

**La Finestra sul
Cortile**
Via in Publicolis 45.
Map 4 F5 & 12 D5.
[683 24 97.

Folkstudio
Via Frangipane 42.
Map 5 B5.
[487 10 63.

Fonclea
Via Crescenzio 82 A.
Map 3 C2.
[689 63 02.

Forte Prenestino
Via F. del Pino.

**Ippodromo
Capannelle**
Via Appia Nuova km.12.
[718 31 43.

K.K.
Piazza in Piscinula 20.
Map 8 D1.
[589 64 21.

Melvyn's
Via del Politeama 8.
Map 4 E5 & 11 C5.
[580 30 77.

Mississippi Blues
Via del Mascherino 65.
Map 3 C2.

Osiris
Largo dei Librari 82 A.
Map 4 E5 & 11 C4.

Palazzo dello Sport
Viale dell'Umanesimo.
[592 51 07.

Palladium
Piazza B. Romano 8.
[511 02 03.

Piper '90
Via Tagliamento 9.
[855 53 98.

**Saint Louis Music
City**
Via del Cardello 13.
Map 5 B5.
[47 45 06.

Shamrock
Via Capo d'Africa 26 D.
Map 9 A1.
[700 25 83.

Stadio Flaminio
Viale Pilsudski.
Map 1 B2.
[323 65 39.

Smile
Via Schiaparelli 29.
Map 2 D3.
[322 1251.

Stadio Olimpico
Viale dei Gladiatori.

Stardust
Vicolo de Renzi 4.
Map 7 C1.

Vicolo 49
Vicolo dei Soldati 47.
Map 4 E3 & 11 C2.
[687 54 40.

**Villaggio Globale Il
Mattatoio**
Lungotevere Testaccio.
Map 8 D4.
[57 30 03 29.

Yes Brazil
Via S. Francesco a Ripa 103.
Map 7 C2.
[581 62 67.

Cinema and Theatre

CINEMA-GOING IS A POPULAR pastime in Rome, with around 40 films on show on an average weekday, while theatre-goers have far less choice.

The great majority of Roman cinemas are *prima visione* (first run) and show the latest international films in dubbed version. The smaller art cinemas are more likely to show subtitled versions of foreign films.

Theatre productions are performed in Italian whether the plays are national classics or by foreign playwrights. The main theatres offer a selection by great Italian playwrights. There are also performances of traditional cabaret, avant-garde theatre and dance theatre. Theatre tickets cost between L10,000 and L70,000 and can generally only be booked in advance by visiting the theatre box office in person, or through agencies such as **Gesman** and **Box Office** *(see p341)*.

PRIMA VISIONE

THERE ARE OVER 80 *prima visione* cinemas in the city. The best cinemas in Rome in terms of decor and comfort are the **Fiamma** (two screens), **Barberini** (three screens) and **Rivoli**.

As a rule, foreign films are dubbed into Italian rather than subtitled (Italian dubbers are considered among the best in the world) but the **Alcazar** has showings in the original language – mainly English – on Mondays.

Tickets for new films generally cost around L10,000 but a few cinemas listed as *prima visione* charge less, namely **Capranichetta**, **Diamante** and **Cinema Roma**. Over 60s and disabled people are normally entitled to a 30% reduction on weekdays. The Comune di Roma sponsors a reduced ticket day (normally it's Wednesday). Check the newspaper or *Trovaroma* for accurate details *(see p340)*.

ART CINEMAS

THERE ARE TWO main types of art cinema in Rome: the *cine-clubs* and the *cinema d'essai*. Both of these are good if you're interested in catching older classics and new foreign films as well as films by some of the con-temporary Italian directors.

The *d'essai* cinemas now and then show films in the original language (indicated by *v.o.* for *versione originale* in the listings). Try the **Azzurro Scipioni** (one of the few to remain open through-out summer) or the **Nuovo Sacher**. Some of the smaller cinemas like the **Labirinto** are called *cine-clubs* and require membership.

The multi-media arts centre **Palazzo delle Esposizioni** usually shows interesting series of international films in the Sala Rossellini (prior booking is advised).

Cartoons and children's favourites are shown at **Dei Piccoli**. The evening showings for adults, often in the original language, are listed as Dei Piccoli Sera.

The **Tibur** is a small cinema with a varied programme and one of the few places where students get a reduction.

ENGLISH-LANGUAGE FILMS

IN ADDITION TO occasional undubbed showings of British, American and Austral-asian films in art cinemas and the **Alcazar**, Rome has its own English-language cinema, the **Pasquino**, in Trastevere. Titles change every few days (tickets cost around L7,000).

SUMMER CINEMA

MANY ROMAN cinemas have roll-back ceilings which are in use during the summer, while the others close down. The **Nuovo Sacher** has an outdoor arena which also is used for summer screenings.

Rome also has two summer cinema festivals: Cineporto and Massenzio. These show several films each night from 9pm until the small hours, with food and drinks on sale and often live music during the intervals. Cineporto (every night, July–September) has a fixed venue in the Parco della Farnesina but Massenzio moves around (see listings).

It's also worth keeping an eye on the listings pages *(see p340)* for retrospectives or avant-garde film seasons at the **Azzurro Scipioni** and the open-air arts festivals like RomaEuropa *(see p341)* and Festa dell'Unità *(see p341)*. Sci-fi enthusiasts should keep an eye out for the Fantafestival (early June), a science fiction, fantasy and horror film festival.

MAINSTREAM THEATRE

THE BACKBONE of Rome's theatrical repertoire are Luigi Pirandello's dramas and comedies by 18th-century Venetian Carlo Goldoni and 20th-century Neapolitan Eduardo de Filippo. Major foreign playwrights are also performed from time to time.

The best classic productions are staged at the **Teatro Argentina**, **Teatro Quirino**, **Teatro Valle**, **Teatro Eliseo** and **Teatro Piccolo Eliseo**. **Teatro Argentina**, originally an opera house, is state-owned and home of Rome's permanent theatre company. The **Quirino** and **Valle** host productions from other Italian cities. The **Valle** alternates between productions of great Italian classics by famous companies and lesser known modernist works. Plays at the **Quirino** often feature famous Italian actors. The **Eliseo** and **Piccolo Eliseo** are among the best of the private theatres. Agatha Christie and Alfred Hitchcock are often on at the **Teatro Stabile del Giallo** which specializes in crime and detective thrillers, and **Teatro Vittoria** goes in for Noël Coward or Raymond Queneau. The programme at

Teatro Sistina usually includes musicals by visiting foreign companies and shows by popular Italian actors.

CONTEMPORARY THEATRE

THE HOME OF contemporary theatre is the **Tordinona**, **Politecnico**, **Ateneo** (inside the university) and in a host of small theatres, ingeniously rigged up in cellars, garages, small apartments or tents. The **Colosseo** and **La Scaletta** host some alternative fringe-type productions (known here as *teatro off*) while the **Tordinona**, the **Politecnico** and the **Ateneo** tend to stage contemporary authors and occasional avant-garde productions. Some of them, like the **Teatro dei Cocci**, put on drama school productions.

FOLK, CABARET AND PUPPET THEATRE

ROMAN AND Neapolitan folk songs and cabaret can be enjoyed in one of Trastevere's traditional lively cabaret restaurants like **Ciceruacchio**, **Fantasie di Trastevere** or **Meo Patacca**.

Puppet theatre is another tradition. Shows generally take place early in the evening at weekends and sometimes during the week at **Teatro Verde**, **Teatro Villa Lazzaroni**, **Teatro Mongiovino** and the **English Puppet Theatre** where puppeteers will recite in English if there is enough demand. In the summer, travelling Neapolitan and Sicilian marionette companies give one-off performances.

OPEN-AIR THEATRE

THE OPEN-AIR summer theatre season usually features Greek and Roman plays at **Ostia Antica** *(see pp270–71)*.

The **Anfiteatro Quercia del Tasso** in the Janiculum park takes its name from the oak tree under which 16th-century poet Tasso used to sit. The theatre has no fixed genre (both Plato and Noël Coward were on recently, for instance), and tickets cost around L20,000.

Nearby is a permanent Neapolitan street puppet theatre booth featuring *Pulcinella* (the Italian original of Punch). Shows are usually on in the afternoons, with morning shows on Sundays; children love them.

DIRECTORY

PRIMA VISIONE

Alcazar
Via Card. Merry del Val 14.
Map 7 C1. **(** 588 00 99.

Barberini
Piazza Barberini 52.
Map 5 B3. **(** 482 77 07.

Capranichetta
Piazza di Montecitorio 125.
Map 4 F3 & 12 E2.
(679 69 57.

Cinema Roma
Piazza Sonnino 37.
Map 7 C1. **(** 581 28 84.

Diamante
Via Prenestina 232.
(29 56 06.

Fiamma
Via Bissolati 45.
Map 5 C2. **(** 482 71 00.

Rivoli
Via Lombardia 23.
Map 5 B2. **(** 488 08 83.

ART CINEMAS

Azzurro Scipioni
Via degli Scipioni 82.
Map 3 C2. **(** 39 73 71 61.

Dei Piccoli
Viale della Pineta 15.
Map 5 B1. **(** 855 34 85.

Labirinto
Via di Pompeo Magno 27.
Map 4 D1. **(** 321 62 83.

Nuovo Sacher
Largo Ascianghi 1.
Map 7 C2. **(** 581 81 16.

Palazzo delle Esposizioni
Via Milano 9A. **Map** 5 B4.
(488 54 65.

Tibur
Via degli Etruschi 40.
(495 77 62.

ENGLISH-LANGUAGE FILMS

Alcazar
See left.

Pasquino
Vicolo del Piede 19.
Map 7 C1. **(** 580 36 22.

MAINSTREAM THEATRE

Teatro Argentina
Largo Argentina 56.
Map 4 F4 & 12 D4.
(68 80 46 01.

Teatro Eliseo
Via Nazionale 183.
Map 5 B4. **(** 488 21 14.

Teatro Piccolo Eliseo
Via Nazionale 183.
Map 5 B4. **(** 488 50 95.

Teatro Quirino
Via M. Minghetti 1.
Map 5 A4 & 12 F2.
(679 45 85.

Teatro Sistina
Via Sistina 129.
Map 5 B2. **(** 482 68 41.

Teatro Stabile del Giallo
Via Cassia 871C.
(30 31 13 35.

Teatro Valle
Via Teatro Valle 23 A.
Map 4 F4 & 12 D3.
(68 80 37 94.

Teatro Vittoria
Piazza S. Maria Liberatrice 8.
Map 8 D3. **(** 574 01 70.

CONTEMPORARY THEATRE

Teatro Ateneo
Viale delle Scienze 3.
Map 6 F3. **(** 49 91 44 35.

Teatro Colosseo
Via Capo d'Africa 5 A.
Map 9 A1. **(** 700 49 32.

Teatro dei Cocci
Via Galvani 69.
Map 8 D3. **(** 578 35 02.

Teatro La Scaletta
Via del Collegio Romano 1.
Map 5 A4 & 12 E3.
(678 31 48.

Teatro Politecnico
Via Tiepolo 13 A.
Map 1 B3. **(** 361 15 01.

Teatro Tordinona
Via degli Acquasparta 16.
Map 4 E3 & 11 C2.
(68 80 58 90.

FOLK, CABARET, PUPPET THEATRE

Ciceruacchio
Via del Porto 1. **Map** 8 D2.
(580 60 46.

English Puppet Theatre
Via di Grotta Pinta 2.
Map 4 E5 & 11 C4.
(589 62 01.

Fantasie di Trastevere
Via di Santa Dorotea 6.
Map 4 D5.
(588 16 71.

Meo Patacca
Piazza dei Mercanti 30.
Map 8 D1. **(** 581 61 98.

Teatro Mongiovino
Via Genocchi 15.
(513 94 05.

Teatro Verde
Circonvall. Gianicolense 10.
Map 7 B4.
(588 20 34.

Teatro Villa Lazzaroni
Via Appia Nuova 522.
Map 10 F5.
(78 77 91.

OPEN-AIR THEATRE

Anfiteatro Quercia del Tasso
Viale Aldo Fabrizi.
Map 3 C5. **(** 575 08 27.

Nightclubs

THE CENTRE OF ROMAN NIGHT LIFE used to be the Via
Veneto area so effectively portrayed by Fellini in
his film *La Dolce Vita*. The place still offers plenty of
venues, but new, less formal and more affordable clubs
have emerged, with a more vibrant atmosphere and
appealing to a younger and more diverse crowd.

With the new clubs come new areas. The picturesque
narrow streets in Trastevere, the Piazza Navona and the
Pantheon areas are becoming more popular. Testaccio
too has become a new mecca for Roman clubbers.

WHAT'S ON

AS IN ANY OTHER major city,
Rome's nightlife is
constantly changing. Roman
club-goers are an extremely
varied group and most clubs
arrange different nights to
appeal to different tastes – so
it's essential to keep up-to-
date on what's happening by
checking in a magazine like
Roma C'E', on newsstands
every Thursday.

For a more direct source of
information, head for the bars
around the Piazza Navona
and Campo de' Fiori areas. At
about 10.30pm the narrow
streets and piazzas swarm
with people and any
interesting event will soon
become common knowledge.
Buoni (free or reduced price
tickets) may be handed out.

PRACTICALITIES

PREFERRED CLUBBING nights
for Romans are Thursday,
Friday and, of course,
Saturday, when you should
expect to pay around L35,000
for entrance. Queues for the
most popular places can be
long but provided you arrive
before midnight you'll avoid
the crush.

Some clubs require a *tessera*
(membership card) which
you can buy on the spot and
which usually replaces the
entrance fee. Your ticket or
tessera usually includes a free
first drink; your second could
well be expensive – as much
as L20,000 in some of the
plusher clubs.

In these smarter places how
you look is all important: a
jacket and tie are a must and
usually you need an invitation
or a personal introduction to
get in. It should not be

difficult to gain entrance to
the traditional discos as long
as you dress in designer casual
wear, but choose your clothes
with care – a black T-shirt
could make you too
alternativo. All-male groups
are never welcome, and in
more exclusive clubs neither
are unaccompanied men.

CLUBS AND BARS

AN ELEGANT NIGHT out could
start in one of the refined
piano bars such as **Le
Cornacchie**, **Giulio Passami
l'Olio** frequented by the
English-speaking community,
or the intimate **Tartarughino**,
popular with politicians and
financiers. Livelier places are
the American-style bars such
as **Hemingway**. If you prefer
the arts world, head for **Bar
del Fico**, **Bar della Pace**, **Cafe'
les Folies** and **La Vetrina**.

To continue, head for
Gilda, a favourite with the
Roman jet set, with two
elegant restaurants, a large
glitzy dancefloor and many
VIPs. The famous nightclub
of the 1960s, **Jackie O**, has
been revamped in lavish style,
with a lush interior and
expensive restaurant. In a
similar vein, and not to be
missed, are **Open Gate**,
Gossip Café and **Club 84**.

The hottest club among the
younger and trendier is **Alien**.
This club offers house, techno
and hip-hop, along with
stages, wild lighting effects
and "happenings". A smaller
dance floor offers a more
mellow music selection.
Equally funky is **Heaven**
which also offers soul and
dance music. At **Groove**, acid
jazz, rap and soul dominate
on Wednesday, Thursday and
Friday nights.

An unforgettable place for
dancing in a blitzkrieg of beat
is **Radio Londra**, designed to
look like a World War II
bunker, where hard dance
music and free entrance attract
huge crowds of jive bombers.
Black out is one of the few
clubs in Rome offering punk
and British rock music, with
the occasional live concert.

The more traditional disco
is at its best at **Piper**, the
oldest and biggest Roman
disco which totally revamps
its interior every season. It's
especially popular with the
younger crowd, as is **Smile**.
Qube is a huge disco laid out
on several floors with various
dance floors playing mainly
rave music. There are some
disco bars worth noting too,
like **B-Side** and **DDT**.

To find out about events in
the more unusual Roman
venues, start the evening at
the **Vineria**. The old abattoir
(il Mattatoio) at Testaccio is
the setting for **Villaggio
Globale**, a social centre
hosting concerts, shows,
discos and parties. **Circolo
degli Artisti** is another social
centre with a large dance floor,
bar, theatre and video room,
situated in the old milk centre.
In the southern suburbs, two
larger venues offer a variety
of concerts and events – the
converted cinema **Palladium**
and **Alpheus**.

GAY

THE GAY SCENE is well
served. Many clubs have
fixed gay nights and one-offs
are arranged, especially
during the Maratona Gay
festival in May. The most
famous gay club is **Alibi**,
where music is a mixture of
underground and 1970s hits.
Angelo Azzurro offers hi-
energy and house in Post-
Modern surroundings. Listen
out for events organized by
**Circolo Mario Mieli di Cul-
tura Omosessuale**, or go to
bars such as **Hangar** for ideas
of what's on. For gay women
Angelo Azzurro has a women-
only night on Thursday, and
New Jolie Cover often has
them on Saturdays.

JAZZ, SALSA AND AFRICAN

THERE ARE many jazz venues *(see p344)*. The following mix live music with dancing and drinking. **Caffè Latino** (membership club) is best at the weekend. For South American music try **Yes Brazil** and **Drink Music** with live bands and lots of people, or **Caffè Caruso** (membership club) for salsa. **Alpheus** is a four-roomed venue where different kinds of music events take place simultaneously.

African clubs like **Fantasy** (free on Fridays) are lively, friendly and cheap.

CLUBBING IN SUMMER

IN SUMMER when everything closes down in the city, head for the Roman seaside resorts. At Fregene, for instance, there are 13 clubs; all pretty much the same, with a dress-code of designer-label casuals. Take along your swimsuit too as much of the fun takes place in and around the pools. Names include **Gilda on the Beach**, **Tattou** and **Miraggio** – the latter two popular with a younger crowd. **Sogno del Mare** features live concerts by well-known bands, a swimming pool and a spacious, pleasant

environment. Most of these seaside clubs have restaurants attached to them as well.

LATE CLUBS

MOST ROMAN clubs stay open until 3am or 4am, but the disco bar **Sol e Luna** (a club that, unusually, is open on Mondays) and the smarter **Decó** both stay open until dawn.

Before heading off to bed, join other die-hard clubbers at any of the city's 24-hour bars for a final drink and make for one of the early-morning bakers to buy sweet *cornetti* hot from the oven.

DIRECTORY

Alibi
Via di Monte Testaccio 44.
Map 8 D4. **[** 574 34 48.

Alien
Via Velletri 13. **Map** 6 D1.
[841 22 12.

Alpheus
Via del Commercio 36/8.
Map 8 D5. **[** 574 78 26.

Angelo Azzurro
Via Card. Merry del Val 13.
Map 7 C1. **[** 580 04 72.

Antico Caffè della Pace
Via della Pace 2/5.
Map 4 E4 & 11 C2.
[686 12 16.

Bar del Fico
Piazza del Fico 26/8.
Map 11 B2.

Black Out
Via Saturnia 18.
Map 9 C3.

B-Side
Via dei Funari 21A.
Map 12 E5.

Cafe' les Folies
Via San Francesco a Ripa
165. **Map** 7 C1.

Caffè Caruso
Via di Monte Testaccio 36.
Map 8 D4. **[** 574 50 19.

Caffè Latino
Via di Monte Testaccio 96.
Map 8 D4. **[** 574 40 20.

Circolo degli Artisti
Via Lamarmora 28.
Map 6 E5. **[** 446 49 68.

Club 84
Via Emilia 84.
Map 5 B2.

Le Cornacchie
Piazza Rondanini 53.
Map 4 F4 & 12 D2.

Déco
Via C. Beccaria 22.
Map 4 E1. **[** 361 12 40.

DDT
Via dei Sabelli 2.
Map 6 F4.

Drink Music
Via Natale del Grande 4.
Map 7 C1. **[** 580 02 86.

Fantasy
Via Alba 42. **Map** 10 F3.
[701 67 41.

Gilda
Via Mario de' Fiori 97.
Map 5 A2 & 12 F1.
[678 48 38.

Guilio Passami l'Olio
Via di Monte Giordano 2.
Map 11 B2.

Gossip Café
Via Romagnosi 11A.
Map 4 E1. **[** 361 13 48.

Groove
Vicolo Savelli 10.
Map 11 C3.

Hangar
Via in Selci 69. **Map** 5 C5.

Heaven
Viale di Porta Ardeatina
118A. **Map** 9 B5.

Hemingway
Piazza delle Coppelle 10.
Map 4 F3 & 12 D2.
[686 44 90.

Jackie O
Via Boncompagni 11.
Map 5 B2.
[488 54 57.

Circolo Mario Mieli di Cultura Omosessuale
Via Ostiense 202.
[541 39 85.

New Jolie Cover
Via Sirte 5.

Open Gate
Via San Nicola da
Tolentino 4. **Map** 5 C2.
[482 44 64.

Palladium
Piazza B. Romano 8.
[511 02 03.

Piper
Via Tagliamento 9.
[855 53 98.

Qube
Via del Portonaccio 21.

Radio Londra
Via Monte Testaccio 67.
Map 8 D4.

Safari
Via Aurelia 601.
[66 41 63 09.

Smile
Via Schiaparelli 29-31.
Map 2 D3.

Sol e Luna
Via Campania 37 A.
Map 5 B1. **[** 482 18 90.

Tartarughino
Via della Scrofa 1.
Map 4 F3 & 12 D2.

La Vetrina
Via della Vetrina 1.
Map 4 E3 & 11 B2.

Villaggio Globale
Lungotevere Testaccio. **Map**
8 D4. **[** 57 30 03 29.

Vineria
Campo de' Fiori 5.
Map 4 E4 & 11 C4.

Yes Brazil
Via S. Francesco a Ripa 103.
Map 7 C2. **[** 581 62 67.

SUMMER CLUBS

Gilda on the Beach
Lungomare di Ponente 11.
[66 56 06 49.

Miraggio
Lungomare di Ponente 95.
[65 56 39 50.

Sogno del Mare
Lungomare di Ponente 25.
[66 56 05 40.

Tattou
Via Francavilla a Mare.
[646 38 38.

Sport

DON'T BE SURPRISED if the peace of a Sunday afternoon in Rome is interrupted by the honking of cars and people shouting. It simply means that one of the home football teams has won at the stadium and the whole town will vibrate with the excitement.

Football is Italy's national sport but other sports also manage to attract a large following and Roman sports fans are never at a loss for varied and well organized events and activities.

You'll find times and venues for most spectator sports listed in *Trovaroma (see p340),* as well as the local sections of *La Gazzetta dello Sport* or *Corriere dello Sport.*

FOOTBALL

AN ITALIAN SOCCER MATCH is an experience not to be missed for the quality of the play, the excitable crowds and fun atmosphere. Football hooligans are rare.

Rome has two teams, Roma and Lazio, and they take it in turns to play at the **Stadio Olimpico** on a Sunday afternoon at 3pm, in the Campionato Italiano (Italian championship league). Seats can be scarce so get tickets in advance from the stadium (L15,000 to L150,000). The cheapest tickets are in the La Tribuna stand; middle-range and most expensive are in Le Catinate and Le Curve respectively.

On Wednesday evenings there are international competitions – the Coppa delle Coppe (European Cup Winners Cup), the UEFA cup and the Coppa dei Campioni (European Championship Cup). In between these, teams battle it out for the national Coppa Italia.

TENNIS

A MAJOR EVENT, the International Championships go on at **Foro Italico** for two weeks in May. The world's top tennis stars thrash it out on clay courts at 1pm and 8.30pm from Tuesday to Friday, and at 1pm only at weekends. Buy tickets in advance either directly from the Foro Italico or from a ticket agency.

If you wish to play yourself, there are now over 350 tennis clubs in Rome. It is often essential to book at least a week in advance and there's usually a moderate court fee.

Clubs where membership is not required are the **Centro Sportivo Italiano** and the **Circolo Stampa** in northern Rome and the **Oasis di Pace**, just off the Via Appia Antica. The big hotels offer tennis for a reasonable price. **St Peter's Holiday Inn** requires a small annual membership fee on top of the court price, which includes the gym and the pool (in the summer).

HORSE-RACING, TROTTING AND LEISURE-RIDING

IMPORTANT RACES include the Derby in June and the Premio Roma in November. There are trotting races at the **Ippodromo di Tor di Valle** and flat races and steeple chases at **Ippodromo delle Capannelle**.

The International Horse Show is held at the end of April and the beginning of May in Piazza di Siena, Villa Borghese *(see p258).* It is one of the most important social and sporting events in the calendar, and the setting makes it a great attraction.

For a hack in the countryside around Rome, try the **Centro Ippico Fiano Romano**. Most riding clubs in the city do not accept short-term members.

GOLF

EVEN THE MOST ELITE golf clubs will accept a touring golfer with a home membership and handicap. Most clubs are shut on Mondays and at the weekend when they host competitions, and when guests cannot play. Prices range from L50,000–80,000.

The **Olgiata Golf Club** is open to everybody from Tuesday to Thursday, and to guests accompanied by a member Friday to Sunday. **Country Club Castel Gandolfo** is the newest club and **Circolo Golf Roma** the oldest and most prestigious. Within the city ring road is the course at the **Sheraton Hotel** (closed Tuesday).

Two of the many important competitions taking place on the various golf courses in and around Rome are the National Championships in October and the Rome Masters in April.

CAR AND MOTORBIKE RACING

FORMULA 1 and Formula 3 races take place on Sundays at **Valle Lunga**; be prepared for some relatively expensive entrance fees. Frequently on Saturdays official trials are open to spectators, and on some non-racing Sundays Italy's car designers show new models.

GREYHOUND RACING

THE **Cinodromo** track has shed its sleazy image, and the entrance fee and bets are inexpensive. There is usually a lively, animated crowd of all ages in attendance. Races are run every Wednesday and Thursday at 6.30pm and on Sundays at 10.15am.

ROWING

IN MID-JUNE an Oxbridge crew challenges the historic Aniene crew to a race taking place alternately on the Thames and the Tiber. The best place to view this from is between the Margherita and the Sant'Angelo bridges. The race usually starts at around 6pm. Another event is the battle between the Roma and Lazio crews, from Ponte Milvio to Ponte Flaminio, on the same variable date as the Roma-Lazio football Derby.

SWIMMING

Swimming pools are few and definitely not geared to the short-term visitor. You often have to pay an expensive membership and on top of that a monthly tariff. It's also essential, in most pools, to produce a medical certificate assuring your good health.

The state-owned pools can be slightly cheaper, but you still have to pay an initial membership fee.

It's better to try the outdoor pools, often part of the big hotels. The **Shangri-La Hotel** opens its pool to non-residents from July to September. For a higher entrance fee, swim at the **Hilton** which also opens its pool in summer. Best deal is on a Sunday when the sports club and swimming pool **La Margherita** opens to non-members 10am–1pm, for a reasonable entrance charge. **Piscina delle Rose** in EUR is an Olympic-sized pool (often deserted in the morning) open from June to September 9am–5.30pm during the week, 9am–7pm at weekends.

HEALTH CLUBS

Just as the swimming pools, Roman health clubs usually require both a membership and monthly payments. For just a short stay in Rome, try the hotel facilities, or, if you are willing to pay, head for one of the private clubs. Use of club facilities may be negotiable – you could be lucky and find that you are waved through for the price of a guest pass.

The **Roman Sports Centre** welcomes daily members for a reasonable price and you can use the swimming pools, the gym and the sauna. The facilities are open 9am–10pm. Wear lycra, as normal shorts are not allowed. The **Centro Internazionale di Danza** (Sep–Jul) offers cheap aerobic and dance classes for non-members on Mondays, Wednesdays and Fridays at 6.30pm; you don't need to book.

JOGGING AND CYCLING

Rome's perfect climate and stunning scenery attract thousands of well-dressed joggers and cyclists into the city's many parks. Early in the morning or on a Sunday you'll find the more popular locations looking rather like a high-speed fashion show than sweat tracks.

Villa Doria Pamphilj (see p267) is an extensive park situated above the Janiculum, where you can choose among three tracks, plenty of open spaces and a network of paths. **Villa Borghese** (see p258) is another vast popular place with a running track.

Alternatively, jog under the acacia trees and palms at Villa Torlonia, on the spot-lit track at Villa Glori, or combine sport with culture, by running the **Via Appia Antica** (see p265) branching off into Parco Caffarella. Other favourites are Viale delle Terme di Caracalla, Circo Massimo, Parco degli Aquedotti and Parco di Colle Oppio.

All of the above are also ideal for cyclists, and you can hire bikes from many places, including **Collalti**, **Via del Corso** and **I Bike Roma**.

Organized bike trips are advertised in *Trovaroma*.

DIRECTORY

FOOTBALL

Stadio Olimpico
Viale dei Gladiatori.
(36 85 75 20.

TENNIS

Circolo Stampa
Piazza Mancini 19.
Map 1 A2.
(323 24 52.

Centro Sportivo Italiano
Lungotevere Flaminio 55.
Map 1 A3. **(** 361 00 36.

Foro Italico
Viale dei Gladiatori 31.
(321 90 64.

Oasis di Pace
Via degli Eugenii 2.
(718 45 50.

St Peter's Holiday Inn
Via Aurelia Antica 415.
(66 42.

HORSE-RACING AND RIDING

Centro Ippico Fiano Romano
Via delle Baiocchelle Fiano Romano.
(0765 45 50 19.

Ippodromo delle Capannelle
Via Appia Nuova 1255.
(718 31 43, 34 56.

Ippodromo di Tor di Valle
Via del Mare km.9.
(529 02 70.

GOLF

Circolo Golf Roma
Via Appianuova 716A.
(780 34 07.

Country Club Castel Gandolfo
Via di Santo Spirito 13.
(931 23 01.

Olgiata Golf Club
Largo dell'Olgiata 15.
(30 88 91 41.

Sheraton Golf Hotel
Viale Parco dei Medici 22.
(655 34 77.

MOTOR RACING

Valle Lunga
Autodromo di Roma,
Via Cassia km 34,500.
(904 10 27.

GREYHOUND RACING

Cinodromo
Via della Vasca Navale 6.
(556 62 58.

SWIMMING

Hilton Hotel
Via Cadlolo 101.
(350 91.

La Margherita
Via Monti Tiburtini 511.
(451 05 52.

Piscina delle Rose
Viale America 20.
(592 67 17.

Shangri-La Hotel
Viale Algeria 141.
(591 64 41.

HEALTH CLUBS

Centro Internazionale di Danza
Via San Francesco di Sales 14. **Map** 4 D5 & 11 A4.
(588 55 28.

Roman Sports Centre
Viale del Galoppatoio 33.
Map 5 A1. **(** 320 16 67.

CYCLING

I Bike Roma
Villa Borghese car park.
Map 5 A1. **(** 322 52 40.

Collalti
Via del Pellegrino 82.
Map 4 E4 & 11 B3.
(68 80 10 84.

Via del Corso
Piazza S. Lorenzo in Lucina. **Map** 4 F3 & 12 E1.

CHILDREN'S ROME

ITALIANS LOVE HAVING children around, and you can be sure yours will be made welcome wherever they go. But there are few special facilities for children, and the heat, crowds and lack of clean public loos mean that Rome is not an ideal city for a holiday with babies or under-sevens. It does, however, have plenty to offer slightly older children, especially those who are keen on

Renaissance cherub from the Villa Farnesina

history or art. The temptation may be to wear yourself and your children out by packing too many sights into one day. Plan in advance and leave plenty of time to wander around the city: looking at the quirkier fountains and monuments, watching knife-grinders at work in the markets, and spending hours agonizing over the choice of ice cream flavours and special pizza toppings.

PRACTICAL ADVICE

IF YOU ARE bringing your children to Rome, try to come in early spring or late autumn, when the weather is good, but not too hot. Easter is best avoided, as the city is more crowded than usual, and you're constantly jostled on packed buses and streets. Where you stay is crucial. A hotel near the Villa Borghese park will give your children plenty of chance to relax and let off steam, though you may end up spending a lot of time and money to get to and from the town centre. A hotel in the old centre is ideal, as you can easily pop back during the day for a rest and a clean bathroom.

Jogging in Villa Borghese

As hygienic toilets and changing facilities are rare within the city, it is really not advisable to bring a baby to Rome unless you are visiting friends or family. As with many historic cities, Rome may not instantly appeal to all children, but there is plenty to inspire their imaginations. Use this book to make the buildings and history come alive. Children might also enjoy learning a few Italian words and phrases so they can order food and buy things by themselves.

If lingering over drinks on the café terraces is what you enjoy best, bring your offspring something to keep them busy once they have finished with their treat: crayons and paper, a computer game or a Walkman. Alternatively, most other adults are very tolerant of children running around and making a noise while they relax and, if yours are reasonably outgoing, they could join in with the local children playing ball games in early evenings on piazzas like Campo de' Fiori.

If you feel the need for a total break, most hotels will be able to provide a babysitter or help you to contact a qualified childminding agency.

In the event of bad luck, see pages 360–61 for information on what to do and a list of emergency numbers.

Fairground in the Villa Borghese park

GETTING AROUND

BUMPY COBBLES, narrow streets without pavements and overcrowded buses make pushing children around in pushchairs tiring work. You will, however, inevitably find some people willing to help you haul a pram up steps in a Metro station or on to a bus. Mothers with young children are usually allowed to jump queues, and may even be offered seats on buses. The Metro is often less crowded. Kids under 1 m (3 ft 3 in) tall travel free on public transport.

Although the city is not good for cyclists, families with older children could hire bikes to ride along the Via Appia Antica, or to take on a regional train into the country. The bike hire hut in the Pincio gardens has free baby seats.

Anyone over the age of 14 can ride a scooter under 50 cc, although Rome is not the best place for novices (see p378).

A hire bike with free baby seat

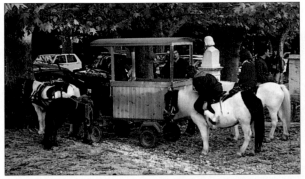
Pony-pulled trains in the Villa Borghese park

EATING OUT

CHILDREN ARE normally warmly welcomed in neighbourhood pizzerias and trattorias, and high chairs are often available for toddlers and babies. If there's no high chair, be prepared for the waiters to improvise for you with armloads of cushions or telephone directories. Most places are perfectly happy to serve half portions, or to let children share meals.

In trattorias it can sometimes be difficult to be exactly sure what a certain dish contains (especially when there is no menu and the dishes of the day are reeled off, usually at top speed, by the waiter), so faddy eaters are likely to be happier in pizzerias *(see pp318–21).* Here they can choose their own topping (remember that *prosciutto,* which is usually translated in menus as ham, is cured). The most entertaining pizzerias for kids are the old-fashioned ones where they can watch the chefs pound, stretch and flip the pizza dough. The best places get busy from around 7.30pm, so it is wise to go early to avoid having to queue. If all else fails, there are three branches of McDonald's.

PICNICS

PICNICS IN THE parks are ideal, and shopping for the food is often half the fun. There's no problem finding small cartons of fruit juice and branded canned drinks, but except in supermarkets (the branch of Standa on Viale Trastevere is the most convenient) they are extremely expensive. The water from drinking fountains is safe, so it's worth carrying plastic cups around.

As well as picnic food from bakeries and markets, there are lots of scrumptious takeaway foods. Many of them are appealingly messy, so it's wise to bring paper tissues. Try deep-fried fruit and vegetables from Cose Fritte on Via di Ripetta and *suppli al telefono,* rice croquettes with a gooey string of mozzarella inside, from *pizza al taglio* outlets. A *tramezzino* comes quite close to an English sandwich and if your kids are miserable without Marmite or peanut butter, you can find them (and other foreign foods) at Ruggieri on Campo de' Fiori.

Feeding pigeons on Piazza Navona

ICE CREAM

ROME, OF COURSE, is famous for ice cream; you and your children are likely to be tempted at every turn. Real ice cream fans may even want to plan their day's sightseeing round one of the best gelaterie *(see pp319–21).* It's far cheaper to buy either a cone or tub of ice cream to eat in the street, but in some of the more traditional places it's worth paying to sit down. At Fassi, they have an old-fashioned ice cream-making machine on display and at Giolitti, you can enjoy gargantuan sundaes in the elegant parlour *(see p109).*

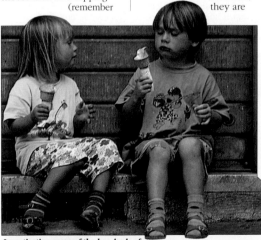
Investigating some of the hundreds of Italian ice cream flavours

Sightseeing with Children

Entrance to the Villa Borghese Zoo

GENERAL TIPS

ROME DOES NOT have many museums with the sort of hands-on exhibits and activities that many other cities lay on for children. Instead, it has other things to entertain visitors. Bernini's marble elephant *(see p108)* and the fat *facchino*, or porter, *(p107)* appeal to children. The Capuchin cemetery at Santa Maria della Concezione *(p254)*, the catacombs *(pp264–7)* and the Mamertine Prison *(p91)* will grab more ghoulish, young imaginations.

Look for details like the dirty toenails on figures in Caravaggio's paintings, the Etruscan votives, which were offered to the gods, at the Villa Giulia *(pp262–3)*, and the illusory collapsing ceiling in the Chiesa Nuova as well as the fake dome of Sant' Ignazio di Loyola *(see p106)*.

Museums your children will enjoy include the Museo delle Arti e Tradizioni Popolari at EUR, with its antique toys, potty and crib scene *(p267)*, and the Museo delle Mura, which explores the length of the Aurelian Wall *(p196)*.

Among the churches, St Peter's, where they can climb to the top of the dome *(see p230)*, and San Clemente, where they can descend to the underground mithreum *(see pp186–7)*, are most fun.

At the Vatican most children will like the statues and mosaics of animals in the Animal Gallery and also the Sistine Ceiling *(p246)*, especially when they get to know that Michelangelo had to paint it hunched up on a scaffolding platform.

ANCIENT RUINS

THE ANCIENT RUINS best appreciated by children are the Colosseum *(see pp92–5)*, and Trajan's Markets *(see pp 88–9)*. You can still make out what both these buildings looked like from their remains. The scant ruins of the Forum and Palatine, on the other hand, may not appeal so strongly. Ostia Antica, where the remains include a theatre, shop and 20-seater public toilet, is much more likely to interest them *(see pp270–71)*.

Mosaic from the Vatican

MOSAICS

THERE ARE SCORES of vivid, sometimes quirky, mosaics in buildings all over Rome. Many of these are particularly appealing to children. Details in the mosaics range from brilliantly coloured flowers, leaves, animals and buildings (in the churches of San Clemente, Santa Prassede and Santa Maria in Trastevere, *see p186, p171 and pp212–13*) to the debris of a banquet (in the Vatican's Museo Gregorio Profano, *see pp234–5*).

Model trains in Villa Borghese

ENTERTAINMENT

ROME'S CULTURAL offerings for children are pretty sparse. To find out what's on, scour the cinema pages of the newspapers and the listings in *Trovaroma (see p340)*. Most theatres and cinemas have reduced entrance tickets for children, although these are only useful if your children are able to speak Italian.

Language is not a barrier in cartoons and puppet shows. There are cartoons at Villa Borghese's Cinema dei Piccoli and traditional puppet shows every afternoon, except Wednesday, up on the Janiculum hill. If your hotel has a TV, you'll find plenty of cartoons there to keep your kids entertained.

Stall at the Befana Christmas toy fair on Piazza Navona

Resting on the kerb side

One of the most appealing times for children to be in Rome is over Christmas, when Piazza Navona hosts the Befana toy fair, where stalls sell toys and sweets.

PARKS

VILLA BORGHESE *(see p258)* has rowing boats to hire and ducks to feed; pony and pony-cart rides; bikes to rent; a mini cinema; a small fun fair; and a zoo. Villa Celimontana *(see p193)* has bike trails, and open-air theatre performances in the summer. The amusement park LUNEUR at EUR *(see p267)* is old-fashioned but can be good fun. The Bomarzo Monster Park, 95 km (60 miles) north of Rome, was built in the 16th century for a mad duke. Children can clamber over its giant stone monsters.

TOYS

A VISIT TO a Roman toyshop can be fun. **Menasci** sells wooden toys, **Città del Sole** has delightful educational toys and games, and **Al Sogno** is a dream for stuffed animals.

Città del Sole
Via della Scrofa 65. **Map** 4 F3 & 12 D2.
687 54 04.

Menasci
Via Napoleone III 72. **Map** 5 A3 & 12 F2. 678 19 81.

Al Sogno
Piazza Navona 53. **Map** 4 E4 & 11 C3.
686 41 98.

CHILDREN'S CLOTHES

Italians adore dressing their children up, and on Sunday afternoons in particular, you are likely to encounter young children dressed as if they had walked straight out of a costume drama: girls in frills and flounces and boys in velvet breeches or knee-length shorts.

Many shops sell beautifully hand-crafted children's shoes and clothes – the downside is that they can often be expensive and impractical: dry-clean-only clothes are common and shoes are not made for mud.

Lavori Artigianili Femminili sells handmade silk and wool clothes for children up to eight. **Succo d'Arancio** sells smart casuals and **Children's Club** offers Italian styles made from classic Liberty fabrics.

Lavori Artigianili Femminili
Via Capo le Case 6. **Map** 5 A3 & 12 F1.
679 29 92.

Succo d'Arancio
Via dell'Arancio 36. **Map** 4 F2 & 12 D1.
687 62 52.

Children's Club
Via della Frezza 61–2. **Map** 4 F2.
322 18 98.

SURVIVAL
GUIDE

PRACTICAL INFORMATION 358-367
GETTING TO ROME 368-373
GETTING AROUND ROME 374-379

PRACTICAL INFORMATION

ROMANS OFTEN SEEM unconcerned by the priceless art treasures and ancient ruins which lie casually among the buildings and workings of their hectic 20th-century city. Visitors nearly always find these wonders very exciting, but it's not always easy to make the most of them. Relaxed local attitudes make for hundreds of variations on opening hours. Most places close for several hours over lunch and reopen in the late afternoon; some museums are open in the mornings only. Bank and shop hours can be just as difficult to pin down. On a more positive note, many of the main sights are within easy walking distance of one another. Start your day early and wear comfortable shoes for the Roman cobblestones. It can be a delightfully informal city to visit; but remember to observe dress rules to cover up in churches, as this is one area where the Italians are very strict.

MUSEUMS AND MONUMENTS

MANY MUSEUMS open only in the mornings and close all day on Mondays. If you are particularly keen to see a specific monument or museum, make sure it's open before you set out. There is usually an admission charge for museums and monuments, though some are free on Sundays. All churches are free, and many contain works of art that are worthy of the world's greatest museums. Some of Rome's sights are accessible only on personal application or by written appointment. Examples include Nero's Aqueduct or the gardens at the Vatican. The *Area by Area* section of this guide gives opening times for each sight and tells you whether there is an admission charge. The **EPT** publishes a useful leaflet called *Musei e Monumenti di Roma* which gives details of current exhibitions at Rome's main museums and galleries.

Museum entry cards are available from museums, tourist offices, or by writing in advance to **L'Associazione Nazionale Museidon**. The cards admit you without extra charge to most museums, galleries and exhibition centres in the city. They are valid for two, four or seven consecutive days and cost from around L15,000 to L50,000.

EPT's guide to current exhibitions

MUSEI e MONUMENTI di ROMA

Typical traffic congestion in Via delle Quattro Fontane

TOURIST INFORMATION

THE SERVICE at the main provincial tourist office (**EPT**) is better than at the crowded station. You should be able to pick up details of special tours here. EPT also help with accommodation *(see p289)*. Besides the official tourist offices, good travel agents such as **CIT**, **Wagons Lits** or the **American Express** office can also be helpful to visitors. For information on Italian cities and areas outside Rome, contact **ENIT** (the National Tourist Board), who have offices in all the main cities.

A word of warning: any information you obtain in Italy should be regarded as only approximate; prices and opening times change often, without warning. Even sights which are normally open for regular hours can be closed for what seem to be unbelievably long periods of restoration *(chiuso per restauro)* or because of a sudden strike *(sciopero)*.

ITALIA®

ENTE NAZIONALE
ITALIANO PER IL TURISMO

ENIT logo

The 119 electric minibus: useful for the historic centre

ENTERTAINMENT INFORMATION

THE WEEKLY *Trovaroma*, in *La Repubblica*, is the main guide to what's on. The bilingual fortnightly *Un Ospite a Roma* (A Guest in Rome) also has entertainment listings and is available free from newsagents. Listings in English are also in *Metropolitan* and *Wanted in Rome*.

Trovaroma

Full entertainment information is on page 340.

GUIDED TOURS

SEVERAL COMPANIES offer tours of Rome with English-speaking guides; these include **CIT**, **American Express**, **Green Line Tours** and **Carrani Tours**. Full-day city tours including lunch cost around L95,000–110,000; half-day tours around L40,000–50,000. Alternatively the No. 110 ATAC bus passes many of the main sights in Rome on a three-hour circuit. The journey will cost you around L6,000. Tour guides can be hired at many of the major sights, such as the Roman Forum *(see pp78–87)*. Employ only the official guides and make sure you establish the fee in advance; on average they charge around L100,000 for a half-day's tour.

ATAC, the Rome bus company

VISITING CHURCHES

MANY OF ITALY'S churches are very dark, but they usually have light meters to illuminate chapels and works of art. The meters are coin-operated (L100, L200 or L500 coins accepted). Recorded information in several languages is often available at coin-operated machines. Dress codes are firmly upheld in Roman churches; St Peter's *(see pp230–33)* is especially strict.

Unacceptable dress in church: both sexes should cover torsos and upper arms

ETIQUETTE

PEOPLE IN ROME are generally courteous and friendly to foreign visitors. Remember to show consideration for local residents and workers.

Italians are delighted at any effort to speak their language, so it's worth learning a few phrases *(see p431)*. Italians tend to drink only with meals and are unlikely to be seen drunk – obvious drunkenness is frowned upon. Smoking is common in bars, restaurants and on streets, but banned on public transport.

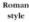

Roman style

TIPPING

FOREIGNERS ARE expected to tip, although Italians themselves don't often do so. Leave a few coins in bars or cafés; in restaurants where service is not included, leave around 10%. Keep L1,000 or L2,000 notes and coins handy for taxi drivers, sacristans, chambermaids, doormen, porters and usherettes.

ROME FOR THE DISABLED

ROME IS not particularly well organized to cater for the disabled. Its uneven cobbles and crowded pavements aren't suitable for those in wheelchairs and even the most agile must be alert when crossing the busy roads. Look before crossing at traffic lights and pedestrian crossings – not all vehicles stop when you expect. The seriously disabled will need to organize help getting around. Ramps, lifts and modified WCs exist in a few places, including Termini station and the Colosseum. If you have no escort, consider a specially-designed package tour, or contact an organization for disabled travellers before you set off. The Vatican Museums, Sistine Chapel and St Peter's are all accessible by wheelchair. The Vatican Museums recently received an EC award for improving accessibility for the disabled, and offer staff help if needed.

WCs

PUBLIC TOILETS are few and far between. There are clean ones by the Colosseum (with facilities for the disabled), at St Peter's and in the Rinascente store *(see p323)*. Most cafés let you use theirs if you ask. Take your own paper.

USEFUL ADDRESSES

American Express
Piazza di Spagna 38. **Map** 5 A2.
℡ 676 41.

Associazione Nazionale Museidon
Via A. Silvani 23, 00139 Rome.

Carrani Tours
Via V. E. Orlando 95.
Map 5 C3.
℡ 488 05 10.

CIT
Piazza della Repubblica 65.
Map 5 C3. ℡ 474 65 55.

ENIT
Via Marghera 2. **Map** 6 E3.
℡ 497 11.

EPT
Via Parigi 5. **Map** 5 C2.
℡ 48 89 92 53.
Open 9am–1.30pm, 2pm–7pm Mon–Sat.

Green Line Tours
Via Farini 5A. **Map** 6 D4.
℡ 481 57 64.

Personal Security and Health

O N THE WHOLE, Rome is a safe, unthreatening place for visitors, but petty street crime is a problem. Don't carry more money than you'll need for the day and leave other valuables or documents in a hotel safe. Cameras are less likely to be snatched if they're in a carrier bag rather than an obvious case. Take particular care in crowded places, such as stations, or on full buses, and steer clear of bands of innocent-looking children – they may be skilful professional pickpockets.

Pharmacy sign

ADVICE FOR VISITORS

T AKE OUT ADEQUATE property insurance before you travel (it is difficult to arrange once you are in Italy), and look after your belongings while you're in Rome. Some hotels now have personal safes in the bedrooms. You can programme these with your own memorable number. (Don't use your date of birth; it's on your passport and registration slip.) To be prepared for all eventualities, keep a separate photocopy of vital documents, such as your passport, to minimize the problem of replacing them, and take a spare photograph or two. Traveller's cheques are the safest way to carry large amounts of cash. Keep the receipts separate from the cheques for a refund in case they do go missing.

Be wary of bag-snatchers on mopeds who operate in quiet streets. You might want to take a discreet money belt or a securely-fastened, long-strapped shoulder bag, while

Mounted police

equipment like video cameras should be disguised. Pickpockets (sometimes children) adopt highly sophisticated distraction techniques with pieces of card or newspaper while they deftly sever you from your possessions in seconds. Take particular care of your valuables in market places or on public transport. Bus route No. 64, which runs between Termini station and the Vatican, is notorious for pickpockets. Thefts from cars

are also rife. Nothing portable like a jacket or bag should be left visible inside a car on Rome's streets, and don't carry luggage on a roof rack. The streets to the east and south of Termini station and around the Colosseum are well-known for prostitution and drug-peddling, and are unsavoury at night.

Women travelling alone (or even in small groups) may need to take extra care. Italian society is male-dominated, and women who are out without male escorts attract more attention than they do in much of the rest of Europe and Northern America.

Beware of unauthorized minicab drivers who are probably not insured and frequently overcharge. They operate in particular near the airport, waiting to profit from

Distinctive *carabinieri* motorcycle

Carabiniere – a member of the military police

Carabiniere in traffic police uniform

Municipal policeman directing traffic

new arrivals. Hotel touts and unofficial tour guides are also best avoided; instead stick to the official tourist agencies *(see p289 and pp358–9)*.

POLICE

THE VIGILI URBANI, or municipal police, wear blue uniforms in winter and white in summer, and can most often be seen regulating traffic. The *carabinieri* are the military police, in red striped trousers. They deal with everything from fine art thefts to speeding offences. *La polizia* (the state police) wear blue uniforms with white belts and berets, and they specialize in serious crime. Any of these should be able to help you.

MEDICAL MATTERS

NO INOCULATIONS are required for Rome, but take mosquito repellent and sun screen in the summer. The Tiber is polluted but the water from the taps and from many street fountains is piped straight from the hills, and is fresh and palatable. EC residents are officially entitled to reciprocal medical care, but the bureaucracy involved can be daunting. Before you travel, pick up form E111 from a post office. This covers you for emergencies – you'll need medical insurance for other needs. Form E111

Police car

Green cross ambulance

Italian fire engine

comes with a booklet of health advice and information on the procedure for claiming free medical treatment. It has to be stamped by a post office to be valid abroad.

Non-EC visitors should take out insurance to cover every-thing, including emergencies.

If you need urgent medical attention, contact the First Aid *(Pronto Soccorso)* department of a main hospital such as **Policlinico Umberto I**, or check the Yellow Pages *(Pagine Gialle)* for a doctor *(medico)* or dentist *(dentista)*. Pharmacists post late-opening rosters on their doors (several stay open all night), and can usually supply the local equiv-alent of foreign medicines. **Farmacia Internazionale Capranica** and **Farmacia Internazionale Barberini** stock American and British pharmaceutical products.

Farmacia Internazionale Barberini
Piazza Barberini 49. **Map** 5 B3.
🔇 482 54 56.

Farmacia Internazionale Capranica
Piazza Capranica 96. **Map** 4 F3 &
12 D2. 🔇 679 46 80.

Policlinico Umberto I
Viale del Policlinico 155. **Map** 6 F2.
🔇 499 71.

Carabinieri **in dress uniform**

LOST PROPERTY

IF YOU WANT to make an insurance claim, report your loss to any police station and get a signed form. For lost passports, go to your embassy or consulate; for lost traveller's cheques, go to the issuing company's office *(see p362)*.

Termini station has a police office on platform 1. Or contact the **Ufficio Stranieri**.

Lost Property on Buses
🔇 581 60 40. **Open** *9am–1pm.*

Lost Property on the Metro
🔇 57 53 36 80.

Ufficio Stranieri
Via Genova 2. **Map** 5 B3.
🔇 46 86 28 29 or 46 86 29 86 *(office hrs)*, English spoken.

Commissariato di Polizia **– a police station**

EMERGENCY TELEPHONE NUMBERS

Ambulance
🔇 55 10.

Automobile Club d'Italia
🔇 116.

Fire
🔇 115.

General SOS
🔇 113. *(Free from any telephone).*

Police
🔇 112. (Carabinieri) or 46 86 (La Polizia).

Samaritans
🔇 70 45 44 44.
Line open *1pm–10pm daily.*

Traffic Police
🔇 676 91.

Banking and Local Currency

Eagle sculpture on the Ministry of Finance

MONEY SERVICES are not always fast in Rome. Transactions can involve considerable paperwork and a lot of waiting around. On the whole, bank exchange rates are more favourable than those in travel agents and hotels – the deal just takes longer to complete. Small change is indispensable – especially the L100, L200 or L500 coins needed for telephones, tips and for illuminating works of art and chapels in churches (*see p359*).

CHANGING MONEY

IT'S BEST to have at least some local currency when you arrive, so you won't have to change money immediately. However, there are increasing numbers of convenient electronic exchange machines at arrival points. There are now several throughout the city too. Multilingual instructions are available. You simply feed in up to 14 notes of the same foreign currency, and should get some lire back. Exchange rates vary from place to place. The Banco di Santo Spirito office at Fiumicino airport offers reasonable rates.

For the best rates, change money at a bank (look for the sign *Cambio*). Hotels tend to give poor rates, even if they charge modest commissions. At the Vatican Museums (*see p235*), you aren't charged any commission. The American Express office (*see p359*) gives good rates and is open on Saturday mornings. Cardholders may withdraw up to $1,000 (or £500) a week from the cash machine, but you have to pay a fee for this service and need to organize a PIN (personal identification number) linked to your account before you travel.

Automatic exchange machine

CREDIT CARDS

CREDIT CARDS, which used to be regarded with great suspicion in Italy, are now much more widely accepted in larger hotels, shops and restaurants in Rome. Some places, however, prefer Eurocheques, which can be cleared faster. All major credit and charge cards (American Express, Access/Mastercard, Visa, Diners Card) are well known. Banks and cash dispensers are more likely to accept Visa cards for cash advances, but Access (Mastercard) is accepted by more retail outlets in Italy. Take both if you have them. Paying for anything in foreign currency will almost always be expensive.

TRAVELLER'S CHEQUES

IF YOU OPT for traveller's cheques, choose a well-known name such as Thomas Cook or American Express, or take those issued through a major bank. Most issuers charge a 1% commission on traveller's cheques. Get some small denominations, so you won't be left with huge amounts of Italian currency at the end of your trip. But don't forget that the minimum commission charged for each transaction (and the amount of time involved) may make changing small amounts of money uneconomical. Always record the traveller's cheque numbers and refund addresses separately from the cheques themselves in case they are stolen. Some places will charge you for each cheque.

Check the exchange rates before you travel and decide whether lire, dollar or sterling cheques are more appropriate. Lire cheques are issued only by Italian banks, and may be more difficult to cash in Italy than dollar or sterling ones.

OPENING HOURS

BANKS ARE USUALLY open 8.30am–1.20pm Mon–Fri. Some larger branches also open from about 3pm to 4.30pm, but opening times vary and banks are closed for public holidays and at weekends. Bureaux de Change have more generous opening times, similar to shop hours. The exchange office at Termini station (*see p372*) is open on Sunday mornings.

USING BANKS

QUEUES IN BANKS can be long and the form-filling involved in changing money can take up a lot of time. You usually have to queue first at the *cambio,* then at the *cassa* to obtain your cash. Take some form of identity with you, such as a passport. Metal objects may set off emergency detectors as you enter.

Exchange office at one of the Italian national banks

One of the major Italian banks

The Bank of Rome, which has branches in other Italian cities

CURRENCY

ITALY'S CURRENCY unit is the *lira* (plural *lire*) and is usually abbreviated L or £. It became the national currency during the unification process in the mid-19th century.

Lira means pound and the English pound is referred to as *lira sterlina* to distinguish it.

Telephone tokens *(gettoni)* are worth L200 and you may get some *gettoni* in your change instead of coins.

Shops and bars are usually not very keen on giving change for a high-value note, so ask for smaller denominations of bank notes when you change money. Coins are often in short supply.

The prospect of carrying around millions of units of currency may at first seem alarming. Plans to alter the basic unit have still not been realized, but you'll find in practice that the last three noughts are often ignored in spoken Italian: *sessanta* will usually mean L60,000 and not, as one may think, L60.

Bank Notes

Italian bank notes come in denominations of L100,000, L50,000, L10,000, L5,000, L2,000 and L1,000, which are easily identifiable by their colours and the historic people portrayed. Notes increase in size progressively according to their value. The lira is never divided into smaller units.

1,000 lire

2,000 lire

5,000 lire

10,000 lire

50,000 lire

100,000 lire

Coins

Coins, shown here at actual size, are in denominations of L500, L200, L100 and L50. Old L100 and L50 coins are still in use and there are L10 and L20 coins of minute value. Telephone gettoni *are worth L200.*

50 lire (new)

100 lire (new)

500 lire

50 lire (old)

100 lire (old)

200 lire

Gettone (200 lire)

Using Rome's Telephones

THE ROME TELEPHONE SYSTEM has recently undergone a major upheaval. Many numbers have been changed and new equipment has been installed alongside older machinery. Until the overhaul is complete you may need a degree of patience when using the phone. At present, telephone numbers can have any number of digits from four to about nine.

Telephone company logo

TELEPHONE OFFICES

TELEPHONE OFFICES (*Telefoni*) are run by Telecom Italia (previously called SIP) and ASST, and offer a convenient way of making long-distance or private calls. At the *Telefono* there will be several metered telephones, each in its own sound-proofed booth. An assistant will assign you a booth, and meter your call once you have been connected to the number you want. You pay on your way out. No premium is charged on this service, but *Telefoni* opening hours rarely

Telephone sign

coincide with Italy's cheapest-rate calling times. The one at the **Palazzo delle Poste** on Piazza San Silvestro is an exception – it stays open 24 hours a day. There are other *Telefoni* throughout Rome, including ones at Fiumicino airport, Termini railway station, other major post offices and in the underground car park at Villa Borghese.

To send international telegrams, go to a post office and dial 186 or call **Telecom**.
Useful information Telecom
573 41; Palazzo delle Poste, Via Calabria 46. **Map** 5 A3 & 12 E1.

CALL CHARGES

THE CHEAPEST times to phone within Italy are 10pm–8am from Monday to Saturday and all day Sunday. If this is inconvenient, it is also relatively inexpensive to call during weekday evenings between 6.30pm and 10pm, or after 1pm on Saturday. But check what time is best if you are making international calls: time variations throughout the world make a difference to cheap rates. Telephoning from hotel rooms is usually expensive and is sometimes marked up by several hundred per cent. In general, telephone calls cost more from Italy than they do from the UK or North America.

USING A SIP COIN AND CARD TELEPHONE

1 Lift the receiver and wait for the dialling tone.

2 If you use coins or *gettoni* insert them in the slot at the top. The slot for telephone cards is lower down.

3 The display shows how much credit is left.

4 Dial the number and wait to be connected.

5 If you still have credit and want to make a second call, press the "follow-on call" button.

6 If your telephone card is about to expire, place a new one in the telephone card slot. When the old card expires, it will feed through automatically.

7 After your call is finished, unused coins or *gettoni* are returned from the left-hand slot. Cards are returned from the slot on the right.

Telephone cards have values of L5,000 or L10,000.

To use a card, break off the marked corner and insert, arrow first.

L500

Gettone

L200

L100

Using Public Telephones

Newer sip payphones, or *interurbani*, are orange, and from these you can dial long-distance and some international calls direct. Payphones take L100, L200 and L500 coins. For longdistance direct-dial calls, have at least L2,000 of change ready. If you don't put enough coins in to start with, the telephone simply retains your money and disconnects you. After a successful call, however, any unused coins are usually returned.

New sign

Old sign for telephone

The most up-todate payphones (pictured opposite) take SIP telephone cards (ask for a *scheda* or *carta telefonica*), costing L5,000 or L10,000, as well as coins. Some payphones will now only accept cards. Cards are available from shops, bars

Reaching the Right Number

• The telephone code for Rome is 06.
• General information on calls within Europe is on 176. Reverse charge and credit card-holder calls are also accepted.
    • European operator assistance is on 15.
    • Intercontinental operator assistance is on 170.
    • General telephone information is on 180.
    • You can dial direct to the operator in Australia, Canada and the US through the Countrydirect service. Dial 172 followed by: 1061 for Australia; 1001 for Canada; 1011 for AT&T, US; 1022 for MCI, US; and 1877 for US Sprint.
    • *See also* Emergency Numbers *p361.*

Gettoni and stamps are available here

and tobacconists displaying the black and white T sign. Break off the marked corner, insert the card arrow first, and the value of the unexpired units will show on a display window. After your call, the card can be retrieved and reused until its value expires.

Older-style phones tend to be found in bars and cafés. These phones will only accept tokens (*gettoni*), costing L200, which can be purchased at shops, bars,

newsagents, post offices or special vending machines. To use these phones insert the *gettone*, dial, wait for an answer and then push the knob to make the token drop; this connects you.

For long-distance calls on older telephones, it is much easier to seek out a *telefono a scatti,* or metered phone. Ask the bar owner if you can phone and the call will be metered. You pay him or her when you have finished.

Sending Letters

The italian postal service is not especially efficient and it is said that letters travelled faster in the days of the old Roman Empire than they do today, in spite of modern technology. For leisurely postcards, the service is usually fine but expect anything sent abroad to take its

Rome letters   Other destinations

Italian state post box

Post Office sign

time; the Italian postal service is particularly slow in August when it can take up to a month for a postcard to reach the UK. For anything urgent or important, it's better to use the more expensive express system, which knocks a day or two off the delivery time, or registered post. Otherwise, you can buy ordinary stamps (*francobolli*) at tobacconists with the black and white T sign as well as in post offices. Sub-post office hours are generally from around 8.30am

until 2pm (8.30am–noon on Saturdays and the last day of the month), but main offices stay open 24 hours a day or well into the evening for some services (such as registered post). Among the 24-hour ones are Piazza San Silvestro, at Termini and at the airport. Italian post boxes are red.

Poste Restante

Letters and parcels which are to be picked up at the post office are sent care of *(c/o)* Palazzo delle Poste, Roma, *Fermo Posta.* Print the surname clearly in block capitals and underline it to make sure the letters are filed correctly. To collect your post, you have to show your passport and pay a small charge. American Express *poste restante* is free to clients.

Vatican post office sign

Vatican postage stamps

Vatican Post

The Vatican postal service costs the same as the state post, but is faster. Buy cards and stamps at the post office near the Vatican Museums entrance, or in Piazza San Pietro. Letters bearing Vatican stamps can only be posted in blue Vatican post boxes.

Postage stamps

Airmail sticker

Additional Information

Fiumicino airport, point of arrival for most visitors to Rome

CUSTOMS AND IMMIGRATION

CITIZENS OF the United States, Canada, Australia, New Zealand or the UK do not need visas for stays of up to three months, but all non-European Community (non-EC) residents require full passports. British citizens may use a Visitor's Card. For longer stays, a visa should be obtained from your nearest Italian embassy or consulate before you travel. You won't usually need any vaccination certificates, but you should check if you have stopped over in tropical or Middle Eastern zones. Duty-free allowances are as follows:

Non-European Community residents are allowed to bring in 400 cigarettes, 100 cigars, 200 cigarillos or 500 grams of tobacco; 1 litre of spirits or 2 litres of wine; 50 grams of perfume. Goods such as watches and cameras may be imported freely for personal or professional use. EC residents no longer have to "declare" goods but random checks are made to guard against the likes of drug traffickers.

The refund system for Value Added Tax (IVA in Italy) for non-EC residents is very complex (see p323) and it is only worth reclaiming if you have spent a lot of money in a single outlet.

Strictly speaking, all visitors to Italy have to register with the police, presenting a passport within three days of their arrival. In practice, the vast majority of visitors have this procedure taken care of for them by their hotels, when they first register. If you are staying elsewhere, contact a local police department for advice, or telephone the **Questura** (police station).

Questura
[C] 46 86.

CATHOLIC SERVICES

FOR MANY CATHOLICS, a visit to Rome means an audience with the pope. General audiences are usually held every Wednesday at 11am (10am in hot weather) in St Peter's square, the Audiences room, or at the summer residence at Castel Gandolfo. To attend an audience, apply to the **Prefettura della Casa Pontificia** before your visit. (Rome travel agencies may be able to arrange an audience as part of a coach tour during your stay.) There is no charge. Mass is held daily in the main churches of Rome (High Mass is on Sunday). Churches where confession is heard include St Peter's (see pp230–33), San Giovanni in Laterano (pp182–3), San Paolo fuori le Mura (p264), Santa Maria Maggiore (pp172–3), the Gesù (pp114–15), Santa Sabina (p204) and Sant'Ignazio (p106). English-speaking Catholic churches include San Silvestro (Piazza San Silvestro) and San Tommaso di Canterbury (Via di Monserrato 45).

Confession box, Gesù

Prefettura della Casa Pontificia
Città del Vaticano, 00120. **Map** 3 B3.
[C] 69 82.

STUDENT INFORMATION

AN INTERNATIONAL Student Identity Card (ISIC) or a Youth International Educational Exchange Card (YIEE) are worth having for reductions on museum and other charges.

Students on the steps of Santa Maria Maggiore

Contact the **Centro Turistico Studentesco** for information. The **Associazione Italiana Alberghi per la Gioventù** (the Italian YHA) has four hostels in the city. **Casa dello Studente** lists student hostels. **Transalpino** is for rail discounts.

ISIC card

Associazione Italiana Alberghi per la Gioventù
Via Cavour 44, 00184. **Map** 3 D3.
[C] 487 11 52.

Casa dello Studente
Viale Ministero degli Affari Esteri 6.

Centro Turistico Studentesco
Via Genova 16. **Map** 5 C3. [C] 467 92 71. (Branches at Via Appia Nuova 434 and Corso Vittorio Emanuele 297.)

Transalpino
Piazza Esquilino 10Z. **Map** 6 D4.
[C] 487 08 70. (Branch at Stazione Termini, in main gallery).

The pope on his balcony at St Peter's

Newspapers available in Rome

NEWSPAPERS, TV, RADIO

ROME'S MAIN newspapers are La Repubblica and Il Messaggero. British and American newspapers are readily available, and the International Herald Tribune is sold on the day of issue. The state TV channels are RAI Uno, Due and Tre; all of them are politically aligned. The advent of satellite and cable TV means there are European channels in many languages, plus sport and CNN news in English. The BBC World Service is broadcast on radio on 15.070MHz (short wave) in the mornings and 648KHz (medium wave) at night. Vatican Radio on 93.3MHz and 105MHz (FM) broadcasts news in English.

EMBASSIES AND CONSULATES

IF YOU LOSE your passport, or need other help, contact your national embassy or consulate as listed below.

Australia
Via Alessandria 215. **Map** 6 E1.
📞 85 27 21.

Canada
Via G.B. De Rossi 27.
📞 44 59 81.

New Zealand
Via Zara 28.
📞 440 29 28.

United Kingdom
Via XX Settembre 80A. **Map** 6 D2.
📞 482 54 41.

United States
Via Veneto 119A/121. **Map** 5 B2.
📞 467 41.

ELECTRICAL ADAPTORS

ELECTRIC CURRENT in Italy is 220V AC, with two-pin round-pronged plugs. Adaptors can be purchased in most countries. In most hotels of three or more stars, there are hair dryers and shaving points in all the bedrooms.

Shaving point in hotel bedroom for 110V or 220V

Standard Italian plug

ROME TIME

ROME IS ONE HOUR ahead of Greenwich Mean Time (GMT). Examples of the time difference with Rome for other major cities are as follows: London: -1 hour; New York: -6 hours; Dallas: -7 hours; Los Angeles: -9 hours; Perth: +7 hours; Sydney: +9 hours; Auckland: +11 hours; Tokyo: +8 hours. These figures can vary slightly for brief periods with local changes in summer. For all official purposes, the Italians use the 24-hour clock.

CONVERSION TABLE

Imperial to Metric

1 inch	= 2.54 centimetres
1 foot	= 30 centimetres
1 mile	= 1.6 kilometres
1 ounce	= 28 grams
1 pound	= 454 grams
1 pint	= 0.57 litres
1 gallon	= 4.6 litres

Metric to Imperial

1 centimetre	= 0.4 inches
1 metre	= 3 feet 3 inches
1 kilometre	= 0.6 miles
1 gram	= 0.04 ounces
1 kilogram	= 2.2 pounds
1 litre	= 1.8 pints

SIGHTSEEING PERMITS

TO VISIT certain sights in Rome, you need to obtain a written permit and book the time of your visit in advance. This applies particularly to archaeological sites, which may sometimes be closed during excavations. Write to:

Comune di Roma Ripartizione X
Piazza Campitelli 7. **Map** 4 F5 & 12 E5.
📞 67 10 20 70. **FAX** 67 10 31 18.

To speed things up, deliver your application in person to the protocollo on the third floor. Once your application has been received, fix a time for your visit by calling Signor Natale of the:

Ufficio Monumenti Antichi e Scavi, Via del Portico d'Ottavia 29.
Map 4 F5 & 12 E5. **Map** 4 F5 & 12 E5.
📞 67 10 38 19, 67 10 20 71 or 67 10 24 75. **FAX** 67 10 31 18.

OTHER RELIGIOUS SERVICES

Anglican
All Saints, Via del Babuino 153.
Map 4 F2. 📞 36 00 18 81.

American Episcopal
St Paul's, Via Napoli 58. **Map** 5 C3.
📞 488 33 39.

Jewish
Sinagoga, Lungotevere Cenci.
Map 4 F5 & 12 D5. 📞 684 00 61.

Methodist
Via Firenze 38. **Map** 5 C3.
📞 481 48 11.

Mosque
Viale della Moschea (Parioli district).
Map 2 F1. 📞 808 21 67.

Presbyterian
St Andrew's, Via XX Settembre 7.
Map 5 C3. 📞 482 76 27.

The Mosque in Parioli

GETTING TO ROME

Alitalia aircraft

MANY NATIONAL AIRLINES, including Italy's Alitalia, fly direct to Rome from most European cities and several in North America and Australia. There are no direct flights from New Zealand, but passengers can catch connections from either Frankfurt or London.

Rome also has train and coach links with the rest of Europe. These take a lot longer than flights (about 24 hours from London, compared with about three), but tend to cost about the same, so are only really worthwhile if you want to travel overland. The trains are often crowded in summer.

Part of the new extension to Fiumicino airport

BY AIR

IF YOU'RE FLYING from the United States, **TWA**, Delta and United Airlines operate regular direct scheduled flights to Rome, with services from about half a dozen cities (including New York, Boston, Washington, Los Angeles and Chicago). Flying time from New York is about eight and a half hours and it's about 13 hours from Los Angeles. **Canadian Airlines** flies from Montreal and Toronto; **Qantas** from

Alitalia flight tickets

Melbourne and Sydney. The Italian state airline, **Alitalia**, also flies between Rome and New York, San Francisco, Philadelphia, Boston, Chicago, Detroit, Washington, Montreal, Toronto and Sydney. It may, however, be considerably cheaper for intercontinental travellers to take a budget flight to London, Paris, Frankfurt or Amsterdam and continue the journey to Rome from there.

British Airways and Alitalia operate direct scheduled flights from London Heathrow to Rome, and you can fly from Manchester. Among the airlines using Rome as an intercontinental transit point are **Philippine Airlines**, Sudan Airways and Ethiopian Airlines: fares are cheaper, but flights tend to be less frequent and are sometimes subject to long delays.

APEX, PEX, or SuperPEX fares generally offer the best value in scheduled flights, but you must purchase them well in advance (for example, 7 or 14 days ahead in the UK; 21 days in the US). They are subject to penalty clauses if you cancel, so it's advisable to take out insurance as soon as you buy your ticket.

The new ticket hall at Ostiense

If you're based in the UK, it's worth looking in the small ads of newspapers for cut-price charters (though even in low season these are becoming increasingly rare). Regular charters run all year round. Most leave from Gatwick and Luton, but there are a couple of flights a week from Manchester and it's usually possible to fly from Glasgow and Birmingham. Fares vary greatly, peaking in summer, and in Holy Week for the Pope's Easter blessing.

If you want to book flights during your stay in Rome, travel agents, such as the **American Express** office, should be able to help.

↖ 📷 Stazione 🚇 – Railway Station
↖ Ⓜ Metropolitana per Termini Underground to Termini
↘ Piazzale dei Partigiani
🚌🚶 Ⓟ 📷 Centro

Easy-to-follow signs at Ostiense

AIRLINE NUMBERS

Alitalia
📞 656 43 (information),
656 42 (international flights).

American Express
📞 676 41.

British Airways
📞 147 85 88 58 (toll free).

Canadian Airlines
📞 655 71 17 or 167 86 22 16 (toll free).

Qantas
📞 48 88 03 20 or 65 01 01 46.

TWA
📞 472 11 or 60 12 49 36.

PACKAGE HOLIDAYS

PACKAGE HOLIDAYS to Rome can be much better value than travelling independently. For European visitors there are weekend packages and two- or three-centre holidays; Rome is frequently packaged with Florence and Venice. Those from further afield can visit the city during Europe-wide tours. Most package companies transport you free of charge from the airport to your hotel in Rome. Many, especially the more expensive ones, include a tour guide.

AIRPORTS

ROME HAS TWO international airports. Leonardo da Vinci – commonly known as Fiumicino – handles most

Ciampino, a more basic airport used by most charter flights

scheduled flights, and is about 30 km (18 miles) south-west of the city. The other airport is Ciampino, about 15 km (9 miles) southeast and used by the majority of charter flights. Major car hire firms have rental offices at both airports, though you may find it less harrowing to get into the city centre on public transport or by taxi.

Shuttle bus to car-hire lots at Fiumicino

From Fiumicino there's a train to Tiburtina station (6.15am–midnight; 25 min journey). If you are lucky the ticket office (which also sells Metro tickets) will be open; if not, you'll have to tackle the automatic ticket machine *(see p373)*. A faster – and more expensive – train leaves Fiumicino each hour, bound for Termini (7.50am–10.05pm, return trains departing hourly 7am–9.15pm).

Ostiense is linked with Piramide Metro by a series of escalators, flyovers and moving pavements. At Piramide Metro you can catch an underground train to the city centre. This Metro line stops at 9pm on weekdays and at 11.30pm on Saturdays and Sundays, though. Taxis can be difficult to find at Ostiense after 9pm, but there's a bus (the No. 95) to Piazza Venezia.

The swiftest way to get to the centre from Ciampino is by bus to Anagnina Metro station, then by underground train to Termini. Taxis from both airports are expensive; only use official cabs and make sure that the fare meter is switched on and showing only the minimum charge before you leave.

One of the overhead walkways linking the air terminal at Ostiense station with Piramide Metro station

KEY

🚌 Coach to Termini

🚉 Railway to Ostiense

🅿 Multistorey car park

――― Future extension

――― New ring road

The Domestic Terminal has a restaurant, shops and three bars.

Taxi rank

Domestic pier

The International Terminal will have better facilities for passengers.

Overhead walkways

THE FUTURE FIUMICINO
Fiumicino airport is currently being extended. The plans include a new international terminal, and improved road access.

From Rome

To Rome

Arriving in Rome

THIS MAP shows the main bus, rail and Metro links used by travellers arriving in Rome. The connections between Rome's two airports and the city centre are shown, as well as links between Rome and the rest of Italy and the international rail routes from neighbouring European countries. Travel information, including details of journey times and service frequency, is listed separately in each box.

FS *National connections*
Links to Flaminio from **Viterbo** (2 hrs), **Bracciano** (90 mins).

Flaminio

FS *Coastal route from Northern Italy*
Links with Termini station. **Marseille** (11 hrs), **Nice** (9 hrs), **Turin** (7 hrs 30 mins), **Genova** (6 hrs), **Pisa** (3 hrs 30 mins).

Lepanto

Ottaviano

Piazza di Spagna

Spagn

Barberin

Vatican

Piazza Navona

Piazza della Rotonda

KEY

✈ Airport *see pp368–9*

FS Railway *see pp368–9*

🚌 Coach & Bus Link *see pp374–7*

M Metro *see pp376–7*

Airport Link *see pp368–9*

State Rail Link *see pp374–5*

Metro Line A *see pp376–7*

Metro Line B *see pp376–7*

•• Walkway *see pp372–3*

San Pietro

Janiculum

Campo de' Fiori

Capitol

Foru

Pala

Trastevere

Ostiense station, linked to Piramide Metro

Circo Massimo

Aventine

Piramide

✈ **LEONARDO DA VINCI (FIUMICINO)**
Direct train links to Ostiense, Tiburtina and Termini. Linked with Piramide Metro station.
FS *Fiumicino–Tiburtina* every 20 mins; *Fiumicino–Termini* every 60 mins.
🚌 *Fiumicino–Lepanto* (via Fregene) every 30 mins.
🚌 *Fiumicino–Ostiense* (via Fiumicino village) every 45 mins.

Trastevere

Ostiense

M *Line B, southbound*
Stops after Piramide are: Garbatella, San Paolo Basilica, Marconi, Magliana, EUR Palasport, EUR Fermi and Laurentina (end station).

International and Northern Italy
Links with Termini. Trains arriving after midnight terminate at Tiburtina.
Paris *(15 hrs),* **Vienna** *(14 hrs),* **Geneva** *(14 hrs),* **Basle** *(13 hrs),* **Munich** *(11 hrs),* **Verona** *(7 hrs),* **Milan** *(5 hrs),* **Bologna** *(3 hrs 30 mins),* **Florence** *(2 hrs).*

Coach connections into Rome
International and national bus links at **Piazza dei Cinquecento** *(in front of Termini). Buses for the Lazio region link at* **Lepanto**. *Connections to the city centre and other parts of Italy link at* **Piazzale Ostiense**.

Coach arriving at Piazzale Ostiense

Piazza Bologna

Policlinico

Castro Pretorio

Tiburtina

ia Veneto

epubblica

uirinal

Roma Termini

Cavour

Esquiline

Vittorio Emanuele

Colosseo

Manzoni

Lateran

San Giovanni

Caracalla

Re di Roma

Tuscolana

Ponte Lungo

Termini Metro station

Line B, northbound
Stops after Tiburtina are: Quintiliani, Monti Tiburtini, Pietralata, Santa Maria del Soccorso, Ponte Mammolo and Rebibbia (end station).

Eastern Italy
Links with Termini station. **Pescara** *(4 hrs),* **L'Aquila** *(3 hrs 30mins).*

Southern Italy
Links with Termini station. **Palermo** *(12 hrs),* **Reggio Calabria** *(9 hrs 30 mins),* **Bari** *(6 hrs 30 mins),* **Naples** *(2 hrs).*

Line A, southbound
Stops after Ponte Lungo are: Furio Camillo, Colli Albani, Arco di Travertino, Porta Furba, Numidio Quadrato, Lucio Sestio, Giulio Agricola, Subaugusta, Cinecittà and Anagnina (end station).

CIAMPINO
Bus link to Anagnina Metro station (on Line A). **Atac bus** *every hour (10–20 mins).* **ACOTRAL bus** *every hour to Anagnina Metro station (10–20 mins). Metro line A links with Termini station.*

Reaching Rome by Train, Coach or Car

Aᴺʏ ᴏᴠᴇʀʟᴀɴᴅ journey to Rome is fastest by train, though there are coach connections to most major European cities. Within Italy, journeys between large cities are usually also best done by train, but when travelling from towns which are not on the main Intercity rail routes, coaches can be quicker. For drivers, the Italian Automobile Club *(see p361)* provides free assistance and excellent maps to members of affiliated automobile clubs from all over the world.

A Pendolino – Italy's fastest train

The foyer of Stazione Termini

STAZIONE TERMINI

Sᴛᴀᴢɪᴏɴᴇ ᴛᴇʀᴍɪɴɪ, Rome's main train station, is also the hub of the urban transport system. Beneath it is the only interchange between the city's two Metro lines, and directly outside, on Piazza dei Cinquecento, is the central bus terminus. Though it is one of Rome's most stunning 20th-century buildings, it also has many unsavoury aspects, so it is unwise to linger longer than necessary.

FS logo

If you arrive late, aim to leave the neighbourhood as swiftly as you can. There are usually taxis (go to the official queue), even in the small hours, and most of the city's night buses start at Termini.

In summer the station gets very crowded, and you can expect long queues at ticket booths, bureaux de change and at both the transport and tourist information offices. There's a left luggage office, a police station where you should report anything lost or stolen on a train or in the station; and a small Citalia office where you can exchange money as well as

get travel information. In the foyer, there is an international telephone office *(see p364)*, a bookshop, a post office and a tobacconist (where you can stock up on bus and Metro tickets). Other facilities at the station include a burger bar, a café, a ticket office for Transalpino and, downstairs in the gloomy Metro subway, a hairdresser and an *albergo diurno* (day hotel), where, for a price, you can freshen up with a bath or shower.

BINARIO 17
Platform sign

← uscita
Exit sign

Of Rome's other stations, four are most likely to be of interest to tourists. They are Ostiense and Trastevere, for trains to Fiumicino airport and Viterbo *(see p271)*; Tiburtina, for some of the trains on the north-south line through Italy; and Roma Nord for trains to Prima Porta.

TRAVELLING BY TRAIN

Iᴛᴀʟɪᴀɴ sᴛᴀᴛᴇ ʀᴀɪʟᴡᴀʏs (Ferrovie dello Stato or FS) have several levels of service, from Locale trains which stop at every station, to the Pendolino, a super-fast and extremely luxurious train, which offers first- and second-class service. The Pendolino runs between Rome and Milan, Turin, Genoa, Bari, Naples and Venice. You have to reserve and you're charged hefty supplements for the privileges of speed, hostess service and free newspapers. You also pay a supplement on Intercity trains. These trains are for fast long distance journeys and have both first- and second-class carriages. They run from Rome to Venice, Milan, Florence and Naples. You should book in high season and at weekends. Booking is obligatory on some services,

Termini, the heart of Italy's rail network and Rome's transport system

An international Eurocity train

which are marked in the timetable by a black R on a white background. Some staff at the **Booking Office** speak English, but it may be easier to go in person to the station, or to a travel agent displaying the FS symbol.

From Rome you can also take international or Eurocity (EC) trains to destinations all over Europe. It's worth reserving a seat, especially during the summer when trains become crowded.

**Stazione Termini
Booking Office**
Via Giolitti 22. (47 75.

MACHINES FOR FS RAIL TICKETS

These self-service machines are easy to use, and most have instructions in four languages on a printed panel.

1 Select your destination.

2

1

2

3 Take your ticket and change.

Date

Length of journey

Price of ticket

2 The price is shown on the display. Insert coins, notes, or an American Express or Diners Club card.

Destination | **Class**

Number of adults and children travelling

COACH TRAVEL

Most regional and long-distance coaches are blue

LONG-DISTANCE coaches terminate at Tiburtina, which is the city's main coach station. Information and tickets for Euroline coaches to European cities are available from **Lazzi Express**. The **Appian Line** offers regular services within Italy. Its itineraries include Florence, Naples, Capri, Sorrento, Pompei, Venice and Assisi. Local buses, serving villages and towns within the Lazio region, are run by **COTRAL**. All bus stations used by COTRAL are linked

to Metro stations. Tickets for COTRAL services are bought on the spot and cannot be booked in advance. Some day trips from Rome by bus are described on pages 268–71.

Appian Line
Piazza dell'Esquilino 6–7. (48 78 61.

COTRAL
(591 55 51.

Lazzi Express
Via Tagliamento 27. (884 08 40.

TRAVELLING BY CAR

TO DRIVE YOUR OWN car in Italy you need an international Green Card (for insurance purposes) and the vehicle registration document. A translation of your driving licence, available at Italian tourist offices abroad, is also useful. Wearing seatbelts is

Blue signs showing A roads and green signs showing motorways

compulsory in Italy. You must also carry a warning triangle in case of breakdown. Main routes to Rome connect with the Grande Raccordo Anulare (GRA), Rome's ringroad.

Tolls are charged on all Italian motorways. You can buy petrol coupons and magnetic motorway toll cards from motoring organizations before entering Italy.

Euroline coach running between Rome and the rest of Europe

GETTING AROUND ROME

Rome's centre is compact and, although walking absolutely everywhere would be over-ambitious, it is a city in which you can spend much of your time on foot. As the main streets in the centre are usually clogged with traffic, driving and cycling cannot be recommended, but courageous motorbike or scooter riders can have

A Roman family's solution to very heavy traffic

great fun buzzing around on a rented Vespa. Travelling by bus and tram can be very slow, so use overland public transport only when you have a long way to go. The Metro, designed to connect the suburbs with the centre, has no stops in the historic city centre near the Pantheon or Piazza Navona, though it is certainly the swiftest way of crossing the city.

WALKING

WANDERING through Rome's old centre is one of the most enjoyable aspects of being in the city. You can take in the architectural details, absorb the streetlife, make diversions at will, and peek into any church, shop or bar that catches your interest. And you can easily visit, or at least see, several of the main tourist sights in a few hours. The Colosseum, for example, is only about 2.5 km (1.5 miles) from the Spanish Steps. Your route could pass by the Forum, Piazza Venezia and several churches; other sights, such as the Trevi Fountain, the Galleria Doria Pamphilj and the Pantheon, are just a short detour away.

Explore the city area by area, using public transport when distances are too far.

Avanti: go! Pedestrians have right of way

Alt: stop! Traffic has right of way

Only very small patches of central Rome are pedestrianized, and a street which is closed to cars will still be used by cyclists and scooter riders. There have been many plans to create more traffic-free zones, and even to ban anything on wheels from some parts of the city – but imposing such measures on a population as insubordinate as Rome's is not easily done.

If you find the summer heat hard to bear, remember that the narrow cobbled streets get little sunlight and remain relatively cool, while walking into an open piazza can be like stepping into a furnace.

During the height of summer, you'll have a more enjoyable time if you follow the example of the Italians. Walk slowly on the shady side of the street; have a long lunch followed by a siesta in the hottest part of the day. You can continue exploring in the late afternoon, when churches and shops reopen and the streets are at their liveliest. Wandering at night is worthwhile, as the streets are cool and many facades floodlit.

Directions for walkers

Pedestrian crossing: only slightly safer than the open road

CROSSING ROADS

FIRST IMPRESSIONS suggest there can be only two sorts of pedestrian in Rome: the quick and the dead. Even if you cross roads by sets of traffic lights and pedestrian crossings strictly in your favour, there are sure to be some van or Vespa hurtling towards you with apparently homicidal intent. Fortunately, Roman drivers have quick reactions. The pious would attribute this to the protection of Santa Francesca Romana *(see p87)*, cynics to the fact that according to Italian insurance law, drivers are responsible for any road accident. Whatever the inspiration, accidents are quite rare. The best tactic is to be as alert and confident

Pedestrian crossing   Watch out for children

as Romans. The roads are very busy. When crossing, try to leave as large a gap as possible between yourself and oncoming traffic. Step purposefully into the road, facing approaching motorists with a determined glare. The trick now is to keep going steadily: don't hesitate, or change your course, and don't run. As long as a driver can see you, he or she should stop, or at least swerve, albeit at the last moment.

Pedestrians and drivers must both take particular care at night, when the traffic lights are switched to a constantly flashing amber, turning the crossings into free-for-alls.

STREET SIGNS

THEORETICALLY, although it may not always seem to be the case, pedestrians have right of way at crossings when the green *avanti* sign is lit up. The red sign *alt* means you must wait. Underground crossings are indicated by a sign reading *sottopassaggio*.

It is easy to get lost in the maze of streets and piazzas that comprise the historic centre. Until you know your way around, you can follow the yellow signs marking routes between the sights and piazzas of particular interest to tourists. Routes leading to general landmarks are indicated by signs on a silver-grey background.

No stopping

continua

No parking

SENSO UNICO

One-way street

strada senza uscita

No through road

DRIVING

DRIVING IN CENTRAL Rome can be an extremely intimidating experience for visitors. The flamboyant aggression of Italian drivers is notorious, pedestrians step out into the roads without warning, and the one-way system operating in much of the centre makes retaining a sense of direction impossible. You'll also find motorists overtaking on the

Directions to parking areas

wrong side, while scooters and Vespas zoom among the lanes of traffic and go the wrong way down one-way streets. One rule to remember is to give way to the right. Unless you are accustomed to driving in Italian cities, leave your car at home – or failing that, in a guarded car park.

Car thefts are rife in Rome, so never leave anything of value in your car, even out of sight: areas such as Campo de' Fiori are patrolled by gangs on the lookout for anyone leaving cameras, fur coats and other costly items in their boots. You should also remove your car radio – you won't be the only person carrying one into a bar, restaurant or disco.

Take extra care if driving late at night. Not only do traffic lights switch to flashing amber, but many Italians are astonishingly cavalier about driving under the influence of drink or drugs.

PARKING

THE MOST convenient car park is below the Villa Borghese. Much of the city centre is reserved for residents with permits and there are thousands of drivers with fake permits, which exacerbates the problem. If you do find a legal place to park, you may return and find you've been hemmed in by double parked cars. Locations of some of the most useful car parks are listed on page 379.

PETROL

PETROL IS very expensive. It can be bought from roadside petrol pumps throughout the city, as well as from regular garages, though the former don't always sell lead-free petrol *(senza piombo)*. In the afternoon and at night many pumps are self-service, operated by banknotes or credit cards. Late-night petrol stations are listed on page 379.

Agip

The state petrol company logo

ILLEGAL PARKING

Rome's traffic police are vigilant. If you've parked illegally, your car may be clamped or (if it's causing an obstruction) towed away, so phone 67 691 to check before reporting it stolen. No-parking zones should be clearly marked, but look carefully, in case the sign is hidden by a tree.

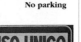

zona rimozione fermata consentita per salita e discesa con conducente a bordo

Signpost for a tow away area *(zona rimozione)*

A tow truck at work

Travelling by Bus, Tram and Metro

R OME'S PUBLIC TRANSPORT system is comparatively
cheap, comprehensive and as efficient as the busy
streets allow. Priests, nuns, tourists, pilgrims, businessmen and pickpockets all pile aboard, transforming the
buses and trams into mobile saunas during the summer.
Short distances are better covered on foot, because
heavy traffic often blocks the roads. Getting off at the
right stop can be difficult, but other passengers will
usually help if you ask for directions. Always keep a
tight hold on your valuables.

Monthly passes

BUSES AND TRAMS

R OME'S PUBLIC bus and tram
company is called **ATAC**
(Azienda Tramvie e Autobus
del Comune di Roma). Scores
of its orange buses and a
handful of rattling trams cover
most parts of the city. They
run from early morning until
about midnight. There are
also a few night buses.

Apart from one electric
minibus (No. 119), no buses
can run through the narrow
streets of the historic centre.
But there are plenty of bus
routes to take you within a
short walk of the main sights
(see map inside back cover).

Rome's new yellow bus
stops comprehensively list the
details of routes taken by all
the buses using that stop.
There are, however, still a
number of old-style bus stops
left. These list only a few of

the streets and
piazzas that the
buses pass and are
mystifying until you
know Rome well.

USING BUSES AND TRAMS

T HE MAIN TERMINUS is on
Piazza dei Cinquecento
outside Termini station, but
there are other major route
hubs throughout the city, most
usefully those at Largo
Argentina, Piazza Venezia and
Piazza del Risorgimento.
Information on public
transport can be obtained from
ATAC kiosks. Tickets can be
bought from automatic
machines found at main bus
stops and also at Metro and
train stations.

Most day buses have only a
driver; night buses usually
also have a conductor who
issues tickets. (You can't buy
tickets on day buses.)

In the day, if you have a
normal ticket, you should
board the bus at the back.
There will be an orange
machine there to time-stamp
your ticket. Timed tickets,
biglietto integrale a tempo
(BIT), are valid for 75
minutes or until the
end of the journey, if
you board before the
end of the 75 minutes.
BIT tickets can be
used on buses and
trams and for one-
way journeys on the
Metro or train.

INFORMATION

ATAC
Piazza dei Cinquecento.
Map 6 D3.
☎ 46 95 44 44;
46 95 22 00.
Open 7.30am-7pm daily.

BIG ticket for one
day's unlimited travel

75-minute BIT tickets

TICKETS

T ICKETS FOR CITY buses, trams
and Metros have to be
bought before you travel. You
can buy them at bars, newsstands and tobacconists, as
well as at Metro stations and
bus termini. Look out for
places displaying ATAC (bus
and tram), COTRAL (Metro)
and FS (train) stickers. Most
of the outlets selling tickets
close by mid-evening but
there are automatic
ticket machines at
main bus stops and
train and Metro
stations which take
both coins and notes
and distribute change.

BIT tickets are
valid for 75 minutes,
during which time
you can hop on and
off as many buses, trams
and Metros as many times as
you like. If you are going to
make four or more
journeys in one day,
it is worth buying a
biglietto integrato

ATAC bus No. 64

Rome–Gubbio bus

FERMATA

**New-style bus stop
listing details of
routes served**

A Roman tram in the orange livery of ATAC

giornaliero (BIG) ticket. These give you a day's travel on the buses, trams and the Metros and one-way on urban train lines, except for Fiumicino airport. There are also available weekly tickets and monthly (calendar month) passes which are valid for the whole transport system, with discounts for students and people over 65. Fare-dodging is common, but incurs a hefty on-the-spot fine.

METROPOLITANA

Rome's underground system, the Metropolitana, has two lines (A and B) which cross the city in a rough X-shape, converging at Termini station *(see inside back cover and pp370-71)*. Line A (red) leads from Ottaviano near the Vatican to Anagnina in the southeast of the city,

where buses go to Ciampino airport. Line B (blue) runs from Rebibbia in the northeast, where you can catch a bus to Tivoli, down to EUR in the southwest, where buses leave for the coast. Stations are clearly marked by the Metro logo, a large white M on a red background.

The system was designed to ferry commuters in from the suburbs, so is not very useful within the centre, but the Metro is a relatively speedy way of crossing the city. Useful stations are Colosseo, Spagna, San Giovanni, Ottaviano and Piramide (for trains to Fiumicino). Metro Line C is due to be completed by 2000, linking St Peter's to the Colosseum. Line A runs from 5.30am–11.30pm and Line B 5.30am–10.30pm.

Metro logo

USEFUL BUS AND TRAM ROUTES

This map shows a selection of buses that go through interesting parts of the city with good views of major sights. The 64 is always full of tourists, since it is the one route from Termini to St Peter's. The other routes are likely to be less crowded. The 30b tram follows a long leisurely route around the southeast of the city, while 23 goes along the Tiber. and the the city

Villa Borghese
Villa Giulia
Piazza del Popolo
M Flaminio
M Spagna
Fontana del Tritone
San Lorenzo fuori le Mura
Mausoleo di Augusto
M Barberini
Castel Sant'Angelo
FS M Termini
Ponte Umberto I
Via del Tritone
Vatican
Piazza Colonna
St Peter's
Pantheon
Porta Maggiore
Gesù
Piazza Venezia
M Colosseo
Villa Farnesina
M San Giovanni
Palazzo Venezia
Trastevere
Teatro di Marcello
M Circo Massimo
Bocca della Verità
Santa Maria in Cosmedin
Pyramid of Caius Cestius
Ostiense FS M Piramide

KEY

FS	Railway station
M	Metro station
▬	Bus route 23
▬	Tram route 30b
▬	Bus route 56
▬	Bus route 64
▬	Bus route 119

BIKE AND MOPED HIRE

ROME'S NARROW streets and heavy traffic, combined with the seven steep hills on which it was built, make it a challenging place for even the most serious of cyclists. However, there are a few areas, such as the Villa Borghese, the banks of the Tiber and some pockets in the historic centre (around the Pantheon and Piazza Navona), where cycling can be a relaxing way to see the city. Make sure that you have a loud bell though – places that are good for cyclists tend to be popular with walkers and strollers too.

Mopeds *(motorini)* and scooters, called Vespas or

Horse-drawn carriages outside the Pantheon

wasps in Italy because of the buzzing noise they make, are an efficient way of getting through the traffic. You may want to stick to quiet streets to begin with, though.

Although motorcyclists have to wear helmets by law, moped riders over 18 don't. However, you can hire helmets from most hire shops in Rome.

Bikes and mopeds can be hired from **Collalti**, **Roma Rent**, **Scoot-a-Long**, **St Peter Moto** and **Scooters for Rent**. **Biciroma** rents from several spots in the old centre and a **telephone hire service** operates in the summer and autumn.

You may have to leave a credit card as deposit when you pick up the bike.

A Vespa scooter and helmet

HORSE-DRAWN CARRIAGES

THESE ARE NOT as popular in Rome as in Florence, but you can hire horse-drawn caleches *(carrozzelle)* for a gentle tour of the historic centre. Carriages carry up to five people and can be hired from many points: Piazza di Spagna, the Colosseum, Trevi Fountain, St Peter's, Via Veneto, Villa Borghese, Piazza Venezia and Piazza Navona. Trips last half an hour, an hour, half a day or a day. They tend to be expensive, but prices for longer rides are negotiable; establish the price before you set off and make sure you understand whether the rate is per person, or for the whole carriage.

TAXIS

OFFICIAL TAXIS in Rome are yellow and must bear the "taxi" sign on the roof. Only use these taxis, not the ones offered by touts at stations and tourist spots; official taxi drivers do not tout for customers. Yellow taxis can be hailed either at specially marked stands or on the street (drivers are not meant to stop in the street but many of them do). You can nearly always find them at the main tourist sights, at

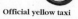

Taxi stand signpost

airports and stations (including Termini and Ostiense). Roman taxi drivers are not renowned for their friendliness and may even refuse to take you too far from the lucrative city centre.

Taxis aren't a particularly cheap way of getting about, so, unless you have heavy luggage or screaming toddlers, public transport is usually a better option. Taxi drivers always charge supplements for baggage, night journeys (10pm–7am) and journeys on Sundays or public holidays. As with taxis elsewhere, the fare meter continues running while you're at a standstill so traffic jams can

Taxis lining up at Fiumicino

become expensive. Drivers may also take suspiciously circuitous routes to your destination. Taxi drivers in Rome expect tips from visitors. Native Romans generally give small amounts or nothing at all, but you'll be expected to give at least 10% of the fare.

You can book in advance from **Cosmos Radio Taxi**, **Società Cooperativa Autoradiotaxi Roma** or **Società la Capitale Radio Taxi**. There is a surcharge for taxis booked in advance.

Official yellow taxi

CAR HIRE

IN ITALY car hire is generally expensive, while petrol is among the highest-priced in Europe. Major international companies (**Avis, Europcar, Hertz** and **Eurodollar**) have rental offices at airports and within the city centre. However, you may get a better deal by booking a car ahead through a travel agent or tour operator before you leave. Local firms (such as **Maggiore**) are generally a lot cheaper, but check that breakdown service and collision damage waiver are included in the hire price.

Prospective renters should be aged 21 or over and have held a driving licence for at least one year. Theoretically you should also hold an international licence (available from your national automobile association) but most car rental firms do not usually insist on this.

Accident rates on Italian roads are very high, so insure yourself to the hilt. It's also a good idea to join an internationally affiliated automobile association (such as the AA in Britain or the AAA in the US). If you break down in Italy, phone for **ACI** (Italian Automobile Club) assistance. They will tow anyone without charge, but only members of affiliated associations get free repairs. There is also a Roman automobile club (**AC Roma**) with its own assistance centre.

Details of current road and traffic conditions (in Italian) are available from a special **Road Conditions** number. You'll find more information on driving and parking in Rome on page 375.

ROMA 69087M

Roman car number plate

Car rental offices at Fiumicino airport

DIRECTORY

BIKE AND MOPED HIRE ADDRESSES

Biciroma
Piazza del Popolo.
Map 4 F1.
Also: Piazza di Spagna.
Map 5 A2.
Also: Piazza San Lorenzo in Lucina.
Map 4 F3 & 11 E1.
Also: Piazza SS. Apostoli.
Map 5 A4.

Collalti
Via del Pellegrino 82.
Map 4 E4 & 11 C4.
☎ 68 80 10 84 *(bikes).*

St Peter Moto
Via fosse di Castello 7.
☎ 687 49 09.

Scoot-a-Long
Via Cavour 302.
Map 5 B5.
☎ 678 02 06 *(mopeds).*

Scooters for Rent
Via della Purificazione 84.
☎ 488 54 85 *(bikes and mopeds).*

TAXI BOOKING NUMBERS

Cosmos Radio Taxi
☎ 881 77.

Società la Capitale Radio Taxi
☎ 49 94.

Società Cooperativa Autoradiotaxi Roma
☎ 35 70.

CAR HIRE ADDRESSES

Avis
Ciampino airport.
☎ 79 34 01 95.
Also: Fiumicino airport.
☎ 65 01 15 79.
Also: Via Sardegna 38A.
Map 5 C1.
☎ 42 82 47 28.

Eurodollar
☎ 167 01 86 68
toll-free.

Europcar
Fiumicino airport.
☎ 65 01 08 79.

Also: Via Lombardia 7.
Map 5 B2.
☎ 487 12 74.

Hertz
Via Gregorio VII, 207.
☎ 39 37 88 07.
Also: Stazione Termini.
Map 6 D3.
☎ 474 03 89.
Also: Fiumicino.
☎ 65 01 14 48.

Maggiore
Stazione Termini.
Map 6 D3.
☎ 488 00 49.
Also: Via Po 8A. **Map** 5 C1.
☎ 854 86 98.

CAR BREAKDOWN SERVICES

ACI
Via Marsala 8.
☎ 499 81 or 4477.

ACI Breakdown
☎ 116.

AC Roma
Via Cristoforo Colombo 261. ☎ 51 49 17.

AC Roma Assistance Centre
☎ 499 81.

Autosoccorso CARA
Veientana Vetere 405.
☎ 332 01 19.
(24-hour rescue service).

Road Conditions
Via Magenta 5. **Map** 6 E3.
☎ 44 77.

MAIN CAR PARKS

Acqua Acetosa station.
Map 2 E1.
Also: Lepanto Metro station. **Map** 4 D1.
Also: Piazza del Popolo.
Map 4 F1.
Also: EUR Palasport Metro station.

USEFUL 24-HOUR PETROL STATIONS

Trastevere
Lungotevere Ripa.
Map 8 D1.

Portuense
Piazza della Radio.
Map 7 B5.

STREET FINDER

MAP REFERENCES given with sights, restaurants, hotels, shops and entertainment venues refer to the maps in this section (*see* How the Map References Work *opposite*). A complete index of the street names and places of interest marked on the maps follows on pages 382–91. The key map below shows the area of Rome covered by the *Street Finder*. This includes the sightseeing areas (which are colour-coded) as well as the whole of central Rome with all the districts important for restaurants, hotels and entertainment venues. Because the historic centre is so packed with sights, there is a large-scale map of this area on pages 11 and 12.

HOW THE MAP REFERENCES WORK

The first figure tells you which Street Finder map to turn to.

Trevi Fountain ❼

Fontana di Trevi. **Map 5 A3** & 12 F2 🚌 52, 53, 58, 60, 61, 62, 71, 95, 492 and many other routes.

The letter and number are a grid reference. You will find the letters at the top and bottom of the map and the numbers at the sides.

The second reference refers to the large-scale maps of central Rome (11 & 12). It is read in exactly the same way as the first.

The map continues on map 8 of the Street Finder.

The key to the abbreviations used in the Street Finder is on page 382.

KEY TO STREET FINDER

▨	Major sight
▨	Places of interest
▨	Railway station
Ⓜ	Metro station
🚌	Bus terminus
🚃	Tram terminus
Ⓟ	Main car parks
ℹ	Tourist information office
✚	Hospital with casualty unit
🛡	Police station
✝	Church
✡	Synagogue
⊠	Post office
=	Railway line
—	One-way street
=	Steps
▬	City wall

SCALE OF MAPS 1–10

0 metres	250	
0 yards	250	1:13,000

SCALE OF MAPS 11 & 12

0 metres	150	
0 yards	150	1:8,000

Street Finder Index

KEY TO ABBREVIATIONS USED IN THE STREET FINDER					
B.go	Borgo	**M.te**	Monte	**Reg.**	Regina
d.	di, del, dell',	**P.**	Piazza	**S.**	San, Sant', Santa
	dello, della, dei,	**P.etta**	Piazzetta	**S. M.**	Santa Maria
	delle, degli	**P.le**	Piazzale	**SS.**	Santi, Santissima
Gall.	Galleria	**Princ.**	Principe	**V.**	Via
L.go	Largo	**P.ta**	Porta	**Vic.**	Vicolo
Lungot.	Lungotevere	**P.te**	Ponte	**V.le**	Viale

A

IV Novembre, Via	5 A4
XVII Olimpiade, Viale	1 B1
XX Settembre, Via	5 B3
XXIV Maggio, Via	5 B4
Abruzzi, Via	5 C1
Acaia, Via	9 C4
Accademia d'America	7 A1
Accademia Britannica	2 D4
Accademia di	5 A3
San Luca	& 12 F2
Acerbi, Via	
Giuseppe	8 D5
Acireale, Via	10 E1
Acqua Acetosa,	
Lungot. dell'	1 C1
Acqua Acetosa,	
Piazzale dell'	2 E1
Acquasparta,	
Via degli	11 C2
Acquedotto	
Neroniano	10 D1
Acqui, Via	10 E3
Addolorata,	
Ospizio dell'	9 B2
Adelaide, Via Maria	4 E1
Adria, Via	10 F3
Adriana, Piazza	4 D3
	& 11 A1
Agnesi, Largo	
Gaetana	5 B5
Agonistica, Via dell'	2 E1
Alba, Via	10 E3
Albalonga, Via	10 D3
Albania, Piazza	8 E3
Albenga, Via	10 E3
Alberico II, Via	3 C2
Alberone,	
Piazza dell'	10 F4
Alberti, Via Leon	
Battista	8 F3
Alberto, Via Carlo	6 D4
Alcamo, Via	10 F2
Aldega, Via G.	2 F5
Aldrovandi, Via	
Ulisse	2 D5
Aleardi, Via	9 C1
Alesia, Via	9 B3
Alessandria, Piazza	6 D1
Alessandria, Via	6 D1
Alessandrina, Via	5 A4
Alessandro III, Via	3 B4
Alfieri, Via	6 D5
Algardi, Via	
Alessandro	7 A2
Alghero, Via	10 F1
Alibert, Via	5 A2
All Saints	4 F2
Allegri, Via Gregorio	2 F5
Allioni, Via Carlo	2 D3
Alpino, Via Prospero	8 F5
Altamura, Via	10 D2
Altemps, Palazzo	4 E4
	& 11 C2
Altieri, Palazzo	4 F4
	& 12 E3
Altino, Via	10 D3

Altoviti, Lungot.	4 D3
degli	& 11 A2
Alunno, Via Niccolò l'	1 A1
Amadei, Via	7 A4
Amari, Via Michele	10 E4
Amatriciani,	
Vicolo degli	11 B2
Amba Aradam,	
Via dell'	9 B2
Amendola, Via	6 D3
Amiterno, Via	9 C2
Ammannati, Via	
Bartolomeo	1 C4
Ancona, Via	6 D1
Anfiteatro Castrense	10 E1
Angelico, Borgo	3 C2
Angelico, Viale	3 C1
Anglona, Via	9 B2
Anguillara, Lungot. d.	8 D1
Anicia, Via	7 C1
Aniene, Via	6 D1
Ankara, Piazzale	1 B3
Annia, Via	9 A1
Annia Faustina, Via	8 E4
Annibaldi, Via degli	5 B5
Antiquarium Forense	5 B5
Antonelli, Via	
Giovanni	2 D3
Antonina, Via	9 A3
Antoniniana, Via	9 A4
Antoniniano, Vicolo	9 A4
Anzani, Largo	7 C3
Aosta, Via	10 E2
Apollodoro, Piazza	1 A2
Appia,	
Circonvallazione	10 D4
Appia Antica, Via	9 B5
Appia Nuova, Via	10 D2
Appio, Piazzale	10 D2
Apulia, Via	9 C3
Aquila, Via l'	10 F1
Aquiro, Via in	12 E2
Aquitania, Via	9 C3
Ara di Conso, Via	8 E2
Ara Pacis	4 F2
Ara Pacis, Via	4 F2
Aracoeli, Piazza d'	5 A5
	& 12 E4
Aracoeli, Via d'	12 E4
Aranciera, Viale dell'	2 D5
Arancio, Via dell'	4 F2
	& 12 D1
Archetto, Via dell'	12 F2
Archimede, Via	1 C3
Arcione, Via in	5 A3
Arco dei Banchi,	
Via dell'	11 A2
Arco della Ciambella,	
Via dell'	12 D3
Arco di Costantino	8 F1
Arco di Dolabella	9 A2
Arco di Druso	9 B4
Arco della Fontanella,	
Via dell'	11 A2
Arco di Gallieno	6 D4
Arco di Giano	8 E1
Arco de' Ginnasi,	
Via dell'	12 E4

Arco del Monte,	
Via dell'	11 C4
Arco della Pace,	
Via dell'	11 C2
Arco di San Callisto,	
Via dell'	7 C1
Arco di Settimio	
Severo	12 F5
Arco di Tito	8 F1
Ardea, Via	10 D2
Area Sacra	4 F4
	& 12 D4
Arenula, Largo	4 F5
	& 12 D4
Arenula, Via	4 F5
	& 12 D4
Argentina, Via	1 C1
Argilla, Via	3 A5
Ariosto, Via Ludovico	9 C1
Aristotele, Viale	3 A1
Armellini, Via	7 B2
Armenia, Piazza	10 D3
Armi, Lungot. delle	1 B5
Arminjon,	
Via Vittorio	3 B1
Arnaldo da Brescia,	
Lungot.	4 E1
Arrigo VII, Largo	8 E2
Artigiani,	
Lungot. degli	7 C4
Artisti, Via degli	5 B2
Ascanio, Via d'	12 D2
Ascianghi, Via	7 C2
Assisi, Via	10 F3
Astalli, Via degli	5 A4
	& 12 E4
Astura, Via	10 D3
Atleta, Vicolo dell'	8 D1
Auditorio di	
Mecenate	6 D5
Augusta, Lungot. in	4 E1
Augusto Imperatore,	
Piazza	4 F2
Aurelia, Via	3 A3
Aurelia Antica, Via	7 A1
Aureliana, Via	5 C2
Aurelio, Piazzale	7 A1
Aurora, Via	5 B2
Austria, Via	1 B1
Aventina, Via	8 F3
Aventino, Lungot.	8 D2
Aventino, Viale	8 E3
Avezzana, Via	
Giuseppe	1 A5
Avezzano, Via	10 F2
Avignonesi, Via degli	5 B3
Azuni, Via	
Domenico Alberto	1 B5

B

Babington's	
Tea Rooms	5 A2
Babuccio, Vicolo del	12 F2
Babuino, Via del	4 F1
continues	5 A2
Baccarini, Via	
Alfredo	10 E4

Baccelli, Viale Guido	8 F2
continues	9 A3
Baccina, Via	5 B5
Bacone, Via Ruggero	1 C3
Baglivi, Via Giorgio	6 F1
Balbo, Via Cesare	5 C4
Baldassini,	4 F3
Palazzo	& 12 D2
Baldini, Via Baccio	7 B5
Balestrari, Via dei	11 C4
Balilla, Via	6 F5
Banca d'Italia	5 B4
Banchi Nuovi,	4 D3
Via dei	& 11 A2
Banchi Vecchi,	4 D4
Via dei	& 11 A3
Banco di S. Spirito,	4 D4
Palazzo del	& 11 A2
Banco di Santo	4 D3
Spirito, Via del	& 11 A2
Barberini (Metro)	5 B2
Barberini, Palazzo	5 B3
Barberini, Piazza	5 B3
Barberini, Via	5 B3
Barbieri, Via dei	12 D4
Barchetta, Via della	11 B4
Bargoni, Via Angelo	7 B3
Barletta, Via	3 C1
Baronio, Piazza	
Cesare	10 F5
Baronio, Via Cesare	10 E5
Barrili, Via Anton	
Giulio	7 A4
Bartoli, Via Daniello	7 A4
Bartolini, Via Paolo	1 B3
Barzellotti, Via	
Giacomo	3 A1
Basilica Aemilia	5 B5
Basilica di Costantino	
e Massenzio	5 B5
Basilica Giulia	5 A5
	& 12 F5
Bassi, Via Ugo	7 B2
Bastione del	
Sangallo	9 A4
Bastioni di	
Michelangelo, Viale	3 B2
Battistero	9 C2
Battisti, Via Cesare	12 F3
Baullari, Via dei	4 E4
	& 11 C4
Beccari, Viale O.	8 F4
continues	9 A4
Beccaria, Via Cesare	4 E1
Bechi, Via Giulio	2 E2
Belgio, Via	1 B1
Belgrado, Largo	1 C3
Belgrado, Via Jacopo	7 A5
Belisario, Via	6 D1
Bellani, Via Angelo	7 B5
Belle Arti, Piazzale	
delle	1 B4
Belle Arti, Viale delle	1 B4
Belli, Piazza	
Gioacchino	8 D1
Belli, Via Gioacchino	4 D2
Bellini, Via Vincenzo	2 F4
Bellotti Bon, Via L.	2 F2

Belsiana, Via 4 F2
Beltrami, Via
  Costantino 8 F4
Belzoni, Via
  Giovanni Battista 8 F4
Benaglia, Via
  Francesco 7 B4
Benedetta, Via 11 B5
Benedetti,
  Via Giambattista 2 E3
Benedetto XIV, Via 3 A3
Benevento, Via 6 F1
Benzoni, Via
  Gerolamo 8 E5
Bergamaschi, Via dei 12 E2
Bergamo, Via 6 D1
Bering, Via 8 E5
Bernadotte, Viale
  Folke 2 D5
Bernardino da Feltre,
  Piazza 7 C2
Berni, Via Francesco 9 C1
Berniero, Via
  Giuseppe 8 E2
Bernini, Piazza Gian
  Lorenzo 8 F3
Bertani, Via Agostino 7 B1
Bertolini, Via Antonio 2 E3
Bettolo, Via Giovanni 3 B1
Bettoni, Via Nicolò 7 B4
Bezzecca, Via 6 D2
Bezzi, Via Ergisto 7 B3
Biancamano, Via
  Umberto 10 D1
Bianchi, Via
  Gustavo 8 D3
Biblioteca del
  Burcardo & 12 D4
Biblioteca
  Nazionale 6 E2
Biella, Via 10 F2
Biondo, Piazza Flavio 7 B4
Biscione, Piazza del 11 C4
Bissolati, Via Leonida 5 B2
Bitinia, Via 9 C5
Bixio, Via Nino 6 E5
Bligny, Piazza 2 F2
Bobbio, Via 10 E3
Bocca di Leone, Via 5 A2
Bocca della Verità,
  Piazza della 8 E1
Boccaccio, Via del 5 B3
Boccherini, Via Luigi 2 F4
Boccioni, Via
  Umberto 2 E2
Bodoni, Via
  Giovanni Battista 7 C3
Boezio, Via 3 C2
Boiardo, Via Matteo 9 C1
Bolivar, Piazzale
  Simone 2 D4
Bolivia, Via 1 C1
Bollette, Vicolo delle 12 F2
Bologna,
  Vicolo del & 11 B5
Bolognesi,
  Via Francesco 7 A2
Boncompagni, Via 5 B2
Bonghi, Via Ruggero 9 B1
Borghese,
  Palazzo & 12 D1
Borghese, Piazza 12 D1
Borghese, Piazzale
  Paolina 2 D5
Borghese, Via 12 D4
Borgi, Via Giovanni 12 D4
Borgo Angelico 3 C2
Borgo Pio 3 C3
Borgo Sant'Angelo 3 C3
Borgo Santo Spirito 3 C3
Borgo Vittorio 3 C3
Borgognona, Via 5 A2
  & 12 E1

Borgoncini Duca,
  Piazza Francesco 3 A5
Borsi, Via Giosuè 2 E2
Borsieri, Via Pietro 3 C1
Boschetto, Via del 5 B4
Boscovich, Via R. 2 E3
Bossi, Via
  Bartolomeo 8 E4
Botero, Via Giovanni 10 F5
Botta, Via Carlo 6 D5
Botteghe Oscure,
  Via delle & 12 D4
Bottego, Piazza
  Vittorio 8 D4
Bove, Via Giacomo 8 E5
Bovio, Via Giovanni 3 A1
Bragadin, Via
  Marcantonio 3 A2
Bramante, Via 8 F3
Branca, Via
  Giovanni 7 C3
Brancaleone, Rampa 3 A5
Braschi, Palazzo 4 E4
  & 11 C3
Bregno, Via 1 A2
Brescia, Via 6 D1
Bresciani, Via dei 11 A3
Bricci, Via Basilio 7 A2
Britannia, Via 9 C3
Brunelleschi, Via
  Filippo 1 A2
Brunetti, Via Angelo 4 F1
Bruno, Via
  Giordano 3 B1
Bruzzesi, Via
  Giacinto 7 A1
Buccari, Via 3 B1
Bufalini, Via Maurizio 6 E1
Bufalo, Via del 5 A3
  & 12 F1
Bulgaria, Via 1 C1
Buonarroti, Via
  Michelangelo 6 D5
Buozzi, Viale Bruno 1 C4
Burrò, Via de' 12 E3
Burrò, Vicolo de' 12 E2
Busiri-Vici, Via Andrea 7 A2

C

Caboto, Via 8 D5
Caccini, Via Giulio 2 F5
Cadamosto, Via
  Alvise 8 F4
Cadolini, Via 7 A1
Cadore, Via 5 B2
Caetani, Via
  Michelangelo 12 E4
Caffarelletta, Via
  della 10 E5
Caffarelli, Piazzale 12 E5
Caffè Giolitti 4 F3
  & 12 D2
Caffè Greco 5 A2
Cagliari, Via 6 E1
Caio Cestio, Via 8 D4
Caio Mario, Via 3 C1
Cairoli, Piazza
  Benedetto 12 D4
Cairoli, Via 6 E5
Calabria, Via 6 D1
Calamatta, Via 4 E2
  Via Luigi & 11 C1
Calandrelli, Via 7 A2
Calderini, Via
  Guglielmo 1 A2
Caltagirone, Via 10 E1
Cameria, Via 9 C4
Camilla, Via 10 F4
Camozzi, Via
  Gabriele 3 C1
Campana, Vicolo
  della 12 D1

Campanella, 4 D3
  Vicolo della & 11 B2
Campanella, Via
  Tommaso 3 A1
Campania, Via 5 B1
Campanile, Vicolo del 3 C3
Campi Sportivi,
  Via dei 2 E1
Campidoglio, 5 A5
  Piazza del & 12 F5
Campitelli, Piazza 12 E5
Campo Boario,
  Viale del 8 D4
Campo de' Fiori 4 E4
  & 11 C4
Campo Marzio, 4 F3
  Via di & 12 D2
Canada, Via 1 B1
Canal, Via Antonio 3 A2
Cancani, Via Adolfo 2 D4
Cancelleria, 4 E4
  Palazzo della & 11 C3
Cancelleria,
  Piazza della 11 C3
Cancellieri, Via F. 3 C2
Cancello, Via del 11 C1
Candia, Via 3 A2
Candida, Viale A. 1 C2
Canestrari, Via dei 11 C3
Canina, Via Luigi 1 B4
Canneto, Via del 2 F3
Canonica, Viale Pietro 2 D5
Canova, Via Antonio 4 F2
Cantore, Via Antonio 1 A4
Capasso,
  Via Bartolomeo 10 E5
Capitan Bavastro, Via 9 A5
Capizucchi, Piazza 12 E5
Capo d'Africa, Via 9 A1
Capo le Case, Via 5 A3
  & 12 F1
Capo di Ferro, Via 11 C4
Capocci, Via 5 C4
Capoprati, Via 1 A1
Caposile, Via 1 A4
Cappadocia, Via 10 D4
Cappella Sistina 3 B3
Cappellari, 4 E4
  Via dei & 11 B3
Cappellini,
  Via Alfredo 6 E4
Capponi,
  Piazza Amerigo 3 C2
Capponi, Via Gino 10 E4
Capranica, 4 F3
  Palazzo & 12 D2
Capranica, Piazza 12 D2
Caracciolo, Via
  Francesco 3 A2
Carcani, Via Michele 7 C2
Carcere Mamertino 5 A5
  & 12 F5
Carcere di Regina 4 D5
  Coeli & 11 A4
Carceri, Via delle 11 A3
Cardelli, Piazza 12 D1
Cardello, Via 5 B5
Cardinal Agliardi, Via 3 B4
Cardinal Consalvi,
  Piazzale 1 A1
Cardinal De Luca, Via 1 B5
Cardinal Merry di
  Val, Via 7 C1
Cardinal Silj, Via 3 A4
Carducci, Via Giosuè 5 C2
Carini, Via Giacinto 7 A2
Carissimi, Via
  Giacomo 2 E4
Carlo Emanuele I, Via 6 F5
  continues 10 D1
Carlo Felico, Viale 10 D1
Caro, Via Annibale 7 A4
Caroncini, Via Alberto 2 E2

Carracci, Piazza dei 1 A2
Carrara, Via Francesco 4 E1
Carrozze, Via delle 5 A2
Carso, Viale 1 A4
Cartari, Via dei 4 D4
  & 11 B3
Casa dei Cavalieri
  di Rodi 5 B5
Casa dei Crescenzi 8 E1
Casa della 4 D5
  Fornarina & 11 B5
Casa di Goethe 4 F1
Casa di Livia 8 E1
Casa di Lorenzo 4 F5
  Manilio & 12 D5
Casa di Romolo 8 E1
Casa delle Vestali 5 B5
Casalmonferrato, Via 10 E3
Caselli, Via Giovanni 7 A5
Caselli, Via Paulo 8 D4
Caserta, Via 6 F1
Casilina, Via 10 E1
Casilina Vecchia, Via 10 F1
Casini, Via Filippo 7 B2
Casino dell'Aurora 5 B2
Casoria, Via 10 E2
Cassini, Via D. 2 E3
Cassiodoro, Via 4 D2
Castaldi, Via Panfilo 7 B4
Castel Sant'Angelo 4 D3
  & 11 A1
Castelfidardo, Via 6 D2
Castelgomberto, Via 1 A4
Castellini, Via
  Gualtiero 2 E3
Castello, Lungot. 4 D3
  & 11 A1
Castore e Polluce 5 B4
Castrense, Viale 10 D2
Castro Pretorio (Metro) 6 E2
Castro Pretorio, Via 6 E3
Castro Pretorio, Viale 6 E2
Castrovillari, Via 10 F2
Catacombe di
  San Panfilo 2 F4
Catalana, Via 4 F5
  & 12 D5
Caterina, Via in 11 B4
Catone, Via 3 C2
Cattaneo, Via Carlo 6 D4
Catullo, Via 4 D2
Caudini, Via dei 6 F3
Caulonia, Via 10 D4
Cava Aurelia,
  Via della 3 A4
Cavalcanti, Via Guido 7 A4
Cavalieri di Malta,
  Piazza dei 8 D2
Cavalli Marini, Viale d. 2 E5
  continues 5 B1
Cavallini, Via Pietro 4 E2
Cavallotti, Via Felice 7 A4
Cave Ardeatine,
  Viale delle 8 E4
Caverni, Via 3 A1
Cavour (Metro) 5 C4
Cavour, Piazza 4 E2
  & 11 B1
Cavour, Via 5 B5
Ceccarelli, Via Ugo 2 E1
Cecchi, Via Antonio 8 D2
Cedro, Vicolo del 7 B1
Cefalo, Vicolo del 11 A3
Celentano, Via
  Bernardo 1 B3
Celimontana, Piazza 9 A1
Celimontana, Via 9 A1
Celio, Parco del 9 A1
Celio, Viale del
  Parco del 9 A1
Celio Vibenna, Via 9 A1
Cellini, Vicolo 11 B3
Celsa, Via 12 E4

Celso, Via Cornelio 6 F1
Cenci, Lungot. dei 4 F5
& 12 D5
Cenci, Palazzo 4 F5
& 12 D5
Cenci, Piazza 12 D5
Cenci, Via Beatrice 12 D5
Ceneda, Via 10 D3
Centuripe, Via 10 D5
Ceracchi, Via
Giuseppe 1 B3
Cerchi, Via dei 8 E1
Cereate, Via 9 C3
Ceriani, Via Antonio 3 A5
Cernaia, Via 5 C3
Cerreto Sannita, Via 10 E2
Cerri, Via 11 B3
Cerveteri, Via 10 D3
Cesalpino, Via Andrea 6 F1
Cesari, Via Antonio 7 A4
Cesena, Via 10 D2
Cesi, Via Federico 4 E2
Cestari, Via dei 4 F4
& 12 D3
Chelini, Via
Domenico 2 D2
Chiari, Via 10 F3
Chiarini, Largo
Giovanni 8 F4
Chiavari, Via dei 4 E4
& 11 C4
Chiesa Nuova 4 E4
& 11 B3
Chiesa Nuova,
Piazza della 11 B3
Chiesa Nuova,
Via della 11 B3
Chigi, Largo 5 A3
Chigi, Palazzo 5 A3
& 12 E2
Chinotto, Via A. 1 A4
Chiodaroli,
Vicolo dei 12 D4
Ciacconio, Via A. 8 E2
Cialdini, Via Enrico 6 E4
Ciancaleoni, Via de' 5 C4
Cibrario, Via Luigi 10 E5
Cicerone, Via 4 D2
Cilicia, Via 9 B5
Cimarosa, Via
Domenico 2 F4
Cimarra, Via 5 B4
Cimatori, Via dei 11 A3
Cimitero Protestante 8 D4
Cino da Pistoia, Via 7 A4
Cinque, Vicolo
del 4 E5
& 11 B5
Cinque Giornate,
Piazza delle 1 B5
Cinque Lune,
Piazza delle 11 C2
Cinque Scole,
Piazza delle 12 D5
Cinquecento,
Piazza dei 6 D3
Cipro, Via 3 A2
Circo Massimo 8 F2
Circo Massimo
(Metro) 8 F2
Circo Massimo,
Parco del 8 F2
Circo Massimo,
Via del 8 E1
Circonvallazione
Appia 10 D4
Circonvallazione
Gianicolense 7 A5
Cirillo, Via Domenico 2 D4
Cisterna, Via d. 7 C1
Citerni, Via Carlo 9 A5
Città Universitaria 6 F3
Cividale del Friuli,
Via 10 E3

Civinini, Via Filippo 2 D3
Claterna, Via 9 C3
Claudia, Via 9 A1
Clementi, Via Muzio 4 E2
Clementina, Via 5 C4
Clementino,
Via di 4 F3
& 12 D1
Col di Lana, Via 1 A5
Cola di Rienzo,
Piazza 4 D2
Cola di Rienzo, Via 3 C2
Colautti, Via Arturo 7 A3
Collazia, Via 9 C3
Collegio Capranica,
Via del 12 D2
Collegio di
Propaganda Fide & 12 F1
Collegio Romano, 5 A4
Palazzo del & 12 E3
Collegio Romano, 5 A4
Piazza del & 12 E3
Collegio Romano,
Via del 12 E3
Colletta, Via Pietro 10 E5
Collina, Via 6 D2
Colombario di
Pomponio Hylas 9 B4
Colombo, Via
Cristoforo 9 A5
Colonna, Piazza 5 A3
& 12 E2
Colonna, Palazzo 5 A4
& 12 F3
Colonna, Via
Marcantonio 4 D1
Colonna, Via Vittoria 4 E2
Colonna Antonina,
Via della 12 E2
Colonna di Foca 5 A5
Colonna
dell'Immacolata 5 A2
Colonna di Marco
Aurelio 12 E2
Colonna Traiana 5 A4
& 12 F4
Colonnelle,
Via delle 12 D2
Colosseo 5 C5
continues 9 A1
Colosseo (Metro) 5 C5
Colosseo, Piazza del 5 C5
continues 9 A1
Colosseo, Via del 5 B5
Commendatore,
Palazzo del 3 C3
Commercio, Via del 8 D5
Conca, Via
Sebastiano 1 B3
Conce, Via delle 8 D4
Conciatori, Via dei 8 D4
Conciliazione,
Via della 3 C3
Concordia, Via 10 D3
Condotti, Via 5 A2
Confalonieri, Via
Federico 1 A5
Confienza, Piazza 6 F3
Conservatori,
Palazzo dei 5 A5
& 12 F5
Conservatorio,
Via del 11 C5
Consolato, Via del 11 A2
Consolazione,
Via della 5 A5
& 12 F5
Consulta, Via della 5 B4
Contarini, Via
Ambrogio 8 F4
Conte Verde, Via 6 E5
Convertendi,
Palazzo dei 3 C3
Convertite, Via delle 12 E1
Coppelle, Piazza
delle 12 D2

Coppelle, Via delle 12 D2
Coppi, Via Antonio 10 E5
Corallo, Via del 11 B3
Corda, Via della 11 C4
Cordonata 12 F5
Corelli, Via Arcangelo 2 F5
Corio, Via B. 10 E5
Cornaro, Via F. 7 A4
Coronari, Via dei 4 D3
& 11 B2
Corpus Domini 6 E1
Correggio,
Via Antonio da 1 B3
Correnti, Via Cesare 10 E5
Corridori, Via dei 3 C3
Corsi, Via dei 6 F4
Corsini, Palazzo 4 D5
& 11 A5
Corsini, Via 4 D5
& 11 A5
Corso, Via del 4 F1
& 12 E1
continues 5 A3
Cortona, Via
Pietro da 1 B3
Cossa, Via Pietro 4 E2
Cosseria, Via 4 D1
Costabella, Via 1 A4
Costaguti, Piazza 12 D5
Costanzi, Via Guido 7 C5
Cottolengo, Via del 3 A4
Crema, Via 10 F2
Crescenzi, Salita de 12 D3
Crescenzio, Via 3 C2
Crescimbeni, Via
Giovanni Mario 9 B1
Criptoportico 8 F1
Crispi, Via Francesco 5 B3
Croce, Via della 4 F2
continues 5 A2
Croce Rosa, Piazza
della 6 E1
Crociferi, Via dei 12 F2
Crocifisso, Via del 3 B4
Crotone, Via 10 F2
Cuboni, Via Giuseppe 2 D4
Cucchi, Piazza
Francesco 7 A2
Cuma, Via 10 D2
Cunfida, Via 3 B1
Curia 5 B5
Curia, Via della 5 A5
Curtatone, Via 6 D2
Cutilia, Via 10 D3

D

Da Ponte, Via Jacopo 1 C4
Dacia, Via 10 D3
Daini, Piazzale dei 2 F5
Dalla Chiesa,
Via Carlo Alberto 3 C1
Dall'Ongaro,
Via Francesco 7 B3
Damiata, Via 4 D1
Dandini, Via
Girolamo 8 F4
Dandolo, Via 7 B2
Danimarca, Via 1 C1
D'Annunzio, Viale
Gabriele 4 F1
Dante, Piazza 6 E5
D'Arezzo, Via Guido 2 F4
D'Arpino, Via Cavalier 1 C3
Dataria, Via della 5 A3
& 12 F2
Dauni, Via dei 6 F3
Daverio, Via
Francesco 7 A2
D'Azeglio, Via
Massimo 6 D3
De Cesare,
Via Raffaele 10 F5

De Coubertin, Via
Pietro 1 B2
De Coubertin, Viale
Pietro 1 B2
De Gasperi, Via Alcide 3 B4
De Mattias,
Via Beata Maria 9 B3
De Nicola, Viale Enrico 6 D3
De Notaris, Via
Giuseppe 2 D4
De Sanctis, Via
Francesco 3 C1
De Saint Bon,
Via Simone 3 B1
Decennia, Via 9 B2
Decii, Via dei 8 E3
Degli Effetti,
Via Antonio 10 E4
Del Grande,
Via Natale 7 C1
Della Valle, Via Pietro 4 D2
Delfini, Via dei 12 E5
Della Porta, Via G. 8 F3
Denina, Via Carlo 10 F5
Denza,
Via Francesco 2 D2
Depretis, Via Agostino 5 C3
Dezza, Via Giuseppe 7 A2
Di Lauria, Via Ruggero 3 A2
Digione, Piazza 2 E2
Dionigi,
Via Marianna 4 E2
Divino Amore,
Vicolo del 12 D1
Dogana Vecchia,
Via della 12 D3
Dolci, Via Carlo 1 B3
Domodossola, Via 10 D3
Domus Augustana 8 F1
Domus Aurea 5 C5
Domus Aurea, Viale 5 C5
Domus Flavia 8 F1
Don Orione, Via 10 E3
Donatello, Via 1 A3
Donizetti, Via Gaetano 2 F5
Donna Olimpia, Via di 7 A4
Dorando Pietri, Via 1 B2
Doria, Via Andrea 3 A1
Doria Pamphilj,
Palazzo & 12 E3
Drusiana, Via 9 B2
Druso, Via 9 A3
Due Macelli, Via 5 A2
& 12 F1
Due Piramidi,
Viale delle 2 E5
Duilio, Via 4 D1
Dunant, Piazzale
Enrico 7 A5
Duse, Via Eleonora 2 F2

E

Ederle, Via Carlo 1 A4
Egerio, Parco 9 A3
Einaudi, Viale 6 D3
Elea, Via 9 C3
Eleniana, Via 10 E1
Elia, Via Enrico 2 D1
Elvezia, Largo 2 D3
Emanuele Filiberto, V. 6 E5
continues 9 C1
Emilia, Via 5 B2
Emo, Via Angelo 3 A2
Emporio, Piazza dell' 8 D2
Enna, Via 10 F2
Epiro, Piazza 9 C3
Equi, Via degli 6 F4
Eraclea, Via 10 D5
Eroi, Piazzale degli 3 A1
Esculapio, Viale 2 D5
Esposizioni, Palazzo
delle 5 B4

Esquilino, Piazza dell' 6 D4
Esquilino, Via dell' 6 D4
Etruria, Via 10 D3
Euclide, Piazza 2 D2
Eudosiana, Via 5 C5
Eufemiano, Via 8 E2
Eurialo, Via 10 F4
Eustacchio, Via
  Bartolomeo 6 F1
Ezio, Via 4 D1

F

Fabbri, Via Edoardo 1 A5
Fabio Numerio, Via 10 F3
Fabrizi, Viale Aldo 3 C5
  continues 7 A1
Fabrizi, Viale Nicola 7 B2
Faenza, Via 10 D2
Fagarè, Via 1 A4
Falco, Via del 3 C2
Falegnami, Via dei 12 D4
Faleria, Via 10 D2
Falisci, Via dei 6 F4
Famagosta, Via 3 B1
Fante, Piazza del 1 A4
FAO 8 F2
Farini, Via 6 D4
Farinone, Vicolo 3 C3
Farnese, Palazzo 4 E5
  & 11 B4
Farnese, Piazza 4 E5
  & 11 C4
Farnese, Via
  Alessandro 4 D1
Farnesi, Via dei 4 E5
  & 11 B4
Farnesina, 4 D5
  Lungot. della & 11 A4
Faro della Vittoria 3 C5
Farsalo, Via 9 C2
Fauro, Via Ruggero 2 E2
Febo, Largo 11 C2
Fedele, Via Pietro 10 E5
Fedro, Via 3 A1
Ferento, Via 10 D3
Fermo, Via 10 F2
Ferrari, Via
  Giuseppe 1 A5
Ferraris, Via Galileo 7 C3
Ferratella in Laterano,
  Via della 9 B2
Ferruccio, Via 6 D5
Fico, Vicolo del 11 B2
Fidenza, Via 10 D2
Fienaroli, Via dei 7 C1
Fienili, Via dei 8 E1
Filangeri, Via Gaetano 1 B5
Filippini, Via dei 11 B3
Finali, Via G. 10 E4
Finlandia, Via 1 C1
Finocchiaro Aprile,
  Piazza 10 F4
Finzi, Via G. 7 C2
Fiocco, Palazzo del 2 D5
Fiore, Via Ruggero 3 A2
Fiorentini, 4 D4
  Lungot. dei & 11 A3
Fiorini, Via Vittorio 10 D4
Fioritto, Largo Enzo 8 F3
Firdusi, Piazzale 2 D5
Firenze, Piazza 12 D1
Firenze, Via 5 C3
Fiume, Piazza 6 D1
Flaminia, Via 1 A2
  continues 4 F1
Flaminio (Metro) 4 F1
Flaminio, Lungot. 1 A3
Flaminio, Piazzale 4 F1
Flaminio, Stadio 1 B2
Flavia, Via 5 C2
Florentini, Largo dei 11 A3
Florida, Via 12 D4

Florio, Via 7 C3
Foligno, Via 10 E2
Fontana, Via
  Domenico 9 C1
Fontana delle Api 5 B1
Fontana del Facchino 12 E3
Fontana dei Fiumi 4 E4
  & 11 C3
Fontana del Mosè 5 C2
Fontana Paola 7 B1
Fontana delle 4 F5
  Tartarughe & 12 D4
Fontana di Trevi 5 A3
  & 12 F2
Fontana del Tritone 5 B3
Fontanella, Via della 4 F1
Fontanella Borghese, 4 F3
  Via della & 12 D1
Fonte Acqua
  Acetosa, Via della 2 D2
Fonte del Fauno,
  Via della 8 E2
Food and Agricultural
  Organization of the
  United Nations 8 F2
Foraggi, Via dei 5 A5
  & 12 F5
Fori Imperiali, 5 A5
  Via dei & 12 F4
Fornaci, Via delle 3 B4
  continues 7 A1
Fornari, Via dei 12 F3
Fornetto, Via del 7 A5
Fornovo, Via 4 D1
Foro di Augusto 5 B5
Foro di Cesare 5 A5
  & 12 F4
Foro di Nerva 5 B5
Foro Piscario,
  Via del 12 E5
Foro Romano 5 A5
  & 12 F5
Foro Romano,
  Via del 12 F5
Foro di Traiano 12 F4
Fortifiocca, Via
  Tommaso 10 F5
Fortis, Via Alberto 1 C3
Fortuny, Via Mariano 1 C5
Foscolo, Via 6 E5
Fossa, Via della 11 C3
Fra' Albenzio, Via 3 A2
Fracastoro, Via
  Gerolamo 6 F1
Fracassini, Via Cesare 1 B3
Francia, Corso di 1 B1
Frangipane, Via 5 B5
Franklin, Via
  Beniamino 7 C3
Fratelli Bandiera, Via 7 B3
Fratelli Bonnet, Via 7 A2
Fratte di Trastevere,
  Via delle 7 C1
Frattina, Via 5 A2
  & 12 E1
Fregene, Via 10 D2
Frentani, Via dei 6 F3
Frescobaldi, Via
  Gerolamo 2 F4
Frezza, Via della 4 F2
Frisi, Via Paolo 2 D2
Frusta, Vicolo della 7 B1
Funari, Via dei 12 E5
Furio Camillo (Metro) 10 F4
Furio Camillo, Viale 10 F4

G

Gabi, Via 10 D2
Gaddi, Palazzo 4 D3
  & 11 A2
Gaeta, Via 6 D2

Gai, Via Francesco 1 A1
Galazia, Via 9 C4
Galeno, Piazza 6 F1
Galeria, Piazza 9 C4
Galileo Galilei, Via 9 C1
Gallarate, Via 10 F1
Galleria Nazionale
  d'Arte Antica 11 A5
Galleria Nazionale
  d'Arte Moderna, 2 D5
Gallia, Via 9 B2
Gallipoli, Via 10 E3
Gallo, Vicolo di 11 C4
Gallupi, Via Pasquale 3 A1
Galoppatoio 5 A1
Galoppatoio, Viale del 5 A1
Galvani, Via 8 D4
Gambero, Via del 5 A3
  & 12 E1
Garibaldi, Piazzale
  Giuseppe 3 C5
Garibaldi, Via 4 D5
  Giuseppe & 11 B5
  continues 7 A1
Gastaldi, Piazza
  Bartolomeo 2 D3
Gatta, Via della 5 A4
  & 12 E3
Gaudini, Via Giulio 1 C2
Gavinana, Via 4 D1
Gazometro,
  Piazza del 8 E5
Gazometro, Via del 8 D5
Gela, Via 10 F3
Gelsomini,
  Largo Manlio 8 D3
Gelsomini, Viale
  Manlio 8 E3
Gelsomino, Via del 3 A4
Gelsomino,
  Vicolo del 3 A5
Generale Gonzaga
  del Vodice, Largo 1 A4
Genova, Via 5 B3
Genovesi, Via dei 8 D1
Gerace, Via 10 E2
Germania, Via 1 B1
Germanico, Via 3 B2
Gessi, Via Romolo 8 D3
Gesù, Il 4 F4
  & 12 E4
Gesù, Piazza del 12 E4
Gesù, Via del 4 F4
  & 12 E3
Gesù e Maria,
  Via di 4 F2
Ghiberti, Via Lorenzo 8 D3
Ghirlandaio, Via 1 B3
Gianicolense,
  Circonvallazione 7 A5
Gianicolense, 4 D4
  Lungot. & 11 A3
Gianicolo 3 C5
Gianicolo, Via del 3 C4
Giannone, Via Pietro 3 A1
Gianturco, Via 1 B5
Giardini, Via dei 5 B3
Giardini del
  Quirinale 5 B3
Giardino Zoologico 2 E4
Giardino Zoologico,
  Piazzale del 2 E5
Giardino Zoologico,
  Viale del 2 D5
Gigli, Piazza
  Beniamino 5 C3
Gigli d'Oro, Via dei 11 C2
Ginori, Via 8 D3
Gioberti, Via 6 D4
Gioia, Via Flavio 7 C3
Giolitti, Via Giovanni 6 D3
Giordano, Via Felice 2 E3
Giotto, Viale 8 E4

Giovagnoli, Via
  Raffaello 7 A3
Giovannelli, Via
  Ruggero 2 F5
Giovanni da
  Castelbolognese, Via 7 C5
Giovanni da
  Empoli, Via 8 D4
Giovio, Via Paolo 10 E5
Giraud, Via
  Giovanni 11 A3
Giubbonari, 4 E5
  Via dei & 11 C4
Giulia, Via 4 D4
  & 11 C4
Giuliana, Via della 3 B1
Giulietti, Via 8 D4
Giulio Cesare, Viale 3 B1
Giusti, Via 6 D5
Giustiniani, Piazza
  Orazio 7 C4
Giustiniani, Via 12 D2
Giustizia, 4 E3
  Palazzo di & 11 B1
Glorioso, Viale 7 B2
Gobetti, Viale Pietro 6 F3
Goethe, Viale 5 B1
Goito, Via 6 D2
Goldoni, Largo Carlo 12 E1
Gonfalone, Via del 11 A3
Governo Vecchio,
  Palazzo del & 11 B3
Governo Vecchio, 4 E4
  Via del & 11 B3
Governo Vecchio,
  Vicolo del 11 B3
Gracchi, Via dei 3 C2
Gramsci, Via Antonio 1 C3
Gran Bretagna, Via 1 C1
Grandi, Via 6 F5
Grattoni, Via 10 D1
Gravina, Via
  Giovanni Vincenzo 1 B5
Grazie, Via 3 C2
Grazioli, Piazza 12 E3
Grazioli Lante, Via
  Riccardo 3 B1
Greca, Via della 8 E1
Greci, Via dei 4 F2
Grecia, Piazzale 1 C1
Gregoriana, Via 5 A2
  & 12 F1
Gregorio VII, Via 3 A5
Gregorovius, Largo 10 D5
Gregorovius, Via 10 D5
Grosseto, Via 10 F1
Grotta Pinta, Via di 11 C4
Grotte, Vicolo delle 11 C4
Guardiola,
  Vicolo della 12 D2
Guastalla, Via 7 A2
Guerrazzi, Via
  Francesco Domenico 7 A3
Guerrieri, Via 8 F3
Guglia, Via della 12 E2
Guidobaldo dal
  Monte, Via 1 C2
Guinizelli, Via Guido 7 A4

H

Hostaria dell'Orso 4 E3
  & 11 C2

I

Iberia, Via 9 C3
Icilio, Via 8 E3
Iglesias, Via 10 F2
Illira, Via 9 C2
Imera, Via 10 D4
Imperia, Via 6 F1
Impresa, Via dell' 12 E1

India, Via	1 C1
Indipendenza, Piazza	6 D2
Induno, Via	
Girolamo	7 C2
Inghirami, Via G.	2 D2
Innocenzo III, Via	3 B4
Insula Romana	12 F4
Ipponio, Viale	9 B2
Irlanda, Via	1 B1
Isernia, Via	10 E2
Iside, Via	9 B1
Isola Tiberina	4 F5
	& 12 D4
continues	8 D1
Isonzo, Via	5 C1
Israele, Via	1 C1
Italia, Corso d'	5 B1
Ivrea, Via	10 E4

J

Jacometti, Largo I.	1 A1
Jugoslavia, Via	1 C1

K

Kircher, Via A.	2 E3

L

La Farina, Via	
Giuseppe	10 E4
La Goletta, Via	3 B2
La Guardia, Viale	
Fiorello	2 D5
Labicana, Via	9 A1
Labriola, Via	
Antonio	3 A1
Lago Terrione,	
Via del	3 B5
Lagrange, Via	2 E3
Lamarmora, Via	6 E5
Lancelotti, Via	11 B2
Lancisi, Via	
Giovanni Maria	6 F1
Lanza, Via Giovanni	5 C5
Larga, Via	11 B3
Lata, Via	12 E3
Laterani, Via dei	9 C2
Laterano, Palazzo	9 C1
Latina, Via	10 D4
Latini, Via dei	6 F4
Laurina, Via	4 F1
Lavatore, Via del	5 A3
	& 12 F2
Lavinio, Via	10 D2
Lazio, Via	5 B1
Lazzerini, Largo	
Carlo	8 F3
Leccosa, Via	12 D1
Leducq, Via Adolfo	7 B2
Leoncino, Via del	4 F3
	& 12 D1
Leone, Via del	4 F3
	& 12 D1
Leone IV, Via	3 B1
Leone IX, Via	3 A4
Leonetto, Vicolo del	11 C1
Leonina, Via	5 B5
Leopardi, Largo	6 D5
Leopardi, Via	6 D4
Lepanto (Metro)	4 D1
Lepanto, Via	4 D1
Leto, Via Pomponio	3 C2
Leutari, Via dei	11 C3
Liberiana, Via	6 D4
Libertà, Piazza della	4 E1
Librari, Largo dei	11 C4
Liburni, Via dei	6 F3
Licia, Via	9 C3
Licinia, Via	8 E2
Lidia, Via	10 D4
Liegi, Viale	2 F3

Ligorio, Via Pirro	8 F3
Liguria, Via	5 B2
Lima, Via	2 F3
Linneo, Via Carlo	2 D4
Lippi, Via Filippo	1 C3
Lisbona, Via	2 F3
Lituania, Piazza	2 F3
Livenza, Via	2 F5
Locchi, Via Vittorio	2 E3
Locri, Via	9 C2
Lodi, Piazza	10 F1
Lombardi,	
Largo dei	4 F2
Lombardia, Via	5 B2
Longhi, Via Martino	1 A1
Lorenesi, Via dei	11 C2
Lubin, Viale David	1 C5
Luca della Robbia,	
Via	8 D3
Lucania, Via	5 C1
Lucchesi, Via di	5 A3
	& 12 F2
Luce, Via della	7 C2
Luceri, Via dei	6 F4
Luciani, Via Luigi	2 D4
Lucina, Via in	12 E1
Lucio Fabio	
Cilone, Via	9 A4
Lucrezio Caro, Via	4 E2
Lucullo, Via	5 C2
Ludovico di	
Savoia, Via	10 D1
Ludovisi, Via	5 B2
Lugo, Piazza	10 F2
Lungara, Via	4 D4
della	& 11 A4
Lungaretta,	
Via della	7 C1
Luni, Via	9 C3
Lupa, Via della	12 D1
Lupo, Vicolo del	4 F2
Lusitania, Via	9 C4
Lutezia, Via	2 F4
Luzio, Via	
Alessandro	10 E5
Luzzatti, Via Luigi	6 F5

M

Macao, Via	6 D2
Macedonia, Via	10 D4
Machiavelli, Via	6 D5
Madama, Palazzo	4 F4
	& 12 D3
Madama	
Letizia, Viale	2 D5
Maddalena, La	4 F3
	& 12 D2
Maddalena, Via	
della	12 D2
Maderno, Via	8 E4
Madonna dei Monti,	
Via della	5 B5
Madonna	
dell'Orto, Via	8 D1
Magalotti, Via	2 E3
Magazzini Generali,	
Via dei	8 D5
Magenta, Via	6 D3
Magna Grecia, Via	10 D2
Magnani, Via Anna	2 F1
Magnolie,	
Viale delle	5 A1
Maioli, Via Cesare	2 D3
Majorana, Via	
Quirino	7 A5
Malpasso, Vicolo del	11 B3
Malpighi, Via	
Marcello	6 E1
Mameli, Via	
Goffredo	7 B1
Mamiani, Via	6 E4
Manara, Via Luciano	7 B1

Mancini, Piazza	
Antonio	1 A1
Mancini, Via Pasquale	
Stanislao	1 B5
Mancino, Via del	12 F3
Mandorlo, Piazzale	
del	2 D1
Manfredi, Via	
Eustachio	2 D3
Mangili, Via	
Giuseppe	2 D4
Manila, Piazzale	1 B3
Manin, Via Daniele	6 D3
Manno, Via	10 E4
Mantegazza, Via	
Laura	7 A5
Mantellate, Via	4 D4
delle	& 11 A4
Mantellini, Via	
Giuseppe	10 E4
Mantova, Via	6 D1
Manunzio, Via Aldo	8 D3
Manzoni (Metro)	9 C1
Manzoni, Viale	6 E5
continues	9 C1
Maratta, Via	8 E4
Marazzi, Via	
Fortunato	1 A4
Marcella, Via	8 E2
Marche, Via	5 B1
Marco Aurelio, Via	9 A1
Marcora, Via	7 C3
Margana, Piazza	12 E4
Margana, Via	12 E4
Margana, Vicolo	12 E4
Marghera, Via	6 E3
Margherita, Palazzo	5 B1
Margutta, Via	4 F1
continues	5 A2
Maria Cristina, Via	4 E1
Marina, Piazza della	1 B5
Marini, Via Luigi	
Gaetano	10 E5
Marino, Via	
Giambattista	7 B4
Mario, Via Alberto	7 A3
Mario de' Fiori,	4 F1
Via	& 12 F1
Mario Riva, Parco	2 F1
Marmorata, Via	8 D2
Maroniti, Via dei	5 A3
Marrucini, Via dei	6 F3
Marruvio, Via	9 C2
Marsala, Via	6 D3
Martelli, Via Nicola	1 C3
Martini, Via	
Giovanni Battista	2 F4
Marzi, Largo	
Giovanni Battista	7 C4
Marzio, Lungot.	4 E3
	& 11 C1
Masaccio, Via	1 A2
Maschera d'Oro,	
Via della	11 B2
Mascherino, Via del	3 C2
Mascherone,	4 E5
Via del	& 11 B4
Masina, Via	
Angelo	7 A1
Massi, Via	
Francesco	7 A4
Massimo, Via Fabio	3 C1
Massimo alle	4 F4
Colonne, Palazzo	& 11 C3
Mastai, Piazza	7 C1
Mastro, Via del	11 B2
Mastro Giorgio, Via	8 D3
Matera, Via	10 E2
Mattei, Piazza	12 D4
Matteucci,	
Via Pellegrino	8 E5
Mattonato, Via del	7 B1
Mauritania, Via	9 C3

Mausoleo di Augusto	4 F2
Mazzarino, Via	5 B4
Mazzini, Piazza	
Giuseppe	1 A5
Mazzini, Viale	
Giuseppe	1 A5
Mecenate, Via	6 D5
Medaglie d'Oro,	
Viale delle	3 A1
Medici, Via Giacomo	7 A1
Melfi, Via	10 F2
Mellini, Lungot. dei	4 E1
Melone, Via del	12 D3
Meloria, Via della	3 A2
Melozzo da Forlì,	
Piazza	1 A3
Menabrea, Via	
Federico	10 D1
Menotti, Via Ciro	1 A5
Mentana, Via	6 E2
Mercadante, Via	
Saverio	2 E4
Mercalli, Via	
Giuseppe	2 D3
Mercanti, Piazza de'	8 D1
Mercantini, Via Luigi	7 A1
Mercati, Via Michele	2 D4
Mercati Traianei	5 B4
Mercede, Via	5 A3
della	& 12 F1
Mercuri, Via	4 E2
Merulana, Via	6 D4
continues	9 C1
Mesopotamia, Via	10 D5
Messina, Via	6 D1
Mestre, Via	10 F3
Metaponto, Via	9 C3
Metastasio, Via	12 D2
Metronio, Piazzale	9 B2
Metronio, Viale	9 B3
Miani, Via Giovanni	8 F4
Micca, Via Pietro	6 F5
Michelangelo, Lungot.	4 E1
Micheli, Via Pietro	
Antonio	2 D3
Mignanelli, Piazza	5 A2
Milano, Via	5 C4
Milazzo, Via	6 E3
Milizie, Viale delle	1 A5
continues	3 B1
Mille, Via dei	6 E3
Milvio, Ponte	1 A1
Minerva, Piazza della	12 D3
Minerva, Via della	12 D3
Minghetti, Via	5 A3
	& 12 E2
Ministeri del Bilancio	
e del Tesoro	6 D2
Ministero dell'	
Agricoltura e delle	
Foreste	5 C2
Ministero della Difesa	
Aeronautica	6 F3
Ministero della	
Difesa Esercito	5 C3
Ministero dei Lavori	
Pubblici	6 E1
Ministero della	
Pubblica Istruzione	7 C2
Ministero dei	
Trasporti	6 E1
Minzoni, Piazzale	
Don Giovanni	2 D4
Mirandola, Via	10 F2
Missione, Via della	12 E2
Missori, Via	
Giuseppe	3 C5
Mistretta, Via	10 F1
Mocenigo, Via	3 A1
Modelli, Vicolo dei	12 F2
Modena, Via	5 C3
Modica, Via	10 F3
Moletta, Via della	8 E5

Entry	Ref
Molise, Via	5 B2
Mompiani, Via	3 C1
Mondaini, Via Gennaro	10 F5
Mondovi, Via	10 E3
Monselice, Via	10 F3
Monserrato, Via	4 D4 & 11 B3
Montanara, Via	12 E5
Montanelli, Via Giuseppe	1 A5
Monte, Via del	7 B4
Monte Brianzo, Via di	4 E3 & 11 C1
Monte dei Cenci, Via	12 D5
Monte della Farina, Via del	4 F4 & 12 D4
Monte del Gallo, Clivo	3 B4
Monte del Gallo, Via del	3 A4
Monte del Gallo, Vicolo del	3 B4 & 12 F3
Monte Giordano, Via di	4 D1 & 11 B2
Monte Grappa, Piazza	1 A4
Monte Oppio, Viale del	5 C5
Monte d'Oro, Via	12 D1
Monte di Pietà, Palazzo del	4 E5 & 11 C4
Monte Tarpeo, Via di	12 F5
Monte Testaccio,	8 D4
Monte Testaccio, Via	8 D4
Monte Zebio, Via	1 A4
Montebello, Via	6 D2
Montecatini, Via	12 E2
Montecchi, Via	7 B3
Montecitorio, Palazzo di	4 F3 & 12 E2
Montecitorio, Piazza di	4 F3 & 12 E2
Montepulciano, Via	10 F2
Monterone, Via	12 D3
Montevecchio, Vicolo	11 C2
Monteverde, Via di	7 A5
Monteverdi, Via Claudio	2 F4
Montevideo, Via	2 F3
Monti, Via Vincenzo	7 A4
Monti Parioli, Via dei	1 C3
Monticelli, Via Teodoro	2 D3
Monticello, Vicolo del	12 F2
Montoro, Via di	11 B4
Monumento a Anita Garibaldi	3 C5
Monumento a Giuseppe Garibaldi	3 C5
Monza, Via	10 E2
Monzambano, Via	6 E3
Mordini, Via Antonio	1 A5
Morelli, Via Alamanno	2 F2
Moretta, Vicolo della	11 B3
Moretto, Via del	12 F1
Morgagni, Via Giovanni Battista	6 F1
Morin, Via Constantino	3 B1
Moro, Piazzale Aldo	3 C5
Moro, Via del	7 C1
Moroni, Vicolo	11 B5
Morosini, Via Emilio	7 C2
Mortana, Via	10 E3
Mortaro, Via del	12 F2
Moschea, Viale della	2 D1
Mura Aurelie, Viale delle	3 C4 / 7 A1
Mura Gianicolensi, Viale delle	7 A1
Mura Latine, Via delle	9 B4
Mura Portuensi, Via delle	7 C2
Mura Vaticane, Clivo delle	3 A3
Muratori, Via Ludovico	9 B1
Muratte, Via della	5 A3 & 12 E2
Muro Torto, Viale del	4 F1
continues	5 A1
Musa, Via Antonio	6 F1
Muse, Piazza delle	2 E2
Musei del Vaticano	3 B2
Museo Borghese	2 F5
Museo Borghese, Viale del	5 B1
Museo delle Cere	5 A4 & 12 E2
Museo del Folklore	7 C1
Museo Keats-Shelley	5 A2
Museo Napoleonico	4 E3 & 11 C1
Museo Nazionale d'Arte Orientale	6 D5
Museo Nazionale Romano	6 D2
Museo degli Strumenti Musicali	10 E1
Musolino, Via Benedetto	7 C3
Mutilati e Invalidi di Guerra, Largo	11 B1
Muziano, Via G.	1 A3
N	
Nadi, Via Nedo	1 B2
Nansen, Via F.	8 E5
Napoleone III, Via	6 D4
Napoli, Via	5 C3
Navi, Lungot. delle	1 B5
Navicella, Via della	9 A2
Navona, Piazza	4 E3 & 11 C3
Nazareno, Via del	12 F1
Nazionale, Via	5 B4
Negri, Via Francesco	8 E5
Nerva, Via	5 C1
Nicastro, Via	10 E2
Niccolini, Via Giovanni Battista	7 A3
Nicolò III, Via	3 B4
Nicolò V, Via	3 A3
Nicosia, Piazza	11 C1
Nicotera, Via Giovanni	1 A5
Nievo, Piazza Ippolito	7 B3
Nievo, Via Ippolito	7 B3
Niso, Via	10 F4
Nizza, Via	6 D1
Nobel, Via Alfredo	7 C5
Nola, Via	10 E1
Nomentana, Via	6 E1
Norico, Via	9 B2
Normanni, Via dei	9 A1
Norvegia, Via	1 B1
Noto, Via	10 F3
Novelli, Via Ermete	2 E2
Novi, Via	10 E4
Nullo, Via Francesco	7 B3
Numa Pompilio, Piazzale	9 A3
Numanzia, Via	10 D4
Numidia, Via	9 B3
Nuoro, Via	10 F1
Nuova delle Fornaci, Via	3 C5
Nuovo, Palazzo	5 A5 & 12 F5
O	
Obelisco di Montecitorio	12 E2
Obelisco di S. Maria sopra Minerva	12 D3
Oberdan, Lungot.	1 A4
Oca, Via dell'	4 F1
Oddone da Cluny, Via	8 E3
Odescalchi, Palazzo	5 A4 & 12 F3
Oderzo, Via	10 E3
Olanda, Via	1 B1
Olbia, Via	9 C2
Olimpionici, Via degli	1 A1
Olmata, Via dell'	6 D4
Ombrellari, Via degli	3 C3
Omodeo, Via	10 F5
Oratoria, Piazza d'	12 F2
Oratorio dei Fillippini	4 D4 & 11 B3
Orazio, Via	4 D2
Orazio Coclite, Via	10 F4
Orbitelli, Vicolo	11 A3
Oreste Regnoli, Via	7 A2
Orfani, Via d'	12 D2
Oriani, Via Barnaba	2 D2
Oristano, Via	10 F1
Orlando, Via Vittorio Emanuele	5 C2
Oro, Piazza dell'	11 A2
Orsini, Via Virginio	4 E1
Orso, Via dell'	4 E3 & 11 C2
Orti d'Alibert, Via degli	4 D4 & 11 A4
Orti di Cesare, Via	7 B5
Orti Farnesiana	8 E1
Orti Giustiniani, Via degli	1 C5
Orti di Trastevere, Via degli	7 C3
Ortigara, Via	1 A4
Orto Botanico del Gianicolo	4 D5 & 11 A5
Orvieto, Via	10 E2
Osoppo, Via	6 F2
Ospedale Britannico	9 B2
Ospedale del Celio	9 A1
Ospedale San Camillo	7 A5
Ospedale San Giacomo	4 F2
Ospedale di San Giovanni	9 B1
Ospedale di Santo Spirito	3 C3
Osti, Vicolo degli	11 C3
Ostia, Via	3 B1
Ostiense, Piazzale	8 E4
Ostiense, Via	8 E4
Ostilia, Via	9 A1
Otranto, Via	3 B1
Ottaviano (Metro)	3 C1
Ottaviano, Via	3 C2
Ovidio, Via	4 D2
Oxilia, Via Nino	2 E3
Ozieri, Via	10 F1
P	
Pace, Via della	11 C3
Pacinotti, Via Antonio	7 B5
Padre Rafmelis, Via	10 F1
Paganica, Via	12 D4
Paganini, Via Nicolò	2 F4
Pagano, Via	5 C2
Paglia, Via della	7 B1
Paisiello, Via Giovanni	2 F4
Palach, Piazza Jan	1 C1
Palazzetto dello Sport	1 B2
Palermo, Via	5 B4
Palestro, Via	6 D2
Pallacorda, Via di	12 D1
Palladio, Via Andrea	8 F4
Pallante, Via	10 F4
Pallaro, Largo di	11 C4
Palle, Vicolo delle	11 A3
Palombella, Via della	12 D3
Pamphilj, Palazzo	4 E4 & 11 C3
Panama, Via	2 F3
Pandosia, Via	9 C3
Panetteria, Via della	5 A3 & 12 F1
Panico, Via di	4 D3 & 11 A2
Panieri, Via dei	7 B1
Panisperna, Via	5 B4
Pannini, Via	1 A2
Pannonia, Via	9 B3
Pantheon	4 F4 & 12 D3
Paola, Via	4 D3 & 11 A2
Paolina, Via	6 D4
Paolo II, Via	3 B4
Paolo III, Via	3 A4
Paolo Emilio, Via	4 D1
Papa, Via Achille	1 A4
Papareschi, Lungot. dei	7 C5
Papareschi, Via	7 C5
Paradiso, Piazza del	11 C4
Paradiso, Via del	11 C4
Paraguay, Via	2 F3
Parboni, Via	7 B3
Parco degli Scipioni	9 B4
Parigi, Via	5 C2
Parioli, Viale dei	2 D1
Parioli, Salita dei	1 B3
Parione, Via di	4 E4 & 11 C3
Parlamento, Piazza del	4 F3 & 12 E1
Parlamento, Via del	12 E1
Parma, Via	5 B4
Parrasio, Via Giano	7 B4
Partigiani, Piazzale dei	8 E4
Paruta, Via Paolo	10 E4
Pascarella, Via Cesare	7 B4
Pasquino	4 E4 & 11 C3
Pasquino, Piazza di	11 C3
Pasquino, Via di	11 C3
Passaglia, Via Carlo	3 A1
Passeri, Via	7 C4
Passetto, Il	3 C3
Pastini, Via dei	4 F4 & 12 D2
Pasubio, Via	1 A4
Pelasgi, Via dei	6 F4
Peligni, Via dei	6 F4
Pellegrino, Via del	4 E4 & 11 B3
Pelliccia, Via della	7 C1
Pellico, Via Silvio	3 C1
Penitenza, Via della	4 D5 & 11 A4
Penitenzieri, Palazzo dei	3 C3

Penitenzieri, Via dei   3 C3
Penna, Via della   4 F1
Pentathlon, Via del   2 E1
Pepe, Via
   Guglielmo   6 E4
Peretti, Via Pietro   8 D1
Pergolesi, Via
   Giovanni Battista   2 F5
Peri, Via Jacopo   2 F5
Perosi, Largo   11 A4
Perugino, Via   1 A1
Peruzzi,
   Via Baldassarre   8 E3
Pesaro, Via   10 F1
Pescara, Via   10 F2
Pessina, Via Enrico   1 B4
Petrarca, Via   6 E5
Petrella, Via Enrico   2 F4
Petrolini, Via Ettore   2 F2
Petroselli, Via   8 E1
Pettinari, Via dei   5 A3
   & 11 C5
Pezzana, Via
   Giacinta   2 F1
Pfeiffer, Via Padre P.   3 C3
Pia, Piazza   4 D3
   & 11 A1
Piacenza, Via   5 B4
Pianciani, Via   6 F5
Pianellari, Via dei   11 C2
Piatti, Via Giovanni
   Battista   10 D1
Piave, Via   6 D1
Picardi, Via Vincenzo   2 E3
Piccola Farnesina   4 E4
   & 11 C3
Pie' di Marmo   12 E3
Pie' di Marmo, Via   12 E3
Piemonte, Via   5 C1
Piero della
   Francesca, Via   1 A2
Pierleoni, Lungot.   8 D1
Pierluigi da Palestrina,
   Via   4 E2
Pietra, Piazza di   12 E2
Pietra, Via di   12 E2
Pietra Papa, Via di   7 B5
Pigafetta, Via
   Antonio   8 F5
Pigna, Piazza della   12 E3
Pigna, Via della   12 D3
Pigneto, Piazza del   10 F1
Pigneto, Via del   10 F1
Pilo, Piazza
   Rosolino   7 A3
Pilotta, Piazza
   della   5 A4
   & 12 F3
Pilotta, Via della   5 A4
   & 12 F3
Pilsudski, Viale
   Maresciallo   1 B3
Pimentel, Via
   Eleonora   1 A5
Pinciana, Via   2 F5
Pincio, Il   4 F1
Pindemonte, Via   7 A4
Pinerolo, Via   10 E2
Pineta, Viale della   5 B1
Pinturicchio, Viale   1 A2
Pio, Borgo   3 C3
Pio XII, Piazza   3 C3
Pio Righetti,
   Palazzo   4 E4
   & 11 C4
Piombo, Vicolo del   12 E3
Piramide (Metro)   8 E4
Piramide di Caio
   . Cestio   8 E4
Piramide Cestia,
   Via della   8 E3
Pirgo, Via   9 C3
Pisacane, Via Carlo   7 A4
Pisanelli, Via   1 B5
Pisani, Via Vittor   3 A2

Pisano, Via Leonardo   1 C3
Piscinula, Piazza in   8 D1
Pistoia, Via   10 E2
Pitagora, Piazza   2 E3
Plana, Via Giovanni
   Antonio   2 D3
Platina, Via
   Bartolomeo   10 E5
Platone, Viale   3 A1
Plauto, Via   3 C3
Plebiscito,
   Via del   5 A4
   & 12 E4
Plinio, Via   4 D2
Po, Via   2 F5
   continues   5 C1
Podgora, Via   1 A4
Poerio, Via
   Alessandro   7 A4
Polacchi, Via dei   12 E4
Poletti, Via Luigi   1 A2
Poli, Via   5 A3
   & 12 F1
Policlinico (Metro)   6 F1
Policlinico,
   Viale del   6 E1
Policlinico
   Umberto 1   6 F2
Politeama,
   Via del   4 E5
   & 11 B5
Poliziano, Via
   Angelo   6 D5
Pollaiolo, Via
   Antonio   1 C3
Pollione, Via Asinio   8 D3
Polo, Viale Marco   8 E4
   continues   9 A5
Polverone,
   Vicolo del   4 E5
   & 11 C5
Pomarancio, Via   1 C4
Pomezia, Via   10 D3
Pompei, Via   9 C3
Pompeo Magno, Via   4 D1
Pomponazzi, Via
   Pietro   3 A1
Ponte Cavour   4 E2
Ponte Cestio   8 D1
Ponte Fabricio   12 E5
Ponte Garibaldi   4 F5
   & 12 D5
Ponte dell'Industria   7 C5
Ponte Lungo (Metro)   10 E3
Ponte Lungo,
   Piazza di   10 F3
Ponte G. Matteotti   1 B5
Ponte G. Mazzini   4 D4
   & 11 A4
Ponte P. Nenni   4 E1
Ponte Palatino   8 D1
Ponte Principe Amedeo
   Savoia Aosta   4 D3
Ponte Regina
   Margherita   4 E1
Ponte del
   Risorgimento   1 B4
Ponte Rotto   8 D1
Ponte Sant'Angelo   4 D3
   & 11 A2
Ponte Sisto   4 E5
   & 11 B5
Ponte Sisto, Via di   11 B5
Ponte Sublicio   8 D2
Ponte Testaccio   7 C4
Ponte Testaccio,
   Piazzale di   7 C4
Ponte Umberto   4 E3
   & 11 C1
Ponte Vittorio
   Emanuele II   4 D3
   & 11 A2
Pontelli, Via   8 E3
Pontremoli, Via   10 D2
Ponzi, Via Giuseppe   2 D3
Ponziani, Piazza dei   3 C3
Ponziano, Via   7 B4

Ponzio, Via   8 F3
Popolo, Piazza del   4 F1
Populonia, Via   9 C4
Porcari, Via Stefano   3 C2
Pordenone, Via   10 E3
Porpora, Via Nicolò   2 F4
Porro,
   Via Giangiacomo   2 E2
Porta, Via Carlo   7 B4
Porta Angelica, Via di   3 C2
Porta Ardeatina   9 A5
Porta Ardeatina, V.le d.   8 E4
   continues   9 A4
Porta Asinaria   10 D2
Porta Capena,
   Parco di   8 F3
Porta Capena,
   Piazza di   8 F2
Porta Cavalleggeri   3 B3
Porta Cavalleggeri, Via   3 A4
Porta Fabbrica, Via di   3 B4
Porta Labicana, Via di   6 F4
Porta Latina   9 C4
Porta Latina, Via di   9 B3
Porta Lavernate,
   Via di   8 D2
Porta Maggiore   6 F5
Porta Maggiore, Via   6 F5
Porta Metronia,
   Piazza di   9 B2
Porta Pia   6 D1
Porta Pia, Piazzale di   6 D1
Porta Pinciana   5 B1
Porta Pinciana,
   Via di   5 B2
Porta del Popolo   4 F1
Porta Portese   7 C2
Porta Salaria   6 D1
Porta San Giovanni,
   Piazza di   10 D1
Porta San Lorenzo,
   Piazza di   6 F4
Porta San Lorenzo,
   Via di   6 F4
Porta San Pancrazio,
   Via di   7 B1
Porta San Paolo,
   Piazza di   8 E4
Porta San Sebastiano   9 B4
Porta San Sebastiano,
   Via di   9 B3
Porta Santo Spirito   3 C3
Porta Settimiana   4 D5
   & 11 A5
Porta Tiburtina,
   Viale di   6 F3
Portico d'Ottavia   4 F5
   & 12 E5
Portico d'Ottavia,
   Via della   4 F5
   & 12 D5
Porto, Via del   8 D2
Porto Fluviale,
   Via del   8 D5
Portoferraio, Via   10 F2
Portogallo, Via   1 B1
Portuense, Lungot.   7 C3
Portuense, Via   7 B5
Pozzetto, Via del   5 A3
   & 12 F1
Pozzo delle
   Cornacchie, Via d.   12 D2
Pozzuoli, Via   10 D2
Prati, Lungot.   4 E3
   & 11 C1
Prati di Quinzio,
   Via dei   7 B5
Prefetti, Via dei   4 F3
   & 12 D1
Prestinari,
   Via Marcello   1 A4
Pretoriano, Viale   6 E3
Prigioni,
   Vicolo delle   11 A3

Principe Amedeo,
   Via   6 D3
Principe Eugenio,
   Via   6 E5
Principe Umberto,
   Via   6 E5
Principessa Clotilde,
   Via   4 F1
Prisco, Via Tarquinio   10 F4
Progresso, Via del   12 D5
Propaganda, Via   5 A2
   & 12 F1
Properzio, Via   3 C2
Provana, Via   10 D1
Publicii, Clivo dei   8 E2
Publicolis, Via in   12 D4
Puccini, Via Giacomo   5 C1
Puglie, Via   5 C1
Pupazzi, Viale dei   2 E5
   continues   5 B1
Purificazione, Via   5 B2

Q

Quadrio,
   Via Maurizio   7 A3
Quattro Cantoni, Via   5 C4
Quattro Fontane, Le   5 B3
Quattro Fontane,
   Via delle   5 B3
Quattro Venti,
   Piazzale dei   7 A3
Quattro Venti,
   Viale dei   7 A2
Querceti, Via dei   9 B1
Quirinale,
   Palazzo del   5 B3
Quirinale, Piazza del   5 B4
Quirinale, Via del   5 B3
Quiriti, Piazza dei   4 D1

R

Radio, Piazza della   7 B5
Radio Vaticana   3 A3
Raffaelli,
   Via Giacomo   7 C5
Ragusa, Piazza   10 F3
RAI Sede   1 A4
Raimondi, Via Pietro   2 F5
Rainaldi, Largo
   Gerolamo   1 A2
Ramni, Via dei   6 F4
Rasella, Via   5 B3
Rattazzi, Via   6 D4
Ravizza, Via
   Giuseppe   7 A5
Re di Roma (Metro)   10 D2
Re di Roma,
   Piazza dei   10 D3
Rea Silvia, Via   10 F4
Recina, Via Elvia   9 C3
Reggio Emilia, Via   6 D1
Regina Elena, Viale   6 F2
Regina Margherita,
   Galleria   5 C3
Regina Margherita,
   Viale   6 E1
Reginella, Via della   12 D5
Regolo, Via Attilio   4 D2
Remuria, Piazza   8 F3
Renella, Via della   7 C1
Reni, Via Guido   1 A2
Repubblica (Metro)   5 C3
Repubblica,
   Piazza della   5 C3
Resistenza dell'8
   Settembre Parco d.   8 E3
Respighi,
   Via Lorenzo   2 E3
Revere, Via Giuseppe   7 A4
Riari, Via dei   4 D5
   & 11 A5

Ricasoli, Via B. 6 E4
Ricci, Largo Corrado 5 B5
Ricci, Palazzo 4 D4
 & 11 B3
Ricci, Via 8 E4
Ricci Curbastro, Via 7 B5
Ricciotti, Via Nicola 1 A5
Rimembranza, Piazzale
 del Parco della 2 D2
Rimini, Via 10 D2
Rinascimento,
 Corso del 4 E3
 & 11 C2
Ripa, Lungot. 8 D1
Ripa, Via 6 D1
Ripa Grande,
 Porto di 8 D2
Ripari, Via 7 B3
Ripetta,
 Passeggiata di 4 E1
Ripetta, Via di 4 F2
 & 12 D1
Risorgimento,
 Piazza del 3 C2
Ristori, Via Adelaide 2 F2
Riva Ostiense 7 C5
Rizzo, Via Luigi 3 A1
Robecchi Brichetti,
 Via 8 F5
Rodi, Via 3 B1
Rogazionisti, Via dei 10 F3
Rolli, Rampa 7 B4
Rolli, Via Ettore 7 B5
Roma Libera, Via 7 C2
Romagna, Via 5 C1
Romagnosi, Via
 Giandomenico 4 E1
Romania, Viale 2 F3
Romano, Via Giulio 1 A1
Romita, Via Giuseppe 5 C3
Roncinotto, Via 9 A5
Rondanini, Piazza 12 D2
Rondinella, Via della 11 B2
Rosa, Via Ercole 8 F3
Rosa, Via Salvatore 8 F3
Rosazza, Via Federico 7 B4
Roselli, Via Pietro 7 A2
Rosmini, Via 6 D4
Rossellino, Via 1 B2
Rossetti, Via Gabriele 7 A2
Rossi, Via Pellegrino 6 D4
Rossini, Viale
 Gioacchino 2 E4
Rosso, Via 10 D1
Rostra 12 F5
Rotonda,
 Piazza della 4 F4
 & 12 D3
Rovere, Piazza della 3 C4
Roverella, Via 3 A5
Rubattino, Via 7 C3
Rubens, Via Pietro
 Paolo 1 C3
Ruffini, Via 1 A5
Rupe Tarpea 12 F5
Rusconi, Via 7 B3
Ruspoli, Via Eugenio 8 E5
Rutoli, Vicolo dei 6 F4

S
Sabelli, Via dei 6 F4
Sabini, Via dei 12 E2
Sacchi, Via Andrea 1 A1
Sacchi, Via Gaetano 7 B1
Sacconi, Via
 Giuseppe 1 A1
Saffi, Viale Aurelio 6 D4
Salandra, Via 5 C2
Salara Vecchia,
 Via della 5 B5
Salaria, Via 6 D1
Salentini, Via dei 6 F4
Salerno, Piazza 6 F1
Saliceti, Via 7 B3

Saliceto, Via
 Guglielmo 6 E1
Sallustiana, Via 5 C2
Sallustio, Piazza 5 C2
Salumi, Via dei 8 D1
Saluzzo, Via 10 E3
Salvi, Via Nicola 5 C5
Salviati, Palazzo 3 C4
Salvini, Via Tommaso 2 F2
Salvo d'Acquisto,
 Lungot. 1 A1
Sant'Agata dei Goti 5 B4
Sant'Agata dei
 Goti, Via 5 B4
Sant'Agnese in
 Agone 4 E4
 & 11 C3
Sant'Agostino,
 Via di 11 C2
Sant'Alberto Magno,
 Via 8 E2
Sant'Alessio,
 Parco di 8 E2
Sant'Alessio, Via di 8 E2
Sant'Ambrogio, Via 12 D5
Santi Ambrogio e
 Carlo al Corso 4 F2
Sant'Andrea delle 5 A3
 Fratte & 12 F1
Sant'Andrea delle 5 A3
 Fratte, Via di & 12 F1
Sant'Andrea al
 Quirinale 5 B3
Sant'Andrea della 4 E4
 Valle & 12 D4
Sant'Angelo, Borgo 3 C3
Sant'Angelo in
 Peschiera, Via 12 E5
Sant'Anna, Via di 12 D4
Sant'Anselmo, Via di 8 E3
Sant'Apollinare 4 E3
 & 11 C2
Sant'Apollonia,
 Piazza 7 C1
Santi Apostoli 5 A4
 & 12 F3
Santi Apostoli,
 Piazza dei & 12 F3
Santi Apostoli, Via 12 F3
Sant'Aurea, Via di 11 B4
Santa Balbina 8 F3
Santa Balbina,
 Piazza di 8 F3
Santa Balbina, Via di 8 F3
San Bartolomeo 8 D1
San Bartolomeo de
 Vaccinari, Via 12 D5
San Bernadino
 da Siena, Via 7 C5
San Bernardo, Piazza 5 C3
San Bernardo alle
 Terme 5 C3
Santa Bibiana 6 F4
Santa Bibiana, Via 6 F4
Santi Bonifacio
 e Alessio 8 D2
San Calepodio, Via 7 A3
San Carlo, Salita di 7 A5
San Carlo ai 4 F5
 Catinari & 12 D4
San Carlo alle
 Quattro Fontane 5 B3
Santa Caterina da
 Siena, Via 12 D3
Santa Cecilia, Piazza 8 D1
Santa Cecilia in
 Trastevere 8 D1
San Cesareo 9 A3
Santa Chiara,
 Via di 12 D3
San Claudio, Piazza 12 E2
San Claudio, Via 5 A3
 & 12 E2
San Clemente 9 B1

San Cosimato, Piazza 7 C1
San Cosimato, Via di 7 C1
San Crisogono 7 C1
Santa Croce in
 Gerusalemme, 10 E1
Santa Croce in
 Gerusalemme,
 Piazza di 10 E1
Santa Croce in
 Gerusalemme, Via d. 6 F5
 continues 10 D1
San Domenico, Via 8 D2
Santi Domenico
 e Sisto 5 B4
San Donà de
 Piave, Piazza 10 E3
Santa Dorotea, 4 D5
 Via di & 11 B5
Sant'Egidio 7 C1
Sant'Elia, Via Antonio 2 D1
Sant'Eligio, Via di 11 B4
Sant'Eligio degli 4 D4
 Orefici & 11 B4
Sant'Erasmo, Via di 9 B2
Sant'Ermete, Via 2 E3
Sant'Eufemia, Via 12 F3
Sant'Eustachio 4 F4
 & 12 D3
Sant'Eustachio,
 Piazza 12 D3
Santi Fabiano e
 Venanzio, Via 10 F2
San Filippo Martire,
 Via 2 F2
San Filippo Neri, Via 4 D4
Santa Francesca
 Romana 5 B5
San Francesco
 a Ripa 7 C2
San Francesco a
 Ripa, Via 7 C1
San Francesco 3 C4
 di Sales, Via & 11 A4
San Francesco 4 D5
 di Sales, Vicolo & 11 A4
San Gallicano, Via 7 C1
San Giacomo, Via 4 F2
San Giorgio in
 Velabro 8 E1
San Giosafat, Via 8 E3
San Giovanni
 (Metro) 10 D2
San Giovanni
 Decollato 8 E1
San Giovanni
 Decollato, Via 8 E1
San Giovanni dei 4 D4
 Fiorentini & 11 A2
San Giovanni in
 Laterano 9 C2
San Giovanni in
 Laterano, Piazza di 9 C1
San Giovanni in
 Laterano, Via di 9 A1
San Giovanni in Oleo 9 B4
Santi Giovanni e
 Paolo 9 A1
San Giovanni a
 Porta Latina 9 B3
San Girolamo 4 E4
 della Carità & 11 B4
San Girolamo della
 Carità, Via di 11 B4
San Giuliano, Vicolo 11 B2
San Grandis, Via 10 D1
San Gregorio,
 Via di 8 F1
San Gregorio Magno 8 F2
Sant'Ignazio di 4 F4
 Loyola & 12 E3
Sant'Ignazio,
 Piazza di 12 E2
Sant'Ignazio, Via 12 E3

Sant'Isidoro, Via 5 B2
Sant'Ivo alla 4 F4
 Sapienza & 12 D3
San Lorenzo
 in Lucina 4 F3
San Lorenzo in
 Lucina, Piazza & 12 E1
Santi Luca e 5 A5
 Martina & 12 F5
San Luigi dei 4 F4
 Francesi & 12 D2
San Macuto,
 Piazza 12 E3
San Marcello, Via 5 A4
 & 12 F3
San Marcello 5 A4
 al Corso & 12 F3
San Marco 12 F4
San Marco, Piazza 5 A4
 & 12 E4
San Marco, Via 5 A5
 & 12 E4
Santa Maria degli
 Angeli 6 D3
Santa Maria 4 E4
 dell'Anima & 11 C2
Santa Maria dell'
 Anima, Via di & 11 C2
Santa Maria in 5 A5
 Aracoeli & 12 F4
Santa Maria de'
 Calderari, 12 D5
Santa Maria in 4 F5
 Campitelli & 12 E5
Santa Maria in 4 F3
 Campo Marzio & 12 D2
Santa Maria della
 Concezione 5 B2
Santa Maria della 5 A5
 Consolazione & 12 F5
Santa Maria in
 Cosmedin 8 E1
Santa Maria in
 Domnica 9 A2
Santa Maria alle
 Fornaci, Via 3 B4
Santa Maria delle
 Grazie, Piazza di 3 A2
Santa Maria
 Liberatrice, Piazza d. 8 D3
Santa Maria Maggiore 6 D4
Santa Maria Maggiore,
 Piazza di 6 D4
Santa Maria Maggiore,
 Via di 5 C4
Santa Maria
 Mediatrice, Via di 3 A4
Santa Maria sopra 4 F4
 Minerva & 12 E3
Santa Maria dei
 Miracoli 4 F1
Santa Maria di 4 E4
 Monserrato & 11 B4
Santa Maria in
 Montesanto 4 F1
Santa Maria dei
 Monti 5 B4
Santa Maria dell'
 Orazione e Morte & 11 B4
Santa Maria della 4 E3
 Pace & 11 C2
Santa Maria
 del Pianto 12 D5
Santa Maria del
 Popolo 4 F1
Santa Maria della 4 D5
 Scala & 11 B5
Santa Maria dei
 Sette Dolori 7 B1
Santa Maria in
 Traspontina 3 C3
Santa Maria in
 Trastevere 7 C1

Santa Maria in Trivio 5 A3
Santa Maria in Via, 5 A3
  Via di & 12 E2
Santa Maria della
  Vittoria 5 C2
San Martino della
  Battaglia, Via 6 E2
San Martino ai Monti 6 D5
San Martino
  ai Monti, Piazza 6 D5
San Martino
  ai Monti, Via 6 D4
Santa Melania, Via 8 E3
San Michele, Via di 8 D2
Santi Nereo e
  Achilleo 9 A3
San Nicola in
  Carcere & 12 E5
San Nicola
  Cesarini, Via di 12 D4
San Nicola da
  Tolentino, Salita di 5 B2
San Nicola da
  Tolentino, Via 5 B2
Sant'Onofrio 3 C4
Sant'Onofrio,
  Salita di 3 C4
Sant'Onofrio, Via 3 C4
San Pancrazio,
  Via di 7 A2
San Paolo del
  Brasile, Viale 5 A1
San Paolo
  della Croce, Via 9 A1
San Paolo alla
  Regola, Via di 11 C5
San Pietro 3 B3
San Pietro, Piazza 3 B3
San Pietro in
  Carcere, Via di 12 F5
San Pietro in Vincoli 5 C5
Santa Prassede 6 D4
Santa Prassede, Via di 6 D4
Santa Prisca, Via di 8 E2
Santa Pudenziana 5 C4
Santi Quattro Coronati 9 B1
Santi Quattro Coronati,
  Via dei 9 A1
San Quintino, Via 10 D1
San Rocco 4 F2
San Saba 8 F3
San Saba, Via di 8 E3
Santa Sabina 8 E2
Santa Sabina, Via di 8 D2
San Salvatore
  in Lauro 4 E3
   & 11 B2
San Salvatore
  in Lauro, Piazza 11 B2
San Silverio, Via 3 A5
San Silvestro,
  Piazza & 12 E1
San Sisto Vecchio 9 A3
Santo Spirito, Borgo 3 C3
Santo Spirito in Sassia 3 C3
Santo Stefano
  del Cacco, Via 12 E3
Santo Stefano
  Rotondo 9 B2
Santo Stefano
  Rotondo, Via di 9 A2
Santa Susanna 5 C2
San Teodoro 8 E1
San Teodoro, Via di 8 E1
Santa Teresa, Via di 5 C1
San Tommaso
  d'Aquino, Via 3 A1
Santissima Trinità
  dei Pellegrini & 11 C5
Sant'Uffizio, Via del 3 C3
San Valentino, Via di 1 B2
San Venanzio, Via 12 E4
San Vincenzo,
  Via & 12 F2

Santi Vincenzo e
  Anastasio 5 A3
San Vitale, Via 5 C3
San Vito, Via 6 D4
Sanatorio Umberto I 9 B2
Sanfelice, Via Luisa 1 A5
Sangallo, Lungot.
  del & 11 A3
Sannio, Via 9 C2
Sannita, Via Cerreto 10 E2
Sanremo, Via 10 F2
Santamaura, Via 3 B1
Santiago del Cile,
  Piazza 2 E3
Santini, Via 8 D1
Santini, Via Luigi 7 C1
Sanzio, Lungot. 4 E5
  Raffaello & 11 B5
  continues 7 C1
Sapri, Via 6 E2
Sardegna, Via 5 B1
Sarti, Largo Antonio 1 B3
Sassari, Piazza 6 F1
Sassia, Lungot. in 3 C3
Sassoferrato, Via 1 C3
Satrico, Via 9 C3
Saturnia, Via 9 C3
Savastano, Via
  Francesco Eulalio 2 D3
Savelli, Vicolo 11 B3
Savoia,
  Via Ferdinando di 4 E1
Savoia,
  Via Ludovico di 4 E1
Savoia Aosta, Galleria
  Principe Amedeo 3 B3
Savona, Via 10 F2
Savonarola, Via
  Girolamo 3 A1
Scala, Via della 4 D5
   & 11 B5
  continues 7 C1
Scala Santa e Sancta
  Sanctorum 9 C1
Scalia, Via Giorgio 3 A2
Scalinata della Trinità
  dei Monti 5 A2
Scarlatti, Via
  Alessandro 2 F4
Scarpellini, Via
  Feliciano 1 C3
Scarpetta, Via 8 D1
Scauro, Clivo di 9 A1
Scavolino, Vicolo 12 F2
Schiaparelli, Via 2 D3
Sciacca, Via 10 D2
Scialoia, Via degli 1 B5
Sciarra, Via 5 A4
   & 12 E2
Scienze, Viale
  delle 6 F3
Scimmia,
  Vicolo della 11 A3
Scipione, Via
  Gaetano 1 C3
Scipione Ammirato,
  Piazza 10 E4
Scipioni, Via degli 3 B2
Sclopis, Via 10 D1
Scrofa, Via della 4 F3
   & 12 D2
Scuderie, Via
  delle 5 A3
Sdrucciolo,
  Vicolo dello 12 E2
Sebeto, Via 5 C1
Secchi, Via Angelo 2 E3
Sediari, Via 12 D3
Segesta, Via 10 D5
Seggiola, Via della 12 D5
Segneri, Via P. 7 B4
Selci, Via in 5 C5
Sella, Via Quintino 5 C2

Seminario,
  Via del & 12 D3
Senatorio, Palazzo 12 F5
Seni, Via 7 A2
Sepolcro di Marco
  Virgilio Eurisace 6 F5
Sergio I, Via 3 A4
Sermide, Via 10 E3
Serpenti, Via dei 5 B4
Serpieri, Via A. 2 D3
Serra, Via 7 C2
Servili, Piazza 8 D3
Sesia, Via 5 C1
Sessoriana, Via 10 D1
Sette Sale, Via delle 5 C5
Settembrini, Via Luigi 1 A5
Sforza, Via 5 C4
Sforza Cesarini,
  Vicolo 11 B3
Sforza Pallavicini,
  Via 4 D2
Sforzesca, Via 6 E2
Siacci, Via Francesco 2 E3
Sibari, Via 9 C2
Sicilia, Via 5 B2
Siculi, Piazzale dei 6 F4
Siena, Piazza di 2 E5
Signorelli, Via Luca 1 A3
Sigonio, Via Carlo 10 F4
Silla, Via 3 C1
Silvagni, Via 7 A4
Silveri, Via
  Domenico 3 B4
Sinagoga 4 F5
   & 12 E5
Sinibaldi, Vicolo 12 D3
Sinuessa, Via 9 C3
Siponto, Via 10 D3
Siracusa, Via 6 F1
Siria, Via 10 D4
Sistina, Via 5 A2
Sisto V, Piazzale 6 F4
Sivori, Via Francesco 3 A2
Slataper, Via Scipio 2 F3
Soana, Via 10 D3
Socrate, Piazzale 3 A1
Soldati, Via dei 11 C2
Solferino, Via 6 D3
Solunto, Via 10 E3
Sommacamp, Via 6 E2
Sommeiller, Via
  Germano 10 D1
Sondrio, Via 10 F1
Sonnino,
  Piazza Sidney 7 C1
Sora, Via 11 B3
Spada, Palazzo 4 E5
   & 11 C4
Spadini, Via
  Armando 1 C4
Spagna (Metro) 5 A2
Spagna, Piazza di 5 A2
Spagnoli, Via degli 12 D2
Spallanzani, Via
  Lazzaro 6 F1
Specchi, Via degli 11 C5
Speri, Via Tito 1 A5
Spezia, Via la 10 D2
Spoleto, Via 10 F2
Spontini,
  Via Gaspare 2 F4
Sprovieri, Via
  Francesco Saverio 7 A2
Stabia, Via 10 E4
Staderari, Via degli 12 D3
Stadio 8 F1
Stadio Flaminio,
  Via dello 1 B2
Stadio Flaminio,
  Viale dello 1 B3
Stamperia,
  Via della & 12 F2
Stanze di Raffaello 3 B3

Stati Uniti
  d'America, Via 1 B1
Statilia, Via 6 F5
  continues 10 D1
Statuto, Via dello 6 D5
Stazione Acqua
  Acetosa 2 E1
Stazione Centrale
  Roma Termini 6 D3
Stazione Ostiense, Via 8 E4
Stazione Roma-Ostia 8 E4
Stazione
  Roma-Ostiense 8 E5
Stazione Roma-Viterbo 4 F1
Stazione di San Pietro 3 B4
Stazione di San Pietro,
  Via 3 B4
Stazione Trastevere 7 B5
Stazione Tuscolana 10 F3
Stazione Tuscolana,
  Piazzale 10 F3
Stazione Tuscolana,
  Via della 10 F3
Stazione Vaticana 3 A3
Stelletta, Via della 12 D2
Sterbini, Via Pietro 7 B3
Stern, Via Raffaele 1 A3
Stoppani,
  Via Antonio 2 E3
Stradivari, Via 7 C4
Stuparich, Via 2 E2
Sudario, Via del 12 D4
Sugarelli, Vicolo 11 A3
Susa, Via 10 E3
Svezia, Via 1 B1
Svizzera, Via 1 B1

T

Tabarrini, Via Marco 10 D4
Tacchini, Via Pietro 2 D3
Tacito, Via 4 D2
Talamone, Via 9 C4
Taramelli, Via
  Torquato 2 D3
Taranto, Via 10 D2
Tartaglia, Via Nicolò 2 E3
Tasso, Via Torquato 6 E5
  continues 9 C1
Tata, Via 8 F4
Taurini, Via dei 6 F3
Tavolacci, Via 7 C2
Tazzoli, Via Enrico 1 A5
Teatro Argentina 4 F4
   & 12 D4
Teatro dell'Opera 5 C3
Teatro di
  Marcello 4 F5
   & 12 E5
Teatro di Marcello, 5 A5
  Via del & 12 E5
Teatro Pace,
  Via del 11 C3
Teatro Valle,
  Via del 12 D3
Tebaldi, Lungot. 4 D4
   & 11 A4
Telesio,
  Via Bernardino 3 A1
Tempietto di San
  Pietro in Montorio 7 B1
Tempio, Via del 12 D5
Tempio di
  Adriano & 12 E2
Tempio di Antonino
  e Faustina 5 B5
Tempio di Castore e
  Polluce 5 A5
Tempio di Cibele 8 E1
Tempio di Claudio 9 A1
Tempio di Diana,
  Piazza 8 E2
Tempio di Diana, Via 8 E2
Tempio d'Esculapio 2 D5

Tempio di Giove	5 A5	Torricelli, Via	7 C3	Valdina, Vicolo	12 D2
	& 12 F5	Tortolini,		Valenziani, Via	6 D1
Tempio di Giove,		Via Barnaba	1 C2	Valeri, Via	9 B2
Via del	12 F5	Tortona, Via	10 E3	Valesio, Via	10 F4
Tempio di Romolo	5 B5	Toscana, Via	5 C1	Valla, Via Lorenzo	7 A4
Tempio di Saturno	5 A5	Tosti, Via Luigi	10 E4	Vallati, Lungot.	4 E5
	& 12 F5	Toti, Via Enrico	10 D1	dei	& 11 C5
Tempio di Venere		Tracia, Via	9 B3	Valle delle	
e Roma	5 B5	Traforo, Via del	5 B3	Camene, Via di	9 A2
Tempio di Vesta	5 B5	Traforo Umberto I	5 B3	Valle Giulia, Viale di	2 D5
Templi del Foro		Traiano, Parco di	6 D5	Vallisneri, Via	
Boario	8 E1	Trani, Via Barisano da	7 C4	Antonio	2 D4
Teramo, Via	10 E1	Trastevere, Viale di	7 B4	Vannucci, Via A.	10 F4
Terme, Stadio delle	9 A3	Traversari, Via		Vantaggio, Via del	4 F1
Terme di Caracalla	9 A3	Ambrogio	7 B4	Vanvitelli, Via	8 D3
Terme di Caracalla,		Travicella, Via della	9 B5	Varchi, Via	
Largo delle	9 B4	Tre Archi, Via dei	11 C2	Benedetto	10 E4
Terme di Caracalla,		Tre Madonne, Via d.	2 E4	Varese, Via	6 E2
Via delle	9 A2	Tre Orologi, Via dei	2 E4	Varisco, Via	
Terme Deciane,		Trenta Aprile, Viale	7 B1	Bernardino	3 A1
Via delle	8 E2	Trevi, Piazza di	12 F2	Varrone, Via	3 C2
Terme di Diocleziano	6 D3	Treviso, Via	6 F1	Vascellari, Via dei	8 D1
Terme di Tito, Via	5 C5	Triboniano, Via	4 D2	Vascello, Via del	7 A1
Terme di Traiano	6 D5		& 11 B1	Vasto, Via	10 D2
Terme di Traiano,		Tribuna di		Vaticano, Lungot.	4 D3
Via delle	6 D5	Campitelli, Via d.	12 E5		& 11 A2
Termini (Metro)	6 D3	Tribuna di Tor		Vaticano, Viale	3 A3
Termini, Stazione	6 D3	de' Specchi, Via	12 E4	Vecchiarelli, Via	11 B2
Terni, Via	10 E2	Tribunali, Piazza dei	11 B1	Veio, Via	9 C2
Testaccio, Lungot.	7 C4	Trinità dei Monti	5 A2	Velletri, Via	6 D1
Testaccio, Parco	8 D4	Trinità dei Monti,		Veneto, Via Vittorio	5 B1
Testaccio, Ponte	7 C4	Viale della	5 A1	Venezia, Piazza	5 A4
Tevere, Fiume	1 A3	Trinità dei Pellegrini,			& 12 F4
continues	4 E3	Via della	11 C5	Venezia, Palazzo	5 A4
	& 11 B1	Trionfale,			& 12 E4
	7 C3	Circonvallazione	3 A1	Venezian,	
Tevere, Via	2 F5	Trionfale, Largo	3 B1	Via Giacomo	7 C1
Thaon di Revel,		Trionfale, Via	3 B1	Venezuela, Via	1 C1
Lungot.	1 A1	Tritone, Via del	5 A3	Veniero, Via	
Thorwaldsen, Piazza	2 D5		& 12 F1	Sebastiano	3 B2
Tibullo, Via	3 C2	Tullio, Via Servio	6 D2	Venosta, Largo	5 C5
Tiburtina, Via	6 F4	Tunisi, Via	3 B1	Venticinque,	
Tiburtino, Piazzale	6 F4	Turati, Via Filippo	6 D4	Via Giulio	3 A1
Tiepolo, Via	1 B3	Turchi, Via Luigi	7 B4	Verbania, Via	10 F3
Tigri, Via Atto	2 D3	Turchia, Via	1 C1	Vercelli, Via	10 E2
Tirone, Via	7 C5	Tuscolana, Via	10 E2	Verdi,	
Tizi, Via dei	6 F4	Tuscolo, Piazza	10 D3	Piazza Giuseppe	2 F4
Tiziano, Viale	1 A1			Vergini, Via delle	12 F2
Toja, Largo A.	7 B4	**U**		Versilia, Via	5 B2
Tola, Via Pasquale	10 E4	Uccelliera, Viale dell'	2 E5	Vesalio, Via Andrea	6 E1
Tolemaide, Via	3 B1	Uffici del Vicario,		Vescia, Via	10 D4
Tomacelli, Via	4 F2	Via degli	12 D2	Vespasiano, Via	3 B2
	& 12 D1	Ughelli, Via		Vespignani,	
Tomba degli		Ferdinando	10 E5	Via Virginio	1 A3
Scipioni	9 B4	Ugo la Malfa,		Vespucci,	
Tommaseo, Via	7 B4	Piazzale	8 E2	Via Amerigo	8 D3
Tommaso da		Ulpiano, Via	4 E2	Vetrina, Via della	11 B2
Celano, Via	10 E4		& 11 C1	Vetulonia, Via	9 C4
Tonelli, Via A.	2 D3	Umbri, Via degli	6 F4	Veturia, Via	10 F4
Toniolo, Largo		Umbria, Via	5 C2	Vibo Valsentia, Via	10 D2
Giuseppe	12 D2	Umiltà, Via dell'	5 A4	Vicario, Vicolo del	3 A5
Tor de Conti, Via	5 B5		& 12 F3	Vicenza, Via	6 D3
Tor Millina, Via di	11 C3	Ungheria, Piazza	2 F3	Vico,	
Tor di Nona,		Unione Sovietica, Via	1 B1	Via Gian Battista	4 F1
Lungot. di	& 11 A2	Unità, Piazza dell'	3 C2	Vidoni, Piazza	12 D4
Tor di Nona,		Università, Viale dell'	6 E3	Vigliena, Via	4 D1
Via di	& 11 A2	Università	5 A4	Vigna Fabbri, Via di	10 F5
Tor Sanguigna,		Gregoriana	& 12 F3	Vigna Filonardi, Via	2 E2
Piazza di	11 C2	Urbana, Via	5 C4	Vignola, Viale del	1 A3
Torino, Via	5 C3	Urbino, Via	10 D2	Vigoni, Via	8 E4
Torlonia, Palazzo	3 C3	Urbisaglia, Via	9 C3	Villa Abamelek	3 B5
Torre, Via Federico	7 A3	Usodimare, Via		Villa Ada	2 F2
Torre Argentina,		Antoniotto	9 A5	Villa Alberici, Via di	3 A3
Largo di	& 12 D4			Villa Aldobrandini	5 B4
Torre Argentina,	4 F4	**V**		Villa Aquari, Via	10 D4
Via di	& 12 D3	Vaccarella,		Villa Borghese	2 E5
Torre delle Milizie	5 B4	Vicolo della	12 D2	continues	5 B1
Torre dell'Orologio	4 D4	Vaccaro, Via del	12 F3	Villa Caffarelli, Via di	12 F5
	& 11 B3	Vacche, Vicolo delle	11 B2	Villa Celimontana	9 A2
Torretta, Piazza	4 F3	Vajna, Via Eugenio	2 E2	Villa Elia	1 C3
della	& 12 D1	Valadier, Via	4 D2	Villa Emiliani, Via di	2 E2
Torretta, Vicolo				Villa Farnesina	4 D5
della	12 D1				& 11 A5

Villa Fiorelli,		
Piazza di	10 F2
Villa Flaminia	1 A2
Villa Fonseca,	
Via di	9 B2
Villa Giulia	1 C4
Villa Giulia, Via di	1 B4
Villa Glori	1 C1
Villa Glori, Viale di	1 C2
Villa Lante	3 C5
Villa Lazzaroni	10 F5
Villa Medici	5 A1
Villa Pamphilj,	
Viale di	7 A4
Villa Patrizi, Via di	6 E1
Villa Pepoli, Via di	8 F3
Villa Peretti,	
Largo di	6 D3
Villa Ruffo	1 C5
Villa San Filippo,	
Via di	2 F2
Villa Sacchetti,	
Via di	2 D4
Villa Sciarra	7 B2
Villa Torlonia	6 F1
Villa Wolkonsky	10 D1
Villani, Via	
Giovanni	10 E5
Villari, Via Pasquale	9 B1
Villini, Via dei	6 E1
Viminale,	
Piazza del	5 C3
Viminale, Via	5 C3
Virgilio, Via	4 D2
Virginia, Via	10 F4
Visconti, Via Ennio	
Quirino	4 D2
Vite, Via della	5 A3
	& 12 E1
Vitelleschi, Via	
Giovanni	3 C2
Viterbo, Via	6 D1
Vittoria, Lungot. della	1 A3
Vittoria, Via	4 F2
Vittoriano, il	5 A5
	& 12 F4
Vittorio, Borgo	3 C3
Vittorio Emanuele	
(Metro)	6 E5
Vittorio Emanuele II,	4 D3
Corso	& 11 A2
Vittorio Emanuele II,	
Piazza	6 E5
Voghera, Via	10 E2
Volpato,	
Via Giovanni	7 B5
Volpe, Vicolo della	11 C2
Volsci, Via dei	6 F4
Volta, Via Alessandro	8 D3
Volterra, Via	10 F2
Volturno, Via	6 D2
Vulci, Via	9 C3
W	
Washington, Viale	4 F1
X	
Ximenes, Via Ettore	1 C3
Z	
Zabaglia, Via	
Nicola	8 D4
Zama, Piazza	10 D4
Zanardelli, Via	4 E3
	& 11 C2
Zingari, Via	5 C4
Zoccolette, Via	4 E5
delle	& 11 C5
Zuccari, Via	8 E3
Zucchelli, Via	5 B2

General Index

A

A Bella Napoli 320
Aalto, Alvar 332
Abruzzi 294, 296
AC Roma 379
Acanto 322, 336, 337
Accademia dei Lincei 218
Accademia Nazionale di San Luca 156, 160
Accessories, shops 328–9
Achilleus, St 194
Achilli al Parlamento 318, 320
ACI 379
Acqua see Aqueducts
Adam, Robert 56
Adoration of the Magi (Pinturicchio) 241
Adrian I, Pope 26
Adrian IV, Pope 26, 192
Adrian VI, Pope, tomb 121
Aedicules 34
Aeneas 17, 87
Aeneas and the Founding of Rome 81
Aesculapius 152, 259
African music 349
Agata e Romeo 311, 315
Agenzia d'Arte Moderna 337
Agnes, St 121, 264
Agrippa, Marcus 52, 110, 111, 140
Air travel 368–9
Airports 370–71
   Ciampino 369, 371
   Fiumicino (Leonardo da Vinci) 66, 368, 369, 370
Al 34 (restaurant) 310, 313
Al Ceppo 311, 317
Al Moro 310, 314
Al Pellegrino Cattolico 334, 335
Al Pompiere 310, 313
Alaric 24
Alba Longa 16
Alberini, Giordanello degli 203
L'Albero del Pane 335
Alberti, Leon Battista 75, 185
Albertoni, Beata Ludovica 211
Albrecht 320
Alcazar 346, 347
Alcohol, duty-free allowances 366
   see also Wine
Aldobrandini family 107, 155, 165, 248
Aldobrandini, Villa 165
Aldrovandi Palace 291, 295, 301, 317
Alemagna 319, 320
Alessio, Sant' 204
Alexander VI, Pope 27, 146, 149, 228
   Porta Settimiana 218
   private apartments in Vatican 242
   Santa Maria Maggiore 172
   Vatican Corridor 229, 249
Alexander VII, Pope 27, 137
   monument to 32, 232
   Porta del Popolo 137

Alexander VII, Pope (cont.)
   Santa Maria della Pace 118
   Spanish Steps 134–5
Alexander Severus, Emperor 19
   statue of 71
Alexanderplatz 344, 345
Alexandra 295, 300
Alfredo a Via Gabi 311, 315
Algardi, Alessandro 75, 150, 232
Alibi 348, 349
Alidosi, Cardinal Francesco 227
Alien 348, 349
Alimandi 295, 300
Alimentari (grocery shops) 319
Alinari 337
Alitalia 368
All Saints 135
Alle Carrete 320
Almacrì 321
Alpheus 340, 344, 345, 348
Altar of Mithras, San Clemente 187
Altar of Peace see Ara Pacis
Altemps, Cardinal Marco Sittico 127, 213
Altemps, Palazzo 127
Altieri, Cardinal
   Giambattista di Lorenzo 107
Altieri family 107
Altieri, Palazzo 105, 107
Amalia 295, 300
Amati e Amati 329, 331
Ambulances 361
American Episcopal Church 367
American Express 358, 359, 362, 368
Ammannati, Bartolomeo 262
Amphiteatrum Castrense 180
Anacletus, antipope 152
Anagni 271
Anagrafe 274
Anastasius II, Pope 25, 26
Ancus Marcius 18
Andrea 311, 317
Andreucci 332, 333
Anfiteatro Quercia del Tasso 347
Angelico, Fra 165, 241
   tomb of 108
   Triptych 217
Angelo Azzurro 348, 349
Angelo della Navicella (Giotto) 233
Anglican Church 367
Anguillara 275
Anguillara, Rodolfo, tomb of 211
Anguillara, Torre degli 209
Aniene waterfalls 268
Animals fights, Colosseum 94–5
Anne of Cleves 255
Annibaldi family 88
Ansuini 329, 331
Antica Zecca see Palazzo del
   Banco di Santo Spirito
Anticaja e Petrella 336, 337
Antico Arco 311, 316
Antico Caffè della Pace 319, 320
Anticoli 329, 331
Antinous 137

Antiquariato Valligiano 336, 337
Antiquarium Forense 48, 81, 87
Antiques
   fairs 58, 60, 339
   shops 336–7
Antoniazzo Romano 108, 203
   Discovery and Triumph of the Cross 181
Antoninus and Faustina,
   Temple of 44, 80, 85
Antoninus Pius, Emperor 19, 85, 106, 249
Antony, Mark 19, 82, 278
Apartments, self-catering 290
Apéritifs 307
Aperol 307
Apollo, Temple of 151
Apollo and Daphne (Bernini) 260, 261
Apollo del Belvedere 236, 237
Apollo of Veio 17
Apollodoro 337
Apollodorus of Damascus 87, 88
Apolloni, W 336, 337
Appian Line 373
Appian Way see Via Appia
Appius Claudius Caecus 265
Apuleius, Quintus, tomb of 285
Aqua see Aqueducts
Aqueducts 20–21, 307
   Acqua Felice 52, 162, 266–7
   Acqua Paola 219, 225, 275
   Acqua Vergine 52
   Aqua Antoniniana 195
   Aqua Appia 20
   Aqua Claudia 184, 185, 266
      Domitian's extension of 279
   Aqua Marcia 266
   Aqua Virgo 159
   Aqueduct of Nero 184, 191, 193, 358
Ar Popi Popi 321
Ara Pacis 22, 140
Aracoeli Staircase 66, 69
Arch of Augustus 278
Arch of Constantine 77, 91
   Tour of Rome's Triumphal Arches 279
Arch of Dolabella 191, 193
Arch of Drusus 195
Arch of Gallienus 169, 174
Arch of Janus 201, 202, 279
Arch of Septimius Severus 83
   Tour of the Forum 79
   Tour of Rome's Triumphal Arches 278
Arch of Titus 23, 34, 87
   Tour of the Forum 81
   Tour of Rome's Triumphal Arches 278–9
Arch of Titus (Cromek) 279
Archaeological Zone 48, 190
Archimede Seguso 333
Architecture 34–5
Architraves 34

Arco *see also* Arch
Arco degli Argentari 201, 279
Ardeatine caves *see* Fosse Ardeatine
Area Archeologica del Teatro
  di Marcello 343
Area Sacra 150
Aria 327, 330
Ariosto 296
Aristotle 243
Armani, Giorgio 133, 322, 326,
  327, 330
Arnaldo di Brescia 29
Arnolfo di Cambio 211, 267
  St Peter 233
Arpino, Cavalier d' 147
Art and antiques, shops 336–7
Art cinemas 346, 347
Art Deco Gallery 336, 337
Art fair 60
Art Nouveau 259
L'Art Nouveau 336, 337
Arte Antica, Galleria Nazionale d'
  see Galleria Nazionale d'Arte Antica
Arte Orientale, Museo Nazionale d'
  see Museo Nazionale
  d'Arte Orientale
Artemide 332, 333
Arteque 333
Arti e Mestieri 334, 335
Artichokes 302
Artisan handicrafts shops 334, 335
Artists in Rome 56–7
Asprucci, Antonio 259
Associazione Italiana
  Alberghi per la Gioventù 291, 366
L'Associazione Nazionale Museidon
  358, 359
ASST 364
Assyrian art
  in Vatican Museums 238
Astor, Lord 260
ATAC 359, 376
Atistia, tomb of 184
Atlante Star 295, 300
Atlante of the Four Gates,
  Vatican Museums 234
L'Attico 337
Auditorium del Foro Italico
  342, 343, 344, 350, 351
Auditorium di Santa Cecilia
  342, 343
Auditorium of Maecenas 175
Augustine, St 192, 271
Augustulus, Romulus, Emperor 19
Augustus, Emperor
  Ara Pacis 140
  Basilica Julia 84
  bust of 67
  Circus Maximus 205
  Forum of Augustus 90
  history 15, 19, 82, 97
  House of Augustus 97
  House of Livia 101
  Mausoleum of Augustus 141, 158
  obelisks 53, 137
  as patron 56

Augustus, Emperor (cont.)
  statue of 239
  sundial 113
  Temple of Julius Caesar 79, 278
  Theatre of Marcellus 151
  Tivoli 268
  Via Appia 265
Aula La Sapienza 342, 343
Aurelian, Emperor 19, 196, 248
Aurelian Wall 196
  Amphiteatrum Castrense 180
  Aqua Claudia 184
  history 23
  Museo delle Mura 354
  Porta Asinaria 180
  Porta Settimiana 218
  Pyramid of Caius Cestius 205
  Sangallo Bastion 196
  Sessorianum 181
Aurelius, Marcus, Emperor 19
  Arch of Constantine 91
  Column of Marcus Aurelius 113
  statue 70
Aurora, Casino dell' *see*
  Casino dell'Aurora
Automobile Club d'Italia 361,
  379
Autosoccorso CARA 379
Autumn in Rome 60
Aventine 198–205
  area map 199
  hotels 288, 295, 299–300
  restaurants 311, 315, 321
  Street-by-Street map 200–201
  Street Finder maps 7, 8
Aventino 295, 299
Averulino, Antonio 231
Avignon
  popes resident in 29, 30, 182
Avis 379
Azienda Agricola 335
Azzurro, Angelo 348, 349
Azzurro Scipioni 346, 347

B

B-Side 348, 349
Babington's Tea Rooms 134, 309,
  319, 320
  Street-by-Street map 131
Bacchus 22
Il Baciccia (Giovanni Battista
  Gaulli) 151
  Gesù frescoes 114, 115
  *Madonna, San Rocco and
  Sant'Antonio with Victims of
  the Plague* 141
  portrait of Bernini 46
Bacillario 327, 330
Baker's Tomb 184
Balbina, Santa 196
Baldacchino 35
Baldassini, Melchiorre 109
Baldassini, Palazzo 109
Balestra, Renato 326, 330
Ballet 343
Banco di Roma 125

Banco di Santo Spirito,
  Palazzo del 125
Bank of Rome 362
Banking 362–3
Baptism of Christ (Raggi) 153
Baptistry of San Giovanni 178–9
  mosaics 280, 281
Bar del Fico 348, 349
Bar del Palazzo del Yogobar 320
Bar della Pace 348, 349
Bar Parnaso 319, 321
Barberini (cinema) 346, 347
Barberini, Cardinal Antonio,
  tomb 254
Barberini family 49, 133, 252, 254, 282
Barberini, Palazzo 108, 251, 255
  Rome's Best Museums and
  Galleries 47, 49
  Street-by-Street map 252–3
Barcaccia fountain 130, 133
Barigioni, Filippo 75
  tomb of Maria Sobieski 233
Baroque architecture 32–3, 34,
  35, 45
Barracco, Baron Giovanni 145, 149
Barroccio 320
Bars 303, 319, 320–21, 348
Basaldella, Mirko
  Fosse Ardeatine gates 266
Basilica Aemilia 79, 81, 82
Basilica Argentaria 91
Basilica of Constantine and
  Maxentius 81, 86
Basilica Julia 78, 84
Basilicas 35, 44
  see also Churches
Bathroom shops 332, 333
Baths of Caracalla 189, 197
  ballet 343
  concerts 342
  disabled visitors 341
  floorplan 197
  mosaics 188, 239
  opera 343
Baths of Diocletian 22–3, 45,
  162, 163
Baths of Otricoli 239
Baths of Trajan 168, 281
Battello Ubriaco 348, 349
Battistoni 326–7, 330
The Battle of the Milvian Bridge
  (Raphael) 242
BBC 367
The Bean Eater (Carracci) 157
Beauvoir, Simone de 292, 296
Beer 306, 307
Beer houses 302, 318, 320–21
Bees, Fountain of the
  see Fontana delle Api
Befana, Piazza Navona 61, 339, 355
Bellarmino, San Roberto
  statue by Bernini 115
Belli, Giuseppe Gioacchino 210
  statue of 209, 275
Bellini, Giovanni
  Pietà 240, 241

Bellotto, Bernardo 110
Beltrami 133, 328, 331
Belvedere Palace 234, 235
Bembo, Cardinal Pietro
 tomb of 108
Benedict, St 271
Benedict IX, Pope 26
Benedict XIV, Pope 113, 172
Benetton 327, 330
Benevento 265
Bergondi, Andrea 204, 260
Berlioz, Hector 57, 135
Bernadette, St 224
Bernardino, St 69
Bernasconi 320
Bernini, Gian Lorenzo 32, 49, 56,
 75, 108, 112, 117, 125, 136, 144,
 201, 260
 Apollo and Daphne 260, 261
 bust of Cardinal Pedro Foix
 de Montoya 148
 David 47, 261
 *Ecstasy of Beata Ludovica
 Albertoni* 211
 Ecstasy of St Teresa 253, 255, 282
 Fontana delle Api 252, 254, 282
 Fontana della Barcaccia 133
 Fontana del Bicchierone 268
 Fontana dei Fiumi 50, 52,
 53, 119, 120, 283
 Fontana del Moro 52, 119, 283
 Fontana del Tritone 252,
 254–5, 282
 monument to Pope
 Alexander VII 32
 Obelisk of Santa Maria
 sopra Minerva 53, 108, 283, 354
 Palazzo Barberini 49, 255, 282
 Palazzo di Montecitorio 112, 283
 Palazzo Odescalchi 156
 Palazzo del Quirinale 158, 282
 Palazzo Spada 147
 Pantheon 110
 Piazza Navona 33, 283
 Piazza San Pietro 224
 Pluto and Persephone 260
 Ponte Sant'Angelo 273, 283
 Porta del Popolo 137
 portraits 32, 46
 Sant'Andrea delle Fratte 132
 Sant'Andrea al Quirinale
 43, 45, 161, 282
 Santa Bibiana 174
 Santa Maria del Popolo 138
 Santa Maria sopra Minerva
 obelisk 50, 104
 Santa Maria della Vittoria 45
 St Peter's 33, 45, 111, 230, 231,
 232, 233, 283
 San Pietro in Montorio 219
 San Roberto Bellarmino 115
 Santi Domenico e Sisto 165
 Walk around Bernini's
 Rome 282–3
Bernini, Pietro 51, 133, 258
Bernini Bristol (hotel) 295, 301

Bersaglieri 36
Bevitoria Navona 318, 320
Biagiotti, Laura 133, 326, 327, 330
Bibbiena, Cardinal Dovizi di 111
Bibbiena, Maria 111
Bibiana, St 174
Biciroma 378, 379
Bicycles 351, 352, 378, 379
Big Mama 344, 345
Bigio, Nanni di Baccio 137
I Bike Roma 351
Bilenchi 336, 337
Birreria Bavarese 318, 320
Birreria Viennese 310, 313, 318,
 320
Birrerie (beer houses) 302, 318,
 320–21
Bizet, Georges 57, 133
Bizzaccheri, Carlo 51, 201
Black Death 29, 69
Black Out 344, 345
Blatumba 345
Boats, rowing 350
Bocca della Verità 202
Bolivar, Simon 259
Bomarzo Monster Park 355
Bonaparte, Pauline 127, 218
 see also Borghese, Pauline
Bonaparte family 127
Boncompagni Sturni 329, 331
Boniface IV, Pope 26, 111
Boniface IX, Pope 249
Boniface VIII, Pope 26, 27, 29,
 182, 266
Bonomo, Alessandra 337
Books
 shops 334, 335
 street markets 338
Borghese, Prince Camillo 127, 258,
 260, 261
Borghese, Pauline
 portrait 49
 statue 55, 261
Borghese, Cardinal Scipione 258,
 260
Borghese, Museo 260–61
 floorplan 260–61
 Rome's Best 47, 49
 timeline 260
Borghese, Palazzo
 see Palazzo Borghese
Borghese, Villa
 see Villa Borghese
Borghese family 43, 49, 225
Borghini 332, 333
Borgia, Cesare 126
Borgia, Lucrezia 268
Borgia, Rodrigo
 see Alexander VI, Pope
Borgia Apartments, Vatican
 Museums 236
Borgia family 159
Borgianni, Orazio 161
The Borgo 228
 hotels 288
Borgognone, 147

Borgognoni (hotel) 294, 298
Borino 328, 331
Borromeo, San Carlo 146, 147, 150
 Palazzina of Pius IV 259
 Santi Ambrogio e Carlo al
 Corso 141
 San Carlo alle Quattro Fontane 161
 San Carlo at Prayer (Reni) 150
 statue of 141
Borromeo, Ortensia 127
Borromini, Francesco 32, 56, 109,
 117, 136
 Collegio Innocenziano 283
 Collegio di Propaganda
 Fide 131, 132
 Oratorio dei Filippini 125
 Palazzo Barberini 255
 Palazzo Falconieri 276
 Palazzo Pamphilj 120
 Palazzo Spada 147
 portrait of 33
 Sant'Agnese in Agone 33, 45, 119,
 120, 121
 Sant'Andrea delle Fratte 131, 132
 San Carlo alle Quattro
 Fontane 33, 45, 161, 282
 San Giovanni in Laterano
 44, 179, 182
 San Giovanni in Oleo 194
 San Girolamo della Carità 144, 148
 Sant'Ivo alla Sapienza 119, 122
 Santa Maria dei Sette
 Dolori 208, 210
 tomb in San Giovanni
 dei Fiorentini 153
 Torre dell'Orologio 118, 125
La Borsa 106
Borsalino 329, 331
Bossa Nova 345
Botanical Gardens 215, 217,
 218
Bottega Artigiana 334, 335
Bottega del Vino da Bleve 320
Botticelli, Sandro
 Punishment of the Rebels 245
 Sistine Chapel frescoes 244, 245
 Temptations of Christ 245
 Youth of Moses 30
Boucher, François 135
Bourbon, Constable of 229
Bowie, Lester 340
Box Office 340, 341, 346
Box 233 (clothes shop) 327, 330
Bozart 329, 331
Bracciano 271
Braccio Nuovo 235
Bramante, Donato 56, 124, 148, 218,
 220, 243
 Cortile della Pigna 225
 Palazzo Caprini 30
 Palazzo dei Convertendi 227
 portrait 235
 San Giovanni in Oleo 194
 Santa Maria della Pace 45, 121
 Santa Maria del Popolo 138
 St Peter's 44, 45, 230

Bramante, Donato (cont.)
Tempietto 30–31, 45, 215, 219
Vatican Museums 234, 235, 239
Via Giulia 153, 276
Braque, Georges 241
Braschi, Palazzo 118, 123
Brawne, Fanny 134
Bregno, Andrea 138, 139, 148
tomb of 108
Bresciano, Prospero 162
Bridges see Ponte
Brighenti 327, 330
Brindisi 265
Brioni 327, 330
British Airways 368
British School at Rome 258, 259
Browning, Elizabeth Barrett 57
Browning, Robert 57
Brueghel, Jan the Elder 49
Bruno, Giordano 32
statue of 143, 146
La Bruschetta 321
Brussels tapestries 107
Brutus, Lucius Junius 16, 17, 18
Brutus, Marcus Junius 22, 90, 268
Buccellati 328–9, 331
Buccone 320
Il Buco 310, 312
Budget accommodation 291
Bulgari 130, 328, 331
Burcardo Theatre Museum 49, 149
Burckhardt, Johannes 149
Bureaux de change 362
Burial and Glory of St Petronilla
(Guercino) 72
Burne-Jones, Edward 135
Buses 376
map 370–71, 377
tickets 376–7
Byron, Lord 133, 134, 266
Celebrated Visitors to Rome 55, 57
statue of 258
Byzantine art 47, 280–81
Byzantine empire 25, 88

C
Cabaret 347
Cabernet grape 307
Caelius Vibenna 189
Caesar, Julius 15, 18, 20, 21, 91
assassination 22, 82, 90, 150
Basilica Julia 78, 84
Curia 82
Forum of Caesar 77, 90–91
Temple of Julius Caesar 79, 278
Caetani family 88, 152, 266, 284
Cafés 319, 320–21
Rome's Best 308–9
types of 302
Caffarelli, Prince 69
Caffè Caruso 344, 345, 349
Caffè Flores 319, 320
Caffè des Folies 344, 345
Caffè Giolitti 109, 308
Caffè Greco 133, 309, 319, 320
Street-by-Street map 130

Caffè Latino 344, 345, 349
La Caffettiera 319, 320
Caius Cestius, Pyramid of 205
Cake shops 319
Caligula, Emperor 19, 97, 238
Calling of St Peter and St Andrew
(Ghirlandaio) 245
Callixtus I, Pope 26, 212, 213
see also Catacombs of San Callisto
Calza e Calze 329, 331
Camerino, Jacopo de 280
Camillians 109
Camillo, San 109
Camilloni 320
Camillus, Marcus Furius 18
Campanile 328, 331
Campidoglio see Capitol
Campidoglio, Piazza del see
Piazza del Campidoglio
Camping 291
Campo de' Fiori 142–53
area map 143
hotels 294, 298–9
market 338
restaurants 302, 310, 313–14, 320
Street-by-Street map 144–5
Street Finder maps 4, 8, 11, 12
Campo de' Fiori (hotel) 292, 294,
298
Camponeschi 310, 314
Camporese 234
Campus Martius 113
Canada (hotel) 295, 299
Canadian Airlines 368
Canaletto, Antonio 68, 178
The Colosseum 95
Cancelleria, Palazzo della 31, 149
concerts 342
Street-by-Street map 145
Canina, Luigi 258, 285
Cannavota 311, 315
Canonica, Pietro 258–9
Canova, Antonio 36, 49, 56, 156, 233
Accademia Nazionale
di San Luca 160
Chiaramonti Museum 239
excavations along
Via Appia Antica 284
statue of Pauline
Borghese 55, 127, 260, 261
tomb of Pope Clement XIV 158, 159
Cantina Cantarini 311, 317
Il Cantiniere di Santa Dorotea 321
Canuti, Domenico 165
Capitol 64–75
area map 65
Capitoline Museums 70–73
Street-by-Street map 66–7
Street Finder maps 5, 12
Capitoline Museums 70–73
Museo Nuovo 74
Palazzo dei Conservatori 66, 72–3
Palazzo Nuovo 67, 70–71
Rome's Best Museums
and Galleries 47, 48, 49
Capitoline Venus 70

Capo di Bove 284
Capo di Ferri, Cardinal 147
Cappella see also Chapel
Cappella Paolina, Santa Maria
Maggiore 172
Cappella di Santa Caterina,
San Clemente 186
Cappella di San Venanzio, San
Giovanni in Laterano 182
Cappella Sistina, Santa Maria
Maggiore 173
Cappella Sistina, Vatican see
Sistine Chapel
Capponi, Luigi 148
Capranica, Cardinal Domenico 113
Capranica, Palazzo 113
Capranichetta 346, 347
La Capricciosa 320
Capucci, Roberto 326, 330
Capuchin cemetery 354
Capuchin friars 254
Carabinieri (police) 360, 361
Caracalla 188–97
area map 189
Street-by-Street map 190–91
Street Finder maps 8, 9
Caracalla, Baths of
see Baths of Caracalla
Caracalla, Emperor 19, 83, 197,
278, 279
Caracalla Festival 340
Caravaggio 32, 45, 46, 48, 56, 72, 354
Palazzo Barberini 255
Palazzo Corsini 218
The Crucifixion of St Peter 138–9
The Deposition 49
Rest during the Flight
into Egypt 107
St John the Baptist 72
St Matthew paintings in San Luigi
dei Francesi 122
Carceri Nuove 276
Il Cardinale 310, 314
Carlo Borromeo, San
see Borromeo, San Carlo
Carmel 295, 300
Carmelite order 210
Carne, Sir Edward, tomb 192
Carnival 61, 137, 339
Carracci, Agostino 56
Carracci, Annibale 56, 158
The Bean Eater 157
Palazzo Farnese 32
San Diego de Alcalá 148
Carrani Tours 359
Carreras, José 38
Carriage (hotel) 293, 294, 297
Cars
breakdowns 379
driving in Rome 373, 375
hiring 379
parking 289, 375, 379
petrol 375
racing 350, 351
Carthage 20, 21
Cartoons 355

Caryatids 34
Casa dei Cavalieri di Rodi 90
Casa dei Crescenzi 200, 203, 274
Casa della Fornarina 208, 210
Casa di Goethe 136
Casa di Lorenzo Manilio 153, 275
Casa dello Studente 366
Casali 337
Casanova, Giacomo 133
Casari, Giorgio 219
Casina di Raffaello 258
Casina of Pius IV 225
Casina Valadier 136, 137
Casino dell'Aurora 252, 254
Casino del Bel Respiro 267
Casino Borghese 258
Casino della Meridiana 258
Cassina 332, 333
Cassius 22, 90, 268
Castel Sant'Angelo 248–9
   architectural features 248–9
   timeline 249
   Vatican Corridor 229
Castellesi, Cardinal Adriano 229
Castelli Romani (wine) 306
Castor and Pollux 157, 158
   Temple of *see* Temple of
   Castor and Pollux
Castriota, Giorgio (Scanderbeg)
   282
Castro, Amedeo di, 336, 337
Castroni 335
Catacombs 25
   of Domitilla 266
   of San Callisto 265
   of San Clemente 187
   of San Panfilo 25
   of San Sebastiano 265
   Via Appia Antica 265
Catanei, Vannozza 146
Catello d'Auria 329, 331
Catherine of Alexandria, St 186
Catherine of Aragon 192
Catherine of Siena, St, tomb of 108
Catholic services 366
Catiline 20
Catullus 56, 97, 268
Cavalieri di Rodi, Casa dei
   see Casa dei Cavalieri di Rodi
Cavallini, Pietro
   Santa Cecilia in Trastevere 44, 211
   San Giorgio in Velabro 202
   Santa Maria in Trastevere 208,
   212, 213
   San Paolo fuori le Mura 267
Cavour 313 (wine bar) 318, 320
Cavour, Count Camillo 36
Ceci, Enzo 327, 330
Cecilia, St 211, 265
   statue of 42
Celestine V, Pope 240
Celian hill
   Street-by-Street map 190–91
Celimontana, Villa 190, 193, 355
Cellas 34
Cellini, Benvenuto 30, 56

Cemeteries
   Capuchin 354
   Prima Porta 60
   Protestant 205
   Verano 60
Cenci, Beatrice 152, 153, 255
Cenci, Davide 327, 330
Cenci, Palazzo 152–3, 275
Centro Internazionale di Danza 351
Centro Ippico Fiano Romano
   350, 351
Centro Macrobiotico 319, 320
Centro Sportivo Italiano 350, 351
Centro Turistico Studentesco 366
Ceramic tiles, shops 332, 333
Ceramiche Musa 332, 333
Cerasi Chapel, Santa Maria
   del Popolo 138
Cerveteri 238, 262, 271
Cervia 295, 299
I Cervone 328, 331
Cesanese grape 307
Cesari 322, 327, 330, 333
Cesena, Biagio da 244
Chalet del Lago 319, 321
Chamber music 342, 343
Chapel *see also* Cappella
Chapel of St Francis Xavier, Gesù 115
Chapel of San Venanzio,
   Baptistry of San Giovanni 179, 280
Chapel of Santa Rufina,
   Baptistry of San Giovanni 178, 280
Chapel of Sant'Ignazio, Gesù 114, 115
Chapel of St Zeno, Santa Prassede
   28, 281
El Charango 345
Charlemagne, Emperor 28, 230, 280
   dalmatic of 29
Charles V, Emperor 31, 68, 122, 181
Charles VIII, King of France 229
Charlie, Bonnie Prince 33
Charly's Saucière 311, 315
Charter flights 368
Checchino dal 1887 311, 315
Cheeses 305
Chemists 361
Chestnuts 60
Chez Albert 310, 312
Chiaramonti Museum 235, 237, 239
Chiesa Nuova 118, 124, 354
Chigi, Agostino 121, 126
   Chigi Chapel 138
   Villa Farnesina 216, 217, 220, 221
Chigi Chapel, Santa Maria del
   Popolo 138, 139
Chigi Vase 262
Children 352–5
   clothes 329, 355
   eating out 353
   entertainments 355
   getting around 352
   in hotels 290
   ice cream 353
   mosaics 354
   parks 355
   picnics 353

Children (cont.)
   practical advice 352
   in restaurants 303
   sightseeing with 354
   toys 355
Children's Club 355
La Chimera 336, 337
Choral music 342, 343
Choses de Cachemire 327, 330
Christ 24, 180, 181
   Christ Child *(Santo Bambino)* in
   Santa Maria in Aracoeli 69
Christian Museum 235
Christianity 15, 24–5
Christina, Queen of Sweden 54, 57
   history 33
   Palazzo Corsini 218
   Palazzo Doria Pamphilj 107
   Palazzo Torlonia 229
   Porta del Popolo 137
   Villa Medici 135
Christmas 61, 355
Churches
   architecture 35
   Baroque 32–3
   Catholic services 366
   early Christian 25
   mosaics 280–81
   music in 342
   other religious services 367
   practical information 359
   Rome's Best 42–5
   All Saints 135
   Baptistry of San Giovanni 280, 281
   Chiesa Nuova 118, 124
   Domine Quo Vadis? 265
   Gesù 32, 45, 105, 114–15, 342, 366
   La Maddalena 109
   Oratorio dei Filippini 118
   Pantheon 25, 29, 110-11, 283
   Sant'Agata dei Goti 165
   Sant'Agnese in Agone 33, 45, 117,
   119, 120, 121
   Sant'Agnese fuori le Mura 25, 264
   Santi Ambrogio e Carlo al
   Corso 141
   Sant'Anastasia 279
   Sant'Andrea delle Fratte 131, 132
   Sant'Andrea al Quirinale 43, 45, '
   161, 282
   Sant'Andrea della Valle 69,
   119, 123
   Sant'Angelo in Pescheria 151,
   152, 274
   Sant'Anselmo 204
   Sant'Apollinare 127, 342
   Santi Apostoli 157, 158–9
   Santa Balbina 196
   Santa Bibiana 174
   San Bartolomeo all'Isola 152, 275
   San Bernardo alle Terme 162
   San Biagio degli Armeni 277
   Santi Bonifacio e Alessio 204
   San Carlo ai Catinari 45, 150
   San Carlo alle Quattro
   Fontane 33, 45, 161, 282

Churches (cont.)
Santa Caterina da Siena 276
Santa Caterina dei Funari 274
Santa Cecilia in Trastevere
42, 44, 211
San Cesareo 194
San Clemente 28, 29, 35, 43, 44,
186–7, 281, 354
Santi Cosma e Damiano 44, 80, 86
Santa Costanza 24, 44, 264
San Crisogono 209, 211
Santa Croce in Gerusalemme
43, 177, 181
Santi Domenico e Sisto 165
Sant'Egidio 208, 210
Sant'Eligio degli Orefici
144, 148, 276
Sant'Eustachio 109
San Filippo Neri 276
Santa Francesca Romana 77, 81, 87
San Francesco a Ripa 211
San Giorgio in Velabro 29, 201,
202, 279
San Giovanni Decollato 201, 203
San Giovanni dei Fiorentini
153, 277
San Giovanni in Laterano 29, 35,
43, 44, 177, 179, 182–3, 280, 342
San Giovanni in Oleo 194
Santi Giovanni e Paolo 190, 192
San Giovanni a Porta Latina 194
San Girolamo della
Carità 144, 148
San Giuseppe dei Falegnami 91
San Gregorio Magno 190, 192, 275
Sant'Ignazio di Loyola 45, 105,
106, 342, 354
Sant'Ivo alla Sapienza 45, 119, 122
San Lorenzo in Damaso 149
San Lorenzo in Lucina 112
San Lorenzo in Miranda 44, 80, 85
San Lorenzo fuori le Mura 264–5
Santi Luca e Martina 79, 82
San Luigi dei Francesi 45, 119, 122
San Marcello al Corso 156, 159
San Marco 66, 75
Santa Maria degli Angeli 45, 163
Santa Maria dell'Anima 119, 121
Santa Maria Antiqua 24
Santa Maria in Aracoeli 67, 69
Santa Maria in Campitelli 151, 274
Santa Maria in Campo Marzio 112
Santa Maria della
Concezione 252, 254, 354
Santa Maria della Consolazione
201, 203
Santa Maria in Cosmedin 35, 42,
44, 200, 202, 274, 275
Santa Maria in Domnica 191,
193, 280
Santa Maria Maggiore 24, 43, 44,
167, 169, 172–3, 366
Santa Maria sopra Minerva 104, 108
Santa Maria dei Miracoli 136
Santa Maria di Monserrato
144, 148

Churches (cont.)
Santa Maria in Montesanto 136
Santa Maria dei Monti 164
Santa Maria dell'Orazione e Morte
144, 147, 276
Santa Maria della Pace 45, 118,
121, 341, 342
Santa Maria del Popolo 45, 138–9
Santa Maria del Priorato 204
Santa Maria della Scala 208, 210
Santa Maria dei Sette Dolori
208, 210
Santa Maria del Suffragio 277
Santa Maria in Traspontina 228
Santa Maria in Trastevere 29, 42,
44, 208, 212–13, 275
Santa Maria in Trivio 156, 160
Santa Maria in Via 156, 282–3
Santa Maria della Vittoria 45, 253,
255, 282
San Martino ai Monti 169, 170, 281
Santi Nereo e Achilleo 194, 266
San Nicola 284
San Nicola in Carcere 21, 152, 274
Sant'Omobono 200
Sant'Onofrio 219
San Paolo fuori le Mura 22, 35, 44,
267, 342
St Peter's 24, 35, 42, 45, 59, 199,
223, 230–33, 342, 354
San Pietro in Montorio 219
San Pietro in Vincoli 45, 168, 170
Santa Prassede 28, 43, 44, 169,
171, 281
Santa Pudenziana 168, 171, 281
Santi Quattro Coronati 44, 185, 281
San Rocco 141
San Saba 35, 205
Santa Sabina 24, 25, 29, 44, 204
San Salvatore in Lauro 126
San Sebastiano 265
San Sisto Vecchio 193
Santo Spirito in Sassia 226
Santo Stefano Rotondo 24, 185, 280
Santa Susanna 253, 255
San Teodoro 201, 202
San Tommaso in Formis 191,
280–81
Santissima Trinità dei Pellegrini
145, 146–7
Santi Vincenzo e Anastasio
156, 160
Tempietto 45
Trinità dei Monti 129, 131, 134, 135
Ciac Musica 344, 345
Ciampini 320
Ciampini al Café du Jardin 319, 320
Ciampino airport 369, 371
Ciarla, Alberto 302, 311, 316
La Cicala 321
Ciceruacchio 347
Cicilardone 311, 315
Cigarettes, duty-free
allowances 366
Il Cigno 321

Cincinnatus, Lucius Quintus 18
Cine-clubs 346
Cinecittà Due Centro Commerciale
323
Cinecittà studios 39, 57
Cinema 39, 57, 346, 347
for children 355
discounts 341
festivals 341
open-air 341
Cinema d'essai 346
Cinema Esperia 346, 347
Cinodromo (greyhound track)
350, 351
Circolo degli Artisti 348, 349
Circolo Golf Roma 350, 351
Circolo Stampa 350, 351
Circus Flaminius 151
Circus Maximus 137, 205, 279
Cisternino Cooperativa fra Produttori
di Latte di Lazio 335
CIT 358, 359
Città Aperta (listings magazine) 340
Città del Sole 355
Claude Lorrain 48, 107
View of the Forum 56
Claudia (Vestal Virgin) 85
Claudio e Laura Moretti 336, 337
Claudius, Emperor 19, 184, 266,
276
Clement, St 26, 186, 187
Clement V, Pope 29
Clement VII, Pope 27, 31, 126, 242
Palazzo Madama 122
portrait 228
tomb of 108
Vatican Corridor 229
Clement VIII, Pope 27, 146, 230
Castel Sant'Angelo 248
Chapel of St Peter 224
San Cesareo 194
Villa Aldobrandini 165
Clement IX, Pope 27, 132
Clement X, Pope 27, 105, 107
Clement XI, Pope 27, 51, 55, 139
Clement XII, Pope 33, 70, 139
Clement XIII, Pope 36
Clement XIV, Pope 115
tomb of 158, 159
Cleopatra 90, 278
Clivo di Scauro 190
Cloaca Maxima 17, 91, 274
Cloister of San Giovanni 178
Clothes
children's 355
fashion 325, 326–7, 330
gloves, hats and hosiery
shops 329, 331
knitwear 327
lingerie 327
sales 322
second-hand 327, 331
size chart 329
Spanish Steps Alta Moda
Fashion Show 339
visiting churches 359

Clothes (cont.)
  young designer wear 327, 330
Club 84 348, 349
CNN 367
Coach travel 373
Coas Tradizione Casa 332, 333
Coccia, Francesco 266
Coffee 307
Coffers 34
Coin 323
Coins 363
Collalti 351, 378, 379
Colle Oppio 167, 281
Collegio di Propaganda Fide 131, 132
Collegio Innocenziano 283
Collegio Romano,
  Palazzo del 105, 106
Colli Albani (wine) 306
Colline Emiliane 310, 314
Colonna, Cardinal Girolamo 158
Colonna, Marcantonio 158, 196
Colonna, Palazzo 157, 158
Colonna dell'Immacolata 131, 132
Colonna family 155, 158
Colonna Palace (hotel) 294, 296
Colonnades 34
Colosseum 77, 92–5
  architectural features 92–3
  for children 354
  fights 94–5
  floorplan 94
  flora 92
  interior features 95
  sea battles 95
  timeline 93
  Visitors' Checklist 93
The Colosseum (Canaletto) 95
Colossus of Nero 93
Columbarium of Pomponius
  Hylas 195
Columbus (hotel) 295, 300
  see also Palazzo dei Penitenzieri
Columbus, Christopher 172
Columns
  caryatids 34
  Column of Marcus Aurelius
    28, 113, 283
  Column of Phocas 78, 83
  Column of Trajan 28, 90
  orders 34
  Piazza Santa Maria Maggiore 173
Commendatore, Palazzo del 227
Commodus, Emperor 19
Comune di Roma 65
Conca, Sebastiano 151
Condotti 294, 297
Congregazione Suore dello
  Spirito Santo 290, 291
Conservatori, Palazzo dei
  see Palazzo dei Conservatori
Constans II, Emperor 111
Constantia, St 264
Constantine I, Emperor 19, 182, 280
  Arch of Constantine 77, 91, 279
  Basilica of Constantine and
    Maxentius 86

Constantine I, Emperor (cont.)
  conversion to Christianity
    24, 25, 170, 185
  San Giovanni in Laterano 43
  San Lorenzo fuori le Mura 265
  St Peter's 230, 232
Constantine II, Emperor 19, 51, 53
  statue of 73
Constantine and Maxentius,
  Basilica of 86
Constantinople 28
Consulates 367
Consuls 18–19
Conte, Jacopino del 107, 203
  Portrait of Michelangelo 126
Conversion table 367
Convertendi, Palazzo dei 227
Il Convivio 310, 312
Corallo 320
Le Corbusier 332
Cordonata 65, 66, 68
Corelli, Arcangelo 57
Corinthian order 34
Coriolano 310, 315
La Cornucopia 311, 316
Coronation of the Virgin
  mosaic (Torriti) 173
Corsi 320
Corsini, St Andrea 182
Corsini, Cardinal Neri 218
Corsini Chapel, San Giovanni
  in Laterano 182
Corsini, Palazzo *see* Palazzo Corsini
Cortile della Pigna 225, 234
Cortona, Pietro da 126, 150
  Chiesa Nuova 124
  Palazzo Barberini 252, 255
  Palazzo Pamphilj 120
  portrait 125
  Rape of the Sabine Women 47
  Santa Maria della Pace 45, 118, 121
  Santi Ambrogio e Carlo al Corso 141
  Santi Luca e Martina 79
  Torre dell'Orologio 125
  *The Triumph of
    Divine Providence* 47
Cose Così 336, 337
Cosmatesque sculpture and mosaics
  35, 186
Cosmati family 29, 35
Cosmos Radio Taxi 378, 379
Costume jewellery 329, 331
COTRAL 373, 376
Cottini 321
Council of Trent 115
Counter Reformation 45, 106, 109,
  114, 124
Country Club Castel Gondolfo
  350, 351
Cozza, Count Adolfo 263
Crafts fair 60

Crafts shops 334, 335
Crassus 18, 21
Crater of the Dawn 262
Craxi, Bettino 297
The Creation of Adam
  (Michelangelo) 246
The Creation of Eve
  (Michelangelo) 247
The Creation of the Sun and Moon
  (Michelangelo) 246
Credit cards 323, 362
Credito Italiano 362
Crescenzi, Casa dei 200, 203, 274
Crescenzi family 203
Crime 338, 360, 375
Crivelli, Giovanni,
  tombstone 69
Croce, Baldassarre 147, 255
Croff (Centro Casa) 323, 333
Cromek, Thomas Hartley
  Arch of Titus 279
  The Theatre of Marcellus 151
Cross of Justin 250
Crucifixion (Van Dyck) 156
The Crucifixion of St Peter
  (Caravaggio) 139
Cryptoporticus 99, 100
C.u.c.i.n.a. 333
Cul de Sac 1 (wine bar) 318, 320
Cul de Sac 2 (restaurant) 311, 316
Curia 79, 82
Currency 362–3
Customs and immigration 366
Cybele, Temple of *see* Temple
  of Cybele
Cycling 351, 378, 379

D

Da Baffetto 318, 320
Da Cocco 321
Da Gildo 321
Da Gino 310, 312
Da Giovanni 320
Da Lucia 311, 316
Da Paris 311, 316
Da Patrizia e Roberto del
  Pianeta Terra 310, 314
Da Vittorio 321
Dafrosa 174
Damasus, Pope 149
Dance 343
D'Annunzio, Gabriele 328
Dante Alighieri 57, 127, 209, 244
D'Arpino, Cavalier 73
  The Horatii and Curatii 72
David (Bernini) 47, 261
DDT 348, 349
De Bach 328, 331
De' Florio Arte 337
De Filippo, Eduardo 346
De Niro, Robert 296
De Rapiza family 187
De Sica, Vittorio 57
Debussy, Claude 57, 135
Degli Effetti 327, 330
Dei Piccoli 346, 347

Del Colle, Raffaellino 242
Del Grande, Antonio 158
Delettré 329, 331
Il Delfino 308, 319, 320
Delicatessens 334–5
Della Porta, Giacomo
  Fontana delle Tartarughe 150–51
  Gesù 115
  Palazzo dei Conservatori 72
  Palazzo Farnese 147
  San Cesareo 194
  San Luigi dei Francesi 122
  Santa Maria dei Monti 164
  Villa d'Este 268
Della Porta, Jacopo 53
Della Rovere, Cardinal
  Domenico 227
Della Rovere, Giovanni, tomb 139
Della Rovere Chapel, Santa Maria
  del Popolo 138, 139
Della Rovere family 107, 227
Delphic Sibyl (Michelangelo) 247
Delphic Sibyl (Pinturicchio) 139
Delta 368
The Deluge (Michelangelo) 247
Demetria 174
Dentists 361
Department stores 323
The Deposition (Caravaggio) 49
Design, interior 332–3
Di Cori 329, 331
Di Ripetta 290
Dialling codes 365
Diamante 346, 347
Dickens, Charles 57, 135
Diego de Alcalà, San (Carracci) 148
Diocletian, Baths of *see*
  Baths of Diocletian
Diocletian, Emperor 19, 22, 82, 163,
  253, 264
Dion Cassius 95
Dioscuri, statues of 68
  see also Castor and Pollux
Disabled visitors
  entertainments 341
  hotels 290
  practical advice 359
  restaurants 303
Discobolus 71
Discoteca Frattina 334, 335
Discount dell'Alta Moda 327, 330
Discount System 327, 330
Discounts
  shopping 323
  theatre tickets 341
Discovery and Triumph of the Cross
  (Antoniazzo Romano) 181
The Dispute over the Holy Sacrament
  (Raphael) 243
Divina 348, 349
Doctors 361
Dolabella, Arch of 191, 193
La Dolce Vita 39, 52, 251
La Dolceroma 320
Dolcetto 307
Dolci e Doni 319, 320

Domenichino 45, 49, 163, 241
  Sant'Andrea della Valle 123
  Santa Maria in Trastevere 213
  Sant'Onofrio 219
Domine Quo Vadis? (church) 265
Domingo, Placido 38
Dominic, St 54, 193
Dominican order 54, 108, 186,
  193, 204
Dominici 328, 331
Domitia 100
Domitia family 139
Domitian, Emperor 19, 97, 239
  Arch of Titus 87
  Curia 82
  Domus Augustana 100
  Domus Flavia 100
  Forum of Caesar 91
  Forum of Nerva 91
  Stadium 120
Domitilla, Catacombs of *see*
  Catacombs of Domitilla
Domus Augustana 98, 100
Domus Aurea *see* Nero's
  Golden House
Domus Aventina 295, 300
Domus Flavia 98, 100
Domus Mariae 290
Donarelli, Palazzo 277
Donatello, Giovanni,
  Crivelli's tombstone 69
Doney 319, 321
Donizetti, Gaetano 282
Doria Pamphilj, Palazzo
  see Palazzo Doria Pamphilj
Doria Pamphilj, Villa
  see Villa Doria Pamphilj
Doric order 34
Dormitory accommodation 291
Doryphoros 239
Il Drappo 310, 314
Drink Music 349
Drinks 306–7
Druid's Den 345
Drusus, Arch of *see* Arch of Drusus
Due Torri 294, 296
Dughet, Gaspare 158, 169, 170
Duphot, General 218
Dürer, Albrecht 147
Duse 321
Duty-free allowances 366
Dying Galatian 71

E

Eagle Fountain 225
Easter 58
Ecstasy of Beata Ludovica Albertoni
  (Bernini) 211
Ecstasy of St Teresa
  (Bernini) 253, 255, 282
Egyptian art in Vatican Museums 238
Ekberg, Anita 52
Electrical adaptors 367
Embassies 367
Emergency telephone numbers 361
Emperors 18–19

Emporio Armani 133, 327, 330
Endymion (Mola) 73
Energie 327, 330
English-language films 346, 347
English Puppet Theatre 347
ENIT 289, 358, 359
Enoteca Buccone 335
Enoteca Corsi 335
Enoteca del Corso 335
Enoteche (wine bars) 302, 318
Entertainment 340–51
  booking tickets 340, 341
  cinema and theatre 346–7
  classical music and dance 342–3
  disabled visitors 341
  nightclubs 348–9
  open-air 341
  practical information 340, 359
  reduced-price tickets 341
  rock, jazz, folk and world
  music 344–5
  sport 350–51
EPT (Roman Provincial Tourist
  Board) 289, 358, 359
Equitius 170
Er Buchetto 319, 320
Er Faciolaro 320
Erasmus 218
Esposizione Universale di
  Roma *see* EUR
Esquiline 166–75
  area map 167
  restaurants 311, 315, 321
  Street-by-Street map 168–9
  Street Finder maps 5, 6
Esquiline Venus 73
Est! Est! Est! 320
Este, Cardinal Ippolito d' 268
Este, Villa d' 53, 268
Etiquette 323, 359
Etro 327, 330
Etruscans 15
  art 48
  Cerveteri 271
  Etruscan Museum 235, 237
  history 16–17
  jewellery 17
  sculpture 17
  Tarquinia 271
  Vatican Museums 238
  Villa Giulia 46, 262–3, 354
Euclide 321
Eudoxia, Empress 170
Eugenius III, Pope 126
Eugenius IV, Pope, monument 126
EUR 267
  gelaterie 319
  light meals and snacks 321
  LUNEUR amusement park 355
  Natale Oggi 339
Eurocheques 362
Eurocity trains 373
Eurodollar 379
Euroline 373
Europcar 379
Eurysaces, tomb of 184

Eventi 327, 330
Excelsior 291, 295, 301
Exchange rates 362
Exekias 239
Expo Tevere 59, 339
The Expulsion of Heliodorus from the Temple (Raphael) 242
Ezekiel, Moses
  bust of Shelley 134

F

Fabric shops 333
Facchino fountain 107
Fairs 338, 339
Falconieri, Palazzo 276
Faliscans 48, 262
Fantasie di Trastevere 347
Fantasy 349
FAO (UN Food and Agriculture Organization) 196
Farmacia Internazionale Barberini 361
Farmacia Internazionale Capranica 361
Farnese (tile shop) 332, 333
Farnese, Cardinal Alessandro 101, 115
Farnese, Ottavio 122
Farnese archway 276, 277
Farnese family 122, 149, 197
Farnese Gardens 101
Farnese, Palazzo 32, 147, 276
Farnesina, Piccola
  see Piccola Farnesina
Farnesina, Villa
  see Villa Farnesina
Farouk, King of Egypt 136
Fascism 38, 152, 267
Fashion
  sales 322
  shops 325, 326–7, 330
  size chart 329
  Spanish Steps Alta Moda Fashion Show 339
Fast food 318–19, 320–21
Faustina 85, 258
Felice Aqueduct 266–7
Fellini, Federico 39, 52, 57, 251, 348
Feltrinelli 334, 335
Fendi 133, 326, 328, 330
Ferdinand II, King of Aragon 219
Ferragamo 133, 328, 331
Ferragosto 59
Ferrara 321
Ferrari, Francesco 192
Ferrata, Ercole 108, 123
Ferrè, Gianfranco 133, 326, 330
Festa della Madonna Immacolata 61
Festa della Madonna della Neve 59
Festa de Noantri 59, 339, 341
Festa della Primavera 58
Festa di Santa Cecilia 60
Festa di Santa Francesca Romana 58
Festa di San Giovanni 59
Festa di San Giuseppe 58
Festa di San Pietro 59

Festa dell'Unità 341
Festivals 341
Fiamma 346, 347
Fiammetta 126
Fiaschetteria Beltramme 310, 313
Ficoroni Cist 263
Fiddler's Elbow 345
Fiera dell'Antiquariato 339
Fieramosca 347
Filarete Door, St Peter's 231
Filetti di Baccalà 308, 319, 320
Filippo Neri, San *see* Neri, San Filippo
Filippini 117, 125
Films *see* Cinema
La Finestra sul Cortile 344, 345
Fiocco di Neve 320
Fior Fiore 320, 335
Firdusi 259
The Fire in the Borgo (Raphael) 243
Fire services 361
Firenze 294, 297
First Aid 361
Fishmonger's Oratory 151
Fiumicino airport 366, 368, 369, 370
Flaminio 291
Flavian dynasty 92
Flea markets 339
Floorplans, churches 44–5
Florentine Quarter, walks 277
Florentines 153
Flos Arteluce 332, 333
Flowers
  Colosseum 92
  Flower Festival 59
  markets 338
Folk music 344–5
Folk theatre 347
Folklore, Museo del
  see Museo del Folklore
Folkstudio 344, 345
Fonclea 344, 345
Fontana *see* Fountains
Fontana, Carlo
  Fontana Paola 219
  Palazzo di Montecitorio 112
  Piazza di Santa Maria in Trastevere fountain 208
  San Teodoro 202
  Santa Maria in Trastevere 212
  Santi Apostoli 159
  Temple of Hadrian 106
Fontana, Domenico 180
  Column of Marcus Aurelius 113
  Lateran Palace 179
  Moses Fountain 162
  Palazzo del Quirinale 158
  Piazza del Popolo 137
  San Giovanni in Laterano 182, 183
  San Luigi dei Francesi 122
  Santa Maria Maggiore 173
  tomb of Pius V 169
Fontana, Francesco 159
Fontana, Giovanni 258
Fontana, Lavinia
  Portrait of Gregory XIII 27
  Self-portrait 160

Fontana, Luigi 241
Fontana Arte 332, 333
La Fonte della Salute 321
Food and Agriculture Organization of the United Nations (FAO) 196
Food and drink
  drinks 306–7
  ice cream 353
  light meals and snacks 318–21
  markets 338–9
  picnics 353
  shops 334–5
  What to Eat in Rome 304–5
  see also Restaurants
Football 350, 351
Formosus, Pope 26, 182
Formula 1 321
La Fornarina (Raphael's mistress) 208, 210, 255, 316
  portrait by Giulio Romano 111
Fornarina, Casa della 208, 210
Il Forno del Ghetto 320
Foro Italico 342, 343, 344, 350, 351
Foro Olitorio (Forum Holitorium) 152, 274
Forte Appio 284
Forte Prenestino 344, 345, 349
Forum 11, 76–95
  area map 77
  for children 354
  hotels 294, 296
  light meals and snacks 320
  Street Finder maps 5, 8, 9
  Tour of the Roman Forum: East 80–81
  Tour of the Roman Forum: West 78–9
  triumphal arches 278–9
  West Forum
Forum (hotel) 294, 296
Forum of Augustus 90
Forum Boarium 203, 274, 279
Forum of Caesar 90–91
Forum Holitorium (Foro Olitorio) 152, 274
Forum of Nerva 91
Forum of Peace 86, 91
Forum of Trajan 89
Fosse Ardeatine 266
Foster, Lady Elizabeth 83
Fountains 50–53
  Acqua Paola 275
  Cortile della Pigna 225, 234
  drinking water 307, 353, 361
  Eagle Fountain 225
  Fontana dell'Acqua Felice *see* Moses Fountain
  Fontana delle Api (Bernini) 252, 254, 282
  Fontana della Barcaccia (Bernini) 51, 52, 130, 133
  Fontana dei Cavalli Marini 52, 53, 258
  Fontana dei Fauni 259
  Fontana dei Fiumi 50, 52, 53, 119, 120, 283

Fountains (cont.)
Fontana del Mascherone 153, 276
Fontana del Moro 52, 117, 119, 120, 259, 283
Fontana delle Naiadi 51, 52, 155, 164
Fontana della Navicella 53
Fontana di Nettuno 120
Fontana dell'Organo 268
Fontana Paola 52, 219
Fontana delle Tartarughe 50, 52–3, 150–51
Fontana del Tritone (Bernini) 52, 252, 254–5, 282
Fontana dei Tritoni (Bizzaccheri) 201
Fontanella del Facchino 105, 107
Fountain of the Amphorae 52
Fountain of the Four Tiaras 52
Galleon Fountain 53, 225
Moses Fountain 52, 162
Neptune Fountain 282
Ovato Fountain 53
Pantheon Fountain 52, 53
Piazza della Bocca della Verità 51
Piazza del Popolo 37, 50, 52
Piazza di Santa Maria in Trastevere 208
Piazza San Pietro 50, 52
Le Quattro Fontane 53, 162, 282
Rome's best 50–53
Santa Sabina 199
Trevi Fountain 33, 36, 51, 52, 156, 159, 160, 282
Villa d'Este 268
Fragonard, Jean Honoré 135
Francesca Romana, Santa 87
Franchi, Pietro 335
Francis of Assisi, St (San Francesco) 207, 211
Franco Maria Ricci 334, 335
Frangipane family 93, 279
Frascati 306
Fratelli Fabbri 335
Fratelli Rossetti 328, 331
Fratelli Tempera 318, 320
Freedmen's Tombs 184
Fregene 341, 349
French Academy 135
Frette 333
FS (Ferrovie dello Stato) 372–3
Fuga, Ferdinando 127, 147, 172, 173, 218
Fulvia 82
Funeral of St Bernardino (Pinturicchio) 67
Funeral urns 17
Furniture shops 332, 333
Fuscus, Hilarius, Tomb of 285

G

Gabinetto delle Stampe, Villa Farnesina 220
Gaddi, Cardinal 126
Gaddi, Palazzo 126
Gagliardi, Filippo 170

Gaius 84
Galilei, Alessandro 179, 182
Galileo 32, 218
Galleon Fountain 53, 225
La Galleria 334, 335
Galleria Colonna 49
Galleria Comunale d'Arte Moderna 164
Galleria Doria Pamphilj 46, 48
Galleria Giulia 337
Galleria Nazionale d'Arte Antica (Palazzo Barberini) 49, 255
Galleria Nazionale d'Arte Antica (Palazzo Corsini) 49, 217, 218
Galleria Nazionale d'Arte Moderna 49, 259
Galleria Spada 46, 49, 147
Galleries, Rome's Best 46–9
see also Museums and Galleries
Gallienus, Emperor, Arch of, 174
Gallori, Emilio, Garibaldi Monument 218
Galtrucco 333
Gardens see Parks and gardens
Garibaldi, Anita, monument to 216
Garibaldi, Giovanni 333
Garibaldi, Giuseppe 36, 37, 215
Garibaldi Monument 216, 218
Gattinoni, Raniero 326
Gaultier, Jean-Paul 326, 327
Gay clubs 348
Gelateria della Palma 319, 320
Gelaterie (ice cream parlours) 319, 320–21
Gemma alla Lupa 310, 314–15
Genio 294, 296
Genny 326, 330
Gente 326, 330
Genzano 59
George, St 202
George's 311, 317
Germalus 100
Gesman (ticket agency) 340, 341, 346
Gesù 45, 114–15
altar carving 32
concerts 342
confession box 366
floorplan 114–15
Street-by-Street map 105
timeline 115
Geta 83, 278, 279
Gettoni (telephone tokens) 363, 364, 365
Gexim 295, 299
Gherardi, Antonio 150, 160
Ghetto 152
restaurants 302
Walk by the Tiber 274–5
Ghirlandaio, Domenico
Calling of St Peter and St Andrew 245
Sistine Chapel frescoes 244, 245
Gibbon, Edward 57
Gift shops 334
Gigli, Romeo 327

Gilda 348, 349
Gilda on the Beach 349
Ginocchi 328, 331
Ginori, Richard 333
Giolitti, Caffè 109, 308, 319, 320
in EUR 321
Giordano, Luca 151
Giotto 182, 228
Angelo della Navicella mosaic 233
Innocent III's Vision of the Church 26
Stefaneschi Triptych 29, 240
Giovanni 311, 317
Giovanni, San see John, St
Giovanni, San (4th-century martyr) 192
Giovanni di Cosma 196
Giulia, Villa see Villa Giulia
Giulia Domna 47
Giuliana 295, 299
Giuliano da Maiano 75
Giulio Passami l'Olio 348, 349
Giulio Romano 69, 121, 242
La Fornarina 111
Giustizia, Palazzo di 229
Gladiators 93, 94
Glass shops 332–3
Glove shops 329, 331
Gobelins tapestries 107
Il Goccetto 320
Goethe, Johann Wolfgang von 54, 57, 133
Casa di Goethe 136
portrait of Goethe in the Roman countryside by Tischbein 136
statue of 258
Goethe, Julius, grave of 205
Golden House see Nero's Golden House
Goldsmiths 329, 331
Golf 350, 351
Good Friday 58
Goths 24, 82, 165, 180, 197
Governo Vecchio, Palazzo del 124
Gozzoli, Benozzo 151, 165
Gracchi brothers 21
Gracchus, Gaius 18
Gracchus, Tiberius 18
I Granai 323
Grand 293, 295, 299
Grande Raccordo Anulare (GRA) 373
Grape festival 60
Gray, Eileen 332
Great Schism 30
El Greco 255
Greco, Emilio 241
Greek art in Vatican Museums 239
Green Cards 373
Green Line Tours 359
Gregorian Etruscan Museum 48
Gregorian Museum of Pagan Antiquities 235, 237
Gregorian Profane Museum 239
Gregorian University 157

Gregoriana (hotel) 290, 294, 297
Gregoriana, Villa 268
Gregorovius, Ferdinand 57
Gregory I (the Great), Pope 25, 26, 90, 190, 192
Gregory III, Pope 26, 111
Gregory IV, Pope 75
Gregory VII, Pope 26, 172, 180
Gregory IX, Pope 26, 139
Gregory XI, Pope 30
Gregory XIII, Pope 27, 69, 106, 124, 158
Gregory XVI, Pope 268
Greyhound racing 350, 351
Groove 348, 349
Grotto of Lourdes 224
Gucci 133, 328, 331
Guercino 49, 107, 147, 254
 Burial and Glory of St Petronilla 72
Guerrini 321
Guibert, antipope 180
Guided tours 359
Guidi, Domenico 146
Guiscard, Robert 180, 186

H

Hadrian, Emperor 19, 223, 268
 Mausoleum (Castel Sant'Angelo) 248, 249
 Obelisk in Pincio Gardens 137
 Ostia Antica 271
 Pantheon 23, 110, 111
 Temple of Hadrian 106
 Temple of Venus and Rome 81, 87, 175
Hadrian's Villa (Tivoli) 34, 71, 238, 257, 269
Handbag shops 328
Handicraft shops 334, 335
Handing over the Keys to St Peter (Perugino) 245
Hangar 348, 349
Hannibal 20, 21, 123, 195
Hannibalianus 264
Hare, Augustus 57
Hassler 293, 294, 298
Hassler Roof Restaurant 310, 313
Hat shops 329, 331
Health 361
Health clubs 351
Heaven 348, 349
Helena (daughter of Constantine I) 264
Helena, St (mother of Constantine I) 43, 180, 181
 statue of 181
Heliogabalus, Emperor 19, 85
Hemingway (bar) 348, 349
Hemingway, Ernest 293, 298
Henry IV, Holy Roman Emperor 180
Henry VII, Emperor 93
Henry VII, King of England 229
Henry VIII, King of England 192, 255
Hepburn, Audrey 326, 340
Heraclitus, Emperor 181
Hermès 133

"Heroic Relief", Tomb of the 284, 285
Hertz 379
Hilton 351
Hiring
 bikes and mopeds 378, 379
 cars 379
History 15–39
Holbein, Hans 255
Holiday Inn Crowne Plaza Minerva 294, 296
Holidays, public 61
Holy Roman Empire 28
Holy Trinity (Reni) 147
Homer 124
Homs 294, 297
Honorius, Emperor 196
Honorius III, Pope 26, 193, 265
Horace 56, 175, 268
The Horatii and Curatii (D'Arpino) 72
Horatius 17
Horses
 horse-drawn carriages 378
 riderless races in Via del Corso 137
 riding 350, 351
 shows 58
 trotting 350
Horti Sallustiani 251
Hosiery shops 329, 331
Hospital of Santo Spirito 226–7
Hospitals 361
Hostaria dell'Orso 127
Hostilius, Tullius 18
Hotel Lord Byron 317
Hotels 288–301
 booking 289
 checking in and out 289
 children in 290
 disabled travellers 290
 exchange rates 362
 facilities 289
 hidden extras 289
 prices 288–9
 residential 290
 Rome's Best 292–3
 safes 360
 telephones 364
Houdon, Jean-Antoine 163
House *see also* Casa
House of Augustus 97
House of Cupid and Psyche 271
House of Diana 271
House of the Dioscuri 271
House of Livia 98, 101
House of the Vestal Virgins 80, 85
Hugo, Victor, statue of 258
Husband and Wife Sarcophagus 262
Huts of Romulus 98, 101
Hylas, Pomponius 195

I

Ibiz 328, 331
Ice cream 353
Ice cream parlours 319, 320–21
Ignatius Loyola, St 114, 115
 see also Sant'Ignazio di Loyola

Ignudi (Michelangelo) 247
Immacolata, Colonna dell' *see* Colonna dell'Immacolata
Imperial Rome
 history 22–3
Imperiale 295, 301
In Trastevere 290
Ine, King of Wessex 28, 226, 228
Inghilterra (hotel) 293, 294, 298
Ingres, Jean Auguste 55, 135
Innocent II, Pope 26, 213
Innocent III, Pope, 26, 226
Innocent III's Vision of the Church (Giotto) 26
Innocent VIII, Pope, 27, 203, 234, 235
Innocent X, Pope 27
 Carceri Nuove 276
 Fontana dei Fiumi 120
 Palazzo Pamphilj 118, 120
 Piazza Navona 283
 portrait 49, 105, 107
 Sant'Agnese in Agone 121
 Villa Doria Pamphilj 267
Inoculations 361, 366
Insula, Roman 66, 68
Insurance
 air travel 368
 cars 373, 379
 medical 361
 property 360
Intercity trains 372
Interior design shops 332–3
International Exhibition (1911) 259
International Herald Tribune 367
International Horse Show 58
International Services 290
International Tennis Championship 58
Ionic order 34
Ippodromo delle Capannelle 344, 345, 350, 351
Ippodromo di Tor di Valle 350, 351
Irish Dominicans 186
Iron Age 80, 97, 101
 history 15, 16
Isabella of Castile 219
Isis, cult of 73, 285
Isola Tiberina (Tiber Island) 10, 152, 275
Istituto Madri Pie 290, 291
Italcable 364
Italian Automobile Club 372
Italian State Tourist Board (ENIT) 289, 358, 359
IVA (Value Added Tax) 323, 366
Ivo 318, 321

J

Jackie O (nightclub) 348, 349
James, Henry 57
James, St, tomb of 159
Janiculum 214–21
 area map 215
 restaurants 311, 316

Janiculum (cont.)
Street Finder maps 3, 4, 7, 11
Tour of the Janiculum 216–17
Janus, Arch of see Arch of Janus
Jazz 344, 349
Jeff Blynn's 348, 349
Jerome, St (Leonardo da Vinci) 237
Jesuits 32, 54, 106, 227
Collegio di Propaganda
Fide 132
Gesù 105, 114–15
Sant'Andrea al Quirinale 161
Sant'Ignazio di Loyola 105
Jewellery
costume 329, 331
goldsmiths and silversmiths
329, 331
shops 328–9, 331
Jews 87
Ghetto 152
synagogues 152, 275, 367
Jogging 351
John, St 194
John the Baptist, St (Caravaggio) 72
John XI, Pope 26
John XII, Pope 26
John Paul II, Pope 38, 39, 121,
342, 366
Jonella 294, 297
Joseph Lending Grain to the
Egyptians
(Théudon) 146
Julia (daughter of Emperor
Augustus) 82, 101, 140, 141
Julian the Apostate, Emperor 19,
174, 192
Julius II, Pope 26, 27, 126, 227,
243, 277
Obelisk of Montecitorio 113
private apartments in
Vatican 242
St Peter's 31, 230
Sistine Chapel 246
tomb 170
Vatican Museums 234, 235, 239
Via Giulia 153, 276
Julius III, Pope 48, 262
Jupiter, Temple of see Temple
of Jupiter
Justin, Emperor, Cross of 25
Juvenal 68

K

Katty 295, 299
Kauffmann, Angelica 156, 160
Self-portrait 56
Keats, John 37, 133, 288, 290
grave 205
portrait of 57
Keats-Shelley Memorial House 49,
131, 134
Kings of ancient Rome 18
Kinson, Portrait of Pauline
Borghese 49
Kitchen shops 332, 333
K.K. 345

Klee, Paul, Town with Gothic
Cathedral 241
Knights of Malta 204
Knights of St John 90
Knitwear 327, 330
Kostka, St Stanislas 161
Krechel 320
Krizia 327

L

Labirinto 346, 347
Laboratorio Scatole 334, 335
Labre, Benoit-Joseph 164
Lagerfeld, Karl 326, 329
Lake Regillus, battle of 84
Lampronti, Cesare 336, 337
Landini, Taddeo 150
Landmark Trust 290
Lanfranco, Giovanni 123, 147
Laocoön 48, 49, 236, 237, 239
Lapidary Gallery, Vatican
Museums 25, 237, 240
Largo della Moretta 276
The Last Judgment
(Michelangelo) 244
Late clubs 349
Lateran 176–87
area map 177
restaurants 311, 315, 321
Street-by-Street map 178–9
Street Finder maps 6, 9, 10
Lateran Palace 177, 180, 182, 183
Street-by-Street map 179
Lateran Treaty (1929) 38
Laterani family 182
Latin language 15
Latins 48
Lavori Artigianili Femminili 355
Lazzi Express 373
Leather goods shops 328, 331
Léger, Fernand 241
Legros, Pierre 146, 161
statue of San Filippo Neri 148
Lella, Sora (restaurant) 310, 314
Leo I, Pope 170
Leo III, Pope 26, 243, 280
Leo IV, Pope 26, 226, 243
Leo X, Pope 26, 27, 30, 229
Palazzo della Cancelleria 149
Palazzo Madama 122
Raphael Rooms 243
San Giovanni dei Fiorentini 153
Santa Maria in Domnica 193
tomb of 108
Leo XI, Pope 27
monument to 232
Leonardo da Vinci 241, 243
St Jerome 237
Leonardo da Vinci airport see
Fiumicino airport
Il Leoncino 320
"Leonine City" 226
Leonine Wall 224
Lepidus, Marcus 19, 82
Lepidus, Marcus Aemilius 82
Leroy, Thomas 149

Les Etoiles 311, 316
Letters, postal service 365
The Liberation of St Peter
(Raphael) 243
Liberius, Pope 26, 172
Liberti 327, 330
Liberty style 336
Libreria Belardetti 334, 335
Libreria Godel 334, 335
Libreria San Silvestro 334, 335
Licinius, Caius, Tomb of 285
Lighthouse, Manfredi 216
Lighting shops 332, 333
Ligorio, Pirro 225, 234, 268
Linens, shops 333
Lingerie shops 327, 330–31
Lippi, Filippino 245
Lippi, Filippo 48, 255
Liszt, Franz 57, 133, 298
Livia 97, 141
House of see House of Livia
Livia's Villa 47, 48
Livy 16, 74
Liz 327, 330
Locarno 289, 294, 297
Loggia of Cupid and Psyche,
Villa Farnesina 221
Loggias 35
Lombard community 141
Lombardi, Pietro 52
Longhi, Martino the Elder
Chiesa Nuova 124
Palazzetto Cenci 153
Palazzo Altemps 127
Santa Maria della
Consolazione 203
Santa Maria in Trastevere 213
Santi Ambrogio e Carlo al Corso 141
Longhi, Martino the Younger 160
Longhi, Onorio 141
Lord Byron (hotel) 295, 301
Loren, Sophia 326
Lorenzetto (Lorenzo Lotti) 111, 138
Lorenzo, San (St Lawrence) 85, 265
Lost property 361
Lotto, Lorenzo 107
Louis, St 119
Louis XIV, King of France 134–5, 160
Loyola, St Ignatius of 54, 105, 106, 125
Luca, San see Luke, St
Lucius 84, 140
Ludovic, St
St Ludovic Kneels Before
Boniface VIII (Martini) 26–7
Ludovisi, Bernardino 147
Ludovisi, Cardinal Ludovico 106, 254
Ludovisi, Prince 112
Ludovisi family 163, 251, 252, 254
Ludwig, King of Bavaria 133
Luke, St 160, 180
Luna e L'altra 327, 330
Lunetta 294, 298
LUNEUR amusement park 355
Lungotevere embankments 274
Walk by the Tiber 276
Luther, Martin 54, 107, 227

Lutyens, Edwin 258, 259
Lydia 294, 297

M

McDonald's 319, 320, 321
Macedonian War 21
Mackintosh, Charles Rennie 332
Madama, Palazzo 119, 122
La Maddalena 109
Maderno, Carlo 56
  Palazzo Barberini 255
  Palazzo del Monte di Pietà 146
  Palazzo del Quirinale 158
  Piazza San Pietro fountains 50
  St Peter's 230
  Sant'Andrea della Valle 123
  San Giovanni dei Fiorentini 153
  Santa Susanna 255
  tomb of 153
Maderno, Stefano 211
  statue of St Cecilia 42
Madonna (the popular singer) 301
Madonna and Child, mosaic in
  Chapel of St Zeno,
  Santa Prassede 28
Madonna della Clemenza, icon in
  Santa Maria in Trastevere 213
Madonna di Foligno (Raphael) 31, 225
Madonna di Guadalupe (statue in
  Vatican Gardens) 224
*Madonna, San Rocco and
  Sant'Antonio with Victims of
  the Plague* (Il Baciccia) 141
Madonna della Strada, painting
  in the Gesù 115
Maecenas 167
  Auditorium of 175
Maga Morgana 327, 331
Magazines
  entertainments listings 340
Magazzini Forma & Memoria 332, 333
Maggiore (car hire firm) 379
Magistretti, Vico 332
Magli, Bruno 328, 331
Mai Visto 327, 331
Maidalchini, Olimpia 120
Mail services 365
Majestic 288, 295, 301
Mambo 345
Mamertine Prison 91, 354
Manasse 336, 337
Mancini, Maria 160
Mancini, Ortensia 160
Mandarina Duck 328, 331
Manfredi 294, 298
Manfredi Lighthouse 216
Manilio, Lorenzo 153
Manuia 318, 321
Maratta, Carlo 141
Marcellinus 264
Marcellus 141
Marcellus, Theatre of
  see Theatre of Marcellus
Marchetti 321
Marcillat, Guillaume de 139
Marco Marinucci 328, 331

Marconi (beer house) 321
Marforio (talking statue) 124
Margani family 274
La Margherita 351
Margherita, Madama of Austria 122
Margherita, Palazzo 254
Margutta 294, 297
Mari 295, 299
Mariani, Camillo 162
Marini, Pasquale 131
Marino 306
Marino Wine Festival 60
Mario alle Vite 310, 313
Marius 18, 20
Marj, Paolo 332, 330
Mark, St 26, 75
  see also San Marco
Markets 338–9
  Rome's Best 324–5
  local 339
  Campo de' Fiori 143, 145,
  146, 322, 338
  Mercato Andrea Doria 338
  Mercato dei Fiori 338
  Mercato delle Stampe 323, 337, 338
  Mercato di Testaccio 325, 338
  Mercato di Via Sannio 180, 339
  Piazza Vittorio Emanuele II
  174, 338
  Porta Portese 339
Markets, Trajan's
  see Trajan's Markets
Marozia 28
Martial 68
Martin V, Pope 27, 30, 75, 158–9
Martini 307
Martini, Simone, *St Ludovic Kneels
  before Boniface VIII,* 26–7
Martyrdom of St Simon
  (Pomarancio) 194
Maruccelli, Paolo 122
Le Maschere 310, 313, 321
Mascherino, Ottaviano 126
Masolino, San Clemente frescoes 186
The Mass at Bolsena (Raphael) 242
Massimo family 123
Massimo, Paolo 123
Massimo alle Colonne,
  Palazzo 118, 123
Massoni 329, 331
Matisse, Henri 241
Mattei family 150, 190, 193, 275
Matteo da Città di Castello 124
Mauro Vigneti Gallery 337
Mausoleum of Augustus 141, 158
Max & Co 327, 330
Maxentius, Emperor 19
  Arch of Constantine 91, 279
  Aurelian Wall 196
  Basilica of Constantine and
  Maxentius 86
Maximus, Quintus Fabius 18
MaxMara 326, 330
Mazzarino, Cardinal Raimondo 160
Mazzini, Giuseppe 36
Medici, Alessandro de' 122

Medici, Caterina de' 122
Medici, Duke Cosimo II de' 277
Medici, Cardinal Ferdinando de' 135
Medici family 122
  see also Leo X, Pope
  and Clement VII, Pope
Medici, Villa 135, 341, 343
Medieval Rome 28–9, 44
Mekong 310, 313
Melchiades, Pope 182
Meli, Giosuè 180
Melvyn's 344, 345
Menasci 355
Men's fashion 326–7, 330
Menus 303
Meo Patacca 347
Merano 295, 300
Mercato Andrea Doria 338
Mercato dei Fiori 338
Mercato Generale 339
Mercato delle Stampe 323, 337, 338
Mercato di Piazza Vittorio 174, 338
Mercato di Testaccio 338
Mercato di Via Sannio 180, 339
Merola 329, 331
Il Messaggero 367
Messalina 184
Metella, Cecilia, tomb of 265, 266
Methodist Church 367
Metro 376–7
  map 370–71
Metropolitan 359
Michael, Archangel 248, 249
Michelangelo 30, 46, 56, 108, 123,
  135, 149, 218, 219, 220, 239, 243
  Cordonata 65, 66
  Farnese archway 276, 277
  The Last Judgment 244
  Moses 45, 162, 170
  Palazzo dei Conservatori 72
  Palazzo Farnese 144, 147
  Palazzo Nuovo 70
  Piazza del Campidoglio 65, 67, 68
  Pietà 31, 233
  portrait of 126
  St Peter's 31, 42, 45, 230, 232
  Santa Maria degli Angeli 45, 163
  Sistine Chapel 31, 241, 244, 245,
  246–7, 354
  tomb of Pope Julius II 170
  Villa Giulia 262
Michiel, Cardinal Giovanni,
  tomb of 159
Midnight Mass 61
Mila Schön 330
Il Millennio 337
Milton, John 57
Milvian Bridge, Battle of the 24
Mimosa 294, 296
Minibuses, electric 358, 376
Minicabs 360–61
Minim's de Paris 319, 320
Ministry of Finance 362
Ministry of Justice 276
Miracle of St Benno (Saraceni) 121
Miraggio 349

Miranda 327, 330
Mississippi Blues 344, 345
Missoni 327
Missoni Donna 330
Missoni Uomo 330
Mithraism 23, 186, 187
Mithras 23
Mola, Pier Francesco, *Endymion* 73
Momix 340
Momo, Giuseppe 235, 241
Mondadori 334, 335
Money 362–3
  security 360
  traveller's cheques 360, 361
Moneychangers' Arch *see* Arco
  degli Argentari
Monnot 71
Montaigne, Michel de 57, 127
Monte Cavallo 158
Monte di Pietà, Palazzo del 145, 146
Monte Testaccio 204
La Montecarlo 318, 320
Montecitorio, Obelisk of
  see Obelisk of Montecitorio
Montecitorio, Palazzo di 33, 112, 283
Montelupo, Raffaele da 108
Montepulciano d'Abruzzo 307
Montoya, Cardinal Pedro Foix de
  144, 148
Monuments
  to Anita Garibaldi 216
  to Garibaldi 216, 218
  Victor Emmanuel 37, 38, 65, 74
Moon 327, 331
Moore, Henry 241
Mopeds 378, 379
Moravia, Alberto 57
Morelli, Cosimo 123
Moro, Aldo 39
Moroni Gioielli 329, 331
Morris, William 135
Mosaics
  Tour of Rome's Best
  Mosaics 280–81
  Baths of Caracalla 188, 239
  Baths of Otricoli 239
  for children 354
  Cosmatesque 35
  Mosaic of the Doves 71
  Museo Borghese 261
  Ostia Antica 271
  Sant'Agnese fuori le Mura 264
  San Clemente 187
  Santa Costanza 24–5
  Santa Maria in Domnica 191
  Santa Maria Maggiore 172, 173
  Santa Maria in Trastevere 29,
  208, 212–13
  Santi Nereo e Achilleo 194
  Santa Prassede 28, 171
  Vatican Museums 46, 237
Moses (Michelangelo) 170
Moses Fountain 52, 162
Mosque 367
Mostra (monumental fountains) 52
Motor racing 350, 351

Motorbike racing 350
Mouth of Truth *see* Bocca della Verità
Movies 39, 57, 346, 347
Mozart (hotel) 294, 298
Mozart, Wolfgang Amadeus 57
Mr Boots 328, 331
Mullooly, Father 186
Multimedia shops 334, 335
Munch, Edvard 241
Muratori, Domenico 159
Murillo, Bartolomé 218
Museo *see* Museums
Museums and galleries
  cafés 319
  for children 354
  practical information 358
  Rome's Best 46–9
  Antiquarium Forense 48, 81, 87
  Burcardo Theatre Museum 49,
  149
  Capitoline Museums 48, 49, 65, 66,
  67, 70–73, 74
  Chiaramonti Museum 235, 237, 239
  Christian Museum 235
  Etruscan Museum 235, 237
  Galleria Colonna 49
  Galleria Doria Pamphilj 46, 48
  Galleria Nazional d'Arte Antica
  at Palazzo Barberini 47, 49, 255
  Galleria Nazional d'Arte Antica
  at Palazzo Corsini 46, 49, 217, 218
  Galleria Nazionale d'Arte
  Moderna 49, 259
  Galleria Spada 49
  Gregorian Etruscan Museum 48
  Gregorian Museum of Pagan
  Antiquities 235, 237
  Gregorian Profane Museum 239
  Keats-Shelley Memorial House 49,
  131, 134
  Museo delle Arti e Tradizioni
  Popolari 354
  Museo Barracco 48, 149
  Museo Borghese 47, 49, 260–61
  Museo delle Cere 49, 156, 159
  Museo del Civiltà Romana 48, 90,
  113, 267
  Museo del Folklore 49, 208, 210
  Museo delle Mura 354
  Museum of Musical
  Instruments 49, 181
  Museo Napoleonico 49, 127
  Museo Nazionale d'Arte
  Orientale 174–5
  Museo Nazionale Etrusco 48, 262
  Museo Nazionale Romano 47, 48,
  155, 163
  Museum of Pagan Antiquities 235
  Museo del Palazzo Venezia 75
  Museo di Roma 123
  Museo Zoologico 259
  Palatine Museum, 99
  Pio-Christian Museum 237, 240
  Pio-Clementine Museum 235,
  237, 239
  Vatican Museums 48, 49, 234–7

Music
  ballet and dance 343
  booking tickets 340
  in churches 342
  contemporary 343
  folk 344–5
  jazz 344, 349
  musicians 57
  open-air 341, 342–3
  opera 343
  orchestral, chamber and choral
  342, 343
  rock 344
  salsa and African 349
  shops 334, 335
  world 345
Musical Instruments, Museum of 181
Mussolini, Benito 38, 53
  Casina Valadier 136
  Museo delle Cere 159
  Obelisk of Axum 196
  Palazzo Venezia 75
Myricae 332, 333
Myron 239

N

Nadia e Davide 321
Napoleon I, Emperor 36
  Museo Napoleonico 49, 127
Napoleon III, Emperor 127
Nardecchia 337
Natale Oggi 339
Navona (hotel) 294, 296
Navona, Piazza *see* Piazza Navona
Nazionale (hotel) 294, 296
Nazis 266
Nel Regno del Re Ferdinando 310, 312
Nemi 271
Neo-Classicism 56
Neo-Realism 57
Neptune Fountain 282
Nereus, St 194
Neri, San Filippo 123, 148
  Chiesa Nuova 117, 118, 124
  Oratorio dei Filippini 125
  Santissima Trinità dei
  Pellegrini 146–7
  statue of 148
  tomb of 124
  Visit of the Seven Churches 193
Nero, Emperor 19, 22, 186
  Aqueduct of 184, 191, 193, 358
  Colossus of 93
  Cryptoporticus 100
  ghost of 138
  Torre delle Milizie 90
Nero's Golden House 92, 100, 175, 281
Nerva, Emperor 19, 88
  Forum of Nerva 91
Nervi, Pier Luigi 224
New Jolie Cover 348, 349
New Life 348, 349
New Year's Eve 61
Newspapers 367
  entertainments listings 340
  shops 334

Nicholas, St 205
Nicholas III, Pope 180
Nicholas IV, Pope 172
Nicholas V, Pope 27, 126
  St Peter's 31, 230
  Santo Stefano Rotondo 185
  San Teodoro 201
  Vatican chapel 241
Nicholas V Receiving a Book 27
Nicolò di Angelo 267
Night buses 376
Night driving 375
Nightclubs 348–9
Noantri, Festa di 59, 339, 341
Nobilor, Marcus Fulvius 82
Normans 29, 185
Numa Pompilius, King 16, 18
Nuovo Sacher 346, 347

O

Oasis di Pace 350, 351
Obelisks
  Rome's Best 50–53
  of Axum 53, 196
  Circus Maximus 205
  Fontana dei Fiumi 120
  Montecitorio 53, 113
  Piazza dell'Esquilino 53, 168, 172
  Piazza del Popolo 50, 53, 137
  Piazza del Quirinale 53, 158, 162
  Piazza di San Giovanni
    in Laterano 51, 53
  Piazza San Pietro 53, 224
  Pincio Gardens 137
  Santa Maria Maggiore 162
  Santa Maria sopra Minerva 50, 53,
    104, 108
  Trinità dei Monti 162
  Villa Celimontana 193
Octavia 101
  Portico of 151, 274
Octavian *see* Augustus, Emperor
Odazzi, Giovanni 159
Oddi e Seghetti 329, 331
Odoacer 18
Odorisio 332, 333
Old Master paintings, shops 336,
  337
Olgiata Golf Club 350, 351
Olive oil 304
Oliver 327, 330
Olympic Games (1960) 39, 267
Open-air concerts 341, 342–3
Open-air theatre 347
Open Gate 348, 349
Opening hours
  banks 362
  museums 358
  restaurants 303
  shops 322
Opera 343
  booking tickets 340
  open-air 341
  Three Tenors Concert 38–9
Opificio Romano 334, 335
Oratorio dei Filippini 118, 125

Oratorio del Gonfalone 277, 342, 343
Orbis 340, 341
Orchestral music 342, 343
Orders, Classical architecture 34
Original Sin (Michelangelo) 247
Orsini family 151
Orso, Bishop Antonio, tomb of 159
Orvieto 60
  wine 306
Osiris 344, 345
Un Ospite a Roma 359
L'Osservatore Romano 224
Ostello del Foro Italico 291
Osteria dell'Antiquario 310, 312
Osteria Picchioni 318, 321
Ostia Antica 270–71, 347, 354
Ostiense station 368, 369
Ottaviano 291
Otto I, Emperor 28
Ottoboni, Cardinal 57
Ouroboros 329, 331
Ovato Fountain 53
Ovid 56
Oxford (hotel) 295, 300

P

Package holidays 369
Paganini 333
Painters 56
Paintings, shops 336, 337
Palace of Justice *see* Palazzo
  di Giustizia
Palace of Septimius Severus 97,
  99, 100
Paladini 319, 320
Palatine 96–101
  area map 97
  for children 354
  Street Finder map 8
  Tour of the Palatine 98–9
Palatine Museum 99
Palatium 100
Palazzetto Cenci 153
Palazzetto dell'Orologio 258
Palazzi, Carlo 327, 330
Palazzina di Pius IV 259
Palazzo Altemps 127
Palazzo Altieri 105, 107
Palazzo Baldassini 109
Palazzo del Banco di Santo
  Spirito 125
Palazzo Barberini 108, 255
  Rome's Best Museums and
    Galleries 47, 49
  Street-by-Street map 252
  Walk around Bernini's Rome 282
Palazzo Borghese 112
Palazzo Brancaccio 174
Palazzo Braschi 118, 123
Palazzo della Cancelleria 31, 149
  concerts 342
  Street-by-Street map 145
Palazzo Capranica 113
Palazzo Caprini 30
Palazzo Cenci 152–3, 275
Palazzo della Civiltà del Lavoro 267

Palazzo Clarelli 277
Palazzo del Collegio Romano
  105, 106
Palazzo Colonna 157, 158
Palazzo del Commendatore 227
Palazzo dei Conservatori 68, 72–3
  floorplan 72–3
  Rome's Best Museums
    and Galleries 47, 49
  Street-by-Street map 66
Palazzo dei Convertendi 227
Palazzo Corsini 218
  Rome's Best 46, 49
  Street-by-Street map 217
Palazzo Donarelli 277
Palazzo Doria Pamphilj 105, 107
Palazzo delle Esposizioni 164,
  346, 347
  café 319, 321
Palazzo Falconieri 276
Palazzo Farnese 32, 147, 276
Palazzo del Freddo di Giovanni
  Fassi 321
Palazzo Gaddi 126
Palazzo di Giustizia 229
Palazzo del Governo Vecchio 124
Palazzo Grazioli 107
Palazzo Madama 119, 122
Palazzo Margherita 254
Palazzo Massimo 163
Palazzo Massimo alle Colonne
  118, 123
Palazzo Misciattelli 127
Palazzo del Monte di Pietà 145, 146
Palazzo di Montecitorio 33, 112, 283
Palazzo Nardini 124
Palazzo Nuovo 33, 68, 70–71
  floorplan 70–71
  Rome's Best Museums
    and Galleries 47
  Street-by-Street map 67
Palazzo Odescalchi 156
Palazzo Pamphilj 118, 120
Palazzo dei Penitenzieri 227
Palazzo Pio Righetti 145, 146
Palazzo delle Poste 364
Palazzo del Quirinale 157, 158, 282
Palazzo Ricci 144, 149, 276
Palazzo Sacchetti 277
Palazzo Senatorio 65, 67, 68
Palazzo Spada 145, 147
Palazzo dello Sport 267, 344, 345
Palazzo Torlonia 229
Palazzo Venezia 75
  Rome's Best 47, 49
  Street-by-Street map 66
Palena, Beato Nicola da Forca,
  tomb of 219
Palestrina 15, 271
Palestrina, Giovanni Luigi da 57
Palladium (sacred statue of Troy) 85
Palladium (club) 344, 345, 348, 349
Pallas Athenae 85
Pallavicini, Cardinal 211
Palombi 321
Pamphilj, Prince Camillo 267

Pamphilj family 107
Pamphilj, Palazzo 118, 120
Panattoni 318, 321
Pannini, Giovanni Paolo
  Interior of the Pantheon 41
  Piazza Navona with Fontana dei
  Fiumi 53
Pannocchi 321
Pantheon 41, 83, 103, 110–11
  architectural features 110–11
  floorplan 44
  history 25
  Rome's Best Churches
  and Temples 42, 44
  Street-by-Street map 104
  timeline 111
  Walk around Bernini's Rome 283
Pantheon Fountain 52, 53
Paolo, San (4th-century martyr) 192
Paolo, San *see* Paul, St
Papà Giovanni 310, 312
Papacy 26–7
Papal Audience Chamber 224
Paper crafts shops 334, 335
Papirus 334, 335
Pappagallo 328, 331
Parco Appio Claudio 266–7
Parking 289, 375, 379
Parks and gardens
  for children 355
  jogging 351
  Botanical gardens 215, 217, 218
  Colle Oppio 281
  Farnese Gardens 101
  Hadrian's Villa 269
  Palazzo Farnese 276
  Parco Appio Claudio 266–7
  Parco del Celio 191
  Pincio Gardens 136–7, 343
  Villa Aldobrandini 165
  Villa Borghese 258–9, 352,
  353, 355
  Villa Celimontana 193
  Villa Doria Pamphilj 60, 267, 341
  Villa d'Este 53, 268
  Villa Giulia 262, 341
  Villa Gregoriana 268
  Villa Sciarra 211
Parmesan 305
Parnassus (Raphael) 48
La Partenopea 321
Paschal candlestick 186
Paschal I, Pope 26
  Chapel of St Zeno 281
  Santa Cecilia in Trastevere 211
  Santa Maria in Domnica 193, 280
Paschal II, Pope 26
  Santa Maria del Popolo 138, 139
  Santa Prassede 171
Pasolini, Pier Paolo 57
Pasquali, Guido 328, 331
Pasquino (talking statue) 120, 124
  Street-by-Street map 118
Pasquino (English-language
  cinema) 346, 347
Passetto *see* Vatican Corridor

Passports 289, 360, 361, 366
Pasta 304, 305
Pasticcerie (pastry shops)
  319, 320–21
Pastry shops 319, 320–21
Paul, St 87, 185, 228
  graffiti in catacombs 265
  history 22, 24, 25
  statue of 113
  tomb of 267
Paul II, Pope 27, 75
Paul III, Pope 27
  Castel Sant'Angelo 249
  coat of arms 277
  Palazzo del Monte di Pietà 146
  Palazzo Farnese 147
  Piazza del Campidoglio 68
  St Peter's 31
  Sangallo Bastion 196
  Sistine Chapel 170, 244
  Paul III Gives his Approval to the
  Capuchin Order (Ricci) 27
Paul IV, Pope 27, 152
Paul V, Pope 27
  Fontana Paola 52, 219
  Galleon Fountain 225
  Palazzo del Banco di Santo
  Spirito 125
  Palazzo Borghese 112
  Santa Maria Maggiore 172
Paul VI, Pope 235, 241
Pavarotti, Luciano 38, 301
PDS 341
Peccati di Gola 311, 316
Peck, Gregory 340
Pedestrian crossings 374
Pediments 34
Pelagius II, Pope 26, 265
Pendolino trains 372
Penitenzieri, Palazzo dei 227
Penni, Giovanni Francesco 242
Perfume, duty-free allowances
  366
Perilli a Testaccio 311, 315
Peroso 329, 331
Perugia 60
Perugino 56, 242
  Handing over the Keys to
  St Peter 245
  Sistine Chapel frescoes 244, 245
Peruzzi, Baldassarre 151
  biography 220
  Palazzo Massimo
  alle Colonne 118, 123
  Sant'Eligio degli Orefici 148
  Santa Maria della Pace 121
  Villa Farnesina 217, 220–21
Peter, St (San Pietro)
  history 22, 24, 25, 26
  legends 91, 171, 185, 194, 265
  relics 87, 168, 228
  San Pietro in Montorio 219
  San Pietro in Vincoli 45, 170
  statues of 31, 90, 233
  tomb of 230, 232
  Vatican 223

Peter of Illyria 204
Petocchi 329, 331
Petrarch 57
Petrol 375, 379
Pharmacies 360, 361
Philip, St, tomb of 159
Philip Neri, St *see* Neri, San Filippo
Philippine Airlines 368
Phocas, Column of *see* Column
  of Phocas
Photographs, antique shops 337
Piacentini, Pio 164
Piazza Belli 209
Piazza della Bocca della
  Verità 51, 200–201
Piazza Campo de' Fiori market 322
Piazza dei Cavalieri di Malta 204
Piazza del Campidoglio 65, 68, 72
  Street-by-Street map 67
Piazza delle Coppelle market 339
Piazza Esedra *see* Piazza
  della Repubblica
Piazza dell'Esquilino
  obelisk 53, 172
  Street-by-Street map 168
Piazza del Fico market 339
Piazza della Minerva obelisk 283
Piazza di Montecitorio obelisk 53,
  113
Piazza Navona 116–27, 353
  area map 117
  Befana 61, 355
  history 33
  hotels 294, 296–7
  restaurants 310, 312, 320
  Street-by-Street map 118–19
  Street Finder maps 4, 11, 12
  walks 283
Piazza Navona with Fontana dei
  Fiumi (Pannini) 53
Piazza della Pilotta 157
Piazza in Piscinula 275
Piazza del Popolo 137
  flower market 58
  fountains 37, 50, 52
  obelisk 53
Piazza di Porta Capena 279
Piazza del Quirinale 158
  obelisk 53, 162
  Street-by-Street map 157
Piazza della Repubblica 155, 164
Piazza della Rotonda 102–15
  area map 103
  hotels 294, 296
  restaurants 310, 312, 320
  Street-by-Street map 104–5
  Street Finder maps 4, 12
Piazza San Cosimato market 339
Piazza di San Giovanni in Laterano
  obelisk 51, 53
  Street-by-Street map 178–9
Piazza di Sant'Ignazio 104, 106
Piazza Santa Maria Maggiore
  173
Piazza di Santa Maria
  in Trastevere 208, 212

Piazza San Pietro 231
  fountains 50, 52
  obelisk 53
  Street-by-Street map 224
Piazza di Siena 258
Piazza di Spagna 128–41
  area map 129
  hotels 294, 297–8
  light meals and snacks 320
  restaurants 310, 313
  Street-by-Street map 130–31
  Street Finder maps 4, 5
Piazza di Spagna (hotel) 294, 297
Piazza Vittorio Emanuele II 174
Piazza Vittorio market 338
Pica, Alberto 320
Picasso (nightclub) 348, 349
Picasso, Pablo 241
Piccola Farnesina 149
  Rome's Best Museums
  and Galleries 48
  Street-by-Street map 145
Piccolo (hotel) 294, 298
Piccolomini family 123
Piceni, Confraternity of the 126
Pickpockets 338, 360
Picnics 353
Pie' di Marmo 105, 108
Pierleoni family 152, 274
Pierleoni Tower 275
Pietà (Bellini) 240, 241
Pietà (Michelangelo) 31, 233
Pietro, San *see* Peter, St
Pilate, Pontius 180, 181
Pilgrims 39, 230
Pincio Gardens 136–7, 343
Pincio hill 135, 136
Pineider 334, 335
Pinturicchio 45, 69, 138, 236
  Adoration of the Magi 241
  Borgia Apartment 241
  Delphic Sybil 139
  Funeral of St Bernardino 67
Pio Righetti, Palazzo 145, 146
Pio-Christian Museum 237, 240
Pio-Clementine Museum 235,
  237, 239
Piombo, Sebastiano del 219
  Santa Maria del Popolo 138, 139
  Villa Farnesina frescoes 220
Piperno 308, 310, 314
Pirandello, Luigi 346
Piranesi, Giovanni Battista 36, 78,
  204
Pirozzi, Anna Maria 328, 331
Pisa, popes in 30
Pisanello 158
Piscina, San Clemente 186
Piscina delle Rose 351
Pius II, Pope 27, 268
  tomb of 123
Pius III, Pope, tomb of 123
Pius IV, Pope 27, 127
  Casina of 225
  Palazzina 259
  Porta del Popolo 137

Pius IV, Pope (cont.)
  Porta Santo Spirito 226
  Sistine Chapel 135
  Via Appia Antica 265
Pius V, Pope 241
  tomb of 169
Pius VI, Pope 113, 123, 218, 235
Pius VII, Pope 239
Pius IX, Pope 37, 227
  Colonna dell'Immacolata 132
  Pio-Christian Museum 240
  portrait of 132
Pius X, Pope 160
Pizzas 302
Pizzeria San Marco 321
Pizzerias 318, 320–21, 353
Plants found in Colosseum 92
Plato 243, 269
Plautus 77
Plaza Minerva 289
Pliny the Elder 239
Plotina 90
Pluto and Persephone (Bernini) 260
Podiums 34
Police 360, 361
  registering with 289, 366
Policlinico Umberto I 361
Polidori Uomo 327, 330
Polidoro da Caravaggio 149
Pollini 328, 331
Polyclitus 239
Pomarancio, Niccolò 185, 208
  Martyrdom of St Simon 194
Pomezia 294, 298
Pomodoro, Giò 241
Pompei 271
Pompeius, Sixtus the Righteous,
  Tomb of 284
Pompey the Great 150, 152, 338
  history 18, 20, 21
  Theatre of Pompey 146, 299
Pomponius Hylas,
  Columbarium of 195
Ponte Cestio 152
Ponte Fabricio 21, 152, 275
Ponte Mazzini 276
Ponte Rotto 200, 274
Ponte Sant'Angelo 126, 132, 152,
  273, 283
Ponte Sisto 209, 210, 275
Pontelli, Baccio 121, 210, 226
Ponti, Giò 333
Pontifex Maximus 80, 85
Ponzio, Flaminio 112, 148, 172, 274
Popes 26–7
  audiences with 366
  see also individual popes
Porchetta stall, Viale Carlo
  Felice 321
Porta Asinaria 179, 180
Porta Maggiore 184
Porta Magica 174
Porta Pia 36–7
Porta Pinciana 253
Porta del Popolo 137
Porta Portese market 324, 339

Porta San Sebastiano 196
Porta Santo Spirito 226
Porta Settimiana 217, 218
Portico of Octavia 151, 274
Porticoes 34
Porto di Ripetta 310, 313
Portoghesi (hotel) 289, 294, 296
Portunus, Temple of *see*
  Temple of Portunus
Post offices 365
Poste restante 365
Il Posto Accanto 310, 314
Postumius 84
Poussin, Nicolas 56, 135
  monument 112
Pozzo, Andrea
  Chapel of Sant'Ignazio,
  Gesù 114, 115
  Pozzo Corridor 32–3
  Sant'Ignazio di Loyola
  ceiling 105
Prefettura della Casa Pontificia
  366
Premiata Fabbrica Birra Peroni
  318, 321
Premiate Gelaterie Fantasia 321
Presbyterian Church 367
Prima Porta cemetery 60
Prima visione cinemas 346, 347
Primoli, Counts 127
Prints 337, 338
Prix de Rome 57
Probus, Emperor 196
Pron'tospettacolo 340, 341
Protestant Cemetery 205
Protezione della Giovane 291
Public holidays 61
Puccini, Giacomo 57, 119, 123
Pudens 171
Pulvillus, Horatius 18
Punic Wars 20, 21
Punishment of the Rebels
  (Botticelli) 245
Puppet shows 347, 355
Putti 35
Pyramid of Caius Cestius 29, 205

Q

Qantas 368
Quadrifoglio 310, 314
Le Quattro Fontane 53, 162, 282
Qube 348, 349
Quiñones, Cardinal, tomb of 181
Quintus Fabius Maximus 123
Quirinal 154–65
  area map 155
  hotels 295, 299
  restaurants 310, 314, 320–21
  Street-by-Street map 156–7
  Street Finder maps 5, 6, 12
Quirinale, Palazzo del, 157, 158, 282

R

Rabelais, François 127
Rabirii freed slaves, tomb of 285
Rabirius 100

Racing
  cars 350, 351
  greyhounds 350, 351
  horses 350, 351
  motorbikes 350
Radio stations in Rome 367
Radio Londra (nightclub) 348, 349
Raffaello Sanzio see Raphael
Raggi, Antonio 114, 165
  Baptism of Christ 153
Raguzzini, Filippo 106
RAI (Italian state TV and
  radio service) 367
Rail services 372–3
  map 370–71
Rainaldi, Carlo
  Palazzo Nuovo 70
  Sant'Agnese in Agone 121
  Sant'Andrea della Valle 119
  Santa Maria in Campitelli 151
  Santa Maria Maggiore 169, 172
  Santa Maria dei Miracoli 136, 137
  Santa Maria in Montesanto
    136, 137
  Santa Maria del Suffragio 277
  Santa Maria in Via 283
  Santi Apostoli 157
Rainaldi, Girolamo 70, 121
Rainfall 60
Ramirez 328, 331
Raniero Gattinoni 330
Rape of the Sabine Women
  (Cortona) 47
Raphael (Raffaello Sanzio) 31, 46, 56,
  135, 160, 208, 219, 227, 277
  The Battle of the Milvian
    Bridge 242
  Casina di Raffaello 258
  Chigi Chapel 45, 138, 139
  The Dispute over the Holy
    Sacrament 243
  The Expulsion of Heliodorus from
    the Temple 242
  The Fire in the Borgo 243
  and La Fornarina 111, 210, 255
  The Liberation of St Peter 243
  Loggia of Cupid and Psyche 221
  Madonna di Foligno 31, 225
  The Mass at Bolsena 242
  Parnassus 48
  Portrait of Julius II 27
  Sant'Eligio degli Orefici 144, 148
  Santa Maria della Pace 45, 121
  St Peter's 230
  The School of Athens 30
  tomb in the Pantheon 110, 111
  Transfiguration 241
  Triumph of Galatea 220
  Vatican frescoes 242–3
  Vatican Loggia 241
  Vatican Museums 235
  Villa Farnesina 216, 217
Raphael (hotel) 292, 294, 297
Raphael Rooms, Vatican 235,
  236, 242–3
  floorplan 242

Raphael Rooms (cont.)
  Hall of Constantine 242
  Room of the Fire in the Borgo 243
  Room of Heliodorus 242–3
  Room of the Segnatura 243
Ravasini 332, 333
Reame, Mino del 153, 212
Red Brigades 39
Red Faun 71
Reformation 244
Regia 80
Regina Coeli prison 276
Regina Hotel Baglioni 290, 295, 301
Regolini-Galassi tomb 238
Relais le Jardin 302
Relais le Jardin dell'Hotel
  Lord Byron 311, 317
Relais la Piscine dell'
  Aldrovandi Palace 311, 317
Religious artefacts, shops 334, 335
Religious institutions,
  staying in 290
Remo 318, 321
Remus see Romulus and Remus
Renaissance 15, 30–31
  architecture 34, 35, 45
Renaissance Quarter 109
Reni, Guido 49, 112, 147, 150, 182,
  218, 241, 255
  Holy Trinity 147
  San Carlo at Prayer 150
La Repubblica (newspaper)
  340, 359, 367
Republic, Roman 20–21
Reservations
  hotels 289
  restaurants 303
Residence Babuino 290
Residential hotels 290
Residenza 295, 300
La Residenza 332, 333
Residenza Universitaria de
  Lollis 291
Resistance in World War II 266
Respighi, Ottorino 57, 258
Rest during the Flight into Egypt
  (Caravaggio) 107
Restaurants 302–17
  booking a table 303
  children in 303, 353
  choosing 310–17
  opening times 303
  prices 303
  reading the menu 303
  Rome's Best 308–9
  tipping 359
  types 302
  vegetarian food 302
  What to Eat in Rome 304–5
  wheelchair access 303
Restivo 295, 299
Retrospettiva 336, 337
Reynolds, Sir Joshua 160
Riario, Cardinal Domenico 218
Riario, Girolamo 127, 245
Riario, Cardinal Raffaele 149

Ricci, Palazzo 144, 149, 276
Ricci, Sebastiano, Paul III Gives his
  Approval to the Capuchin Order 27
Ricimer the Suevian 88
Ricordi 334, 335
Riding 350, 351
Rienzo, Cola di 29, 68, 69, 172
La Rinascente 323
Rinascimento (hotel) 294, 298
Rinascita 340, 341
I Rioni 320
Ripa 290
Ripartizione X 367
Risorgimento museum 74
Ristoro della Salute 321
Rivoli 346, 347
Rizzio, Abbondio 107
Rizzoli 334, 335
Road information 379
Road signs 373, 374, 375
Rock music 344
Rococo 106
Rodriguez, Cardinal, tomb of 173
Roffi Isabelli 320, 335
Roma (goddess) 87
Roma C'E' 348
Roma Jazz Festival 344, 345
Roma Rent 378, 379
RomaEuropa 343
Roman Empire
  art 239
  Christianity in 24
  history 15, 18–19, 22–3
Roman Forum see Forum
Roman Insula 66, 68
Roman Sports Centre 351
Romanesque architecture 34, 35
Romantik Barocco 295, 301
Rome, Treaty of (1957) 39
Rome Provincial Tourist Board (EPT)
  289, 358, 359
Rome's Birthday 58
Romolo nel Giardino della
  Fornarina 308, 311, 316
Romulus (son of Emperor
  Maxentius) 265
Romulus and Remus 18, 74, 93, 97,
  202, 276
  Huts of Romulus 101
  legends 16, 17
  She-Wolf bronze 73
  Temple of Romulus 80, 86
  tomb of Romulus 228
Rooms of St Ignatius, Pozzo
  Corridor 32–3
Rosati 319, 320
Rosati, Rosato 45
La Rosetta 310, 312
Rospigliosi family 211
Rosselli, Cosimo, Sistine
  Chapel frescoes 244, 245
Rossellini, Roberto 57
Rossi, Antonio de 112
Rossi, Giovanni Antonio de 151
Rossini, Gioacchino 150
Rosticcerie 302, 318–19

Rostra 78, 82
Rowing 350
Rubens, Peter Paul 72
  Chiesa Nuova 124
  Palazzo Corsini 46, 218
  Palazzo Spada 49, 147
  visitor to Rome 56
Rughesi, Fausto 124
Rulers of ancient Rome 18–19
Rusticated masonry 35
Rusuti, Filippo 281
Rutelli, Mario
  Fontana delle Naiadi 164
  Monument to Anita Garibaldi 216

S

Sabine War 74
Sabines 16
Sacchetti 321
Sack of Rome (1527) 31
Safari 349
Safety, pickpockets 338
Sagra dell'Uva 60
Saints *see under individual saints'*
  names and under Churches
Saint Louis Music City 344, 345
St Peter Moto 379
St Peter's 59, 199, 230–33
  architectural features 230–31
  Baldacchino 35, 111, 232
  for children 354
  concerts 342
  floorplan 45, 232–3
  historical plan 232
  history 24, 30, 31, 32
  Rome's best 42, 45
  Street-by-Street map 224
  timeline 230
  Visitors' Checklist 231
  walks 283
St Peter's Holiday Inn 350, 351
St Peter's square 58
  see also Piazza San Pietro
Sala Accademica di Via dei Greci
  342, 343
Sala Baldini 342, 343
Salato, Raphael 328, 331
Sales 322
Salomé (Titian) 46
Salsa music 349
Salvi, Nicola 51, 126, 159
Salviati, Francesco 126, 149, 159, 203
Samaritans 361
Sant'Agata dei Goti 165
Sant'Agnese in Agone 117, 120, 121
  history 33
  Rome's Best 45
  Street-by-Street map 119
Sant'Agnese fuori le Mura 25, 264
Santi Ambrogio e Carlo al Corso 141
Sant'Anastasia 279
Sant'Andrea delle Fratte 131, 132
Sant'Angelo in Pescheria 151,
  152, 274
Sant'Andrea al Quirinale 43, 45,
  161, 282

Sant'Andrea della Valle 69, 119, 123
Sant'Anselmo 204
Sant'Anselmo (hotel) 292, 295, 299
Sant'Apollinare 127, 342
Santi Apostoli 157, 158–9
Santa Balbina 196
Santo Bambino 69
San Bartolomeo all'Isola 152, 275
San Benedetto (restaurant) 311, 317
San Bernardo alle Terme 162
San Biagio degli Armeni 277
Santa Bibiana 174
Santi Bonifacio e Alessio 204
San Callisto, Catacombs of
  see Catacombs of San Callisto
San Carlo ai Catinari 45, 150
San Carlo alle Quattro Fontane 33,
  45, 161, 282
Santa Caterina dei Funari 274
Santa Caterina da Siena 88, 276
Santa Cecilia in Trastevere 42, 44, 211
San Cesareo 194
Santa Chiara (hotel) 294, 296
San Clemente 186–7
  floorplan 186–7
  history 29
  mithreum 354
  mosaics 28, 281
  Rome's Best Churches 43, 44
  tabernacle 35
  timeline 186
Santi Cosma e Damiano 44, 80, 86
Santa Costanza 24, 44, 264
San Crisogono 209, 211
Santa Croce in Gerusalemme 43,
  177, 181
Santi Domenico e Sisto 165
Sant'Egidio 208, 210
Sant'Eligio degli Orefici 144, 148, 276
Sant'Eustachio 109
Sant'Eustachio (café) 319, 320
San Filippo (café)321
San Filippo Neri 276
San Francesco a Ripa 211
Santa Francesca Romana 77, 81, 87
San Giorgio convent 126
San Giorgio in Velabro 29, 202
  Street-by-Street map 201
  Walk by the Tiber 279
San Giovanni Decollato 201, 203
San Giovanni dei Fiorentini 153, 277
San Giovanni in Laterano 177, 182–3
  architectural features 182–3
  concerts 342
  history 29
  mosaics 280
  nave 35
  Rome's Best Churches 43, 44
  Street-by-Street map 179
  timeline 182
San Giovanni in Oleo 194
Santi Giovanni e Paolo 190, 192
San Giovanni a Porta Latina 194
San Girolamo della Carità 144, 148
San Giuseppe dei Falegnami 91
San Gregorio 275

San Gregorio Magno 190, 192
Sant'Ignazio di Loyola 106, 354
  concerts 342
  Rome's Best Churches 45
  Street-by-Street map 105
Sant'Ivo alla Sapienza 122
  floorplan 45
  Rome's Best Churches 45
  Street-by-Street map 119
San Lorenzo area,
  restaurants 302
San Lorenzo in Damaso 149
San Lorenzo in Lucina 112
San Lorenzo in Miranda 44, 80, 85
San Lorenzo fuori le Mura 264–5
Santi Luca e Martina 79, 82
San Luigi (restaurant) 311, 317
San Luigi dei Francesi 45, 119, 122
San Marcello al Corso 156, 159
San Marco 66, 75
Santa Maria degli Angeli 45, 163
Santa Maria dell'Anima 119, 121
Santa Maria Antiqua 24
Santa Maria in Aracoeli 67, 69
Santa Maria in Campitelli 151, 274
Santa Maria in Campo Marzio 112
Santa Maria della Concezione 252,
  254, 354
Santa Maria della Consolazione
  201, 203
Santa Maria in Cosmedin 202
  Cosmatesque work 35
  Rome's Best Churches 42, 44
  Street-by-Street map 200
  Tiber walk 274, 275
Santa Maria in Domnica 193
  mosaics 280
  Street by-Street map 191
Santa Maria Maggiore 167,
  172–3, 366
  architectural features 172–3
  history 24
  legend of the snow 172
  Rome's Best Churches 43, 44
  Street-by-Street map 169
  timeline 172
Santa Maria sopra Minerva 108
  obelisk 50, 53, 104, 108
  Street-by-Street map 104
Santa Maria dei Miracoli 136
Santa Maria di Monserrato 144, 148
Santa Maria in Montesanto 136
Santa Maria dei Monti 164
Santa Maria dell'Orazione e Morte 147
  Street-by-Street map 144
  Via Giulia walk 276
Santa Maria della Pace 121
  concerts 341, 342
  Rome's Best Churches 45
  Street-by-Street map 118
Santa Maria del Popolo 138–9
  floorplan 138–9
  Rome's Best Churches 45
  timeline 139
Santa Maria del Priorato 204
Santa Maria della Scala 208, 210

Santa Maria dei Sette Dolori 208, 210
Santa Maria del Suffragio 277
Santa Maria in Transpontina 228
Santa Maria in Trastevere 212–13
  architectural features 212–13
  floorplan 212–13
  mosaics 29
  Rome's Best Churches 42, 44
  Street-by-Street map 208
  timeline 213
  Walk by the Tiber 275
Santa Maria in Trivio 156, 160
Santa Maria in Via 156, 282–3
Santa Maria della Vittoria 255
  Rome's Best Churches 45
  Street-by-Street map 253
  Bernini walk 282
San Martino ai Monti 170
  mosaics 281
  Street-by-Street map 169
Santi Nereo e Achilleo 194, 266
San Nicola (on Via Appia) 284
San Nicola in Carcere 21, 152, 274
Sant'Omobono 200
Sant'Onofrio 219
San Panfilo, Catacombs of see
  Catacombs of San Panfilo
San Paolo fuori le Mura 22, 35, 44,
  267, 342
San Pietro see St Peter's
San Pietro in Montorio 219
San Pietro in Vincoli 45, 168, 170
Santa Prassede 171
  mosaics 28, 281
  Rome's Best Churches 43, 44
  Street-by-Street map 169
Santa Pudenziana 171
  mosaics 28
  Street-by-Street map 168
Santi Quattro Coronati 44, 185, 281
San Rocco 141
San Saba 35, 205
Santa Sabina 204
  Crucifixion 25
  fountain 53, 199
  history 24
  Rome's Best Churches 44
  tabernacle 29
San Salvatore in Lauro 126
San Sebastiano 265
San Sebastiano, Catacombs of
  see Catacombs of San Sebastiano
San Sisto Vecchio 193
Santo Spirito, Hospital of
  see Hospital of Santo Spirito
Santo Spirito in Sassia 226
Santo Stefano Rotondo 24, 185, 280
Santa Susanna 253, 255
San Teodoro 201, 202
San Tommaso in Formis
  mosaics 280–81
  Street by-Street map 191
Santissima Trinità dei
  Pellegrini 145, 146–7
Santi Vincenzo e Anastasio 156, 160
Sancta Sanctorum 180

Sanctis, Francesco de 135
Sanctis, Guglielmo de 127
Sangallo, Antonio da the Younger
  Palazzo del Banco di Santo
    Spirito 125
  Palazzo Clarelli 277
  Palazzo Farnese 147
  Palazzo Sacchetti 277
  Piccola Farnesina 149
  Porta Santo Spirito 226
  San Giovanni dei Fiorentini 153
  San Giovanni in Oleo 194
  Santa Maria della Pace 121
  St Peter's 230
  Santo Spirito in Sassia 226
  Sangallo Bastion 196
Sangallo, Giuliano da 172
  Sangallo Bastion 196
Le Sans Souci 311, 317
Sansovino, Andrea 138, 139
Sansovino, Jacopo 148, 277
  Palazzo Gaddi 126
  San Marcello al Corso 159
  tomb of Cardinal Quiñones 181
Santen, Jan van 260
Santini, Fausto 328, 331
Saraceni, Carlo, Miracle of
  St Benno 121
Saracens 28, 226
Sarto, Andrea del 147
  Visitation 46
Sartre, Jean-Paul 292, 296
Saturn, Temple of
  see Temple of Saturn
Saturnalia 83
Savelli family 151
Scala Quattordici 327, 330
Scala Santa 179, 180
Scalinata di Spagna (hotel)
  293, 294, 298
Scanderbeg 282
Schön, Mila 326
The School of Athens (Raphael) 30
Schostal 327, 330
Sciarra, Villa 211
Scipio Africanus, Publius Cornelius
  history 18, 21
  Tomb of the Scipios 195
Scipio Barbatus, Cornelius 195
Scipios, Tomb of the see Tomb of
  the Scipios
Scoot-a-Long 378, 379
Scooters 352, 378
Scooters for Rent 378, 379
Sculptors 56
Sculpture, Cosmatesque 35
Second-hand clothes 327, 331
Secondinus, Tiberius Claudius,
  tomb of 285
Security 360–61
Selarum 319, 321
Self-catering accommodation 290
Selva, Attilio
  statue of San Carlo
    Borromeo 141
Semidivino 321

Senate (Italian parliament) 122
Senate (Roman) 150
Seneca, tomb of 284
Sergius III, Pope 182
Sermoneta 329, 331
Servian Wall 17, 20, 169, 174
Servilius, Marcus, tomb of 284
Servius Tullius, King 17, 18
Sessorianum 181
Seven hills of Rome 16
Severn, Joseph 134
  grave 205
  Portrait of Keats 57
Severus, Septimius, Emperor 19, 93
  Arch of Septimius Severus 83, 278
  Arco degli Argentari 201, 279
  Palace of 97, 100
Sforza, Ascanio, tomb of 139
Sforza, Countess Caterina Nobili 162
Sforza Cesarini family 150
Shakespeare, William 82
Shamrock 344–5
Shangri-La Hotel 351
She-wolf 17
  statue in Capitoline Museums 73
Shelley, Percy Bysshe 55, 57
  bust of 134
  grave of 205
  Keats-Shelley Memorial
    House 131, 134
Sheraton Golf Hotel 350, 351
Shoes
  sales 322
  shops 328, 331
  size chart 329
Shops 322–39
  art and antiques 336–7
  artisan handicrafts 334, 335
  best buys 322
  books 334, 335
  costume jewellery 329, 331
  department stores and shopping
    centres 323
  etiquette 323
  fashion 325, 326–7, 330
  food 334–5
  gloves, hats and hosiery 329, 331
  goldsmiths and silversmiths
    329, 331
  how to pay 323
  interior design 332–3
  jewellery 328–9, 331
  knitwear 327, 330
  leather goods 331
  lingerie 327, 330–31
  multimedia and music 334, 335
  Rome's Best 324–5
  sales 322
  second-hand clothes 327, 331
  shoes and accessories 328–9, 331
  souvenirs and religious
    artefacts 334, 335
  stationery and paper
    crafts 334, 335
  street markets 338–9
  toys 355

Shops (cont.)
VAT exemption 323
wine 335
see also Markets
Siena 276
Sightseeing permits 367
Il Sigillo 333
Signorelli, Luca,
Sistine Chapel frescoes 244, 245
Silanus, Caius Junius 193
Silversmiths 329, 331
Silvestri, Wilma 327, 331
Simon Magus 87
Simonetti, Michelangelo 238
stairway in Vatican Museums 235
Il Simposio di Piero Costantini 321
Single 333
SIP 364–5
Siragusa (jeweller's) 329, 331
Sirni 328, 331
Sisley 327, 330
Sistine Chapel 235, 236
ceiling 31, 241, 246–7, 354
Rome's Best Museums
and Galleries 45
wall frescoes 244–5
Sixtus III, Pope 172
Sixtus IV, Pope 27, 127, 141, 226, 234
Capitoline museums 70
Hospital of Santo Spirito 226–7
Ponte Sisto 209, 210
Santa Maria della Pace 121
Santa Maria del Popolo 138, 139
Santi Apostoli 159
Sistine Chapel 235, 244, 245
Via dei Coronari 126
Sixtus V, Pope 27, 32, 158, 160,
162, 266
Capitoline museums 70
Column of Marcus Aurelius 113
Felice Aqueduct 267
Moses Fountain 52, 162
Piazza dell'Esquilino
obelisk 168, 172
Piazza del Popolo 137
San Giovanni in Laterano 183
Santa Maria Maggiore 173
Santo Spirito in Sassia 226
Scala Sancta 180
Size chart, clothes 329
Skin (leather goods shop) 328, 331
Sleeping Hermaphrodite 260
Smeraldo 294, 299
Smile 348, 349
Smoking 359
Snacks 318–21
Sobieski, Maria, tomb of 233
Soccer 350, 351
Società Cooperativa Autoradiotaxi
Roma 378, 379
Società la Capitale Radio Taxi
378, 379
Society of Jesus *see* Jesuits
Sodoma, Giovanni Antonio Bazzi,
*The Wedding of Alexander
and Roxanne* 221

"Sofas of Via Giulia" 277
Sofitel Roma 295, 301
Al Sogno 355
Sogno del Mare 349
Sogo-Asahi 310, 313
Sole (hotel) 294, 299
Sole al Pantheon 292, 294, 296
Sole e Luna 349
Soprintendenza Comunale 367
Sora Lella 309
Sorelle Fontana 326, 330
Soria, Giovanni Battista 150, 192
Sormani, Leonardo 162
Soul II Soul 348, 349
Souvenir shops 334, 335
Spada, Cardinal Bernardino 49, 147
Spada, Cardinal Virginio 147, 148
Spada Chapel, San Girolamo
della Carità 144, 148
Spada family 148
Spada, Palazzo 145, 147
Spagnoli, Luisa 327, 330
Spanish Steps 33, 129, 133, 134–5
Street-by-Street map 131
Spanish Steps Alta Moda Fashion
Show 339
Spartacus 21
Spazio Sette 332, 333
Sperone 337
Spinario 73
Spiral ramp, Vatican Museums 235
Spiriti (pizzeria) 320
Sport 350–51
Spring in Rome 58
Stadio Flaminio 344, 345
Stadio Olimpico 344, 345, 350, 351
Stadium on the Palatine 99, 100
Stadium of Domitian 120
Stained glass, Santa Maria del
Popolo 139
Stallone, Sylvester 301
Stamps, postage 365
Standa 323
Stardust 344, 345
Statilii freedmen, tombs of 184
Stationery shops 334, 335
Statues
Belli, Giuseppe Gioacchino 209
Bruno, Giordano 143, 146
Byron 258
Castor and Pollux 157, 158
Dioscuri 68
Madonna of Guadalupe 224
Marforio 124
Palazzo Nuovo 70–71
Pasquino 118, 120, 124
St Helena 181
San Carlo 141
Sant'Agnese 121
Vatican Museums 234–41
see also Monuments
Stazione Termini 372, 373
Stefaneschi, Bertoldo 213
Stefaneschi, Cardinal Jacopo 29, 240
Stefaneschi, Cardinal Pietro,
tomb of 213

Stefaneschi Triptych (Giotto) 29, 240
Le Stelle 349
Stephen VI, Pope 182
Stildomus 332, 333
Stilvetro 333
Strauss, Richard 136
Street, GE 135
Street fairs 338, 339
Street markets 338–9
Street signs 374, 375
Stuart, Charles
(Bonnie Prince Charlie) 33
Stuart, James 55, 233
Stuart monument (Canova) 233
Student information 366
Studio Punto Tre 332, 333
Subiaco 271
Suburra 167
Succo d'Arancio 355
Suetonius 101, 175
Suisse 294, 297
Sulla 265
history 18, 20
Summer cinema 346
Summer in Rome 59
Sunshine 59
Surdis, Cardinal Stefanus de,
tomb of 196
Sutherland, Graham 241
Svizzera Siciliana 321
Swimming 351
Sylvester I, Pope
Raphael Room frescoes 242
San Giovanni in Laterano 182, 280
San Martino ai Monti 170, 281
Santi Quattro Coronati
frescoes 185
Symmachus, St 170
Synagogue 152, 367
Walk by the Tiber 275

T

Tabernacles 35
Tacitus 175
Tad 336, 337
Il Tajut 318, 321
Takeaway food 302, 318–19
Talking statues 118, 120, 124
Talone, Piero 336, 337
La Tana del Grillo 311, 315
Taranto 265
Tarpeia 16, 74
Tarpeian Rock 67, 74, 203
Tarquin family 16
Tarquinia 17, 271
Tarquinius Priscus, King 17, 18
Tarquinius Superbus 16, 18
Tartarughino 348, 349
Tasso, Torquato 57, 216, 219
Tasso's Oak 216
Tattou 349
La Taverna 310, 312
La Taverna di Bambù 311, 316
Taverna Cestia 321
Taverna Negma 345
Tavola calda 302, 303, 319

Tavola D'Oro 311, 316
Tax, Value Added (VAT) 323, 366
Taxis 369, 378, 379
Tazza d'Oro 309, 319, 320
  Street-by-Street map 104
Tea rooms 319, 320–21
Teatro Argentina 150, 346, 347
Teatro Ateneo 347
Teatro Brancaccio 343
Teatro dei Cocci 347
Teatro Colosseo 347
Teatro Eliseo 346, 347
Teatro Ghione 342, 343
Teatro Mongiovino 347
Teatro Olimpico 342, 343
Teatro dell'Opera 340, 341, 342, 343
Teatro Piccolo Eliseo 346, 347
Teatro Politecnico 347
Teatro di Pompeo 292, 294, 299
Teatro Quirino 346, 347
Teatro La Scaletta 347
Teatro Sistina 347
Teatro Stabile del Giallo 346, 347
Teatro Tordinona 347
Teatro Valle 346, 347
Teatro Vascello 343
Teatro Verde 347
Teatro Villa Lazzaroni 347
Teatro Vittoria 346, 347
Teichner 320
Telegrams 364
Telephones 364–5
  call charges 364
  dialing codes 365
  emergency numbers 361
  telephone cards 364, 365
  telephone offices 364
  tokens 363, 364, 365
  using public telephones 365
Television 367
Temperature chart 61
Tempi Moderni 329, 331
Tempietto 219
  architectural features 30–31
  Rome's Best Churches 45
Il Tempio della Pizza 321
Temple of Antoninus and Faustina
  44, 85
  Tour of the Forum 80
Temple of Apollo 151
Temple of Castor and Pollux 20, 79,
  84, 278
Temple of Claudius 191, 192
Temple of Cybele 98, 101
Temple of Diana 258
Temple of Faustina 258
Temple of Fortune 15
Temples of the Forum Boarium
  200, 203
Temple of Hadrian 66, 104, 106
Temple of Hercules 200
Temple of Julius Caesar 79, 278
Temple of Juno 21
Temple of Jupiter 16, 17, 65, 74
  Street-by-Street map 67
Temple of the Magna Mater 98

Temple of Portunus 200, 203
Temple of Romulus 80, 86
Temple of Saturn 21, 78, 83
Temple of Venus and Rome 81, 87
Temple of Vespasian 78
Temple of Vesta 20, 84–5
  Street-by-Street map 80
Temples
  architecture 34
  Area Sacra 150
  Etruscan 263
  Rome's Best Churches
  and Temples 42–5
Temptations of Christ (Botticelli) 245
Tennis 58, 350, 351
Tentativo 311, 316
Termini
  hotels 288, 295, 299
  restaurants 302, 310, 314–15, 321
Tessera (membership cards) 348
Testa 327, 330
Testaccio 204
  market 325
  restaurants 302
Tevere see Tiber, River
Theatre of Marcellus 151, 274
The Theatre of Marcellus
  (Cromek) 151
Theatre of Pompey 146
Theatres 346–7
  booking tickets 340, 341
  Burcardo Theatre Museum 149
  for children 355
  open-air 341
Theft 338, 360, 375
Theodora (medieval tyrant) 28
Theodora (mother of Pope Paschal II),
  mausoleum 171
Theodoric, King of the
  Ostrogoths 100
Theodosius, Emperor 19, 24
Théudon, Giovanni Battista
  Joseph Lending Grain to the
  Egyptians 146
  Triumph of Faith Over Heresy 114
Thorvaldsen, Bertel 56
  statue of Byron 258
Tibaldi, Pellegrino 159, 249
Tiber, River
  Ostia Antica 270
  pollution 361
  rowing 350
  Walk by the Tiber 274–5
  see also Bridges
Tiber Island 152, 275
Tiberius, Emperor 19, 24, 97
  Mausoleum of Augustus 141
  Temple of Castor and Pollux 84
Tibur 346, 347
Tiburtini hills 268
Tickets
  air travel 368
  buses 376–7
  for entertainments 340–41
  Metro 376–7
  rail services 373

Tile shops 332, 333
Timberland 327, 330
Time zones 367
Tintoretto 72
Tipping 289, 359
Tiroler Keller 321
Tischbein, Johann, Portrait of Goethe
  in the Roman countryside 136
Titian 48, 49, 72, 107, 241
  Salomé 46
Titus, Emperor 19, 92, 175, 184
  Arch of Titus 23, 87
Tivoli 268
Toilets, public 359
Tomassini 327, 331
Tombs
  Columbarium of Pomponius
  Hylas 195
  Freedmen's 184
  Protestant Cemetery 205
  Pyramid of Caius Cestius 205
  Tomb of Caius Licinius 285
  Tomb of Cecilia Metella 265,
  266, 284
  Tomb of the Festoons 285
  Tomb of the Frontispiece 285
  Tomb of the "Heroic Relief"
  284, 285
  Tomb of Hilarius Fuscus 285
  Tomb of Marcus Servilius 284
  Tomb of Pope St Urban 285
  Tomb of Quintus Apuleius 285
  Tomb of the Rabirii freed
  slaves 285
  Tomb of the Scipios 195
  Tomb of Seneca 284
  Tomb of Sixtus Pompeus the
  Righteous 284
  Tomb of Tiberius Claudius
  Secondinus 285
  see also Catacombs
Torlonia, Giovanni 229
Torlonia, Palazzo 229
Torquemada, Cardinal Juan de 108
Torre degli Anguillara 209
Torre di Capo di Bove 284
Torre dei Capocci 169
Torre Ercolana 307
Torre delle Milizie 88, 90, 221
Torre dell'Orologio 118, 125
Torriti, Jacopo 173, 280, 281
Tosca 248
Totila 180
El Toulà 310, 312
Tourist information offices 358
  hotel bookings 289
Town with Gothic Cathedral
  (Klee) 241
Toyshops 355
Traffic lights 374, 375
Traffic police 360, 361
Trains 372–3
  maps 370–71
Trajan, Emperor 19, 175, 219, 268
  Column of Trajan 90
  Curia 82

Trajan, Emperor (cont.)
  Forum of Caesar 91
Trajan's Forum 36
Trajan's Markets 88–9
  for children 354
Trams 376, 377
  Celian hill 191
  map 377
  tickets 377
Transalpino 366
Transfiguration (Raphael) 241
Trastevere 206–13
  area map 207
  cafés 303
  Festa de Noantri 59, 339, 341
  hotels 288, 295, 300
  restaurants 302, 311, 316, 321
  Street-by-Street map 208–9
  Street Finder maps 4, 7, 8, 11
  Walk by the Tiber 275
Trattoria 302, 353
Trattoria Monti 311, 315
Travel
  air 368–9
  arriving in Rome 370–71
  bicycles 352, 378, 379
  buses 376–7
  cars 373, 375, 379
  children 352
  coaches 373
  electric minibuses 358, 376
  horse-drawn carriages 378
  Metro 376–7
  minicabs 360–61
  mopeds 378, 379
  package holidays 369
  rail services 372–3
  taxis 378, 379
  trams 191, 376, 377
Traveller's cheques 360, 361, 362
Tre Scalini 319, 320
Trebbiano grape 306
Trevi Fountain 159, 160
  history 33, 36
  Rome's Best Fountains 51, 52
  Street-by-Street map 156
  Bernini Walk 282
Tribune 18
Triclinio Leoniano (banqueting
  hall of Pope Leo III) 179, 280
Triclinium, San Clemente 187
Trilussa 210, 275
Trimani Wine Bar 318, 321
Trinità dei Monti 129, 134, 135
  Street-by-Street map 131
Trinitarians 161
Triton Fountain *see* Fontana
  del Tritone
Triumph of the Cross mosaic 187
The Triumph of Divine Providence
  (Cortona) 47
Triumph of Faith Over Heresy
  (Théudon) 114
Triumph of Galatea (Raphael) 220
Triumph of the Name of Jesus
  (Il Baciccia) 115

Triumphal arches 35
  Tour of Rome's Triumphal
  Arches 278–9
Trotting 350
Trussardi 326, 327, 330
Tullio 311, 317
Tupini 333
Tuscany 307
TWA 368

U

Uccelliera 258
Ufficio Stranieri 361
Umberto I, King, statue of 258
Umberto II, King 38
UN Food and Agriculture
  Organization (FAO) 196
Underground railway *see* Metro
Unification of Italy 36–7
Uniform (clothes shop) 327, 330
United Airlines 368
Università degli Acquaroli 107
University of Rome 122, 217, 218
Uonna 344, 345
Upim 323
Urban I, Pope 26
  tomb of 285
Urban VIII, Pope 27
  Fontana della Barcaccia 133
  Fontana del Tritone 254
  Fontana delle Api 254
  Palazzo Barberini 255, 282
  Pantheon 111, 283
  St Peter's 231, 232
  Tapestries showing 27, 32
Urbino, Dukes of 165, 227

V

Vaccinations 361, 366
Vaga, Perin del 16, 149
  Castel Sant'Angelo 249
  San Marcello al Corso 159
Valadier, Giuseppe 52, 141
  Pincio Gardens 136
  Piazza del Popolo 137
Valadier (hotel) 294, 298
Valentino 39, 133, 326, 327, 330
Valentino, Mario 328, 331
Valentino Uomo 326, 330
Valextra 328, 331
Valle Lunga 350, 351
Value Added Tax (VAT) 323,
  366
Valvassori, Gabriele 107
Valzani 321
Van Dyck, Sir Anthony 49, 72
  Crucifixion 156
  Galleria Nazionale d'Arte
  Antica 46, 218
Vandals 24
Vanvitelli, Gaspare,
  View of the Tiber 228
Vanvitelli, Luigi 163
Vasari, Giorgio 149, 203, 262
Vassalletto, Pietro 267
Vassalletto family 182, 267

Vatican 222–49
  area map 223
  for children 354
  history 28
  hotels 295, 300
  Library 240
  postal service 365
  restaurants 311, 316–17, 321
  Street-by-Street map 224–5
  Street Finder maps 3, 4
Vatican Corridor 228–9, 248, 249
Vatican Council, Second 39
Vatican Gardens 225
Vatican Museums 234–47
  architectural features 234–5
  Borgia Apartment 241
  early Christian and
  medieval art 240
  Egyptian and Assyrian art 238
  Etruscan and other
  pre-Roman art 238
  exchange rates 362
  15th- to 19th-century art 240–41
  floorplan 236–7
  Greek and Roman art 239
  Lapidary Gallery 25, 237, 240
  modern religious art 241
  Pio-Christian Museum 240
  Raphael Rooms 242–3
  Raphael's last painting 241
  Rome's Best Museums 46, 48, 49
  Sistine Chapel 244–7
  Street-by-Street map 225
  timeline 235
  Visitors' Checklist 235
Vatican Radio 367
Vatican Railway Station 224
Vecchia Roma (restaurant)
  309, 310, 314
Vegetarian food 302, 319
Veio 17, 20
Velázquez, Diego 49, 56, 107
  portrait of Pope Innocent X 105
Venantius, St (San Venanzio) 43,
  179
Venezia, Palazzo 75
  Rome's Best Museums 47, 49
  Street-by-Street map 66
Venini 332, 333
Venus Genetrix 90
Venus and Rome, Temple of *see*
  Temple of Venus and Rome
Verano cemetery 60
Veccia Locanda 310, 312
Vercingetorix 91
Verdi, Giuseppe 37, 150
Veronese, Paolo 72
Verschaffelt, Pieter,
  Archangel Michael 249
Versus by Versace 330, 326
Vertecchi 334, 335
Vespasian, Emperor 19, 175, 239
  Arch of Titus 87
  Colosseum 77, 92, 175
  Forum of Peace 86, 91
  Porta Maggiore 184

Vespignani, Virginio 213
Vestal Virgins
  House of the Vestal Virgins 85
  Temple of Vesta 20, 80, 84–5
Vesuvius, Mount 271
Vetreria Murano Veneto 332–3
La Vetrina 348, 349
Via Alessandria market 339
Via Appia Antica 196, 265, 279
  catacombs 265, 266
  history 20
  jogging 351
  restaurants 302
  Walk along the Via Appia 284–5
Via del Babuino, shops 325
Via Balbo market 339
Via Biberatica 88
Via Borgognona, shops 325
Via dei Cappellari, shops 324
Via delle Carrozze 130
Via dei Chiavari 40 327, 331
Via Cola di Rienzo, shops 324
Via Condotti 61, 130, 133
Via dei Coronari 126
  shops 324
Via dei Coronari 193 (jeweller's)
  329, 331
Via del Corso 137
Via del Corso (bicyle hire) 351
Via Flaminia 21, 137
Via dei Fori Imperiali 90
Via della Gatta 105, 107
Via Giulia 153
  street fairs 339
  Walk along Via Giulia 276–7
Via Giulia (tile shop) 332, 333
Via del Governo Vecchio 124
  Street-by-Street map 118
Via Labicana 184
Via Margutta, shops 325
Via Margutta Art Fair 339
Via Milazzo market 339
Via del Pellegrino, shops 324
Via dei Pettinari 80 329, 331
Via Prenestina 184
Via delle Quattro Fontane 358
Via Recta 126
Via Sacra 78, 81, 278
Via di San Gregorio 279
Via Sannio market 339
Via Veneto 240–55
  area map 251
  hotels 288, 295, 300–301
  restaurants 311, 317, 321
  Street-by-Street map 252–3
  Street Finder map 5
Vicolo 49 (jazz club) 344, 345
Vicolo del Piede 209
Victor Emmanuel II, King 74, 111, 174
  history 36
Victor Emmanuel Monument 74
  history 37, 38
  Street-by-Street map 66

Victoria (hotel) 295, 301
View of the Tiber (Vanvitelli) 228
Vigée-Lebrun, Elisabeth 160
Vignola, Giacomo Barozzi da
  Farnese Gardens 101
  Gesù 115
  Palazzina of Pius IV 259
  St Peter's 231
  Villa Giulia 48, 262
La Vignola 190
Villa Aldobrandini 165
Villa Borghese 258–9
  children in 352, 353, 355
  Cinema dei Piccoli 355
  hotels 295, 301
  jogging 351
  restaurants 311, 317
  Zoo 354
Villa Borghese (hotel) 293, 295, 301
Villa Celimontana 193, 355
  Street by-Street map 190
Villa Doria Pamphilj 60, 267
  concerts 341, 343, 344
  jogging 351
Villa d'Este 53, 268
Villa Farnesina 31, 220–21
  architectural features 220–21
  children in 352
  Street-by-Street map 217
  Walk along Via Giulia 276
Villa Giulia 262–3
  concerts 341, 342
  Etruscan art 257, 259, 354
  floorplan 262–3
  Rome's Best Museums 46, 48
  timeline 262
Villa Gregoriana 268
Villa Lante 216
Villa Medici 135
  concerts 343
  RomaEuropa festival 341
Villa San Pio 289, 295, 299
Villa Sciarra 211
Villa Wolkonsky 185
Villaggio Globale 348, 349
Villaggio Globale
  Il Mattatoio 344, 345
Vineria 348, 349
Vineria Reggio 318, 320
Vino e cucina 302
Vino Novello tasting 60
Virgil 23, 56, 175
Virgin Mary 172, 224
  Colonna dell'Immacolata 131, 132
Visas 366
Visitation (Sarto) 46
Vitalinis, Pomponia 195
Viterbo 60, 271
Viti, Timoteo 121
Vitruvius 263
Vittoria 290
Il Vittoriano see Victor
  Emmanuel Monument

Vittorio Emanuele II
  see Victor Emmanuel II
Volpato, Giovanni 159
Volterra, Daniele da 219
  Trinità dei Monti 135
  San Marcello al Corso 159

W
Wagner, Richard 133
Wagons Lits 358, 359
Walks 272–85, 374–5
  Bernini's Rome 282–3
  River Tiber 274–5
  Rome's Best Mosaics 280–81
  Triumphal Arches 278–9
  Via Appia Antica 284–5
  Via Giulia 276–7
Wanted in Rome (English language
  magazine) 359
Warhol, Andy 328
Water, drinking 306, 307, 353
Waxworks, Museo delle Cere 49,
  156, 159
WCs 359
Weather in Rome 58–61
The Wedding of Alexander and
  Roxanne (Sodoma) 221
Wheelchair access see
  Disabled visitors
Winckelmann, JJ 57
Wine 303, 306–7
  festivals 60
  shops 335
  wine bars 318, 320–21
Winter in Rome 61
Wolkonsky, Villa 185
Women
  fashion 326–7, 330
  hostels 291
  safety 360
World Cup (1990) 39
World music 345
World War I 38
World War II 38
Writers in Rome 56–7

X
Xavier, St Francis 115

Y
Yes Brazil 345, 349
Young Women's Christian
  Association (YWCA) 291
Youth hostels 291
Youth of Moses (Botticelli) 30

Z
Zaga, Domenico 248
Zamora, Muñoz de, tomb
  204
Zodiaco 319, 321
Zoo, Villa Borghese 259, 354
Zuccari, Taddeo 148

Acknowledgments

DORLING KINDERSLEY would like to thank the following people whose contributions and assistance have made the preparation of this book possible.

MAIN CONTRIBUTORS

Olivia Ercoli is an art historian and tour guide, who has lived all her life in Rome. Bilingual in English and Italian, she lectures on art history and writes on a range of subjects for English and Italian publications.

Travel writer Ros Belford conceived the idea of the Virago Woman's Guides, of which she is now series editor, and wrote the *Virago Woman's Guide to Rome*. She has travelled widely in Europe and as well as writing guide books contributes to a variety of publications including *The Guardian*.

Roberta Mitchell heads the editorial section of the UN's Publishing Division in Rome, where she has lived for many years. An experienced writer and editor with extensive knowledge of the city, she has contributed to a number of guides to Rome including the *American Express Guide to Rome*.

CONTRIBUTORS

Sam Cole, Mary Jane Cryan Pancani, Daphne Wilson Ercoli, Laura Ercoli, Lindsay Hunt, Adrian James, Christopher McDowall, Davina Palmer, Rodney Palmer, Debra Shipley.

DORLING KINDERSLEY wishes to thank the following editors and researchers at Websters International Publishers: Sandy Carr, Matthew Barrell, Siobhan Bremner, Serena Cross, Valeria Fabbri, Annie Galpin, Gemma Hancock, Celia Woolfrey.

ADDITIONAL PHOTOGRAPHY

Andy Crawford, Philip Enticknap, Steve Gorton, Neil Mersh, Poppy, David Sutherland.

ADDITIONAL ILLUSTRATIONS

Anne Bowes, Robin Carter, Gillie Newman, Chris D Orr.

ADDITIONAL PICTURE RESEARCH

Sharon Buckley.

CARTOGRAPHY

Advanced Illustration (Cheshire), Contour Publishing (Derby), Euromap Limited (Berkshire). Street Finder maps: ERA Maptec Ltd (Dublin) adapted with permission from original survey and mapping from Shobunsha (Japan).

CARTOGRAPHIC RESEARCH

James Anderson, Donna Rispoli, Joan Russell.

RESEARCH ASSISTANCE

Janet Abbott, Flaminia Allvin, Licia Bronzin, Lupus Sabene.

DESIGN AND EDITORIAL ASSISTANCE

Hilary Bird, Vanessa Courtier, Claire Edwards, Simon Farbrother, Vanessa Hamilton, Marcus Hardy, Sasha Heseltine, Sally Ann Hibbard, Stephanie Jackson, Steve Knowlden, Mary Lambert, Janette Leung, Jane Middleton, Fiona Morgan, Helen Partington, Naomi Peck, Carolyn Pyrah, Salim Qurashi, Jane Shaw, Clare Sullivan, Andrew Szudek, Daphne Trotter, Diana Vowles.

SPECIAL ASSISTANCE

Dottore Riccardo Baldini, Signor Mario di Bartolomeo of the Soprintendenza dei Beni Artistici e Storici di Roma, Belloni, Dorling Kindersley picture department, David Gleave MW, Debbie Harris, Emma Hutton and Cooling Brown Partnership, Dottoressa Todaro and Signora Camimiti at the Ministero dell'Interno, Trestini.

PHOTOGRAPHY PERMISSIONS

DORLING KINDERSLEY would like to thank the following for their kind permission to photograph at their establishments: Bathsheba Abse at the Keats-Shelley Memorial House, Accademia dei Lincei, Accanto, Aeroporti di Roma, Aldrovandi Palace, Alpheus, Banco di Santo Spirito at Palazzo del Monte di Pietà, Rory Bruck at Babington's, Caffè Giolitti, Caffè Latino, Comune di Roma (Ripartizione X), Comunità Ebraica di Roma, Guido Cornini at Monumenti Musei e Gallerie Ponteficie, Direzione Sanitaria Ospedale di Santo Spirito, Dottoressa Laura Falsini at the

Soprintendenza Archeologica di Etruria Meridionale, Hotel Gregoriana, Hotel Majestic, Hotel Regina Baglioni, Marco Marchetti at Ente EUR, Dottoressa Mercalli at the Museo Nazionale di Castel Sant'Angelo, Ministero dell'Interno, Plaza Minerva, Ristorante Alberto Ciarla, Ristorante Filetti di Baccalà, Ristorante Romolo, Signor Rulli and Signor Angeli at the Soprintendenza Archeologica di Roma, Soprintendenza Archeologica per il Lazio, Soprintendenza per i Beni Ambientali e Architettonici, Soprintendenza per i Beni Artistici e Storici di Roma, Daniela Tabo at the Musei Capitolini, Villa d'Este, Villa San Pio, Mrs Marjorie Weeke at St Peter's.

PICTURE CREDITS

t = top; tl = top left; tc = top centre; tr = top right; cla = centre left above; ca = centre above; cra = centre right above; cl = centre left; c = centre; cr = centre right; clb = centre left below; cb = centre below; crb = centre right below; bl = bottom left; b = bottom; bc = bottom centre; br = bottom right.

Every effort has been made to trace the copyright holders and we apologize in advance for any unintentional omissions. We would be pleased to insert the appropriate acknowledgments in any subsequent edition of this publication.

Works of art have been reproduced with the permission of the following copyright holders: © DACS: Città con Cattedrale Gotica, 1925 by Paul Klee 241b.

The publishers are grateful to the following individuals, companies and picture libraries for permission to reproduce their photographs:

ACCADEMIA NAZIONALE DI SAN LUCA, Rome: 160b; AFE: 57b, 61cr; Sandro Battaglia 59c, 61clb, 61br, 324br; Louise Goldman 157t; G La Malfa 251t; AGENZIA SINTESI: Fabio Fiorani 360br, 361t, 361b; Antonella di Girolamo 361c; Marco Marcotulli 360bc; R Venturi 360bl; ALITALIA: 368t, 369cl; ALLSPORT: David Cannon 39br; ANCIENT ART AND ARCHITECTURE: 16bl, 20tl, 21tl, 25bc, 34crb, 35tc, 44cl; ARTOTHEK, Stadelsches Kunstinstitut Frankfurt, Goethe in the Roman Campagna by JHW Tischbein 136t.

BIBLIOTECA REALE, Torino: 28–29c; BRIDGEMAN ART LIBRARY: 18br, 37tr; Agnew & Sons, London 51tr; Antikenmuseum Staatliches Museum, Berlin 19bl; Biblioteca Publica Episcopal, Barcelona/Index 114bl; Bibliothèque da la Sorbonne 28c, British Museum, London 27ctr; Chateau de Versailles, France/Giraudon 33tr, 54cl; Christie's, London 40, 55tr, 68b, 95t; The Fine Art Society, London 151tr, 279tl; Galleria degli Uffizi, Florence 31bl; Greek Museum, University of Newcastle-upon-Tyne 16br; King Street Galleries, London 33br; Louvre, Paris/Lauros-Giraudon 56br; Louvre, Paris/Giraudon 26br; Roy Miles Gallery, 29 Bruton St, London 228t; Musée des Beaux-Arts, Nantes 53t; Museo e Gallerie Nazionali di Capodimonte, Naples, Detail from the predella of San Ludovico by Simone Martini 26tr; Musée Condé, Chantilly f.71v Très Riches Heures, 26tc; Museum of Fine Arts, Budapest 110bl; Museo Archeologico di Villa Giulia 48cl; Museo Poldi Pezzoli, Milan 54tr; Palazzo Doria Pamphilj, Rome 107b; Piacenza Town Hall, Italy/Index 27br; Private Collection 19br, 22bl, 24br, 27tr, 178b; Pushkin Museum, Moscow 111t; Sotheby's, London 18bl; Spink & Son Ltd., London 163b; Vatican Museums & Galleries 41ca, 237tr.

CEPHAS PICTURE LIBRARY: Mick Rock 306tr; VANESSA COURTIER: 355t.

CM DIXON: 17bl, 24c, 268b, 269t, 269b.

ECOLE NATIONALE SUPERIEURE DES BEAUX-ARTS: 21cr, 22–23, 248tl, 284–285b; ENTE NAZIONALE ITALIANO PER IL TURISMO: 358cl, cr; ET ARCHIVE: 14, 17tr, 17clb, 18tr, 19tc, 23t, 27cl, 28tl, 31br, 32br, 37br, 48tl, 306tl; MARY EVANS PICTURE LIBRARY: 9, 18cl, 23cl, 24cl, 29br, 30cb, 30b, 31t, 34tl, 34cr, 34bl, 54tl, 56tl, 67bl, 74t, 81b, 91t, 92b, 94bl, 127c, 135t, 135b, 213b.

CORALDO FALSINI: 38–39c, 340b, 341t, 341c; WERNER FORMAN ARCHIVE: 17cr, 20bl, 22tl, 23cr, 23bl, 23br, 47tr, 155t, 163tr, 175c; FOLKLORE MUSEUM, Rome: 210br.

GARDEN PICTURE LIBRARY: Bob Challinor 172cb; GIRAUDON: 15b, 28br, 36br, 55tl; RONALD GRANT: 52br, 340t.

SONIA HALLIDAY: 19c, 22br, 25cl; Laura Lushington 24bl; ROBERT HARDING PICTURE LIBRARY: 23cra, 32bl, 79cr, 177t, 268c, 353c; Mario Carrieri 35tr; Caffè Greco, Rome by

Ludwig Passini 309tr; John G Ross 38tl, 59cl, 341b; Sheila Terry 39cl; G White 59br; MICHAEL HOLFORD: 70b; HULTON DEUTSCH: 36tl, 38bc, 57cr, 63, 175b, 287c, 357c.

MAGNUM: Erich Lessing 15t, 17tl, 89br; MANSELL COLLECTION: 19tr, 25bl, 26bc, 31cl, 54bc, 55tc, 56cl, 57cl, 75cl, 75cr, 78tc, 93b, 112c, 122t, 125tr, 126tl, 132br, 133cr, 136bl, 139bl, 139br, 162tr, 172bl, 172 br, 183br, 192bl, 196bl, 210c, 220bl, 227cr, 229cr; Alinari 80br, 141bl, 160tl, 174t, 254b; Anderson 78cr, 138bl, 163tl, 228b; MORO ROMA: 36cl, 37cl, 38br, 39tr, 39bl.

NATIONAL PORTRAIT GALLERY, London: 55cr, 55b, 56tr, 57tr; © NIPPON TELEVISION NETWORK CORPORATION, Tokyo 1992: 244t, 245t, 245bl, 245br.

LA REPUBBLICA TROVAROMA: 359tl; REX FEATURES: Sipa 366br; Today 39cr.

SCALA: 94t, 278cl, Casa di Augusto 97t, Chiesa del Gesù 115t, Galleria Borghese 32cla, 260tr, Galleria Colonna 157b, Galleria Doria Pamphilj 46br, 105cr, Galleria Spada 46cl, Galleria degli Uffizi 16–17, 27bl, Museo d'Arte Orientale 174t, 174br, Musei Capitolini 47bl, Museo della Civiltà Romana 48tr, 48b, Museo delle Terme 21tr, Museo Napoleonico 49cr, Museo Nazionale, Napoli 21cl, Museo Nazionale, Ravenna 22cl, Museo del Risorgimento, Milano 36clb, 36–37c, Museo del Risorgimento, Roma 37tl, Museo di San Marco 54bl, Palazzo Barberini 253bl, Palazzo Ducale 8, 19tr, Palazzo della Farnesina 220ct, Palazzo Madama 20cl, Palazzo Venezia 47cr, 66bl, San Carlo alle Quattro Fontane 33cl, 33cr, Santa Cecilia in Trastevere 32tl, San Clemente 35bl, Santa Costanza 24–25c, Santa Maria Antiqua 24tl, Santa Maria dell'Anima 121t, Santa Maria Maggiore 43tr, Santa Maria del Popolo 139tr, 139c, Santa Prassede 26bl, 28bl, Santa Sabina 25tc, 29cl, Vatican Museums 19bc, 25t, 25cr, 25cra, 27cr, 29tl, 29cr, 30tl, 30ct, 31cr, 31bc, 32cr, 32clb, 41tr, 46tl, 48cr, 49bl, 224bl, 225cr, 235t, 238tl, 238br, 240t, 240b, 241t, 241c, 241b, 242tl, 242c, 242b, 243t, 243c, 243b, 244–245c, 246cl, 246cr, 246b, 247tl, 247c, 247cr, 247b; TONY STONE: Richard Passmore 1c.

TOPHAM PICTURE SOURCE: 38cl.

ZEFA: 2, 39tl, 230cl, 231br, 356–7, 358t, 372t; Eric Carle 58t; Kohlhas 231t.

Thanks also to Dottoressa Giulia De Marchi of L'ACCADEMIA NAZIONALE DI SAN LUCA, Rome for 160b, Rettore Padre Libianchi of LA CHIESA DI SANT'IGNAZIO DI LOYOLA for 106t, ENTE NAZIONALE PER IL TURISMO, HASSLER HOTEL, Rome for 293tl, GRAND HOTEL, Rome for 293crb and to LA REPUBBLICA TROVAROMA.

Phrase Book

IN EMERGENCY

Help!	**Aiuto!**	*eye-yoo-toh*
Stop!	**Fermate!**	*fair-mah-teh*
Call a doctor	**Chiama un medico**	*kee-ah-mah oon* **meh**-*dee-koh*
Call an ambulance	**Chiama un' ambulanza**	*kee-ah-mah oon am-boo-lan-tsa*
Call the police	**Chiama la polizia**	*kee-ah-mah lah pol-ee-tsee-ah*
Call the fire brigade	**Chiama i pompieri**	*kee-ah-mah ee pom-pee-air-ee*
Where is the telephone?	**Dov'è il telefono?**	*dot-eh eel teb-leb-foh-noh?*
The nearest hospital?	**L'ospedale più vicino?**	*loss-peh-dah-leh pee-oo vee-chee-noh?*

COMMUNICATION ESSENTIALS

Yes/No	**Sì/No**	*see/noh*
Please	**Per favore**	*pair fah-vor-eh*
Thank you	**Grazie**	*grah-tsee-eh*
Excuse me	**Mi scusi**	*mee skoo-zee*
Hello	**Buon giorno**	*bwon jor-noh*
Good bye	**Arrivederci**	*ah-ree-veh-dair-chee*
Good evening	**Buona sera**	*bwon-ah sair-ah*
morning	**la mattina**	*lah mat-tee-nah*
afternoon	**il pomeriggio**	*eel poh-meh-ree-joh*
evening	**la sera**	*lah sair-ah*
yesterday	**ieri**	*ee-air-ee*
today	**oggi**	*oh-jee*
tomorrow	**domani**	*doh-mah-nee*
here	**qui**	*kwee*
there	**la**	*lah*
What?	**Quale?**	*kwah-leh?*
When?	**Quando?**	*kwan-doh?*
Why?	**Perchè?**	*pair-keh?*
Where?	**Dove?**	*doh-veh*

USEFUL PHRASES

How are you?	**Come sta?**	*koh-meh stah?*
Very well, thank you.	**Molto bene, grazie.**	*moll-toh beh-neh grah-tsee-eh*
Pleased to meet you.	**Piacere di conoscerla.**	*pee-ah-chair-eh dee coh-noh-shair-lah*
See you soon.	**A più tardi.**	*ah pee-oo tar-dee*
That's fine.	**Va bene.**	*va beh-neh*
Where is/are ...?	**Dov'è/Dove sono ...?**	*dot-eh/doveh soh-noh?*
How long does it take to get to ...?	**Quanto tempo ci vuole per andare a ...?**	*kwan-toh tem-poh chee voo-oh-leh pair an-dar-eh ah ...?*
How do I get to ...?	**Come faccio per arrivare a ...?**	*koh-meh fah-choh pair arri-var-eh ah..?*
Do you speak English?	**Parla inglese?**	*par-lah een-gleb-zeh?*
I don't understand.	**Non capisco.**	*non ka-pee-skoh*
Could you speak more slowly, please?	**Può parlare più lentamente, per favore?**	*pwoh par-lah-reh pee-oo len-ta-men-teh pair fah-vor-eh?*
I'm sorry.	**Mi dispiace.**	*mee dee-spee-ah-cheh*

USEFUL WORDS

big	**grande**	*gran-deh*
small	**piccolo**	*pee-koh-loh*
hot	**caldo**	*kal-doh*
cold	**freddo**	*fred-doh*
good	**buono**	*bwoh-noh*
bad	**cattivo**	*kat-tee-voh*
enough	**basta**	*bas-tah*
well	**bene**	*beh-neh*
open	**aperto**	*ah-pair-toh*
closed	**chiuso**	*kee-oo-zoh*
left	**a sinistra**	*ah see-nee-strah*
right	**a destra**	*ah dess-trah*
straight on	**sempre dritto**	*sem-preh dree-toh*
near	**vicino**	*vee-chee-noh*
far	**lontano**	*lon-tah-noh*
up	**su**	*soo*
down	**giù**	*joo*
early	**presto**	*press-toh*
late	**tardi**	*tar-dee*
entrance	**entrata**	*en-trah-tah*
exit	**uscita**	*oo-shee-ta*
toilet	**il gabinetto**	*eel gah-bee-net-toh*
free, unoccupied	**libero**	*lee-bair-oh*
free, no charge	**gratuito**	*grah-too-ee-toh*

MAKING A TELEPHONE CALL

I'd like to place a long-distance call.	**Vorrei fare una interurbana.**	*vor-ray far-eh oona in-tair-oor-bah-nah*
I'd like to make a reverse-charge call.	**Vorrei fare una telefonata a carico del destinatario.**	*vor-ray far-eh oona teh-leh-fon-ah-tah ab kar-ee-koh dell dess-tee-nah-tar-ree-oh*
I'll try again later.	**Ritelefono più tardi.**	*ree-teh-teh-foh-noh pee-oo tar-dee*
Can I leave a message?	**Posso lasciare un messaggio?**	*poss-oh lash-ah-reh oon mess-sah-joh?*
Hold on	**Un attimo, per favore**	*oon ah-tee-moh, pair fah-vor-eh*
Could you speak up a little please?	**Può parlare più forte, per favore?**	*pwoh par-lah-reh pee-oo for-teh, pair fah-vor-eh?*
local call	**la telefonata locale**	*lah teb-leb-fon-ah-ta lob-kab-leh*

SHOPPING

How much does this cost?	**Quant'è, per favore?**	*kwan-teh pair fah-vor-eh?*
I would like ...	**Vorrei ...**	*vor-ray*
Do you have ...?	**Avete ...?**	*ah-veh-teh..?*
I'm just looking.	**Sto soltanto guardando.**	*stoh sol-tan-toh gwar-dan-doh*
Do you take credit cards?	**Accettate carte di credito?**	*ah-chet-tah-teh kar-teh dee creb-dee-toh?*
What time do you open/close?	**A che ora apre/ chiude?**	*ah keh or-ah ah-preh/kee-oo-deh?*
this one	**questo**	*kweb-stoh*
that one	**quello**	*kwell-oh*
expensive	**caro**	*kar-oh*
cheap	**a buon prezzo**	*ah bwon pret-soh*
size, clothes	**la taglia**	*lah tah-lee-ah*
size, shoes	**il numero**	*eel noo-mair-oh*
white	**bianco**	*bee-ang-koh*
black	**nero**	*neh-roh*
red	**rosso**	*ross-oh*
yellow	**giallo**	*jal-loh*
green	**verde**	*vair-deh*
blue	**blu**	*bloo*
brown	**marrone**	*mar-roh-neh*

TYPES OF SHOP

antique dealer	**l'antiquario**	*lan-tee-kwah-ree-oh*
bakery	**la panetteria**	*lah pah-net-tair-ree-ah*
bank	**la banca**	*lah bang-kah*
bookshop	**la libreria**	*lah lee-breh-ree-ah*
butcher's	**la macelleria**	*lah mah-chell-eh-ree-ah*
cake shop	**la pasticceria**	*lah pas-tee-chair-ee-ah*
chemist's	**la farmacia**	*lah far-mah-chee-ah*
department store	**il grande magazzino**	*eel gran-deh mag-gad-zee-noh*
delicatessen	**la salumeria**	*lah sah-loo-meh-ree-ah*
fishmonger's	**la pescheria**	*lah pess-keh-ree-ah*
florist	**il fioraio**	*eel fee-or-eye-oh*
greengrocer	**il fruttivendolo**	*eel froo-tee-ven-doh-loh*
grocery	**alimentari**	*ah-lee-men-tah-ree*
hairdresser	**il parrucchiere**	*eel par-oo-kee-air-eh*
ice cream parlour	**la gelateria**	*lah jel-lah-tair-ree-ah*
market	**il mercato**	*eel mair-kah-toh*
news-stand	**l'edicola**	*leb-dee-koh-lah*
post office	**l'ufficio postale**	*loo-fee-choh pos-tah-leh*
shoe shop	**il negozio di scarpe**	*eel neb-goh-tsioh dee skar-peh*
supermarket	**il supermercato**	*su-pair-mair-kah-toh*
tobacconist	**il tabaccaio**	*eel tab-bak-eye-oh*
travel agency	**l'agenzia di viaggi**	*lah-jen-tsee-ah dee vee-ad-jee*

SIGHTSEEING

art gallery	**la pinacoteca**	*lah peena-koh-teh-kah*
bus stop	**la fermata dell'autobus**	*lah fair-mah-tah dell ow-toh-booss*
church	**la chiesa**	*lah kee-eh-zah*
	la basilica	*lah bah-seel-i-kah*
garden	**il giardino**	*eel jar-dee-no*
library	**la biblioteca**	*lah beeb-lee-oh-teb-kah*
museum	**il museo**	*eel moo-zeb-oh*
railway station	**la stazione**	*lah stah-tsee-oh-neh*
tourist information	**l'ufficio turistico**	*loo-fee-choh too-ree-stee-koh*
closed for the public holiday	**chiuso per la festa**	*kee-oo-zoh pair lah fess-tah*

STAYING IN A HOTEL

Do you have any vacant rooms?	Avete camere libere?	ab-**veh**-teb **kab**-mair-eb **lee**-bair-eb?
double room	una camera doppia	oona **kab**-mair-ab **dob**-pee-ab
with double bed	con letto matrimoniale	kon **let**-tob mab-tree-mob-nee-**ab**-leb
twin room	una camera con due letti	oona **kab**-mair-ab kon **doo**-eb **let**-tee
single room	una camera singola	oona **kab**-mair-ab **sing**-gob-lab
room with a bath, shower	una camera con bagno, con doccia	oona **kab**-mair-ab kon **ban**-yob, kon **dot**-chab
porter	il facchino	eel fab-**kee**-nob
key	la chiave	lab kee-**ab**-veh
I have a reservation.	Ho fatto una prenotazione.	ob **fat**-tob oona preb-nob-tab-tsee-**ob**-neb

EATING OUT

Have you got a table for ...?	Avete una tavola per ... ?	ab-**veh**-teb oona **tab**-vob-lab pair ...?
I'd like to reserve a table.	Vorrei riservare una tavola.	vor-**ray** ree-sair-**vab**-reb oona **tab**-vob-lab
breakfast	colazione	kob-lab-tsee-**ob**-neb
lunch	pranzo	**pran**-tsob
dinner	cena	**cheb**-nab
The bill, please.	Il conto, per favore.	eel **kon**-tob pair fab-**vor**-eb
I am a vegetarian.	Sono vegetariano/a.	**soh**-nob veb-jeb-tar-ee-**ab**-nob/nah
waitress	cameriera	kab-mair-ee-**air**-ab
waiter	cameriere	kab-mair-ee-**air**-eb
fixed price menu	il menù a prezzo fisso	eel meb-**noo** ab pret-sob **fee**-sob
dish of the day	piatto del giorno	pee-**ab**-tob dell **jor**-no
starter	antipasto	an-tee-**pass**-tob
first course	il primo	eel **pree**-mob
main course	il secondo	eel seb-**kon**-dob
vegetables	il contorno	eel kon-**tor**-nob
dessert	il dolce	eel **doll**-cheb
cover charge	il coperto	eel kob-**pair**-tob
wine list	la lista dei vini	lab **lee**-stab day **vee**-nee
rare	al sangue	al **sang**-gweh
medium	al puntino	al poon-**tee**-nob
well done	ben cotto	ben **kot**-tob
glass	il bicchiere	eel bee-kee-**air**-eb
bottle	la bottiglia	lab bot-**teel**-yab
knife	il coltello	eel kol-**tell**-ob
fork	la forchetta	lab for-**ket**-tab
spoon	il cucchiaio	eel koo-kee-**eye**-ob

MENU DECODER

apple	la mela	lab **meb**-lab
artichoke	il carciofo	eel kar-**choff**-ob
aubergine	la melanzana	lab meb-lan-**tsab**-nab
baked	al forno	al **for**-nob
beans	i fagioli	ee fab-**job**-lee
beef	il manzo	eel **man**-tsob
beer	la birra	lab **beer**-rab
boiled	lesso	**less**-ob
bread	il pane	eel **pab**-neb
broth	il brodo	eel **brob**-dob
butter	il burro	eel **boor**-ob
cake	la torta	lab **tor**-tab
cheese	il formaggio	eel for-**mad**-job
chicken	il pollo	eel **poll**-ob
chips	patatine fritte	pab-lab-**teen**-eb **free**-teb
baby clams	le vongole	leb **von**-gob-leb
coffee	il caffè	eel kab-**feb**
courgettes	gli zucchini	lyee dzoo-**kee**-nee
dry	secco	**sek**-kob
duck	l'anatra	lab-nab-trab
egg	l'uovo	loo-**ob**-voh
fish	il pesce	eel **pesh**-eb
fresh fruit	frutta fresca	froo-tab **fress**-kab
garlic	l'aglio	**labl**-yob
grapes	l'uva	loo-vab
grilled	alla griglia	ab-lab **greel**-yab
ham	il prosciutto	eel pro-**shoo**-tob
cooked/cured	cotto/crudo	**kot**-tob/**kroo**-dob
ice cream	il gelato	eel jel-**lab**-tob
lamb	l'abbacchio	lab-**back**-kee-ob
lobster	l'aragosta	lab-rab-**goss**-tab
meat	la carne	la **kar**-neb

milk	il latte	eel **labt**-teb
mineral water	l'acqua minerale	**lab**-kwab mee-nair-**ab**-leb
fizzy/still	gasata/naturale	gab-**zab**-tab/nab-too-**rab**-leb
mushrooms	i funghi	ee **foon**-gee
oil	l'olio	**loll**-yob
olive	l'oliva	lob-**lee**-vab
onion	la cipolla	lab chee-**poll**-ab
orange	l'arancia	lab-ran-chab
orange/lemon juice	succo d'arancia/ di limone	**soo**-kob dab-**ran**-chab/ dee lee-**mob**-neb
peach	la pesca	lab **pess**-kab
pepper	il pepe	eel **peb**-peb
pork	carne di maiale	**kar**-neb dee mab-**yab**-leb
potatoes	le patate	leb pab-**tab**-teb
prawns	i gamberi	ee **gam**-bair-ee
rice	il riso	eel **ree**-zob
roast	arrosto	ar-**ross**-tob
roll	il panino	eel pab-**nee**-nob
salad	l'insalata	leen-sab-**lab**-tab
salt	il sale	eel **sab**-leb
sausage	la salsiccia	lab sal-**see**-cbab
seafood	frutti di mare	**froo**-tee dee **mab**-reb
soup	la zuppa, la minestra	lab **tsoo**-pab, lab mee-**ness**-trab
steak	la bistecca	lab bee-**stek**-kab
strawberries	le fragole	leb **frab**-gob-leb
sugar	lo zucchero	lob **zoo**-kair-ob
tea	il tè	eel **teb**
herb tea	la tisana	lab tee-**zab**-nab
tomato	il pomodoro	eel pob-mob-**dor**-ob
tuna	il tonno	**ton**-nob
veal	il vitello	vee-**tell**-ob
vegetables	i legumi	ee leb-**goo**-mee
vinegar	l'aceto	lab-**cheb**-tob
water	l'acqua	**lab**-kwab
red wine	vino rosso	**vee**-nob **ross**-ob
white wine	vino bianco	**vee**-nob bee-**ang**-kob

NUMBERS

1	uno	**oo**-nob
2	due	**doo**-eb
3	tre	treb
4	quattro	**kwat**-rob
5	cinque	**ching**-kweb
6	sei	**say**-ee
7	sette	**set**-teb
8	otto	**ot**-tob
9	nove	**nob**-veb
10	dieci	dee-**eb**-chee
11	undici	**oon**-dee-chee
12	dodici	**dob**-dee-chee
13	tredici	**tray**-dee-chee
14	quattordici	kwat-**tor**-dee-chee
15	quindici	**kwin**-dee-chee
16	sedici	**say**-dee-chee
17	diciassette	dee-chab-**set**-teb
18	diciotto	dee-**chot**-tob
19	diciannove	dee-chab-**nob**-veb
20	venti	**ven**-tee
30	trenta	**tren**-tab
40	quaranta	kwab-**ran**-tab
50	cinquanta	ching-**kwan**-tab
60	sessanta	sess-**an**-tab
70	settanta	set-**tan**-tab
80	ottanta	ot-**tan**-tab
90	novanta	nob-**van**-tab
100	cento	**chen**-tob
1,000	mille	**mee**-leb
2,000	duemila	**doo**-eb mee-lab
5,000	cinquemila	**ching**-kweb **mee**-lab
1,000,000	un milione	oon meel-**yob**-neb

TIME

one minute	un minuto	oon mee-**noo**-tob
one hour	un'ora	oon **or**-ab
half an hour	mezz'ora	medz-**or**-ab
a day	un giorno	oon **jor**-nob
a week	una settimana	oona set-tee-**mab**-nab
Monday	lunedì	loo-neb-**dee**
Tuesday	martedì	mar-teb-**dee**
Wednesday	mercoledì	mair-kob-leb-**dee**
Thursday	giovedì	job-veb-**dee**
Friday	venerdì	ven-air-**dee**
Saturday	sabato	**sab**-bab-tob
Sunday	domenica	dob-**meb**-nee-kab